Abbreviations

1 absolute, absolutely	2 adminis-trate, ion	3 advertise	4 America, n	5 amount	6 and	7 approximate, approxi-mately	8 April	9 associate	10 August
11 avenue	12 average	13 boulevard	14 bureau	15 capital, capitol	16 catalog	17 certify, certificate	18 child	19 children	20 Christmas
21 company	22 corporation	23 credit	24 day	25 December	26 department	27 discount	28 doctor	29 East	30 envelope
31 establish	32 February	33 federal	34 feet, foot	35 figure	36 Friday	37 government	38 inch	39 independent	40 intelligent, intelligently, intelligence
41 invoice	42 January	43 July	44 June	45 junior	46 magazine	47 manufacture	48 March	49 maximum	50 May
51 memorandum	52 merchandise	53 mile	54 minimum, minute	55 miscel-laneous	56 Monday	57 month	58 mortgage	59 North	60 November
61 number	62 October	63 ounce	64 page	65 paid	66 pair	67 parcel post	68 percent	69 place	70 popular
71 post office	72 pound	73 president	74 question	75 railroad	76 railway	77 represent, represent-ative	78 room	79 Saturday	80 second, secretary
81 senior	82 September	83 signature	84 South	85 square	86 street	87 subscribe, subscription	88 Sunday	89 superin-tendent	90 telephone
91 Thursday	92 total	93 Tuesday	94 vice-president	95 volume	96 warehouse	97 Wednesday	98 week	99 West	100 year
101	102	103	104	105	106	107	108	109	110

Speedwriting® EDITIONS

LANDMARK SERIES COLLEGE EDITION

PRINCIPLES OF *Speedwriting*

Speedwriting WORKBOOK

Speedwriting DICTATION AND TRANSCRIPTION

Speedwriting DICTIONARY

Speedwriting® *Dictation and Transcription*

LANDMARK SERIES

COLLEGE EDITION

THE *Speedwriting* DIVISION OF

The Bobbs-Merrill Company, Inc.

INDIANAPOLIS

Printed in the United States of America

The Bobbs-Merrill Company, Inc.
4300 West 62nd Street
Indianapolis, Indiana 46268

First Edition
First Printing 1977

Library of Congress Catalog Card Number: 76-41046
ISBN 0-672-98051-7

CONTENTS

INTRODUCTION vii

How to Use This Textbook 1

UNIT 1 LEISURE TIME 2

Taking Dictation 14

UNIT 2 PHOTOGRAPHY 15

Building Your Speed 28

UNIT 3 COMMUNICATIONS 29

Phrasing 40

UNIT 4 INSURANCE 41

Estimating Length of Letter 53

UNIT 5 ADVERTISING 54

Letter Placement 67

UNIT 6 AUTOMOTIVE 68

Expanding and Condensing Letters 81

UNIT 7 MANUFACTURING 82

What Is a Mailable Letter? 96

UNIT 8 BANKING 97

Proofreading 113

UNIT 9 MEDICAL 115

Where Errors Are Frequently Undetected 130

UNIT 10 EMPLOYMENT 131

Techniques of Proofreading 145

UNIT 11 TRANSPORTATION 147

Correcting Errors 159

UNIT 12 BUSINESS LAW 161

Correction Techniques 175

UNIT 13 FINANCE 176

Enclosures 190

UNIT 14 TRAVEL 191

Submitting Letters for Signature 205

UNIT 15 DECORATING AND DESIGN 206

Folding and Inserting Letters 221

UNIT 16 HOBBIES/HANDCRAFTS 222

Dictionaries 236

UNIT 17 DATA PROCESSING 237

References 250

UNIT 18 GENERAL BUSINESS 251

Word Division 264

UNIT 19 SECRETARIAL CHECKLIST 265

APPENDIX A SUMMARY OF PRINCIPLES 279

APPENDIX B SUMMARY OF BRIEF FORMS 287

APPENDIX C SUMMARY OF STANDARD ABBREVIATIONS 291

APPENDIX D SUMMARY OF GEOGRAPHICAL TERMS 293

APPENDIX E SUMMARY OF PUNCTUATION RULES 299

APPENDIX F KEY TO SHORTHAND PLATES 305

INTRODUCTION

Now that you have completed your lessons in *Principles of Speedwriting*, you are ready to develop your ability to take dictation on new material and to transcribe this material on the typewriter. *Speedwriting* is designed to provide the necessary reviews and drills to enable you to develop this ability. In front of each unit is a one-page discussion on some aspect of secretarial duties and skill.

Each of the nineteen units concentrates on a specific business; for example, Unit I relates to businesses in the leisure-time industry. In this way you will get a taste of the kinds of dictation one is likely to encounter in the various types of businesses. Each unit consists of five parts, and each part contains the following: (1) **Theory Review;** (2) **Transcription Skill Building;** (3) **Speed Building;** (4) **Vocabulary Building.**

The theory reviews provide reinforcement of all the principles you have learned as well as the brief forms, abbreviations, phrasing, and word-building techniques. Each review is introduced by a sound indicated by italicized type, such as *er,* or by labels such as **"Brief Forms"** or **"Abbreviations,"** and is followed by a key.

The transcription skill building exercises are designed to develop your mastery of punctuation and spelling. The speed building letter is a short letter containing many high-frequency words. The vocabulary building letters and/or articles are designed to assist you in expanding your vocabulary and developing your understanding of words.

The six appendices make up the reference section: Appendix A summarizes the principles; Appendix B, the Brief Forms; Appendix C, the Standard Abbreviations; Appendix D, geographical terms; and Appendix E, the high-frequency rules of punctuation. Appendix F is a key for all of the shorthand plates.

The letters in *Speedwriting Dictation and Transcription* are counted in groups of 20 standard words. Each superscript number represents 20 standard words. To dictate at 60 words a minute, dictate each 20-word group in 20 seconds; to dictate at 80 words a minute, dictate each 20-word group in 15 seconds; to dictate at 100 words a minute, dictate each 20-word group in 12 seconds; and to dictate at 120 words a minute, dictate each 20-word group in 10 seconds.

HOW TO USE THIS TEXTBOOK

1. Read the outlines in the Theory Review, checking with the key that follows the exercise. If you need further review for any principle, refer to Appendix A, the Summary of Principles.

2. Read the letter in the Transcription Skill Building exercise. Then transcribe the letter, inserting the correct punctuation marks. Check the transcript carefully with the Key, Appendix F. Each exercise is followed by a guide to help you decide upon the needed marks of punctuation. If you need to review any of these punctuation rules, refer to Appendix E.

3. Read the Speed Building letter using your key when necessary. Copy this letter three times. You must be able to write automatically every word dictated to reach your peak in speed.

4. Read the Vocabulary Building material and copy once in shorthand, checking with your key when necessary. Then read your notes to make sure that you know all of your outlines.

UNIT 1

LEISURE TIME

1.1 THEORY REVIEW

1. Final *er*
2. Final *ter*
3. Brief forms
4. Abbreviations
5. *for* derivations

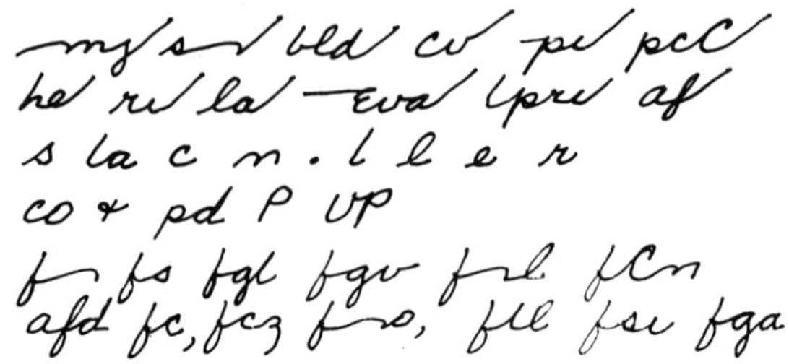

KEY 1. manager; summer; builder; cover; prior; picture 2. heater; writer; later; elevator; typewriter; after 3. is, his; that; can; in, not; the; to, it; will, well; we; are, our, hour 4. company; and; paid; president; vice-president 5. form; force; forget; forgive; formal; fortune; afford; forecast; foreclose; foremost; foretell; foresight; forgave

1.2 TRANSCRIPTION SKILL BUILDING

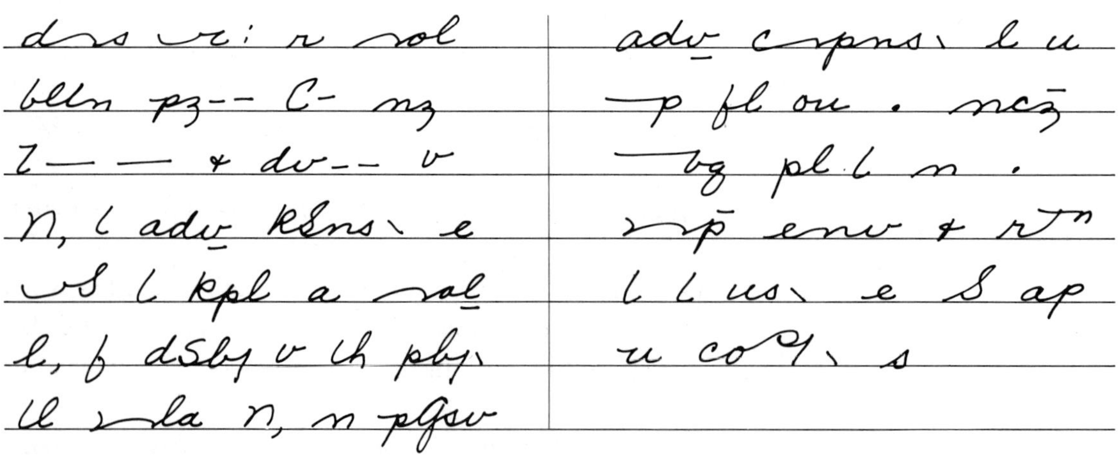

GUIDE Insert four series commas.

1.3 SPEED BUILDING

ms Srl Mn 28-06
Cl sl T-n NJ 18619
ds Mn: er hpe
lnf u la uv ln
T, pz n r kl,
pns f a v rf
3 vk vcj v b d

Tu . acre Tl apl
ly r s u .
dny + ly r avlb
ldsc ne gs u a
v . ncz Cc f
250d s lcv ne
nsd-l xpl s

1.4 VOCABULARY BUILDING

v u ks . fc la T
r 110 adjl ds v vcj
n eC y? Tr 52
vke a y C
gvs u 104 ds ps
r 6 nyl hlds la s
a rl bnnza v lz
lu vo b a a J
u dsc du . vc
d ed lc u lSa
u lz lu v us
r ez ca a Jas +
s Slas r nsl
n. flhls v . pcnos

ez breC b cr
bs o Tn . ousd u
do r y r acv
sce is sca hc
glf s b
f + C so r
s-rl ly s . sepl
f u + u nb l
sz r snc br as
bk . hgou f r lnaz
ll us So u h l
Tn u vke
nl fn ds . rd r
Tlu + pcC usl +

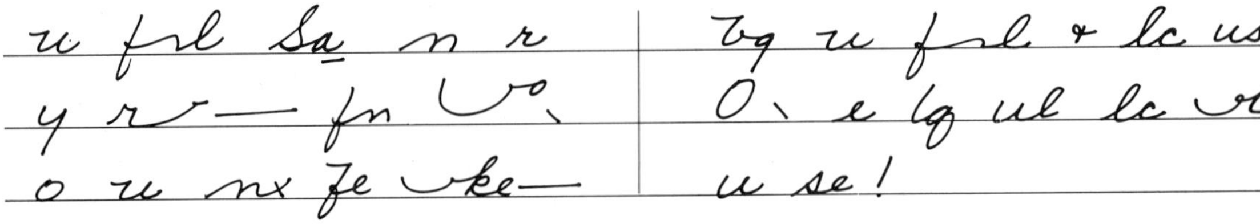

2.1 THEORY REVIEW

1. Medial *vowel-r* 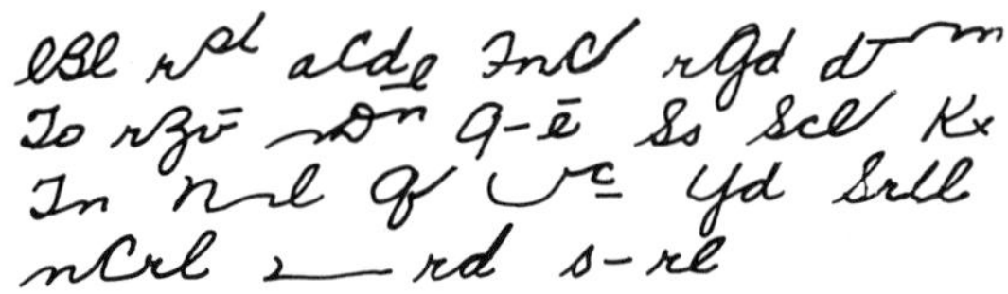

2. Brief forms 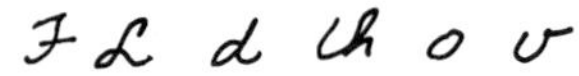

3. Abbreviations 

4. *in* derivations 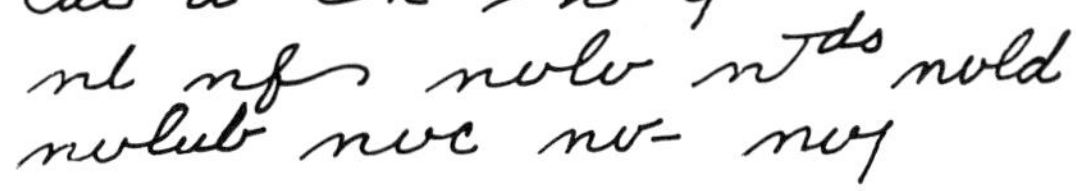

KEY 1. liberally; report; accordingly; furniture; regard; determine; thorough; reserved; modern; guaranteed; source; circular; commercial; turn; normal; quarter; working; yard; shortly; natural; standard; central 2. firm; letter; would; this; on; have, of, very 3. catalog; day; week; month; year 4. into; inform; involve; introduce; invalid; invaluable; invoke; invent; invention

2.2 TRANSCRIPTION SKILL BUILDING

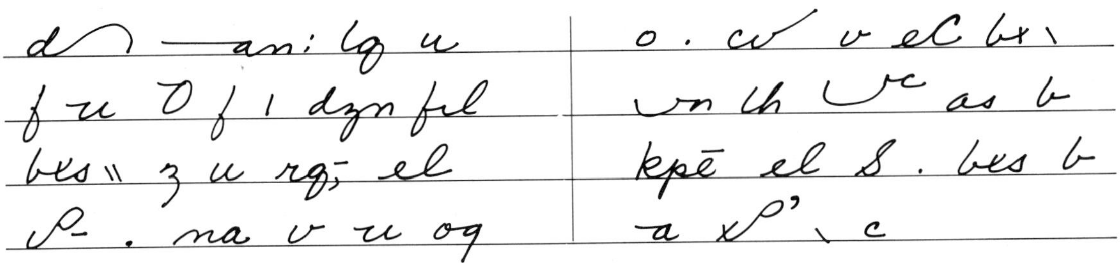

GUIDE Insert two introductory commas.

2.3 SPEED BUILDING

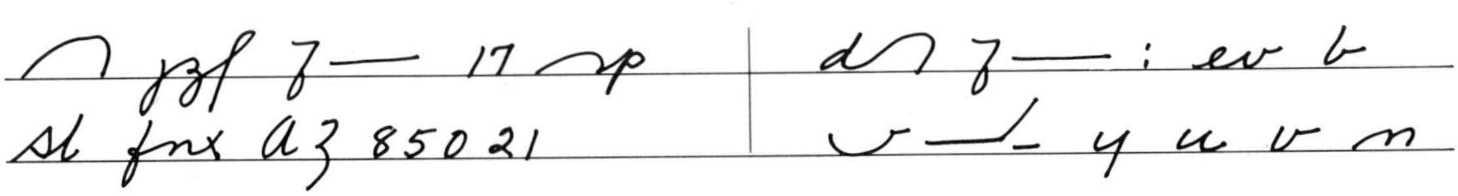

uz u cr Cd rs-l»
s pp sv l Cds 1,
f Twl b acCul ly r
a q kunl n u dl
lf, r sol sa--
l gv u a kpe
rCd v u pCs,
ll u cr Cd
f u, su

2.4 VOCABULARY BUILDING

s rsn dyl 685
hds- pl kgsn MA
01522 ds dyl:
ev sc r hd ksl
pal fC lcl u
& se v u ldsc'
Zqs N, n S—
. sl a cp cga,
pal l So u —sds
v. cpGr——
& s v. acv»
v l, ys cpl»
cp cga as b a
sl ho f bys f
37 ys & er prd
v r rply v of-
.b, v ca lr cpl»
. cp s lcā ne
2 lcs of- xl-
opls f cnu bs
s & fS, ev
—pn hc Tals &
r cpl ofn v.
opl lle cp f a
fuds l —sep ou
n. op, a Lm
frpl ne. m hal
s. gt- pl f oudo
sgs & Nln- v vy
nC» z ul se 7
r —sds e of
al. acv» xpc n

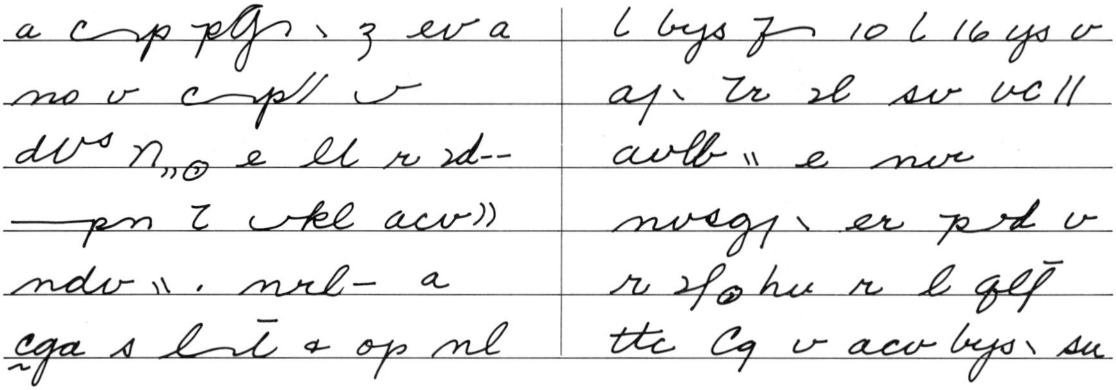

3.1 THEORY REVIEW

1. Initial *combination-r* 
2. Brief forms 
3. Salutations 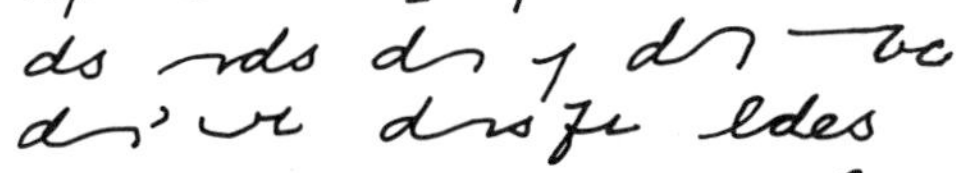
4. *can* derivations 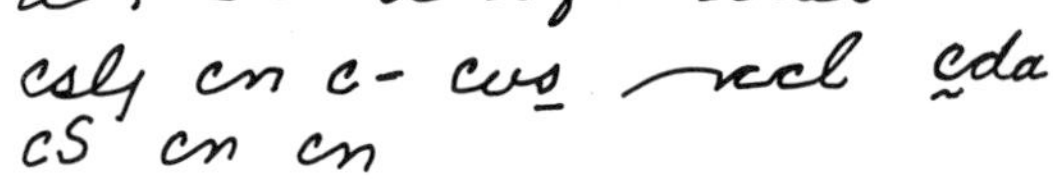

KEY 1. brief; crisis; drawback; erroneously; fragment; grievances; irrational; ordinance; prominent; shrinkage; thrive; troublesome; urgently 2. help; like; be, by, buy, but, been; during; why; ask 3. Dear Sir; My dear Sir; Dear Madam; Gentlemen; Dear Mr. Black; Dear Miss White; Dear Mrs. Fry; Ladies 4. cancellation; cannot; can't; canvassing; mechanical; Canada; canister; canon; canyon

3.2 TRANSCRIPTION SKILL BUILDING

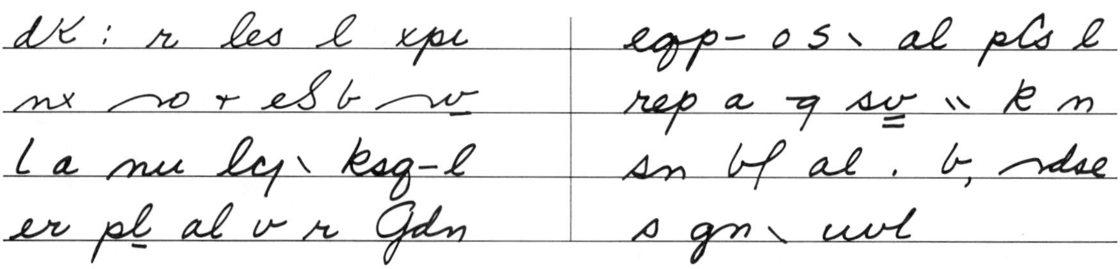

GUIDE Insert one conjunction comma, one introductory comma, and one parenthetical comma.

3.3 SPEED BUILDING

gs lsn 39-38 scro
di Sv LA 71101
d lsn: z a lg l
sub l. S Hld eno
udu n - l '
vn i Su vl ur o
vq" bf u gl nvl
n. pc rS 1, sun
, ofx nlfc f +
l, u ral aD' so
ul n ' i Su " ll
us b rs/b f al,
dlls elhol u bl
ul u r Z u
vq su

3.4 VOCABULARY BUILDING

' rla K// apl 12
snesd 235-618
snesd di l/ mI
48905 d ' K//: er
p l fl r o,
rs- bcll ab Tvl
kdys n zp ec of
u a vru) v Tps
dp o, arl v
l ul v avlb f u
vq" s v r lus
r ba, o vzl 5 f
s)) + 5 apx 3 ds
n eC s) s pp
pf lvzl nl i o
2 f aas + lu
los aas n dll
af esl rzd/ a i
hll lh avyds,
nsl v pc + upc
zlz s v, pbs
v pC d- C//" a
, pz-l cs v,
nyl ekx sul e
fl du) b l
avz r c-- la

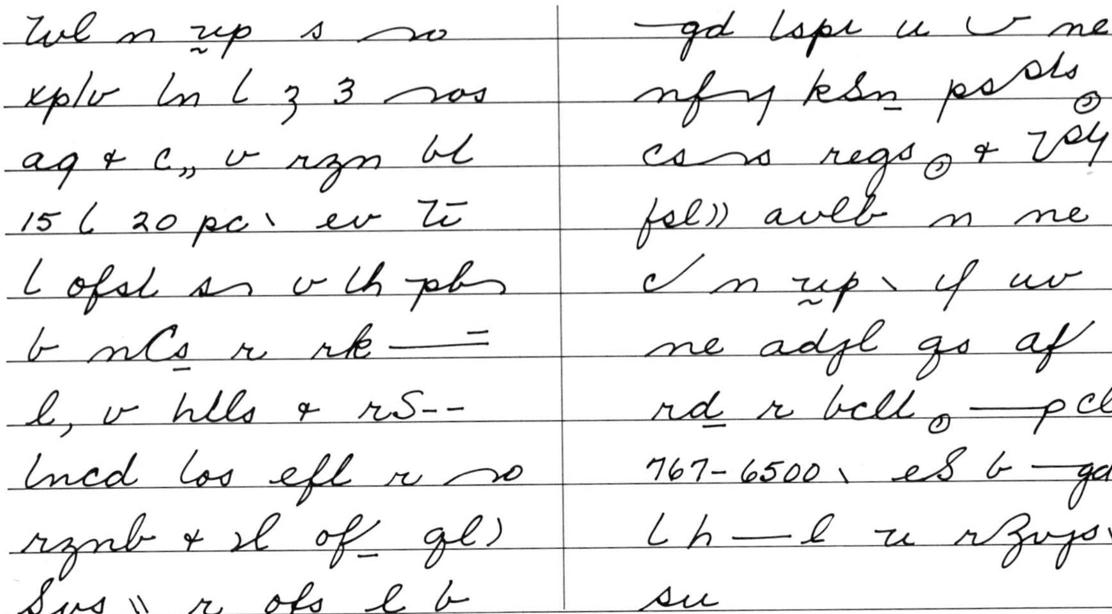

4.1 THEORY REVIEW

1. Final *āte*
2. Final *ēet*
3. Final *īte*
4. Final *ōte*
5. Final *ūte*
6. Brief forms
7. Abbreviations

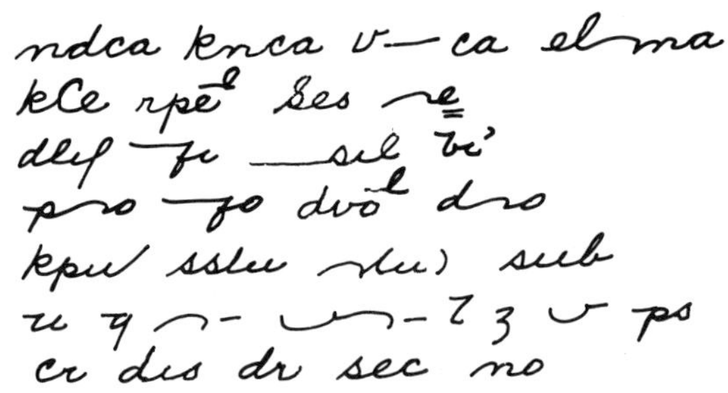

KEY 1. indicate; communicate; vindicate; eliminate 2. concrete; repeatedly; sheets; meetings 3. delightful; flight; slightly; brightness 4. promote; float; devotedly; demote 5. computer; substitute; maturity; suitable 6. your; great; man; woman; their, there; as, was; with, were; price 7. credit; discount; doctor; secretary, second; number

4.2 TRANSCRIPTION SKILL BUILDING

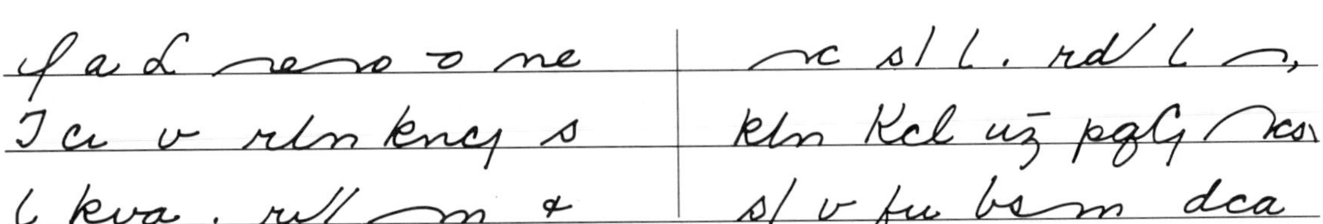

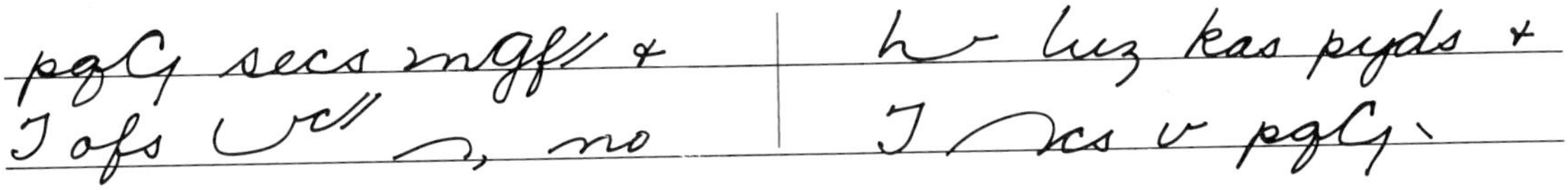

GUIDE Insert two introductory commas, six series commas, and one possessive apostrophe.

4.3 SPEED BUILDING

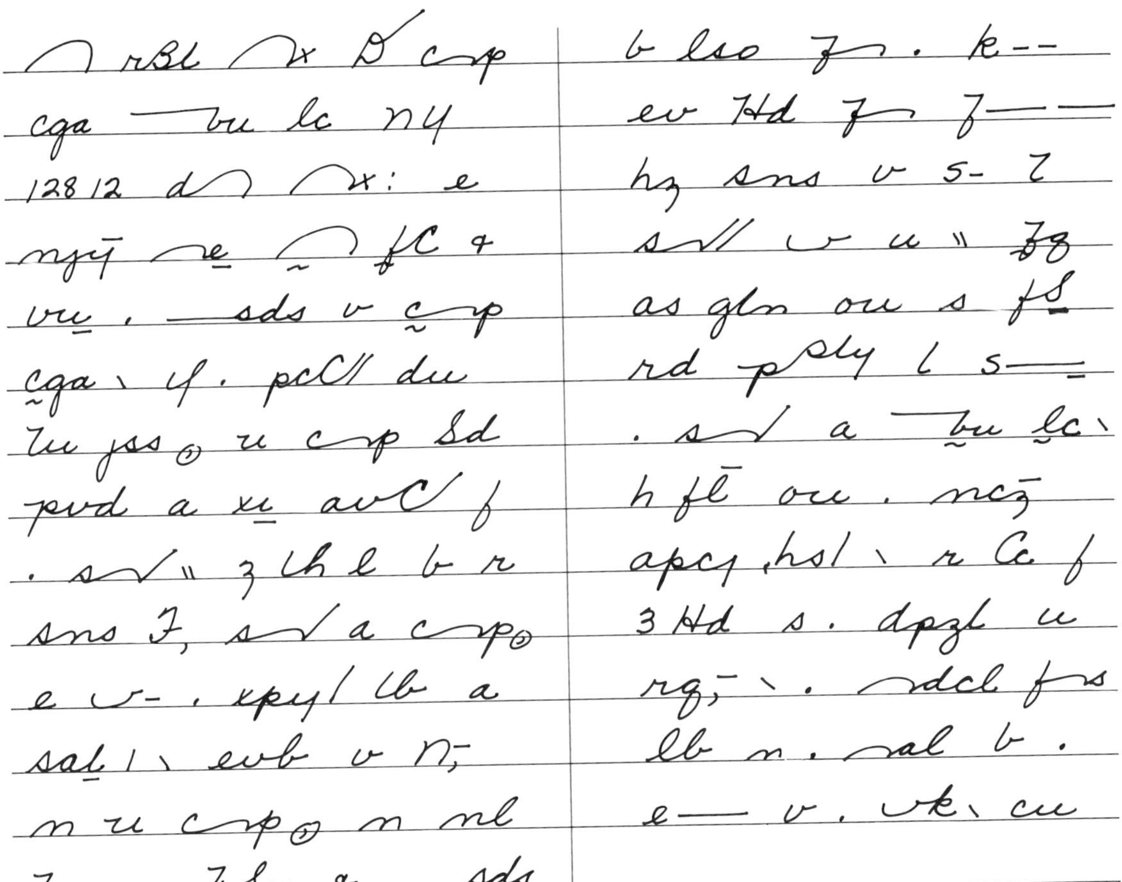

4.4 VOCABULARY BUILDING

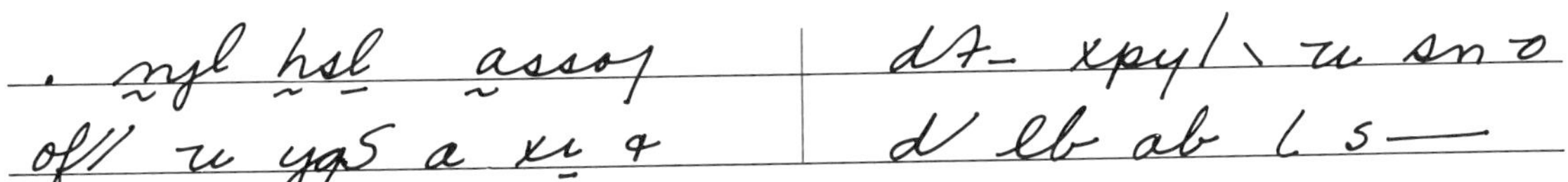

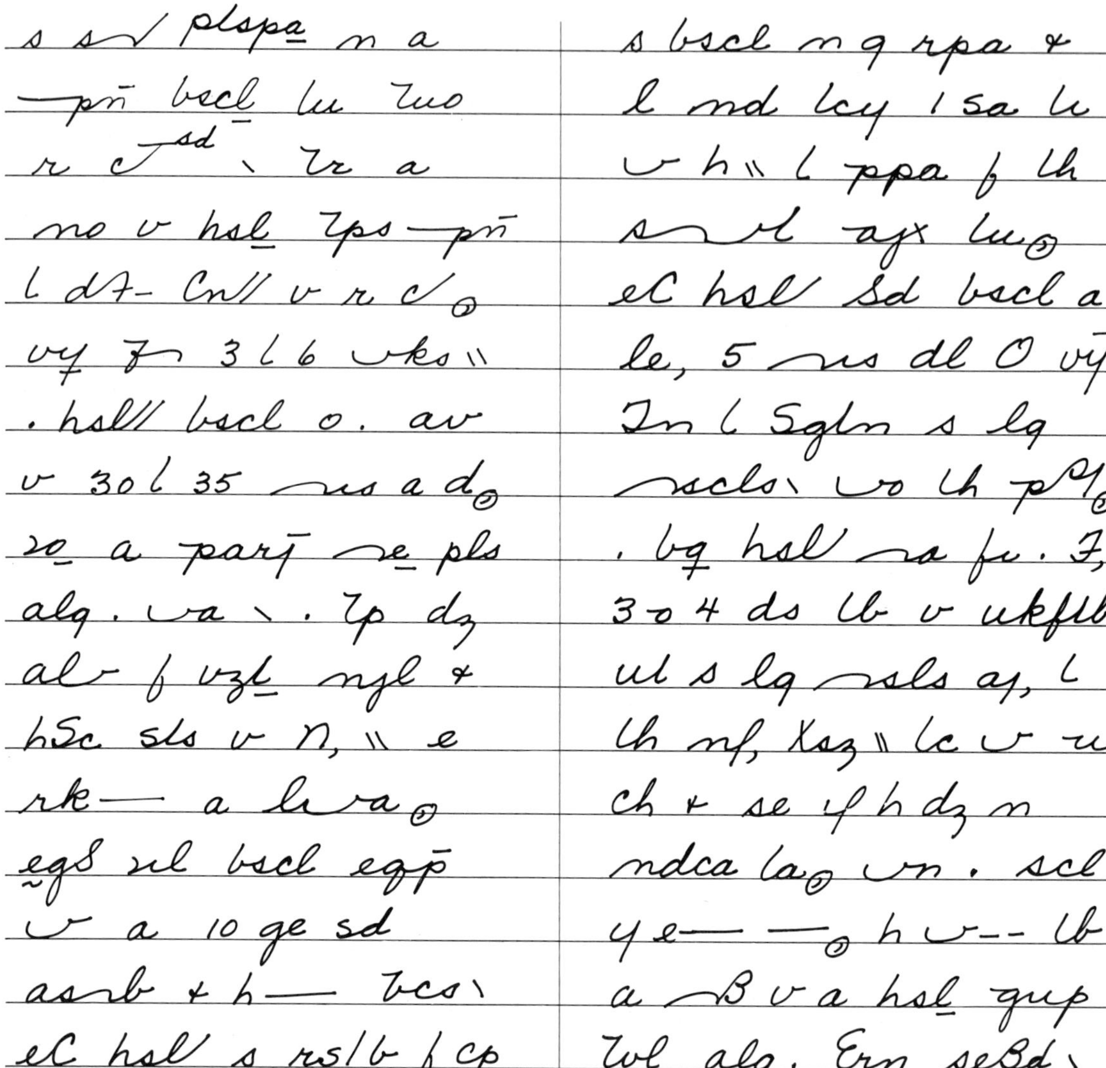

5.1 THEORY REVIEW

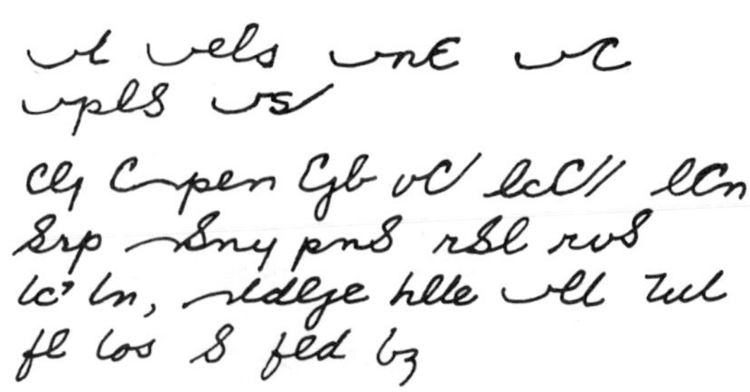

1. *wh*
2. *ch*
3. *sh*
4. *th*
5. Brief forms

6. Compound words

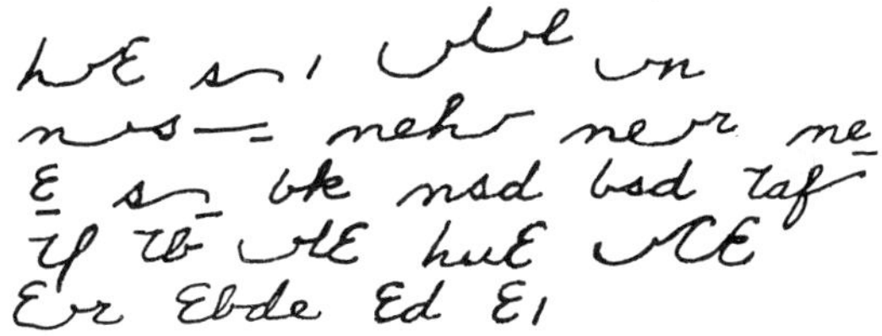

KEY 1. what; wheels; whenever; which; whiplash; whisper 2. challenge; champion; changeable; venture; lectures; luncheon 3. sharp; machinery; punish; rashly; ravish 4. thickness; thinnest; methodology; healthy; wealth; truth 5. fail, feel; those; she, shall, ship; field; busy 6. however; someone; worthwhile; within; notwithstanding; anyhow; anywhere; anything; everything; something; became; inside; beside; thereafter; therefore; thereby; whatever; whoever; whichever; everywhere; everybody; everyday; everyone

5.2 TRANSCRIPTION SKILL BUILDING

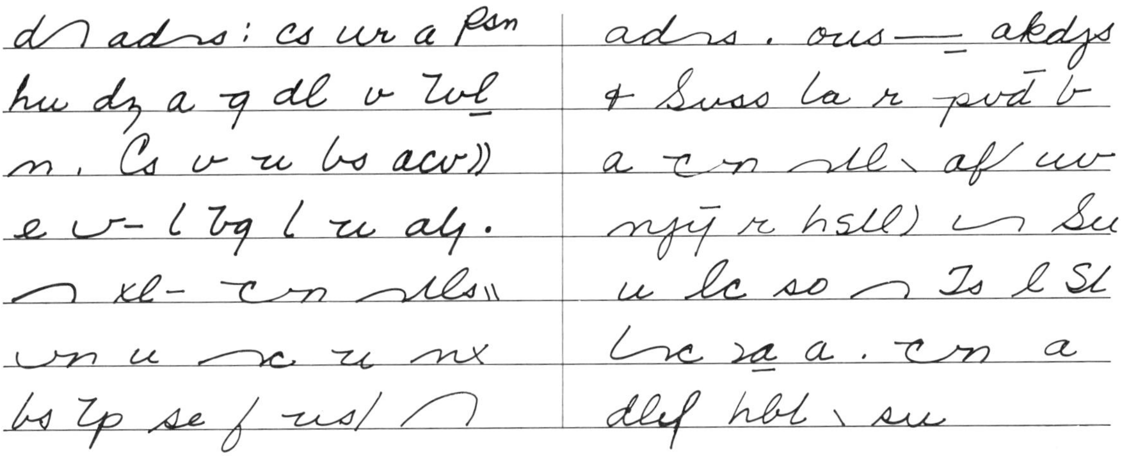

GUIDE Insert three introductory commas and four parenthetical commas.

5.3 SPEED BUILDING

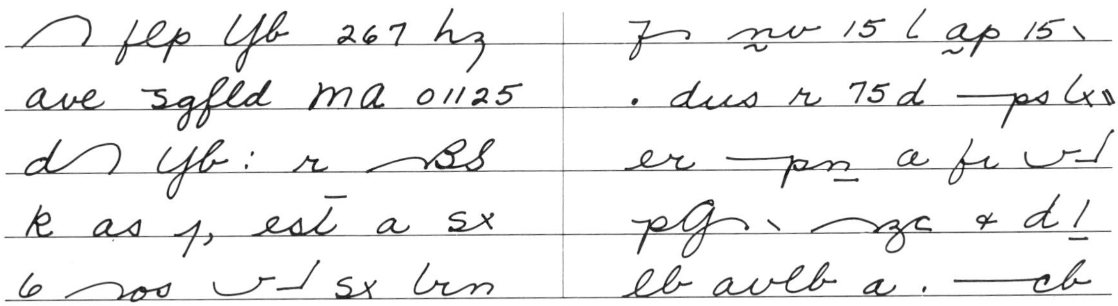

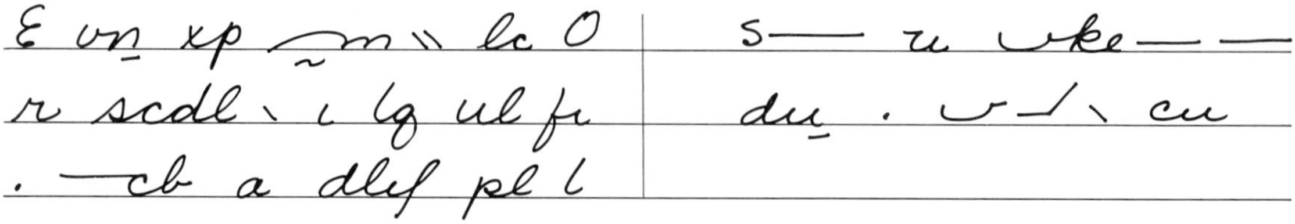

5.4 VOCABULARY BUILDING

(A)

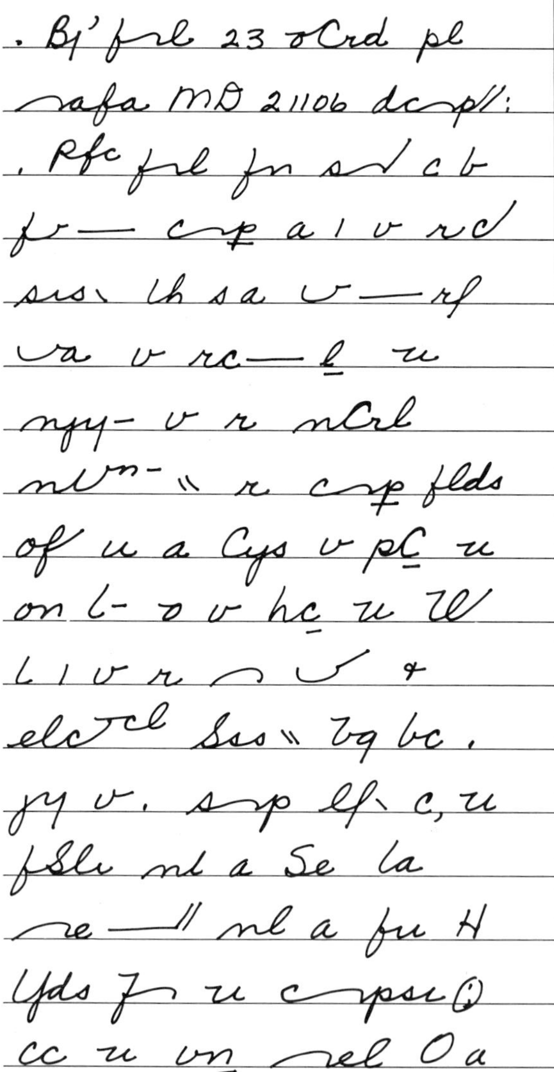

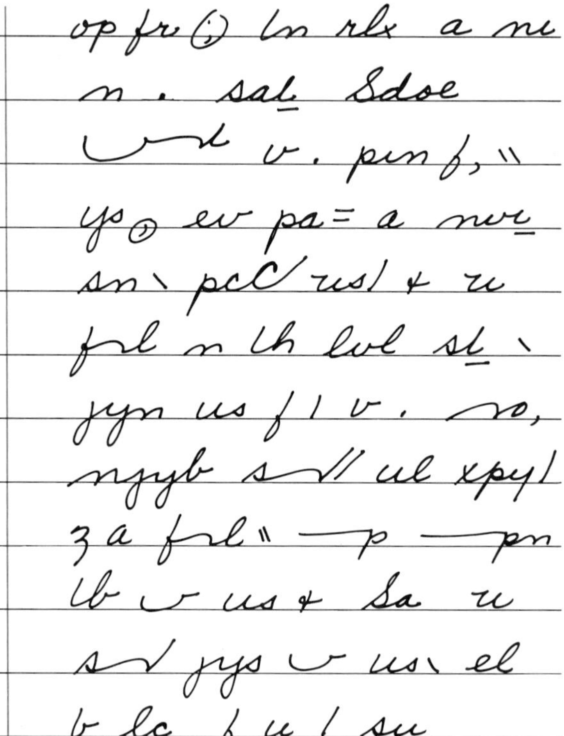

(B)

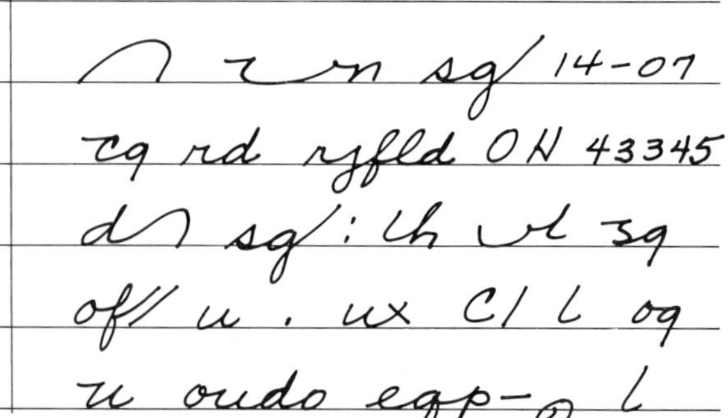

—pn u nec pCs.
l Cg l. & lw l
dē ɩda, n lh ra.
ul b ppā f. F, fu
ke— n lh
rne sl s O" rlfs
St gs S c spu u
fu gl). ullyn
gs C Sd l, f ys
U Nsl sls & usj,
f xp. r nln l--

r dzin zp
— os & do fps
C c b gcl sel̄
l plc u Fs. E--,
lz l-- r bu oj &
ezl nlsb n. dep
ds" 2de r Xo
sans, ev Hs v
req lns la l
ad l u fC q ls,
uc

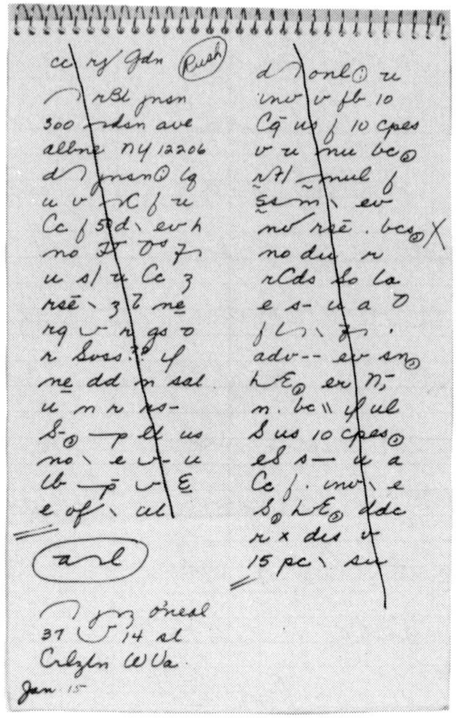

TAKING DICTATION

Don't make corrections until after you have finished taking dictation. The dictator will not wait for you, and taking time to cross out and rewrite can leave you hopelessly behind. Write something for everything that is dictated. For unfamiliar words, try to write all of the sounds you hear. If you can't, try to write the beginning sound, and the context of the material will help you fill in the correct word. If you're unable to write anything, leave a blank space and continue writing. Often the context alone will enable you to supply an acceptable word.

UNIT 2

PHOTOGRAPHY

1.1 THEORY REVIEW

1. Final *ed*
2. Final *ing*
3. Final *thing*
4. Brief forms
5. Abbreviations
6. *self* derivatives

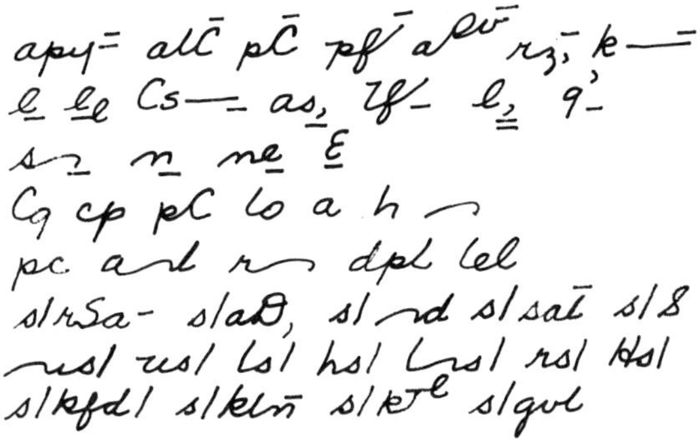

KEY 1. appointed; attached; purchased; preferred; approved; resisted; commanded 2. willing; willingly; corresponding; assisting; transferring; listings; guessing 3. something; nothing; anything; everything 4. charge; keep; purchase; too, thought; at, an; he, had, him; am, many 5. percent; amount; room; department; telephone 6. self-restraint; self-addressed; self-made; self-satisfied; selfishness; myself; yourself; itself; himself; themselves; ourselves; herself; self-confidence; self-contained; self-control; self-government

1.2 TRANSCRIPTION SKILL BUILDING

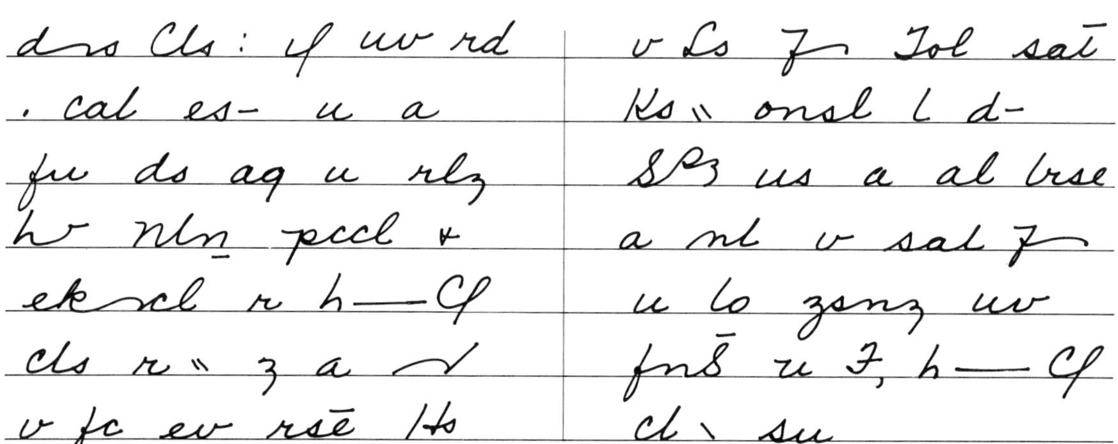

GUIDE Insert three introductory commas, two series commas, two parenthetical commas, and one contraction apostrophe.

1.3 SPEED BUILDING

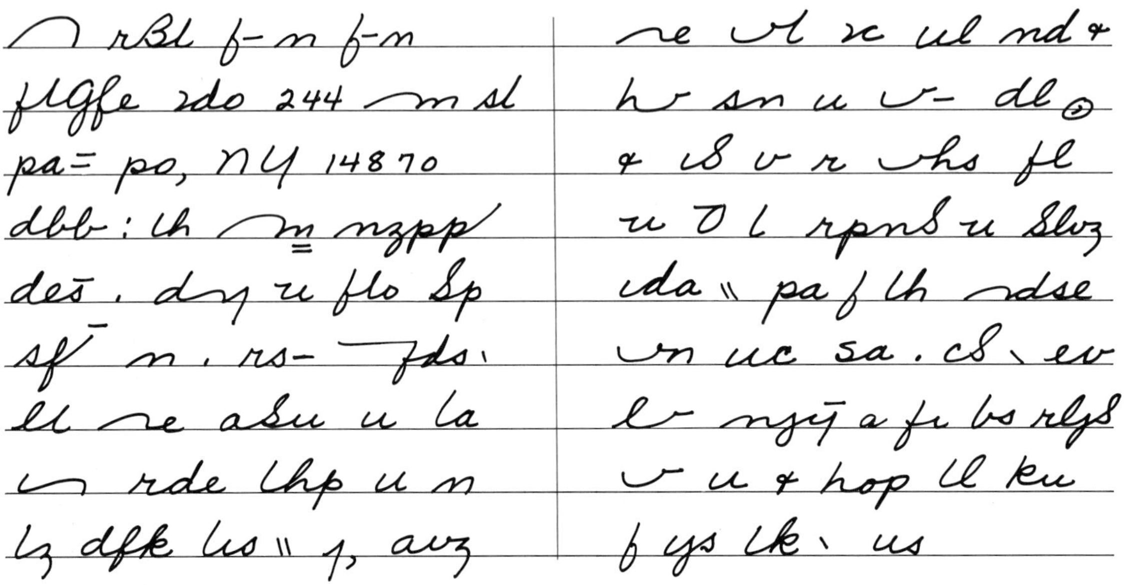

1.4 VOCABULARY BUILDING

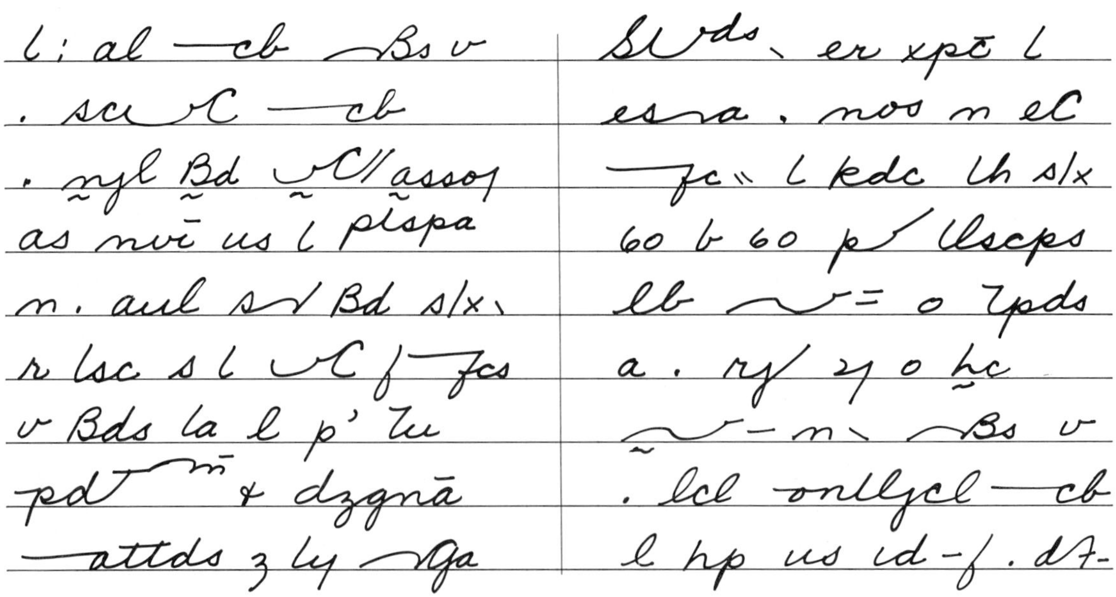

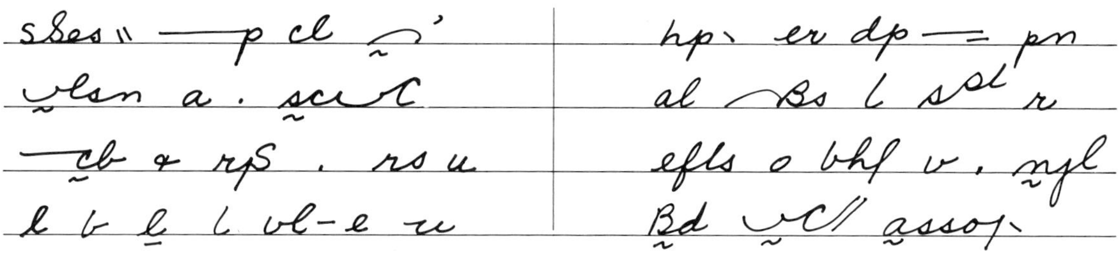

2.1 THEORY REVIEW

1. Final *ss*
2. Final *ness*
3. Final *ssness*
4. Brief forms
5. Abbreviations
6. *over* derivatives

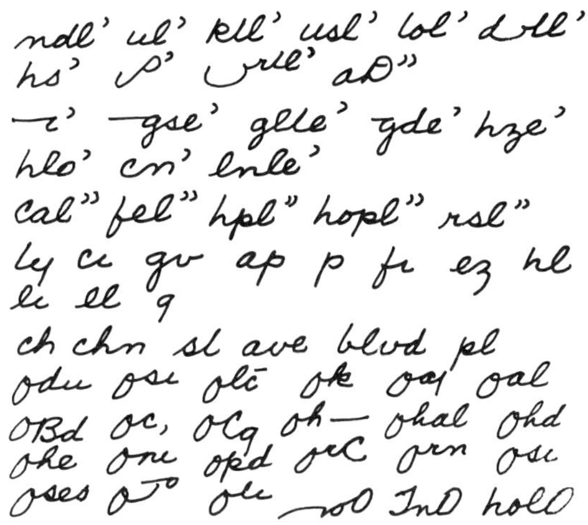

KEY 1. needless; unless; countless; useless; thoughtless; doubtless; hostess; impress; worthless; addresses 2. illness; glossiness; guiltiness; greediness; haziness; hollowness; keenness; loneliness 3. carelessness; fearlessness; helplessness; hopelessness; restlessness 4. they; kind; given; appreciate; put, up; fine, find; easy; held; line; little; go, good 5. child; children; street; avenue; boulevard; place 6. overdue; oversight; overlooked; overcome; overage; overall; overboard; overcast; overcharge; overhand; overhaul; overhead; overhear; overnight; overpaid; overreach; overrun; oversight; overseas; overthrow; overtime; moreover; turnover; holdover

2.2 TRANSCRIPTION SKILL BUILDING

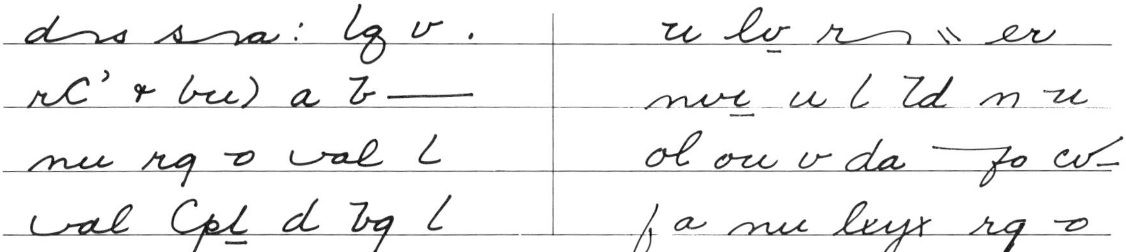

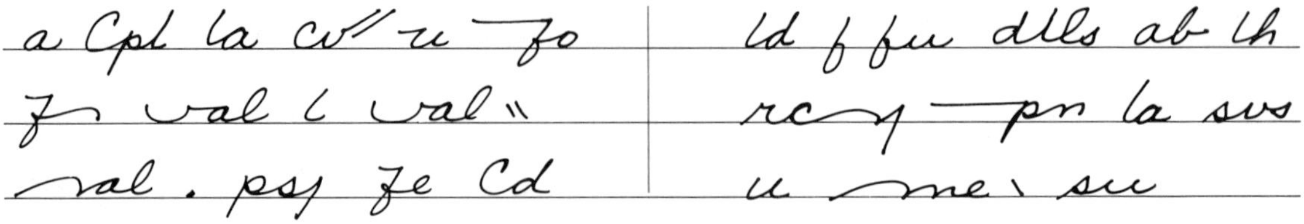

GUIDE Insert five compound adjective hyphens and two adjective commas.

2.3 SPEED BUILDING

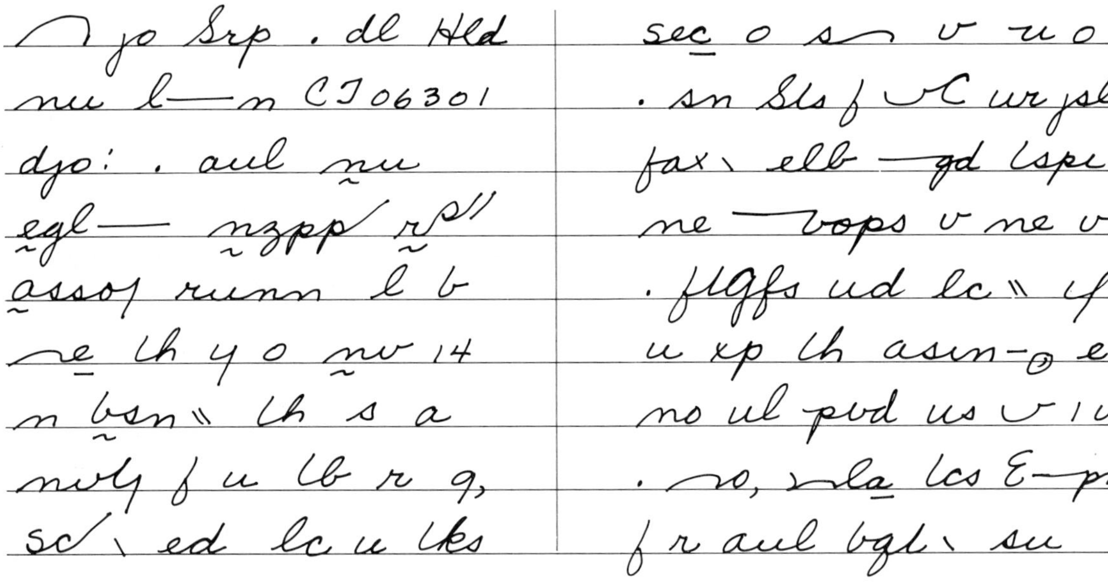

2.4 VOCABULARY BUILDING

(A)

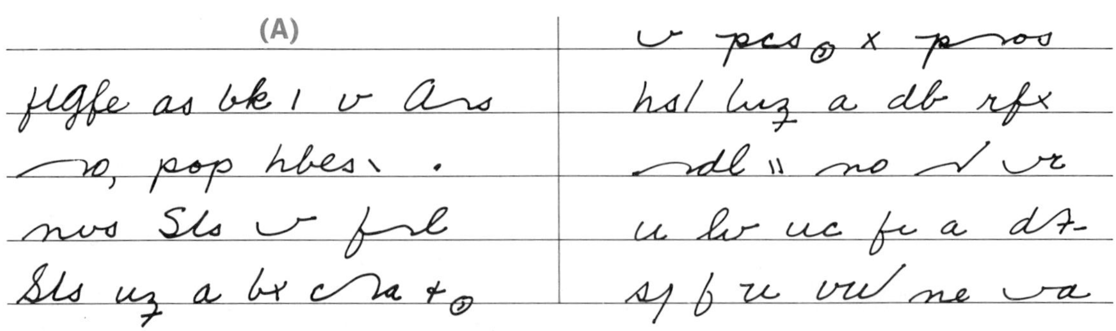

u In, du u lv n
. s)? lr n x xu
sys avlb, f xpo uc
Su sCy n ze
Gdns chn a pa
pp n al pzs Ss b
uld a sp f-n
n a Pc o u u
sl a Ggyl PC o a
rflp, eC G v szn
lgs a nu sn lb
cl b . c a, . l,
v sys s e—l'"
rs l sp b z
u sde u flos l
d h l sv
u flGfc lcnc, u
pcC// l dle u, v
nys"

(B)

s pal gas 278 aDsn
ave onela NY 13820
ds gas: r u St l

pn u hld gf l,?
r u SC u u
f. gf la s d7-? r
u Tu l avyd . x? d
u lc l S s, sx
v a yl pa= v s
fVl flGf?? ec slv
u gf pb f u, er
. ojna// v pa= 7
pcC//, ec pds rC
go yl pa= 7 a
fVl pcC, . ld s
gi sp b s lu ksu"
e c a nDj dpcl
v u pcC, . oul v
. sj s pjc nl
lC cvslc ylj,
ln r scl al" api
yl pa- l lh oul,
. l v . cl// v
. rnbo lq u fVl
pcC l lf" kl
r sdo + ll us So

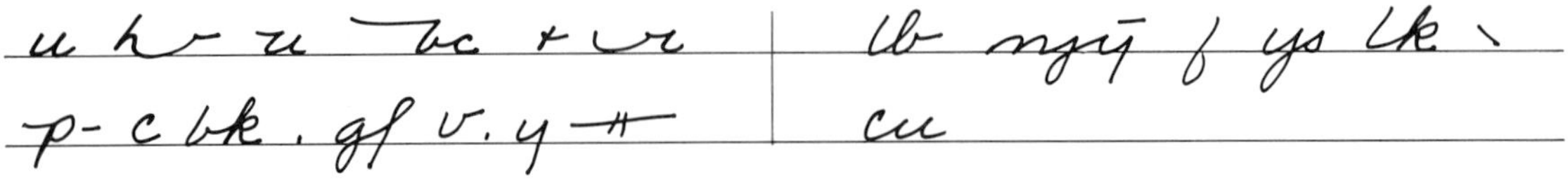

3.1 THEORY REVIEW

1. *oi*
2. *ow*
3. *kw*
4. *nk*
5. Brief forms
6. Days of week
7. Months of year
8. *ship* derivatives

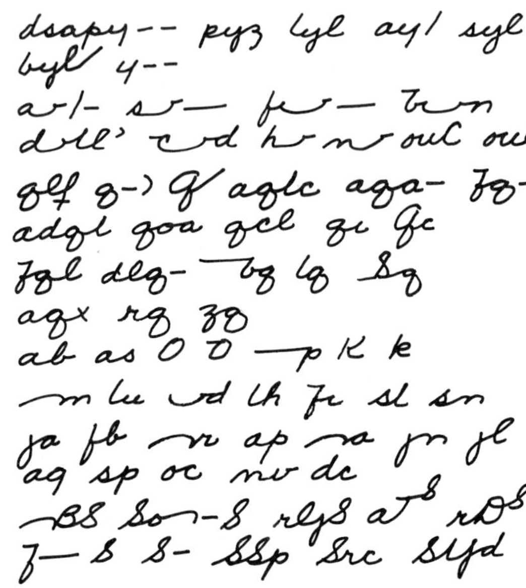

KEY 1. disappointment; poise; toil; annoyance; soil; boiler; ointment 2. announcement; sound; found; brown; doubtless; crowd; how; now; ouch; owl 3. qualifying; quantity; quarter; aquatic; acquaint; frequent; adequate; quota; quickly; quite; quirk 4. frankly; delinquent; blank; think, thank; shrink; anxious; rank; zinc 5. about; has; over; order; please; customer; come, came, committee 6. Monday; Tuesday; Wednesday; Thursday; Friday; Saturday; Sunday 7. January; February; March; April; May; June; July; August; September; October; November; December 8. membership; showmanship; relationship; authorship; readership; friendship; shipment; shipshape; shipwreck; shipyard

3.2 TRANSCRIPTION SKILL BUILDING

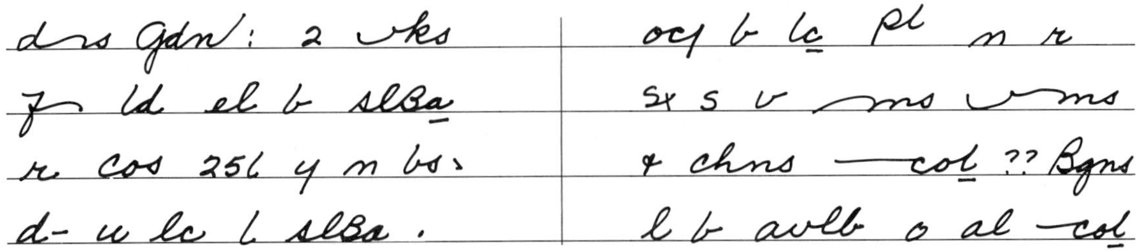

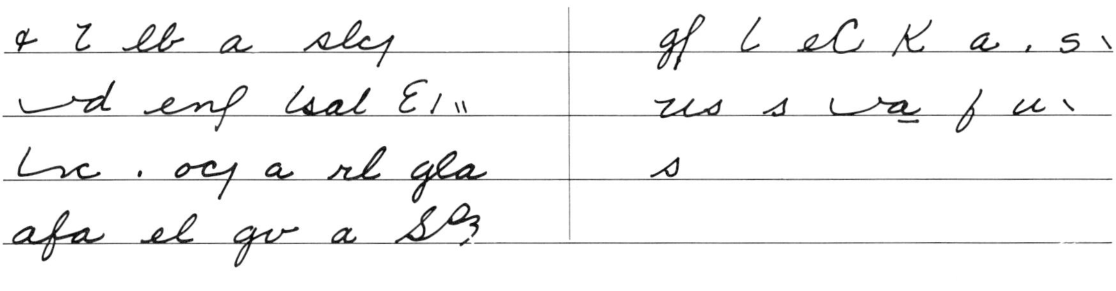

GUIDE Insert four possessive apostrophes, one contraction apostrophe, two series commas, one conjunction comma, and one introductory comma.

3.3 SPEED BUILDING

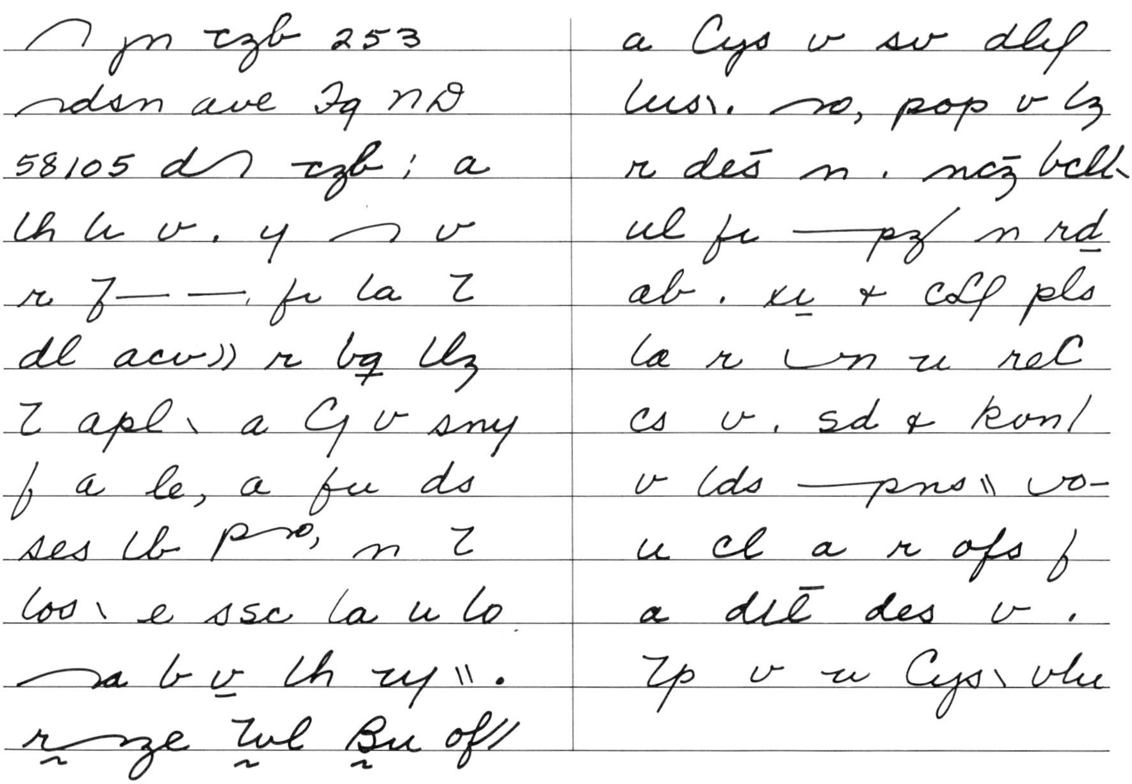

3.4 VOCABULARY BUILDING

(A)

(B)

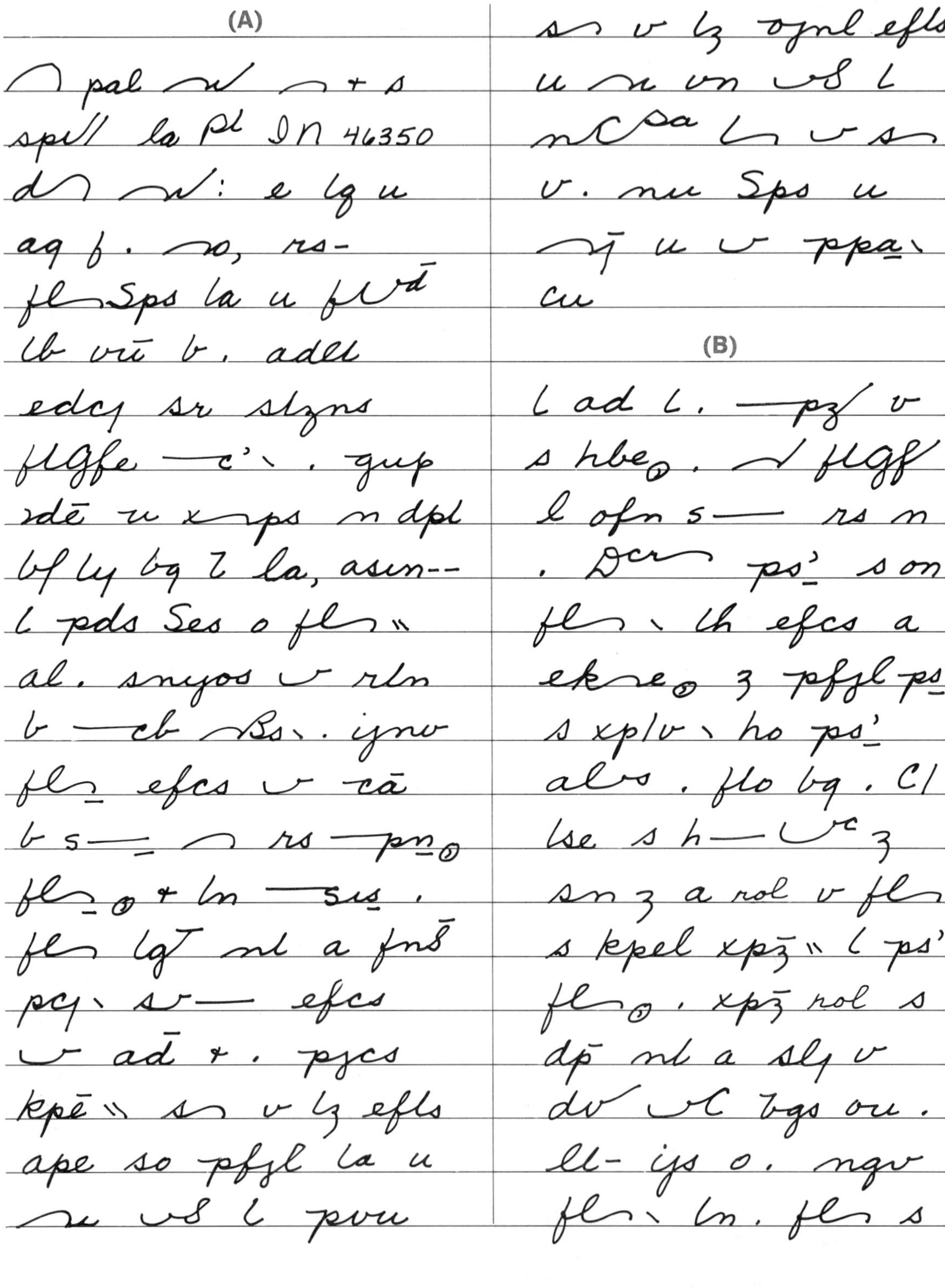

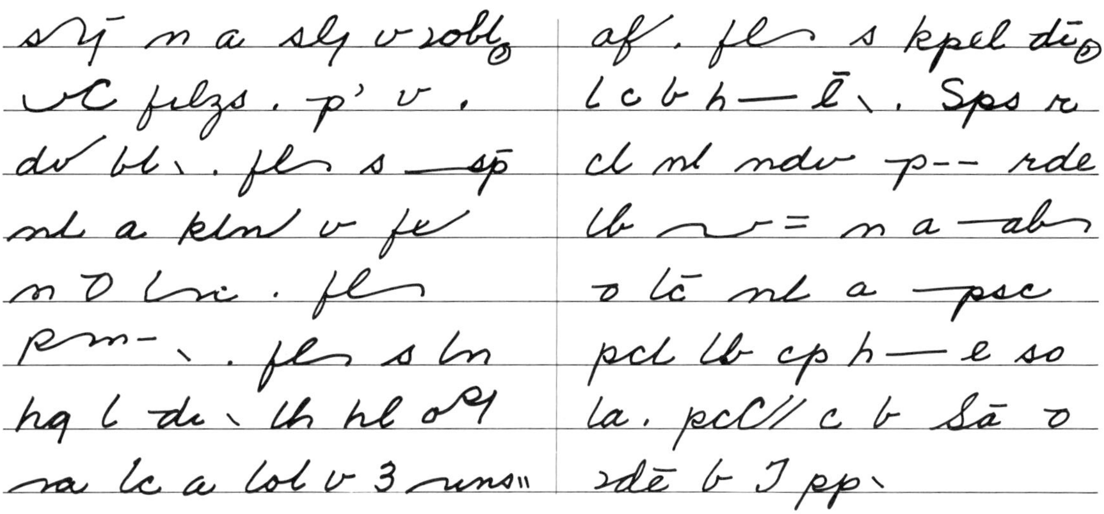

4.1 THEORY REVIEW

1. Final *āve*
2. Final *ēve*
3. Final *īve*
4. Final *ōve*
5. Final *ūve*
6. Brief forms
7. Abbreviations
8. *out* derivatives

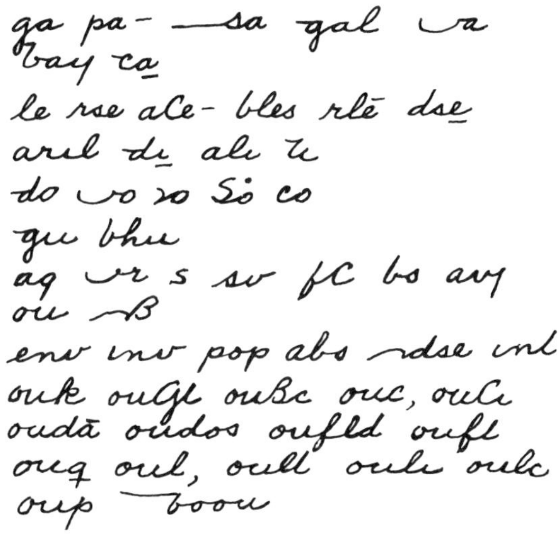

KEY 1. gave; pavement; slave; gravely; wave; bravery; craving 2. leave; receive; achievement; believes; relieved; deceiving 3. arrival; driving; alive; thrive 4. drove; wove; stove; strove; cove 5. groove; behoove 6. again, against; where; sale; save; future; business; advantage; out; member 7. envelope; invoice; popular; absolute, absolutely; merchandise; intelligent, intelligence, intelligently 8. outcome; outgrowth; outbreak; outcast; outcry; outdated; outdoors; outfield; outfit; outgoing; outlast; outlet; outline; outlook; output; blowout

4.2 TRANSCRIPTION SKILL BUILDING

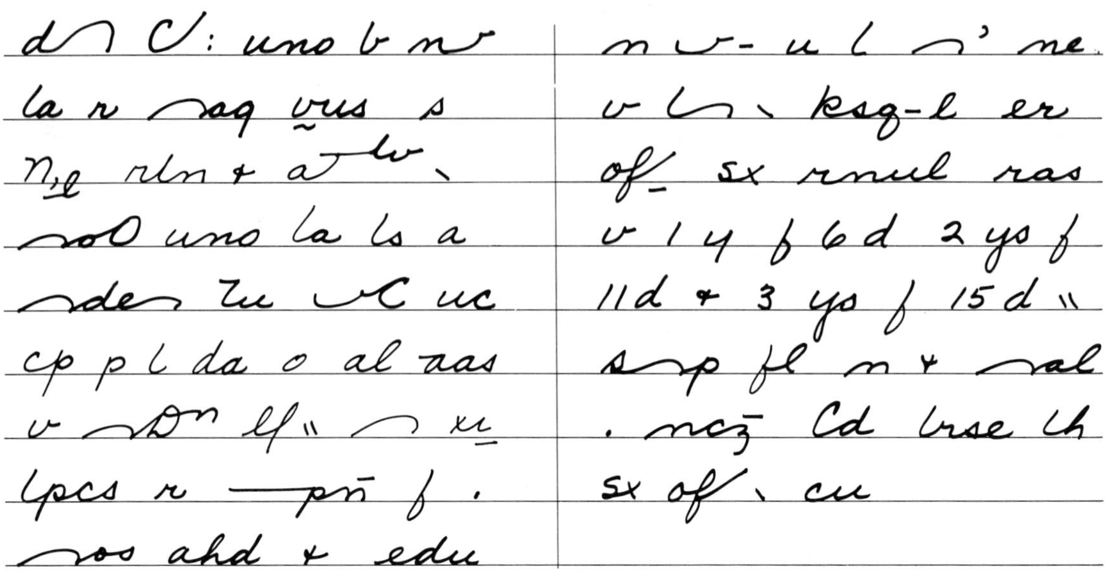

GUIDE Insert two apposition commas, one conjunction comma, two introductory commas, and two series commas.

4.3 SPEED BUILDING

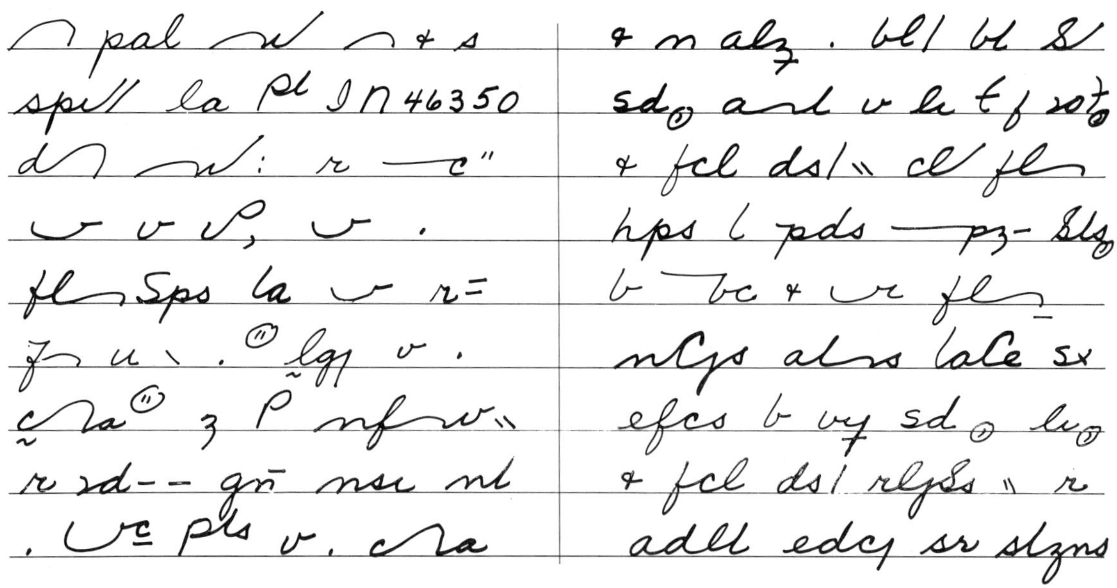

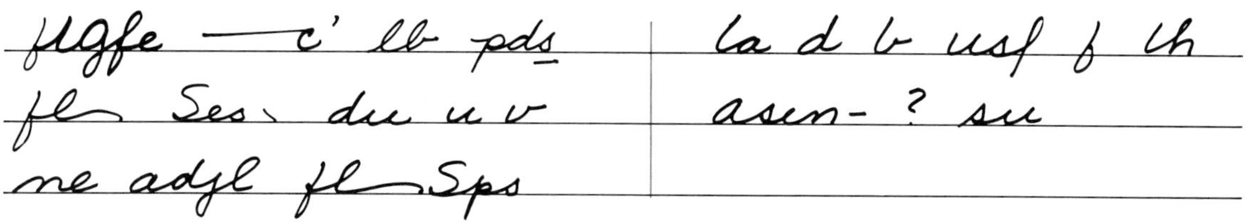

4.4 VOCABULARY BUILDING

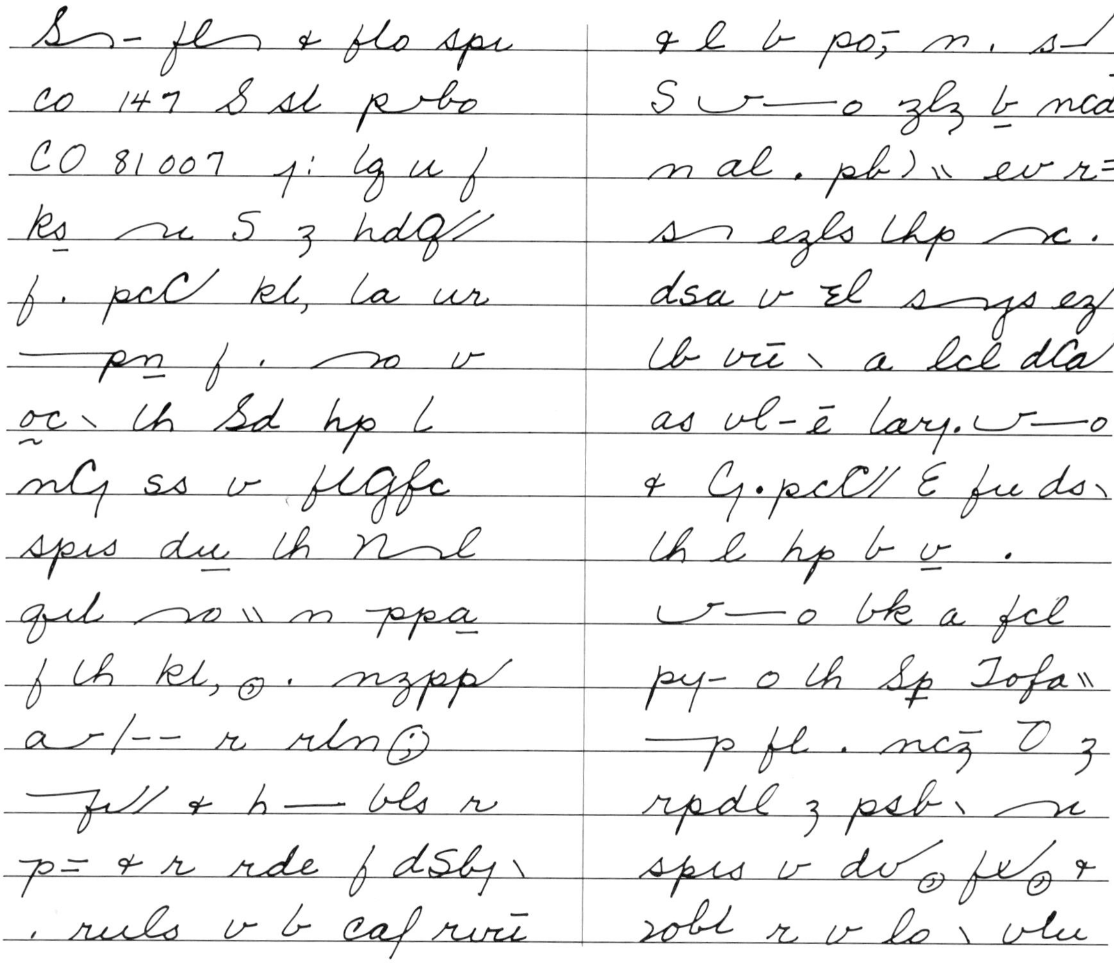

5.1 THEORY REVIEW

1. Medial and final *nd* 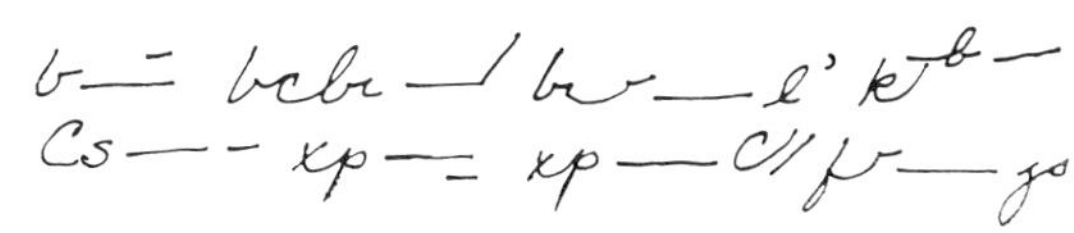

2. Final *tee*

3. *nse*

4. *nsy*

5. Brief forms

6. *up* derivatives

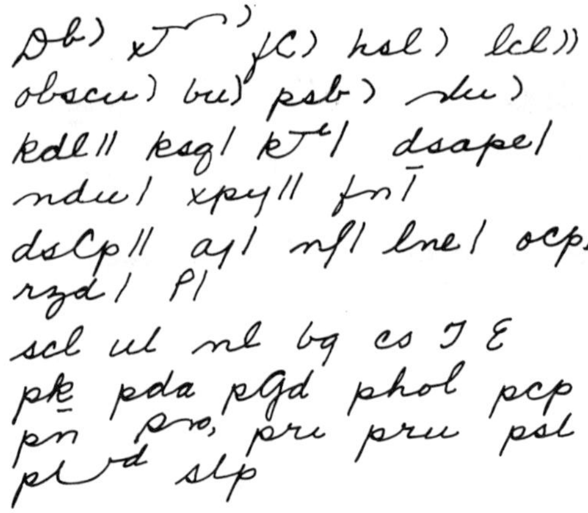

KEY 1. bonded; bookbinder; boundless; contraband; correspondent; expanding; expenditures; foundations 2. durability; extremity; futurity; hostility; localities; obscurity; beauty; possibility; maturity 3. condolences; consequence; contrivance; disappearance; endurance; experiences; financed 4. discrepancies; agency; infancy; leniency; occupancy; residency; presidency 5. school; until; only; begin, began; because; other; ever, every 6. upcoming; update; upgrade; uphold; upkeep; upon; uppermost; upright; uproot; upset; upward; setup

5.2 TRANSCRIPTION SKILL BUILDING

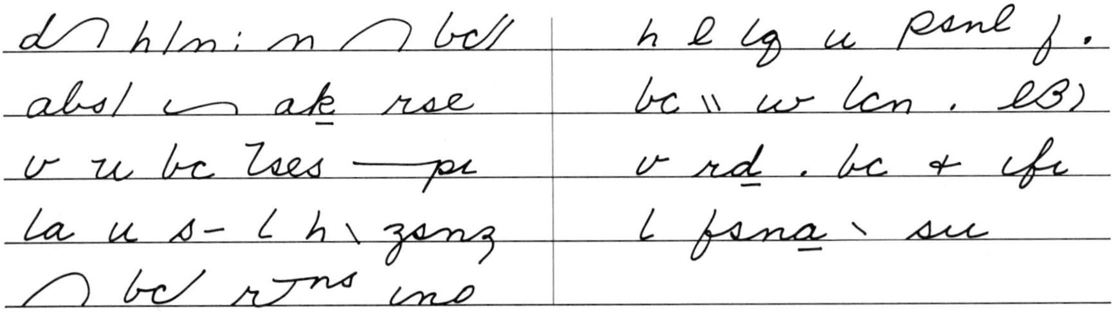

GUIDE Insert two possessive apostrophes, two apposition commas, two introductory commas, and one conjunction comma.

5.3 SPEED BUILDING

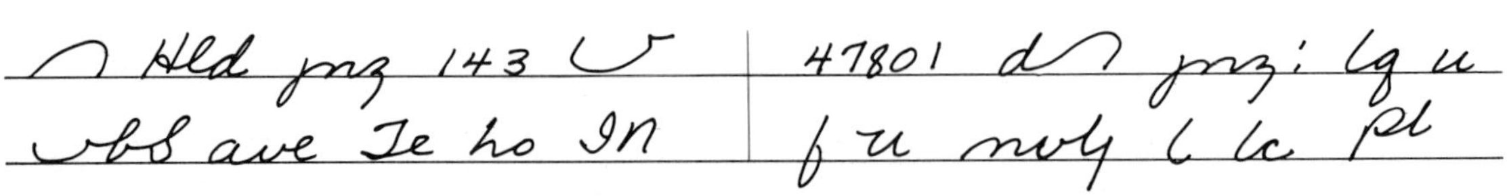

n u kTl o flGfe. (c) hpe l xp⊙ b iS n b ab lgv u a dfn da ul nx so|| ic dfn sa

la il k o eT fn 20 o ag 2. il ru u ag zsnz (c) ab ttl u (c)C da s psb. su

5.4 VOCABULARY BUILDING

. nu s) flGf// —cb s —p l a-/ la U sV ls 15l aul flGfe kl, . kl, s op l ne/ hu (c)Ss l sd nTes|| eC r/S- lb gv a kls- no⊙ + h sa r/S pl 7 nTes|| —bc + (c)r nTes l b jT s Sll Fn cl/ p--. al nTes l b clGz U

-y hd sC z sl lfs⊙ chn⊙ pp⊙ als⊙ aclC/⊙ l— scps⊙ o sescps|| al nTes -, b rsē b vd⊙ fn 14⊙ a nn. ly l b p o dsa f pb vu a . —cb bld o oCrd sl|| pzs + rbns l b al/d o sl⊙ fn 17⊙ bl 3+5 p||

BUILDING YOUR SPEED

If you always take dictation at speeds that you can write easily, you will make little progress. To build your speed, you must push yourself to practice dictation at speeds beyond the rate you are now writing.

When you find yourself getting behind, hang on as long as you can. The dictator may pause or there may be an easy spot in the dictation enabling you to catch up.

If you fall so far behind that you can't possibly catch up, forget what has not been written and pick up the dictation again.

Never stop writing!

UNIT 3

COMMUNICATIONS

1.1 THEORY REVIEW

1. *āne*
2. *ēen*
3. *īne*
4. *ōwn*
5. *ūne*
6. Brief forms
7. *time* derivatives

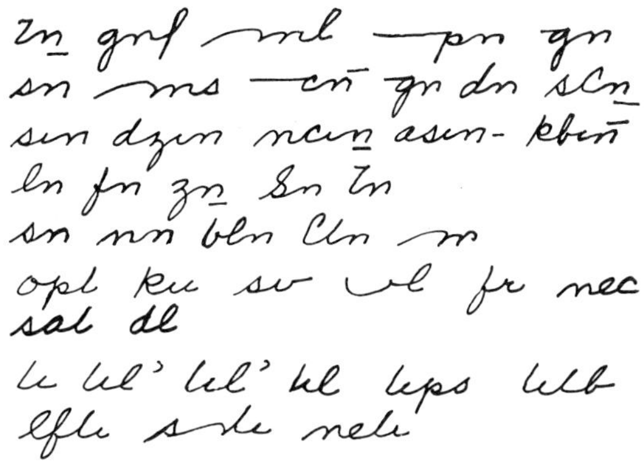

KEY 1. training; gainful; mainly; plane; grain 2. seen; means; cleaned; green; dean; screening 3. sign; design; inclining; assignment; combined 4. loan; phone; zoning; shown; throne 5. soon; noon; balloon; cartoon; moon 6. opportunity; continue; several; while; fire; necessary, necessarily; satisfy, satisfaction, satisfactory; deal, deliver, delivery 7. time; timeless; timeliness; timely; timepiece; timetable; lifetime; sometime; anytime

1.2 TRANSCRIPTION SKILL BUILDING

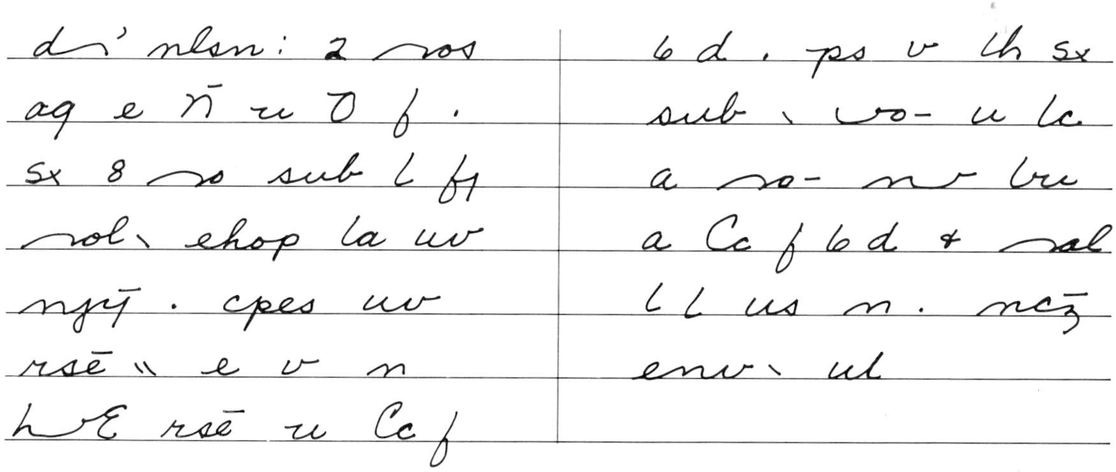

GUIDE Insert one compound adjective hyphen, three parenthetical commas, and one contraction apostrophe.

1.3 SPEED BUILDING

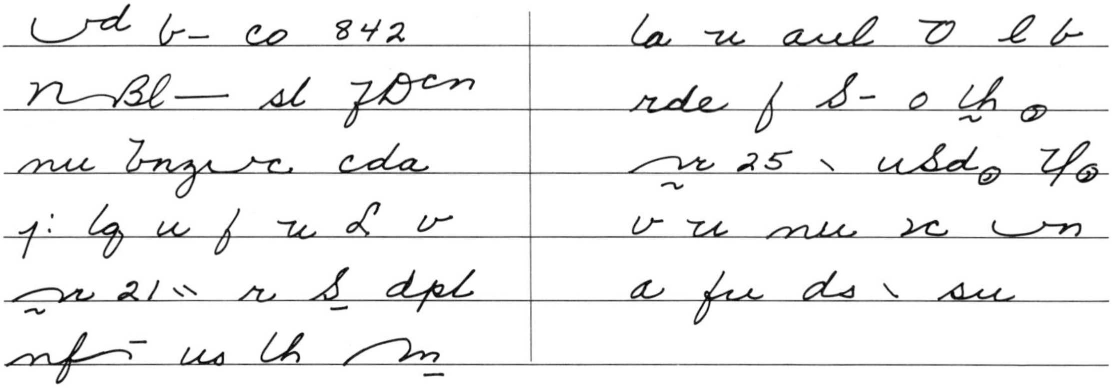

1.4 VOCABULARY BUILDING

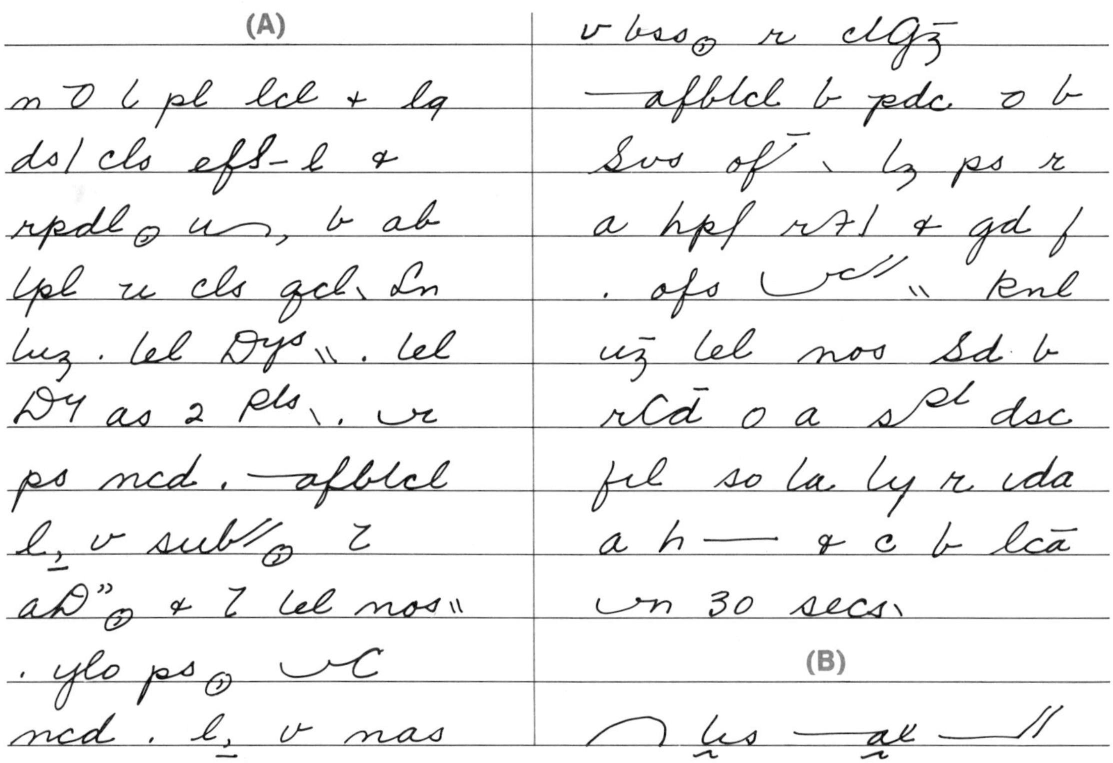

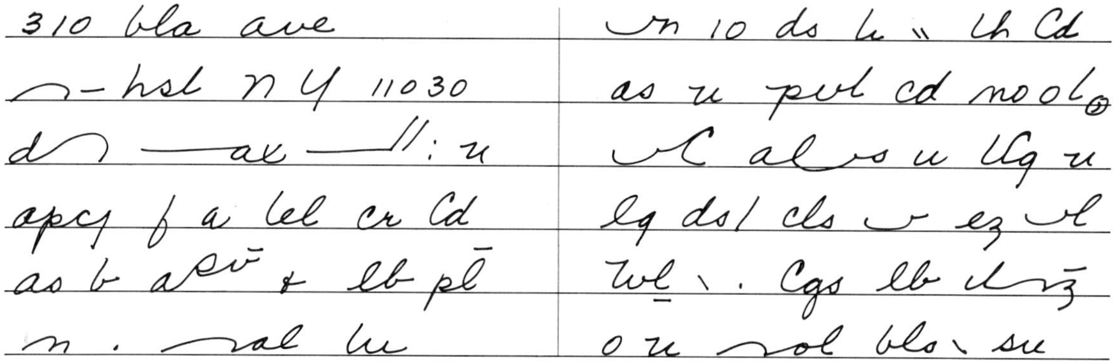

2.1 THEORY REVIEW

1. Initial vowels
2. Final vowels
3. Brief forms
4. Abbreviations
5. *home* derivatives

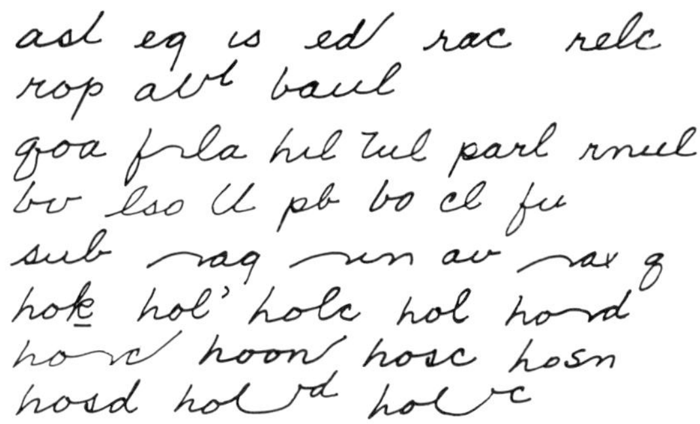

KEY 1. asset; ego; ice; editor; react; reelect; reopen; avert; biannual 2. quota; formula; highly; truly; payroll; renewal 3. above; also; under; public, publish; both; call; full, fully 4. subscribe, subscription; magazine; minimum; average; maximum; question 5. homecoming; homeless; homelike; homely; homemade; homemaker; homeowner; homesick; homespun; homestead; homeward; homework

2.2 TRANSCRIPTION SKILL BUILDING

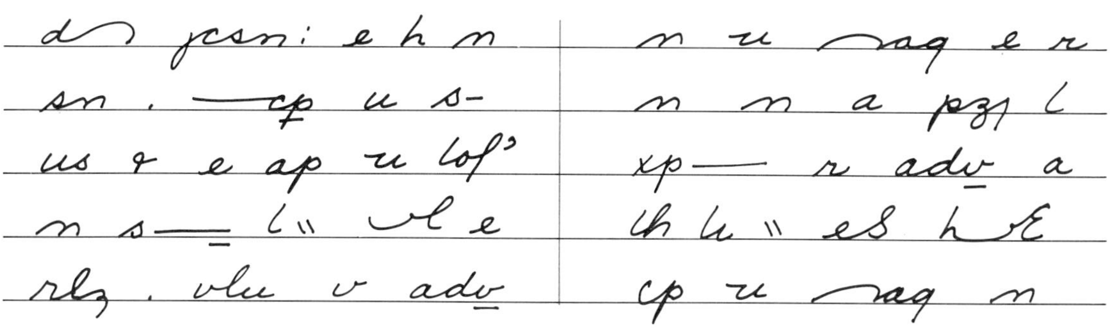

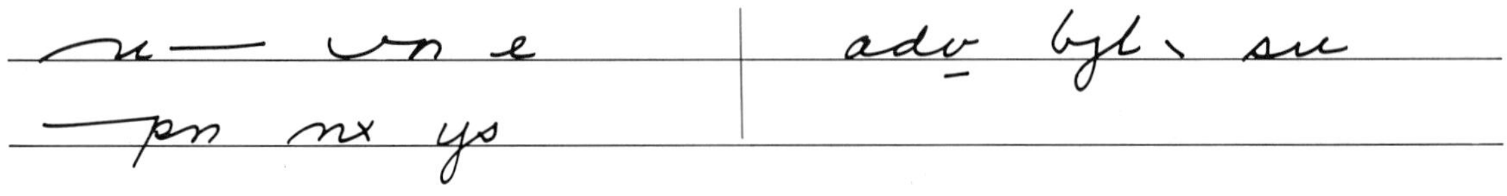

GUIDE Insert one conjunction comma, one introductory comma, two parenthetical commas, and one possessive apostrophe.

2.3 SPEED BUILDING

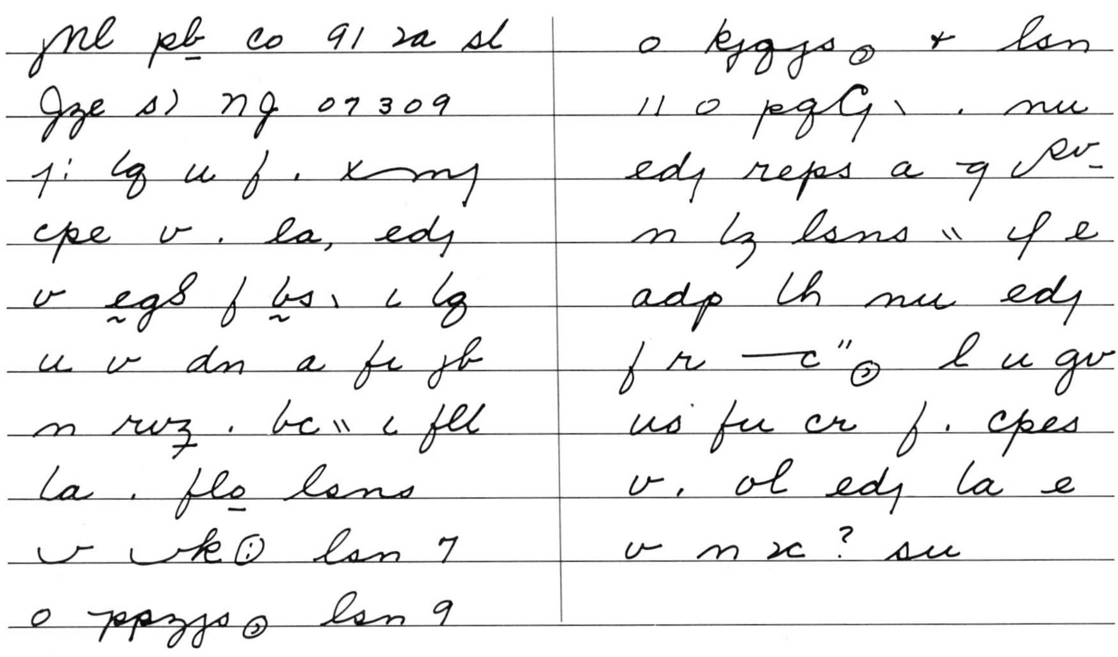

2.4 VOCABULARY BUILDING

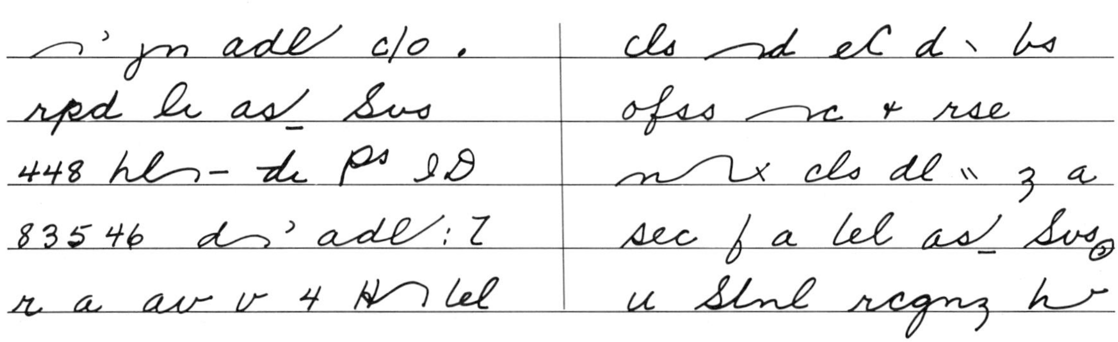

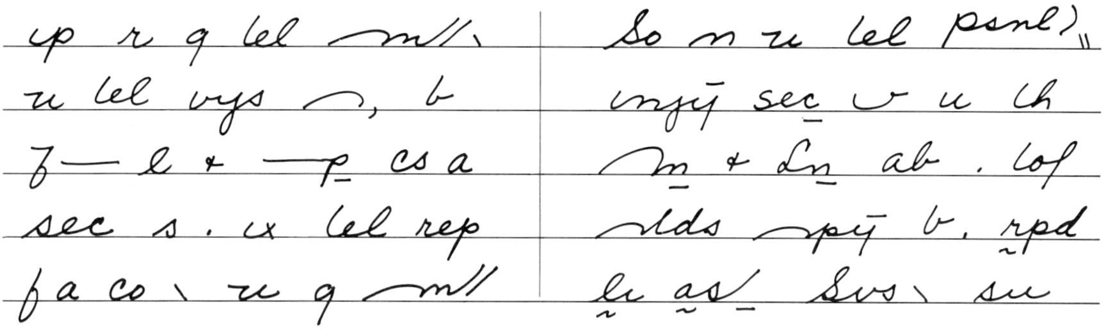

3.1 THEORY REVIEW

1. Plurals

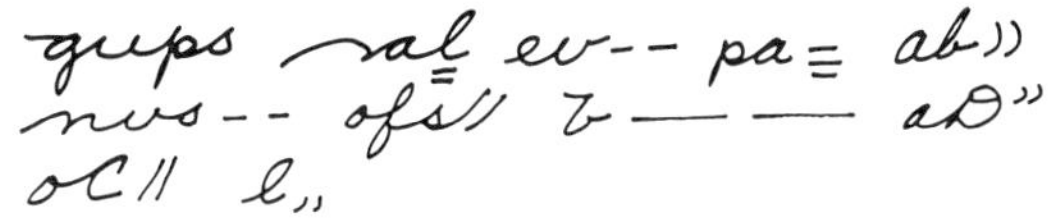

2. Brief forms

3. Abbreviations

4. *under* derivatives

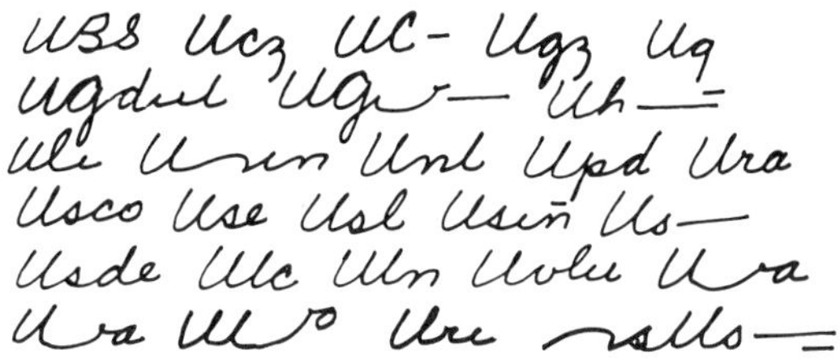

5. Complimentary closings

KEY 1. groups; mailings; events; paintings; abilities; investments; officers; brands; addresses; occurrences; lists 2. note; correct, contract; direct; benefit; even; evenings; consider; upon 3. Christmas; certificate, certify; advertise 4. underbrush; underclothes; undercurrent; underglaze; undergo; undergraduate; underground; underhanded; underline; undermine; underneath; underpaid; underrate; underscore; undersea; undersell; undersigned; understand; understudy; undertake; undertone; undervalue; underway; underwear; underworld; underwrite; misunderstanding 5. Sincerely yours; Very truly yours; Yours truly; Yours very truly; Cordially yours; Respectfully yours

3.2 TRANSCRIPTION SKILL BUILDING

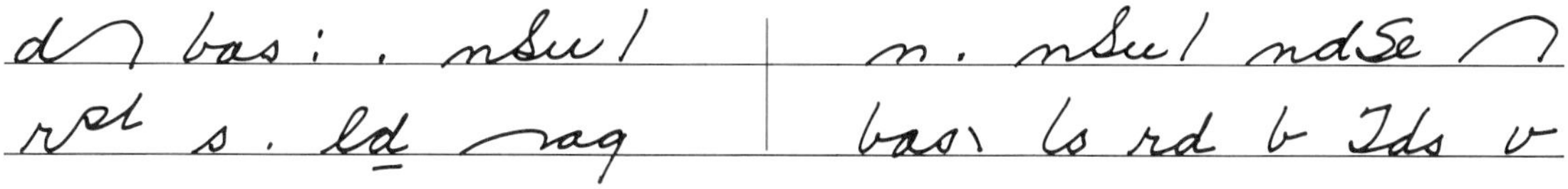

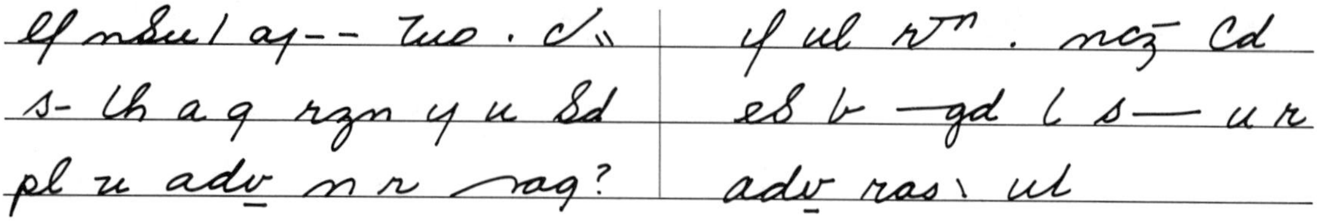

GUIDE Insert one parenthetical comma, one introductory comma, and one contraction apostrophe.

3.3 SPEED BUILDING

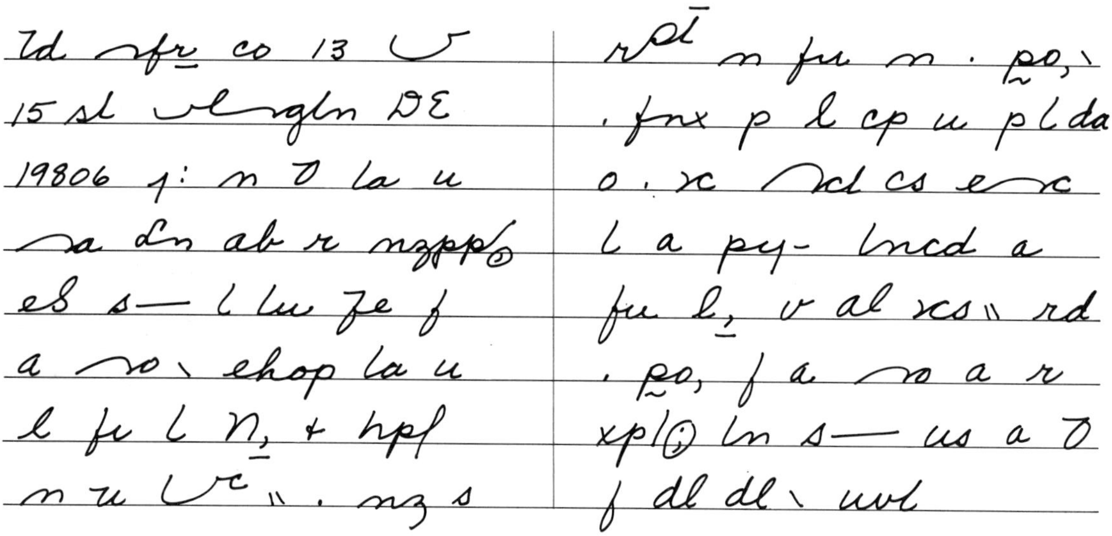

3.4 VOCABULARY BUILDING

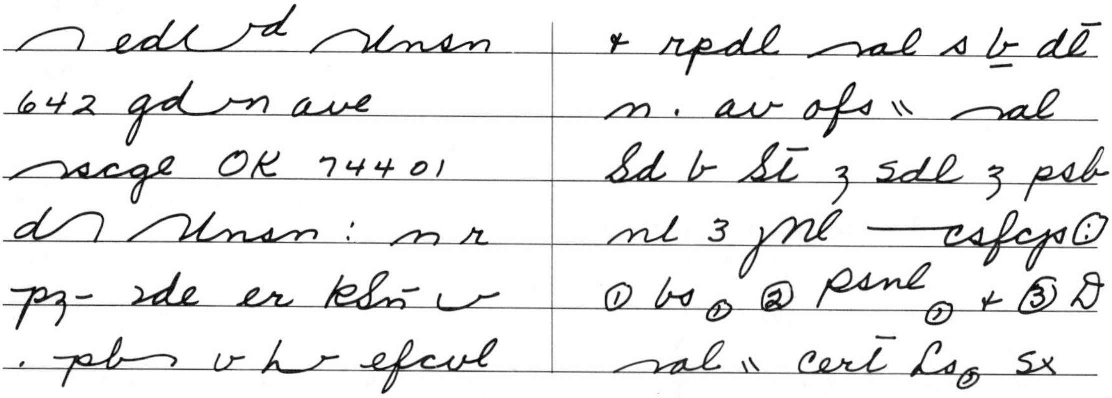

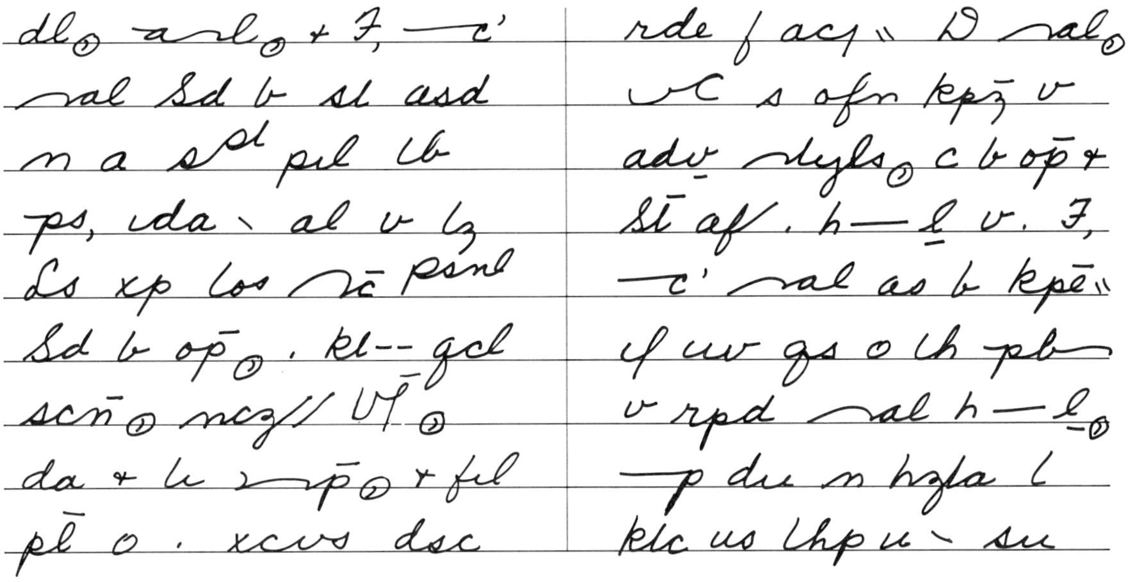

4.1 THEORY REVIEW

1. *zh*
2. Final *lee*
3. Medial and final *ake*
4. Brief forms
5. Abbreviations
6. *direct* derivatives

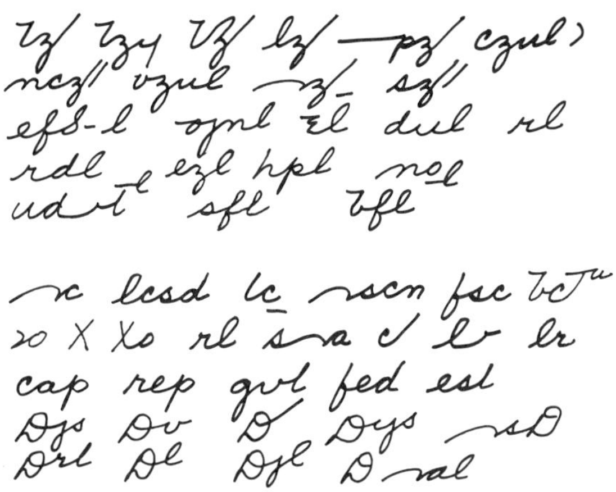

KEY 1. treasure; treasury; treasurer; leisure; pleasure; casualty; enclosures; visual; measuring; seizures 2. efficiently; originally; early; duly; hourly; readily; easily; happily; knowingly; undoubtedly; safely; briefly 3. make; lakeside; taking; mistaken; forsake; breakthrough 4. stop; extra; extraordinary; real, really; small; country; always; already 5. capital; represent, representative; government; federal; establish 6. directions; directive; director; directories; misdirect, directorate; directly; directional; direct mail

4.2 TRANSCRIPTION SKILL BUILDING

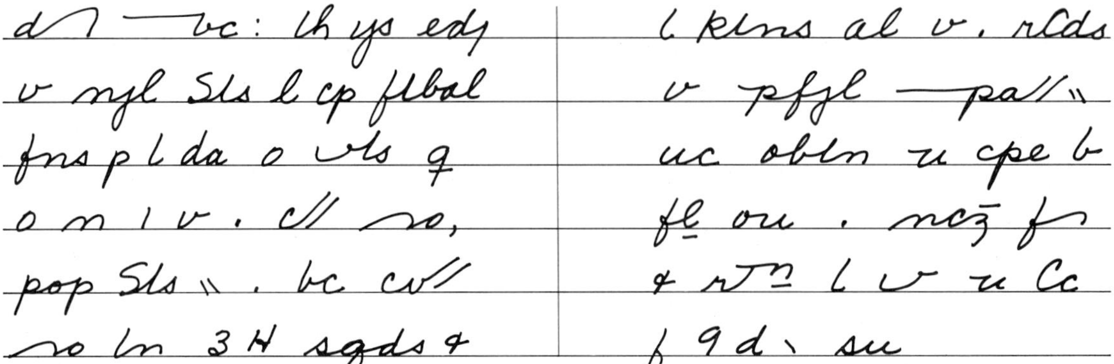

GUIDE Insert two possessive apostrophes, one contraction apostrophe, and one conjunction comma.

4.3 SPEED BUILDING

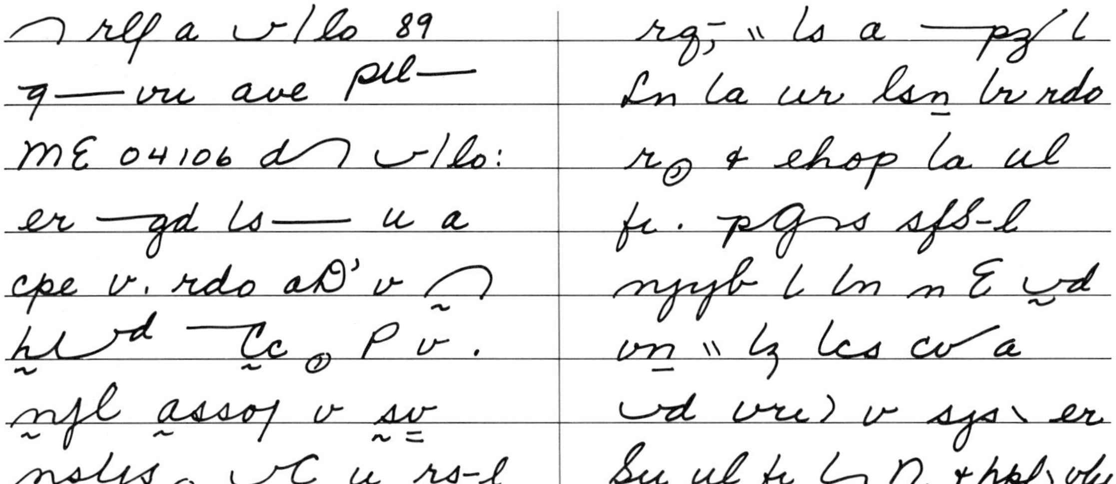

4.4 VOCABULARY BUILDING

(A)

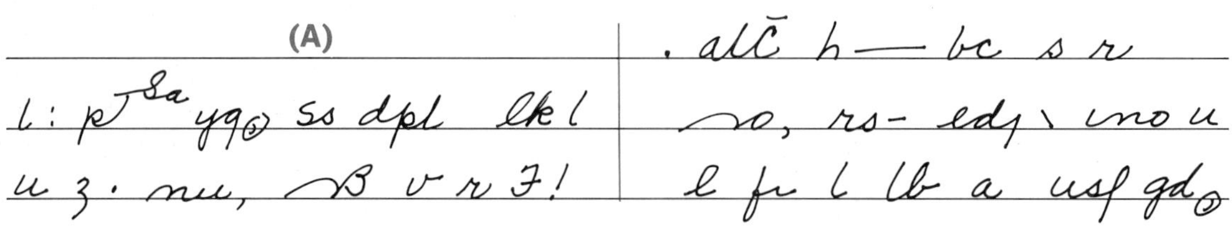

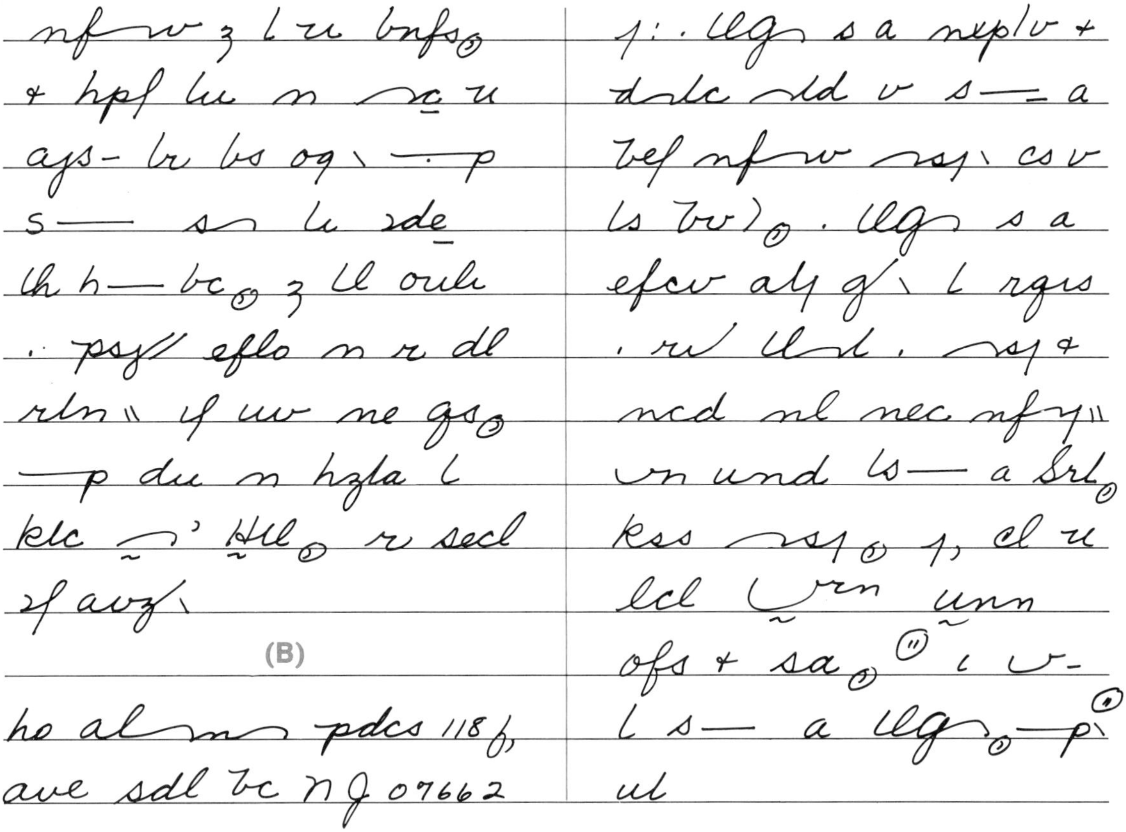

(B)

5.1 THEORY REVIEW

1. Medial and final *shun*
2. Medial and final *ashun*
3. Medial and final *eshun*
4. Medial and final *ishun*
5. Medial and final *oshun*
6. Medial and final *ushun*
7. Medial and final *nshun*
8. Brief forms

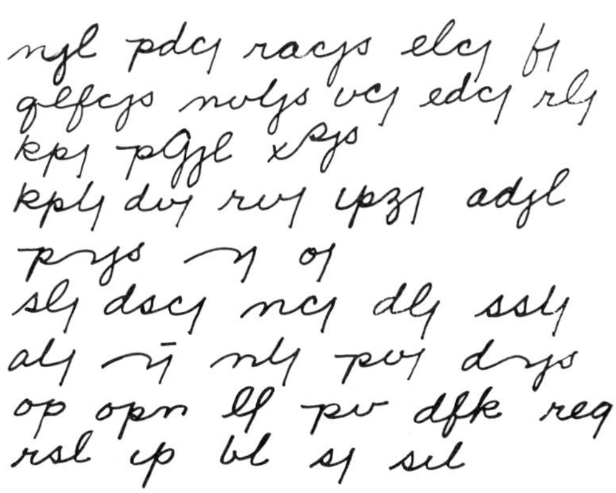

KEY 1. national; production; reactions; election; fashion 2. qualifications; invitations; vacation; education; relation 3. completion; progressional; expressions 4. competition; division; revision; imposition; additional 5. promotions; motion; ocean 6. solution; discussion; inclusion; delusion; substitution 7. attention; mentioned;

intention; prevention; dimensions 8. open; opinion; life; prove; difficult, difficulty; regular, regulation, regularly; result; important; between; subject; situation

5.2 TRANSCRIPTION SKILL BUILDING

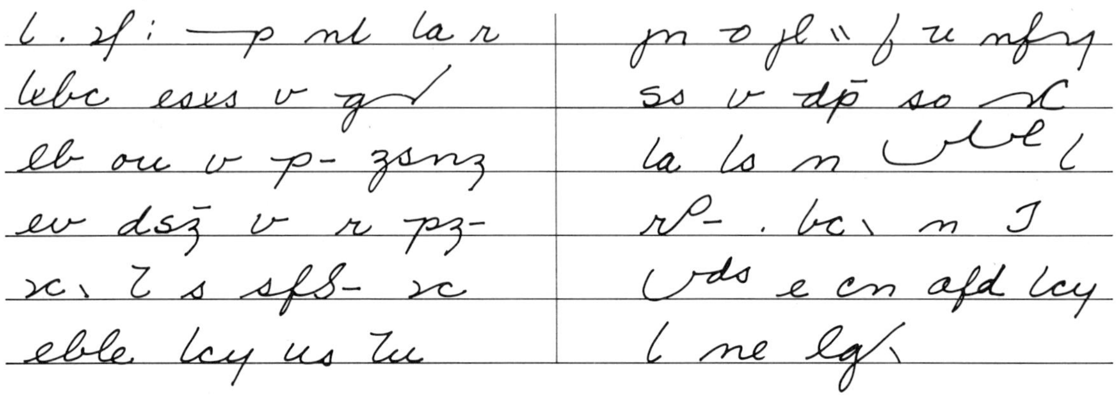

GUIDE Insert two apposition commas, two parenthetical commas; and two introductory commas.

5.3 SPEED BUILDING

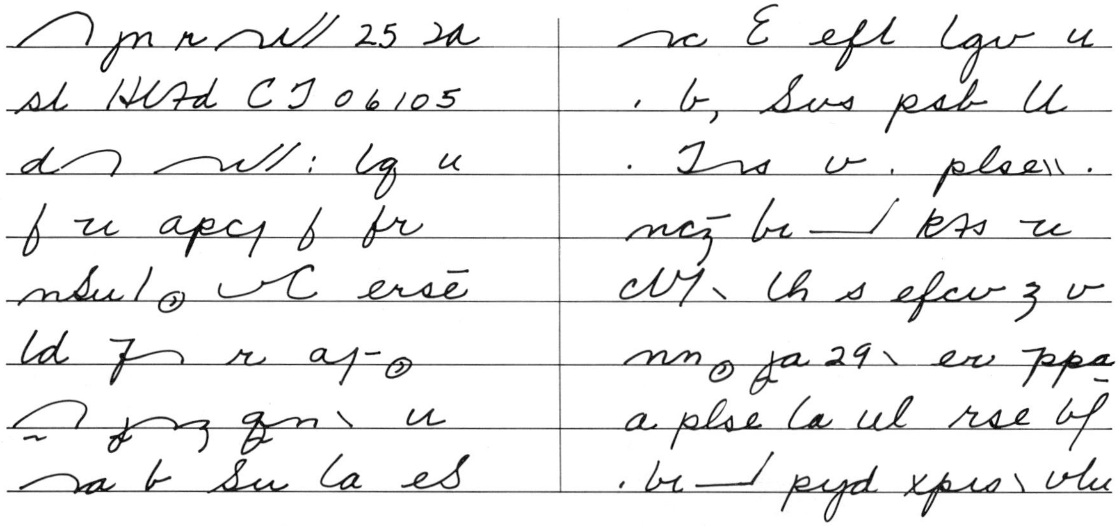

5.4 VOCABULARY BUILDING

(A)	(B)
l: al Bs v secs	elna ruf co 17-08
Nnfl vn u sl	pza rd dfd TX
dn a u lpr/l	78619 j: eno ul b
Ucb u spyl dcj	p̄ brse, rvz psl
u v- eC L lah sins	mul v. unī zas
Uc lc a pcC/n a	po dpl v C xpns
Ja" , va lb Su u	n dll. psl Svss
Ucb̄ slyl l b l	avlb, lh mul l"
cC s lcp u lpr/	. Cgs + sal c" f al
nq rpa, u Ls l	c" v sal, adyl
lc pfyl f. lpr/	er ncd a pp/bv
ryo r cn + vn	cpe v zp cd l, e
vn Sc, as + os Sd	no u sec l fu lh
b op Scls # nq	a h e rA1 + l
fl̄ Sdoe Ls" 5 uns	ncd a zp cd o E L
s- o mn m gcl	S sals f u" f u v
bS + cn u lpr/	ne qs n cv̄ b. psl
l hp u pds sal cpe	mul du n hzla
al vk lq,	lcl u lcl ps S, cu

PHRASING

Some writers think that all they have to do to increase their shorthand speed is to devise shortcuts wherever possible. Shortcuts are not the answer to speed development!

Shortcuts are valuable only if the words represented occur with a high degree of frequency in your dictation. If they are not used often, the shortcuts will hinder rather than develop your speed. If a shortcut is not used frequently, you will not be able to write the outline automatically. The moment you hesitate for even a fraction of a second, you are regressing rather than progressing in speed development.

You will be wise to follow the advice of experienced shorthand writers and write everything in accordance with your shorthand principles.

UNIT 4
INSURANCE

1.1 THEORY REVIEW

1. Initial *combination-l*
2. Medial *combination-l*
3. Final *bul* and *blee*
4. Final *pul* and *plee*
5. All other final *combination-l*
6. Brief forms

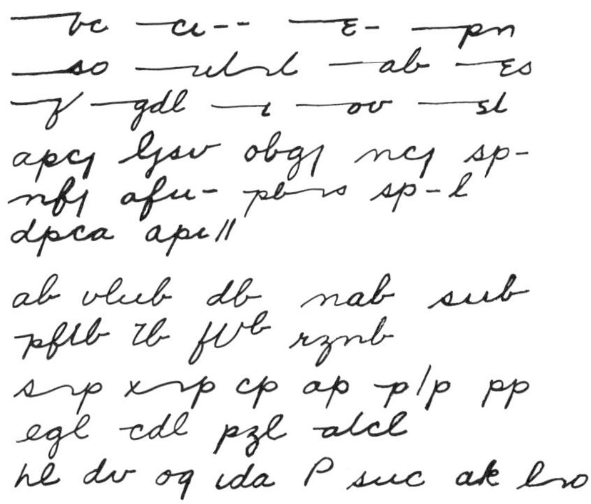

KEY 1. block; clients; element; plan; slow; ultimate; alibi; else; flatter; gladly; ill; olive; split 2. application; legislative; obligation; inclusion; supplement; inflation; affluent; problems; supplemental; duplicate; appliances 3. able, ably; valuable, valuably; double, doubly; enable; suitable, suitably; profitable, profitably; trouble; favorable, favorably; reasonable, reasonably 4. simple, simply; example; couple; apple; principle, principally; people 5. eagle; cradle; puzzle; article 6. whole; develop; organize, organization; immediate, immediately; particular, particularly; success, successful, successfully; acknowledge; almost.

1.2 TRANSCRIPTION SKILL BUILDING

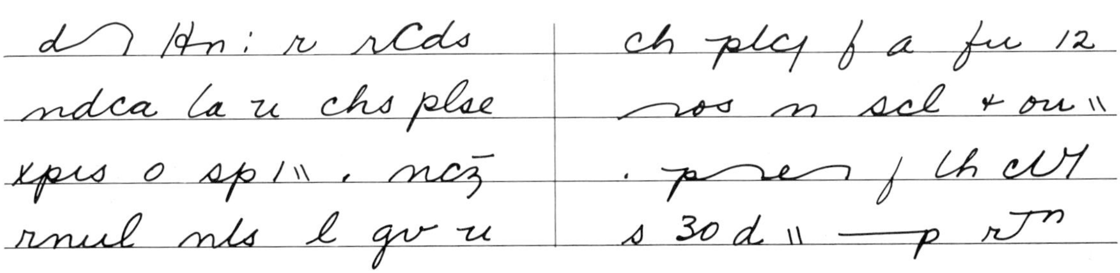

. rnul nls lgT
v u Cc n .

ncz eno \ su

GUIDE Insert three parenthetical commas and one possessive apostrophe.

1.3 SPEED BUILDING

dvd rl 36-05 hu
sl s-a fa NM 87501
ds: du u v dfk rB
vT uv pd. prens
o u nSul plses?
du u rse nlss
la ur o u 30 ds v
gas ?? er ppa a
sny rCd f eC v

r Ks so la Ch l no
lg b a pb \ u
sec l b ab l pvd u
v rde nfy pn u
rg, 3 l pren pa-
das + ards " Ch s 4, 1
v. hpf uds el nSa f
u vn ur plē b r
nyrd nSul og \ su

1.4 VOCABULARY BUILDING

nSul ra b csf
n 2 bd grps \ Psnl
nSul ncds lf kd-
dsab) hll + sx nSul \
p) nSul cv/ l" 7
fr Mo czul) l'
7 pa- lib) dScy
v p) Bgy + Arbl

cas" a ndv o bs
pCs nSul + rses a
plse vC s a rln
Kc bl . b + . nSul
co \ . b s cē a
plschol + . nSul co
s cē . Urv ". plschol
rcs reg pa-- l .

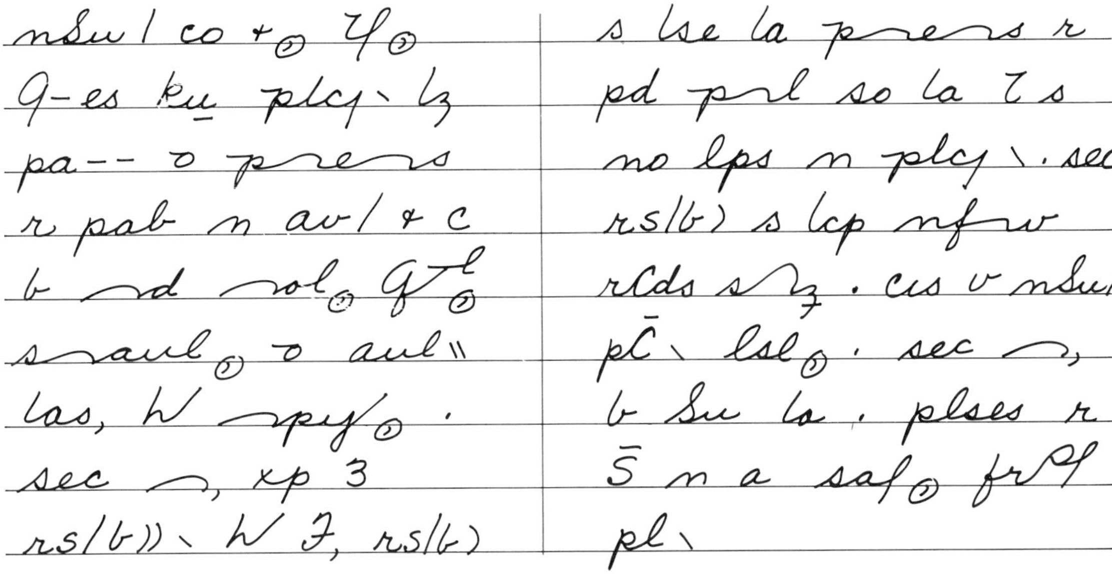

2.1 THEORY REVIEW

1. Final *āme*
2. Final *ēem*
3. Final *īme*
4. Final *ōme*
5. Final *ūme*
6. Brief forms
7. Abbreviations

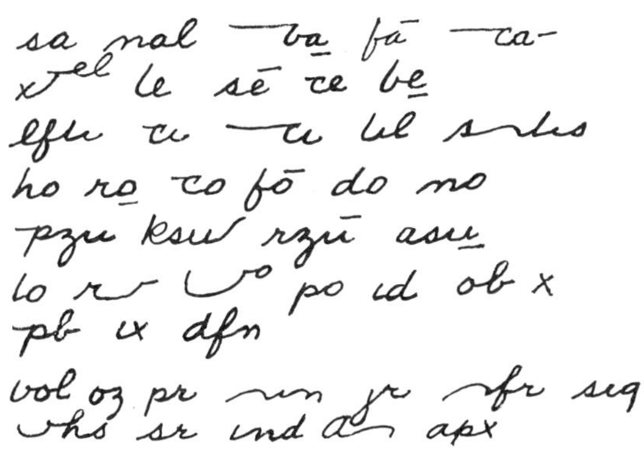

KEY 1. same; namely; blaming; famed; claimant 2. extremely; team; seemed; cream; beaming 3. lifetime; crime; climb; timely; sometimes 4. home; roaming; chrome; foamed; dome; gnome 5. presume; consumer; resumed; assuming 6. thought; around; world; poor; idea; object; usual, usually; probable, probably; initial, initially; definite, definitely 7. volume; ounce; pair; minute; junior; manufacture; signature; warehouse; senior; independent; America, American; approximate, approximately

2.2 TRANSCRIPTION SKILL BUILDING

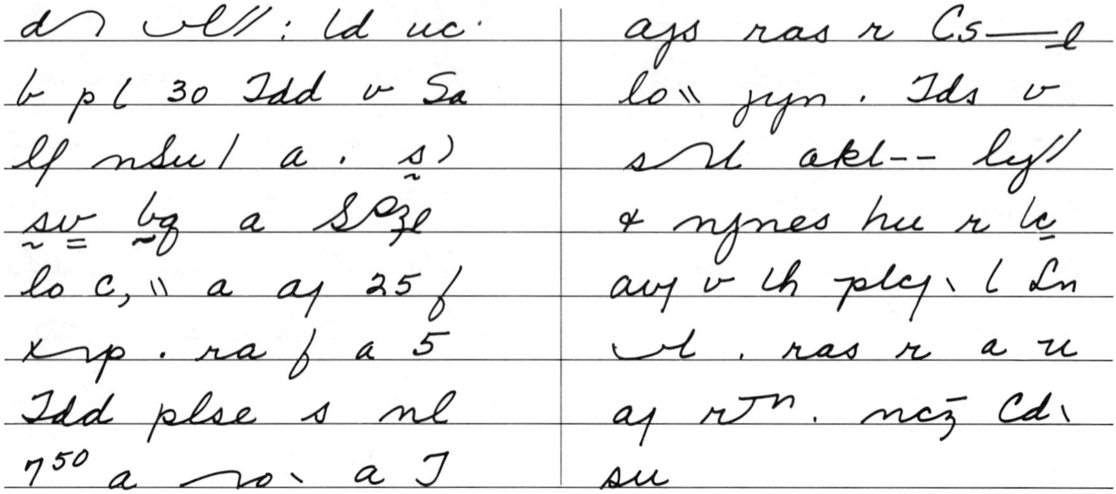

GUIDE Insert two numbers commas, two parenthetical commas, two introductory commas, and two series commas.

2.3 SPEED BUILDING

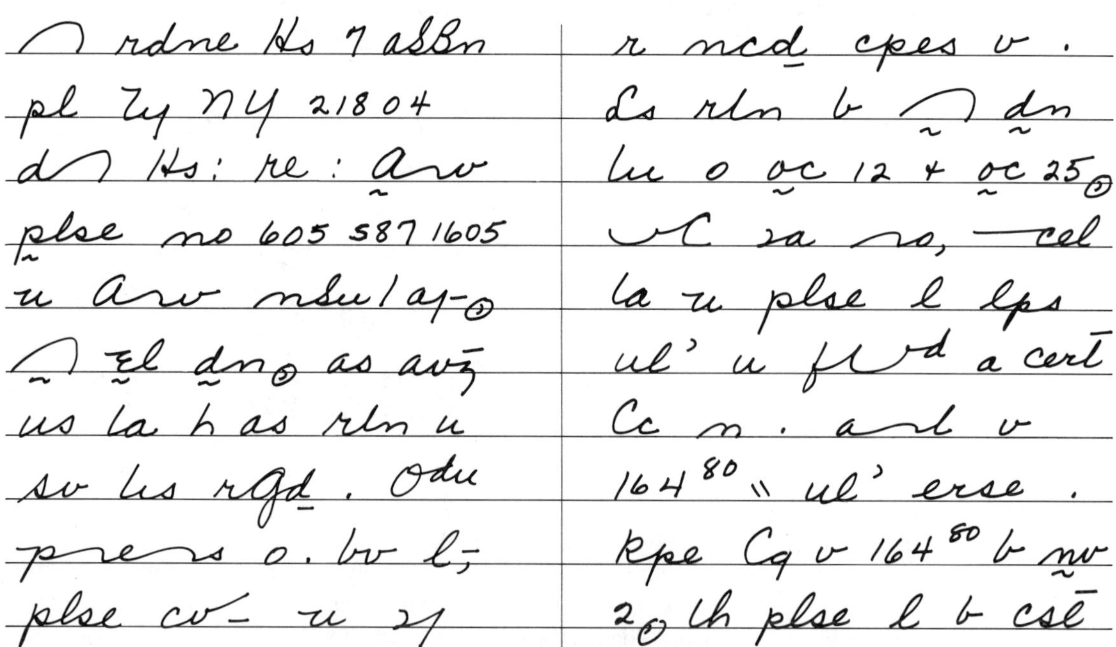

2.4 VOCABULARY BUILDING

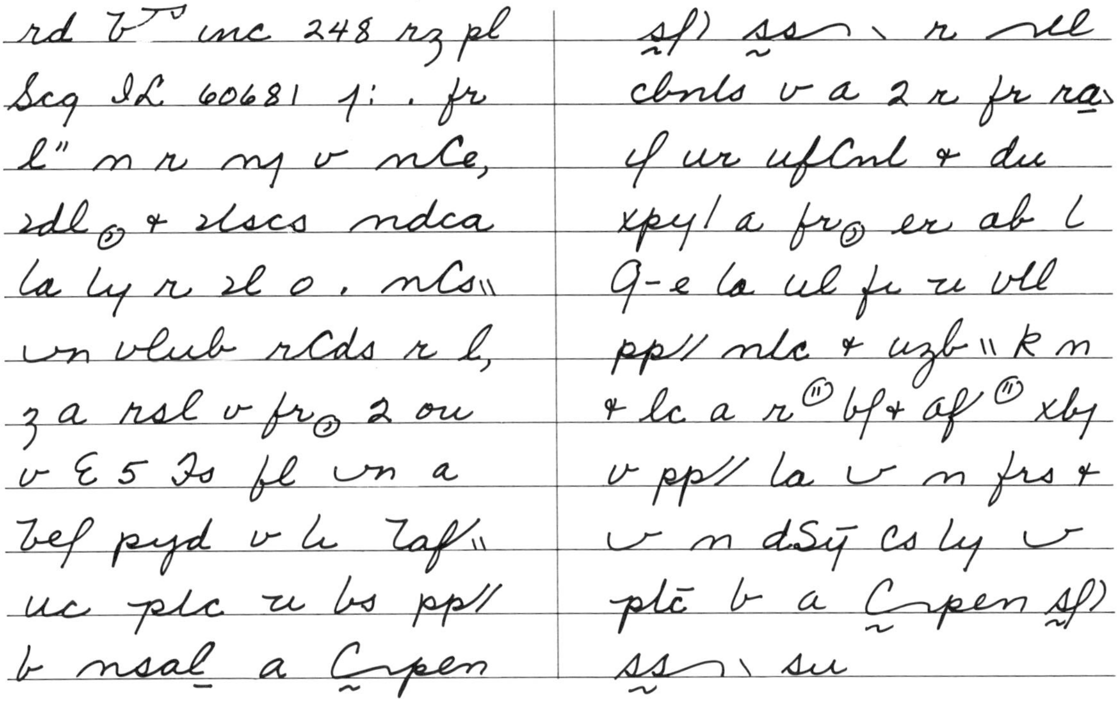

3.1 THEORY REVIEW

1. *old*
2. Initial and final *aw*
3. Final *awl*
4. Brief forms
5. Abbreviations
6. *sale* derivatives

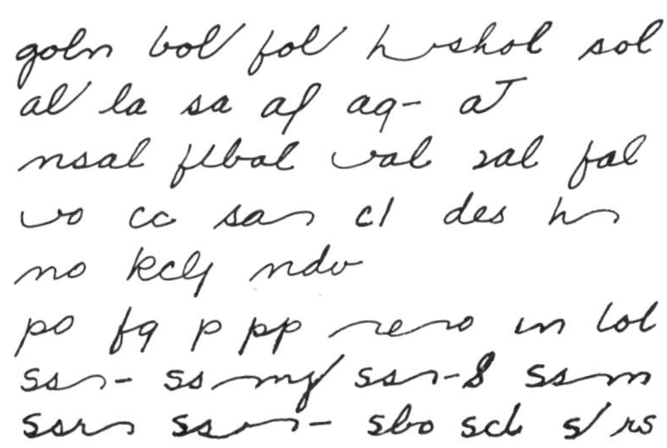

KEY 1. golden; bolder; folder; household; sold 2. alter; law; saw; awful; augment; author 3. install; football; wall; stall; fall 4. without; collect; sample; once, circumstance; describe, description; whom; known; conclusion; individual, individually 5. post office; figure; page; parcel post; memorandum; inch; total 6. salesman; sales manager; salesmanship; salesmen; salesroom; saleswoman; sailboat; sailcloth; sailor; resale

3.2 TRANSCRIPTION SKILL BUILDING

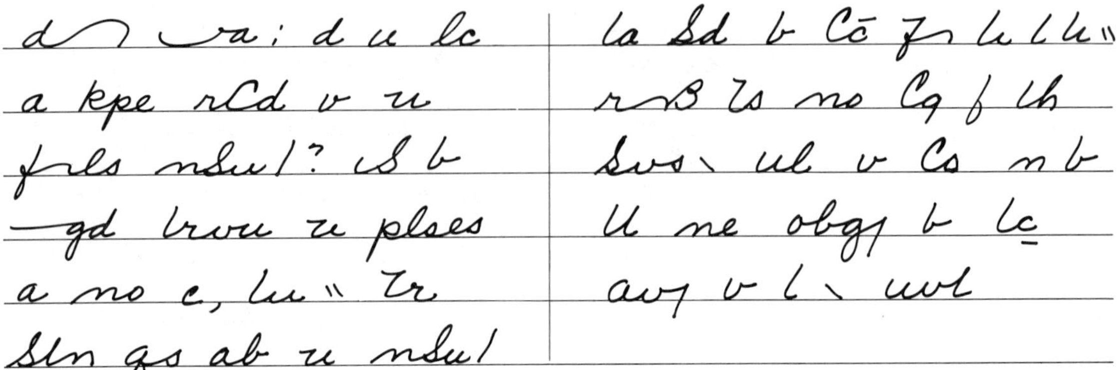

GUIDE Insert one introductory comma, two parenthetical commas, and one possessive apostrophe.

3.3 SPEED BUILDING

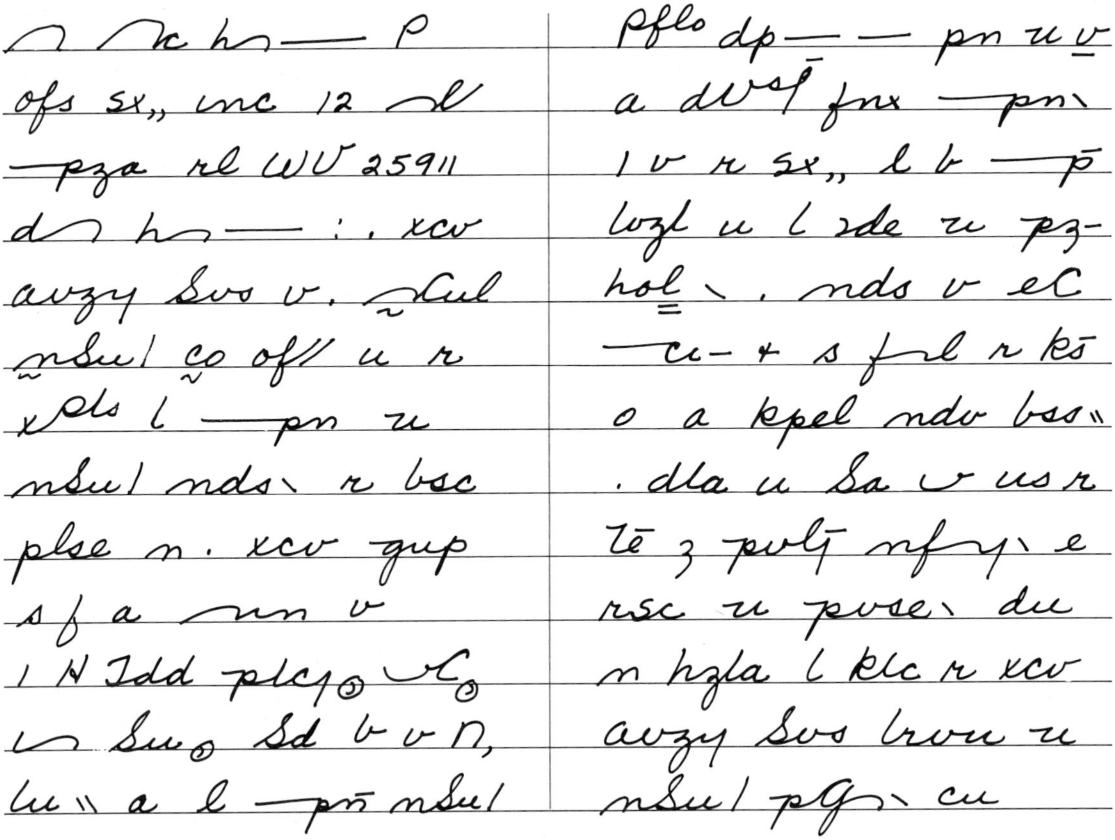

3.4 VOCABULARY BUILDING

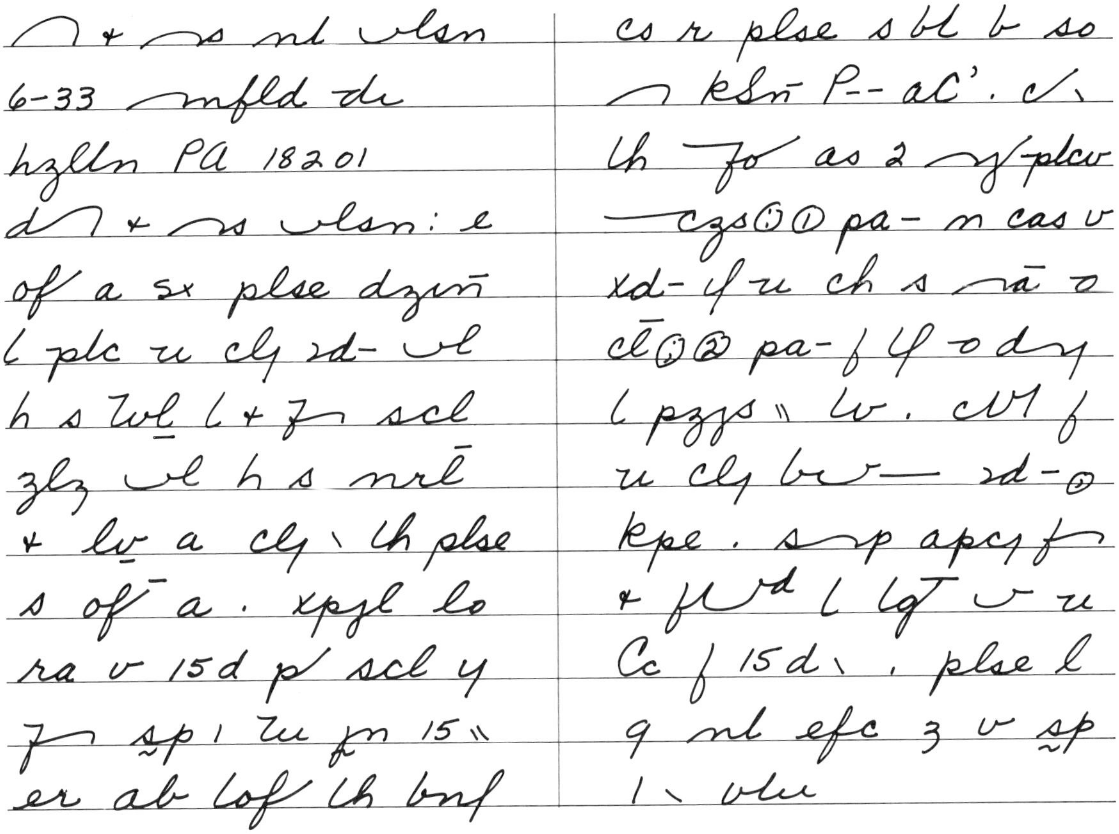

4.1 THEORY REVIEW

1. Final *air*
2. Final *eer*
3. Final *ire*
4. Final *ore*
5. Final *ure*
6. Brief forms
7. Abbreviations

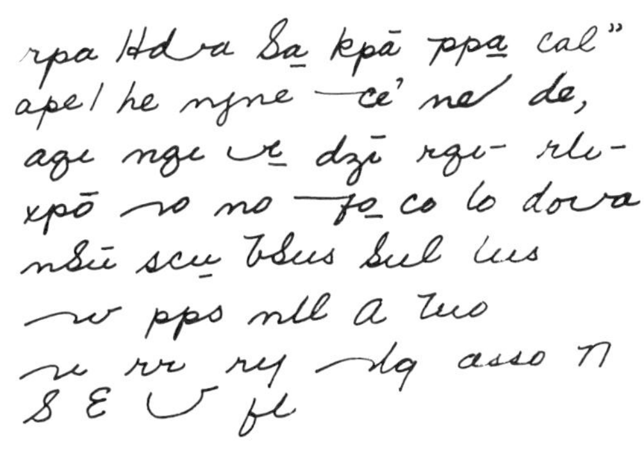

KEY 1. repair; hardware; sharing; compared; preparing; carelessness 2. appearance; here, hear; engineer; clearness; nearer; dearest 3. acquire; inquire; wiring; desired; requirement; retirement 4. explored; more; nor; flooring; core; tore; doorway 5. insured; securing; brochures; surely; tours 6. move; perhaps; entitle; auto;

throughout 7. mile; railroad; railway; mortgage; associate; north; south; east; west; feet, foot

4.2 TRANSCRIPTION SKILL BUILDING

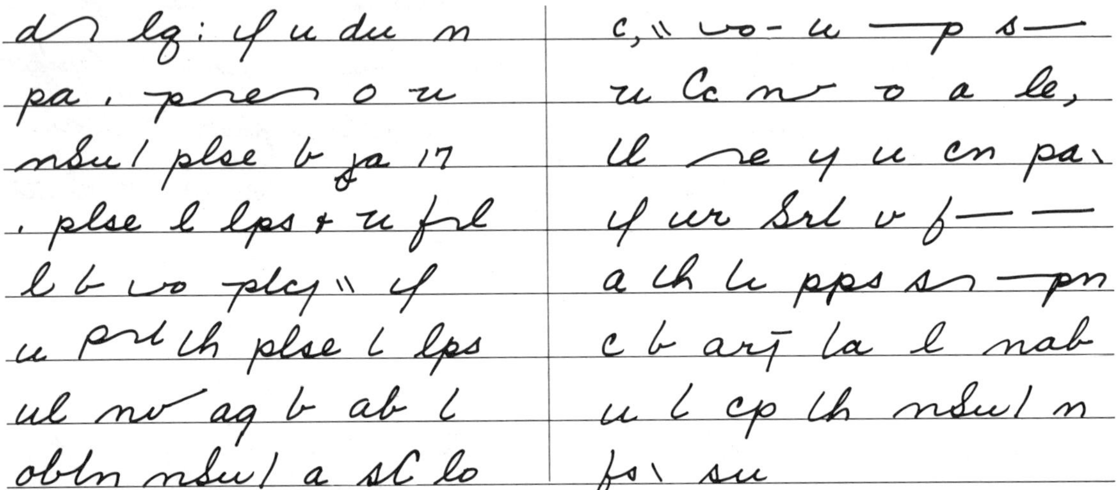

GUIDE Insert three introductory commas, one conjunction semicolon, and one contraction apostrophe.

4.3 SPEED BUILDING

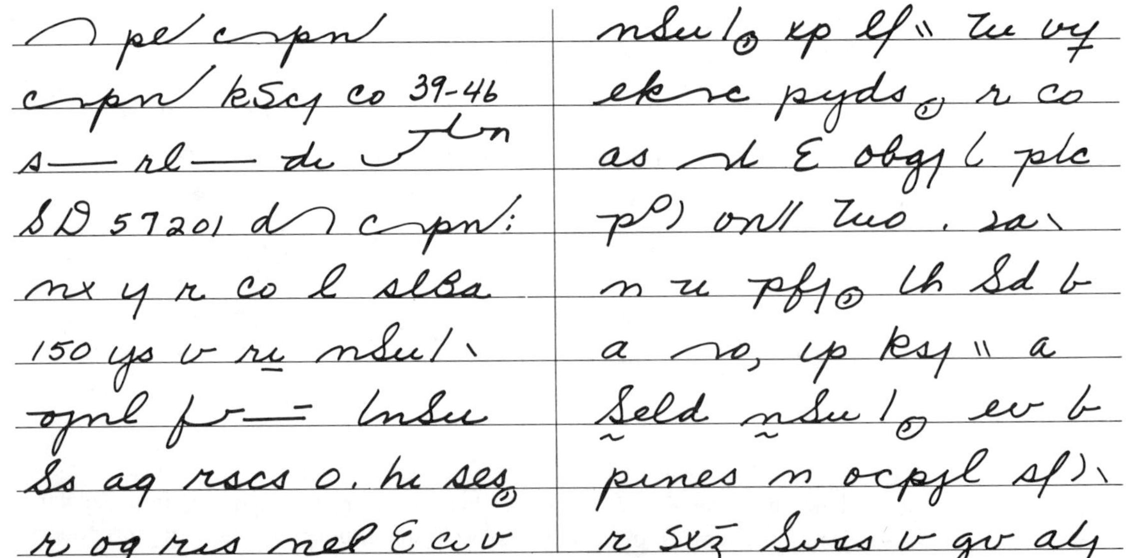

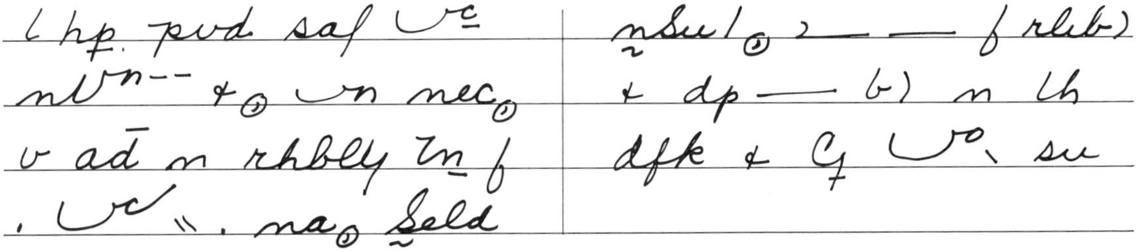

4.4 VOCABULARY BUILDING

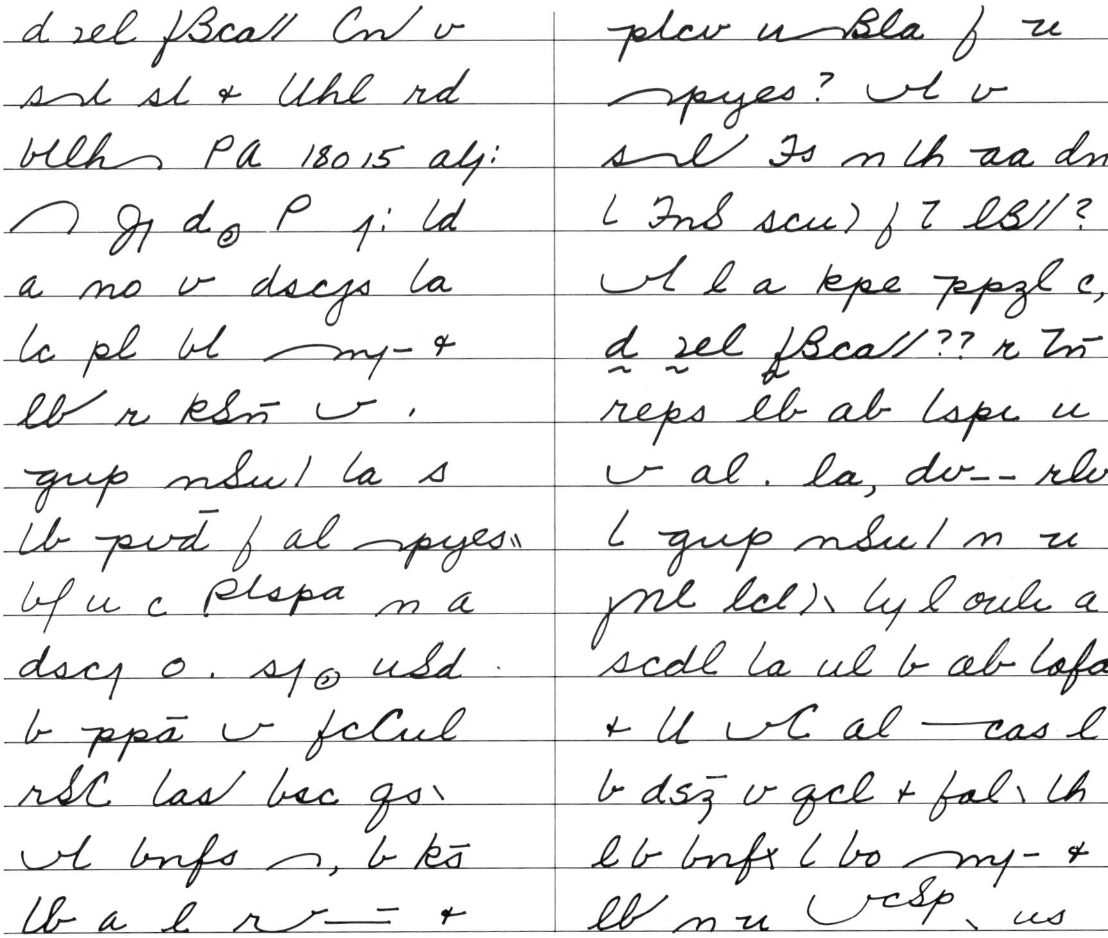

5.1 THEORY REVIEW

1. Initial and final *st*

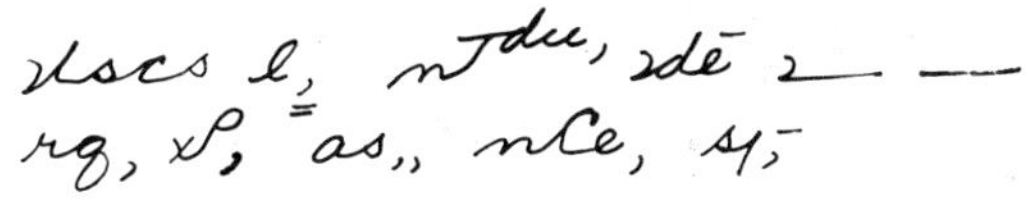

2. Medial *st*
3. Final *ful*
4. Final *fully*
5. Final *fy*
6. Money
7. *head* derivatives

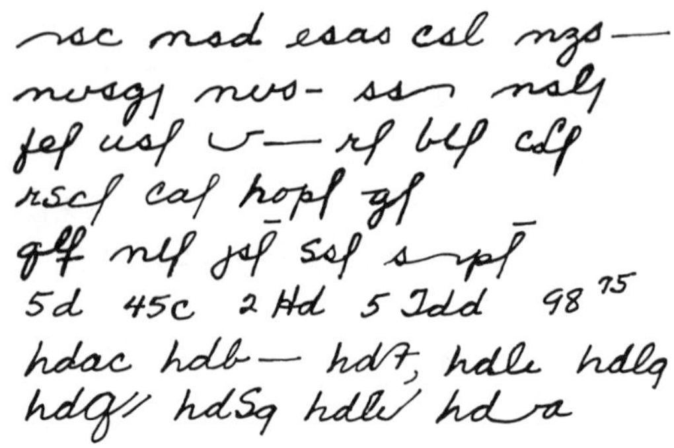

KEY 1. statistics; listings; introduced; studied; stands; request; expressed; assists; increased; suggested 2. mistake; instead; estates; cancel; newsstand; investigation; investment; system; installation 3. fearful; useful; wonderful; beautiful; colorful 4. respectfully; carefully; hopefully; gratefully 5. qualifying; notify; justified; specify; simplified 6. \$5; 45 cents; \$200; \$5,000; \$98.75 7. headache; headband; headfirst; headlight; headlong; headquarters; headstrong; headliner; headway

5.2 TRANSCRIPTION SKILL BUILDING

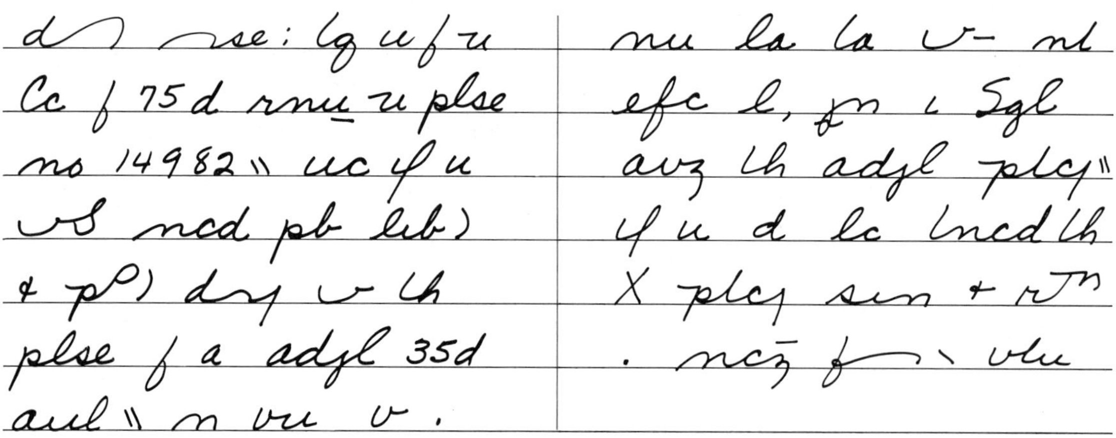

GUIDE Insert two parenthetical commas and two introductory commas.

5.3 SPEED BUILDING

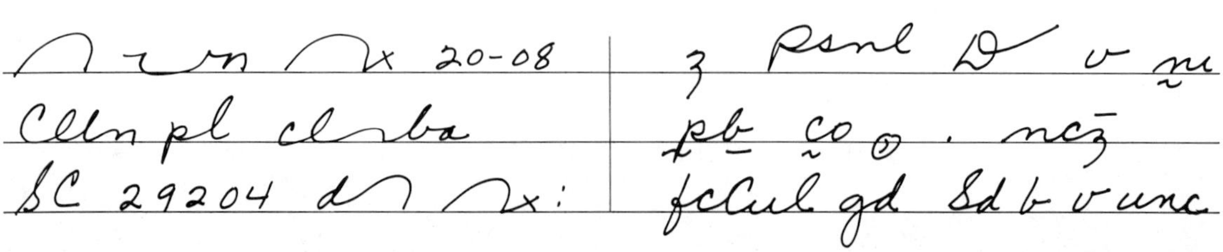

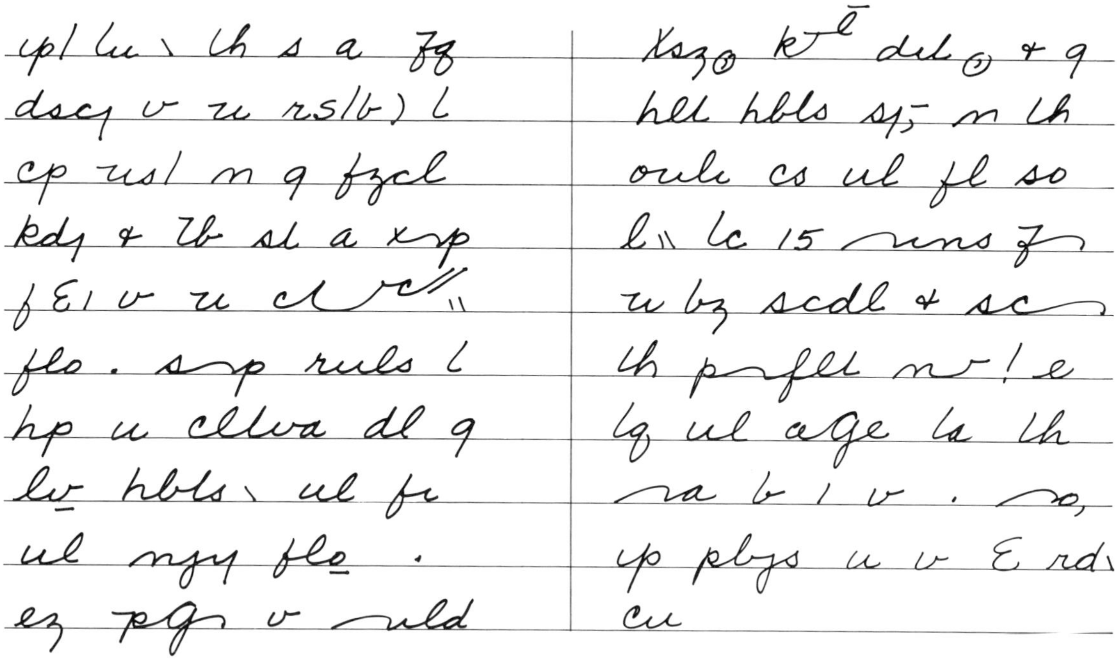

5.4 VOCABULARY BUILDING

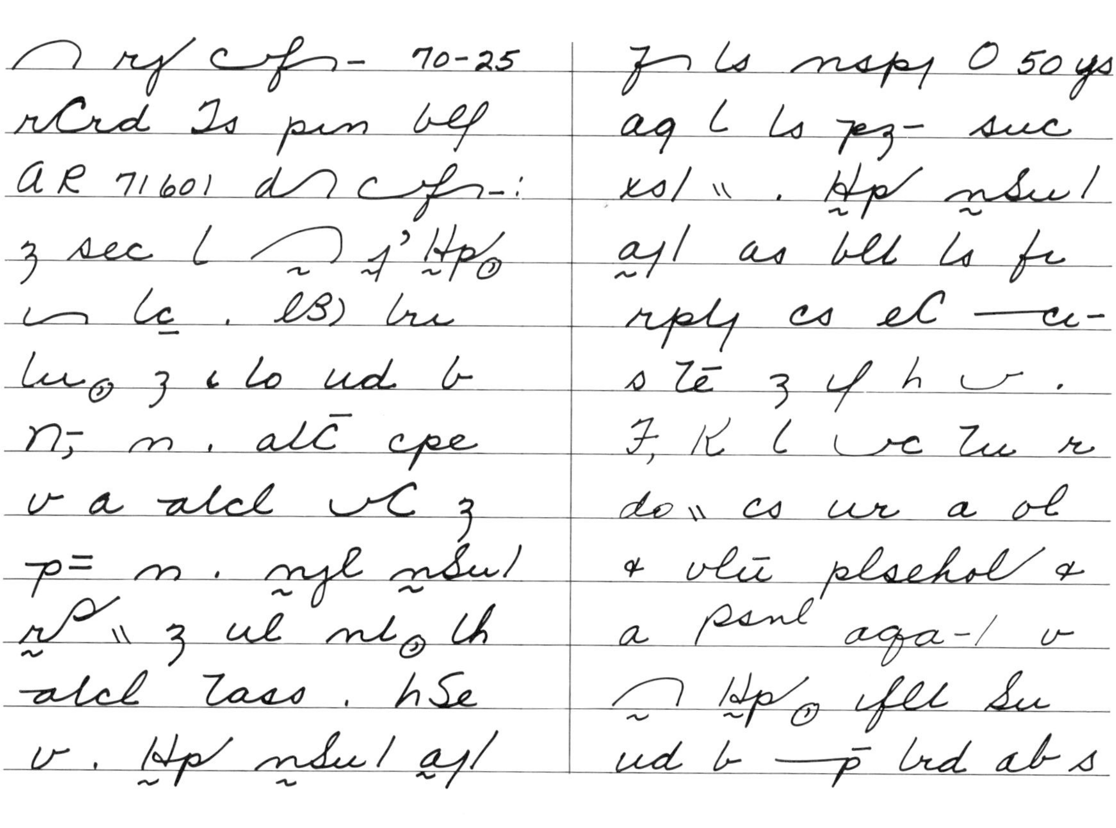

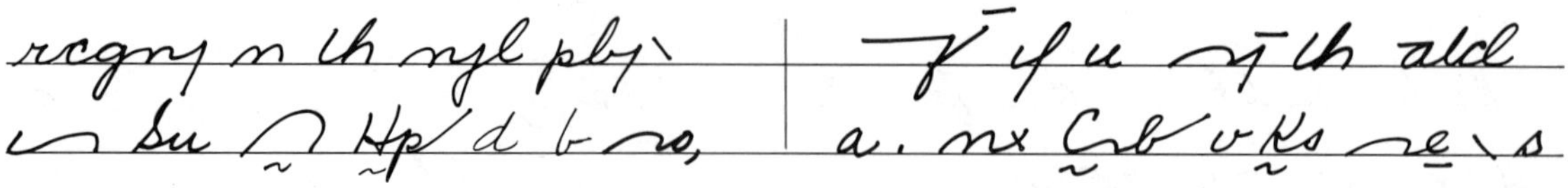

ESTIMATING LENGTH OF LETTER

One of the requirements for a mailable letter is attractive appearance. The letter is a goodwill ambassador, and it should make a good impression on the person to whom it is addressed.

Experienced stenographers learn to place letters by judgment rather than using a letter-placement chart. They glance at their notes to estimate the length of the letter. Then they set the margins by judgment.

How much space did you need for your shorthand notes for the letter on page 49 of the text? The body of this letter contains 173 words.

Using this letter as a guide, estimate the length of the letters you write for homework and check your estimate with the word count at the end of each letter in the key.

UNIT 5

ADVERTISING

1.1 THEORY REVIEW

1. Initial *ĭm*
2. Initial *ŭn*
3. Initial *ĕm*
4. Initial *ĕn*
5. Initial *sub*
6. Initial *trans*
7. Abbreviations

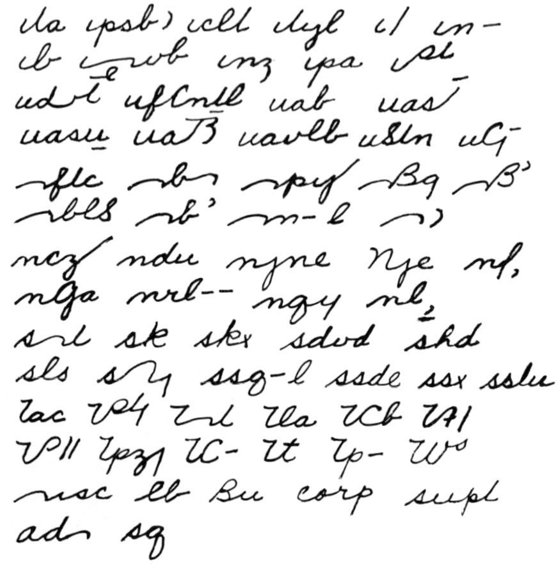

KEY 1. imitate; impossibility; immaculate; immaterial; immense; imminent; immobile; immovable; immunize; impair; impart; 2. undoubtedly; unfortunately; unable; unanswered; unassuming; unauthorized; unavailable; uncertain; unchanged 3. emphatic; emblem; employer; embargo; embarrass; embellish; emboss; eminently; empty 4. enclosure; endure; engineer; energy; enforced; engrave; enrollments; enquiry; enlisting 5. submit; subcommittee; subconscious; subdivide; subhead; sublease; submerge; subsequently; subsidy; substantial; substitute 6. transact; transportation; transmit; translate; transcribe; transference; transparencies; transposition; transient; transit; transplant; transverse 7. miscellaneous; pound; bureau; corporation; superintendent; administrate, administration; square

1.2 TRANSCRIPTION SKILL BUILDING

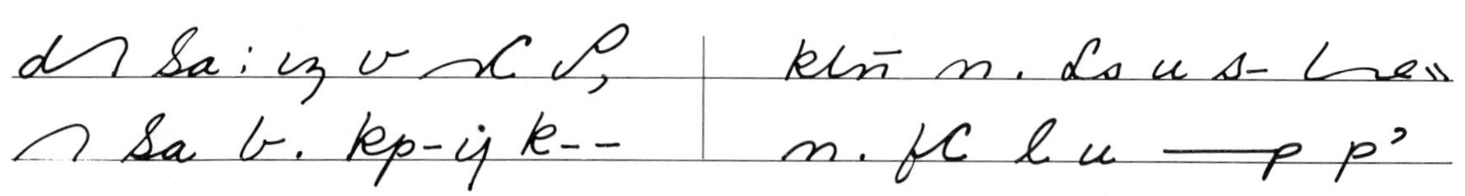

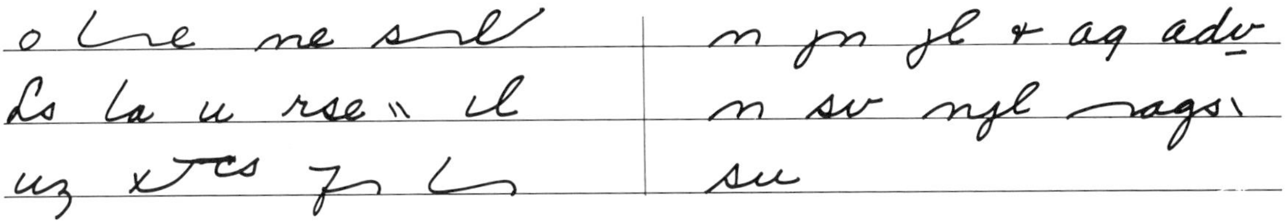

GUIDE Insert one introductory comma, two series commas, and two parenthetical commas.

1.3 SPEED BUILDING

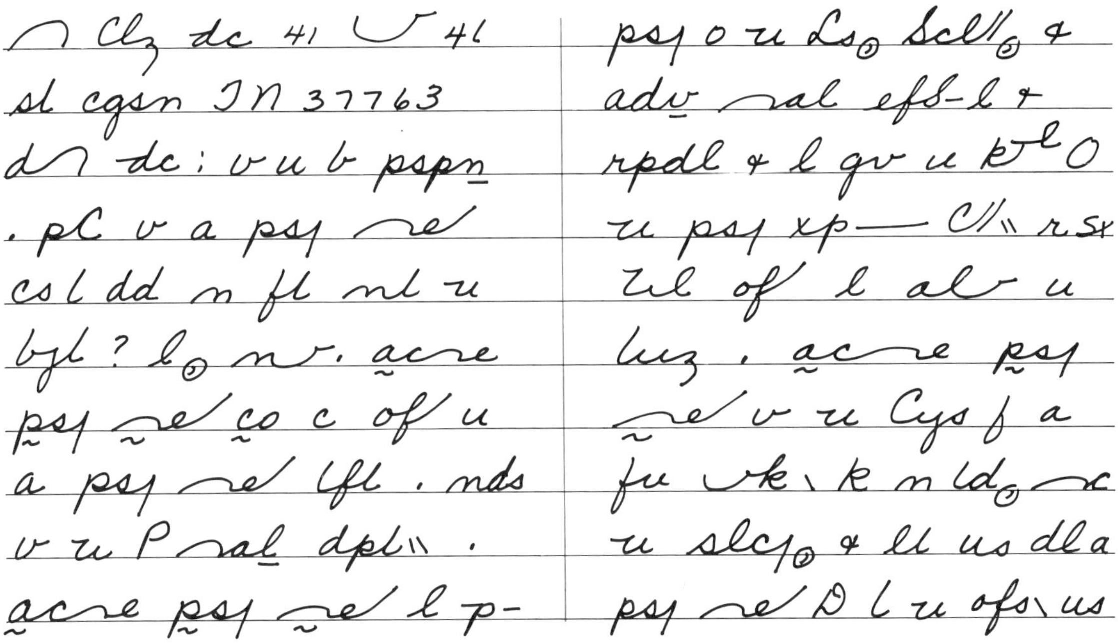

1.4 VOCABULARY BUILDING

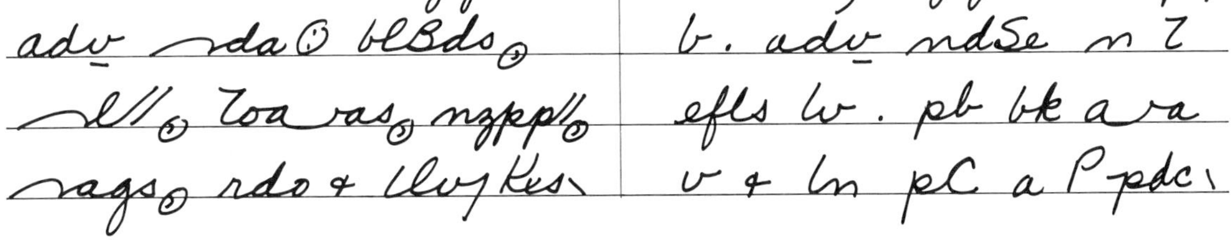

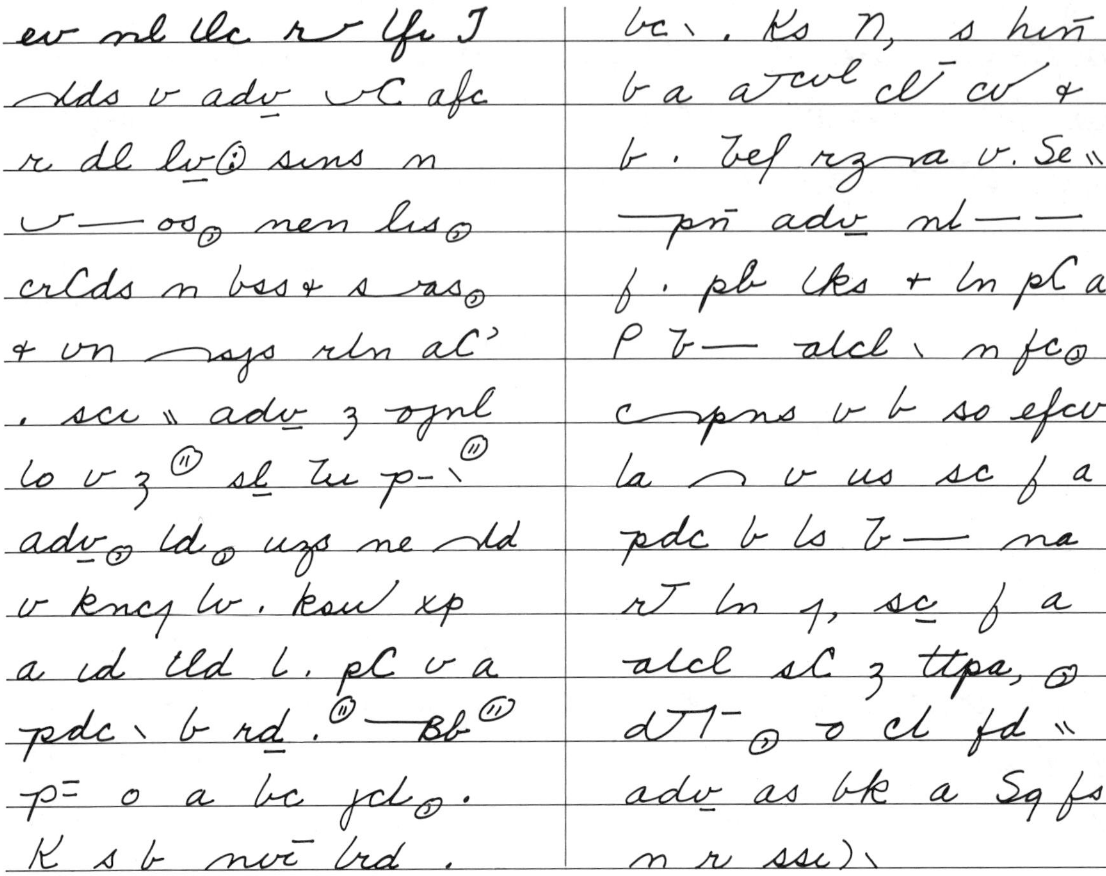

2.1 THEORY REVIEW

1. Medial and final *āde*
2. Medial and final *ēde*
3. Medial and final *īde*
4. Medial and final *ōde*
5. Medial and final *ūde*
6. Brief forms
7. *continue* derivatives
8. *count* derivatives

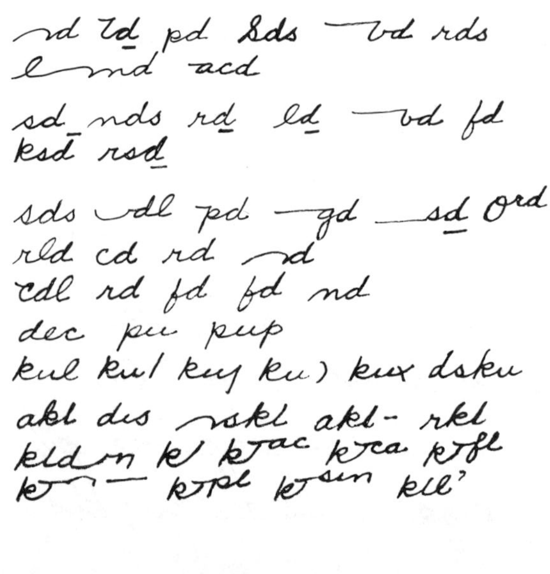

KEY 1. made; trading; paid; shades; blade; raids; lemonade; arcade 2. cede; needs; reading; leading; bleed; feed; conceded; receding 3. sides; widely; pride; glide; sliding; override 4. reload; code; rode; mode 5. crudely; rude; food; feud; nude 6. declare; pull; pupil 7. continual; continuance; continuation; continuity; continuous; discontinue 8. account; discount; miscount; accountant; recount; countdown; counter; counteract; counterclaim; counterfeit; countermand; counterpart; countersign; countless

2.2 TRANSCRIPTION SKILL BUILDING

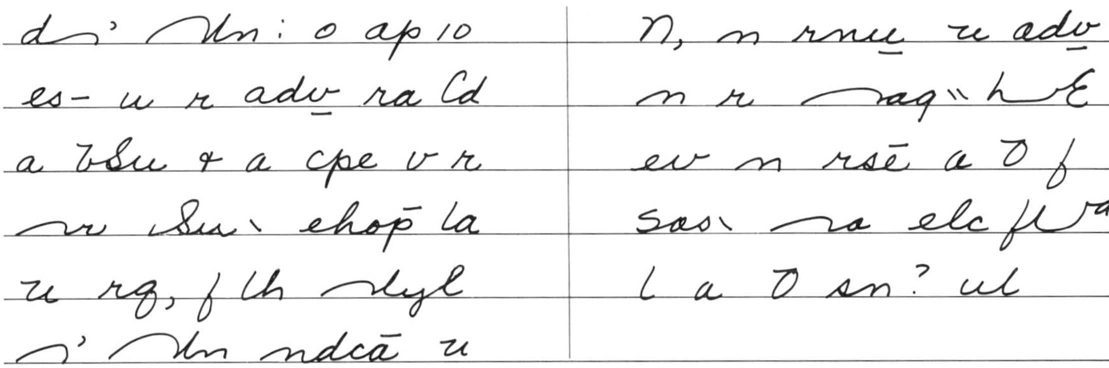

GUIDE Insert two series commas, one introductory comma, and two parenthetical commas.

2.3 SPEED BUILDING

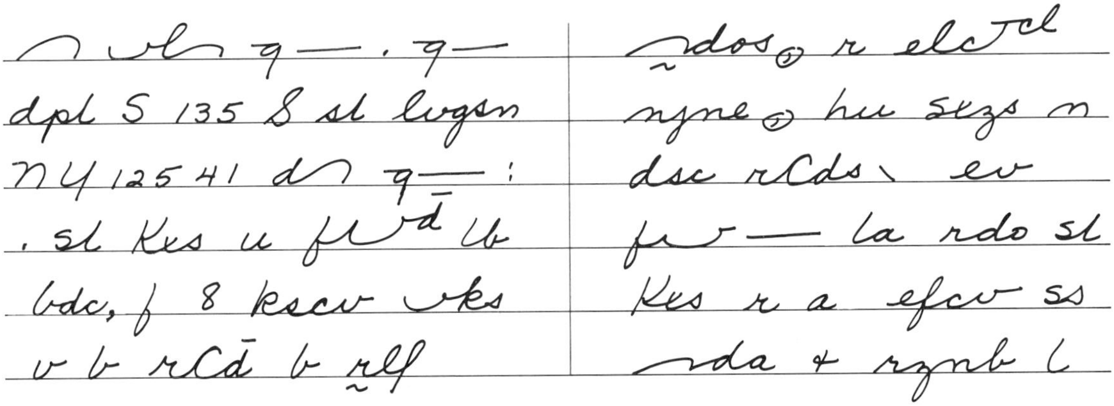

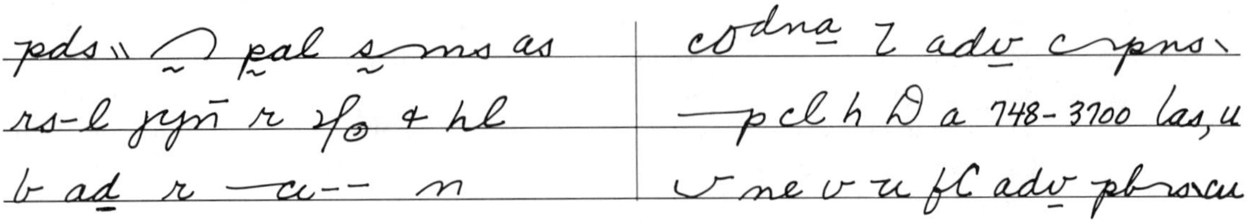

2.4 VOCABULARY BUILDING

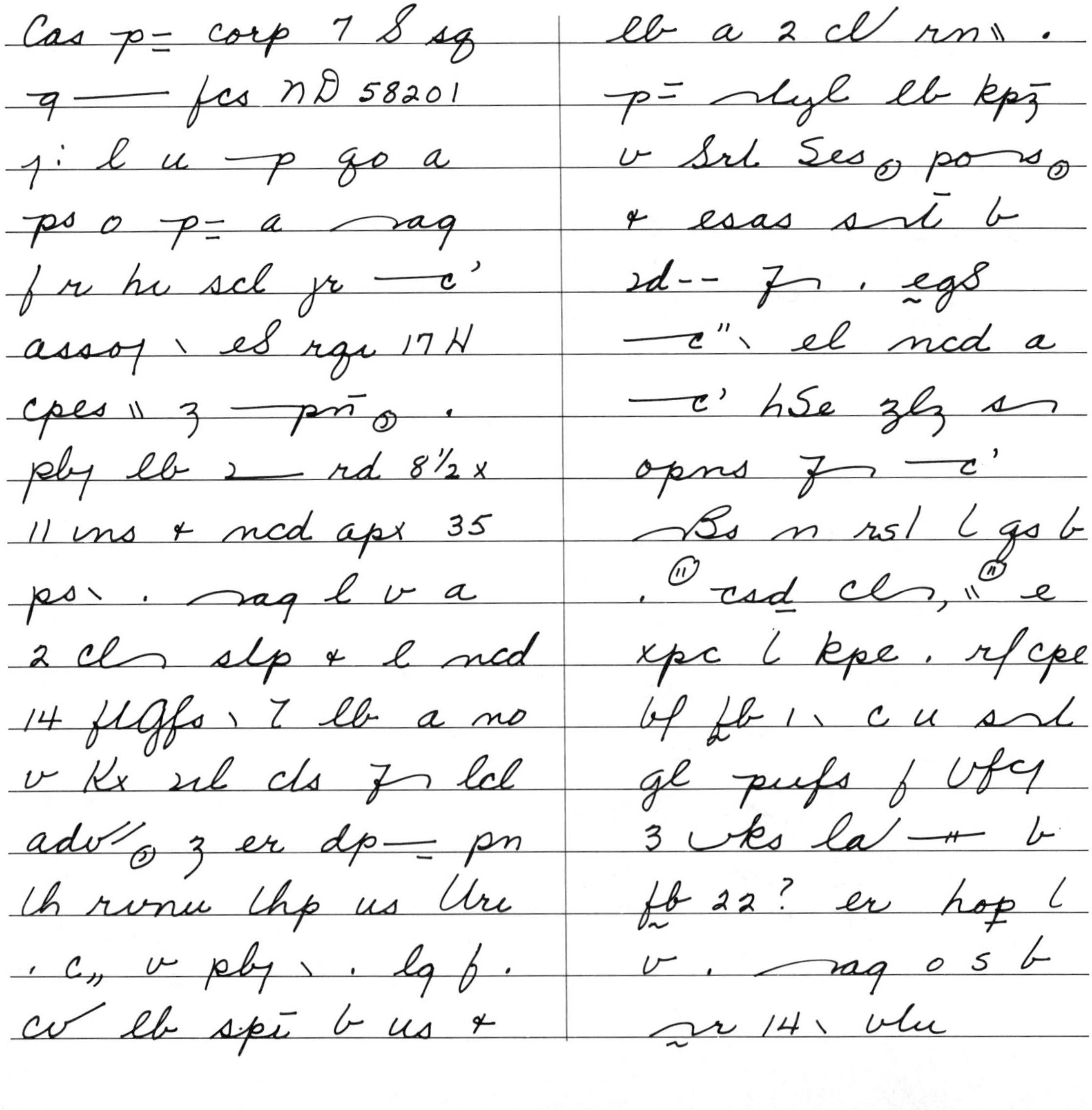

3.1 THEORY REVIEW

1. *aks*
2. *eks*
3. *iks*
4. *oks*
5. *uks*
6. *thing* derivatives
7. *less* derivatives
8. *serve* derivatives

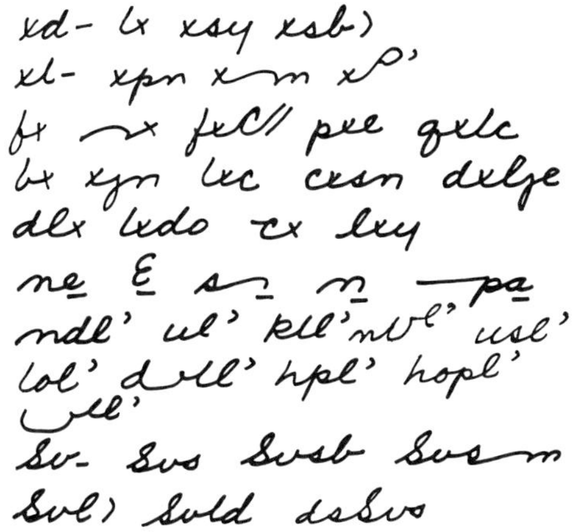

KEY 1. accident; tax; accessory; accessibility 2. extent; explain; examine; express 3. fix; mix; fixtures; pixie; quixotic 4. box; oxygen; toxic; coxswain; doxology 5. deluxe; tuxedo; crux; luxury 6. anything; everything; something; nothing; plaything 7. needless; unless; countless; nevertheless; useless; thoughtless; doubtless; helpless; hopeless; worthless 8. servant; service; serviceable; servicemen; servility; servitude; disservice

3.2 TRANSCRIPTION SKILL BUILDING

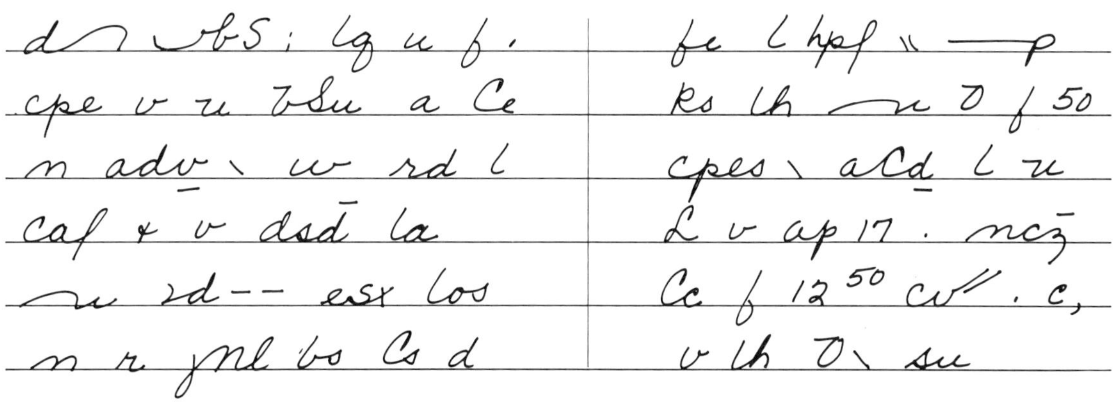

GUIDE Insert one apposition comma, two parenthetical commas, and one introductory comma.

3.3 SPEED BUILDING

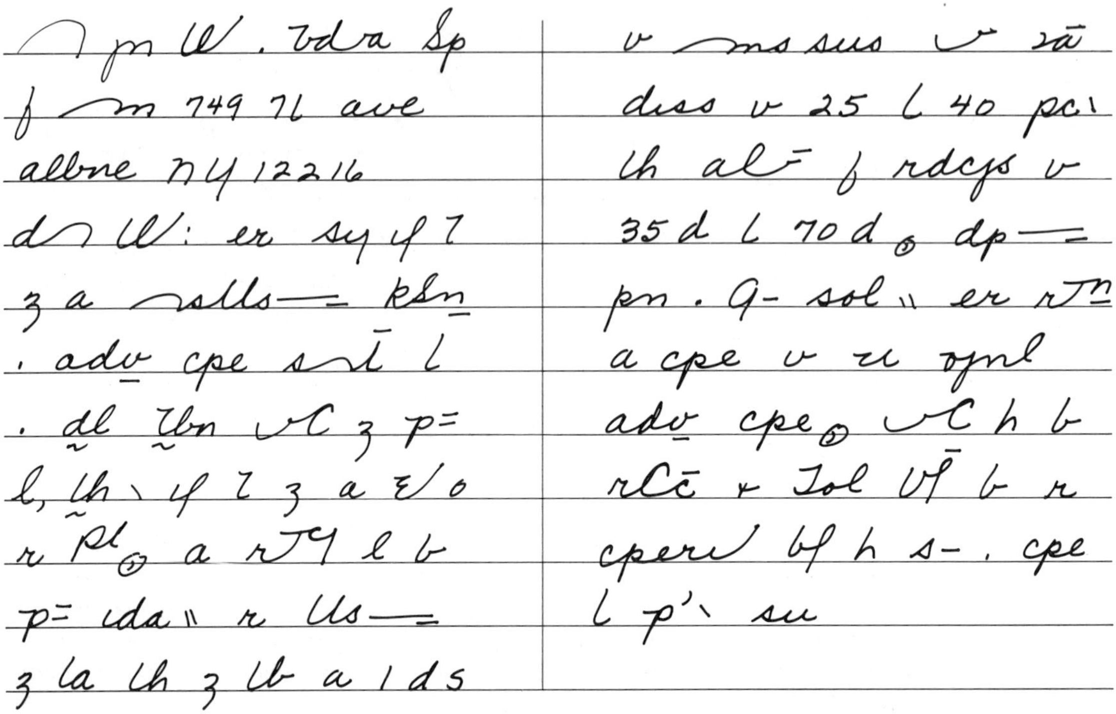

3.4 VOCABULARY BUILDING

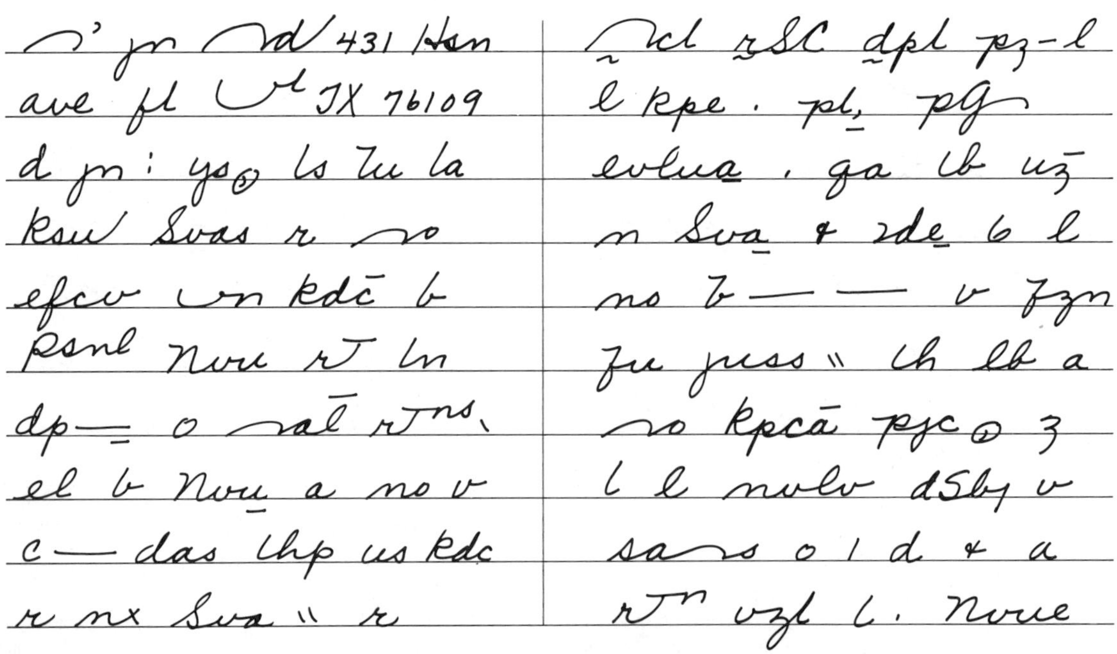

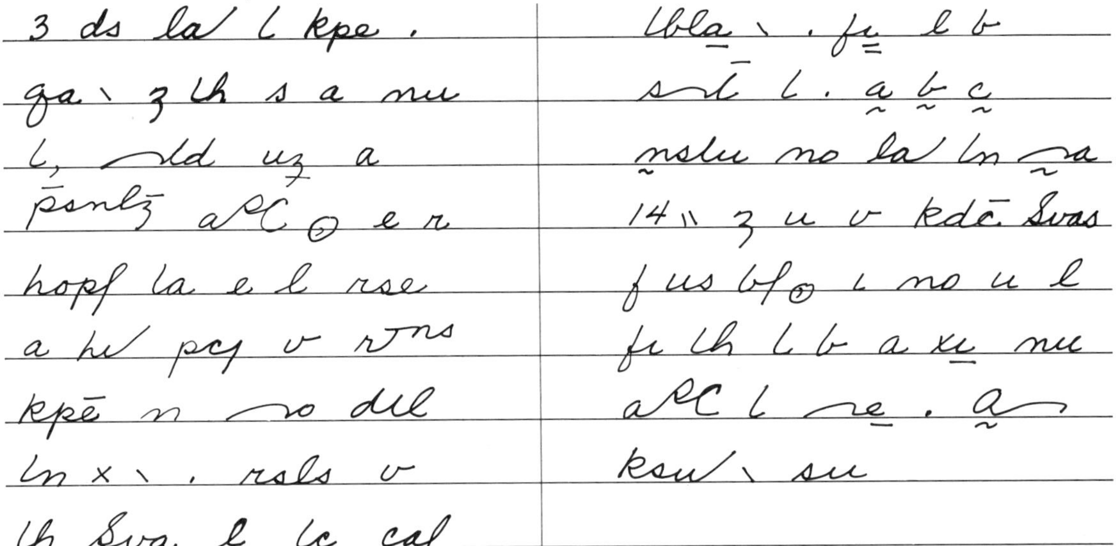

4.1 THEORY REVIEW

1. *sp*

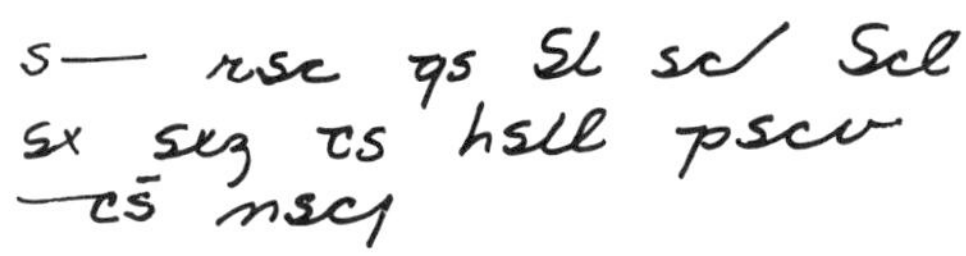

2. Initial *spr*

3. Initial *spl*

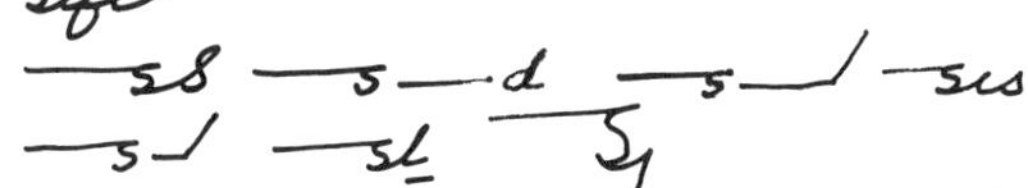

4. *hood* derivatives

5. *man* derivatives

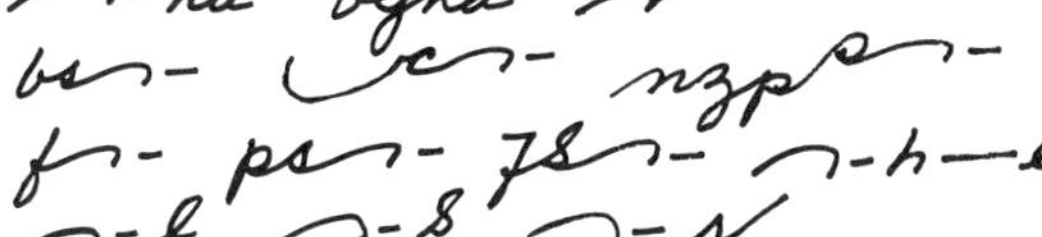

6. *ward* derivatives

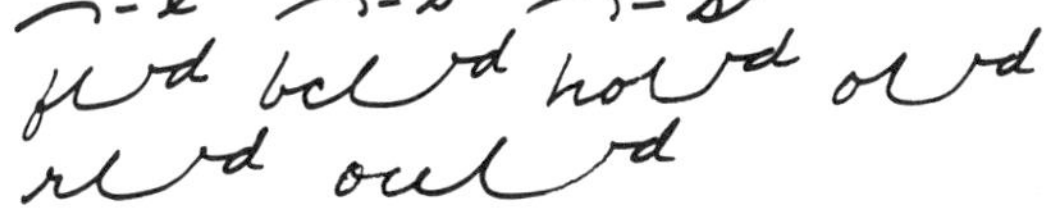

KEY 1. spend; respect; grasp; sport; speaker; sparkle; spacious; specialize; crisp; hospital; prospective; clasped; inspection 2. spring; spread; sprightly; sprain; sprint; sprinkler 3. splash; splendid; splendor; splice; splinter; splitting; splurge 4. neighborhood; childhood; parenthood; likelihood; manhood; boyhood; motherhood 5. businessman; workman; newspaperman; foreman; postman; freshman; manhandle;

manly; mannish; manslaughter 6. forward; backward; homeward; onward; reward; outward

4.2 TRANSCRIPTION SKILL BUILDING

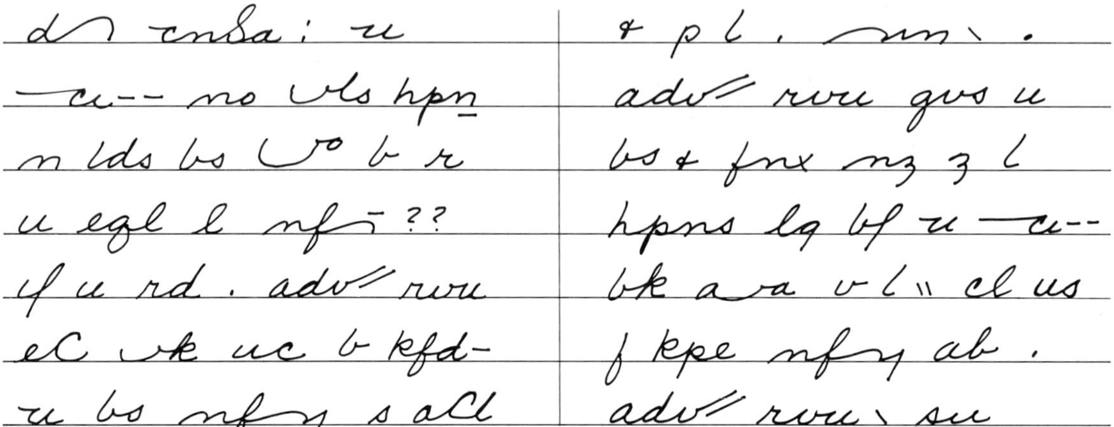

GUIDE Insert one contraction apostrophe, four possessive apostrophes, one conjunction comma, one parenthetical comma, and one introductory comma.

4.3 SPEED BUILDING

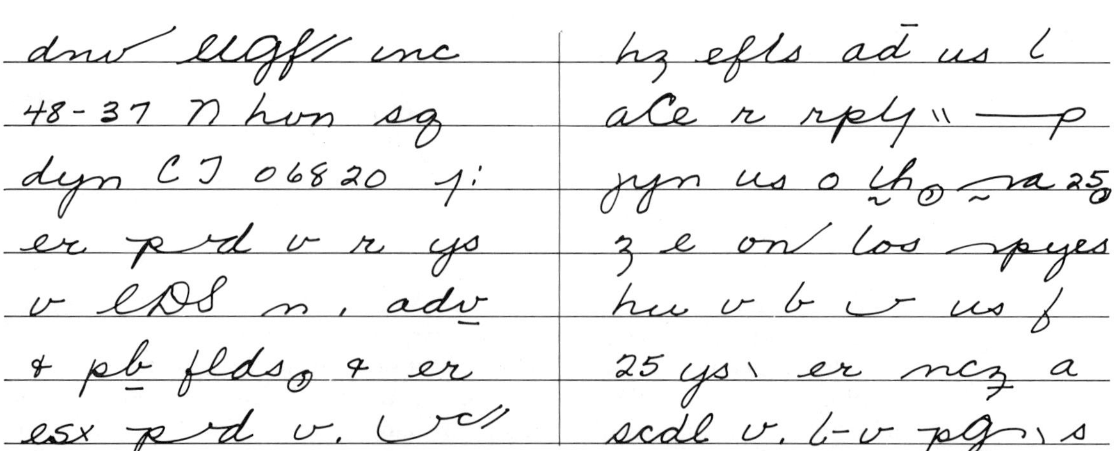

4.4 VOCABULARY BUILDING

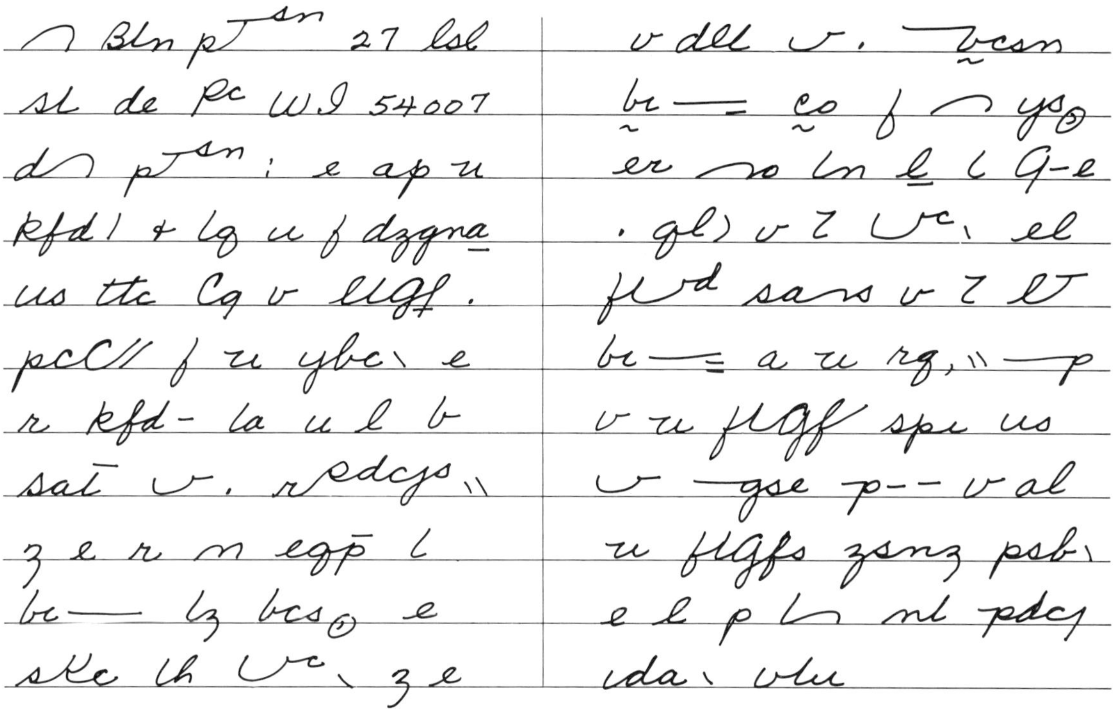

5.1 THEORY REVIEW

1. *k* 

2. *con* 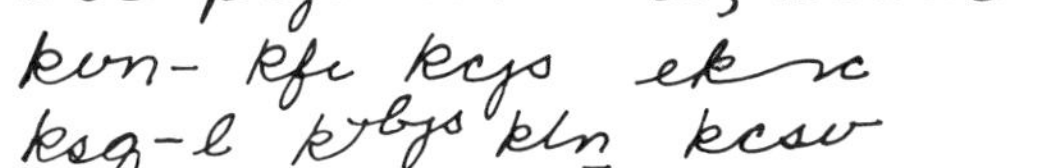

3. *com* 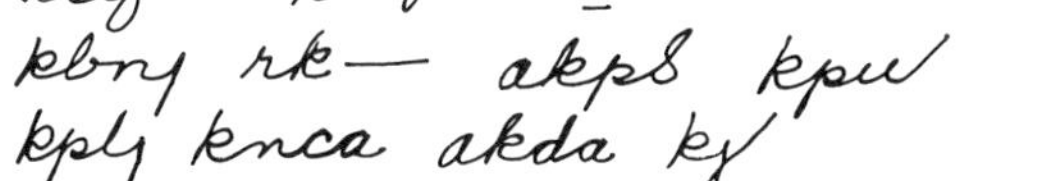

4. *coun* 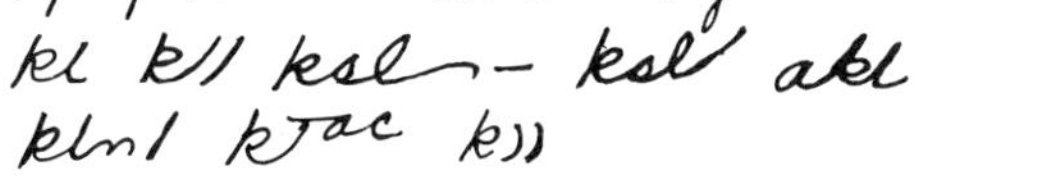

5. *grand* derivatives 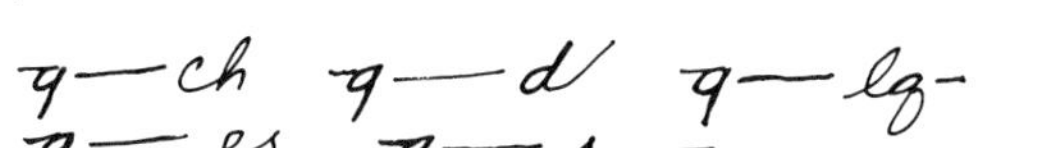

6. *gram* derivatives 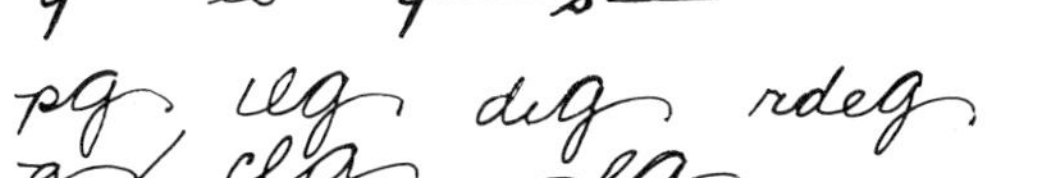

7. *point* derivatives 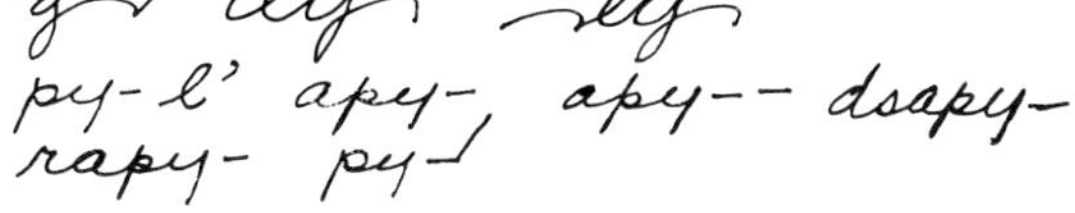

KEY 1. cashier; keynote; booklet; walk; cause; back; book; desk; packages; cabinet; kindest; actual 2. convenient; confine; connections; economic; consequently; contributions; containing; conclusive 3. combination; recommend; accomplish; computer; competition; communicate; accommodate; commissioner 4. count; counters; councilman; counselor; account; continence; counteract; counties 5. grandchild; granddaughter; grandiloquent; grandiose; grandstand 6. program; telegram; diagram; radiogram; grammar; kilogram; milligram 7. pointless; appoint; appointment; disappoint; reappoint; pointer

5.2 TRANSCRIPTION SKILL BUILDING

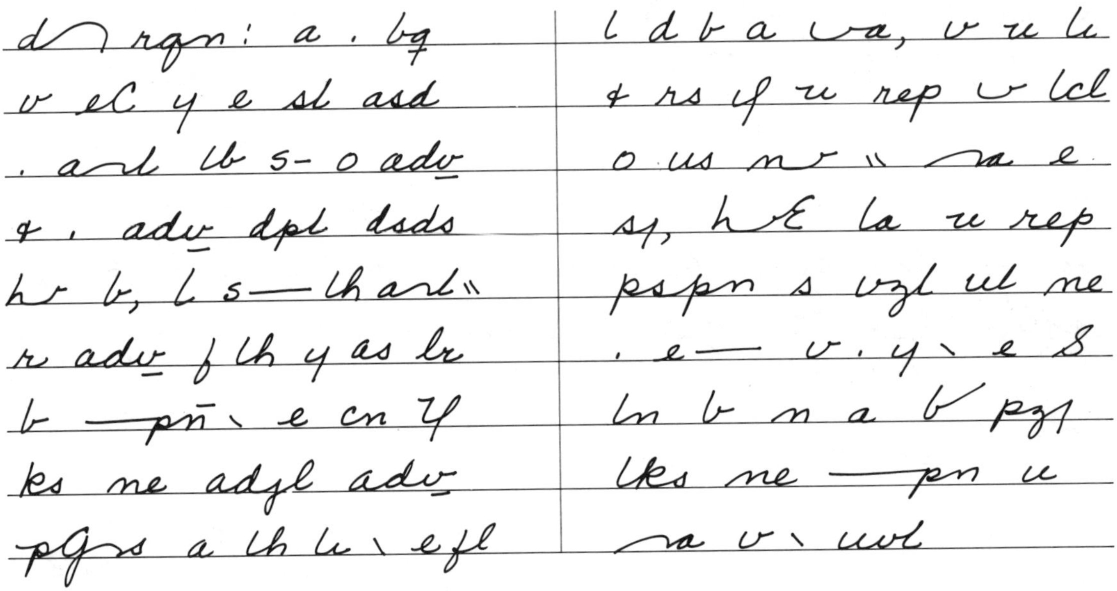

GUIDE Insert one conjunction comma and four parenthetical commas.

5.3 SPEED BUILDING

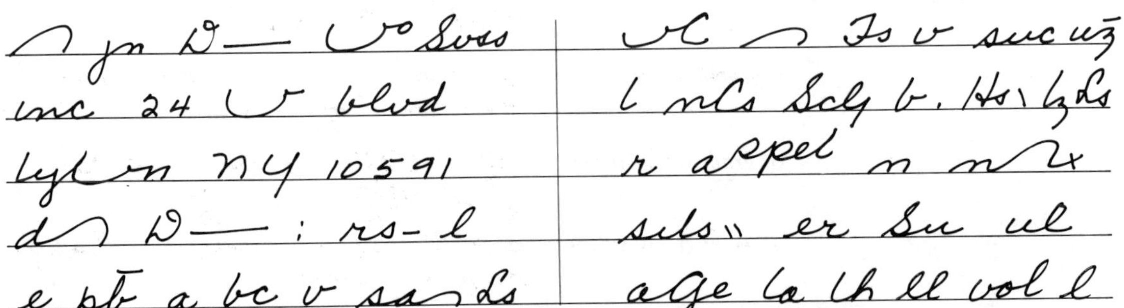

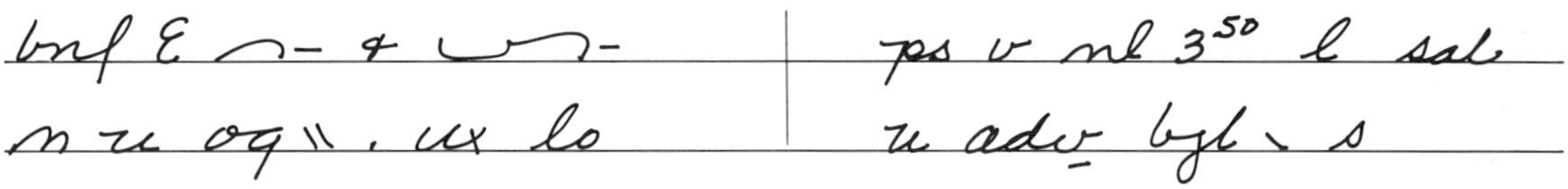

5.4 VOCABULARY BUILDING

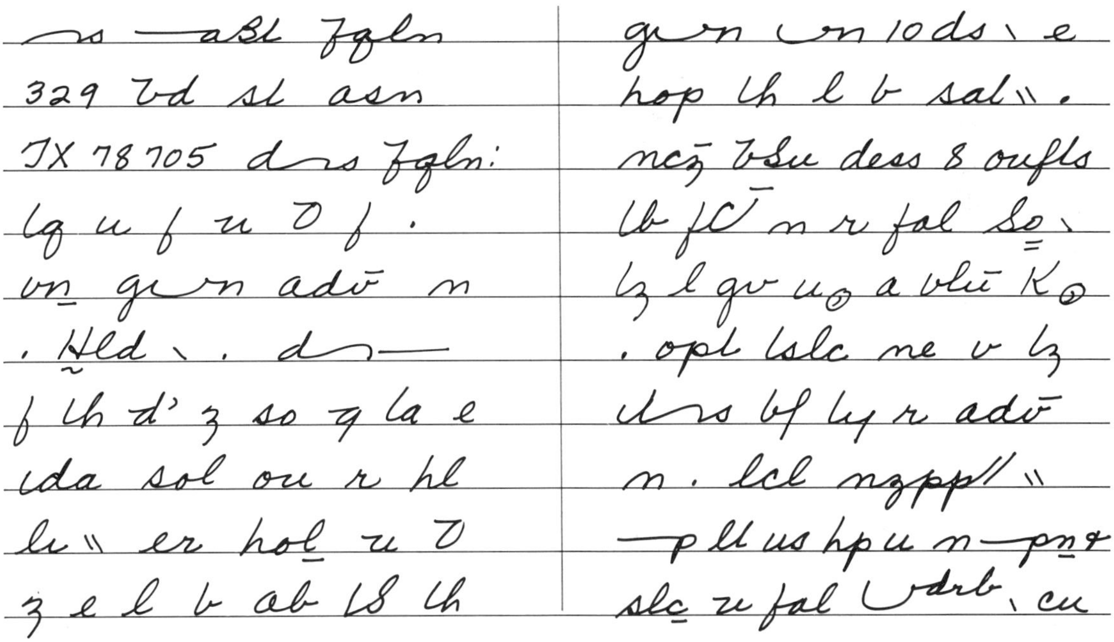

LETTER PLACEMENT

The average business letter today is short—a letter of approximately 100 words. If you will follow these suggestions, you will be able to arrange a short letter attractively on the letterhead:

1. Assuming that your typewriter has elite type, allow right and left margins of about two inches.
2. Type the date line two lines below the last line of the letterhead.
3. Start the inside address about ten lines below the date.

Transcribe a short letter from your notes and examine the placement. Make any necessary alterations to these three steps to correct the placement on the letterhead.

If you will always follow these revised steps, your short letters will always be attractively arranged on the letterhead.

UNIT 6

AUTOMOTIVE

1.1 THEORY REVIEW

1. Medial and final *āze*
2. Medial and final *ēze*
3. Medial and final *īze*
4. Medial and final *ōze*
5. Medial and final *ūze*
6. *come* derivatives
7. *side* derivatives
8. *book* derivatives

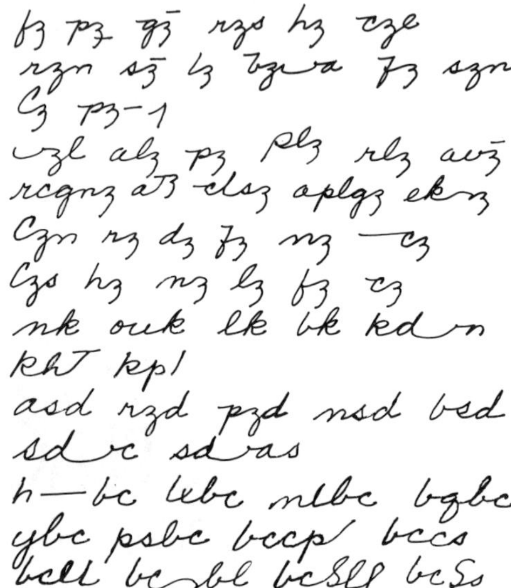

KEY 1. phase; praising; grazed; raises; haze; crazy 2. reason; seized; these; breezeway; freeze; seasonal; cheese; presentation 3. wisely; analyze; prize; paralyze; realize; advised; recognize; authorize; criticize; apologize; economize 4. chosen; rose; doze; froze; nose; close, clothes 5. chooses; whose; news; lose; fuse; cruise 6. income; outcome; welcome; become; comedown; comehither; comeuppance 7. aside; reside; preside; inside; beside; sidewalk; sideways 8. handbook; textbook; notebook; bankbook; yearbook; passbook; bookkeeper; bookcase; booklet; bookmobile; bookshelf; bookstores

1.2 TRANSCRIPTION SKILL BUILDING

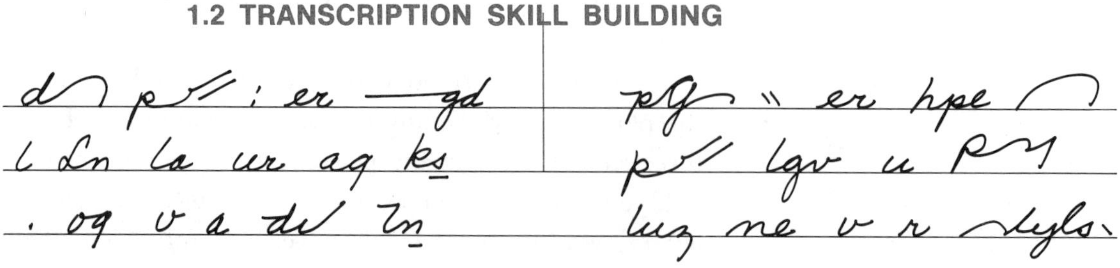

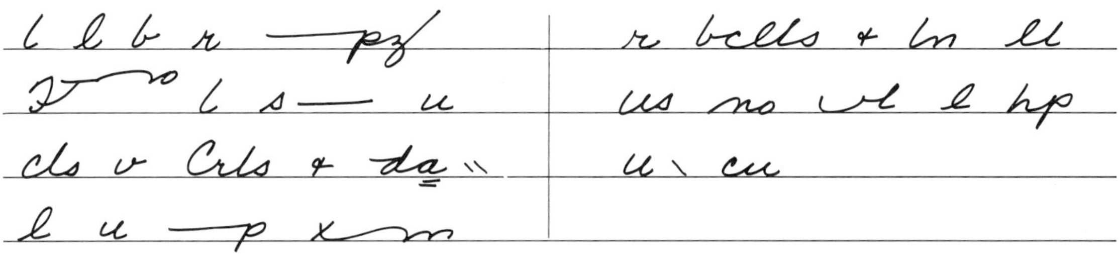

GUIDE Insert one compound adjective hyphen and four parenthetical commas.

1.3 SPEED BUILDING

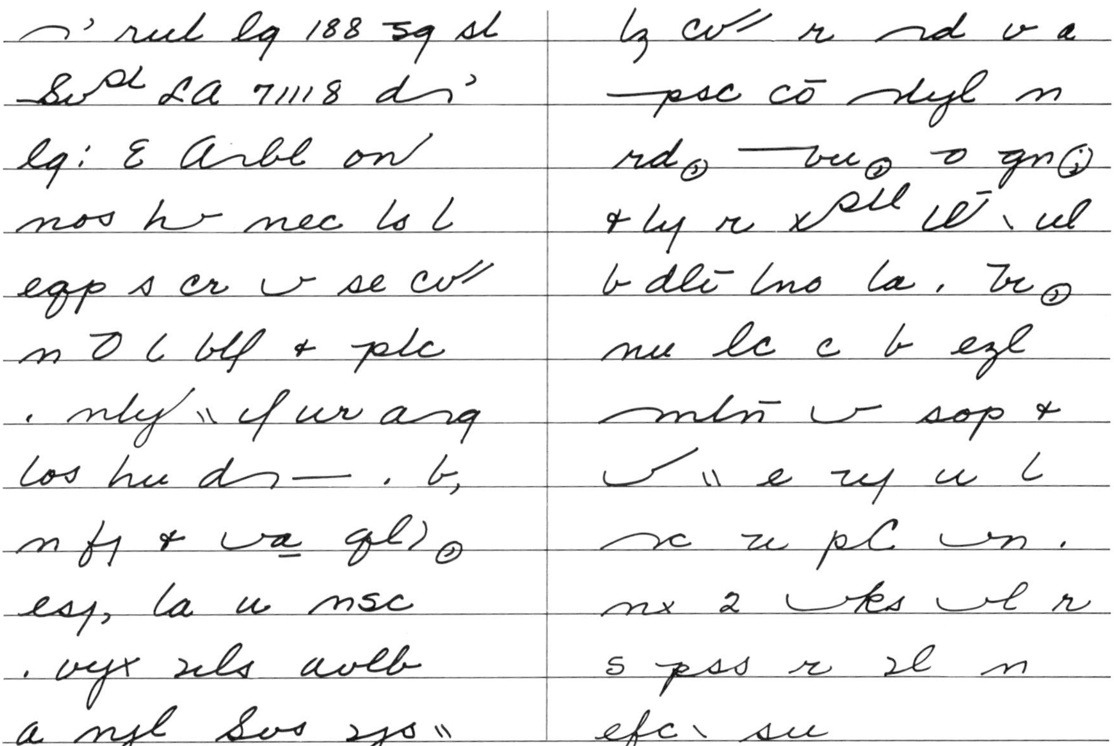

1.4 VOCABULARY BUILDING

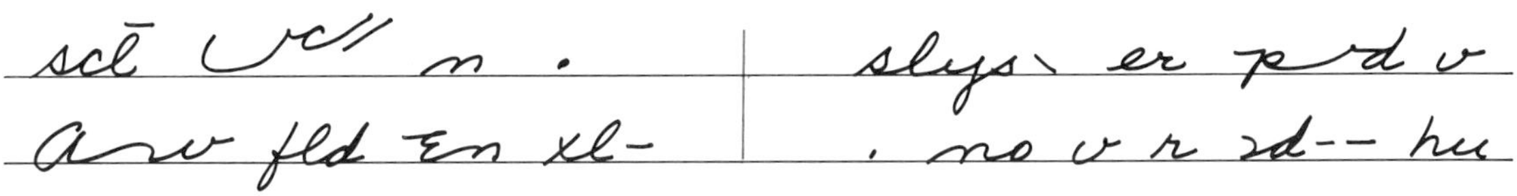

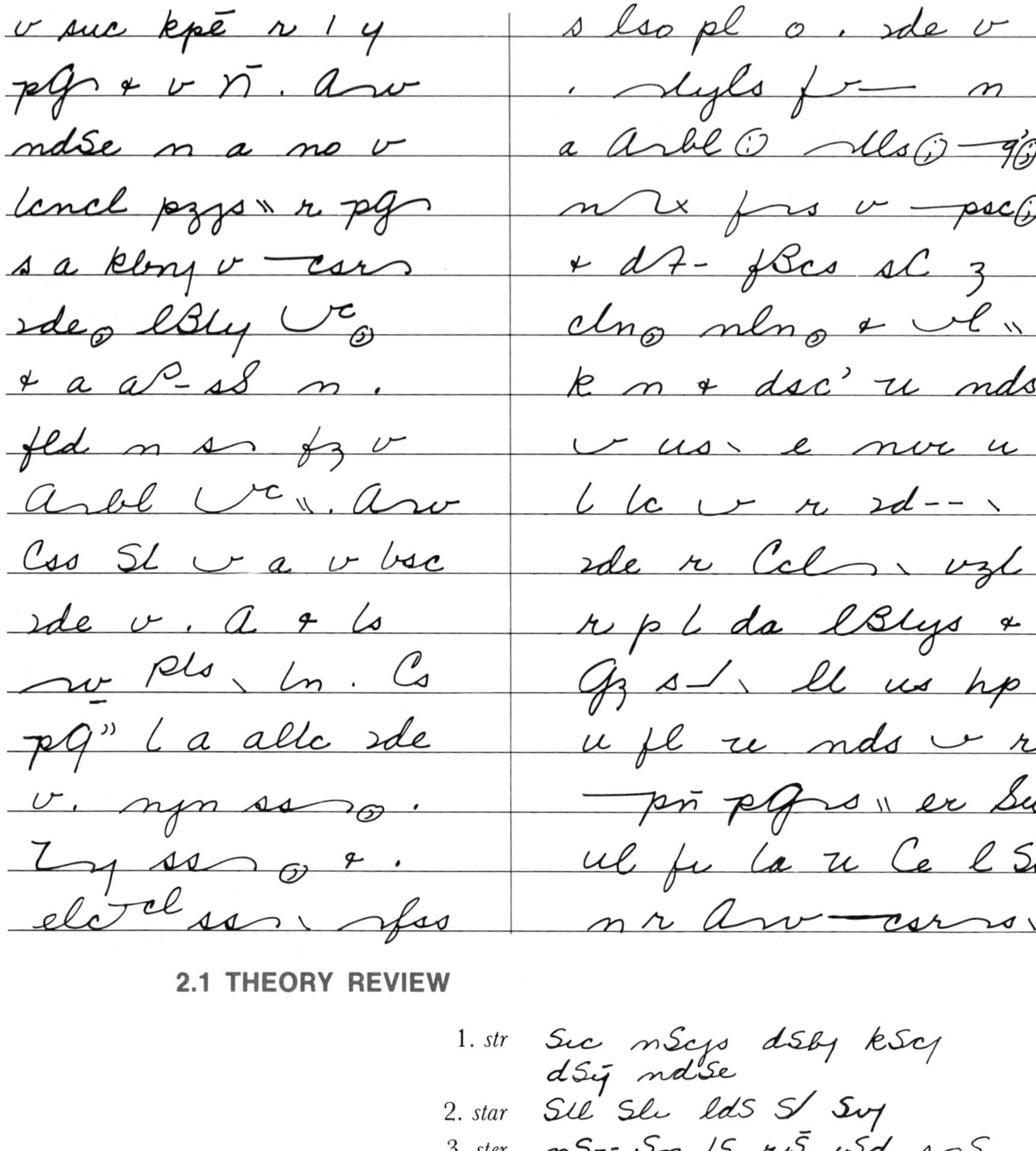

2.1 THEORY REVIEW

1. *str*
2. *star*
3. *ster*
4. *stor*
5. *prove* derivatives
6. *long* derivatives
7. *post* derivatives

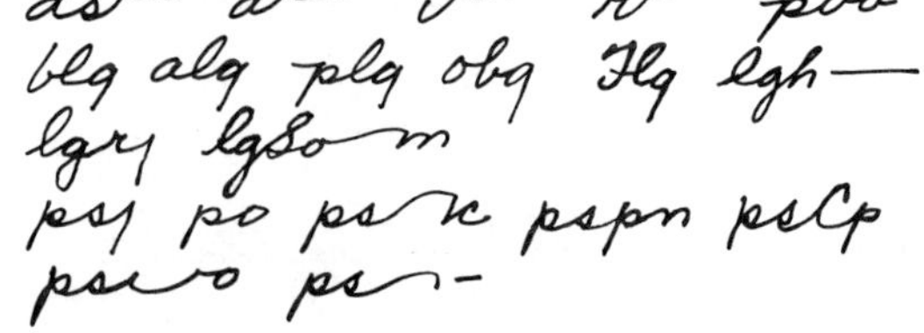

KEY 1. strike; instructions; distribution; construction; destroyed; industry 2. startle; starlight; lodestar; starter; starvation 3. instruments; stern; faster; registered; yesterday; semester 4. storage; storm; history; storeroom; story 5. disprove; approval; improvement; reprove; provable 6. belong; along; prolong; oblong; furlong; longhand; long-range; longshoremen 7. postage; post office; postmark; postpone; postscript; postwar; postman

2.2 TRANSCRIPTION SKILL BUILDING

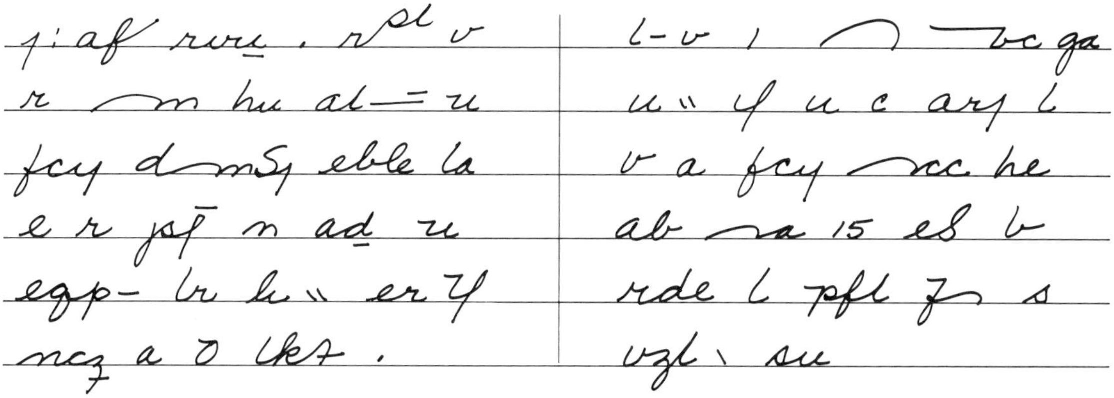

GUIDE Insert two introductory commas and two parenthetical commas.

2.3 SPEED BUILDING

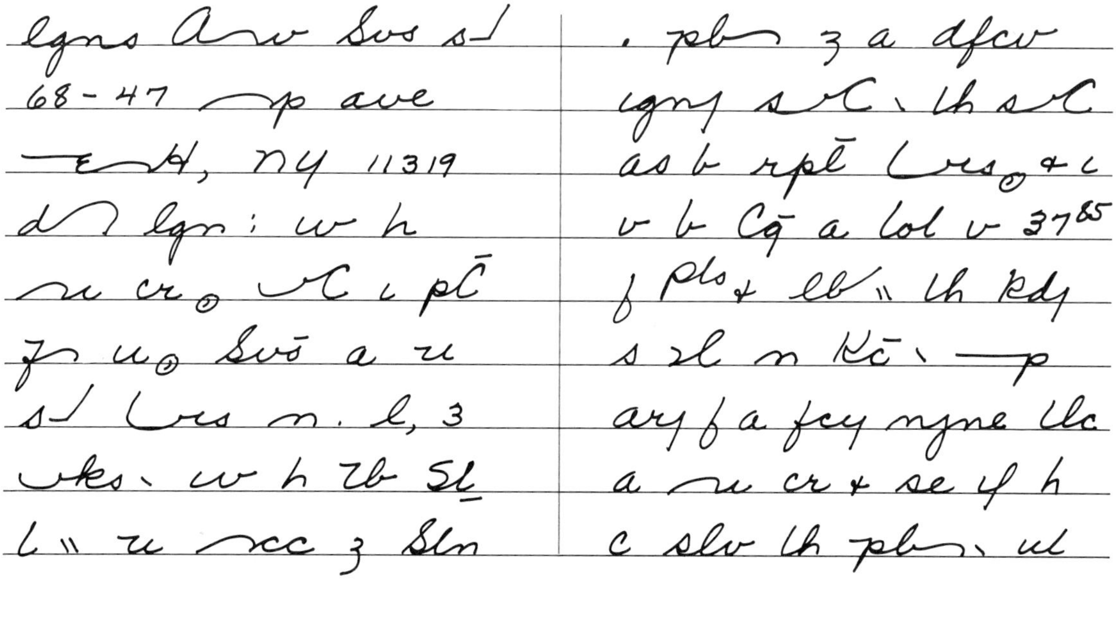

2.4 VOCABULARY BUILDING

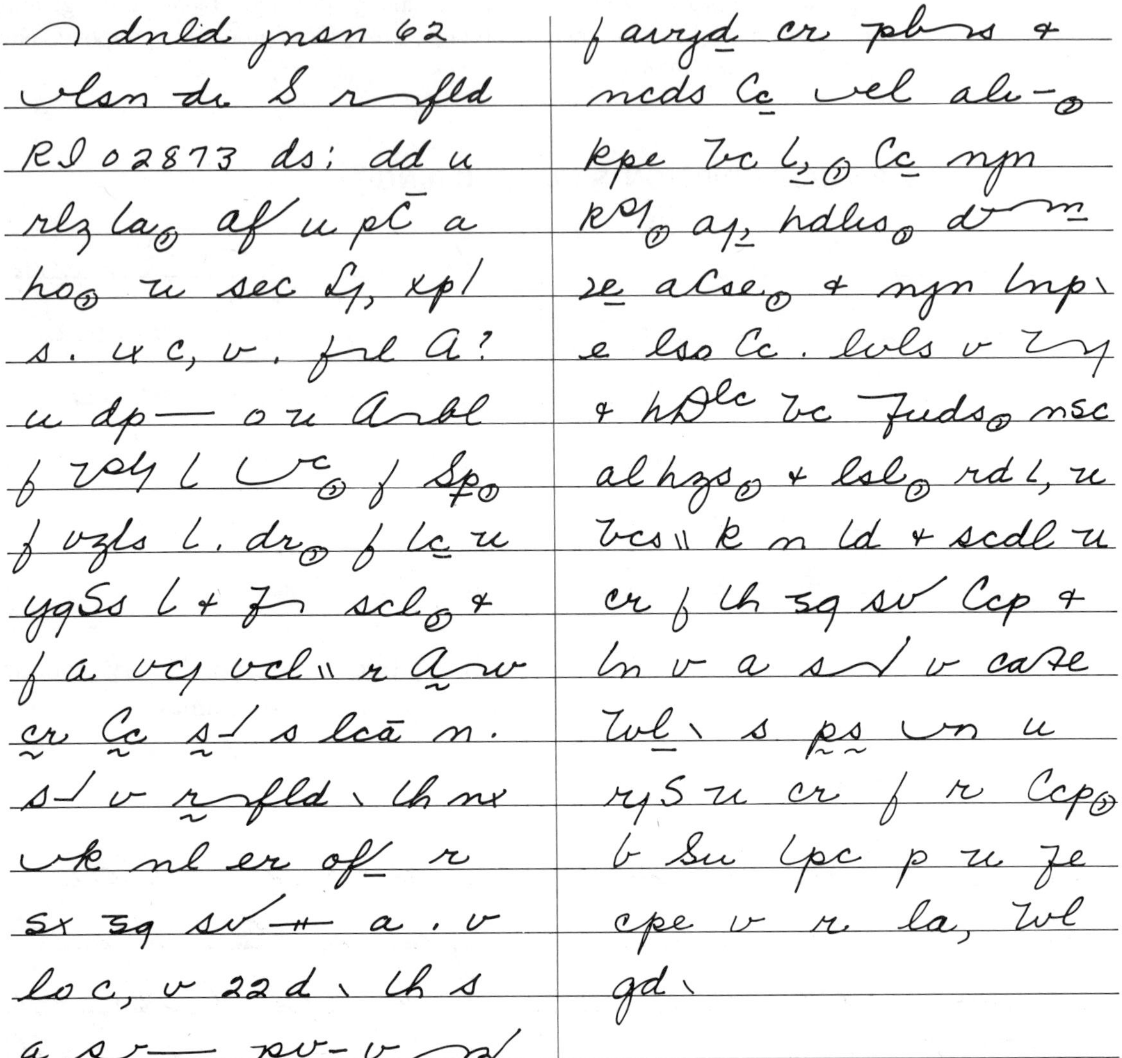

3.1 THEORY REVIEW

1. *us-ly*
2. *shus-ly*
3. *shul-ly*
4. *nshul-ly*
5. *vent* derivatives

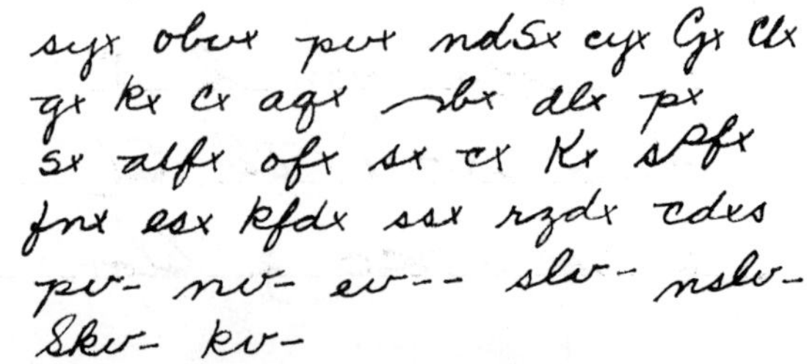

6. Compound words

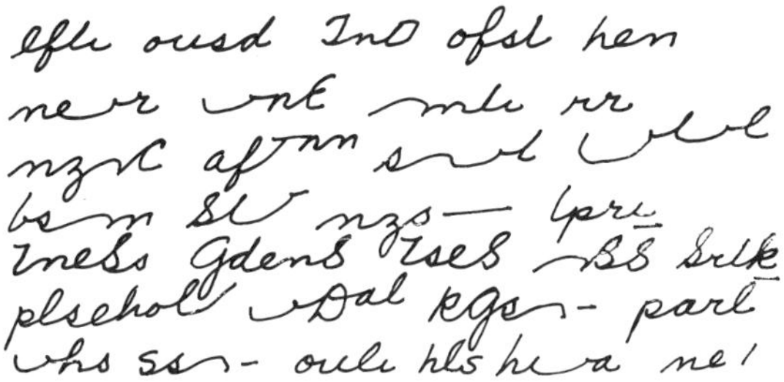

KEY 1. serious, -ly; obvious, -ly; previous, -ly; industrious, -ly; curious, -ly; courageous, -ly; courteous, -ly 2. gracious, -ly; conscious, -ly; cautious, -ly; anxious, -ly; ambitious, -ly; delicious, -ly; precious, -ly 3. special, -ly; artificial, -ly; official, -ly; social, -ly; crucial, -ly; commercial, -ly; superficial, -ly 4. financial, -ly; essential, -ly; confidential, -ly; substantial, -ly; residential; credentials 5. prevent; invent; events; solvent; insolvent; circumvent; convent 6. lifetime; outside; turnover; offset; herein; anywhere; whenever; meantime; railroad; inasmuch; afternoon; somewhat; worthwhile; businessmen; southwest; newsstand; typewriting; traineeships; guardianship; trusteeship; membership; shortcoming; policyholder; withdrawal; congressman; payroll; warehouse; salesman; outline; wholesale; highway; anyone

3.2 TRANSCRIPTION SKILL BUILDING

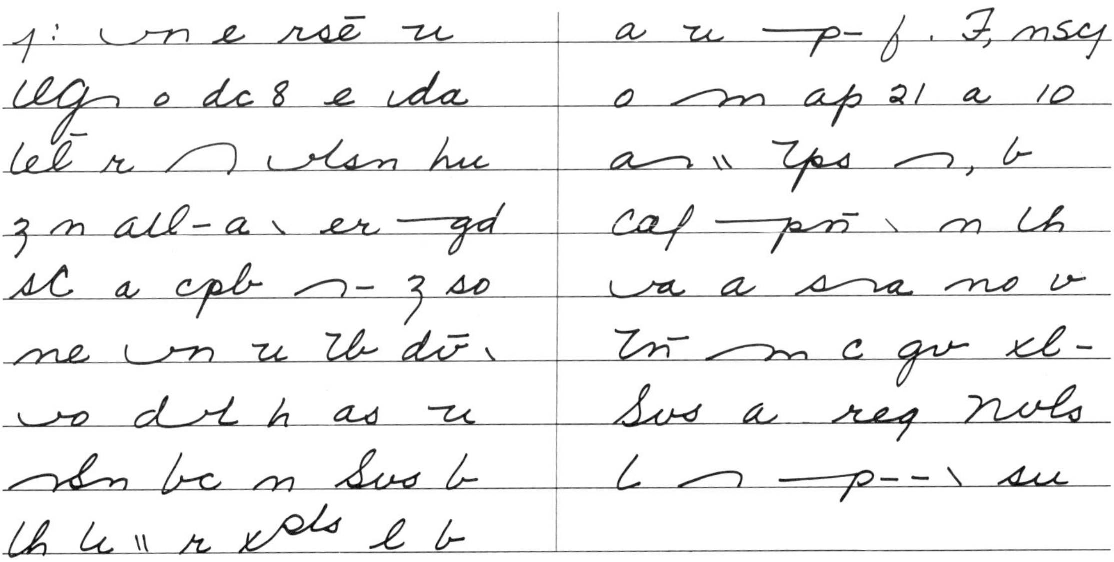

GUIDE Insert two introductory commas, one parenthetical comma, and two apposition commas.

3.3 SPEED BUILDING

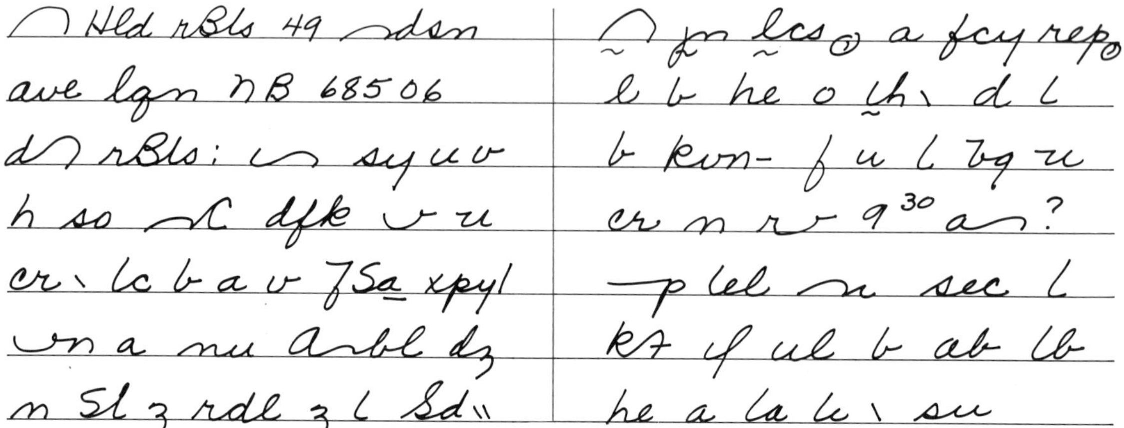

3.4 VOCABULARY BUILDING

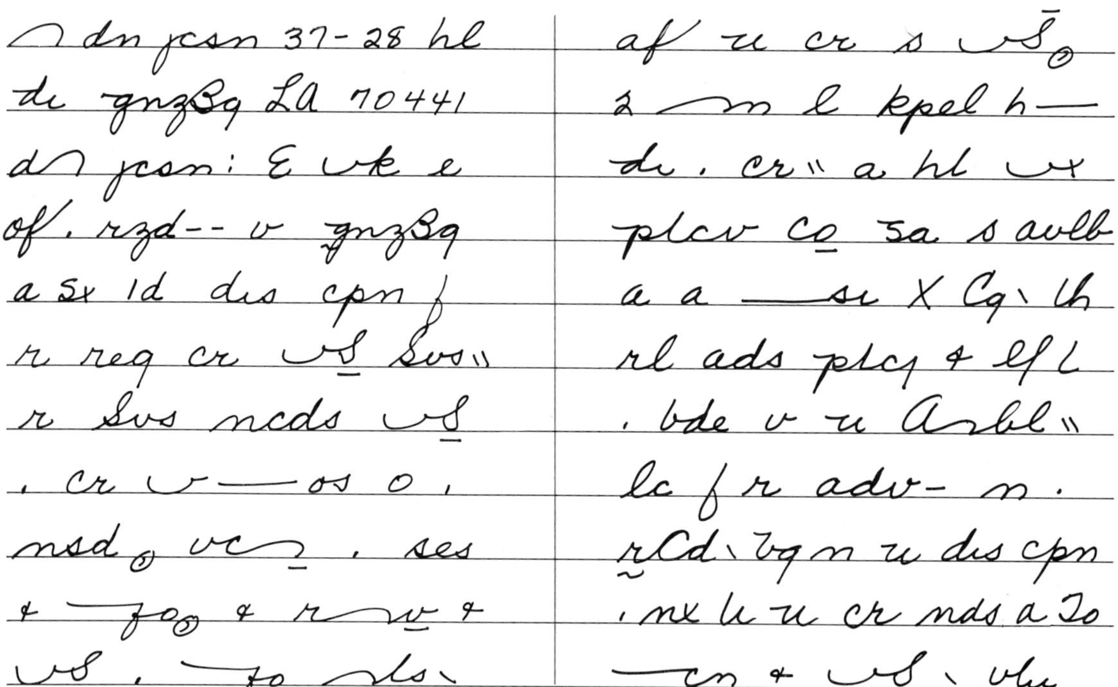

4.1 THEORY REVIEW

1. Final *ther* 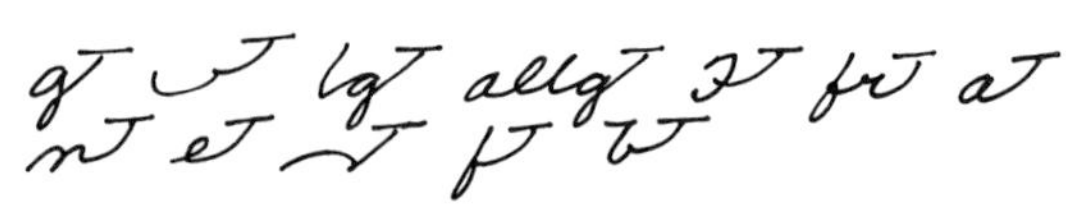

2. *kt*
3. *pt*
4. *ft*
5. *xt*
6. *mpt*

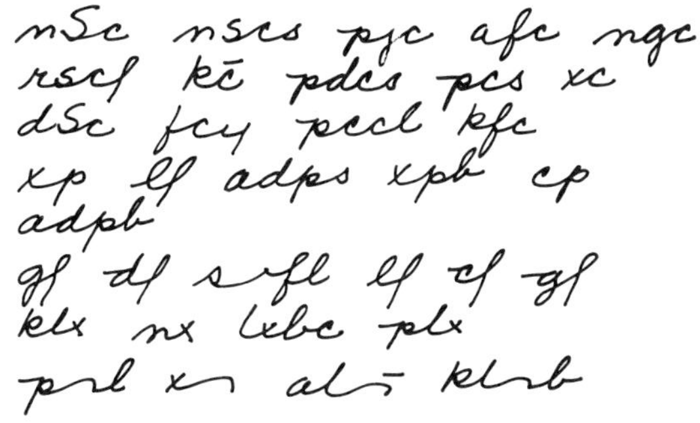

KEY 1. gather; whether, weather; together; altogether; further; farther; another; neither; either; mother; father; brother 2. instruct; inspects; project; affect; neglect; respectful; connected; products; practice; exact; district; factory; practical; conflict 3. except; lift; adopts; acceptable; kept; adaptable 4. gift; draft; swiftly; left; craft; graft 5. context; next; textbook; pretext 6. promptly; exempt; attempted; contemptible

4.2 TRANSCRIPTION SKILL BUILDING

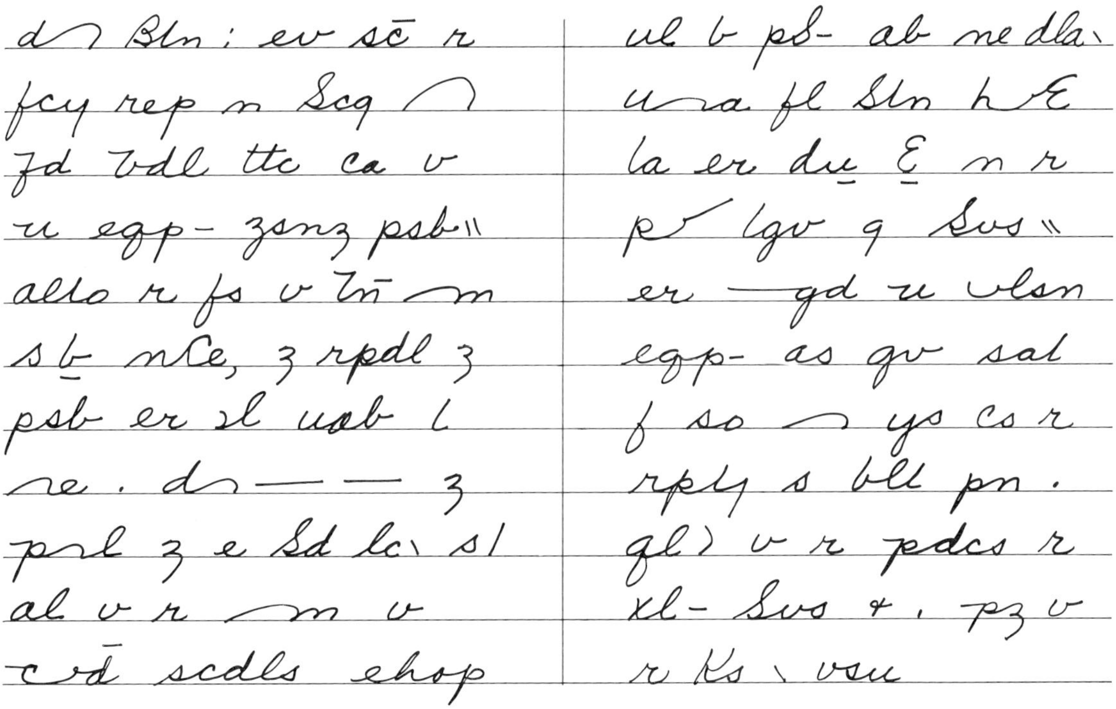

GUIDE Insert two apposition commas, two introductory commas, two parenthetical commas, and two series commas.

4.3 SPEED BUILDING

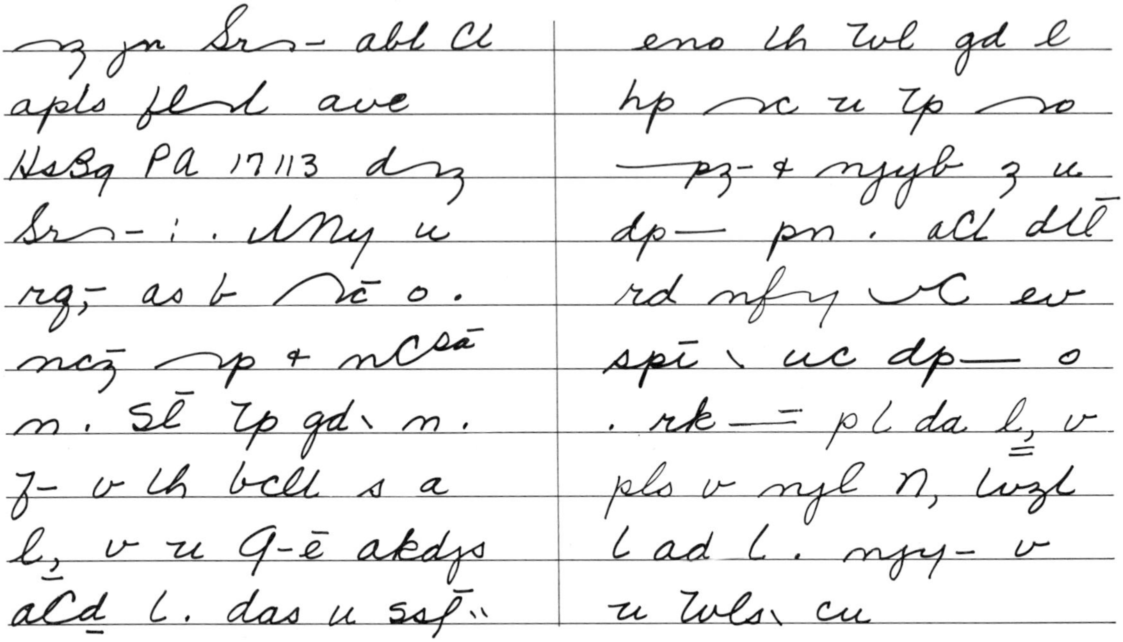

4.4 VOCABULARY BUILDING

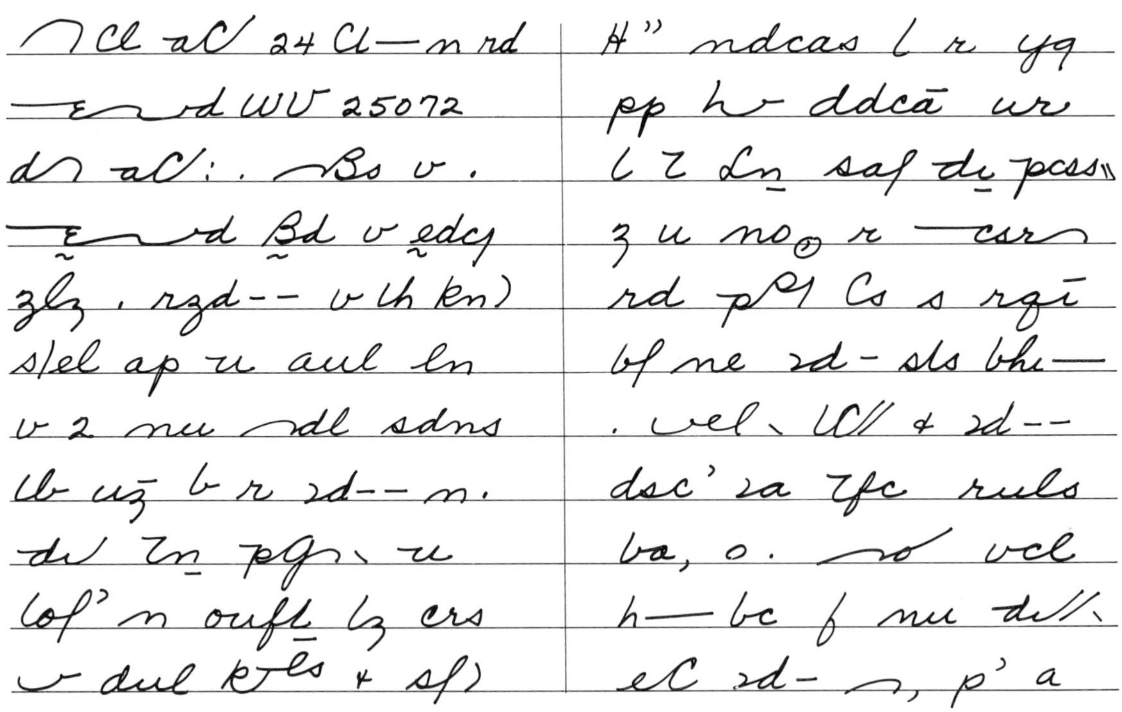

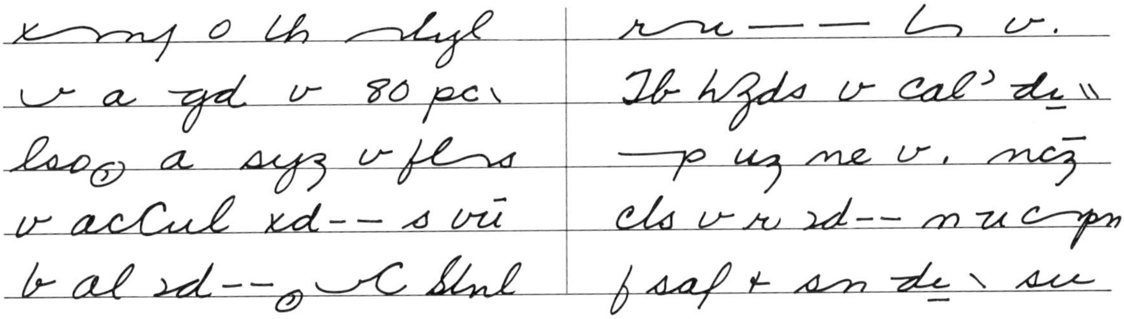

5.1 THEORY REVIEW

1. *dm*
2. *dv*
3. *ng*
4. *nj*
5. *nch*
6. *fine* derivatives
7. *place* derivatives

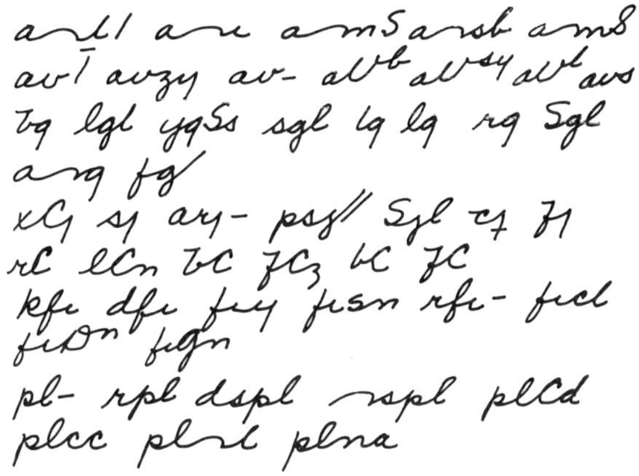

KEY 1. admittance; admire; administer; admissible; admonish 2. advanced; advisory; advent; adverb; adversary; advert; advice 3. bring; length; youngsters; single; thing; long; wrong; strongly; among; finger 4. exchange; singe; arrangement; passengers; strangely; cringing; fringe 5. ranch; lunchcon; branch; franchise; bench; French 6. confine; define; finery; finespun; refinement; fine-cut; fine-drawn; fine-grain 7. placement; replace; displace; misplace; placecard; place kick; placemat; place-name

5.2 TRANSCRIPTION SKILL BUILDING

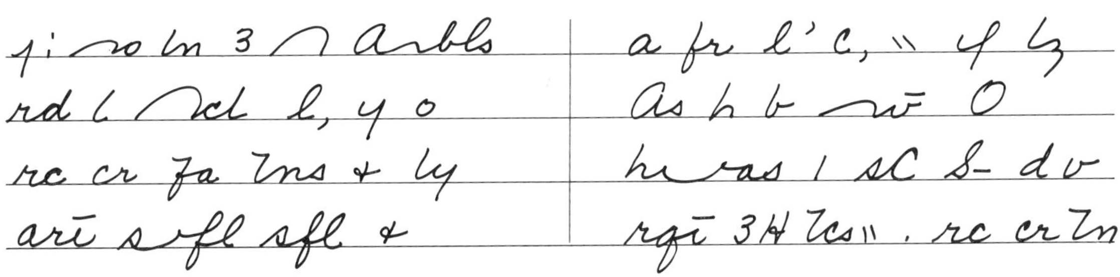

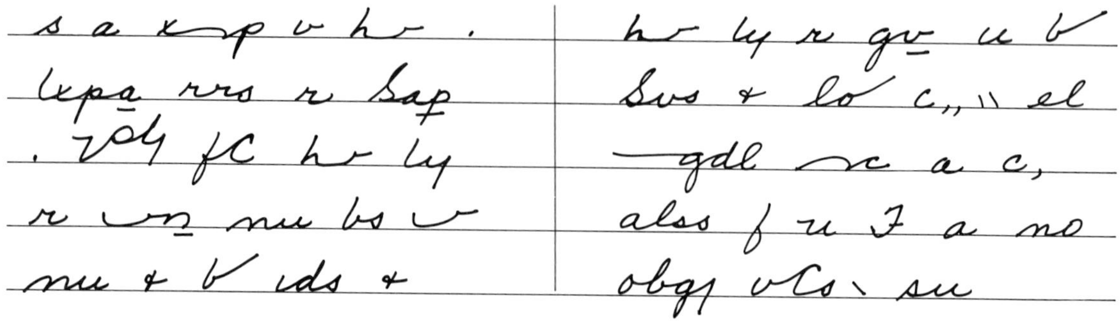

GUIDE Insert one internal punctuation semicolon, four series commas, one introductory comma, one parenthetical comma, and two compound adjective hyphens.

5.3 SPEED BUILDING

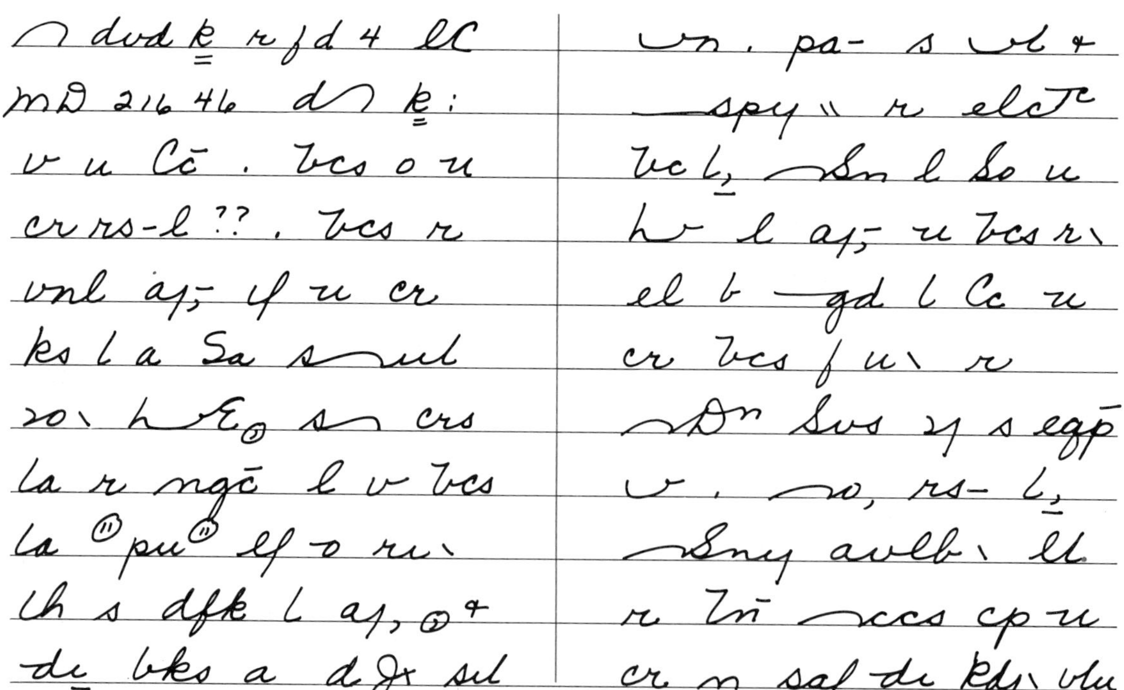

5.4 VOCABULARY BUILDING

(A)

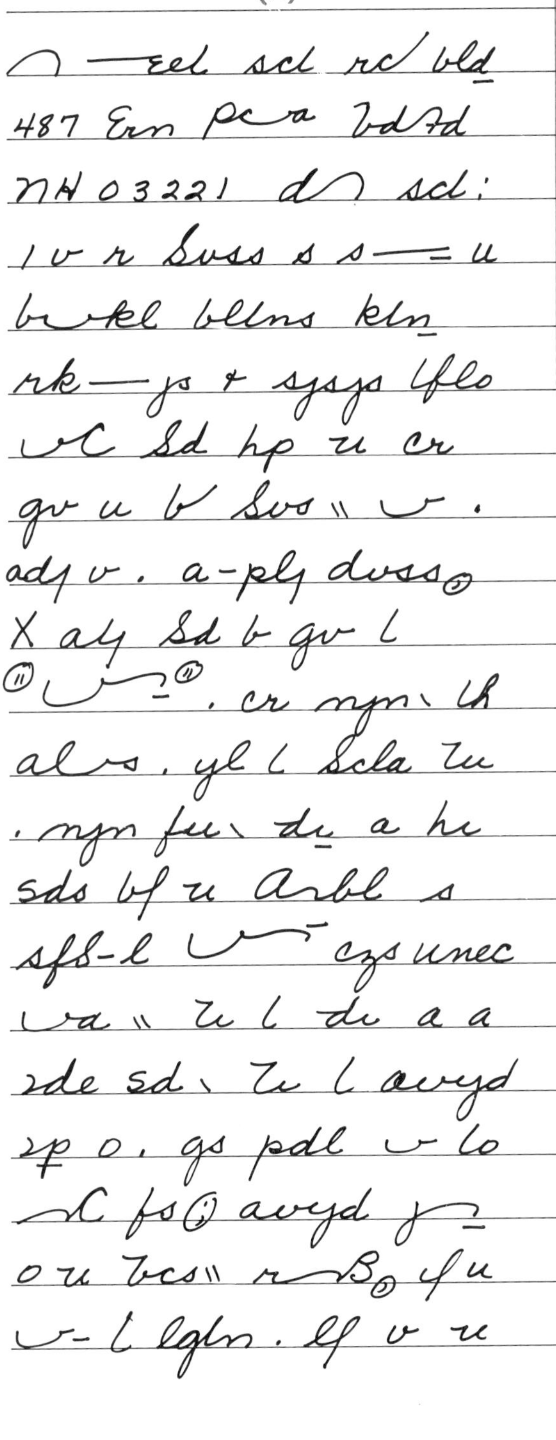

(B)

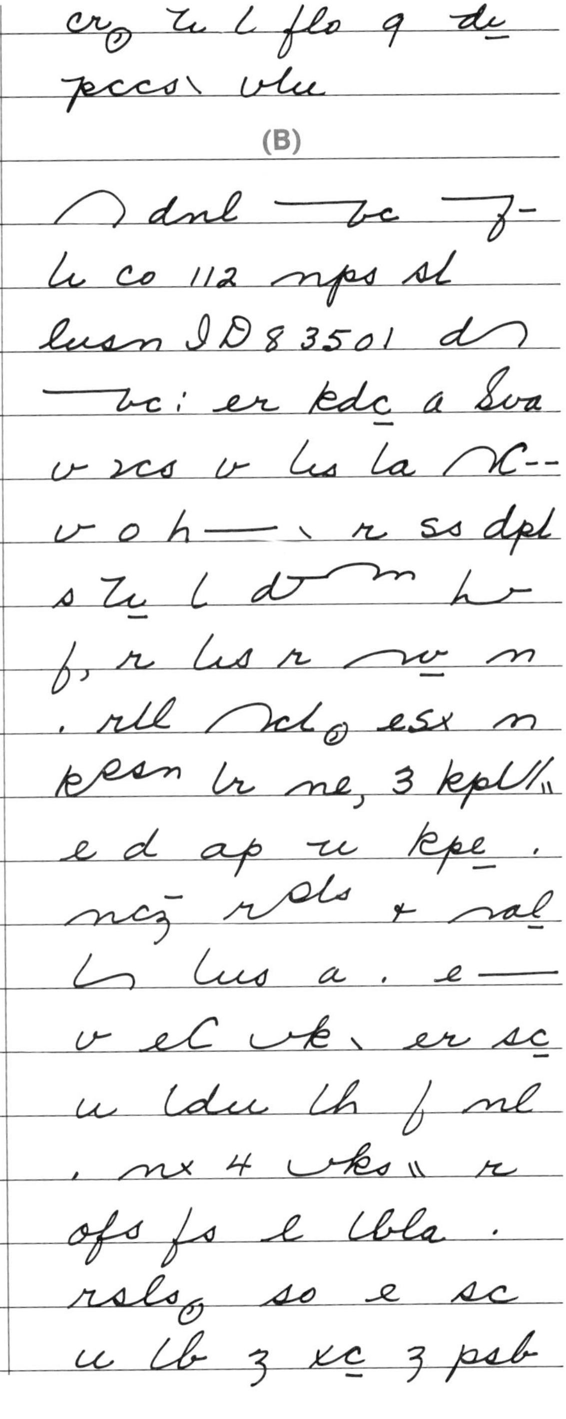

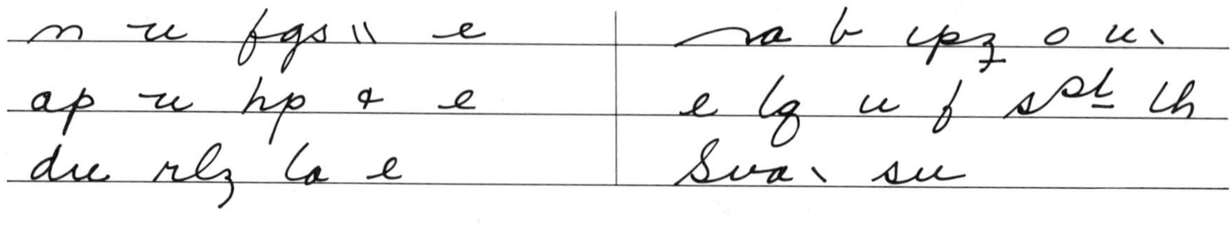

EXPANDING AND CONDENSING LETTERS

If the typist realizes that she has misjudged the length of a letter after she has started it, she need not always start the letter over again. The following pointers will compensate for errors in judgment. To lengthen a very short letter, use one or more of these techniques:

1. Lower the date line three to five lines.
2. Allow additional blank lines between the date and the inside address.
3. Use 10- or 15-space paragraph indentations.
4. Double-space the body of the letter.
5. Using the variable linespacer, leave one and a half blank lines rather than one blank line between parts of the letter.
6. Allow six blank lines for the pen-written signature.
7. Type the dictator's name and official title on separate lines.
8. Lower the reference initials one or two lines.

To shorten a long one-page letter, any one or a combination of the following techniques may be used:

1. Raise the date one or two lines.
2. Allow only two or three blank lines between the date and the inside address.
3. Omit the company name in the closing line.
4. Allow only two blank lines for the penwritten signature.
5. Type the reference initials on the same line as the last line of the closing of the letter.

UNIT 7

MANUFACTURING

1.1 THEORY REVIEW

1. *ārē*
2. *ērē*
3. *īrē*
4. *ōrē*
5. *ūrē*
6. *z*
7. *s*
8. Numbers

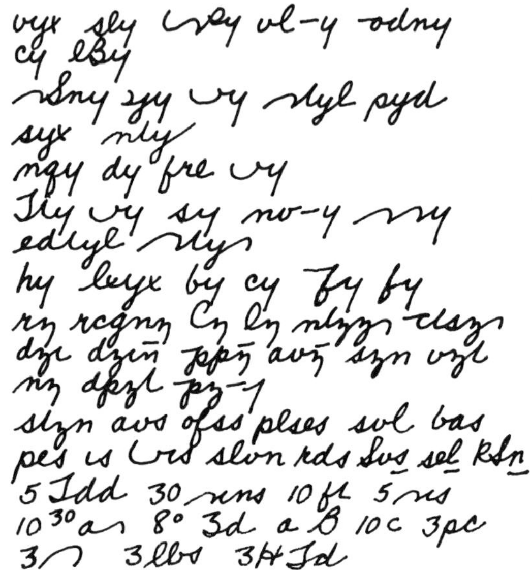

KEY 1. various; salary; temporary; voluntary; ordinary; carry; library 2. machinery; stationery; weary; material; period; serious; interior 3. inquiry; diary; fiery; wiry 4. territory; worry; sorry; inventory; memory; editorial; moratorium 5. hurry; luxurious; bury; curry; flurry; fury 6. rise; recognize; cheese; lose; enthusiasm; criticism; desire; designed; proposed; advised; season; visit; news; deposit; presentation 7. citizen; advice; offices; policies; civil; base; piece; ice; twice; civilian; reduce; servicing; ceiling; concerning 8. $5,000; 30 minutes; 10 feet; 5 miles; 10:30 a.m.; 8 o'clock; third; a billion; 10 cents; 3 percent; 3,000,000; 3 pounds; 300,000

1.2 TRANSCRIPTION SKILL BUILDING

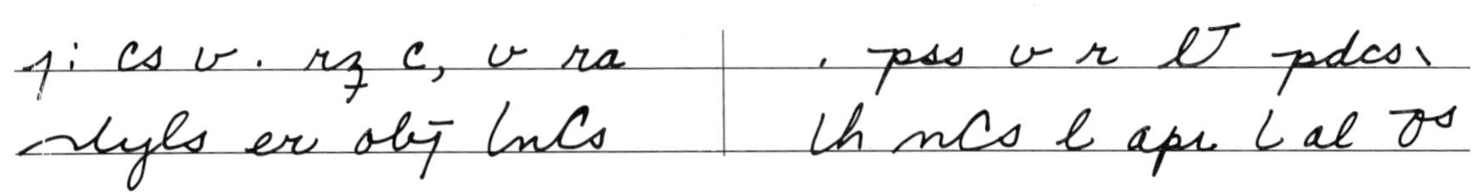

rsē af/ —r 1\ so la
u—a lc avj v lh
opl lsv —me er
s— u av/ nls\ e
sj, Uf la u pl u O
vl, C- lo/ pss
r sl n efc\ a Lj

vol v bs l no dl
reC us bf, e— v nx
no + Z —a b a dla n
s— v r dls\ vo-u
dT m u rgi-- vn.
nx 10 ds + ll usfl u
nds a c/\ ul

GUIDE Insert two introductory commas, two parenthetical commas, one conjunction comma, and one contraction apostrophe.

1.3 SPEED BUILDING

l: dSc —nf/ 8 dSc
—pn sjs r b pjc
f, sos v ap + —a\
Zdjl ss dCs du ,
s/ sos\ ls xpc
la v —dfcjs +
rScC v r ss pjs
ecd Cj lh Z—\ r
pz- Sq ekre l lso
nCj ksu/ s— \ a
r —pn sjs xp

ld// n —cl lcncs
l lc o sC lpcs z
(11) hv l rds Ohd c (11)
+ (11) ip-j v ss pjs\ (11)
lu lb alt f a g
+ as/ pjd\ lf lb
scu b. s-rl
rZvjs —Cc\ l-v
scdls r b dpca
+ l b dSbu nx
vk\

1.4 VOCABULARY BUILDING

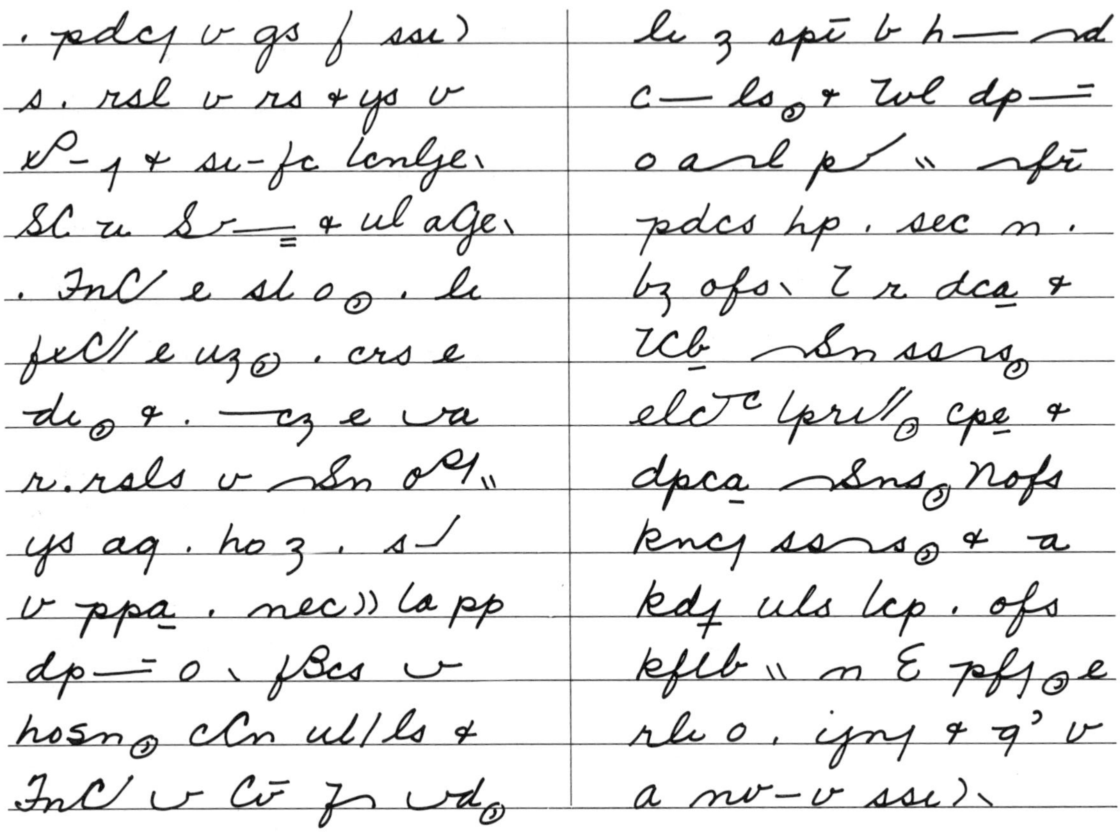

2.1 THEORY REVIEW

1. Medial and final *tiv*

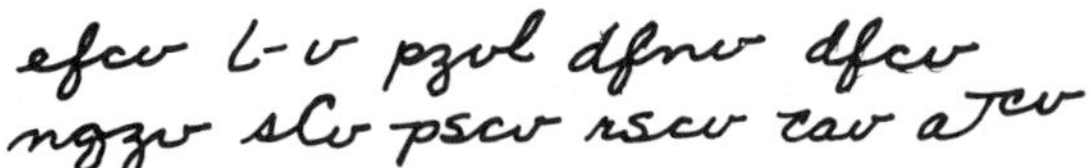

2. Medial consecutive vowels

3. Final consecutive vowels

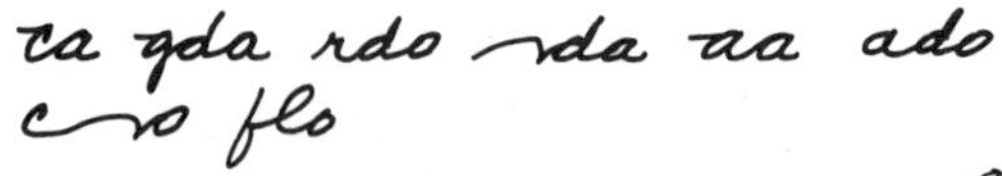

4. Writing vowels

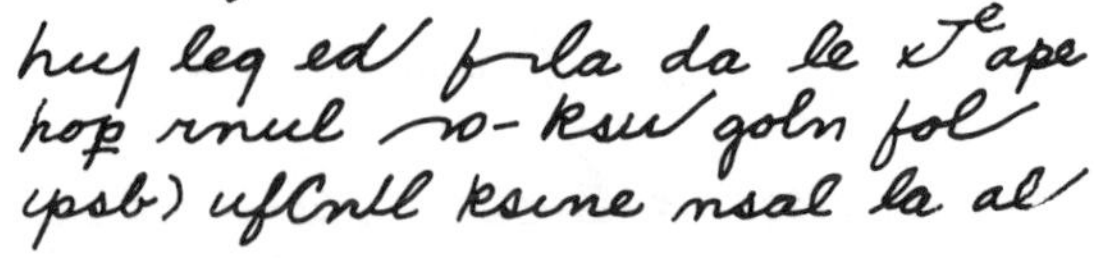

5. Omitting vowels

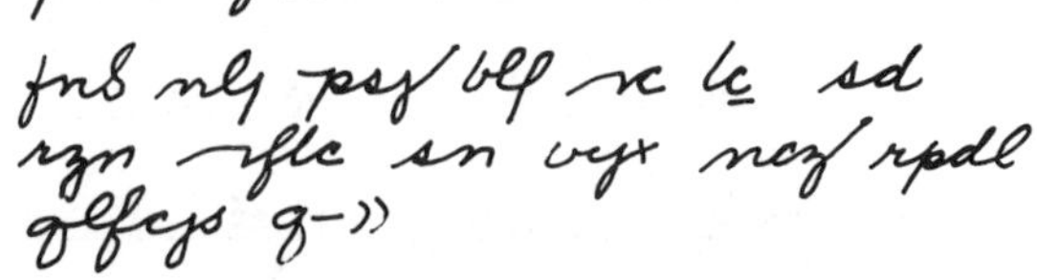

6. *company* derivatives 

7. *firm* derivatives 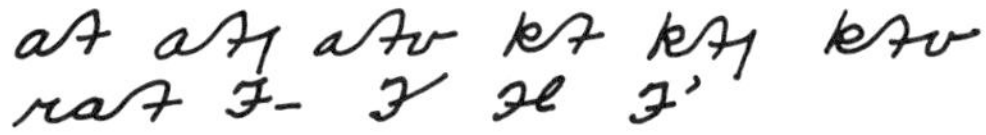

KEY 1. effective; tentative; positively; definitive; defective; inquisitive; secretive; prospective; respective; creative; attractive 2. trial; annual; diameter; mutual; fuel; gradual; actual; ruin; manual 3. create; graduate; radio; media; area; audio; cameo; folio 4. huge; league; editor; formula; date; leave; extreme; appear; hoping; renewal; moment; consumer; golden; folder; impossibility; unfortunately; consignee; install; law; alter 5. finish; knowledge; procedure; belief; make; taking; side; reason; emphatic; soon; various; enclosure; rapidly; qualifications; quantities 6. companies; accompany; accompanied; accompanies; accompaniment; accompanist; accompanying 7. affirm; affirmation; affirmative; confirm; confirmation; confirmative; reaffirm; firmament; firmer; firmly; firmness

2.2 TRANSCRIPTION SKILL BUILDING

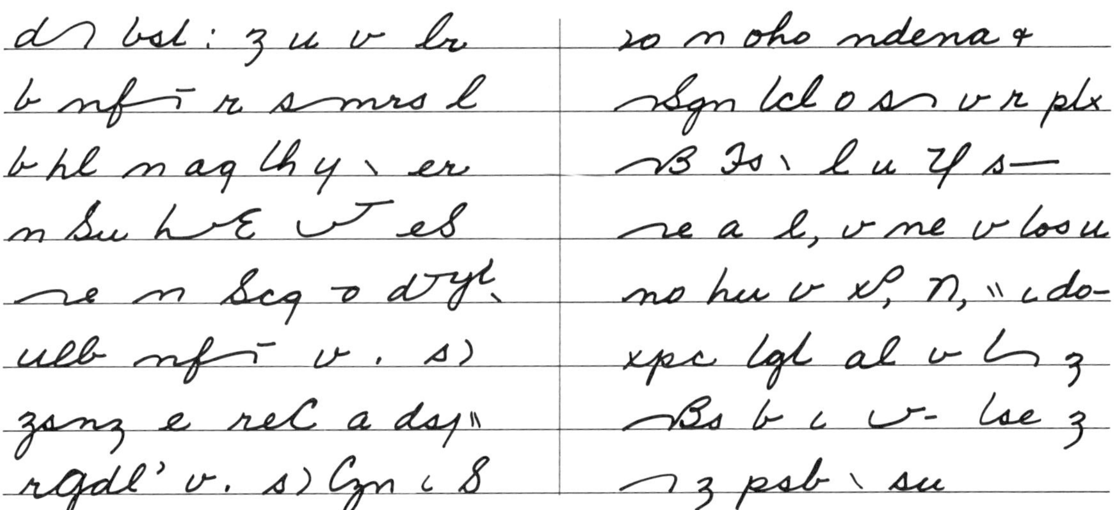

GUIDE Insert two introductory commas, four parenthetical commas, two series commas, and one conjunction comma.

2.3 SPEED BUILDING

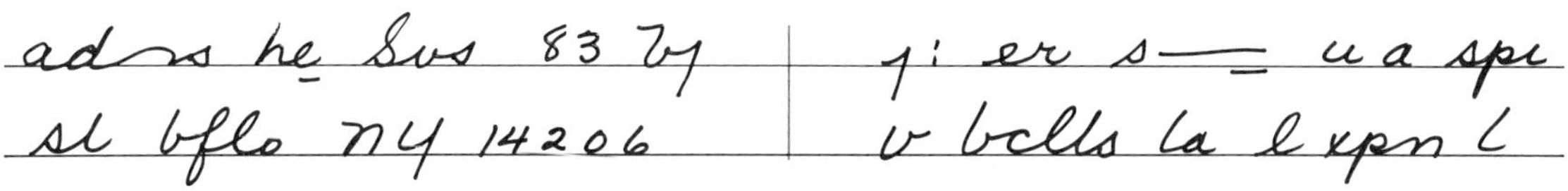

u Ks hv supl s l
Dnz l hos v
pc eqp-. eS b
gd, vCs, l Wc
ou h pa- pns l
se. nds v . Ks.

er eg ldu E e c
l bg kfl + ekre
l . hos v u Ks
Cs e ble Dn hos
r . b, nvs-- n.
nf . su

2.4 VOCABULARY BUILDING

(A)

Crb v Ks mCS
NH 0311 ; u W +
l r sec a lcl zn f
h ndSe . e nl—
l Sl a nl sl.
mCS s ne a no
v ndSelz kn)) +
yl dz n v a Ovl
no v fcys da of
. plx lb fs el nd.
e xpc lpy 180 pp
a lp cps) . er rde
a fu aas la cd of
us a l Se bld, kCe
Fo, kln ab 5 H Id
sq fl . . sl s, b
nkp, b enf l— l
alv f xpl, + el nd
pc fsl)) f r spyes.
er lso dp—- pn a
rde spi v v . duu
v ne rk— js? ul

(B)

sul us b+
1172 s-rl 2/ Scq IL
60628 d us; u
L ngu ab a ndSel
su reC us a a
oDln h . ec s/, 2

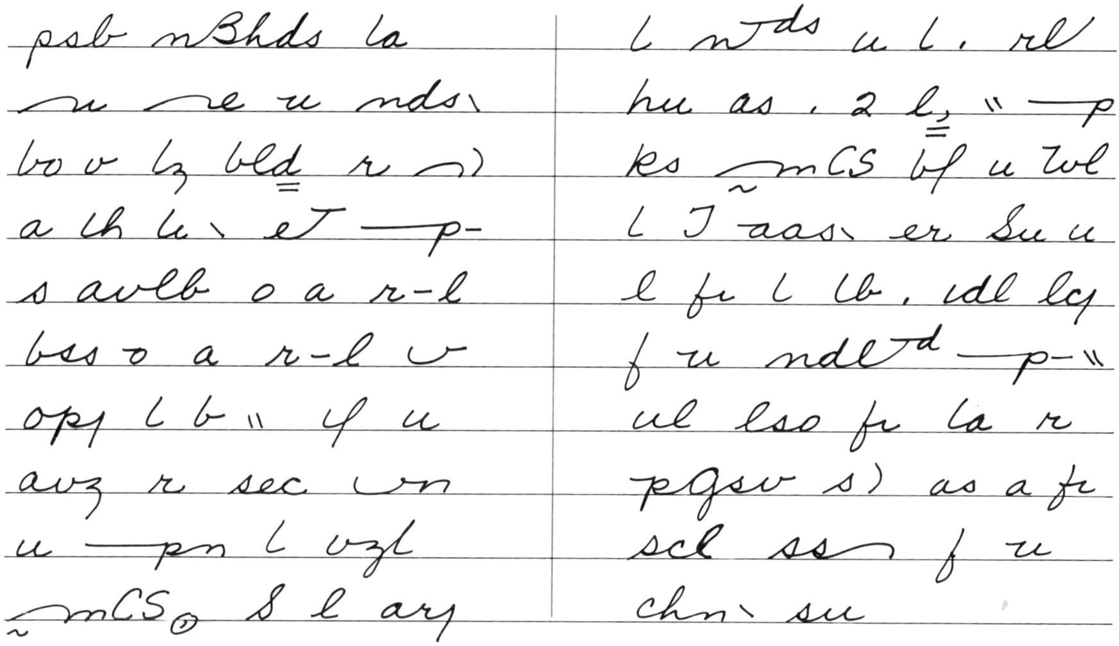

3.1 THEORY REVIEW

1. *ingly*
2. *ings*
3. *enter*
4. *inter*
5. *entr*
6. *intr*

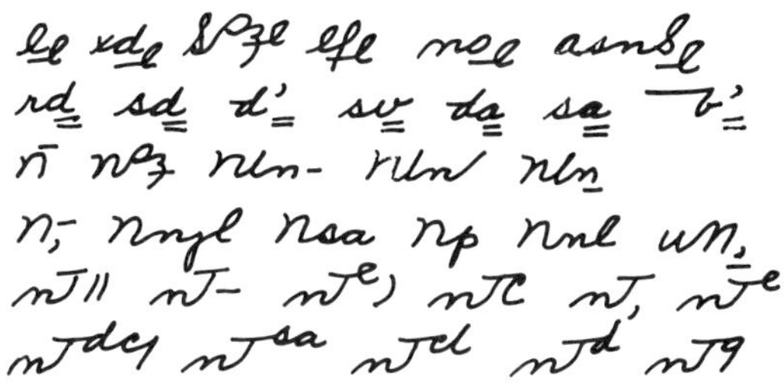

KEY 1. willingly; exceedingly; surprisingly; laughingly; knowingly; astonishingly 2. readings; sidings; dressings; savings; drawings; sayings; blessings 3. entered; enterprising; entertainment; entertainer; entertaining 4. interested; international; interstate; interrupt; internal; uninteresting 5. entrances; entrant; entreaty; entrench; entrust; entry 6. introduction; intrastate; intricate; intrude; intrigue

3.2 TRANSCRIPTION SKILL BUILDING

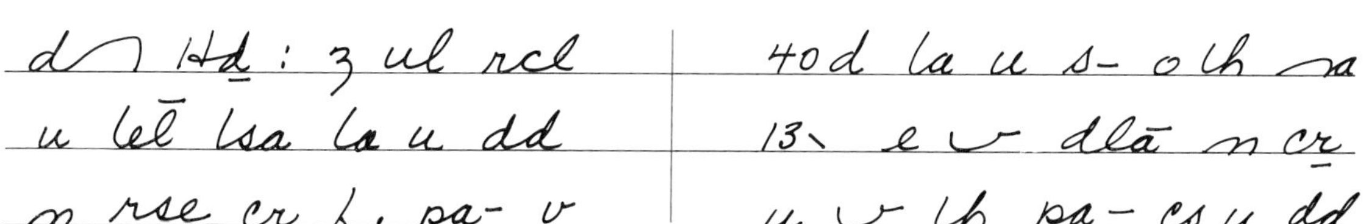

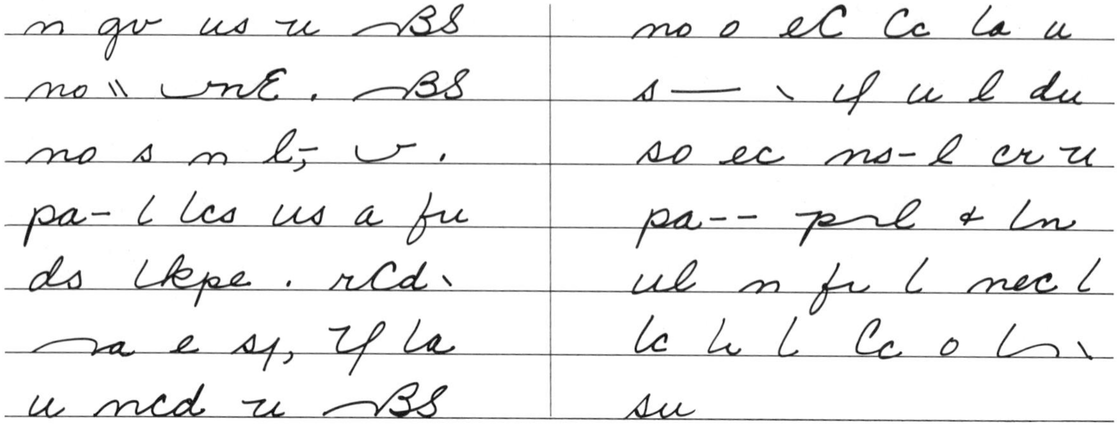

GUIDE Insert three introductory commas, two parenthetical commas, one internal punctuation semicolon, and one apposition comma.

3.3 SPEED BUILDING

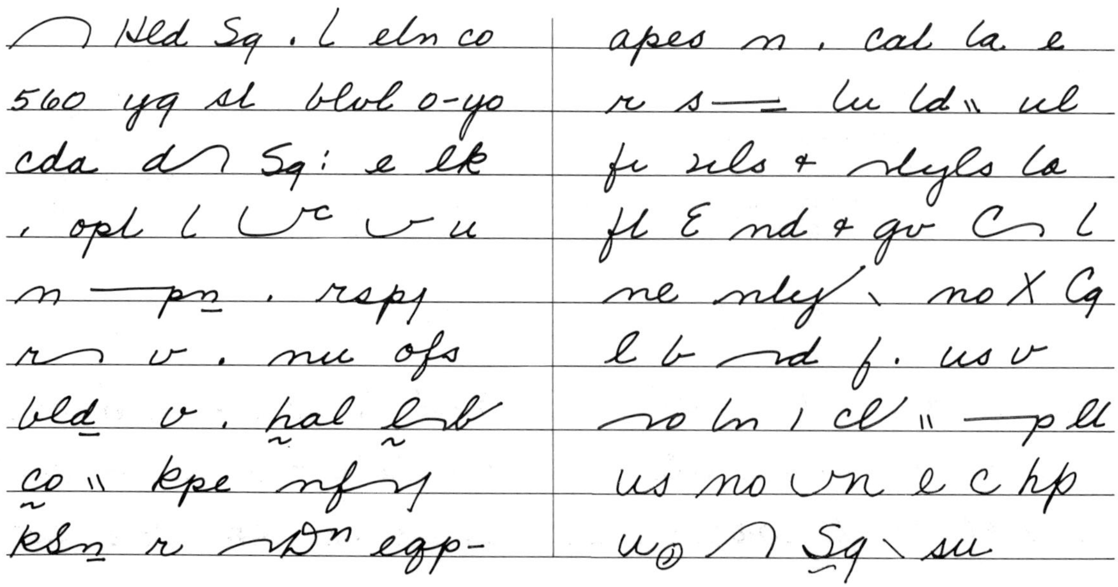

3.4 VOCABULARY BUILDING

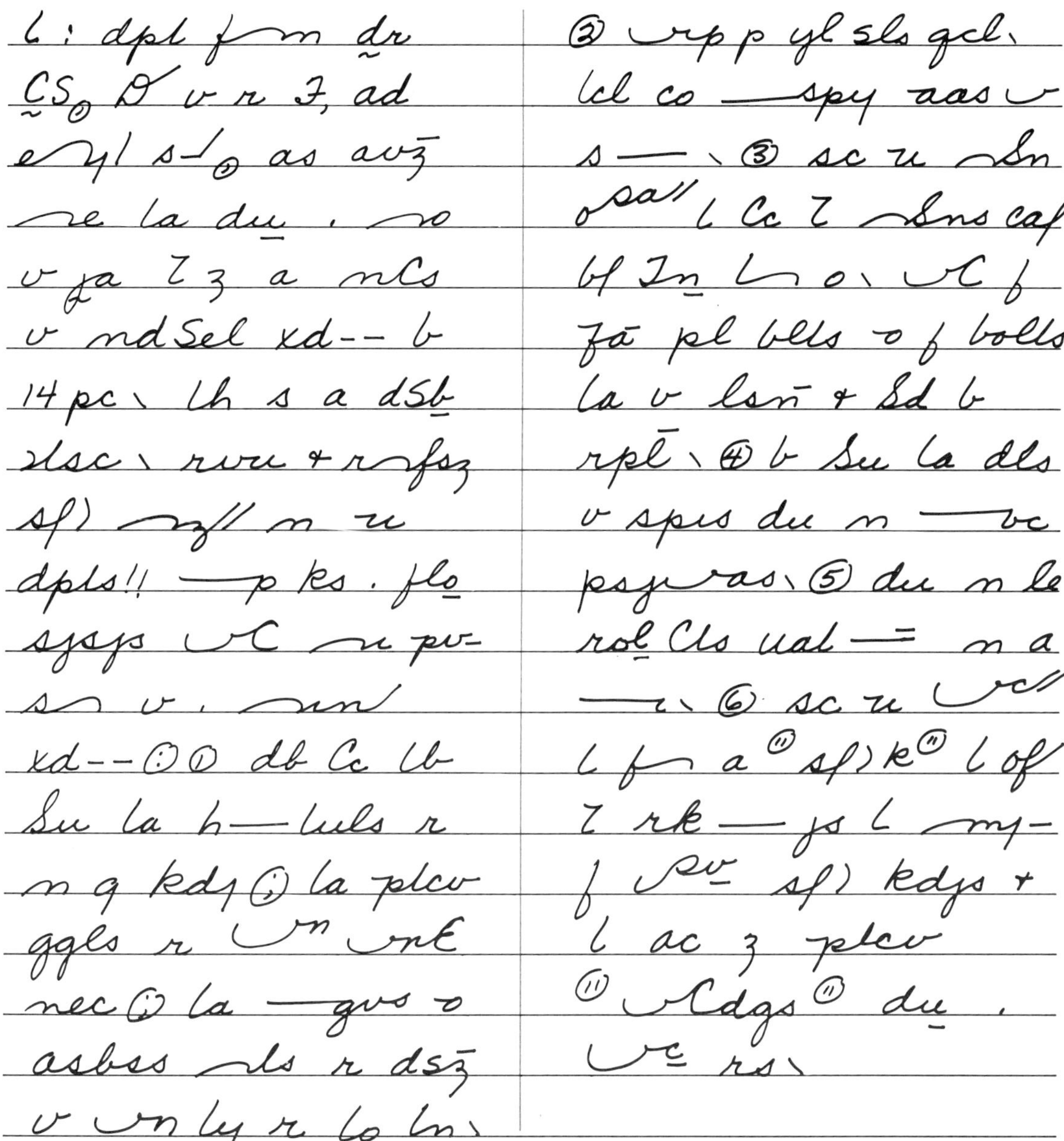

4.1 THEORY REVIEW

1. *nse*

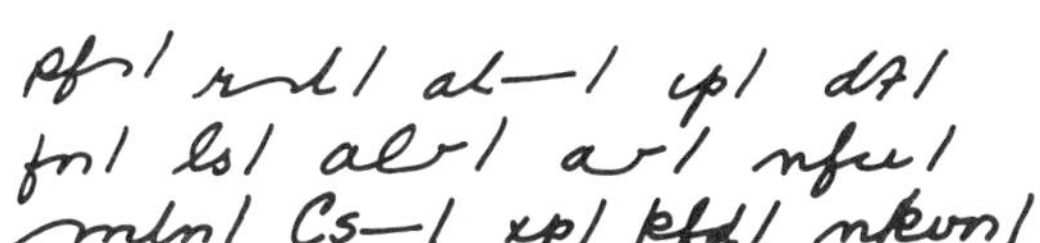

2. *shun*

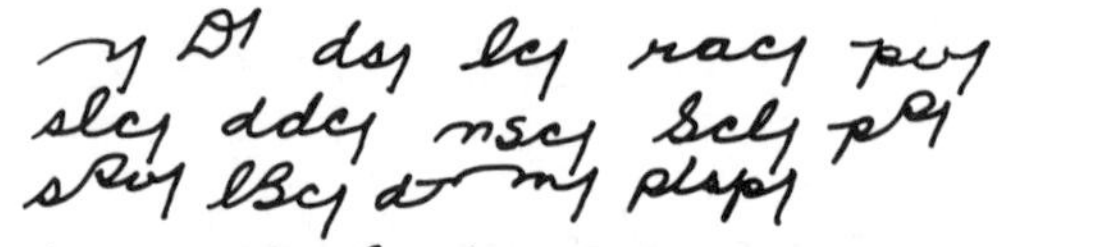

3. *ake*

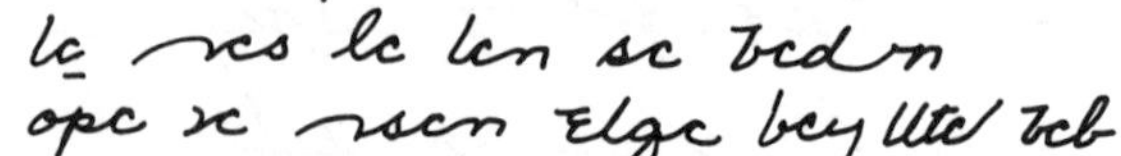

4. *st*

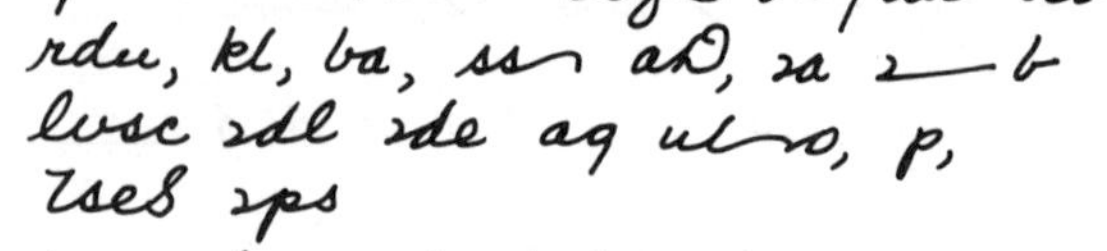

5. *ow*

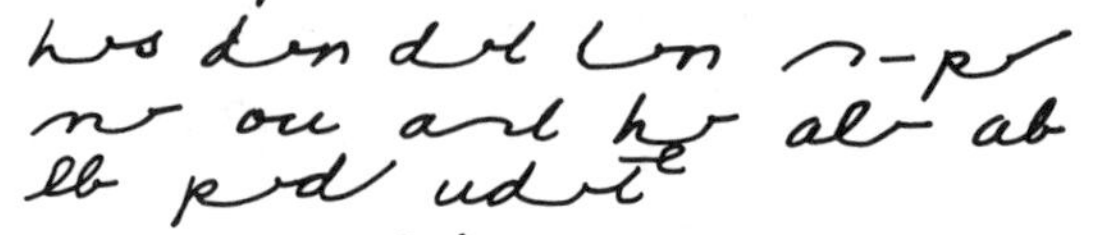

6. *cher*

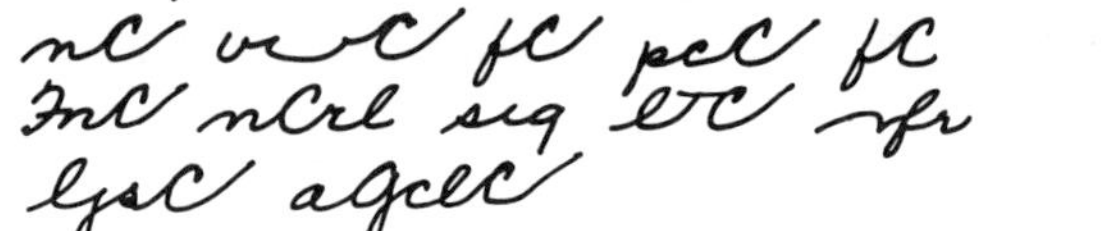

KEY 1. performance; remittance; attendance; importance; difference; finance; license; allowance; announce; influence; maintenance; correspondence; acceptance; confidence; inconvenience 2. motion; direction; decision; location; reaction; provision; selection; dedication; inspection; circulation; preparation; supervision; lubrication; determination; participation 3. taking; makes; lake; taken; sake; breakdown; opaque; stake, steak; mistaken; earthquake; bakery; undertaker; breakable 4. reduced; contest; based; system; addressed; state; standby; livestock; steadily; study, steady; against; utmost; past, passed; trusteeship; steps 5. house; down; doubt; town; manpower; now; out; amount; how; allow; about; pound; powder; undoubtedly 6. nature; voucher; feature; picture; future; furniture; natural; signature; literature; manufacture; legislature; agriculture

4.2 TRANSCRIPTION SKILL BUILDING

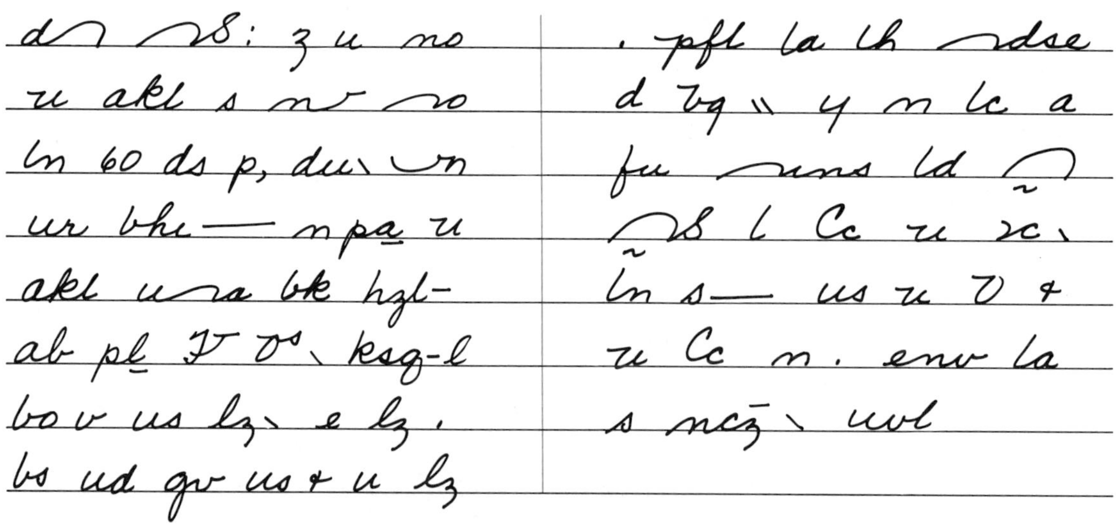

GUIDE Insert three introductory commas, one conjunction comma, and two parenthetical commas.

4.3 SPEED BUILDING

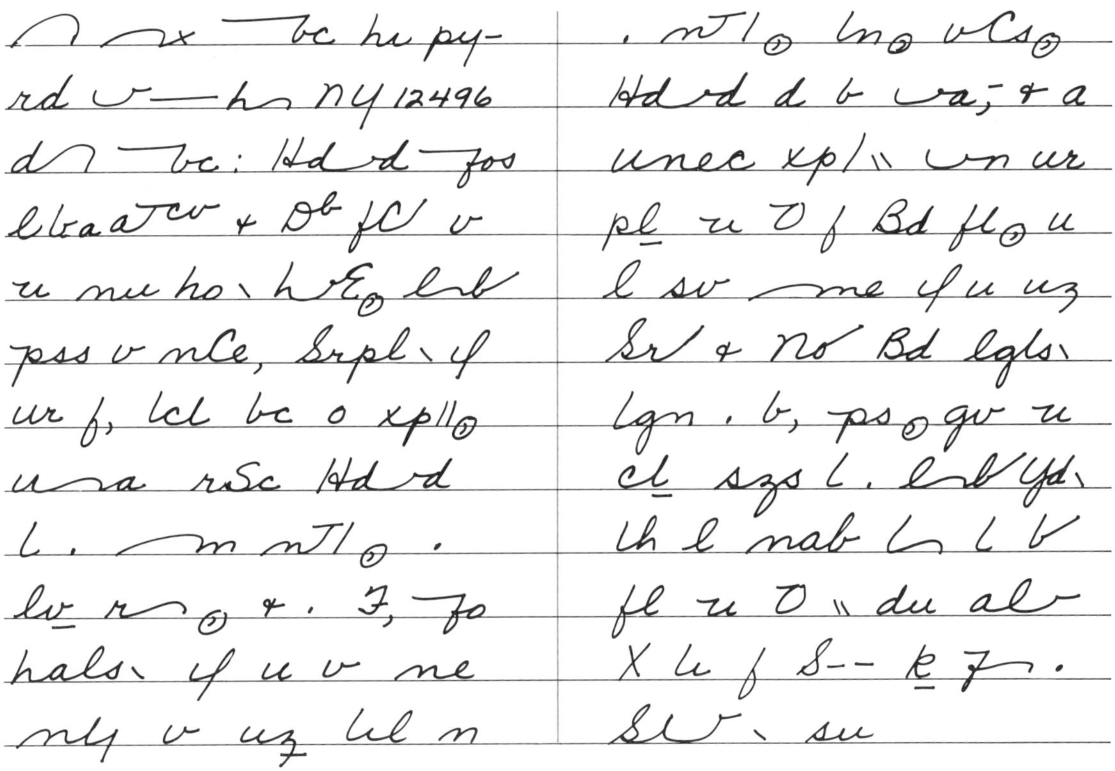

4.4 VOCABULARY BUILDING

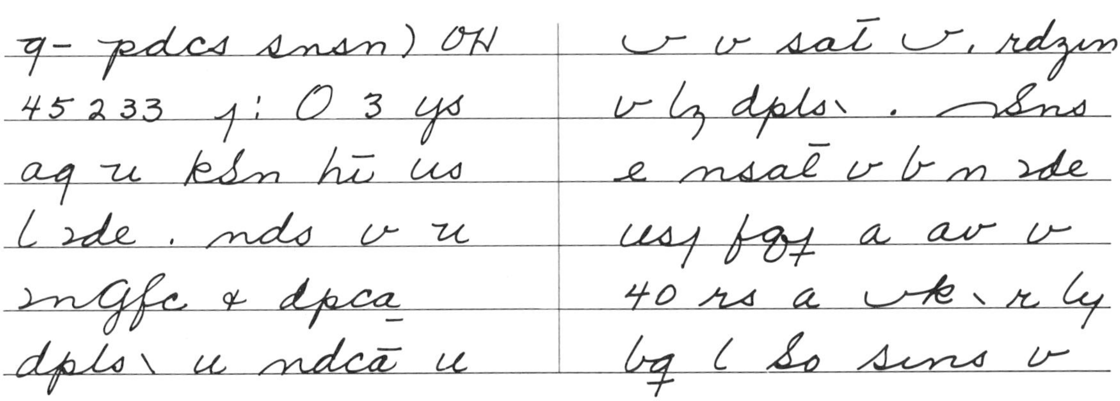

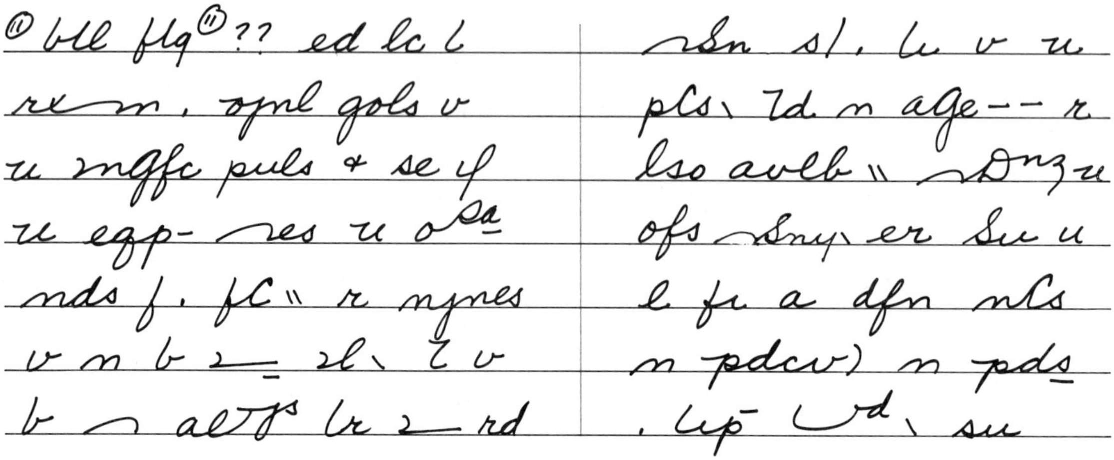

5.1 THEORY REVIEW

1. *ch*

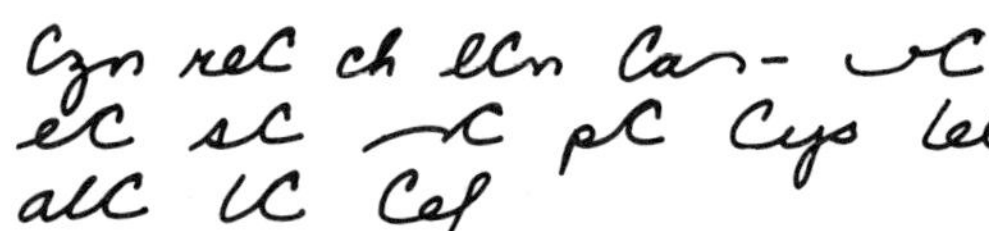

2. Final *tee*

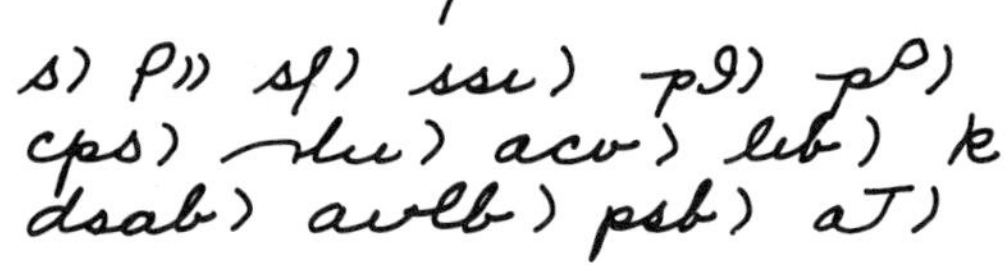

3. Final *lee*

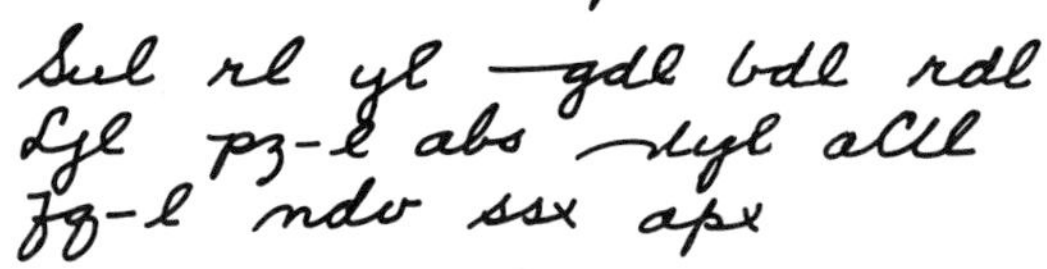

4. *ment*

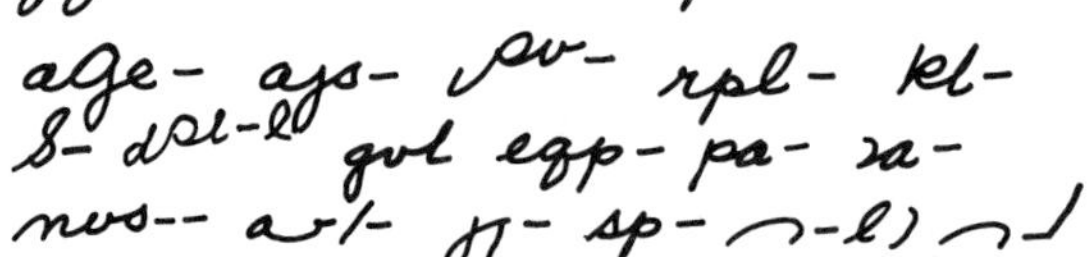

5. Final *ter*

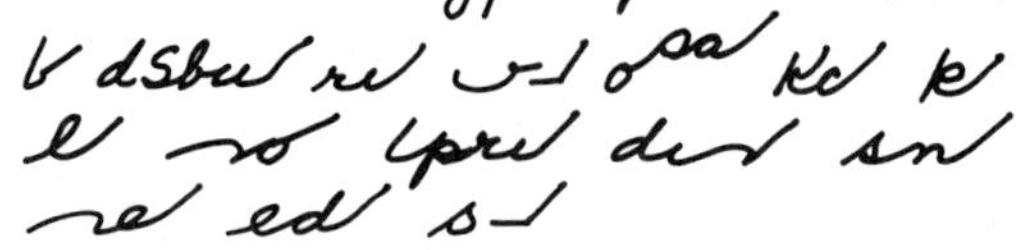

KEY 1. chosen; reach; child; luncheon; chairman; which, watch; each; such; much, match; purchase; choice; teach; attach; touch; cheerful 2. city; parties; safety; society; priority; property; capacity; maturity; activity; liability; committee; disability; availability; possibility; authority 3. surely; really; yearly; gladly; badly; readily; largely; presently; absolutely; materially; accurately; frequently; individually; substantially; approximately 4. agreement; adjustment; improvement; replacement; commitment; shipment; departmental; government; equipment; payment; statement; investments; announcement; judgment; supplement; mentality; mentor 5. better;

distributor; writer; winter; operator; contractor; counter; latter; motor; typewriter; diameter; senator; meter; editor; center

5.2 TRANSCRIPTION SKILL BUILDING

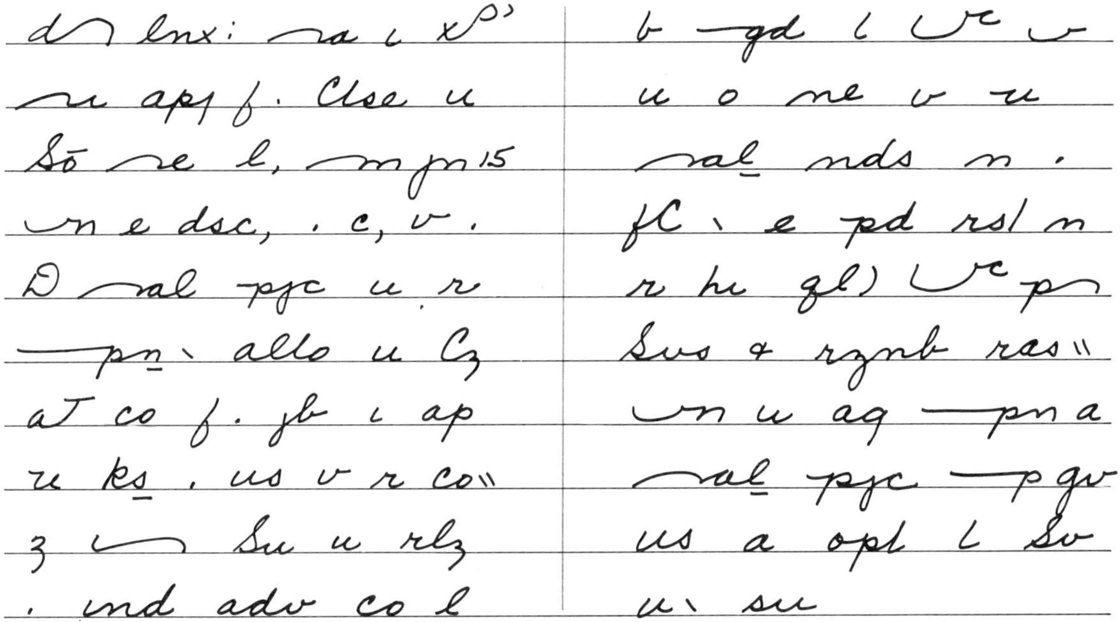

GUIDE Insert two apposition commas, three introductory commas, and two series commas.

5.3 SPEED BUILDING

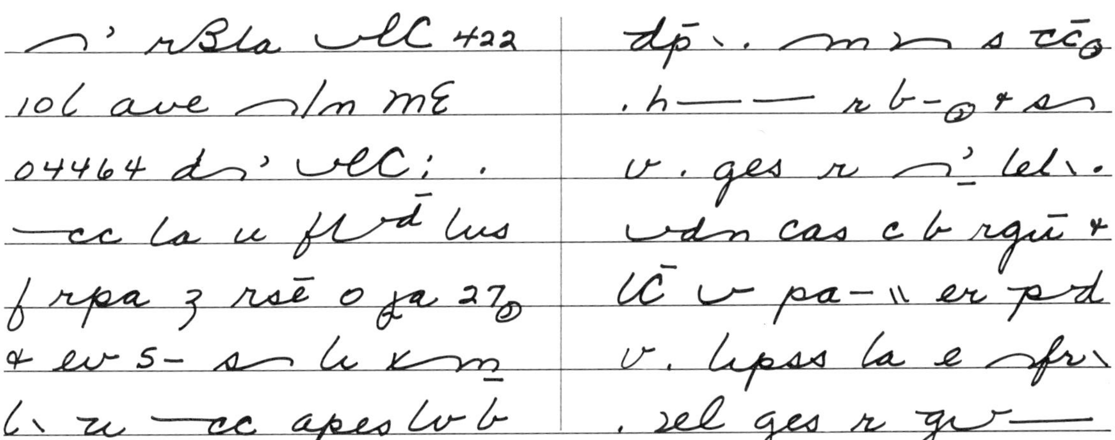

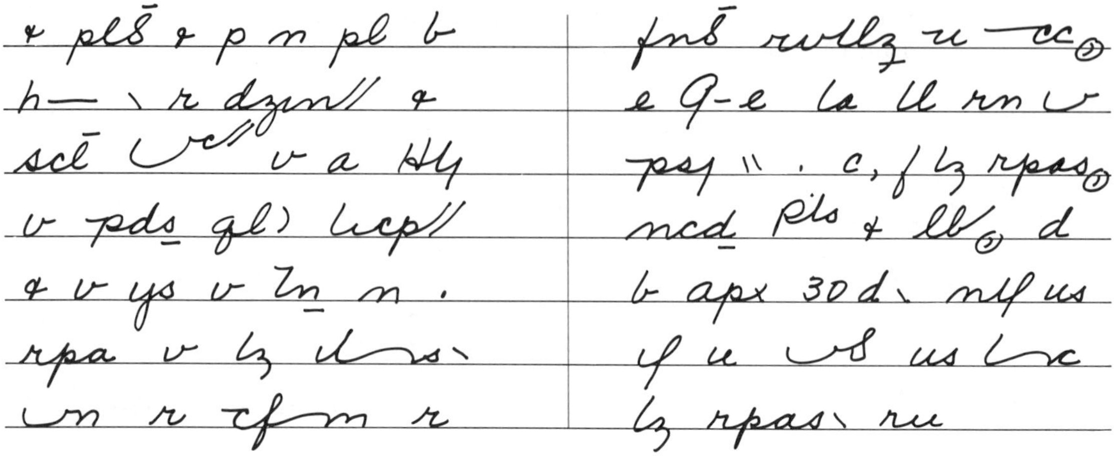

5.4 VOCABULARY BUILDING

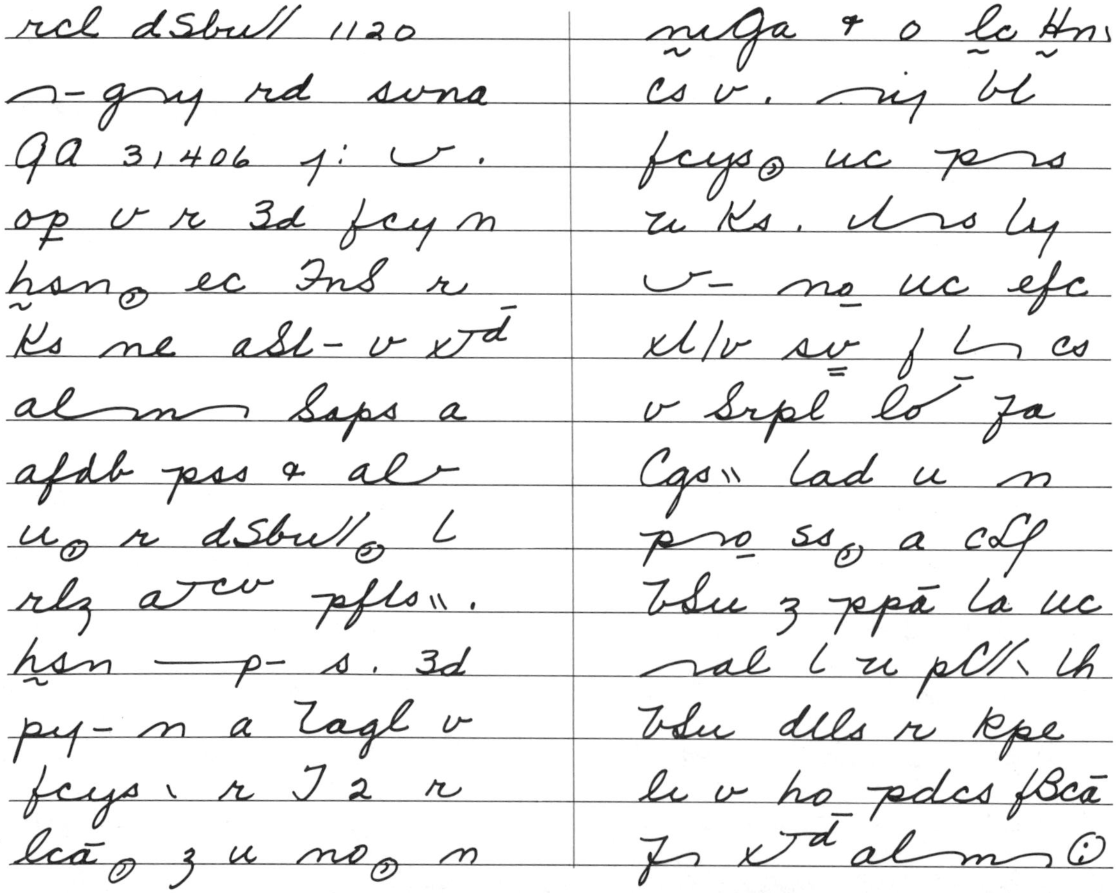

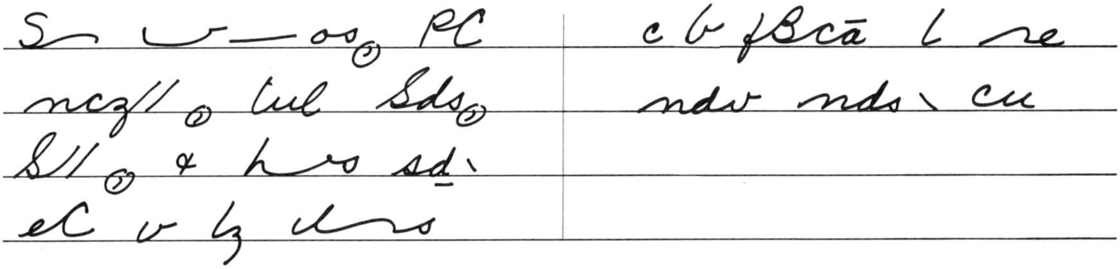

WHAT IS A MAILABLE LETTER?

Whether or not your transcript is mailable depends on:

Appearance:

1. Is the letter arranged attractively on the page?
2. Are the original and carbon copies clean?
3. Are the corrections difficult to detect?

Directions:

1. Is the envelope addressed?
2. Have I made the correct number of carbon copies?
3. Are the enclosures included?
4. Have I made special mailing notations?
5. Are there any other special directions?

Accuracy:

1. Have I transcribed my notes accurately?
2. Have I checked all numbers, names, addresses, etc.?

Sense:

1. Does my transcript make sense?
2. Have I omitted any words, lines, or sentences?

Spelling:

1. Are any words misspelled?
2. Have I used the dictionary to check words about which I am uncertain?
3. Are words correctly divided at the ends of lines?

Proper Usage:

Have I checked grammar, punctuation, capitalization, and figures to be sure all words and forms are correct?

UNIT 8

BANKING

1.1 THEORY REVIEW

1. *nd*
2. *j*
3. *nt*
4. *per* and *ser*
5. *con* and *com*

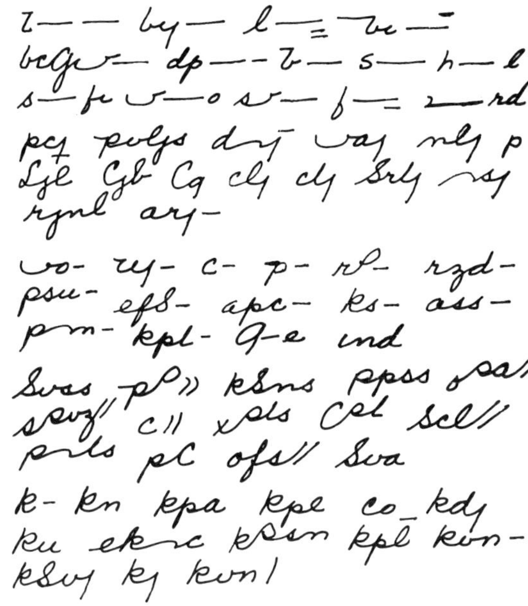

KEY 1. trends; beyond; landings; blinded; background; dependent; brand; spend; handle; send; find; window; sound; funding; standard 2. packaging; privileges; damaged; wage; knowledge; page; largely; changeable; charge; college; cottage; shortage; message; regional; arrangement 3. won't; urgent; can't; print; reprint; resident; pursuant; efficient; applicant; constant; assistant; permanent; competent; guarantee; independent 4. services; properties; concerns; purposes; operators; supervisors; circumstances; experts; corporate; circulars; permits; purchase; officers; survey 5. comment; common; compare; complete; company; condition; continue; economic; comparison; compelled; convenient; conservation; commission; convenience

1.2 TRANSCRIPTION SKILL BUILDING

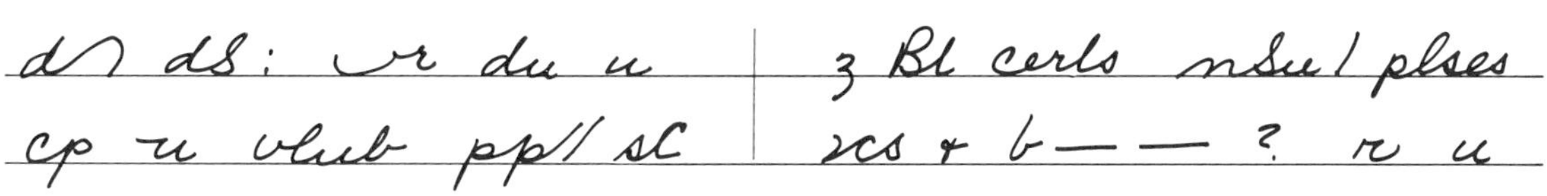

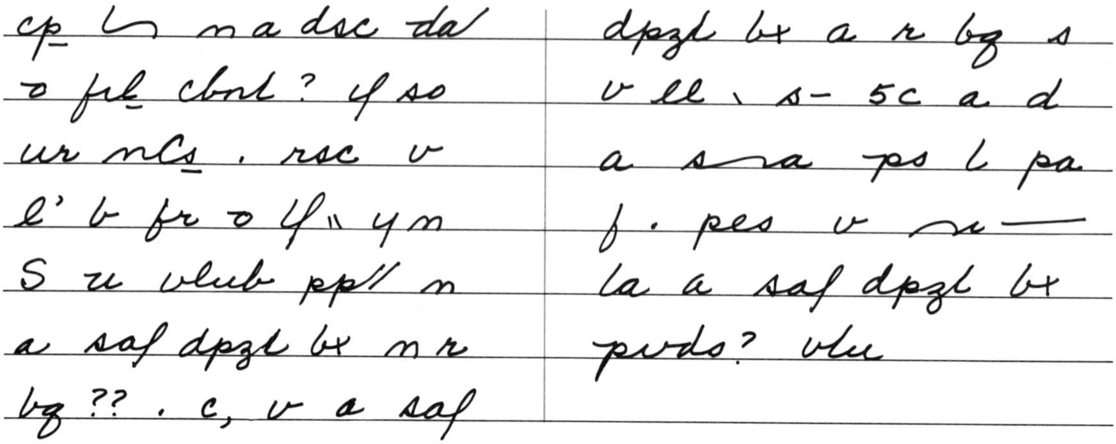

GUIDE Insert three series commas, one introductory comma, three compound adjective hyphens, and one contraction apostrophe.

1.3 SPEED BUILDING

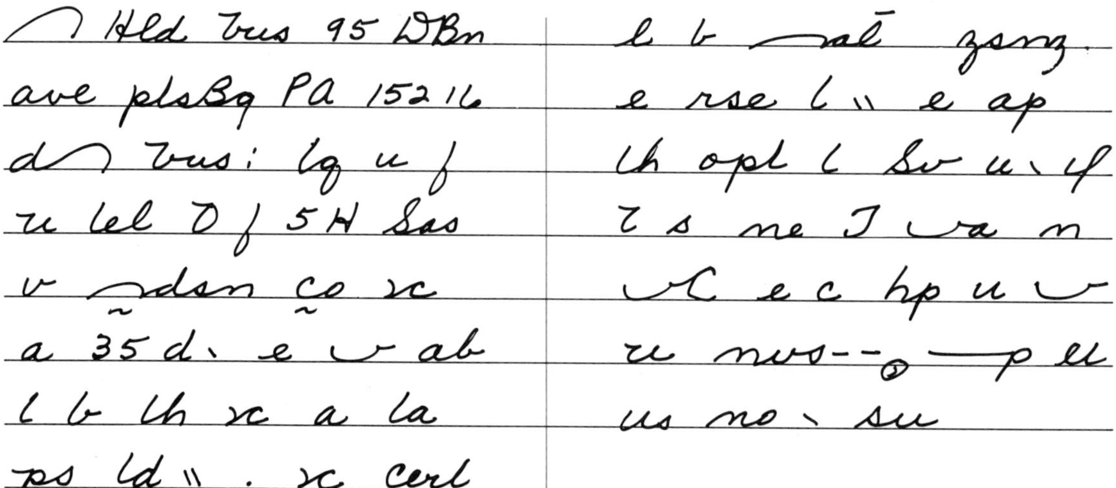

1.4 VOCABULARY BUILDING

(A)

frl nk s 15 Idd o
ro ul glf f l v r
nu edcyl lns, uc
Bo pl 20 Idd a ne
l u ls— u ch l. a
edcyl nsly vTl
b —E-y secy
psly vcyl ocly,
uc Sd rol rpa--
O zlgz 7 ys" Z r
2 sclsc —pns f
u lCz Fs, l —pn
hps u re C-edcyl
bls, U lh —pn y
ur U 60 ur —Eyb
lrse lf nSul cVl
a no X c, " r J
—pn l cv a fu 4
y pyd, y, esra
u lol nds esl a
lu v cr + ln eC y
f 4 ys ul Acl rse
. fn! u nd f. ard
u arj f" nSul a a
lo ra s avlb vC
plcs u ch b G-e la h
lv ne lkpe s edcy
n. ev- v u dl, y, avz
us vC —pn N" u, .
frs r n kpx, s

(B)

. undl Kx bq 10 Pc va
Ice W I 53221
y: w h xsv dfk al
l rksl u bq sa--
ba, o u 3 ro gc
Cc akl, n rse a
sa-E ro s a nsl
+ cas a dfn Hds,
u akl s evd-l
lo acv lku uz. gc
Cc ss" i Kc
n ble la. undl Kx
bq rqs a bl/ v 4Hd
n a req Cc akl? y
lh kdy zl pvls il

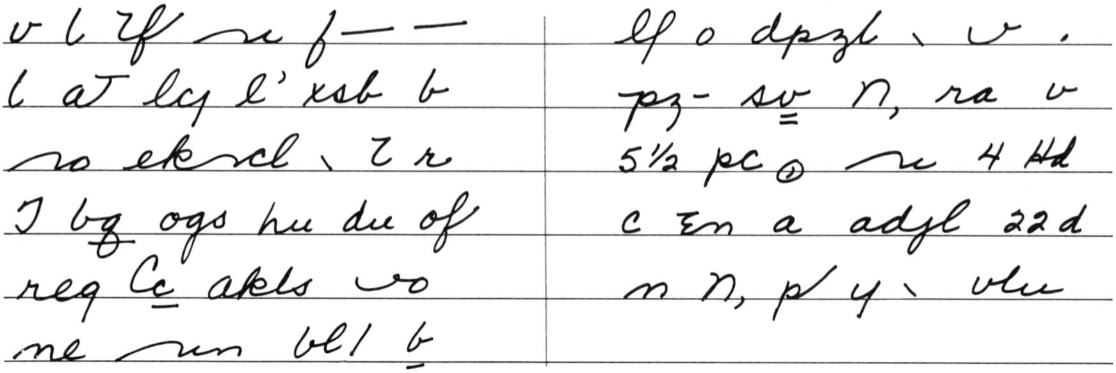

2.1 THEORY REVIEW

1. *combination-l*

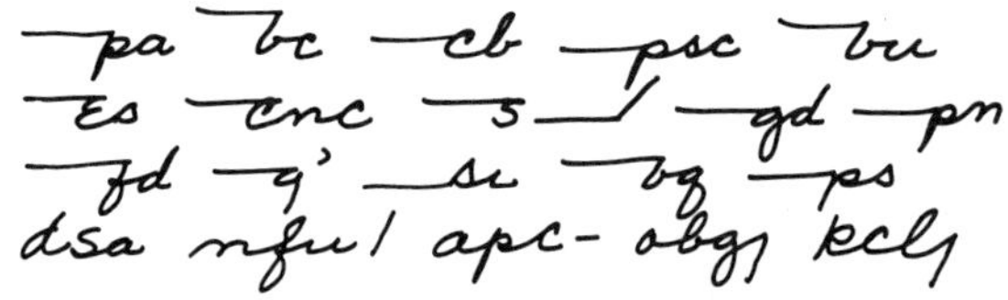

2. *st*

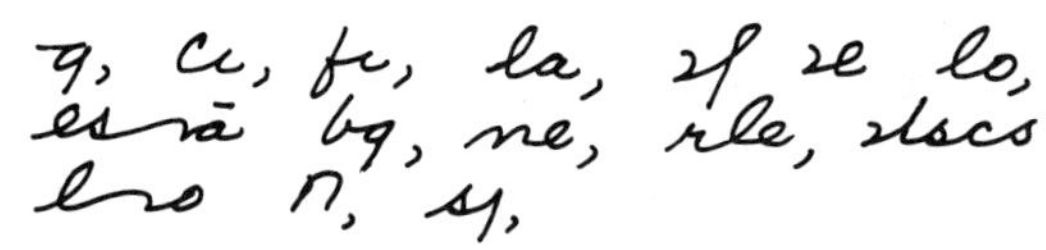

3. *str*

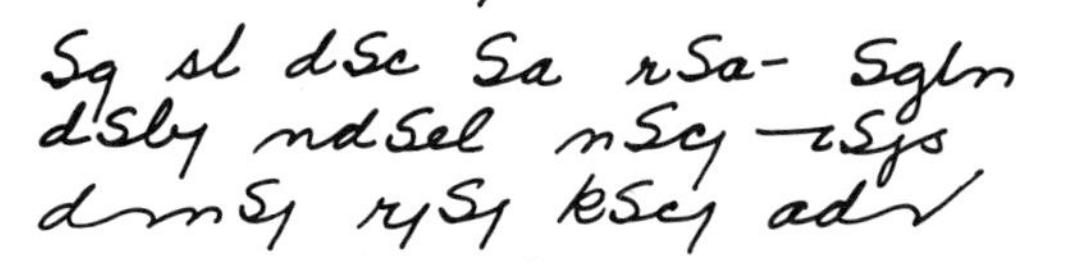

4. *ad*

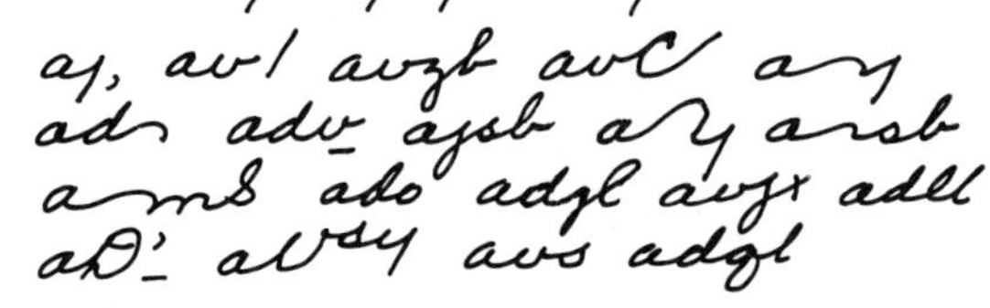

5. *sub*

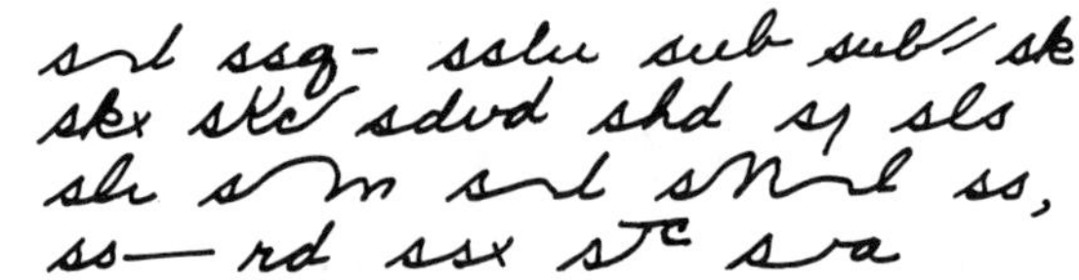

KEY 1. play; black; club; plastic; blue; else; clinic; splendor; glad; plan; flood; glass; slight; blank; plus; display; influence; applicant; obligation; conclusion 2. greatest; kindest; finest; latest; staff; steam; lowest; estimated; biggest; nearest; released; statistics; almost; interest; suggest 3. strong; street; district; straight; restraint; strengthen; distribution; industrial; instruction; illustrations; demonstration; registration; construction; administrator 4. adjust; advance; advisable; adventure; admission; administrate, administration; advertising; adjustable; admiration;

admissible; admonish; adore; additional; advantageous; adult; addressing; adversary; advice; adequate 5. submit; subsequent; substitute; subscribe, subscription; subscribers; subcommittee; subconscious; subcontractor; subdivide; subhead; subject; sublease; sublime; submarine; submit; subnormal; subsist; substandard; substantial; subtract; subway

2.2 TRANSCRIPTION SKILL BUILDING

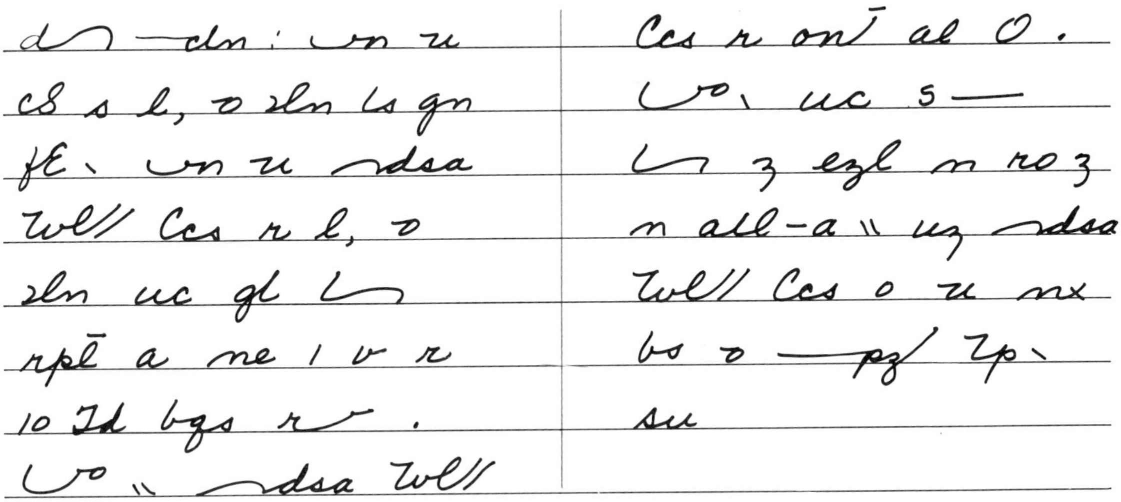

GUIDE Insert two introductory commas, three possessive apostrophes, and one number comma.

2.3 SPEED BUILDING

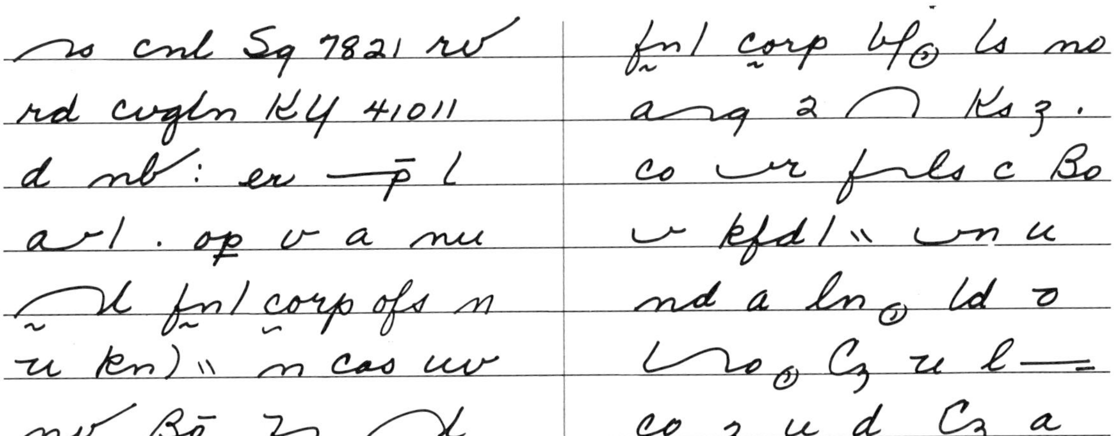

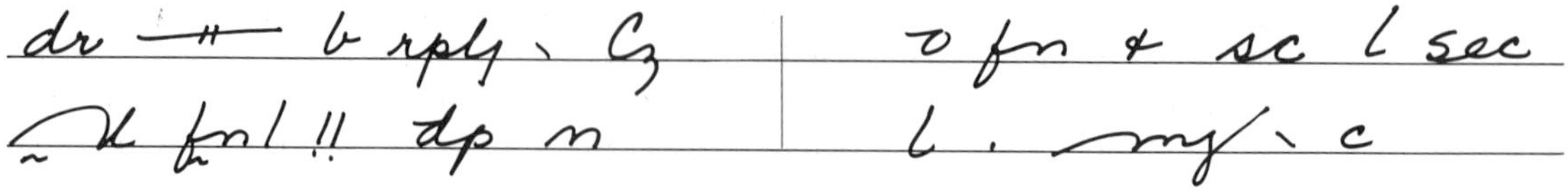

2.4 VOCABULARY BUILDING

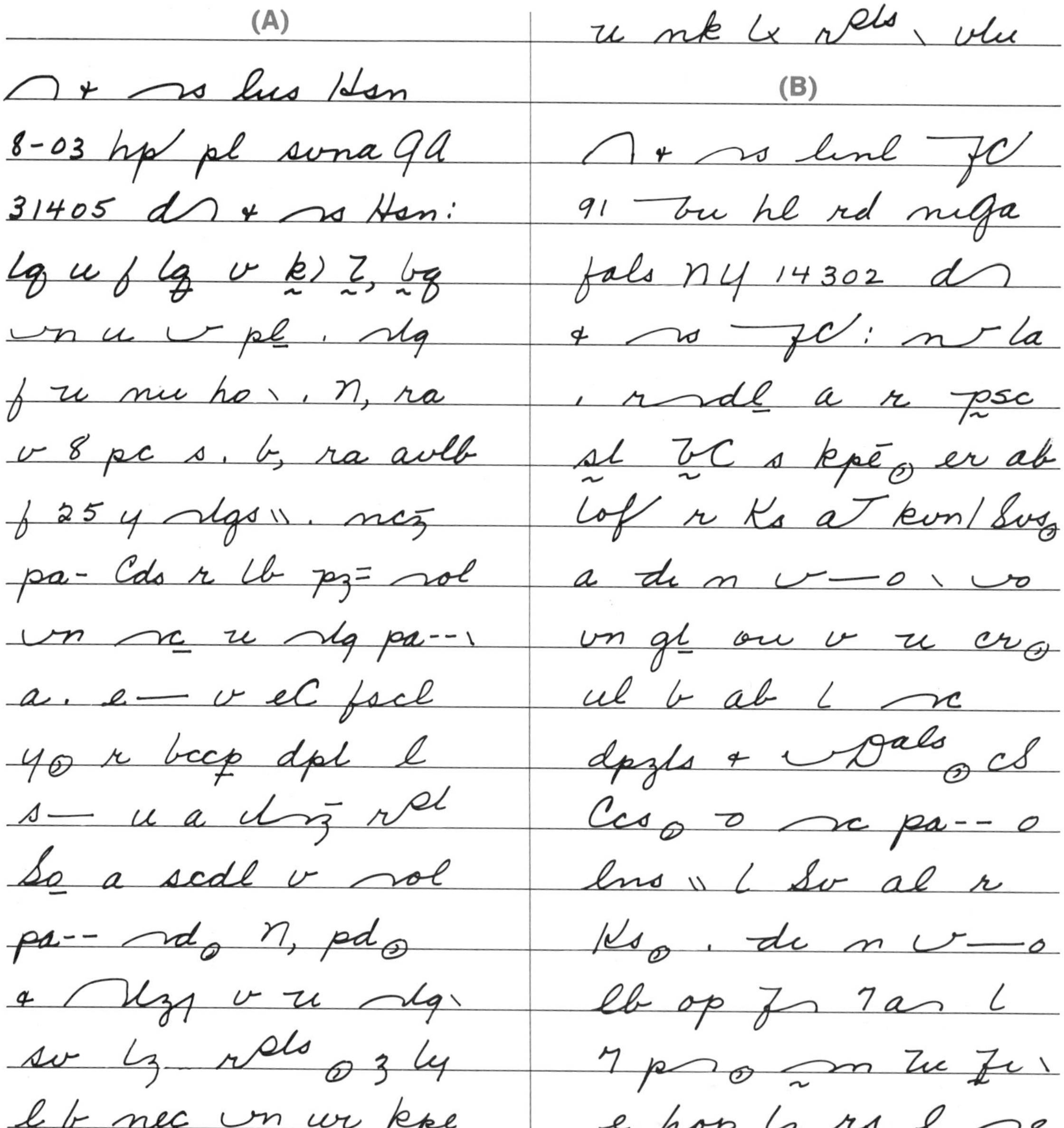

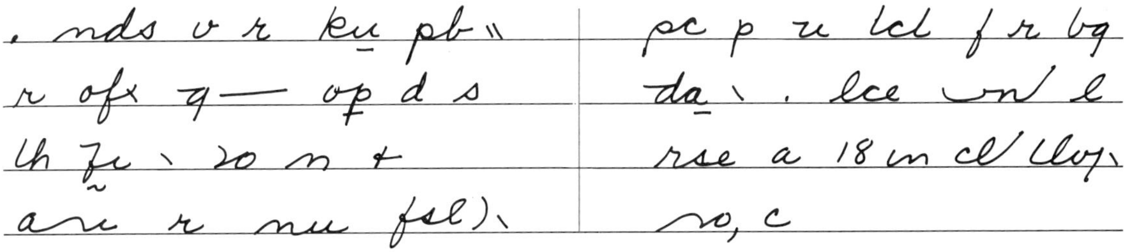

3.1 THEORY REVIEW

1. *self* 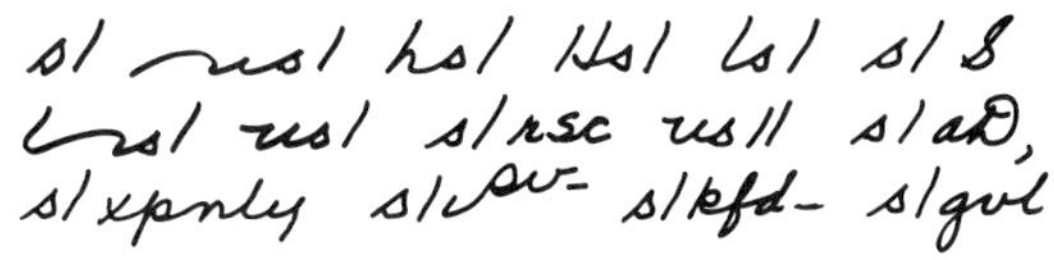

2. *f* 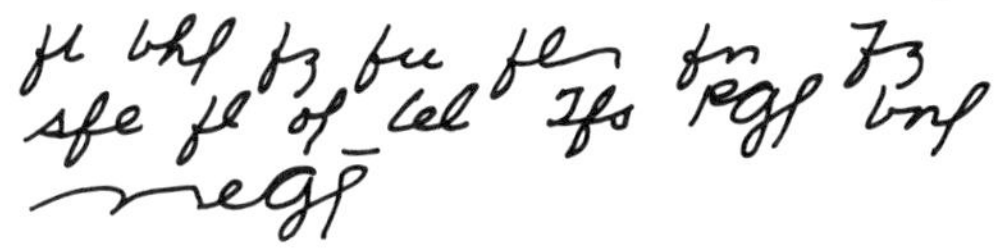

3. *āne* 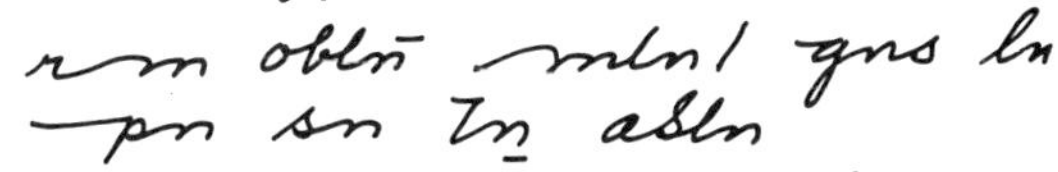

4. *short* 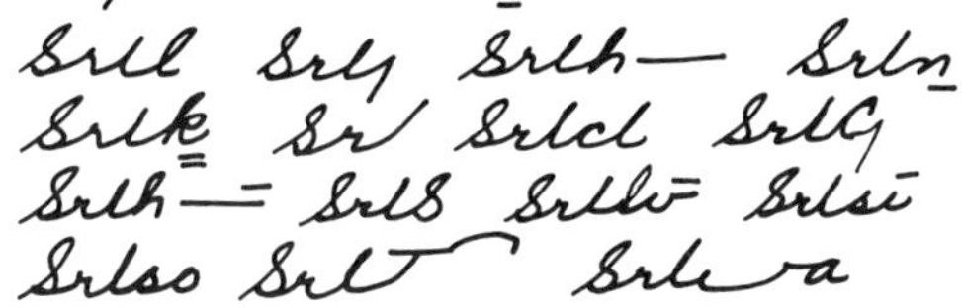

5. *ship* 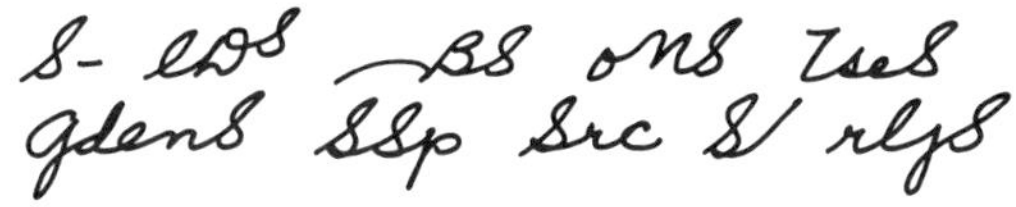

KEY 1. self; myself; himself; herself; itself; selfish; themselves; yourself; self-respect; yourselves; self-addressed; self-explanatory; self-improvement; self-confident; self-government 2. foot; behalf; phase; few; film; phone; phrase; sphere; feel; off; telephone; tariffs; paragraph; benefit; mimeographed 3. remain; obtained; maintenance; grains; lane; plain; sane; training; ascertain 4. shortly; shortage; shorthand; shortening; shortcomings; shorter; shortcut; short-change; shorthanded; shortish; short-lived; shortsighted; shortstop; short-term; shortwave 5. shipment; leadership; membership; ownership; trusteeship; guardianship; shipshape; shipwreck; shipper; relationship

3.2 TRANSCRIPTION SKILL BUILDING

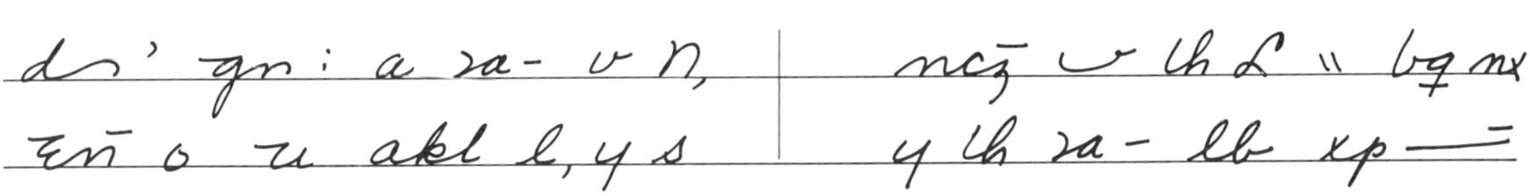

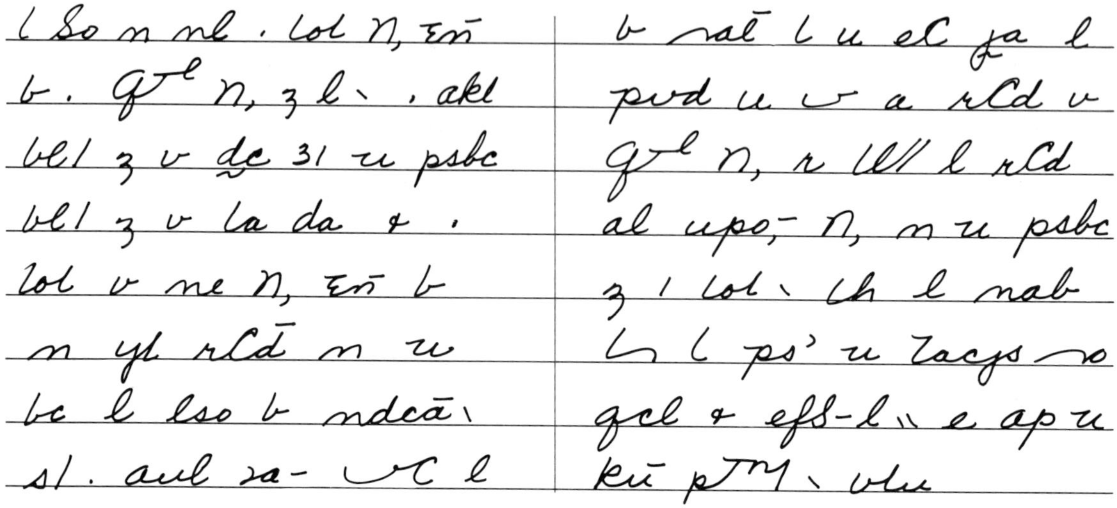

GUIDE Insert two introductory commas, two series commas, and two parenthetical commas.

3.3 SPEED BUILDING

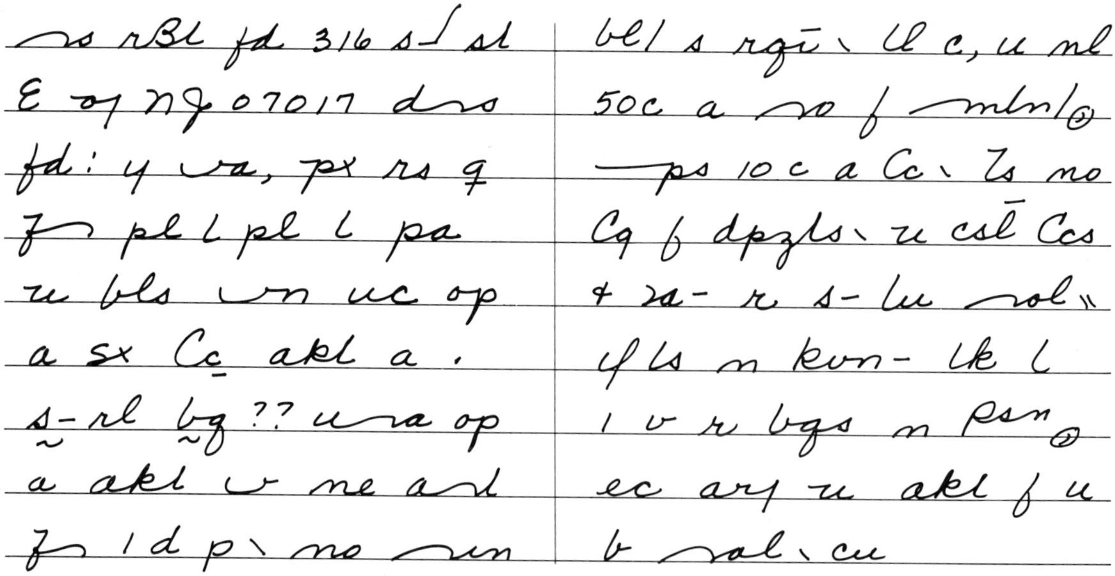

3.4 VOCABULARY BUILDING

(A)

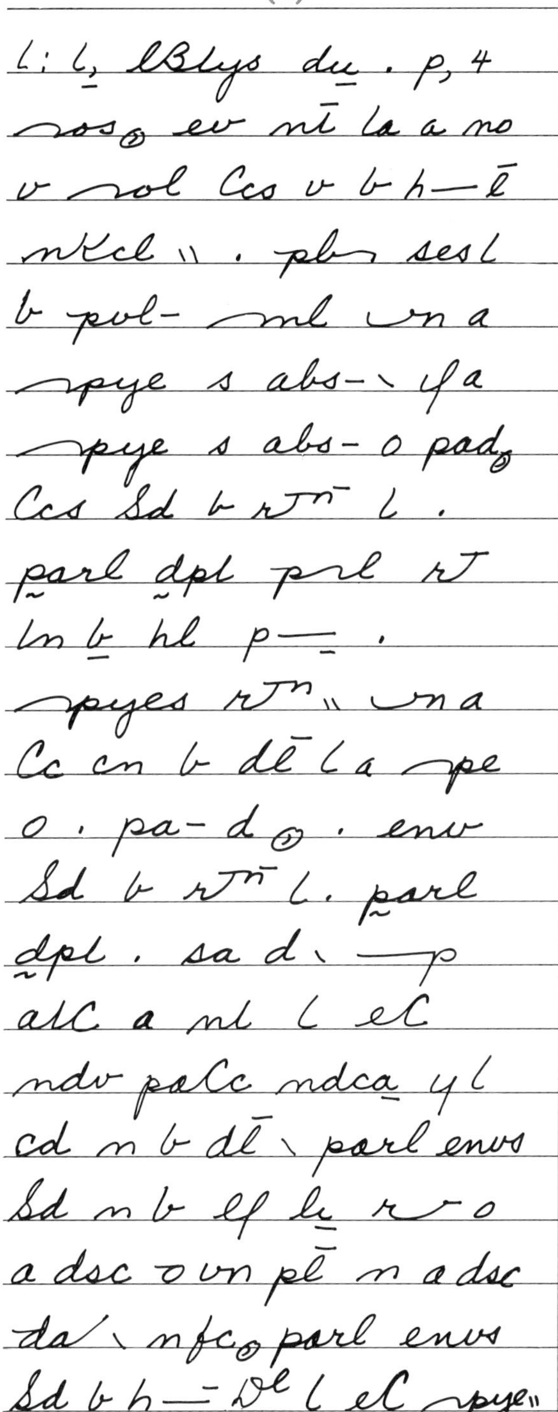

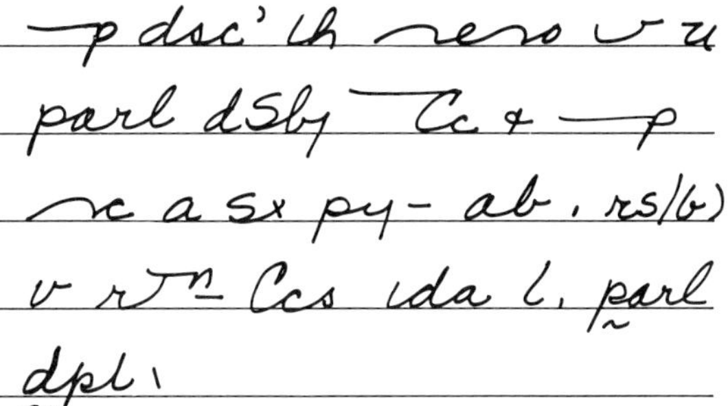

(B)

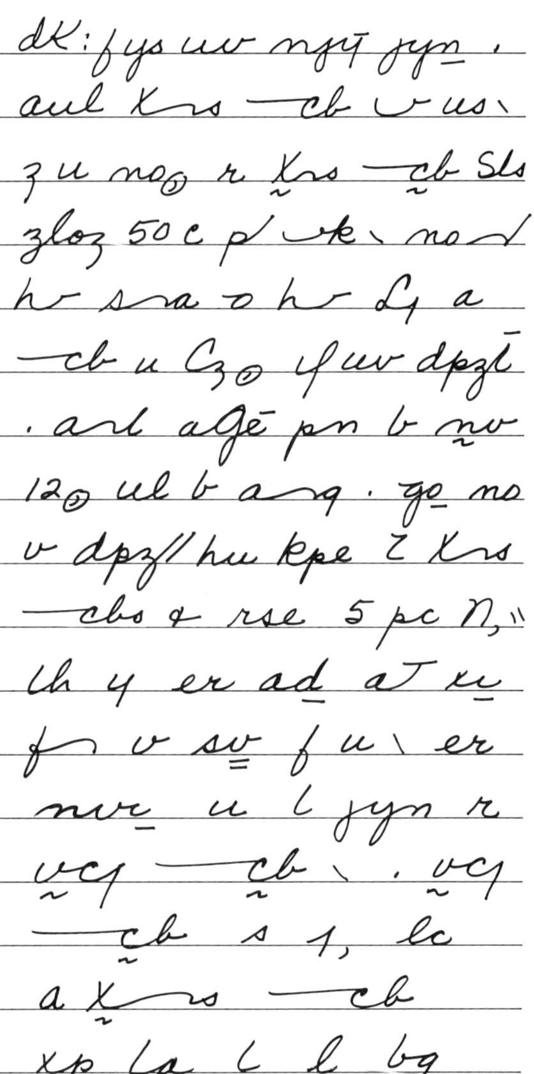

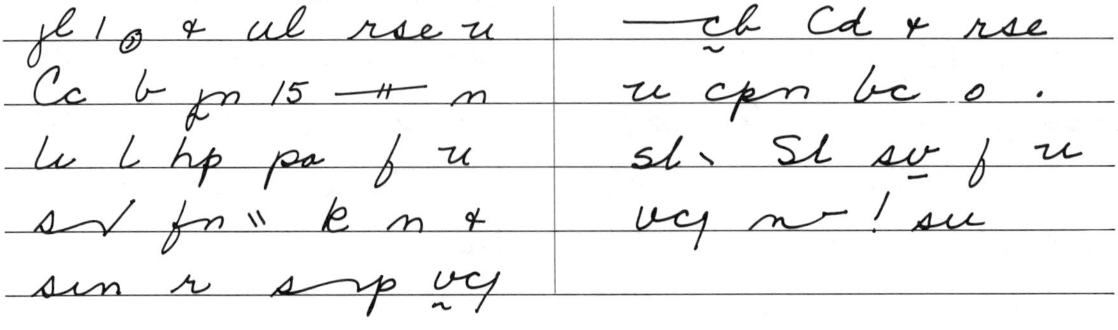

4.1 THEORY REVIEW

1. *trans*
2. *inter*
3. *ĭm*
4. *ăm*
5. *ĕm*

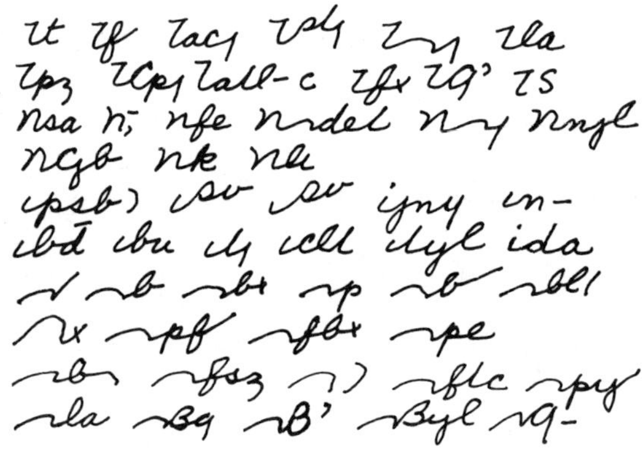

KEY 1. transit; transfer; transaction; transportation; transmission; translate; transpose; transcription; transatlantic; transfix; transgress; transistor 2. interstate; interested; interfere; intermediate; intermission; international; interchangeable; intercom; interline 3. impossibility; imperative; improve; imaginary; imminent; imbedded; imbue; imitation; immaculate; immaterial; immediate 4. amateur; amble; ambitious; ample; amber; ambulance; amorous; amplifier; amphibious; ampere 5. emblem; emphasize; empty; emphatic; employer; emulate; embargo; embarrass; embroil; emigrant

4.2 TRANSCRIPTION SKILL BUILDING

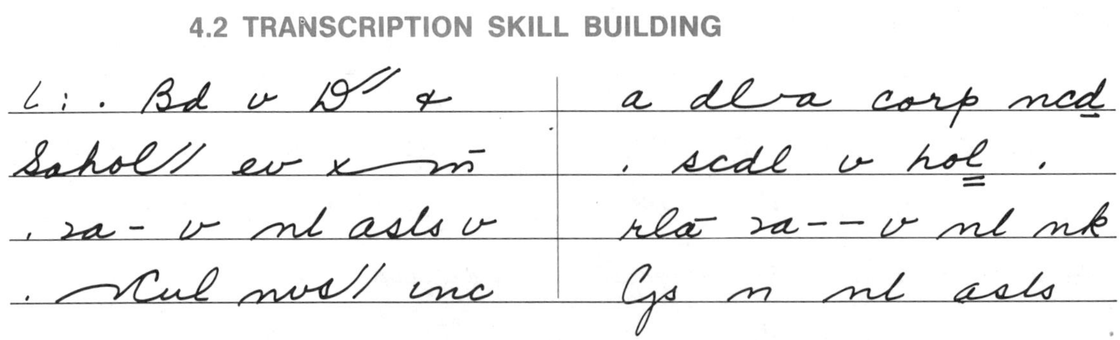

+ sp-4 nf y f.
4" n r opn. ncz
za-- pz- fal.

fnx pzj v. co o dc
31 +. rsls v lz oSjs
f. y ln e—=.

GUIDE Insert three parenthetical commas, three series commas, and one introductory comma.

4.3 SPEED BUILDING

Cl bv 316 s-/ sl
eds-n —aBla cda
d bv: du u v-
lnc Su la u do-
lz u —me? if
u du he r 3 zps
l flo①① avyd cy
dj a-ls v cb.

② avyd xpz u —me
n pb. ③ pa u bls
b Cc" if u flo lz 3
zps ul dCs. hzds
la ld l. l'v —me"
Cc akls r avlb a
r bq. envi ul 20
n l Ln ab r Svss. cu

4.4 VOCABULARY BUILDING

(A)

dnld gsn 247 rSl
pcva gy IN 46401
d gsn: l v. pbs
uSd b fas s —pn.
dSbj v u esa zlz

na u xcu P if u
v —un aj Chn.
dp— o. szv u
esa. xcu// jb c b
a Bdn + n a on f
a Psnl z— ". vlsn

mfl Ɩ, c fq, 3 u
xcu/ o cxcu/ \ if u
sde. ncz pfl
ul fu la. du » v a
xcu/ c b qi upz \
ev 5x Ɩn pfjls ldl
v nvs- lx Ɩ,
& esa Svs \ fu ndvs
pz'. xplz la ec of \
ls up f u lv avs n
O l gn fu lx rlf
al= a dl » e mf
nel 4 Bd Ul v ndv
Ɩ„ & esas \ r Ɩ, dpl
ofs// r kpel fl
v. pbns v esa
lxf \ ul fu. ofs/n
Cq v u flo lb
lls— & cpb v qv
u Rx nlfb f—— »
. Svss v. bq r lv
avlb & fscl aklb \ r
kf c„ f xcu/ Svss r lx

ddcb f e esa
o nHl/ lxs \ vlu

(B)

vls cnde 95
hlln ave -gy
AL 36100 d cnde:
. sf, va l lc cS o
u Ɩp s n. f v
Tvl// Ccs \ . avf v
Tvl// Ccs s la ly r
xpb n lno al pls
n. Uo \ . no, kn
anls v Tvl// Ccs r
x n 10 d o 20 d
vcs \ . Cq f lh Svs
s l d p 1 Hd Ul v
Ccs pC » if ur—pn
llca n 1 aa f a lq
pyd v lu uv
pf e a bq df o a
cSes Cc \ lz c b
cS a ne bq \ lh
f v plcf s qi

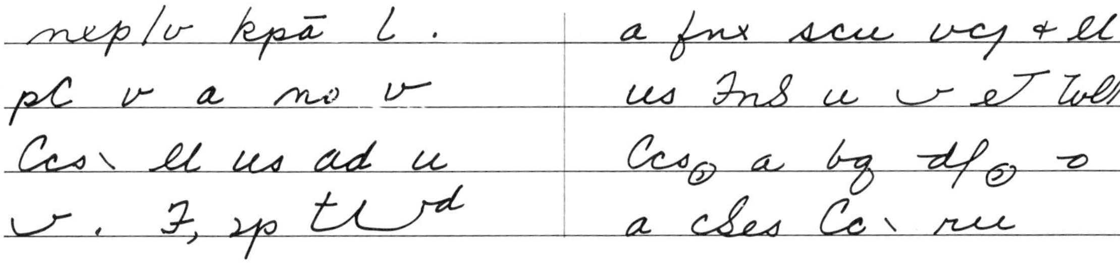

5.1 THEORY REVIEW

1. *old* 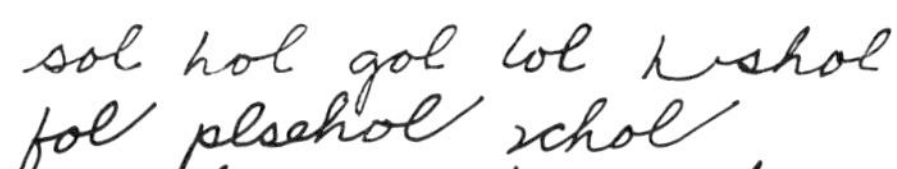

2. *ward* 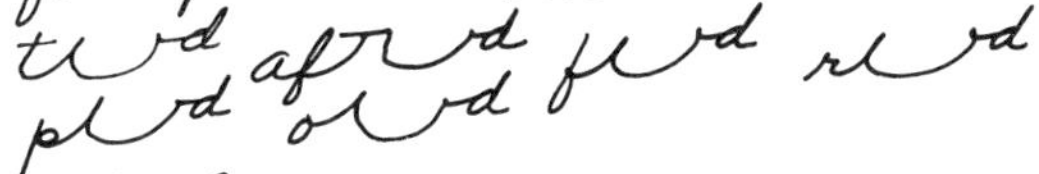

3. *sh* 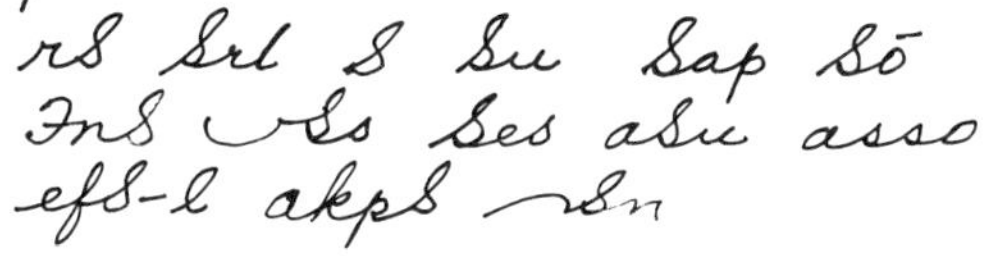

4. *zh* 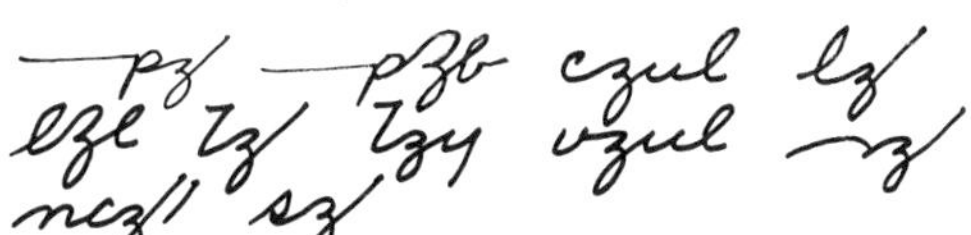

5. *aw* 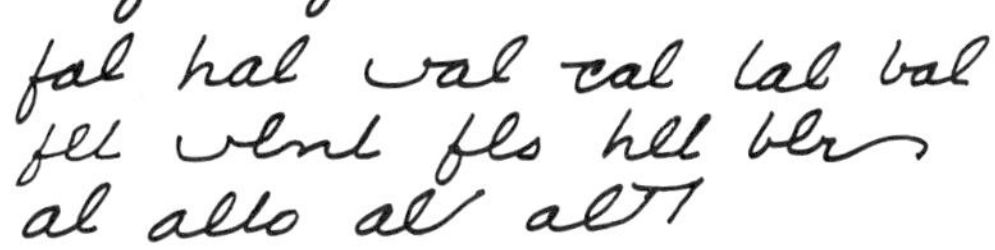

KEY 1. sold; hold; gold; told; household; folder; policyholder; stockholder 2. toward; afterward; forward; reward; upward; onward 3. rush; short; ship; sure; shape; showed; furnish; wishes; sheets; assure; associate; efficiently; accomplish; machine 4. pleasure; pleasurable; casual; leisure; leisurely; treasure; treasury; visual; measure; enclosures; seizure 5. fall; hall; wall; crawl; tall; ball; fault; walnut; false; halt; ballroom; all; although; alter; alteration

5.2 TRANSCRIPTION SKILL BUILDING

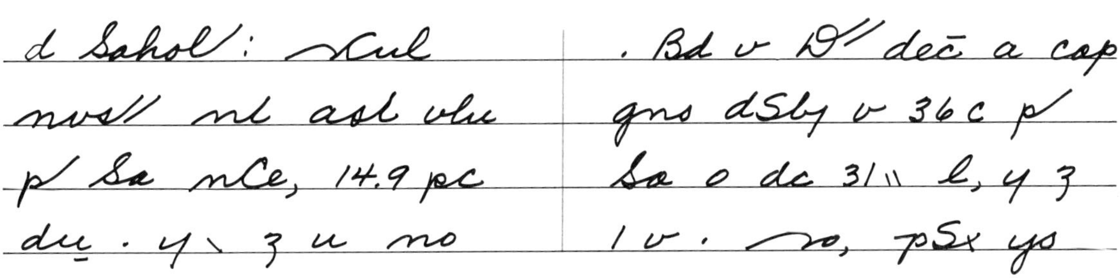

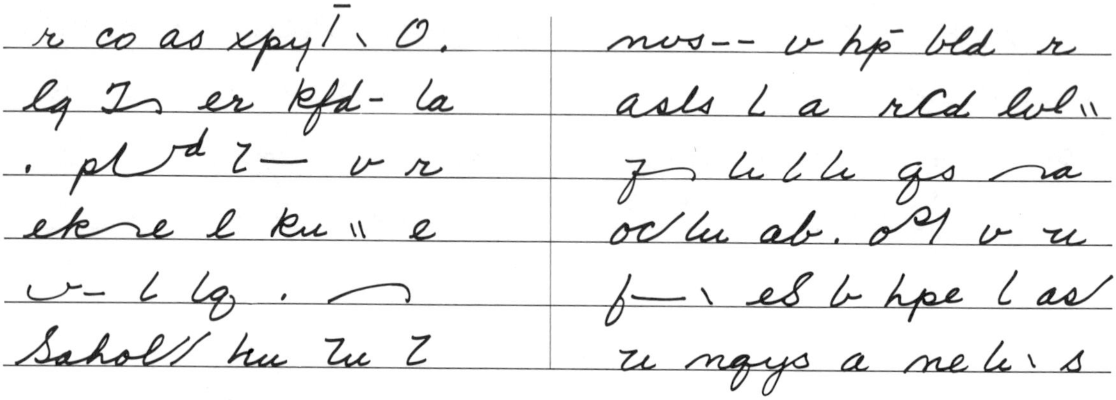

GUIDE Insert three introductory commas, two parenthetical commas, and one possessive apostrophe.

5.3 SPEED BUILDING

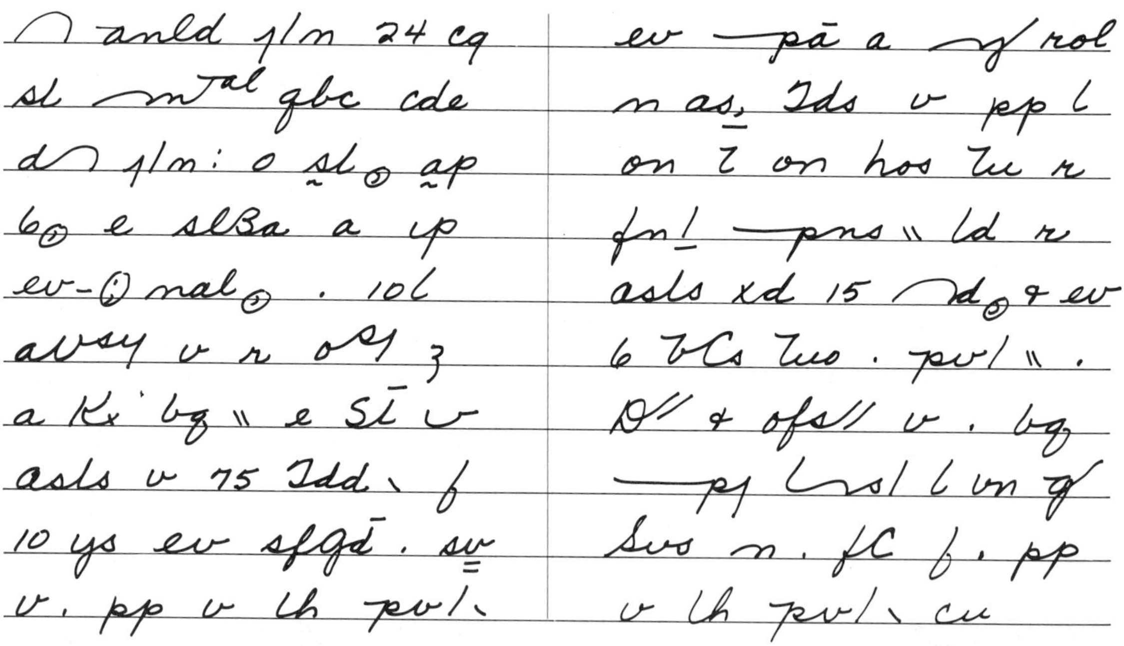

5.4 VOCABULARY BUILDING

(A)

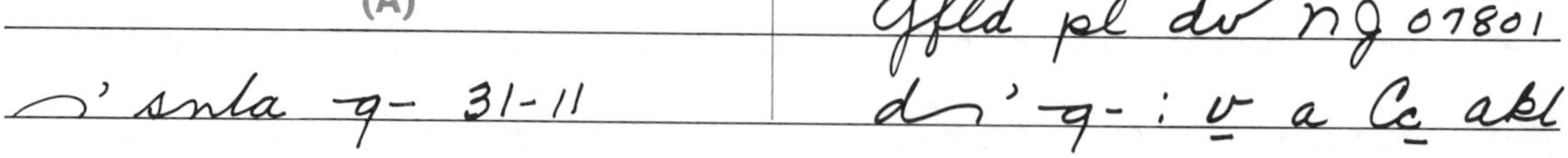

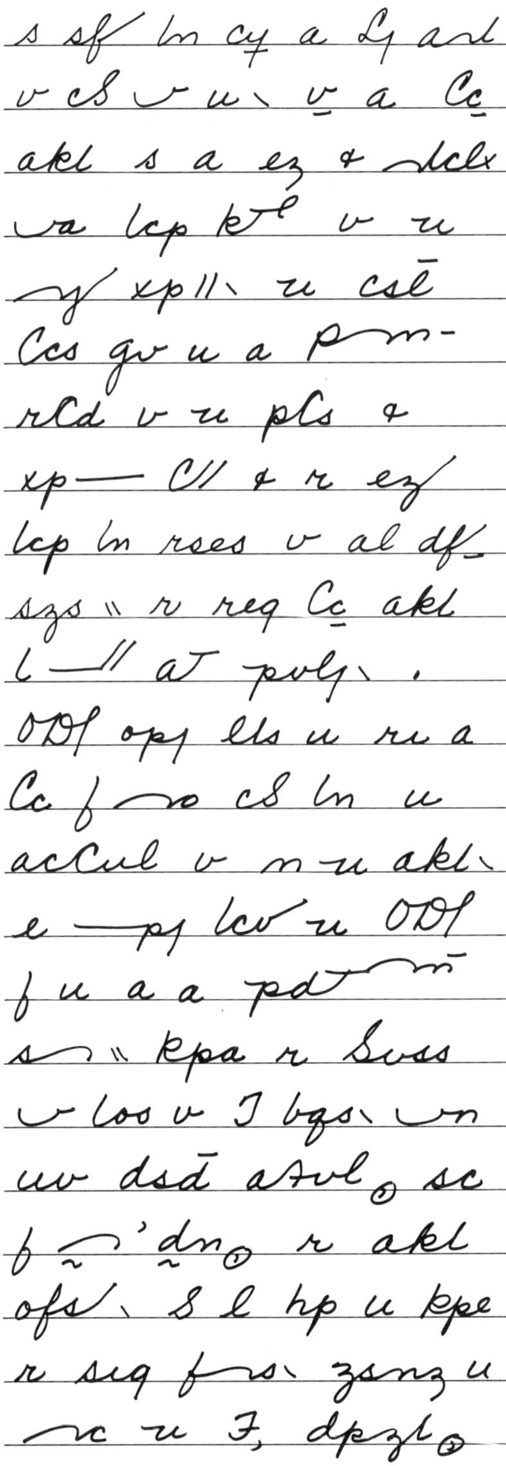

(B)

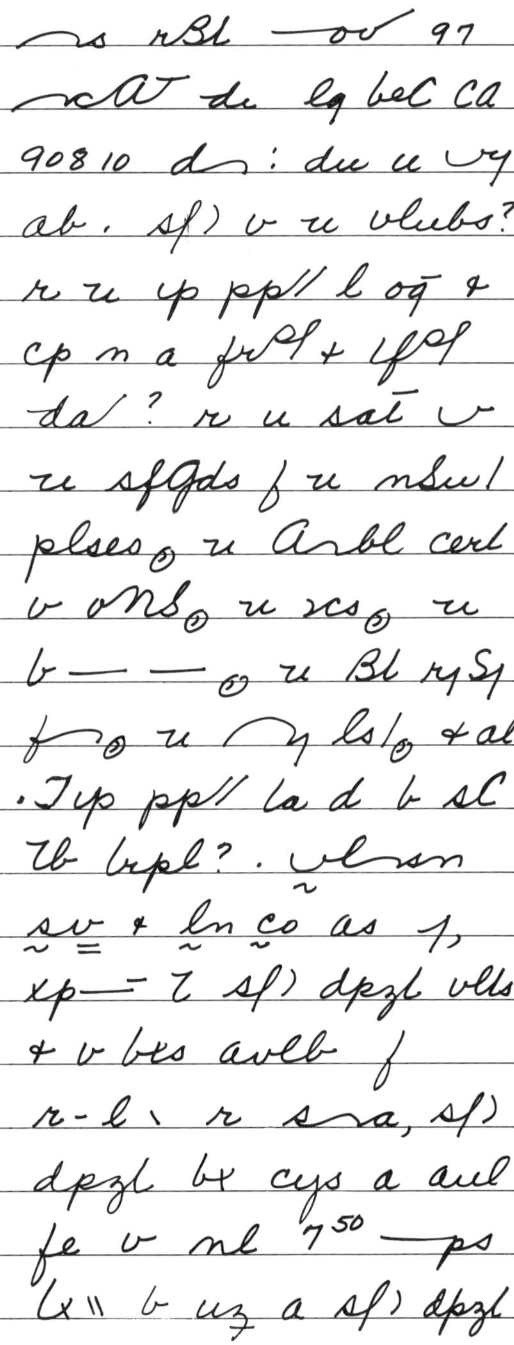

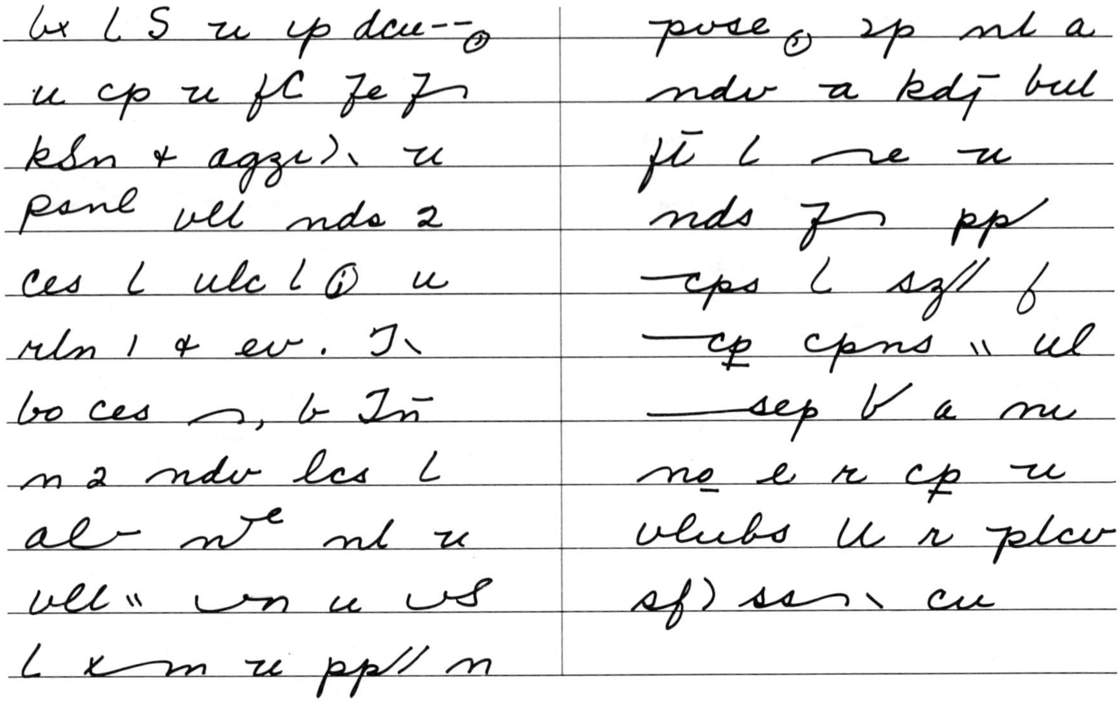

PROOFREADING

Everyone must learn to proofread work carefully. Proofreading includes more than the detection of "typos" such as *hte* for *the.* Some types of errors such as *then* for *than* and *to* for *two* cannot be detected unless the proofreader is reading for thought. This is also true of word omissions and word additions.

Proofreading and correcting errors consume nearly one-fourth of the transcriber's time. If the errors are corrected neatly and quickly, there is no great problem involved. Far too often, however, not all errors are detected.

There are certain errors that everyone tends to make and possibly overlook (see list on page 130). If you are aware of these pitfalls, you have taken a step toward becoming an efficient proofreader.

Everyone must develop the ability to proofread if he expects to produce mailable copy. The final goal of your shorthand training is a mailable transcript of the dictated material.

UNIT 9

MEDICAL

1.1 THEORY REVIEW

1. Plurals
2. *kw*
3. Final *y*
4. *ive*
5. Final *lee*

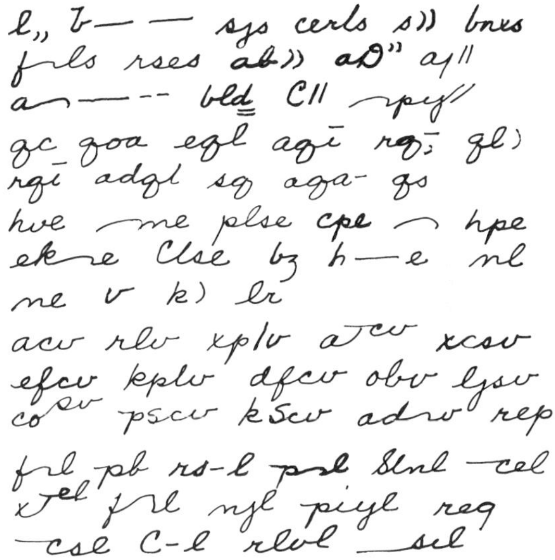

KEY 1. lists; brands; subjects; certificates; cities; bonuses; families; receipts; abilities; addresses; agencies; amendments; buildings; chances; employers 2. quick; quota; equal; acquired; requested; quality; required; adequate; square; acquaint; questions 3. heavy; money; policy; copy; many; happy; economy; courtesy; busy; handy; only; any; very; county; already 4. active; relative; expensive; attractive; exclusive; effective; competitive; defective; objective; legislative; cooperative; prospective; constructive; administrative; representative 5. family; probably; recently; promptly; certainly; clearly; extremely; formerly; nationally; primarily; regularly; closely; currently; relatively; slightly

1.2 TRANSCRIPTION SKILL BUILDING

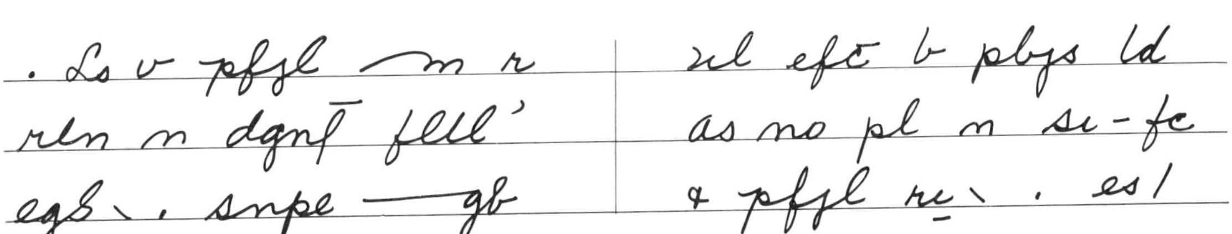

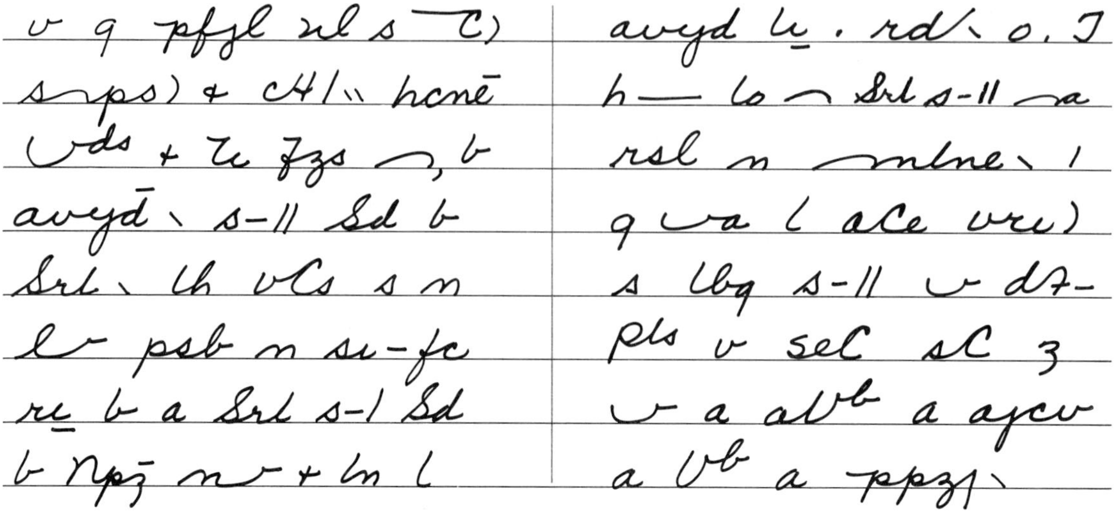

GUIDE Insert two adjective commas, five series commas, two parenthetical commas, one introductory comma, and one internal punctuation semicolon.

1.3 SPEED BUILDING

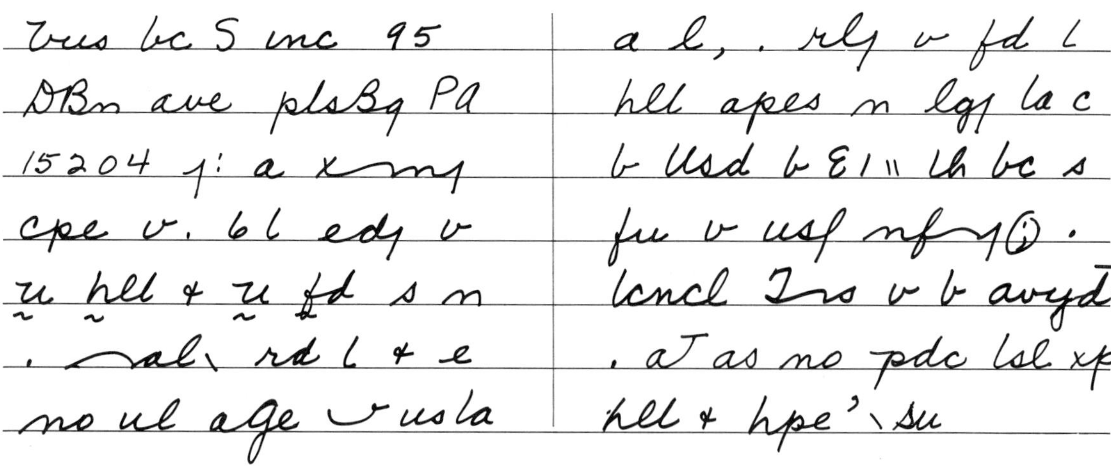

1.4 VOCABULARY BUILDING

(A)

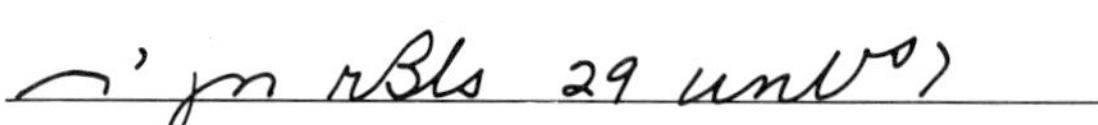

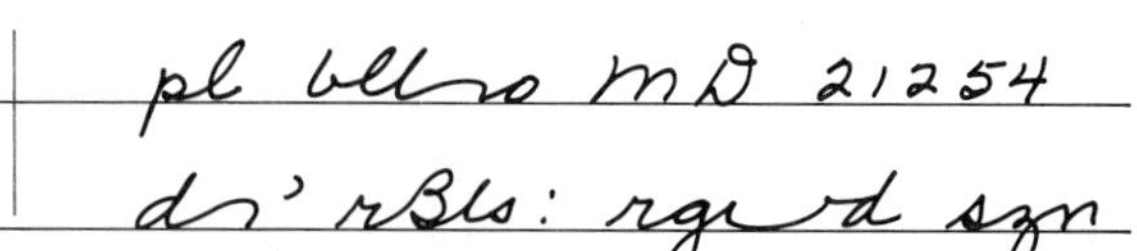

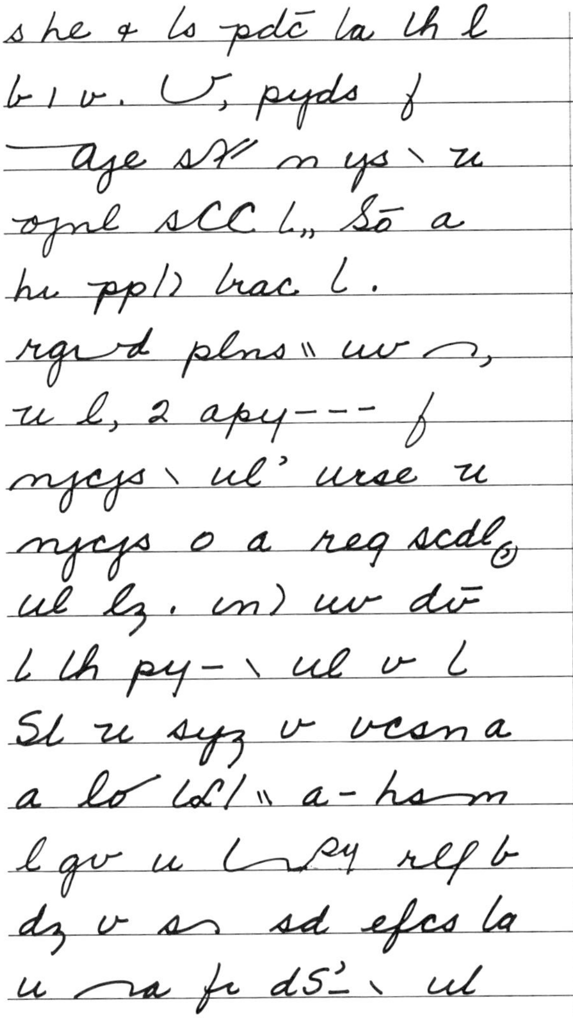

(B)

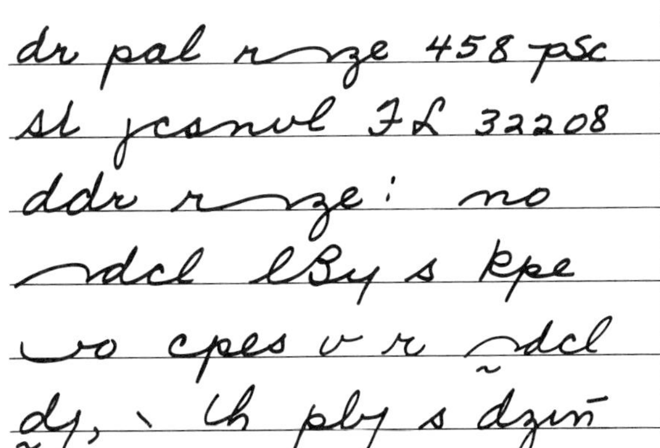

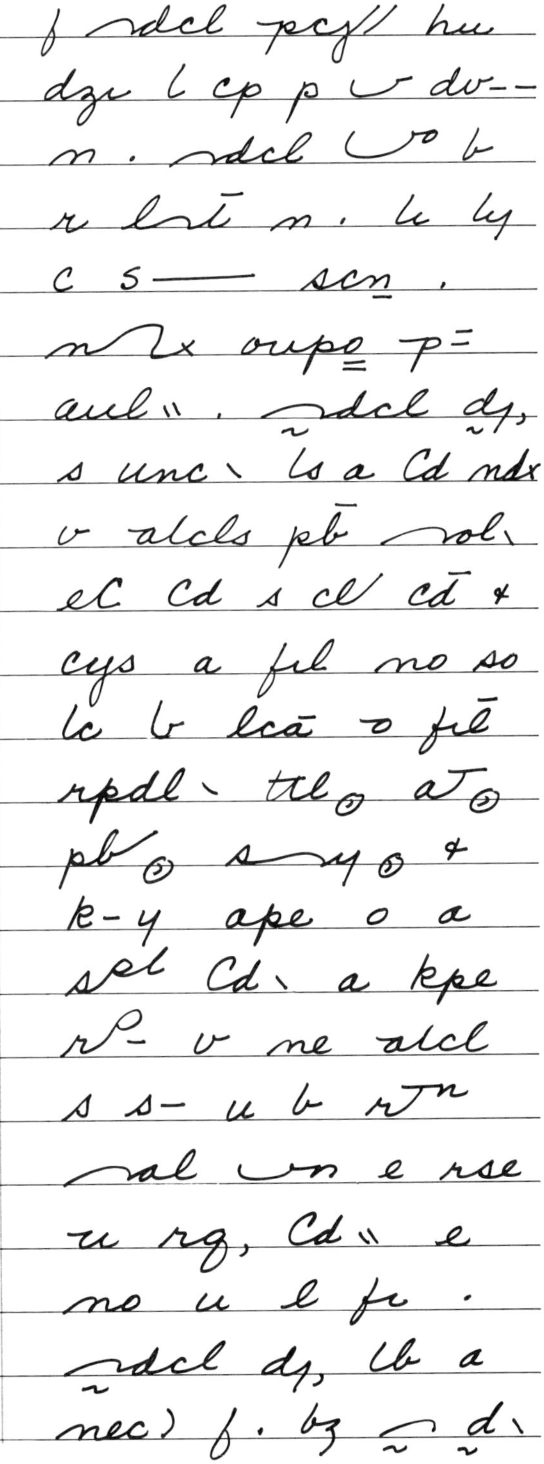

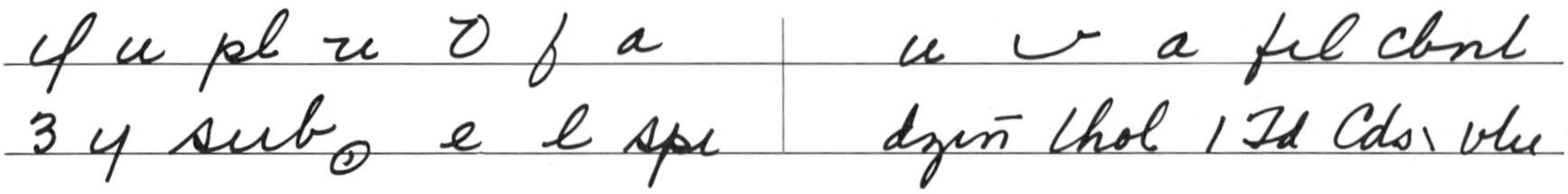

2.1 THEORY REVIEW

1. *nse*
2. *ic*
3. *ate*
4. *ful fully*
5. *ng*

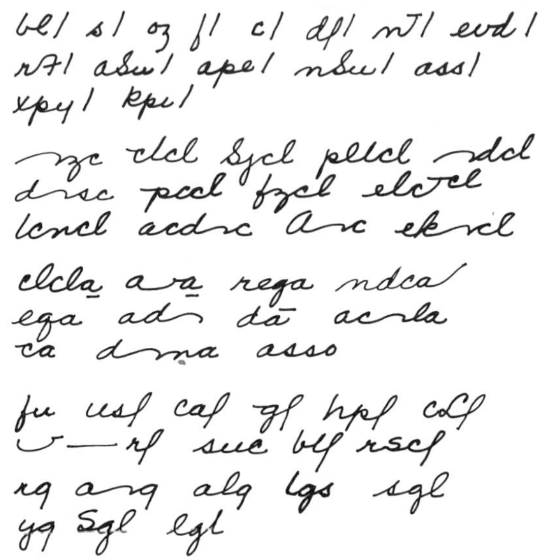

KEY 1. balance; since, sense; ounce; fence; once; defense; entrance; evidence; reference; assurance; appearance; insurance; assistance; experience; compliance 2. music; critical, ly; surgical, ly; political, ly; medical, ly; domestic; practical, ly; physical, ly; electrical, ly; technical, ly; academic; automatic; economical, ly 3. calculating; awaiting; regulate; indicator; equate; administrate; dated; accumulate; create; dominate; associate 4. full, ly; useful, ly; careful, ly; grateful, ly; helpful, ly; colorful, ly; wonderful, ly; successful, ly; beautiful, ly; respectful, ly 5. ring, wrong; among; along; things; single; young; strongly; length

2.2 TRANSCRIPTION SKILL BUILDING

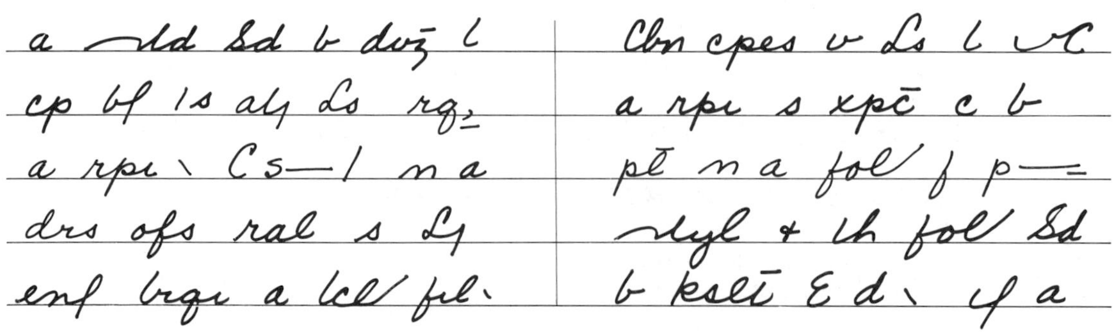

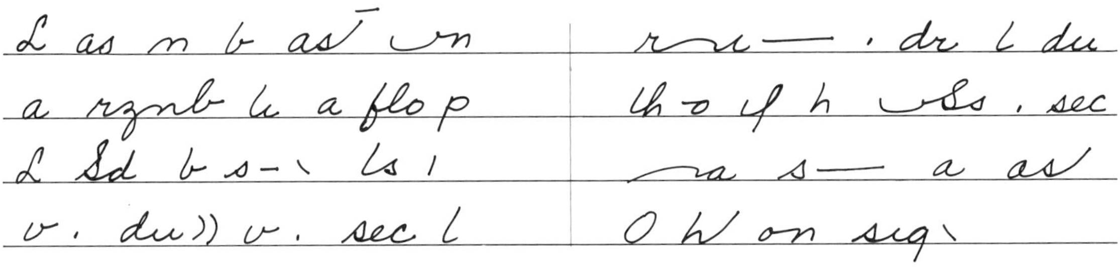

GUIDE Insert two possessive apostrophes, one conjunction comma, one introductory comma, two parenthetical commas, one compound adjective hyphen, and one internal punctuation semicolon.

2.3 SPEED BUILDING

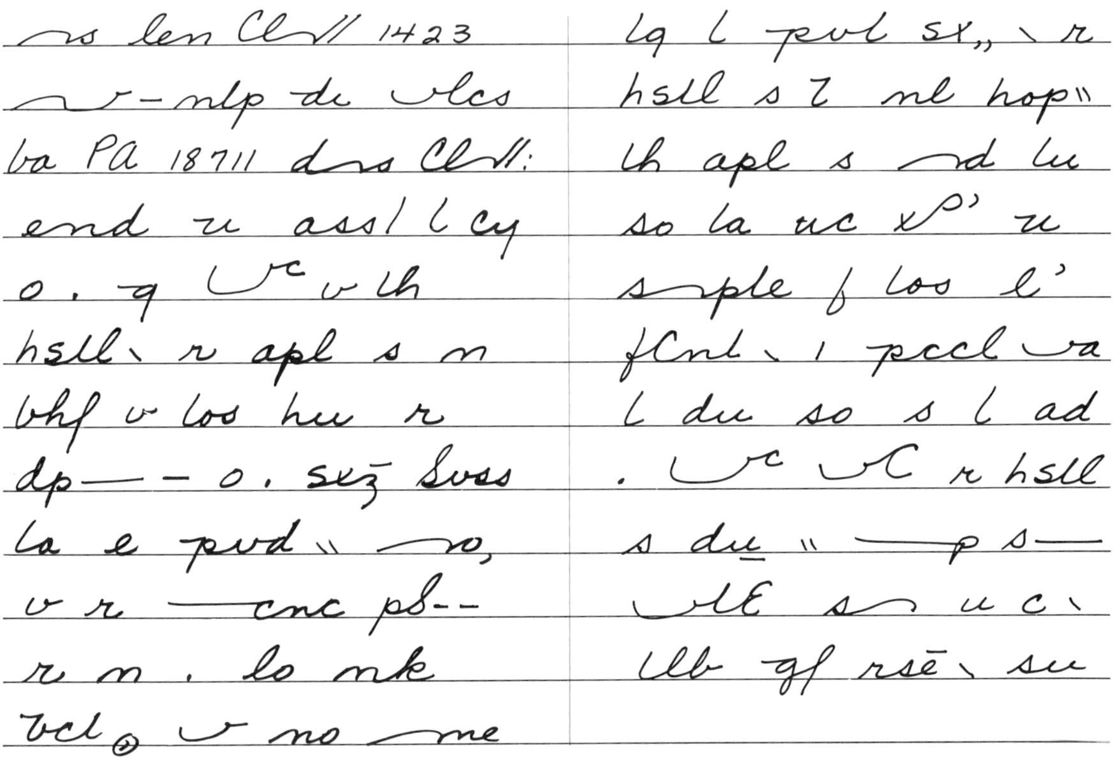

2.4 VOCABULARY BUILDING

(A)

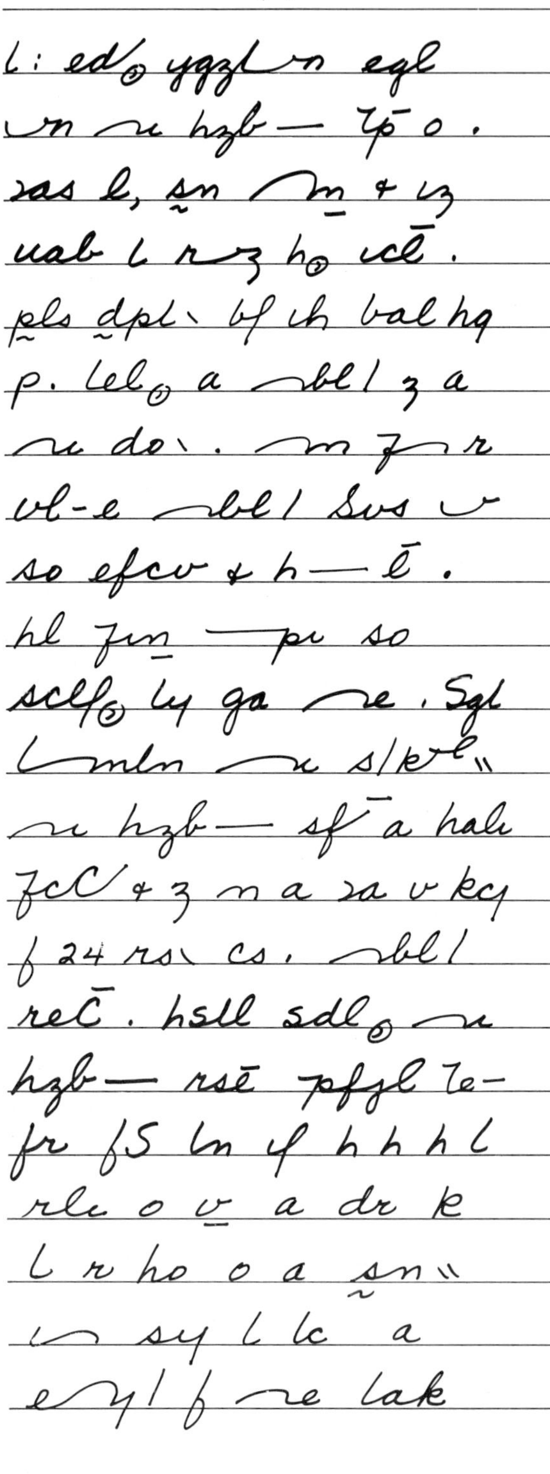

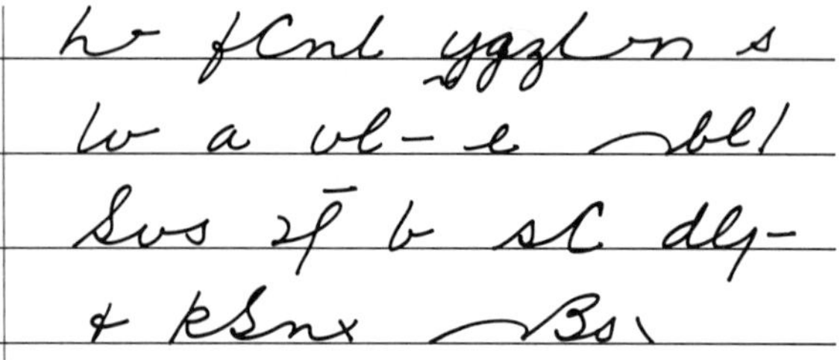

(B)

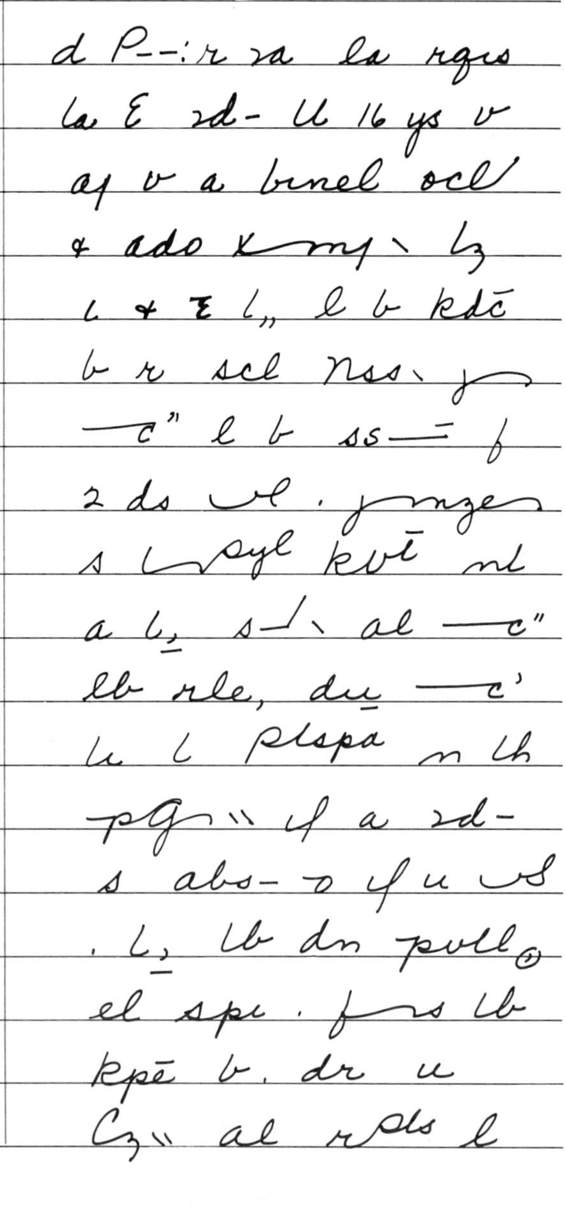

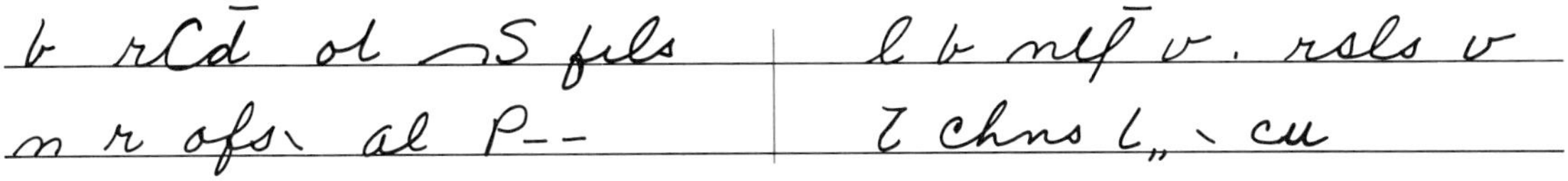

3.1 THEORY REVIEW

1. *nk*
2. *able*
3. *ss*
4. *nt*
5. *ēd*

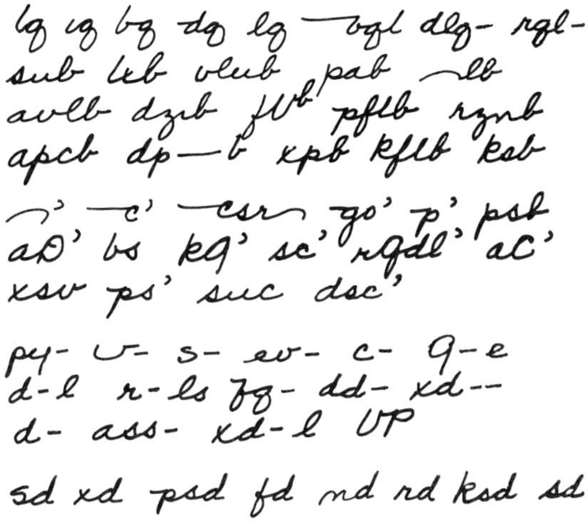

KEY 1. think, thank; ink; bank; drink; link; blanket; delinquent; wrinkled 2. suitable, ly; taxable; valuable, ly; payable; mailable; available; desirable; favorable, ly; profitable, ly; reasonable, ly; applicable; dependable; acceptable; comfortable, ly; considerable, ly 3. mass, miss; class; classroom; gross; press; possible, ly; address; business; congress; sickness; regardless; across; excessive; process; success; discuss 4. point; want, went; spent; event; can't; guarantee; dental; rentals; frequent; didn't; accidents; wouldn't; assistant; accidental; vice-president 5. speed; exceed; proceed; feed; need; read; concede; seed, cede.

3.2 TRANSCRIPTION SKILL BUILDING

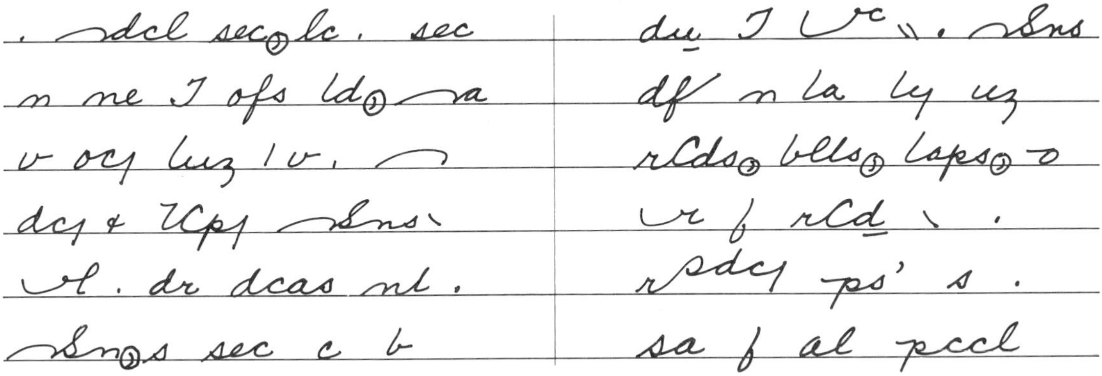

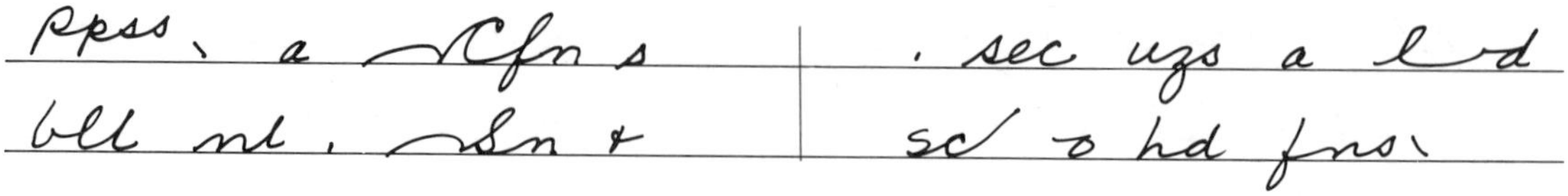

GUIDE Insert two parenthetical commas, one introductory comma, three series commas, one conjunction comma

3.3 SPEED BUILDING

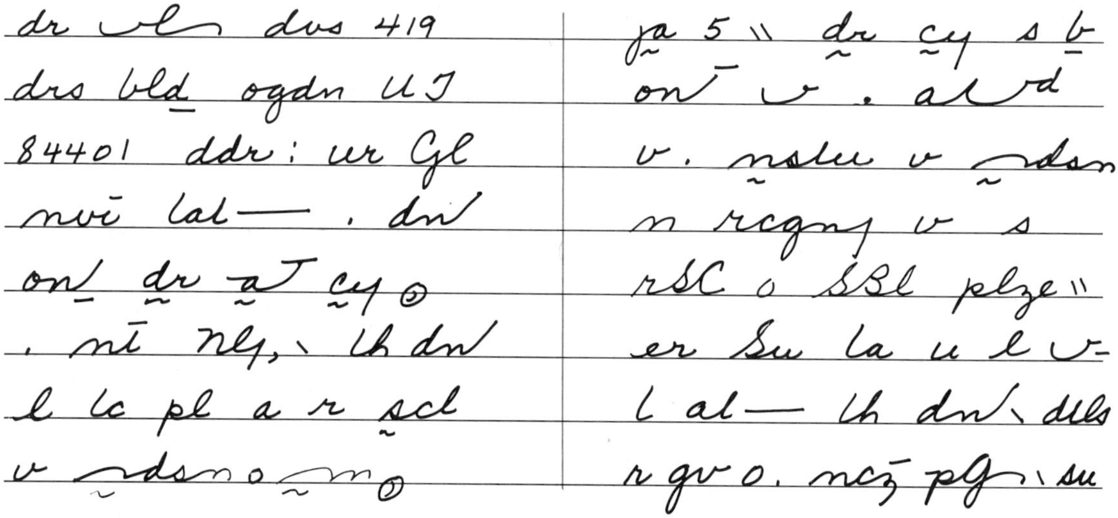

3.4 VOCABULARY BUILDING

(A)

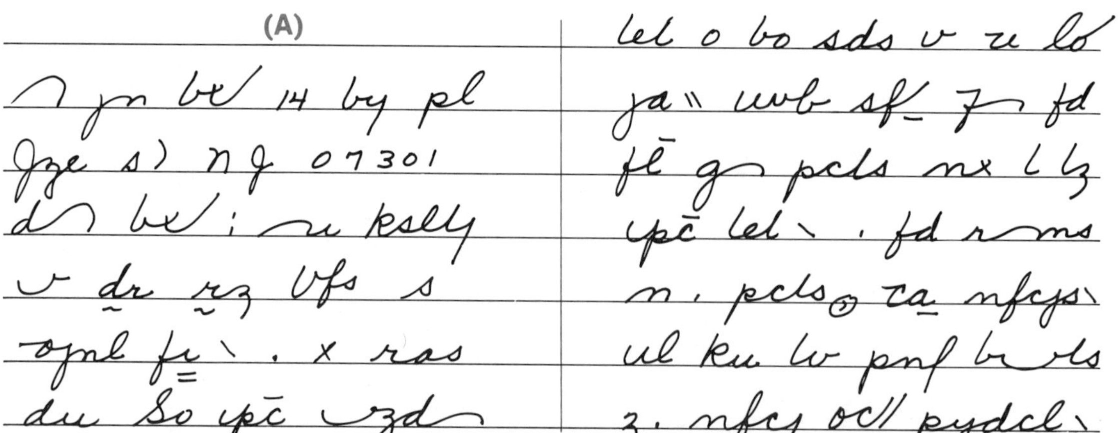

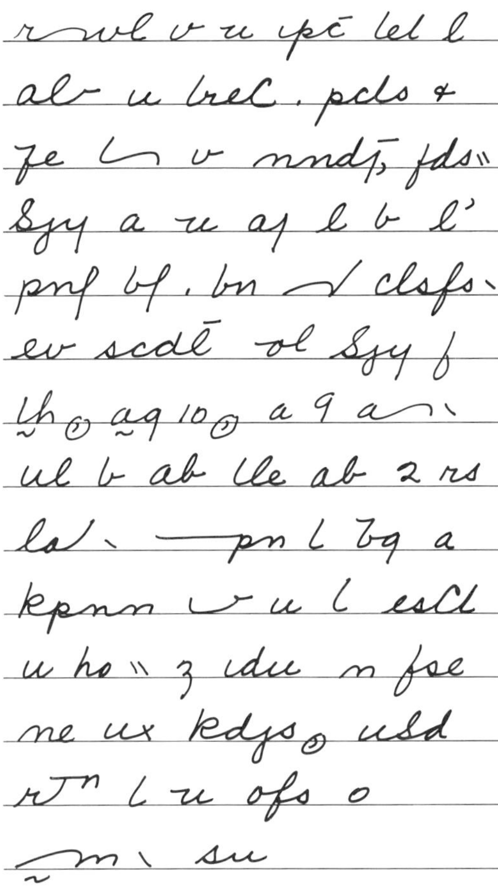

(B)

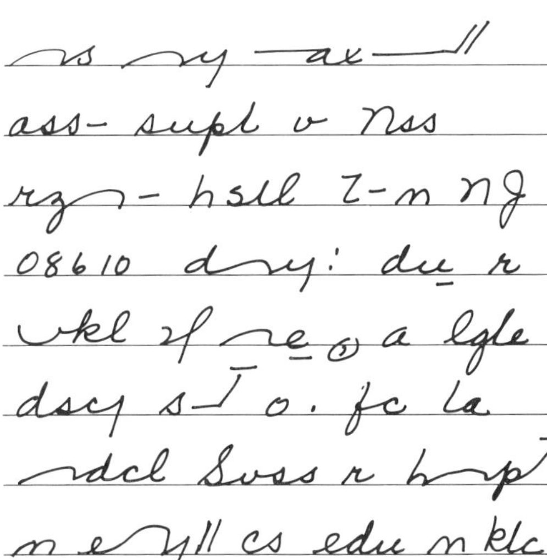

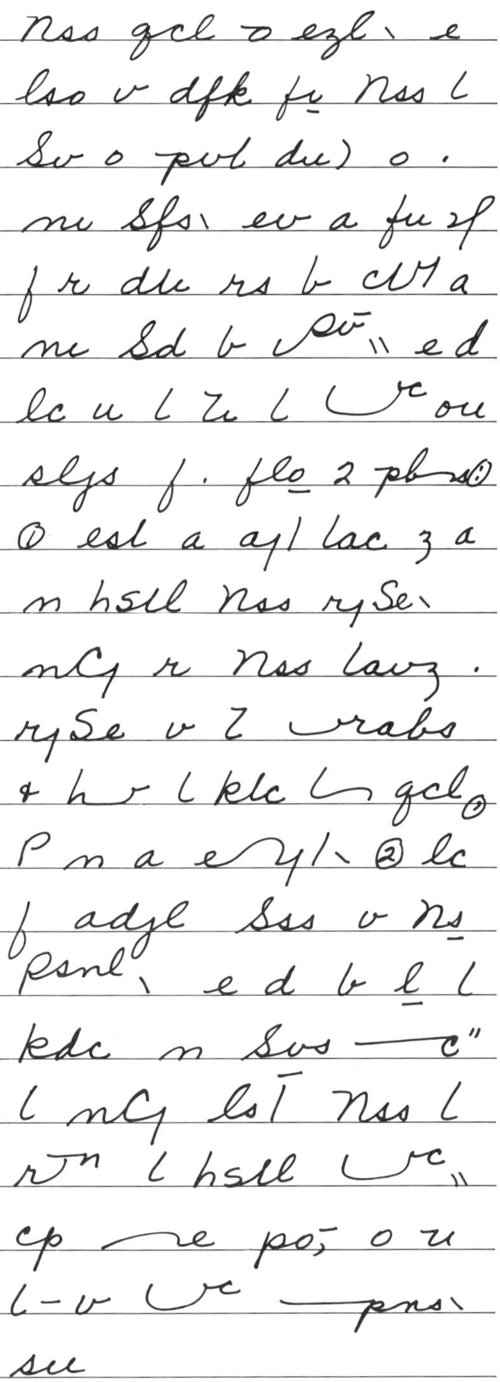

4.1 THEORY REVIEW

1. *sp*

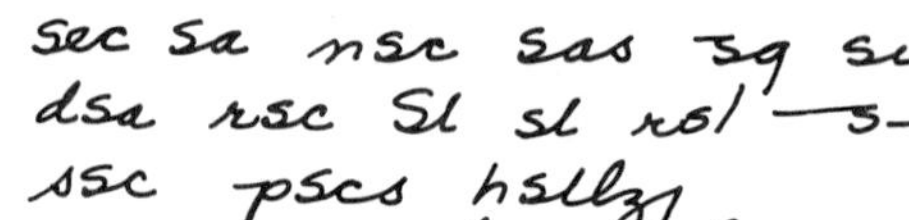

2. *per*

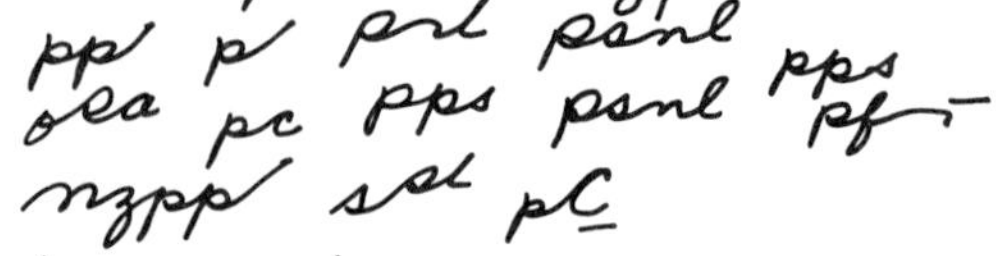

3. *us*

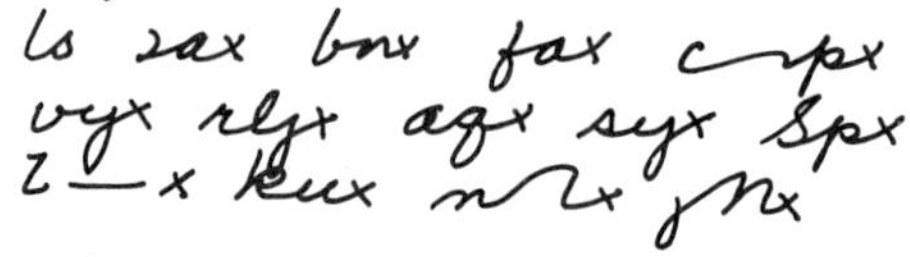

4. *ex*

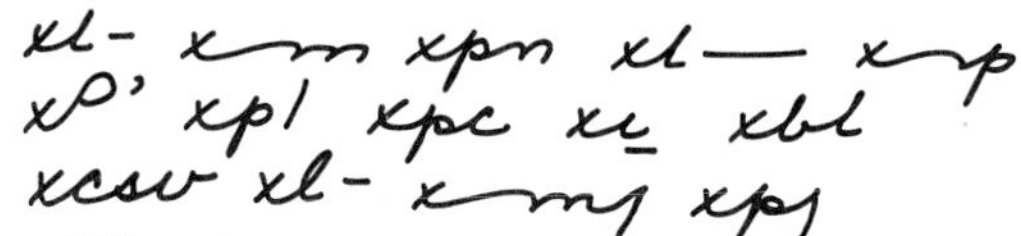

5. *ăn*

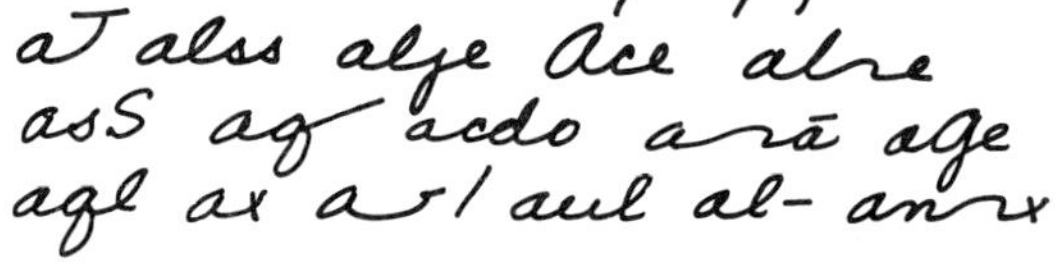

KEY 1. speak; spare; inspect; space; spring; spire, spite; display; respect; spirit; spot; response; splendid; suspect; prospects; hospitalization 2. paper; per; permit; personal; perhaps; operate; percent; purpose; personnel; performed; newspaper; separate; purchasing 3. thus; status; bonus; famous; campus; various; religious; anxious; serious; surplus; tremendous; continuous; numerous; generous 4. extent; examine; explain; extend; example; express; expense; expect; exiting; exhibit; exclusive; excellent; examination; expansion 5. another; analysis; analogy; anarchy; anatomy; ancestor; anchor; anecdote; animated; angry; ankle; annex; announce; annual; annulment; anonymous

4.2 TRANSCRIPTION SKILL BUILDING

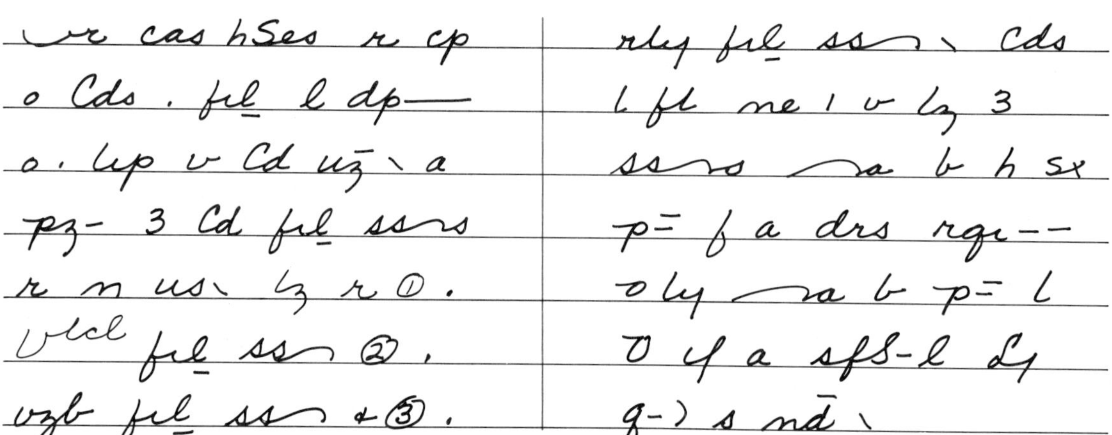

GUIDE Insert two introductory commas, two series commas, one conjunction comma, one enumeration colon, and one possessive apostrophe.

4.3 SPEED BUILDING

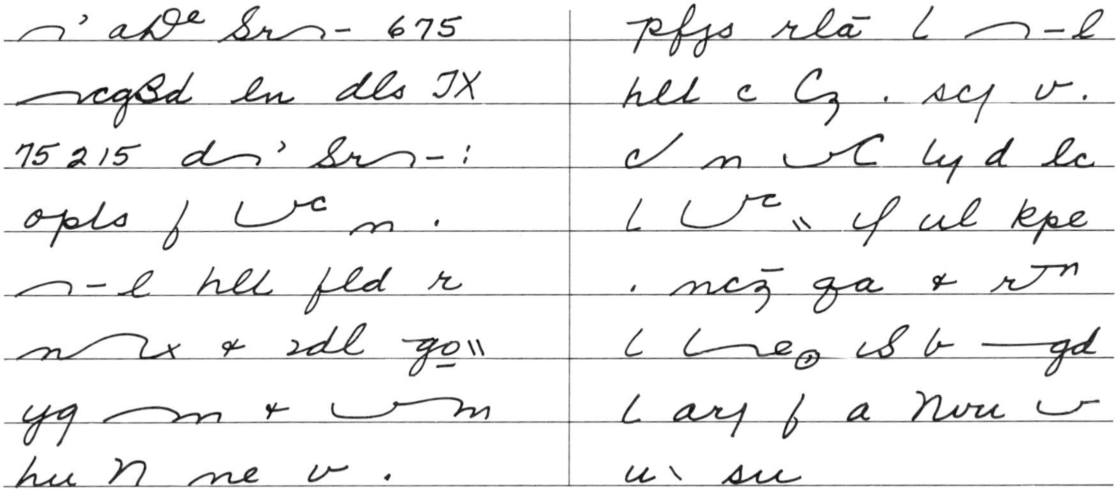

4.4 VOCABULARY BUILDING

(A)

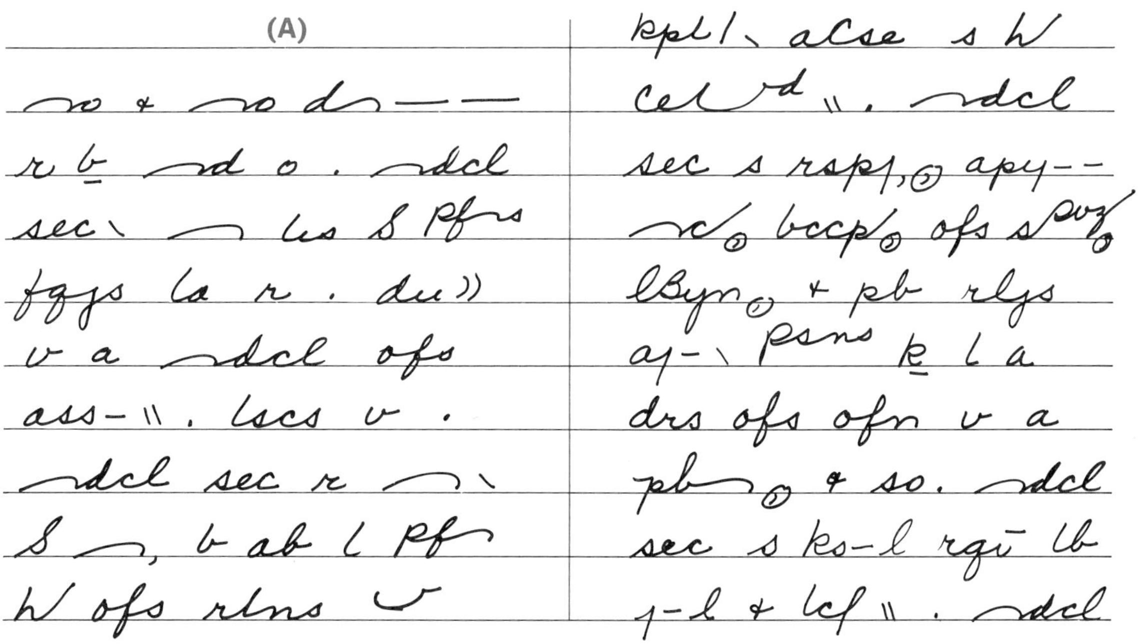

sec ⌒, r⌒ n
fu kTl v Hs/ no ⌒
vl Tdc kdys ⌒u
pvl. W c⌒ ⌒n
raSus W cl Vcl/ &
pS--.

(B)

l: dr —aBl ng sdel
D oho fNl hsll n
sde. cas hSes v.
eYl r⌒ f. p, 6
⌒os e nt la T as
b a nCs v 17 pc v
ndSel Bn pS--. a u
rq, e Utc a sde l
—pn h⌒ ecd b, uz.
hsll fsl)) lcop ⌒
fC nCss" e dT ⌒
la —aca adjl sas
f. scpl v vsln d'
& pSu d' z ⌒=.
elso nd X bd sas
n a isla aa ⌒r
Bn pS-- cd b ⌒C f
rSly kpcys ⌒C d
rqu eT pl- n a
xyn l- o a Tcelre
oSl. nTvnx fd
d b O f svel
Bn pS--. rpl-
v —fuds s clcl
n. 24 l 48 r pyd
af rse. Bn"
if T s a ku nCs
v ndSel Bn
vc⌒s r sdcl
fsl) l b OBdn.
h ⌒E if T s ne
Sl v ⌒' dzS
e du v adqt
spis l nslu
ida bsc F, ad
psf/ f Bn
pS--.

5.1 THEORY REVIEW

1. *pr*
2. *kr*
3. *gr*
4. *br*
5. *fr*

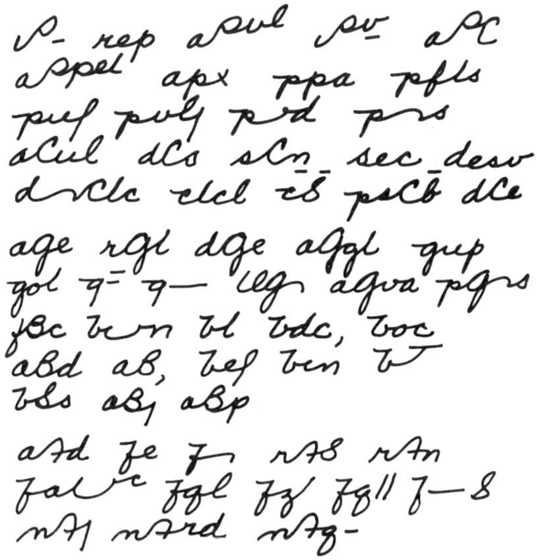

1. imprint; represent; approval; improving; approach; appropriate; approximately; prepare; profits; proof; privilege; proud; promise 2. accrual; decrease; screening; secretary; descriptive; democratic; critical; crashed; prescribed; decree 3. agree; regret; degree; aggregate; group; growth; granted; grand; telegram; aggravate; programs 4. fabric; brown; brought; broadcast; broke; abroad; abreast; brief; brighten; brother; brushes; abridge; abrupt 5. afraid; free; from; refresh; refrain; framework; frankly; freezer; frequencies; friendship; infringe; infrared; infrequent

5.2 TRANSCRIPTION SKILL BUILDING

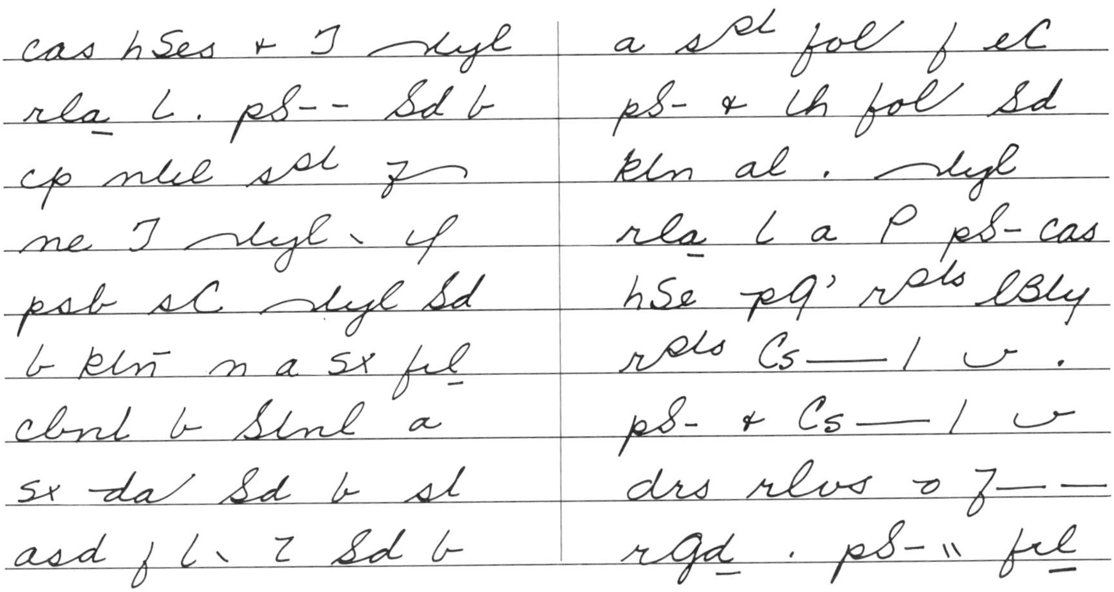

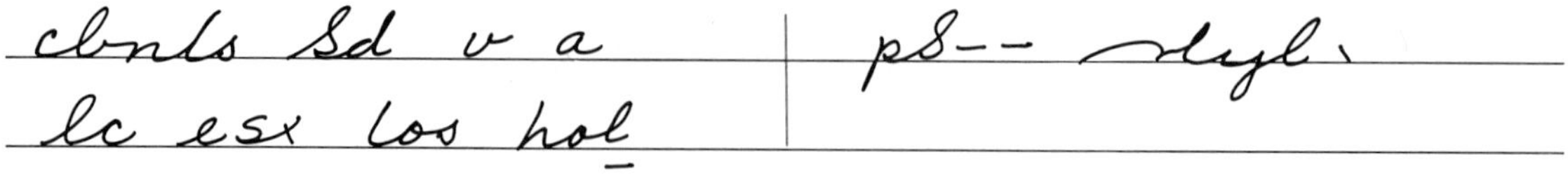

GUIDE Insert one introductory comma, one conjunction comma, six series commas, one parenthetical comma, one internal punctuation semicolon, one enumeration colon, and one possessive apostrophe.

5.3 SPEED BUILDING

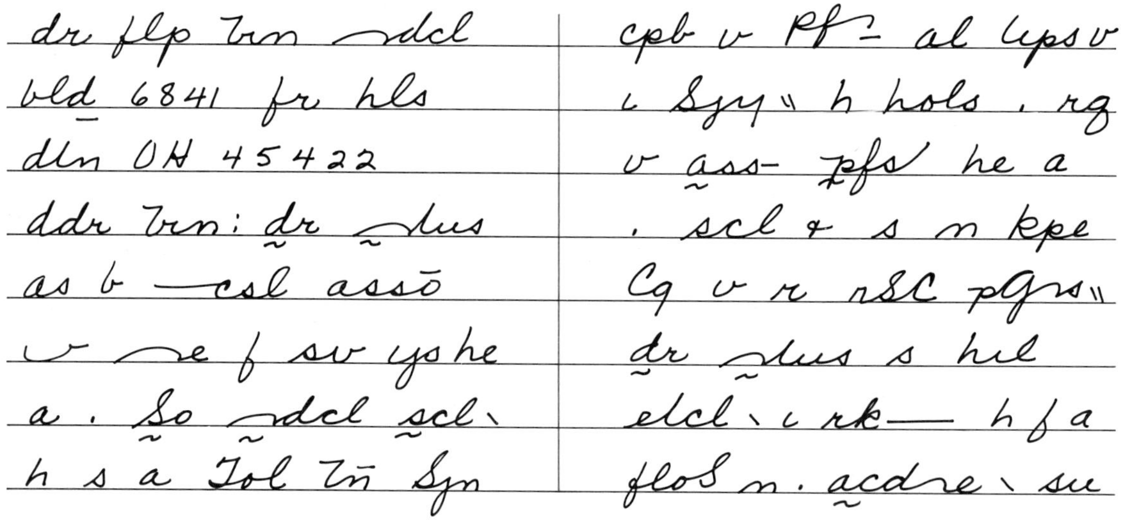

5.4 VOCABULARY BUILDING

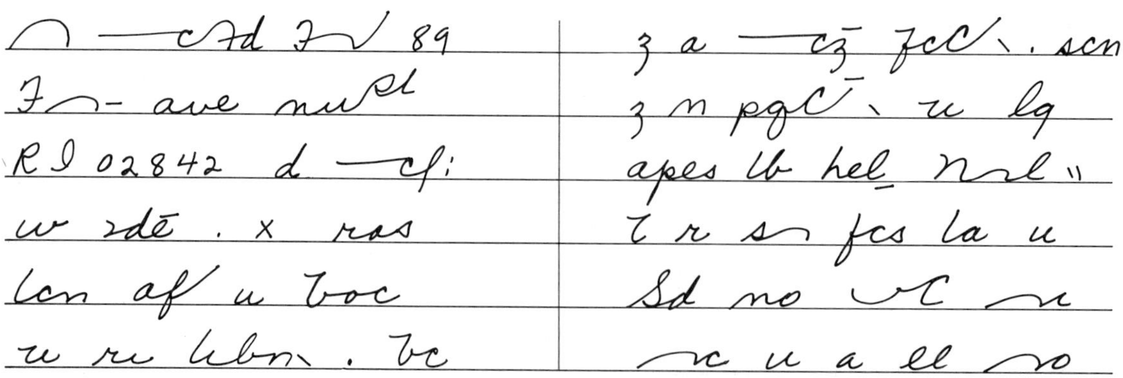

cx nsd v Olx- u bde.
. fr/ s. L1, lq, + Sq,
v al bns + cys. no,
bde va. u bns kln
Vcul al v. bdes
nl spi + no,
v. vr bd sls
vC plc u Fn
nfcj r pdu, vn
. bn no. u bns S +
rls clsen nl .
bdSe n xc + kl
anls" du chhd
r bns sd r bde +
lso ku l go. z e
aj Cllj fns a.
e— — v eC bn. z
. Cllj bl bns Hdns
no I gol s psb"

. aPC l Ze bcn bns
as Cj rdcl. no lg
dz a bcn lq n
a lq rcPl pyd n
bd. olpdc Sjns Zu lv
l pS-- fgl z Nrl z
psb. ly uz pns
sCus — pas alfr
jy-- + l nsal a
nu bal + scl if nec"
n la. ur n u
nd 20s u bns v reC
l pec dl) + Sgl. n.
bn Sgl dmSs a a v
so ra. . nls S
n. bn no bg l
dmS lso. u bns
r go l' rq. gv
l so rsc. s

WHERE ERRORS ARE FREQUENTLY UNDETECTED

Some errors are common to all, while others are strictly individual.

Here is a list of the spots where errors are most frequently undetected:

1. Headings and subheadings
2. Beginning or ending of a line
3. Recurring long words
4. Bottom of the page
5. Additions or omissions of copy
6. Transpositions
7. Computations and footnotes
8. Proper nouns
9. Vertical enumeration (1-2-3-3-4)
10. Number combinations

Train yourself to be especially careful in proofreading in these ten situations. Then analyze your own individual types of errors so that you will be able to watch for them as you proofread.

UNIT 10

EMPLOYMENT

1.1 THEORY REVIEW

1. *oi*
2. *shul*
3. *ēn*
4. *kt*
5. *ther*

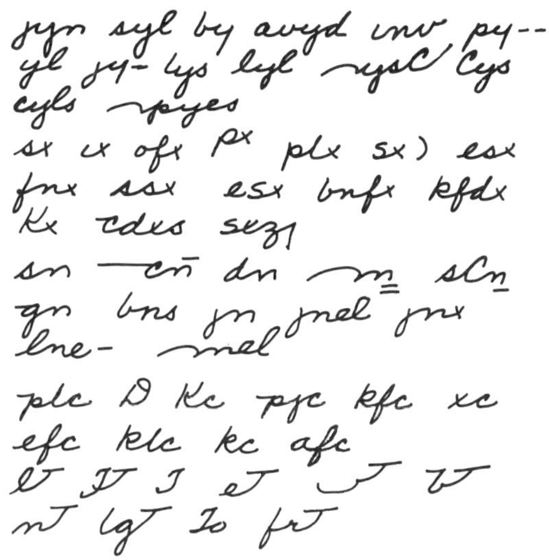

KEY 1. join; soil; boy; avoid; invoice; points; oil; joint; toys; loyal; moisture; choice; coils; employees 2. social, ly; initial, ly; official, ly; partial, ly; potential, ly; specialty; essential, ly; financial, ly; substantial; especial, ly; beneficial; confidential; commercial; credentials; specialization 3. seen; cleaned; dean; meanings; screening; green; beans; gene, jean; genial; genious; lenient; menial 4. protect; direct; correct; project; conflict; exact; effect; contact; connect; affect 5. leather; further; other; either; weather, whether; brother; neither; together; thorough; farther

1.2 TRANSCRIPTION SKILL BUILDING

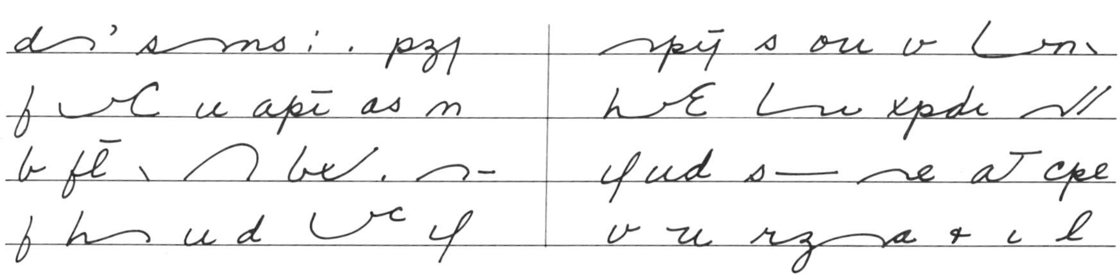

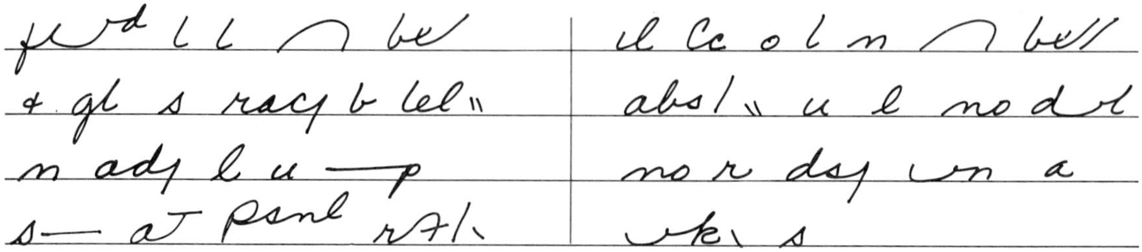

GUIDE Insert four parenthetical commas, two introductory commas, one internal punctuation semicolon, and one possessive apostrophe.

1.3 SPEED BUILDING

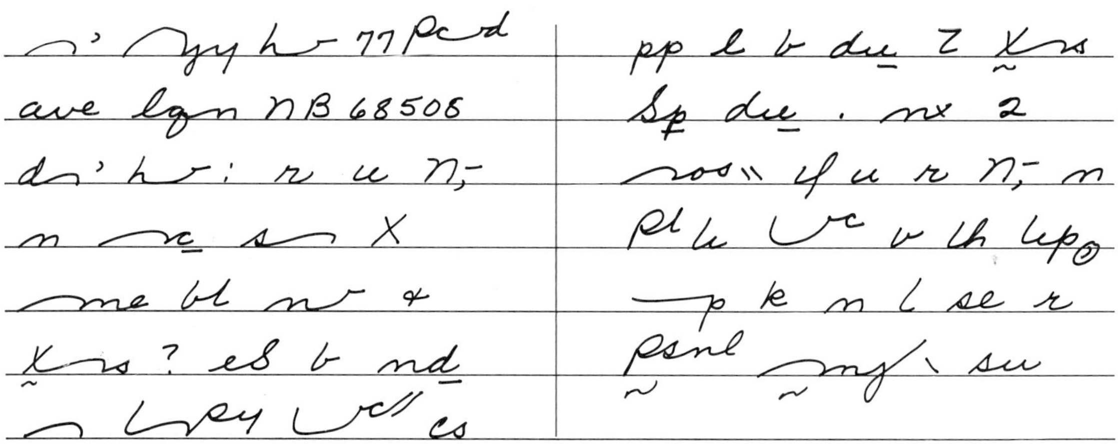

1.4 VOCABULARY BUILDING

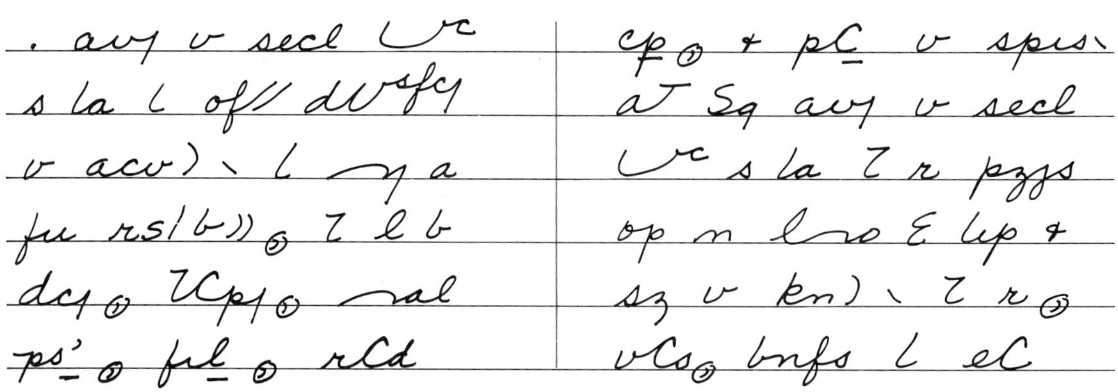

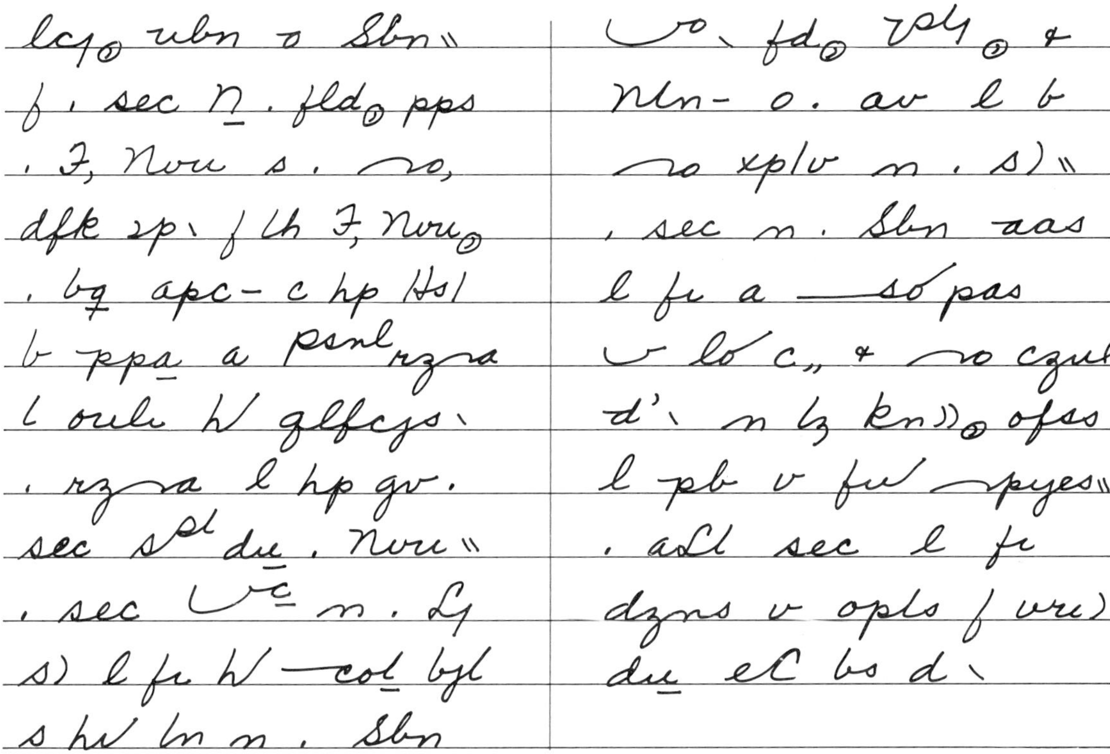

2.1 THEORY REVIEW

1. *īve*
2. *ēry*
3. Final *fy*
4. *ster*
5. Compound words

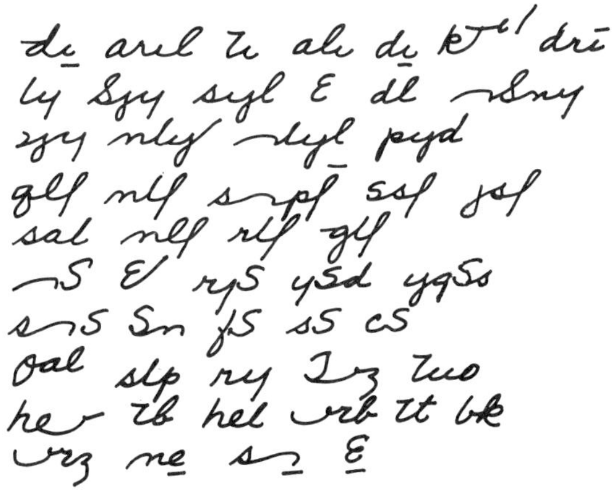

KEY 1. driving; arrival; thrive; alive; diving; contrivance; derived 2. theory; surgery; serial, cereal; every; delivery; machinery; stationery; interior; material; period 3. qualify; notify; simplified; specify; justify; satisfy; nullify; ratify; gratify 4. master; Easter, register; yesterday; youngsters; semester; stern; faster; sister; canister

5. overall; setup; railway; otherwise; throughout; herewith; thereby; hereto; whereby; thereto; become; whereas; anything; something; everything

2.2 TRANSCRIPTION SKILL BUILDING

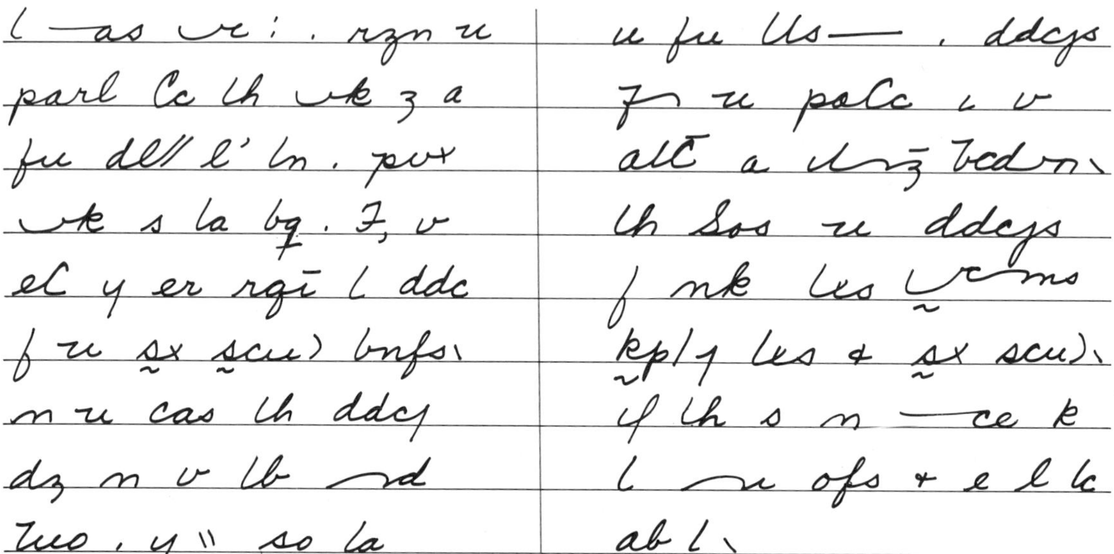

GUIDE Insert three introductory commas, two series commas, and one possessive apostrophe.

2.3 SPEED BUILDING

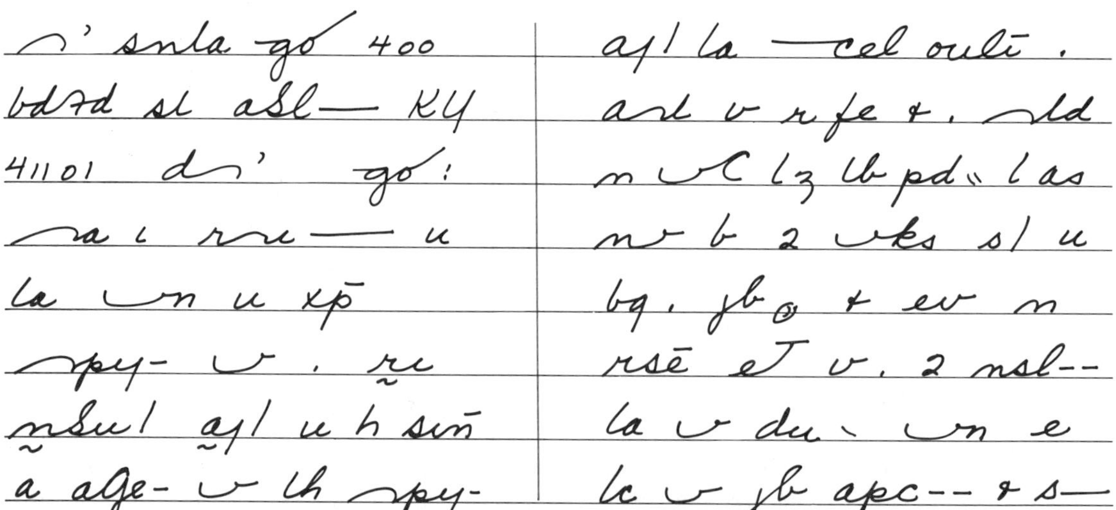

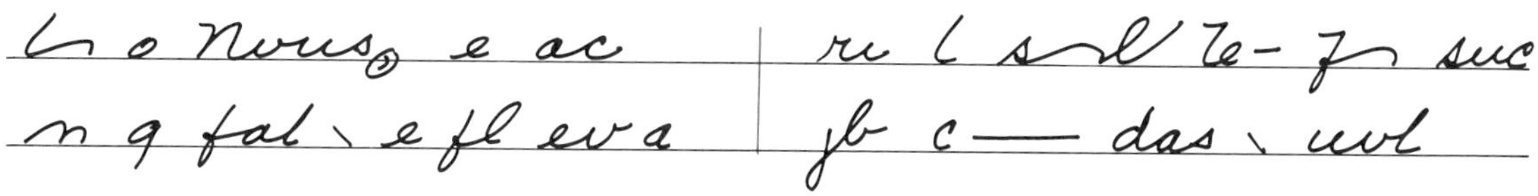

2.4 VOCABULARY BUILDING

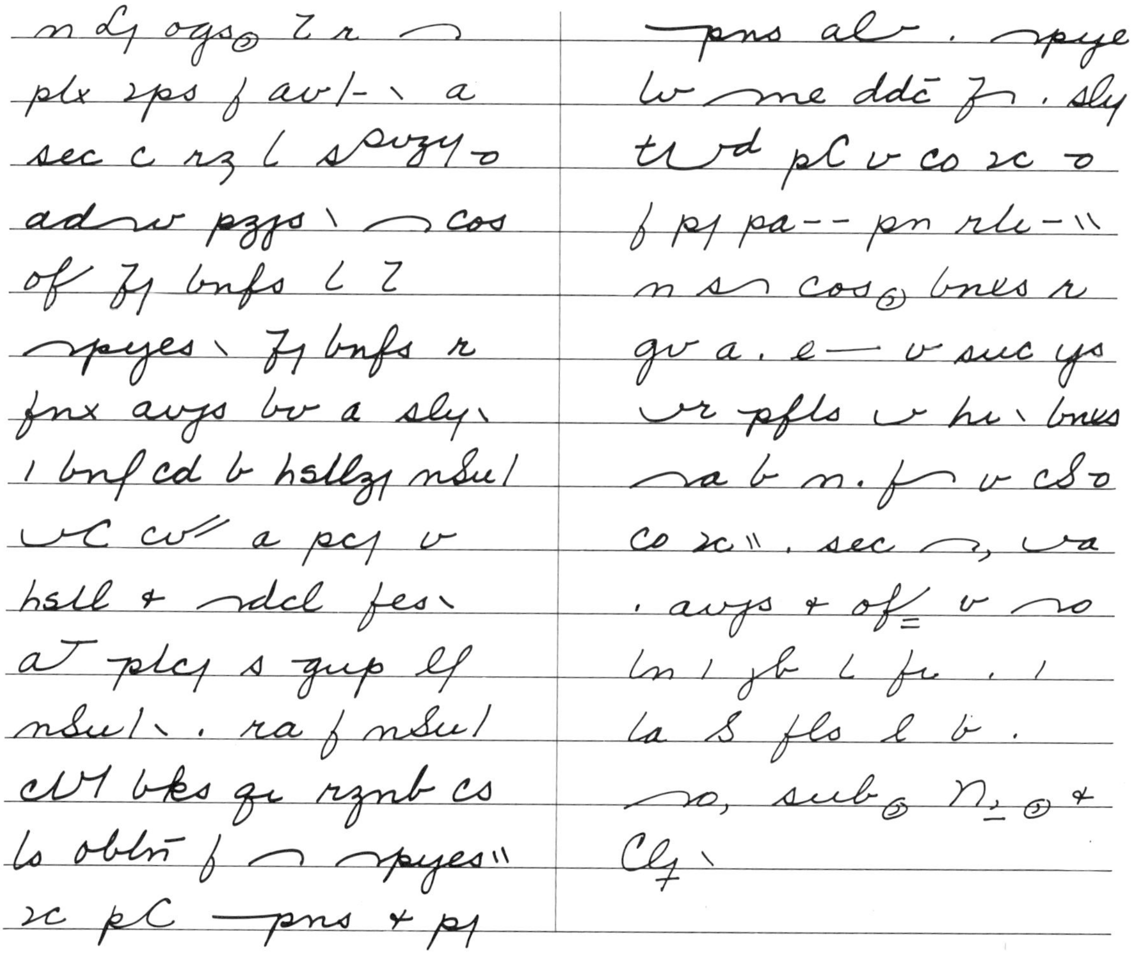

3.1 THEORY REVIEW

1. *shun*

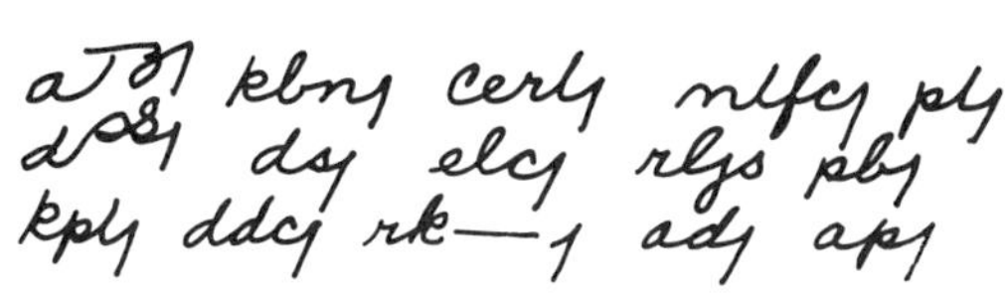

2. *st*

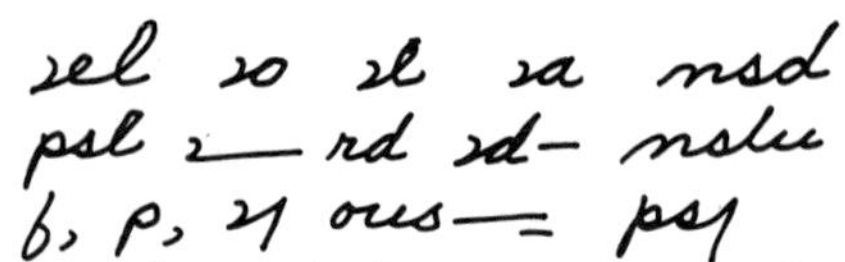

3. Final *tee*

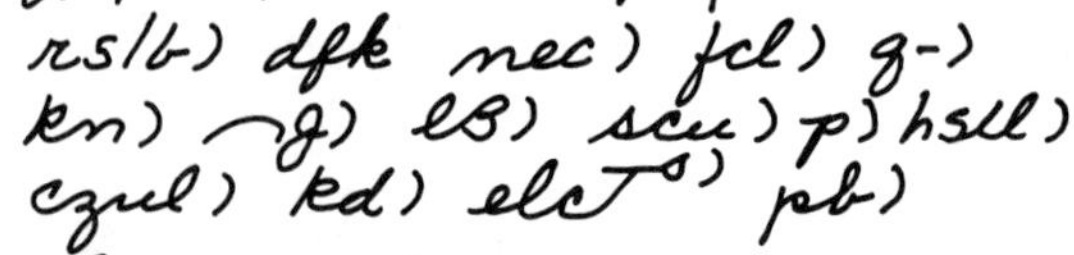

4. *ēte*

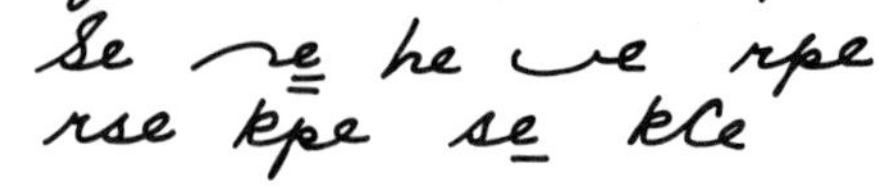

KEY 1. authorization; combination; certification; notification; petition; depreciation; decision; election; relations; publication; competition; deduction; recommendation; addition; appreciation 2. steel, steal; stop; still; state; instead; postal; standard; student; institute; listed; fast, forced; past, passed; station; outstanding; passage 3. responsibility; difficulty; necessity; faculty; quantity; community; majority; liberty; security; pretty; hospitality; casualty; commodity; electricity; publicity 4. sheet; meetings; heat; wheat; repeat; receipt; complete; seating; concrete

3.2 TRANSCRIPTION SKILL BUILDING

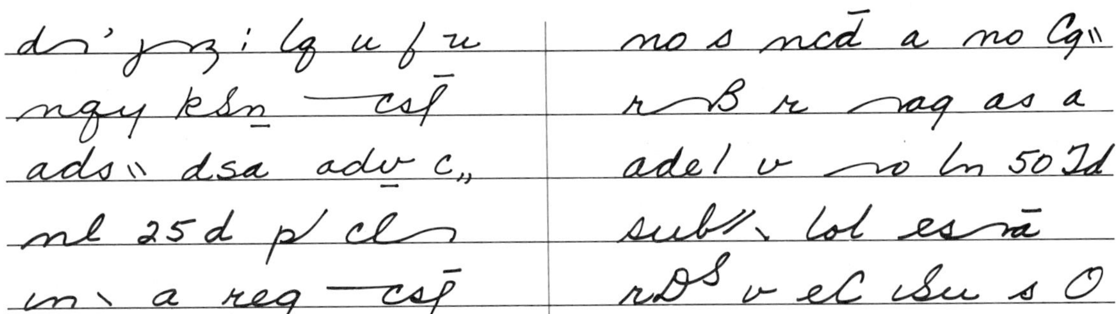

GUIDE Insert two parenthetical commas, two introductory commas, three compound

adjective hyphens, and two numbers commas.

3.3 SPEED BUILDING

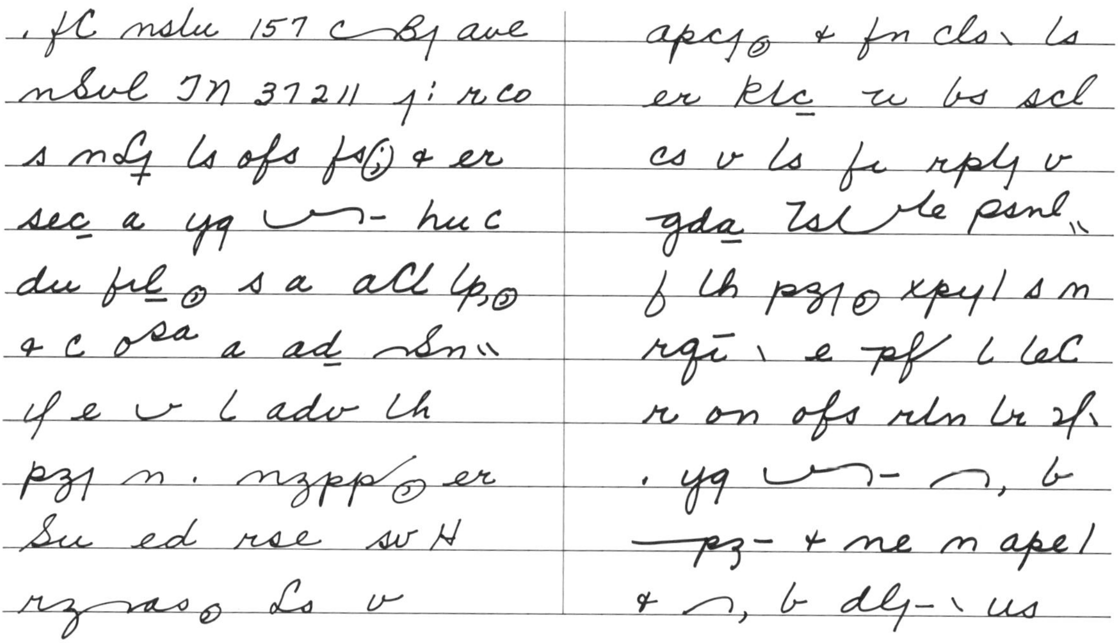

3.4 VOCABULARY BUILDING

(A)

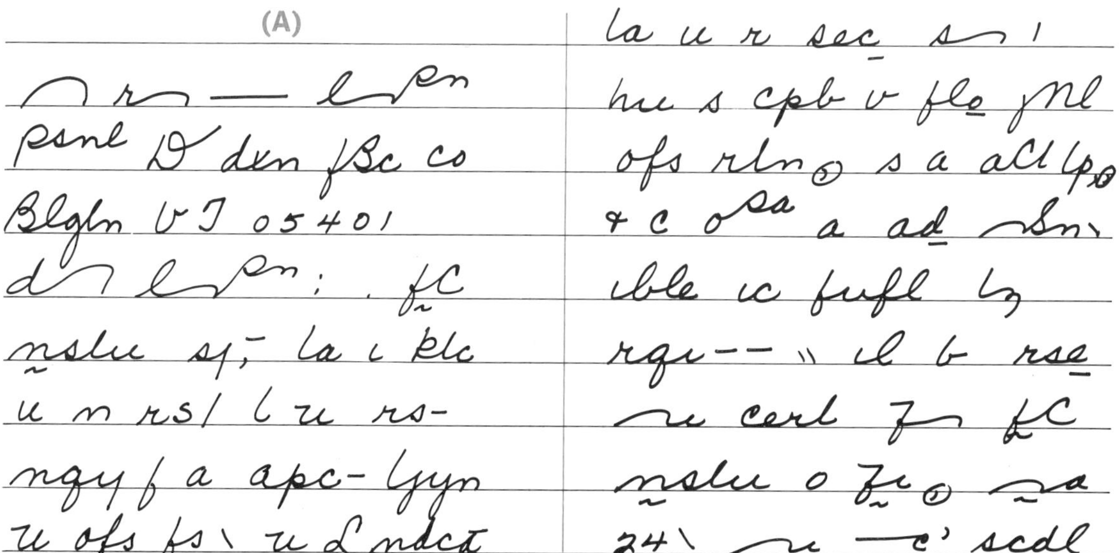

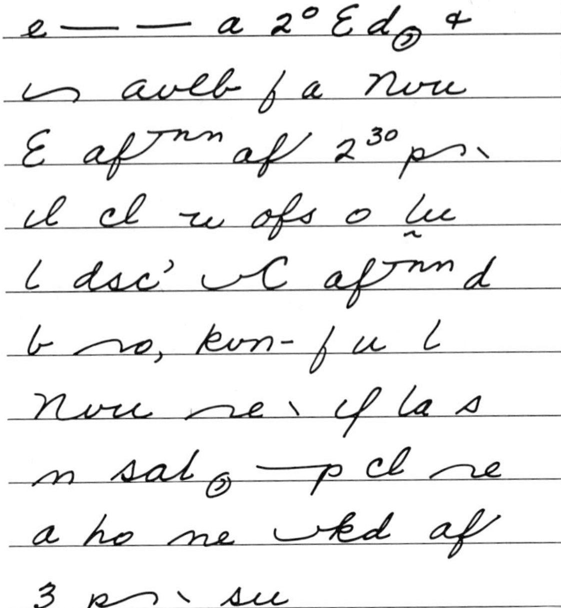

(B)

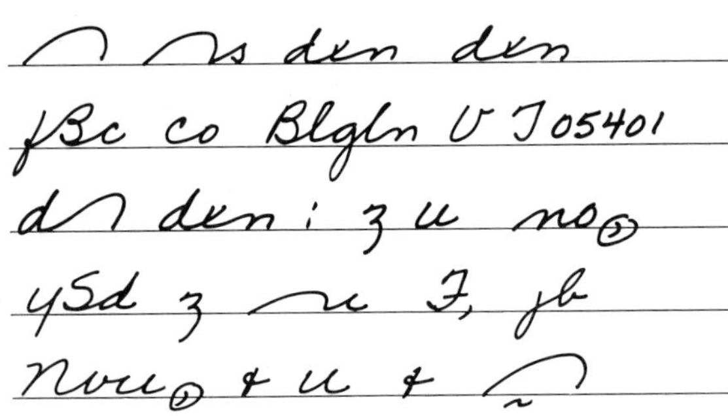

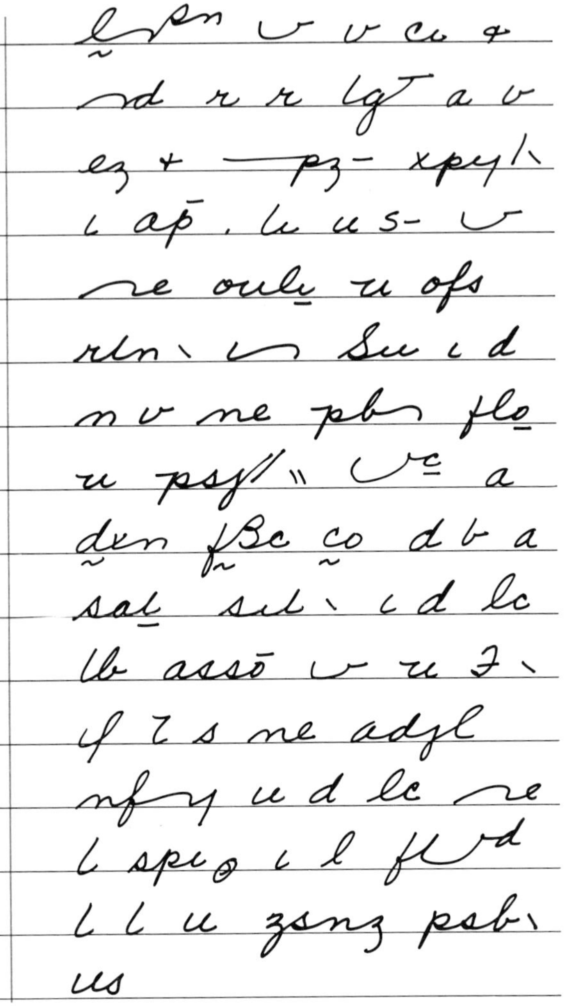

4.1 THEORY REVIEW

1. *stor*

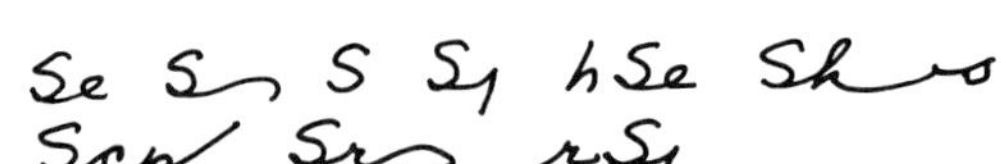

2. *ŭn*

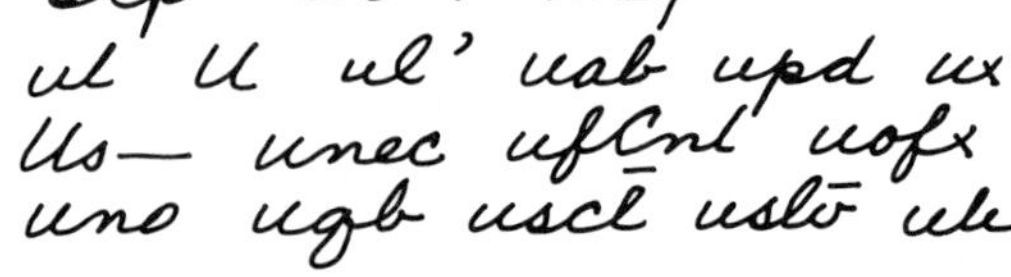

3. *fl*

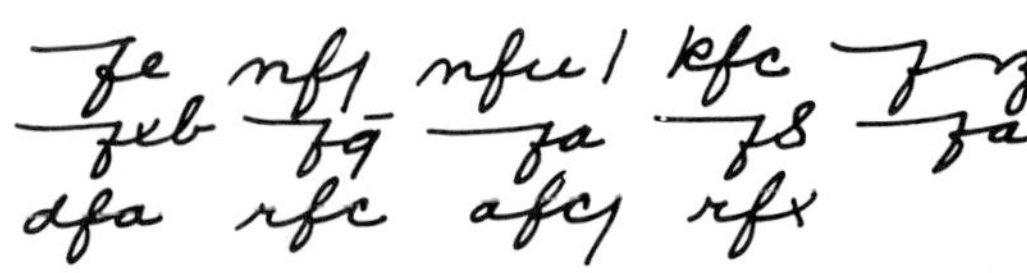

4. *ft*
5. Compound words

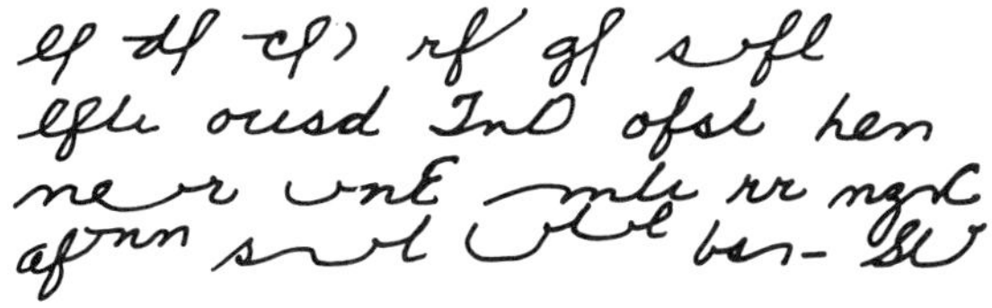

KEY 1. story; storm; store; storage; history; storehouse; storekeeper; storeroom; restoration 2. until; under; unless; unable; unpaid; unusual; understand; unnecessary; unfortunate; unofficial; unknown; unquestionable; unskilled; unsolved; untimely 3. fleet; inflation; influence; conflict; flimsy; flexible; flagged; flame; flash; flawless; deflate; reflect; affliction; reflex 4. left; draft; crafty; rafter; gift; swiftly 5. lifetime; outside; turnover; offset; herein; anywhere; whenever; meantime; railroad; inasmuch; afternoon; somewhat; worthwhile; businessmen; southwest

4.2 TRANSCRIPTION SKILL BUILDING

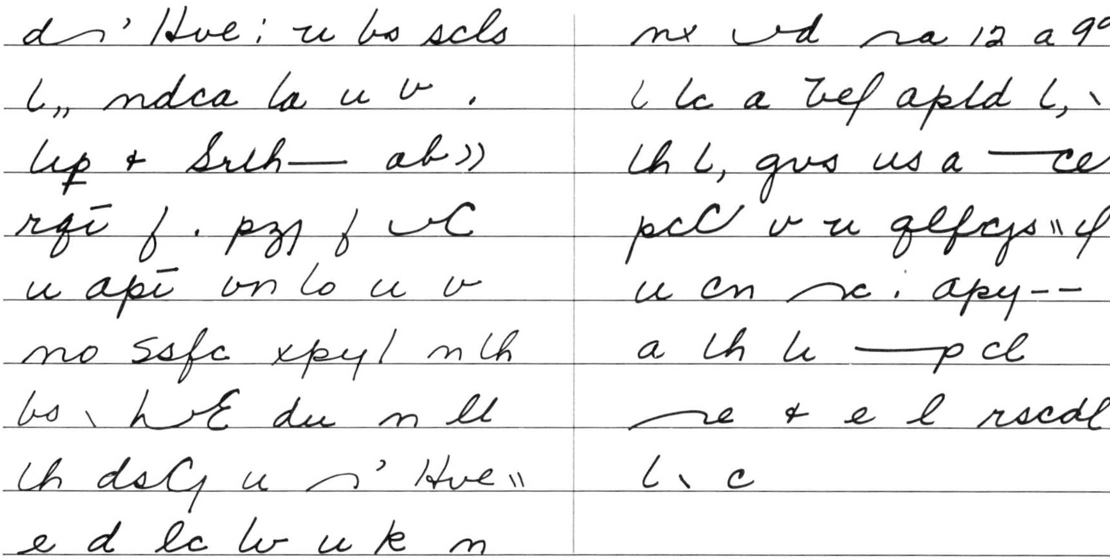

GUIDE Insert two parenthetical commas, two introductory commas, and two apposition commas.

4.3 SPEED BUILDING

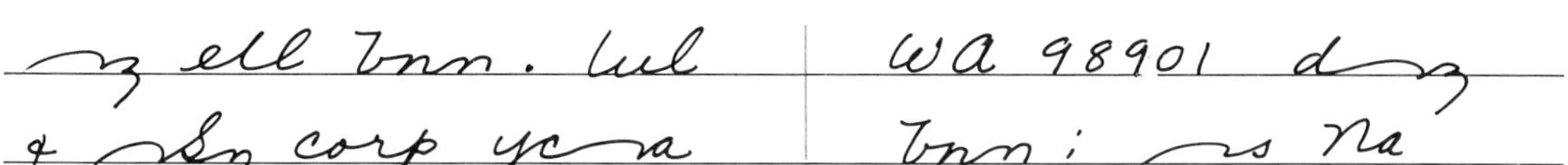

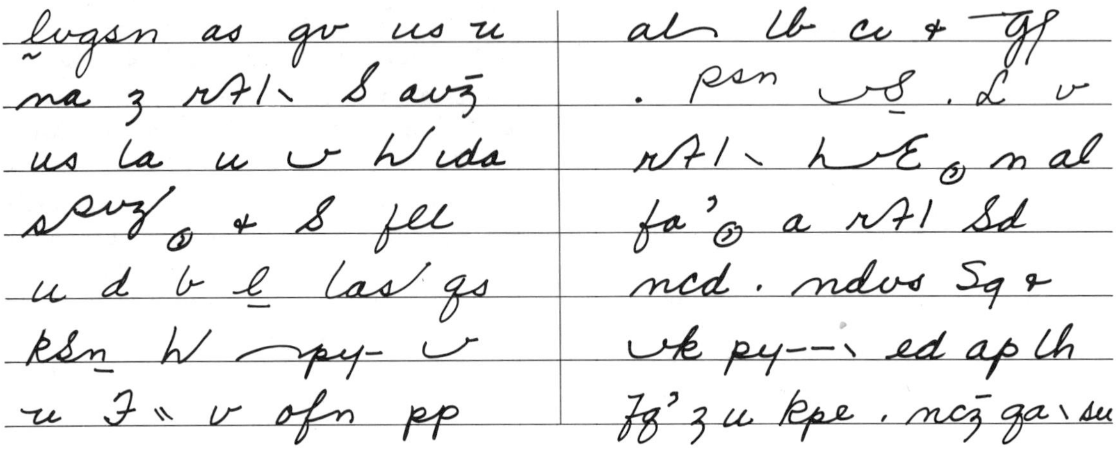

4.4 VOCABULARY BUILDING

(A)

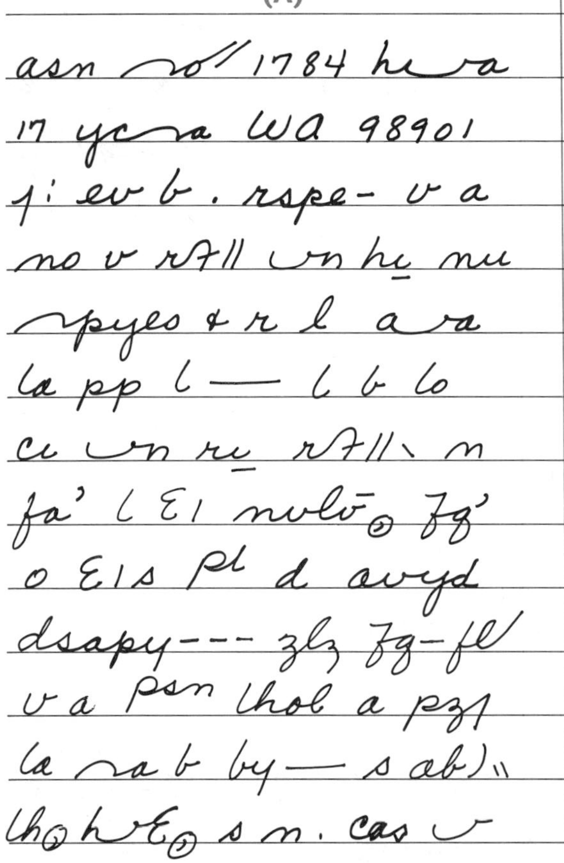

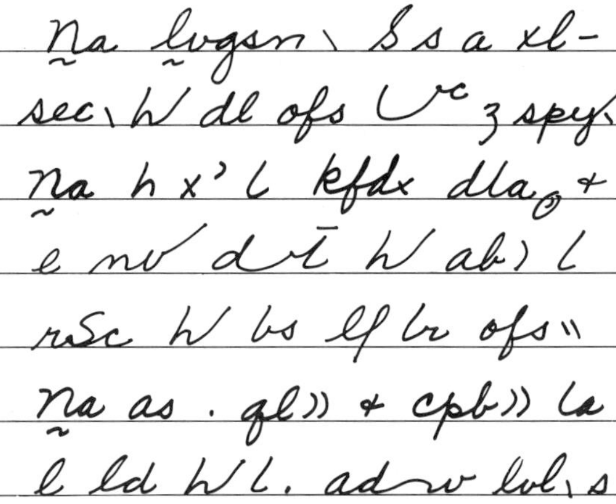

(B)

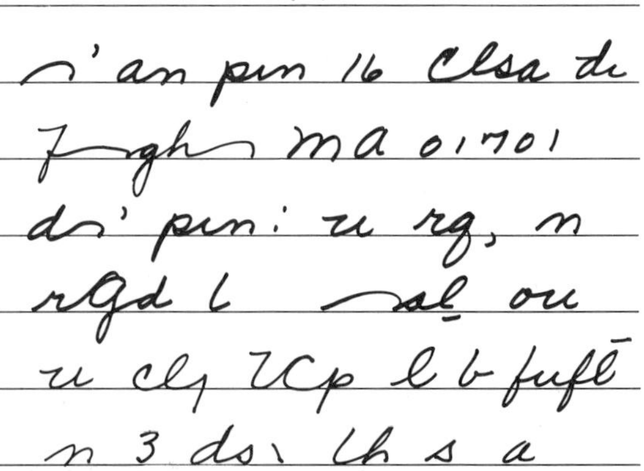

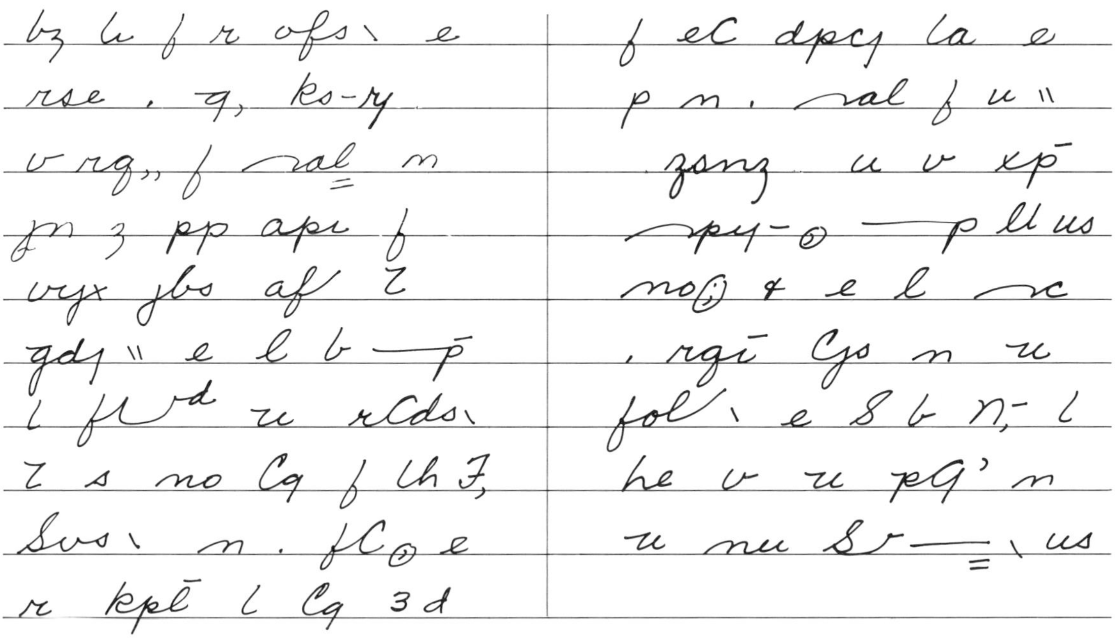

5.1 THEORY REVIEW

1. *s*
2. *ment*
3. *j*
4. *star*
5. *bl*

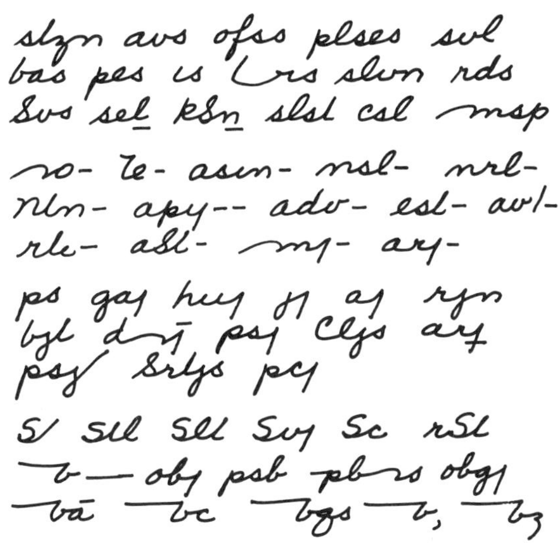

KEY 1. citizen; advice; offices; policies; civil; base; piece; ice; twice; civilian; reduce; service; ceiling; concerning; solicit; cancel; municipal 2. moment; treatment; assignment; installment; enrollment; entertainment; appointment; advertisement; establishment; advancement; retirement; assortment; management; arrangement 3. pages; gauge; huge; judge; age; region; budget; damaged; passage; challenges; arranging; passenger; shortages; package 4. starter; startle; starlet; starvation; stark;

restart 5. bland; oblige; possible; problems; obligation; blamed; black; blanks; blast; blaze

5.2 TRANSCRIPTION SKILL BUILDING

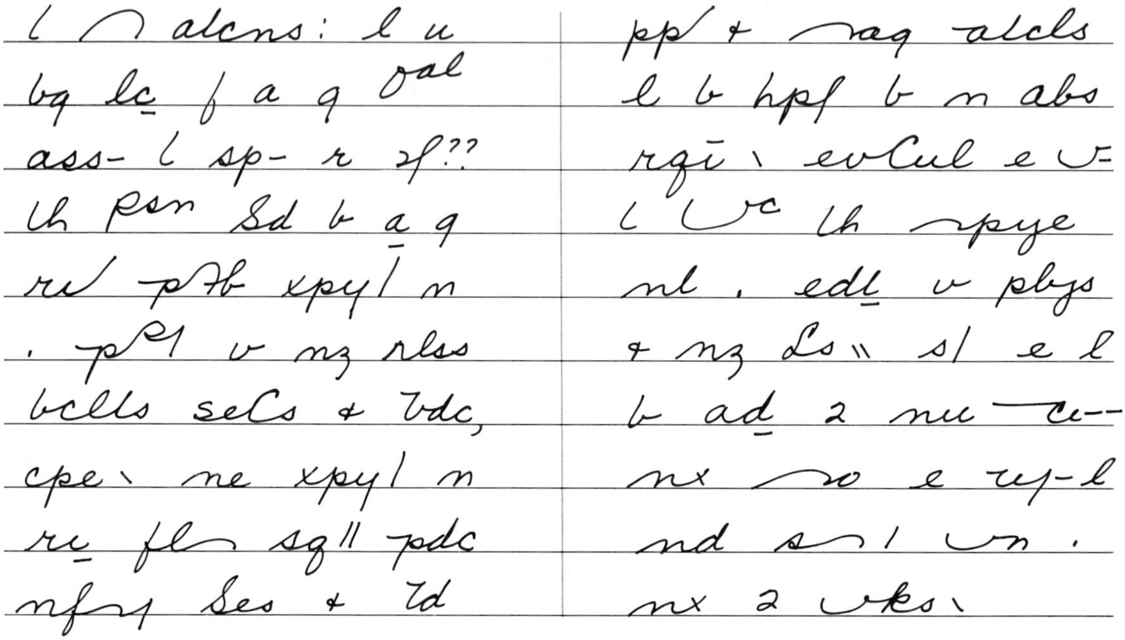

GUIDE Insert two parenthetical commas, five series commas, and two introductory commas.

5.3 SPEED BUILDING

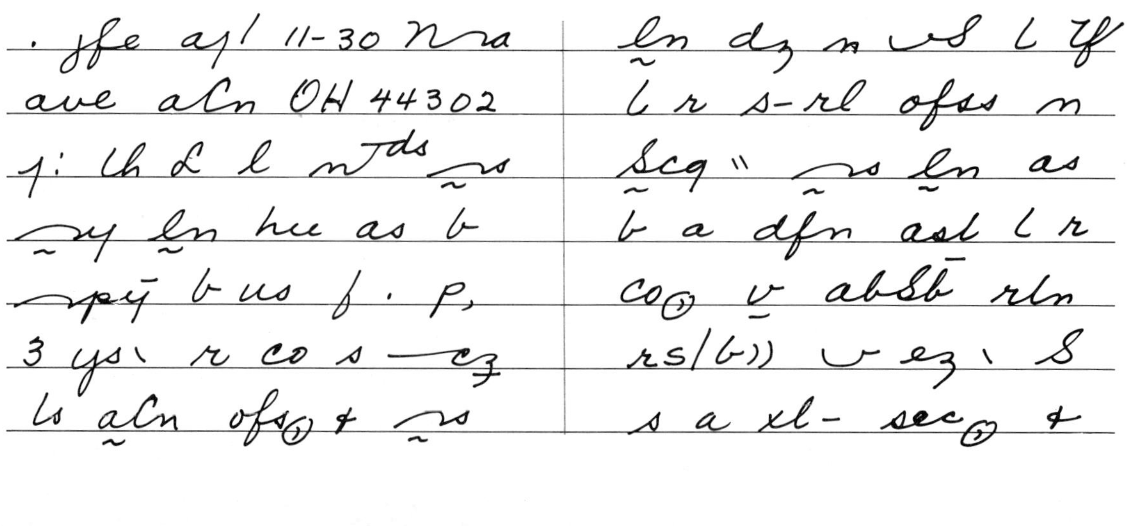

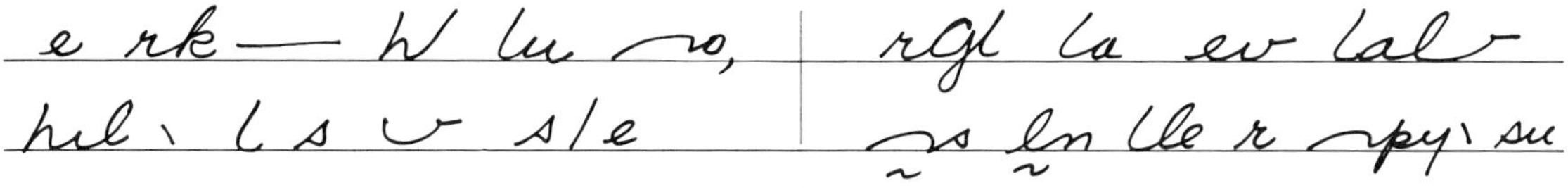

5.4 VOCABULARY BUILDING

(A)

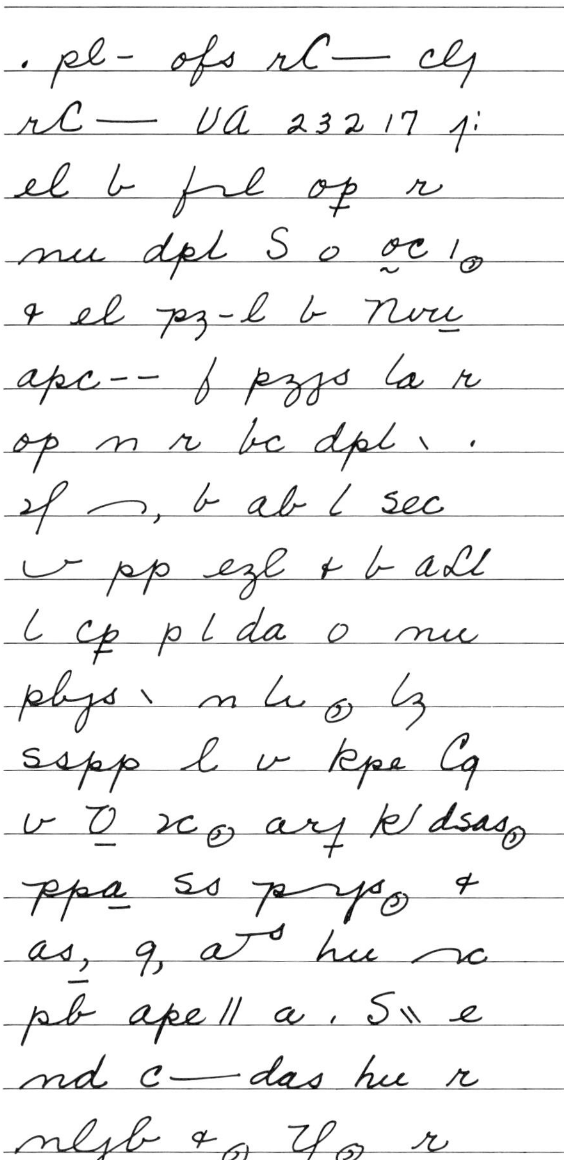

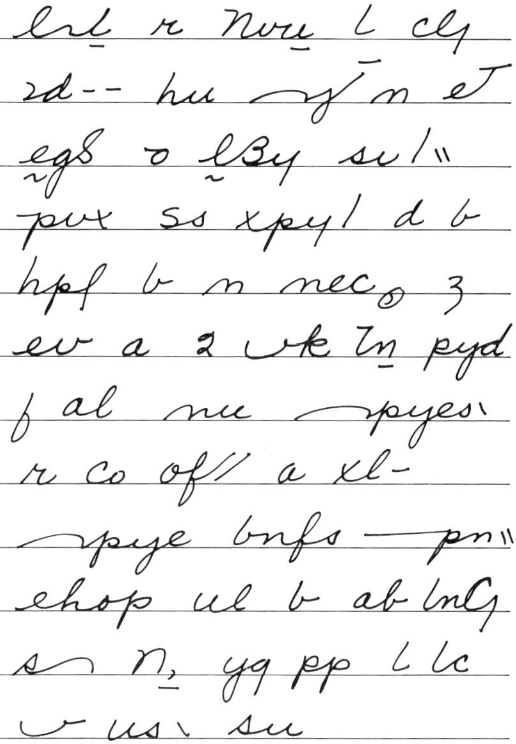

(B)

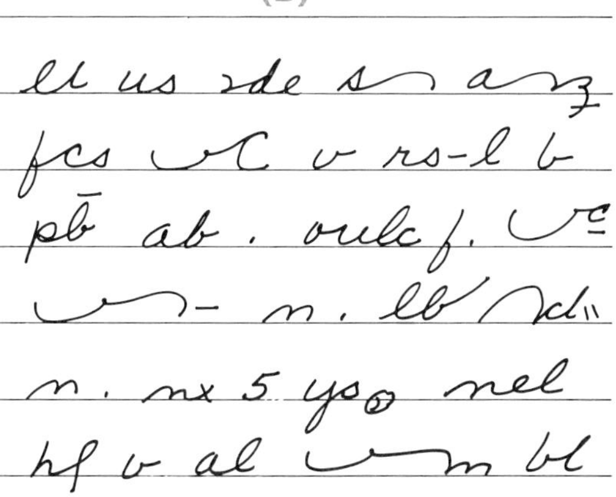

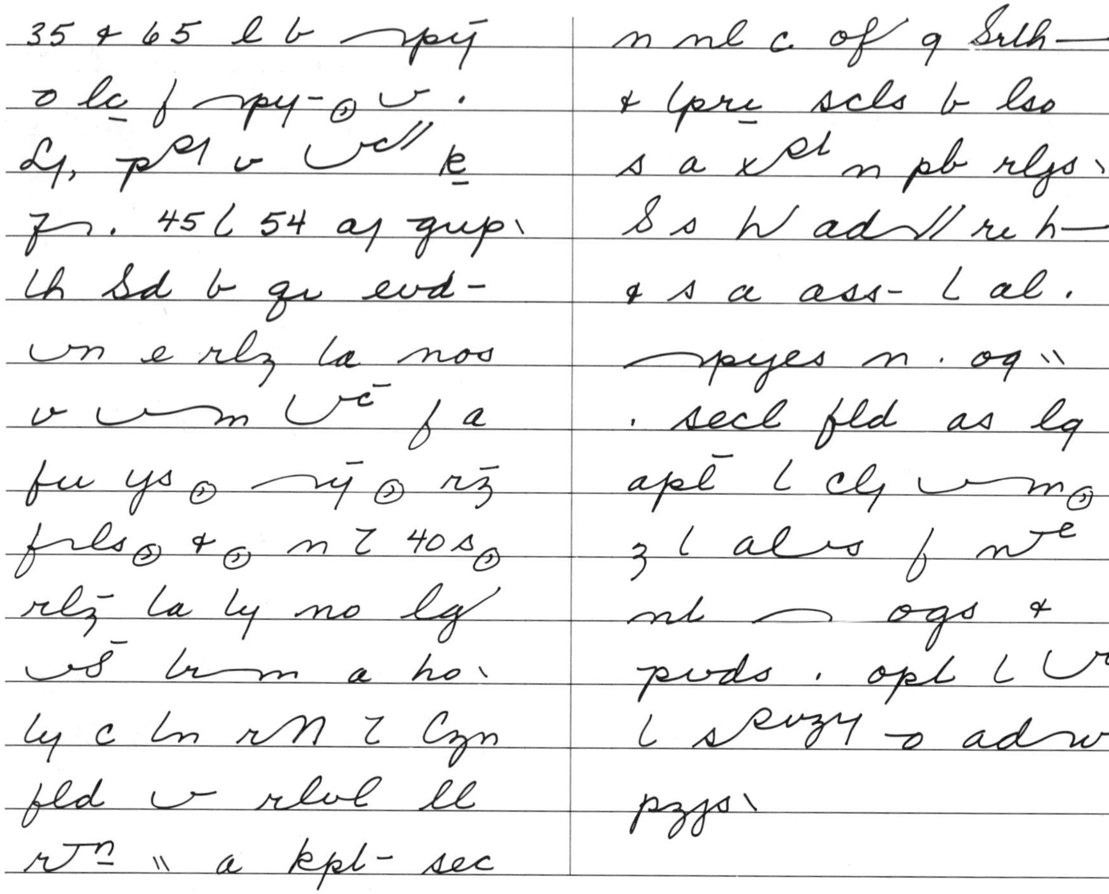

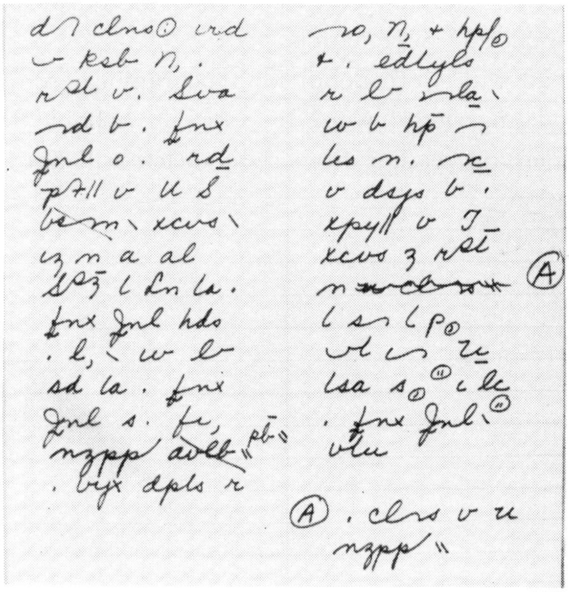

TECHNIQUES OF PROOFREADING

There are two stages in proofreading—preview and postview.

The review stage is editing your shorthand notes. Write in the corrections for errors in grammar, check spelling and correct usage, verify accuracy of figures and dates, check instructions.

In the postview stage do not scan, do not trust to memory, and do not be careless and indifferent. Use the paper bail to allow the line being read to be separated from the rest of the material. Then follow these three steps while the material is in the typewriter:

1. Look at the material as if it were a picture. Are spacing, margins, placements, indentions, and enumerations correct?

2. Read the material orally, concentrating on meaning, grammar, and punctuation.

3. Reread with word detail for typographical errors and misspelling. Read word by word or syllable by syllable. Perhaps reading from right to left will aid in concentration.

UNIT 11

TRANSPORTATION

1.1 THEORY REVIEW

1. *in*
2. *al*
3. *pt*
4. *āme*
5. *ēde*

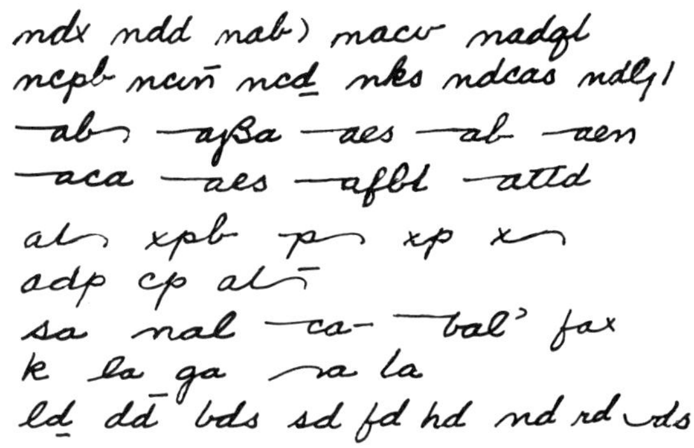

KEY 1. index; indeed; inability; inactive; inadequate; incapable; inclined; including; incomes; indicates; indulgence 2. album; algebra; alias, alibi; alien; allocate; alleys; alphabet; altitude 3. attempt; acceptable; prompt; except; exempt; adopt, adapt, adept; kept; attempted 4. same; namely; claimant; blameless; famous; came; lame; game; maim; tame 5. leading; deeded; beads; cede, seed; feed; heed; need; read; weeds

1.2 TRANSCRIPTION SKILL BUILDING

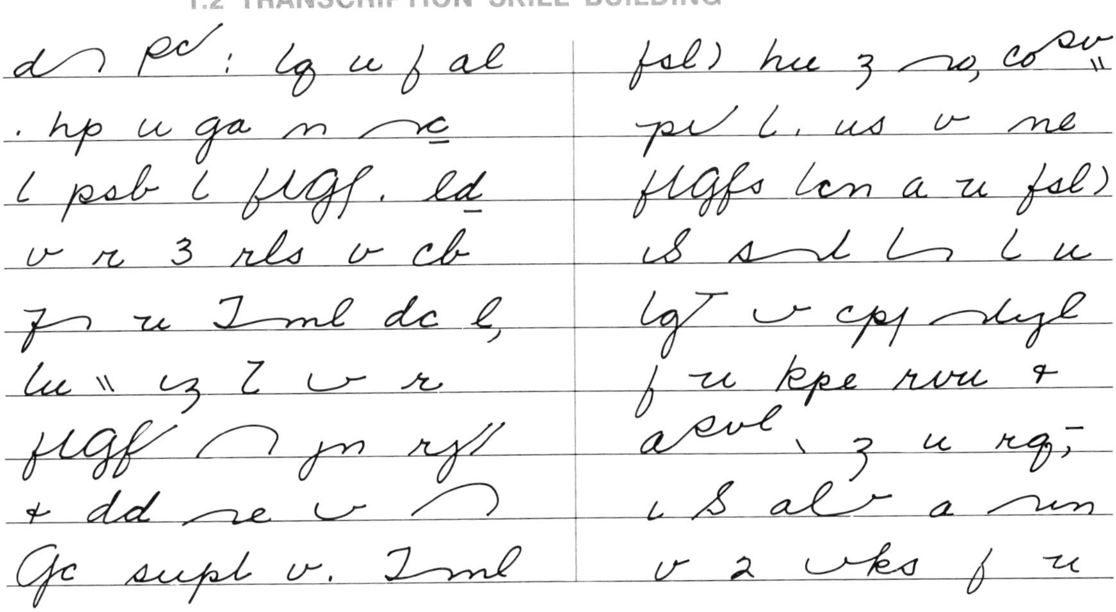

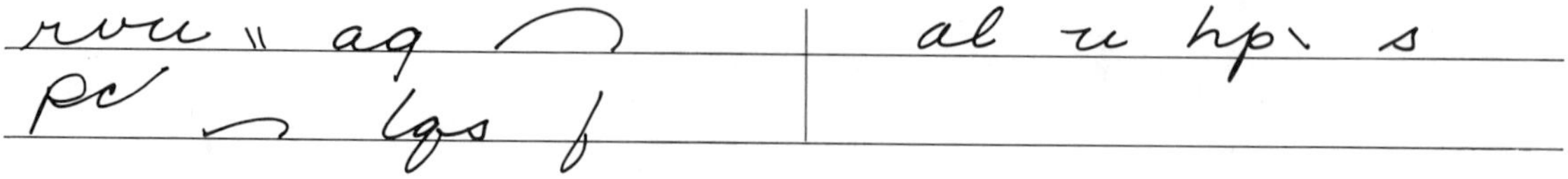

GUIDE Insert four apposition commas, two introductory commas, and four parenthetical commas.

1.3 SPEED BUILDING

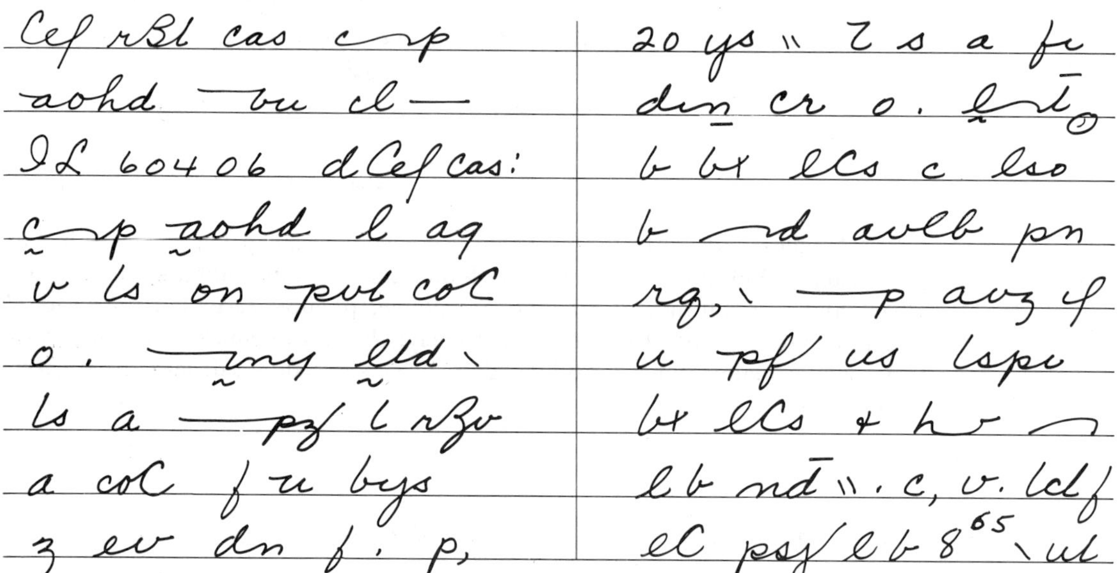

1.4 VOCABULARY BUILDING

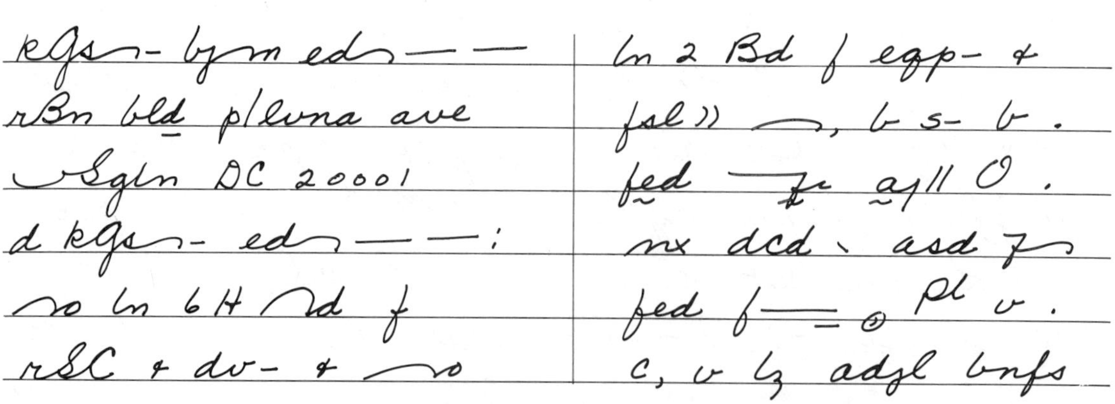

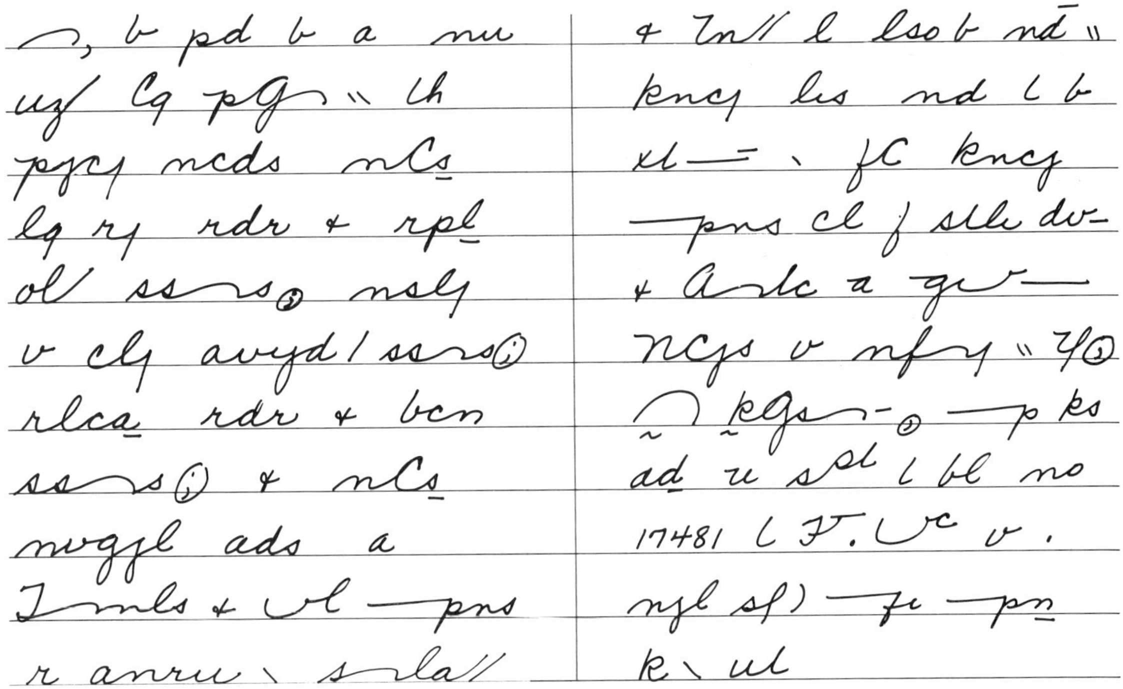

2.1 THEORY REVIEW

1. *ōte* 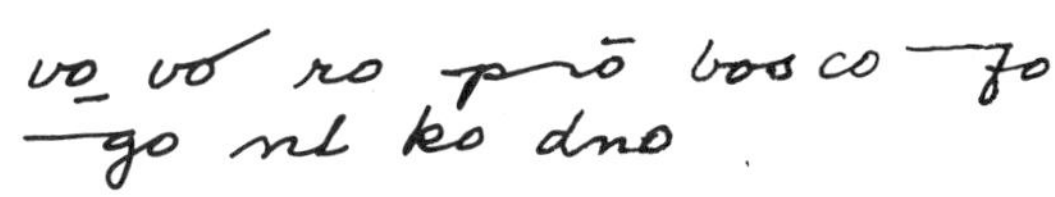

2. *īde* 

3. *ēme* 

4. *ēve* 

5. initial *ar* 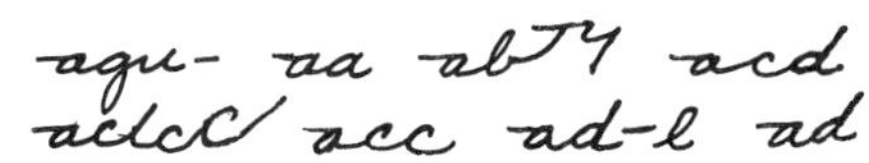

KEY 1. voting; voter; wrote; promoted; boats; coat; float; gloat; note; connote; denote 2. guide; pride; widely; aside; besides; side; inside; decide; ride; tides 3. seemingly; teamwork; cream; beam; reams; extremely 4. leaving; believer; received; deceive; conceive; retrieve 5. argument; area; arbitrary; arcade; architecture; arctic; ardently; arid

2.2 TRANSCRIPTION SKILL BUILDING

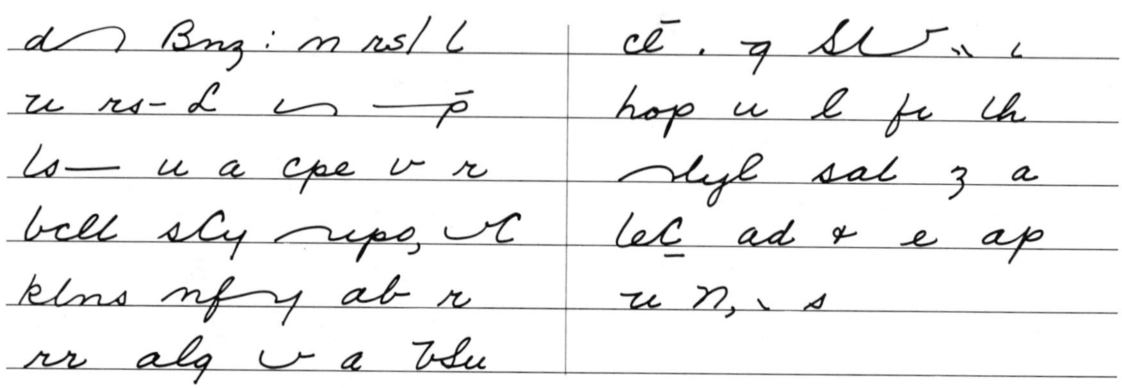

GUIDE Insert one introductory comma, one parenthetical comma, two apposition commas, one conjunction comma, and four title quotation marks.

2.3 SPEED BUILDING

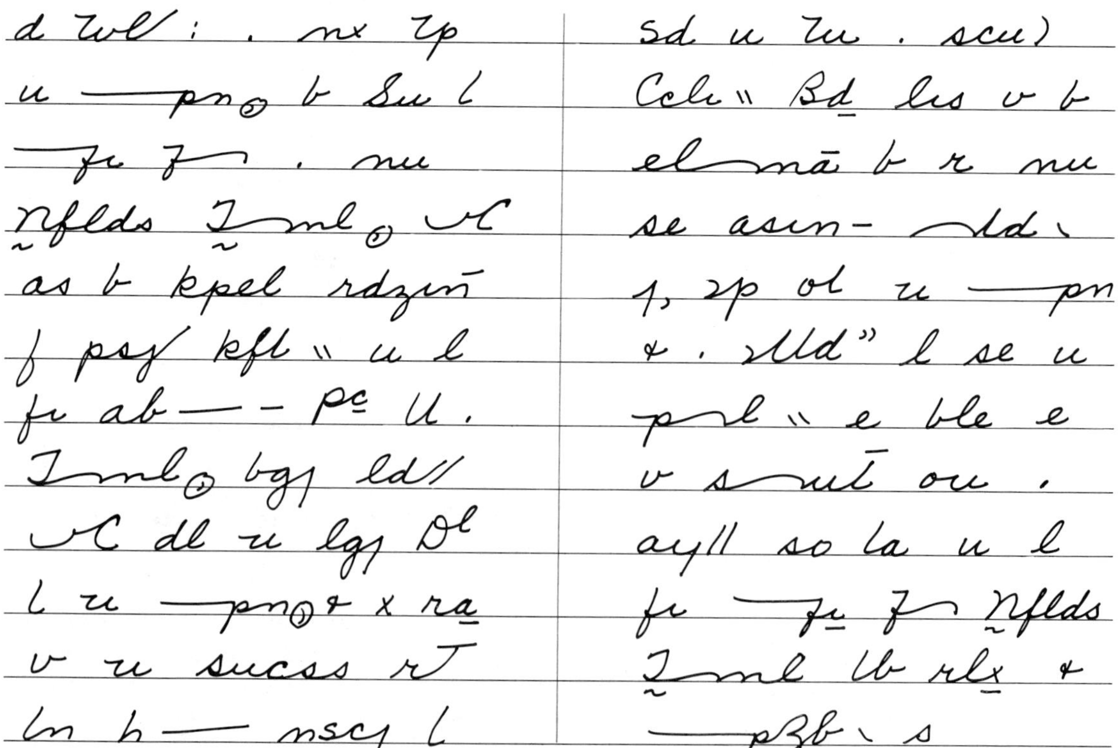

2.4 VOCABULARY BUILDING

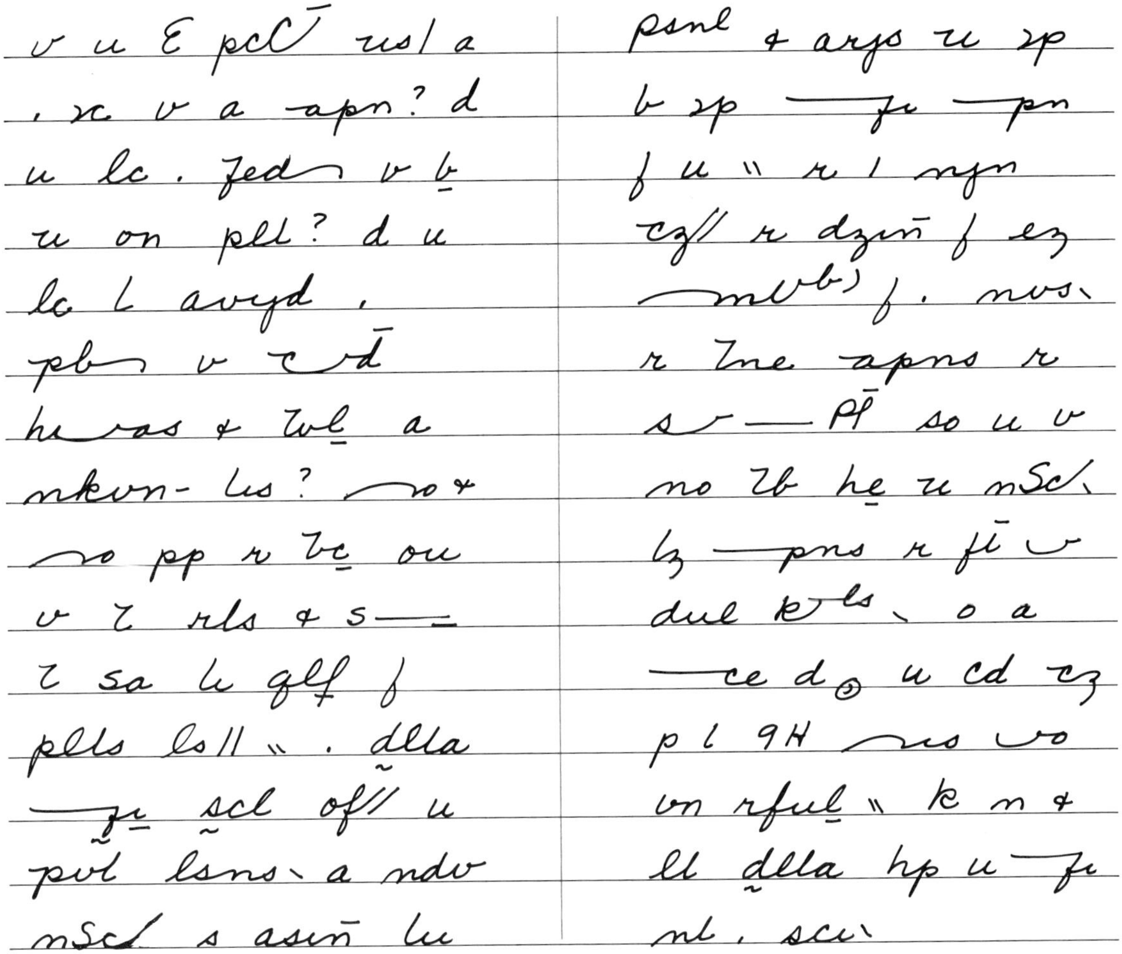

3.1 THEORY REVIEW

1. *en*
2. *īme*
3. Initial *er*
4. *air*

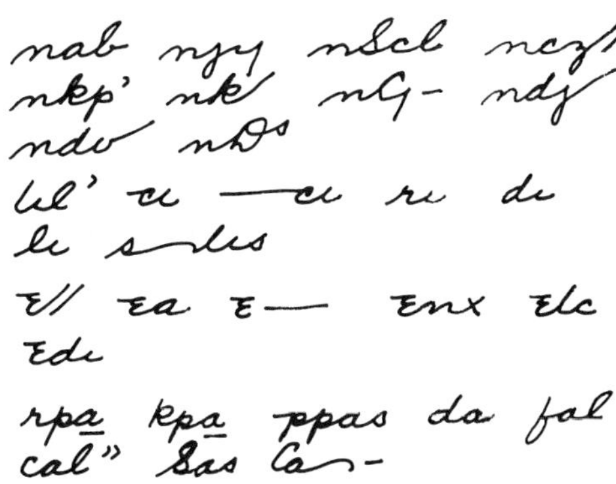

5. *ight* 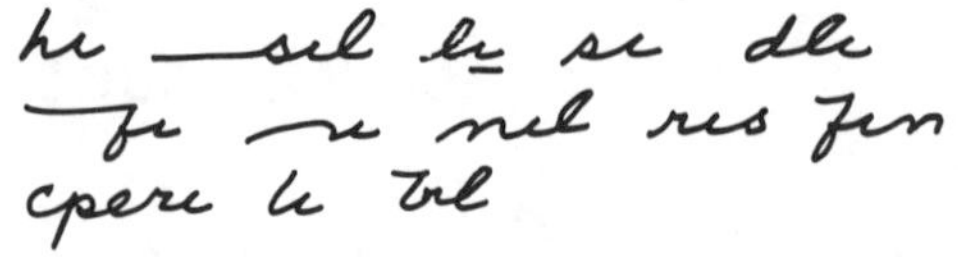

KEY 1. enable; enjoy; encircle; enclosures; encompass; encounter; encouragement; endanger; endeavor; endorse 2. timeless; crime; climb; rhyme; dime; lime; sometimes 3. errors; era; errand; erroneous, ly; erratic; erudite 4. repairing; comparing; prepares; dare; fairly; carelessness; shares; chairman 5. height; slightly; lighting; sight; delighted; flight; might; nightly; rights; frighten; copyright; tight; brightly

3.2 TRANSCRIPTION SKILL BUILDING

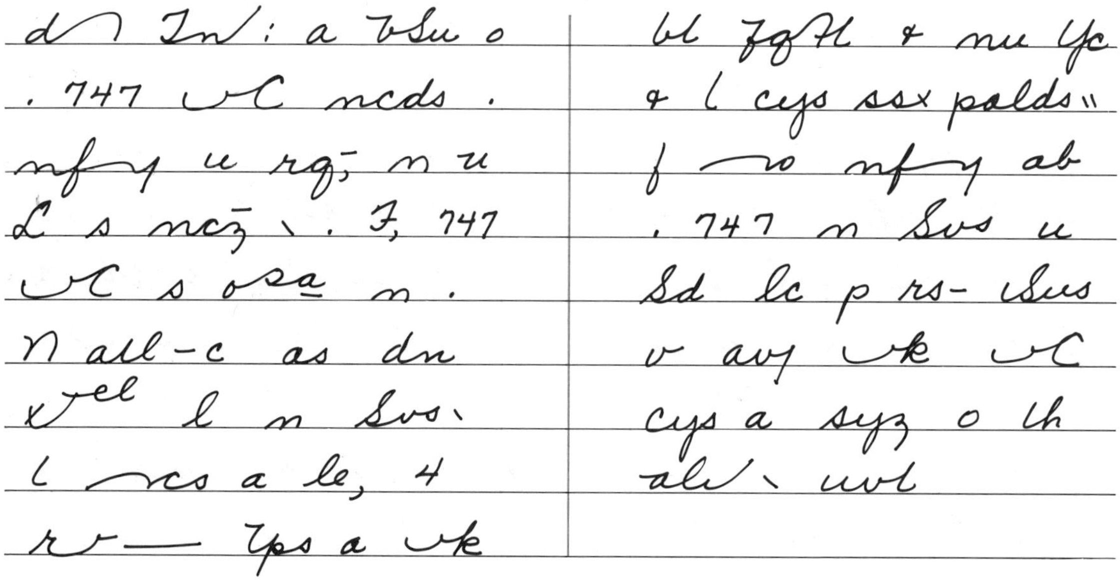

GUIDE Insert five parenthetical commas, one conjunction comma, and one introductory comma.

3.3 SPEED BUILDING

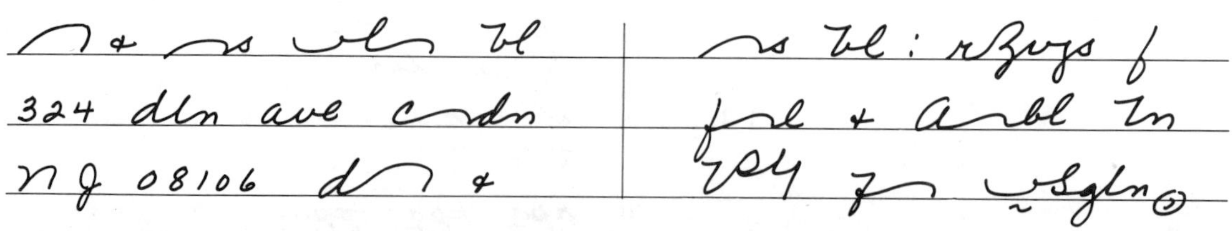

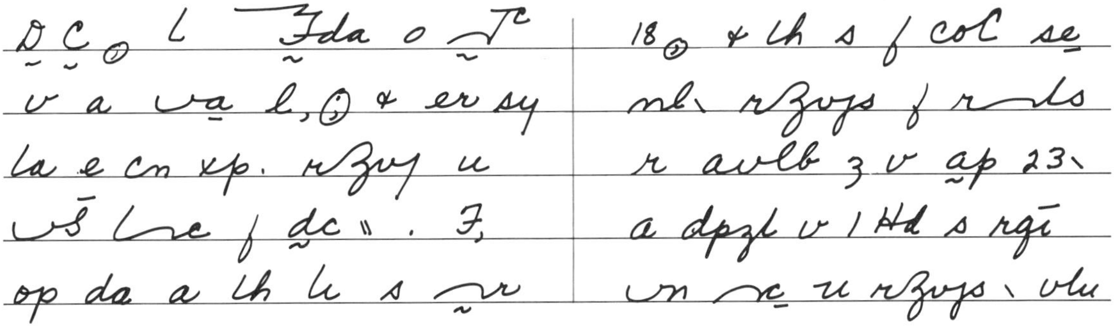

3.4 VOCABULARY BUILDING

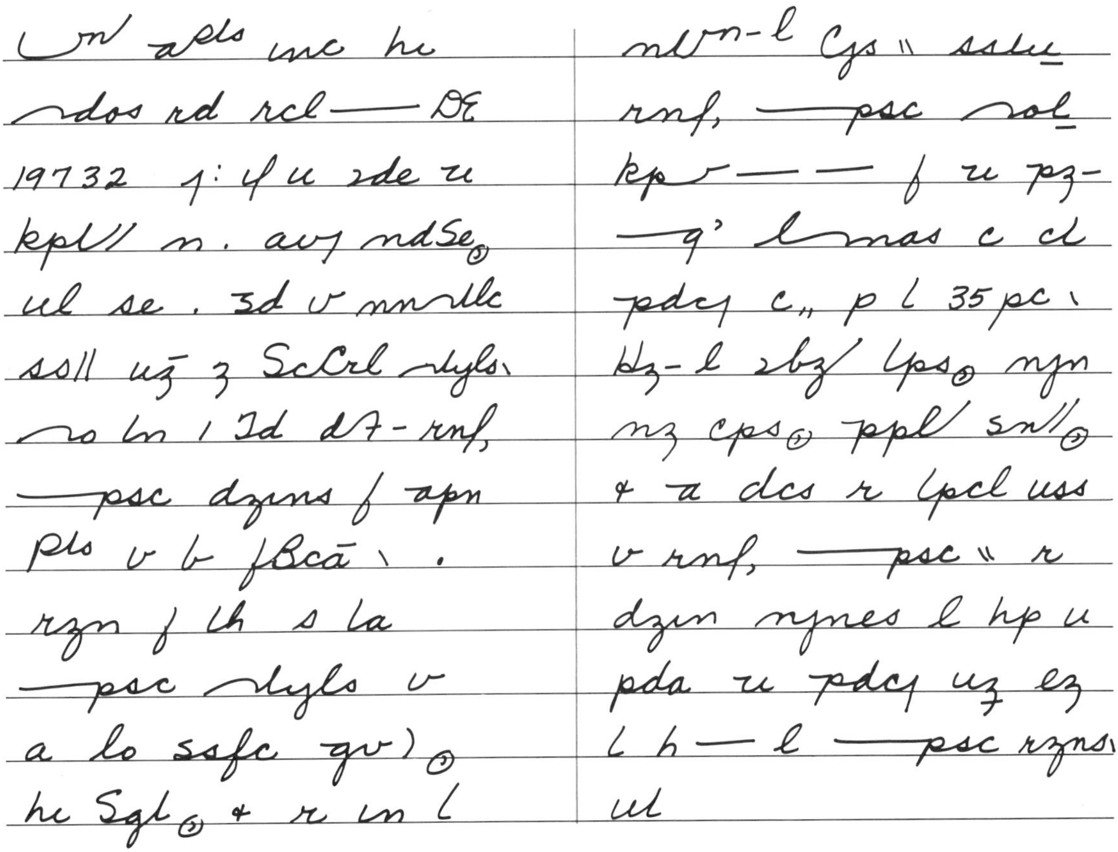

4.1 THEORY REVIEW

1. *ūte*
2. *awe*

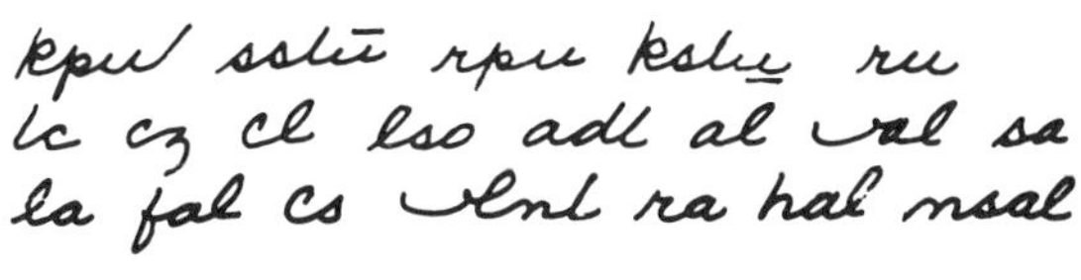

3. *pl*

4. *ōme*

5. Initial *ir*

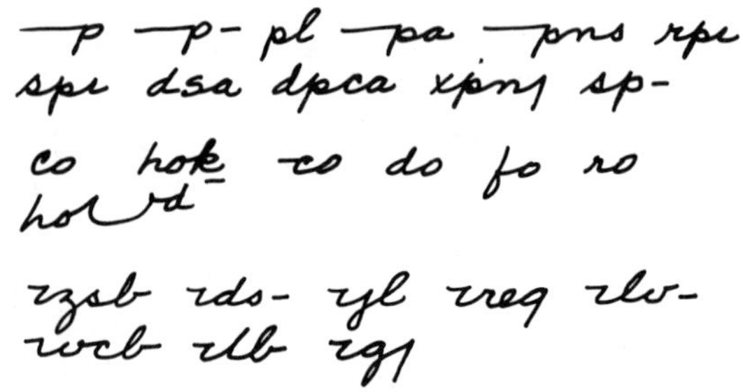

KEY 1. computer; substituted; repute; constituting; route 2. talk; cause; call; also; audit; all; wall; saw; law; fall; because; walnut; raw; hall; install 3. please; plant; place; play; plans; reply; supply; display; duplicate; explanation; supplement 4. comb; homecoming; chrome; dome; foam; roam; homeward 5. irresistible; iridescent; irrational; irregular; irrelevant; irrevocable; irritable; irrigation

4.2 TRANSCRIPTION SKILL BUILDING

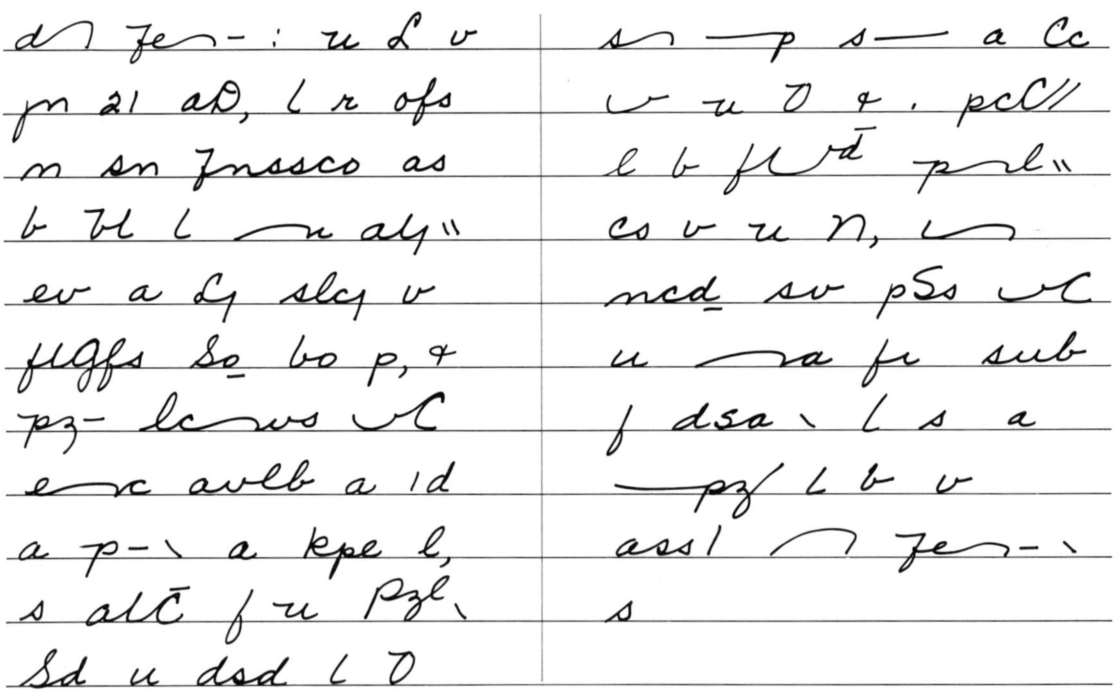

GUIDE Insert five parenthetical commas, two introductory commas, and one internal punctuation semicolon.

4.3 SPEED BUILDING

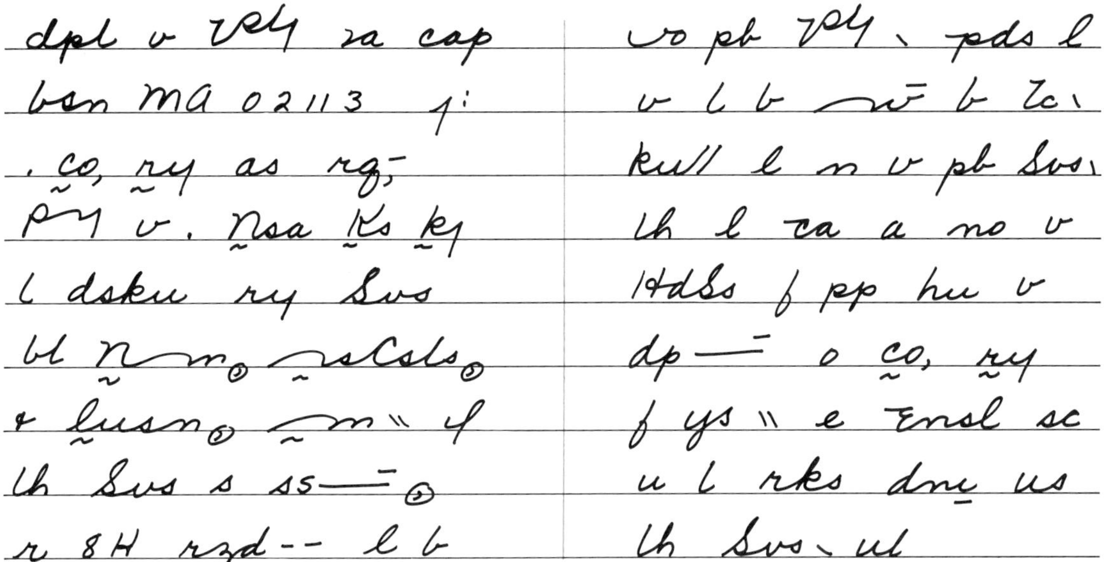

4.4 VOCABULARY BUILDING

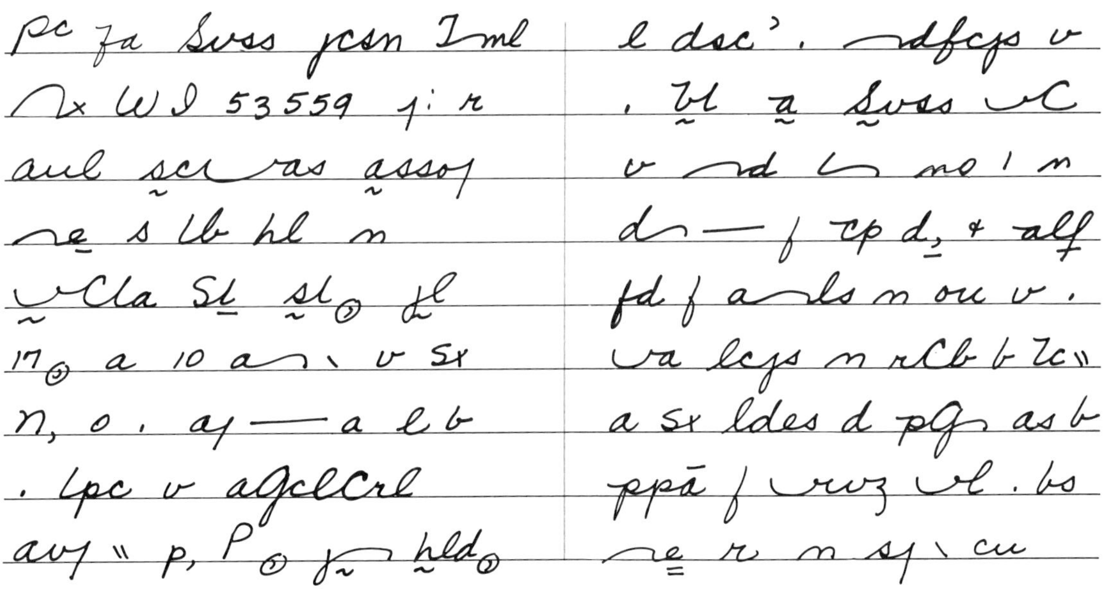

5.1 THEORY REVIEW

1. Final *er*

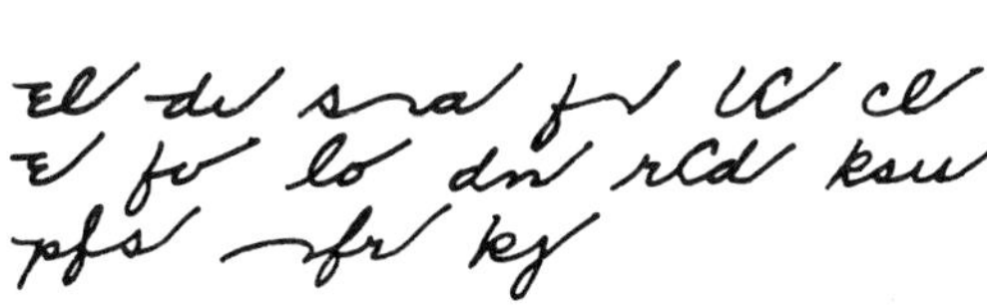

2. *ūde*

3. *āry*

4. *str*

5. *kl*

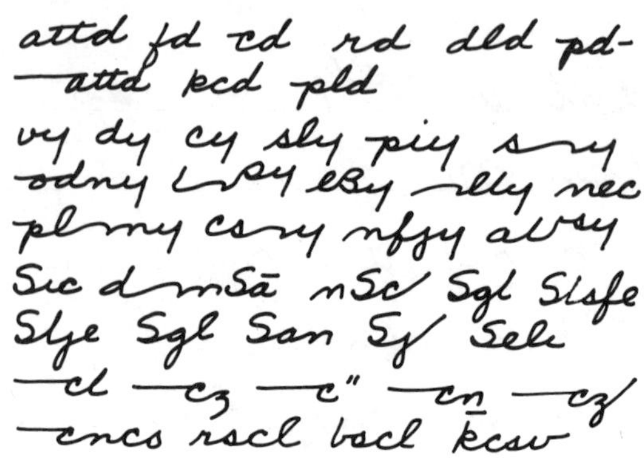

KEY 1. earlier; driver; smaller; former; teacher; color; error; favor; lower; dinner; recorder; consumer; professor; manufacturer; commissioner 2. attitude; food, feud; crude; rude; delude; prudent; altitude; conclude; prelude 3. vary; dairy; carry; salary; primary; summary; ordinary; temporary; library; military; necessary; preliminary; customary; inflationary; adversary 4. strike; demonstrated; instructor; strength; stratosphere; strategy; strongly; straighten; stranger; streamline 5. cloth; close, clothes; classes; cleaning; closure; clinics; recycle; bicycle; conclusive

5.2 TRANSCRIPTION SKILL BUILDING

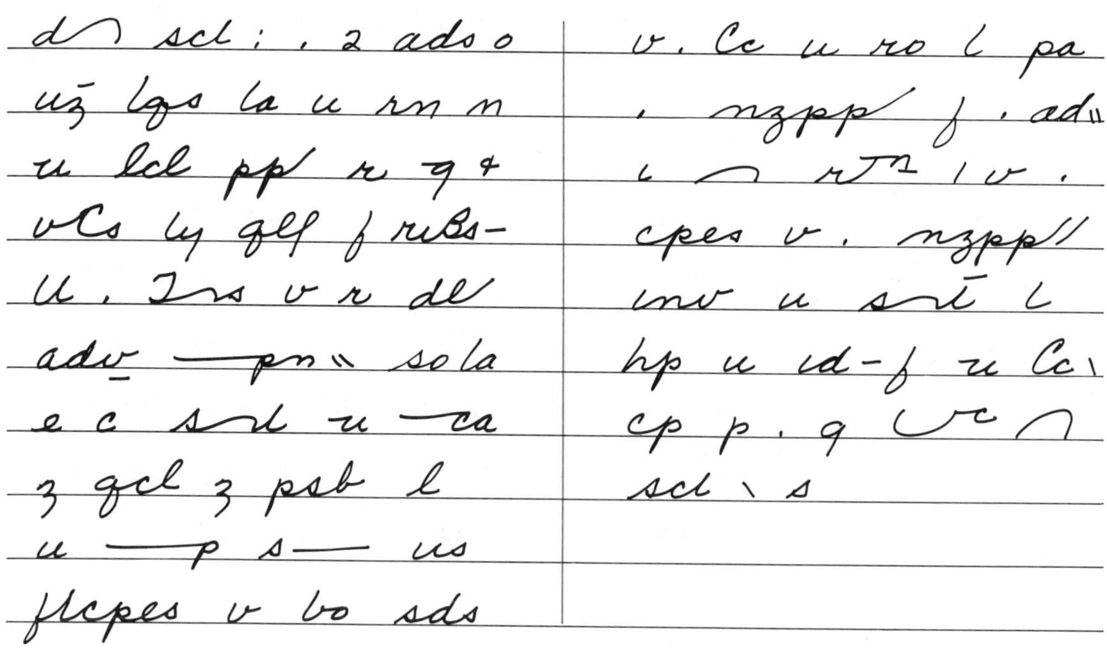

GUIDE Insert three parenthetical commas, one introductory comma, one possessive apostrophe, and one internal punctuation semicolon.

5.3 SPEED BUILDING

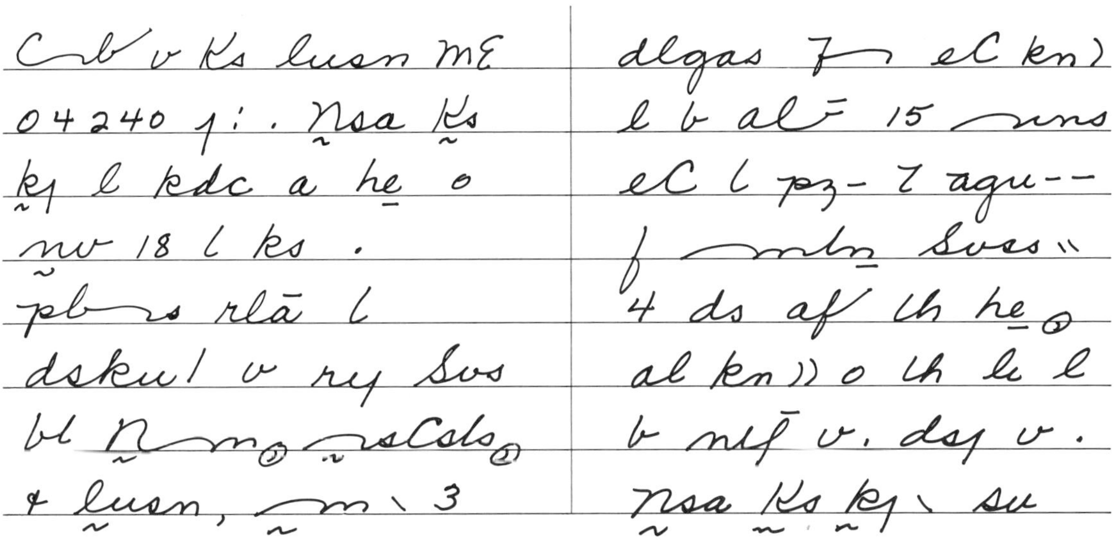

5.4 VOCABULARY BUILDING

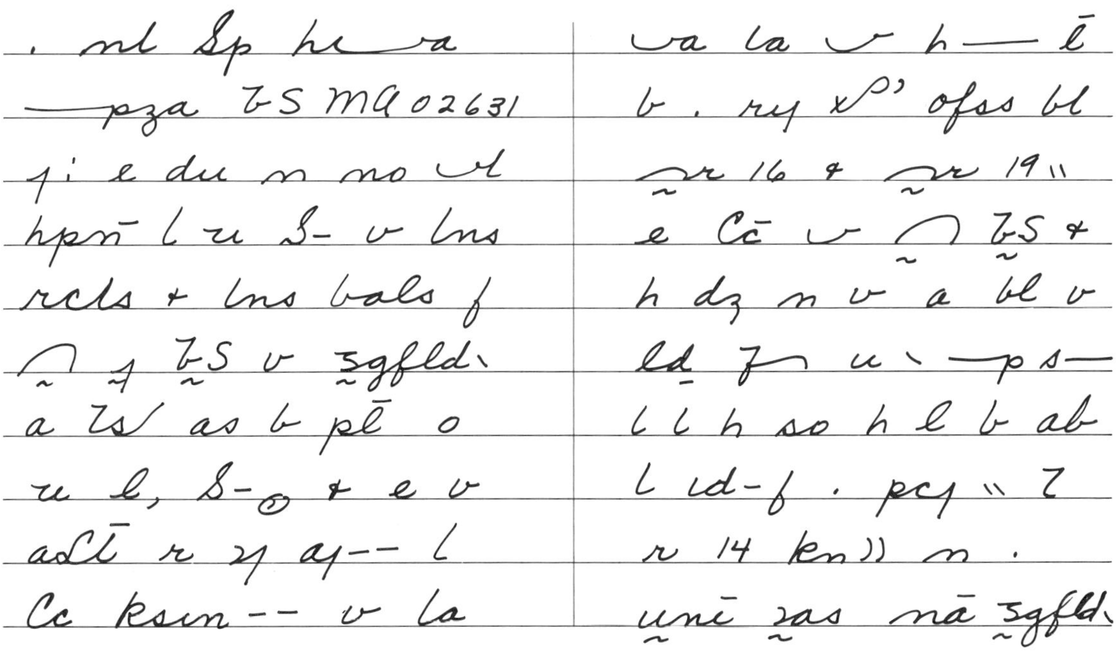

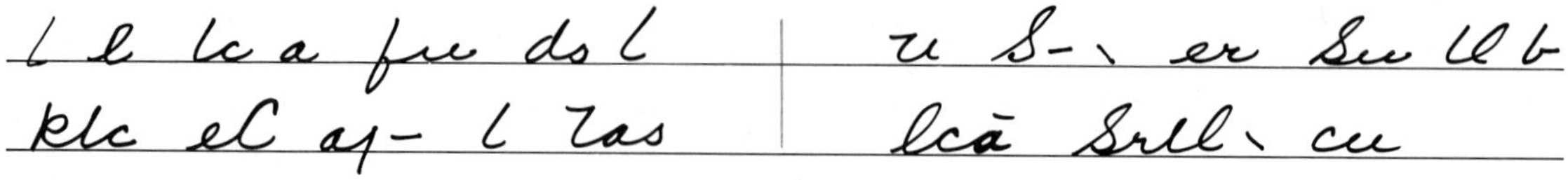

CORRECTING ERRORS

When a secretary is aware that he has made an error, he should correct it immediately.

When a page is being proofread after it has been typed, the secretary should complete the proofreading of the whole page before making the corrections.

The weight, the finish, the grain, and the quality of paper influence the selection of tools with which to make corrections. Here are some helpful hints:

Use a razor blade to delete stray strokes from hard-finished paper and to delete stubborn punctuation marks.

Abrasive erasers are available in the stick type and the wheel type. These are used for original copies.

Pencil erasers are used for carbon copies, whether bond or onionskin paper. They may be used for original copies on easy-erase paper.

Art gum is used for removing smudges or fingerprints on copy.

To clean erasers, use a piece of sandpaper or an emery board. Erase with the grain of the paper. Corrections may also be made with correction fluids, correction tapes, and plastic type cleaners.

UNIT 12

BUSINESS LAW

1.1 THEORY REVIEW

1. *ter*
2. *īne*
3. Initial *or*
4. *ear*
5. Consecutive pronounced vowels

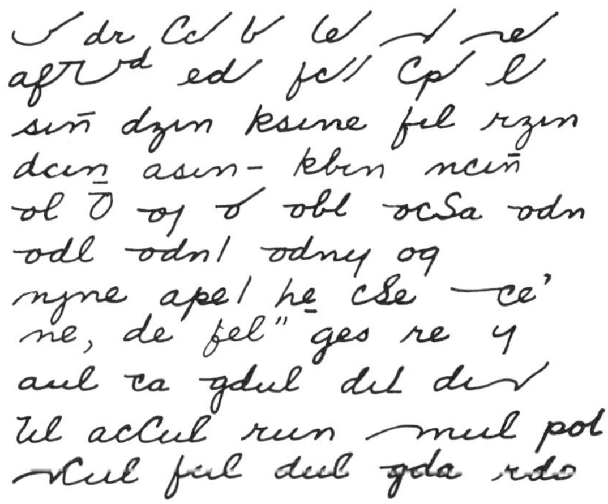

KEY 1. water; doctor; character; better; theater; matter; meter; afterward; editor; factors; chapter; latter 2. signed; design; consignee; final; resign; declining; assignment; combine; inclined 3. oral; order; orange; orator; orbit; orchestra; ordain; ordeal; ordinance; ordinary; organization 4. engineer; appearance; hearing; cashier; clearness; nearest; dear; fearlessness; gears; rear; year 5. annual; create; gradual; diet; diameter; trial; actual; ruin; manual; poet; mutual; fuel; dual; graduate; radio

1.2 TRANSCRIPTION SKILL BUILDING

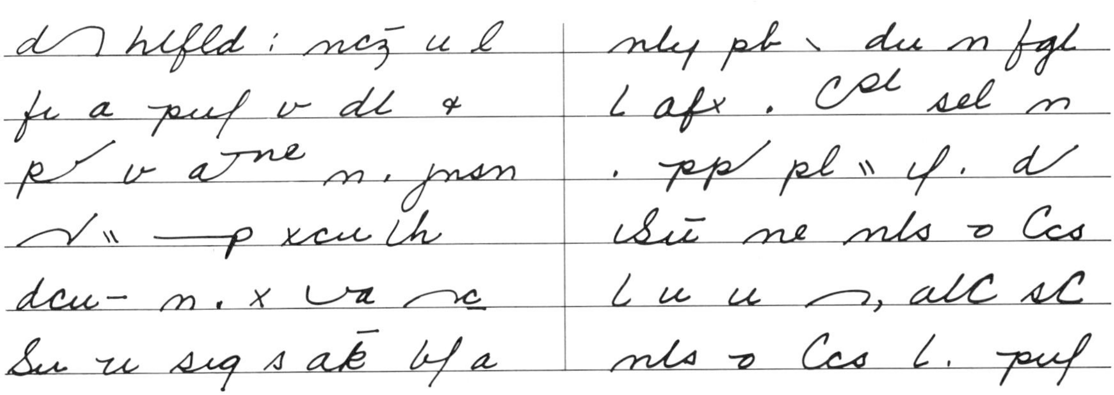

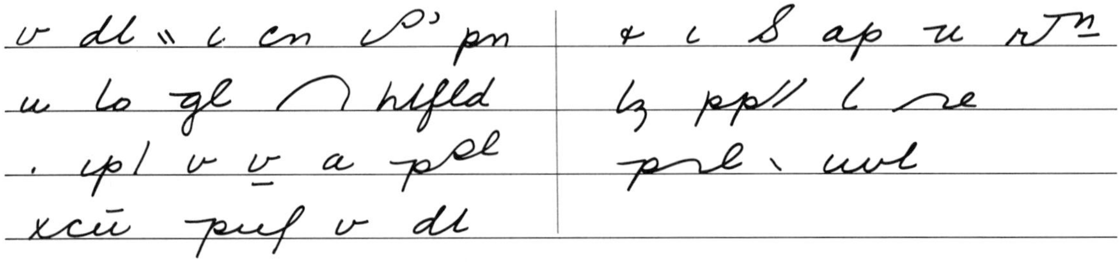

GUIDE Insert three parenthetical commas, one introductory comma, and one internal punctuation semicolon.

1.3 SPEED BUILDING

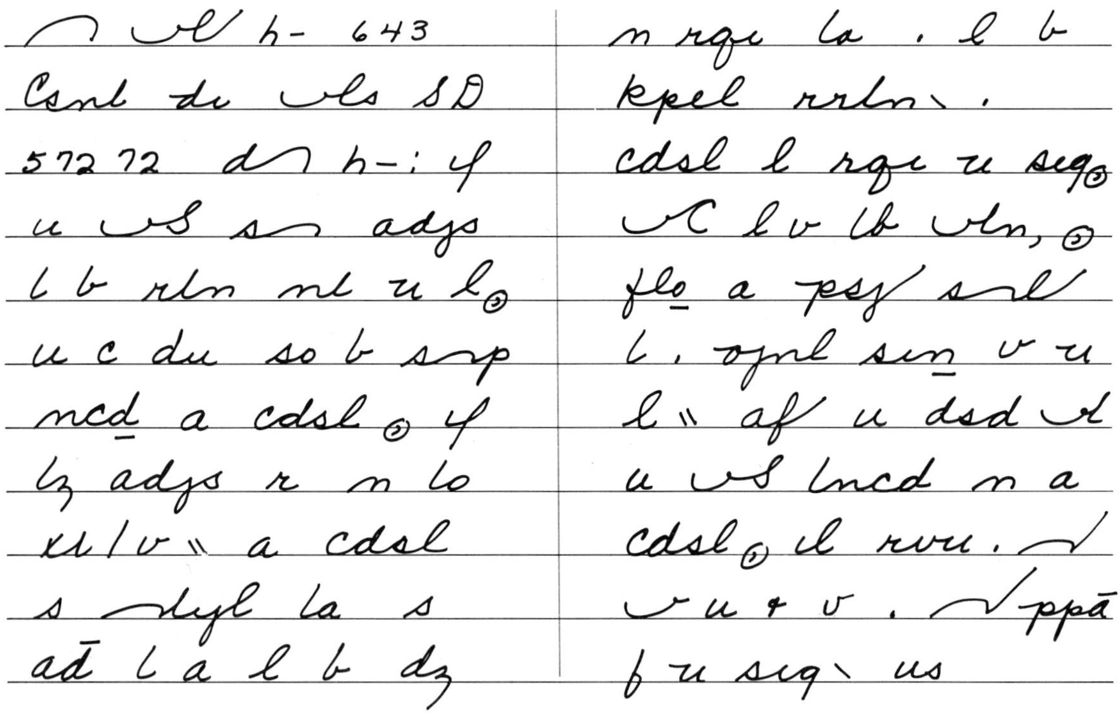

1.4 VOCABULARY BUILDING

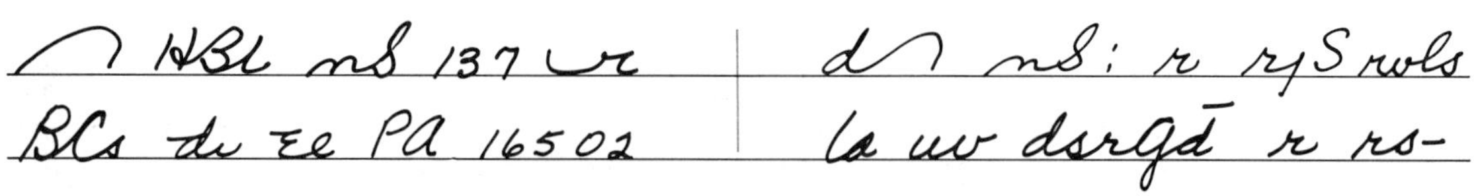

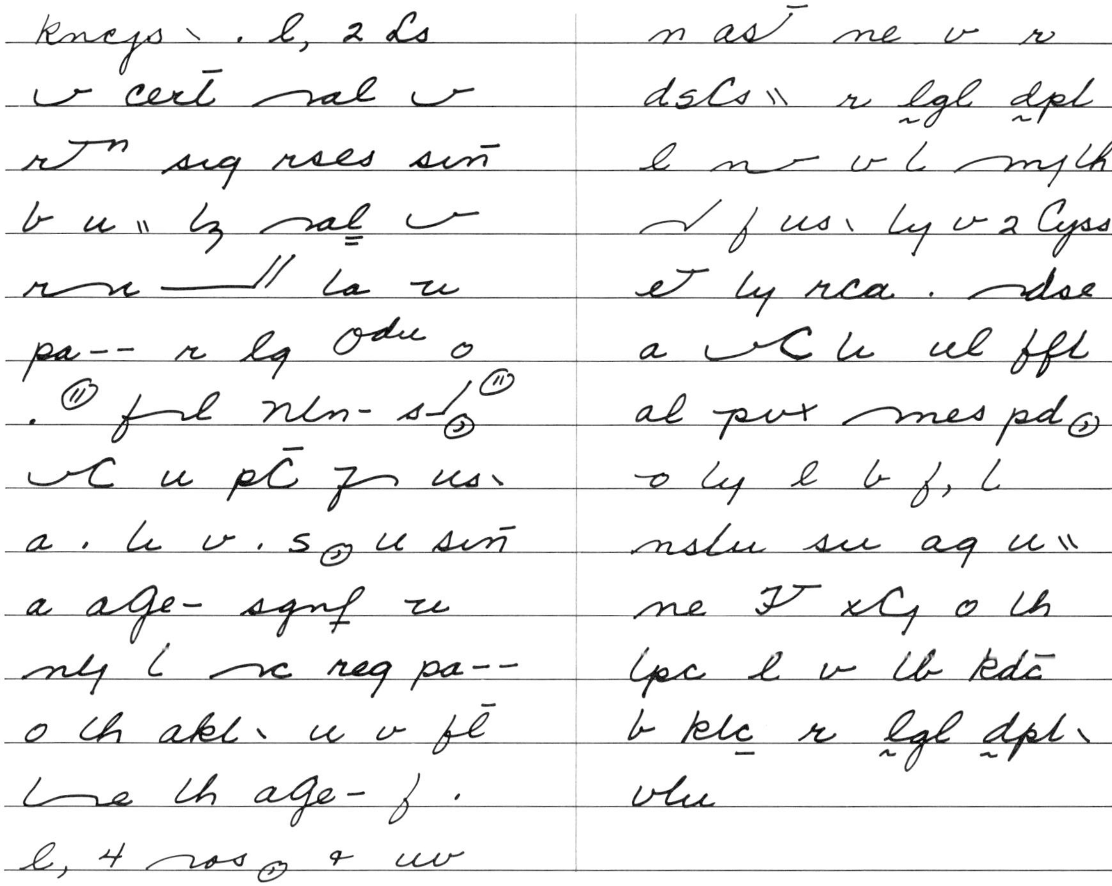

2.1 THEORY REVIEW

1. *ōne*
2. *ūry*
3. Initial *ur*
4. *īre*
5. *sl*

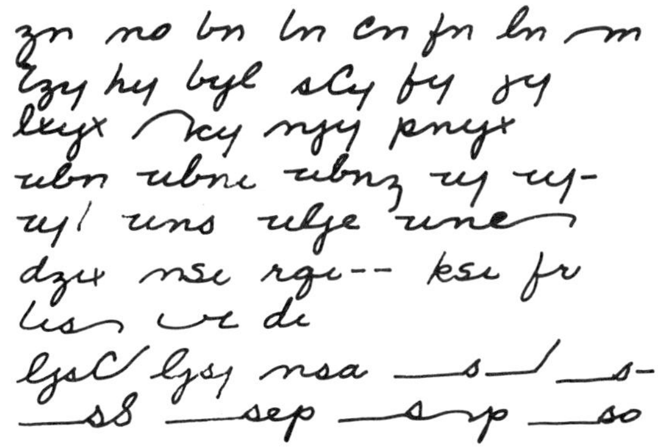

KEY 1. zone; known; bone; tone; cone; phone; lone, loan; moan 2. treasury; hurry; burial; century; fury; jury; luxurious; mercury; injury; penurious 3. urban; urbanite;

urbanize; urge; urgent; urgency; urns; urology; uranium 4. desirous; inspire; requirements; conspire; fire; tiresome; wire; dire 5. legislature; legislation; enslave; slander; slant; slash; sleep; slump; slow

2.2 TRANSCRIPTION SKILL BUILDING

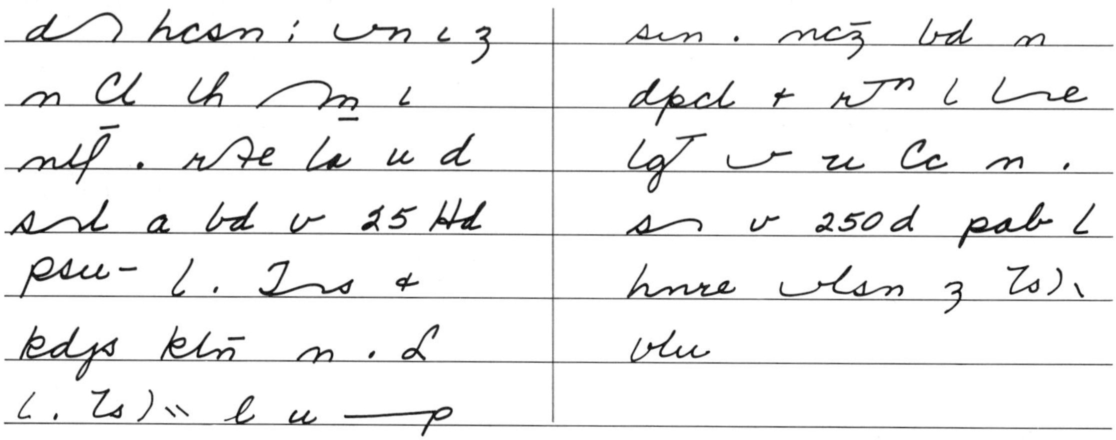

GUIDE Insert one introductory comma, one parenthetical comma, and one numbers comma.

2.3 SPEED BUILDING

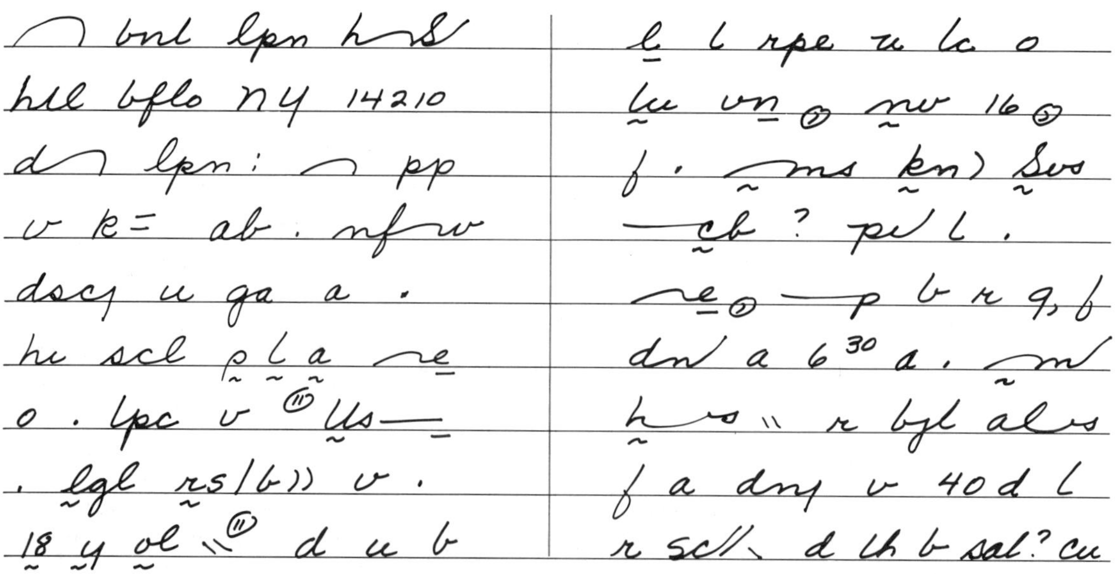

2.4 VOCABULARY BUILDING

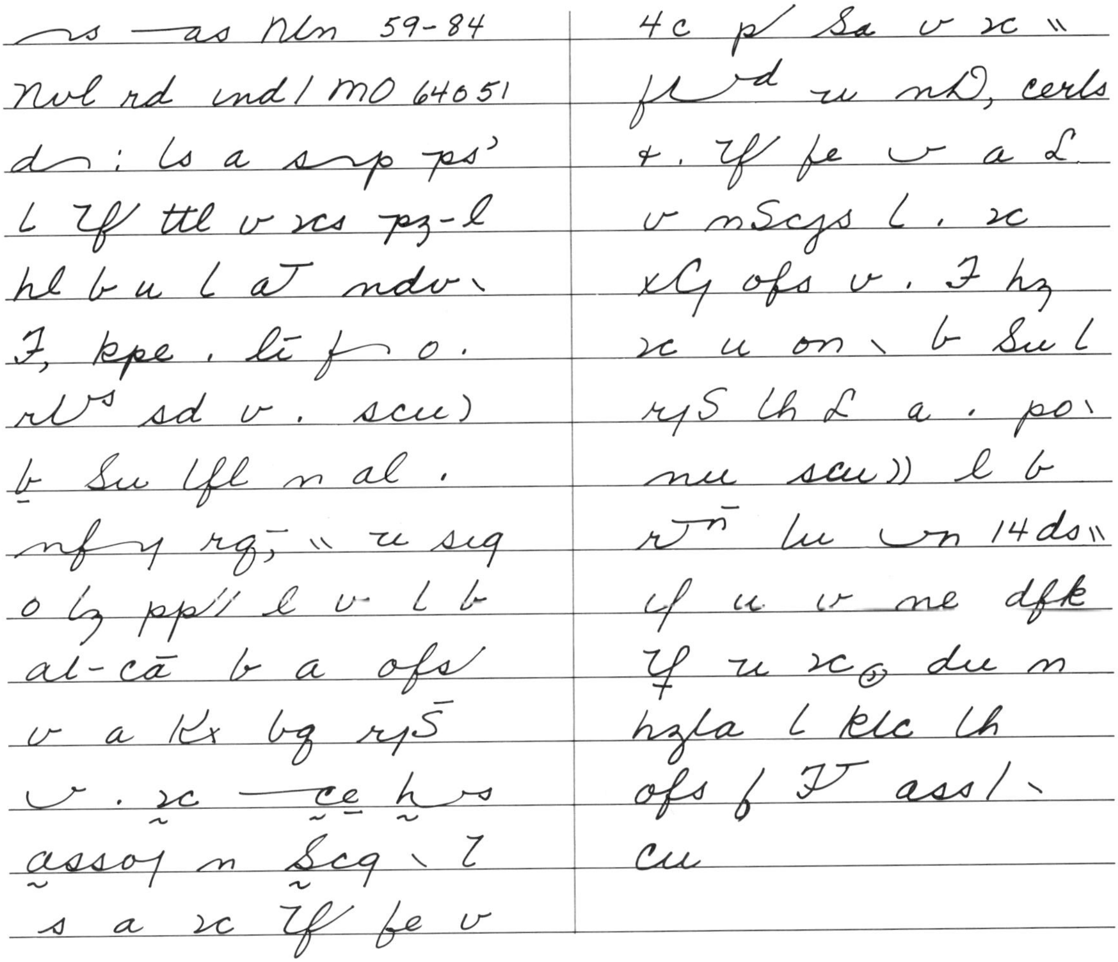

3.1 THEORY REVIEW

1. *sh* 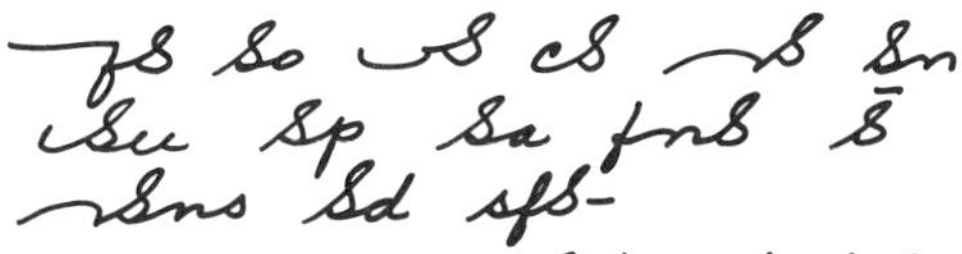

2. *for* 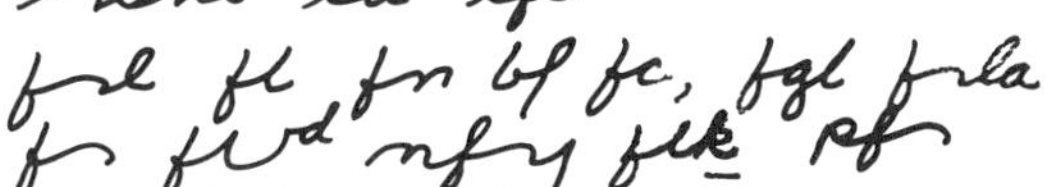

3. *xt* 

4. Initial *br* 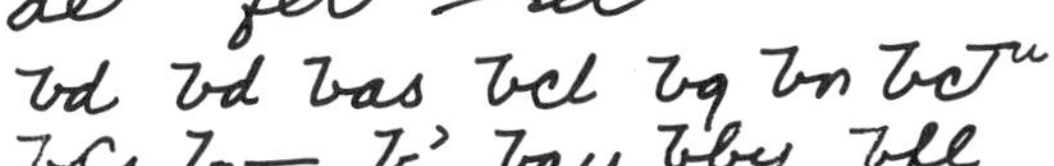

5. *ore* 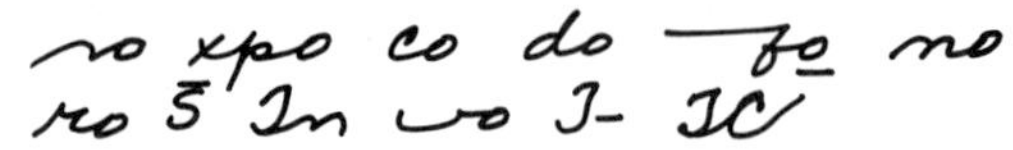

KEY 1. flash; show; wish; cash; mash; shown; issue; shop; share; finish; shipped; machines; should; sufficient 2. formal; forth; foreign; before; forecast; forget; formula; form; forward; information; forthcoming; perform 3. next; textbook; pretext; context; sexton; dextrose; fixture; mixture 4. bread; broad; brace; bracket; bring; brain; breakthrough; branches; branding; brass; bravery; bribery; briefly 5. more; explore; core; door; flooring; nor; roar; stored; torn; wore, war; torrent; torture

3.2 TRANSCRIPTION SKILL BUILDING

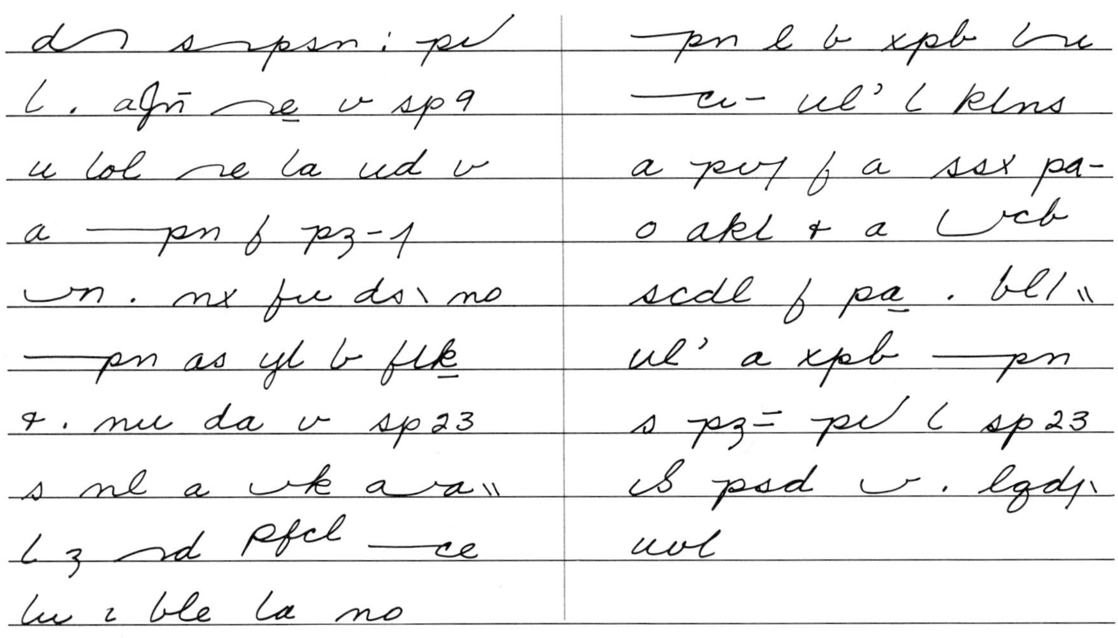

GUIDE Insert two introductory commas, one conjunction comma, and two parenthetical commas.

3.3 SPEED BUILDING

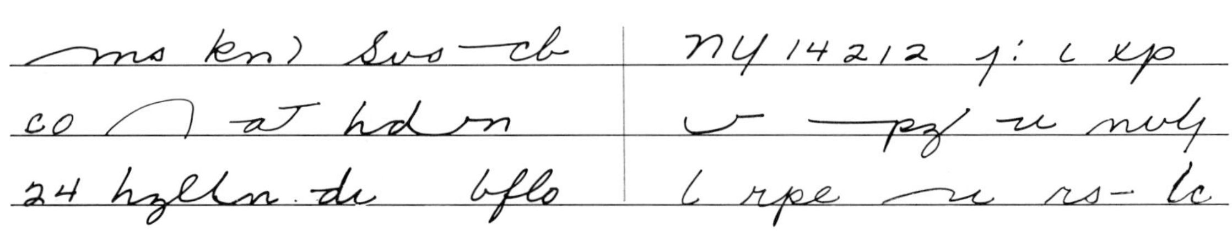

ab (11) Us—. lgl
rs/b)) v. 18 y ol.
. vn v nv 16 l
b rZv f u, +
i l b —p l jyn
u a. mn hs
f dn. rT ln pa
re ne sc/ fe,
—p dna. 40d l
. SA- lgl ofs
sCva o —cv sl.
lz dvo yg lgl pcy
nd al. sPl ec
gv l. s

3.4 VOCABULARY BUILDING

? + rs gs p ly
20-48 ll— rd
lgn NB 68504
d + rs p ly:
u jy- ls v b ppā
+ r rde f u sigs.
ln ncz a flcpe
v. ls. —p rde lz
Ses lb Sln u l
fas u fu nlys.
if ur sat v.
flcpes + v no ida
adys o Kcys, —p
lel ru sec f a
apy-- f a ofs sin.
af uv sin u
ls + u sigs v b
vln, b 2 adlls,
el cal + ln fil 1
cpe v eC dcu-
n r frPl vll. u
l rln 2 cpes. i
sy, 1 v. cpes Sd
b pt n a frPl
saf. s

4.1 THEORY REVIEW

1. *ūme*

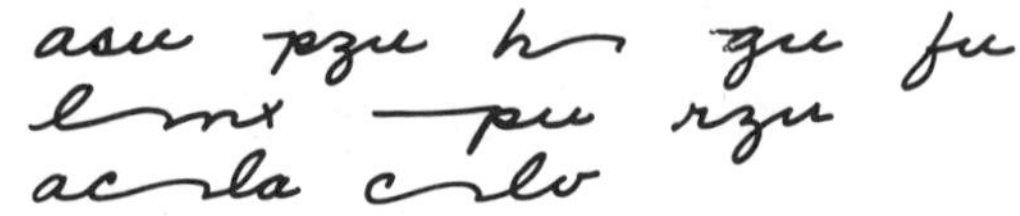

2. *āde*

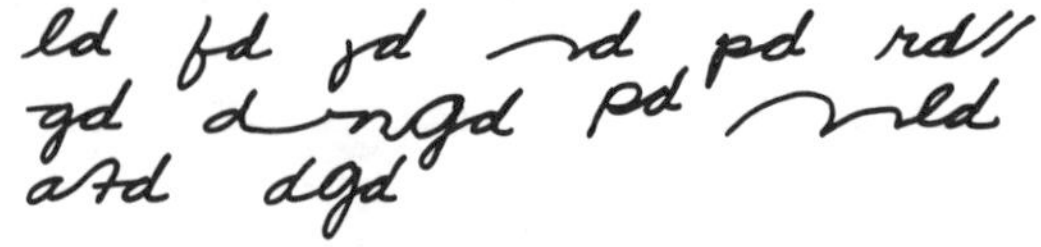

3. *nd*

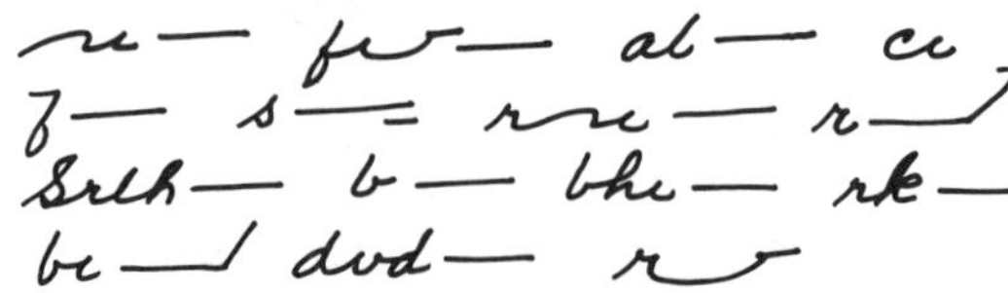

4. *lee*

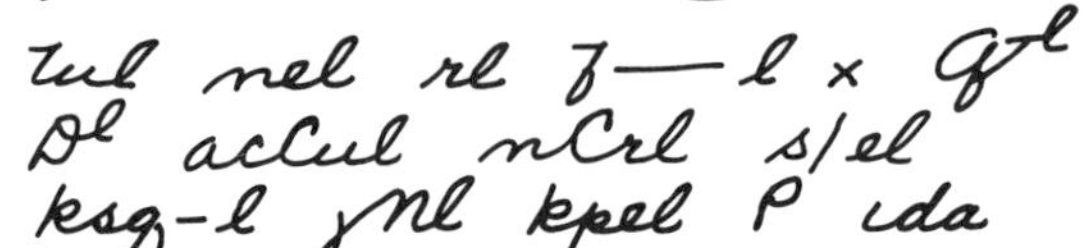

5. Compound words

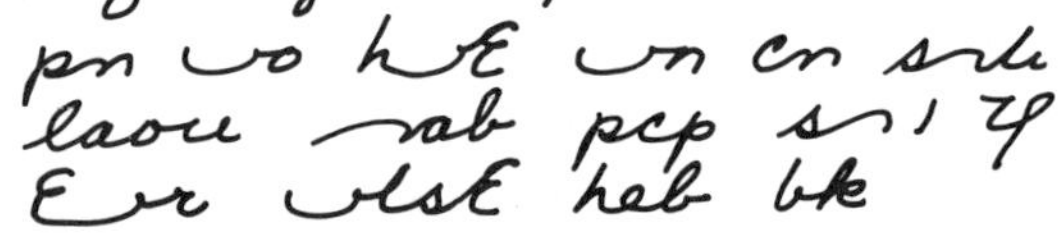

KEY 1. assume; presume; whom; groom; fume; luminous; plume; resume; accumulate; cumulative 2. laid; fade; jade; maid, made; paid; raiders; grade; downgrade; parade; marmalade; afraid; degrade 3. mind; found; attend; kind; friend; sending; remind; rendered; shorthand; band; behind; recommend; binder; dividend; around 4. truly; nearly; really; friendly; usually; quarterly; directly; actually; naturally; sincerely; consequently; generally; completely; particularly; immediately 5. upon; without; however; within; cannot; sometime; layout; maybe; pickup; someone; therefore; everywhere; whatsoever; hereby; become, became

4.2 TRANSCRIPTION SKILL BUILDING

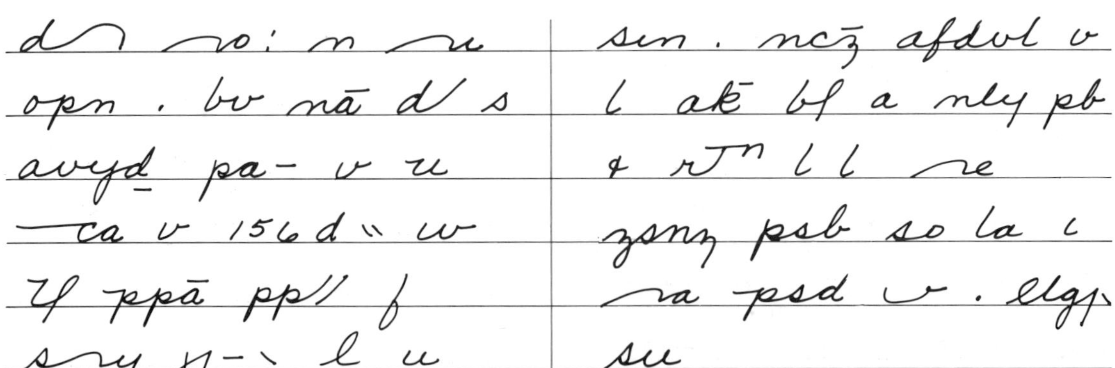

GUIDE Insert one compound adjective hyphen, two parenthetical commas, one introductory comma, and two series commas.

4.3 SPEED BUILDING

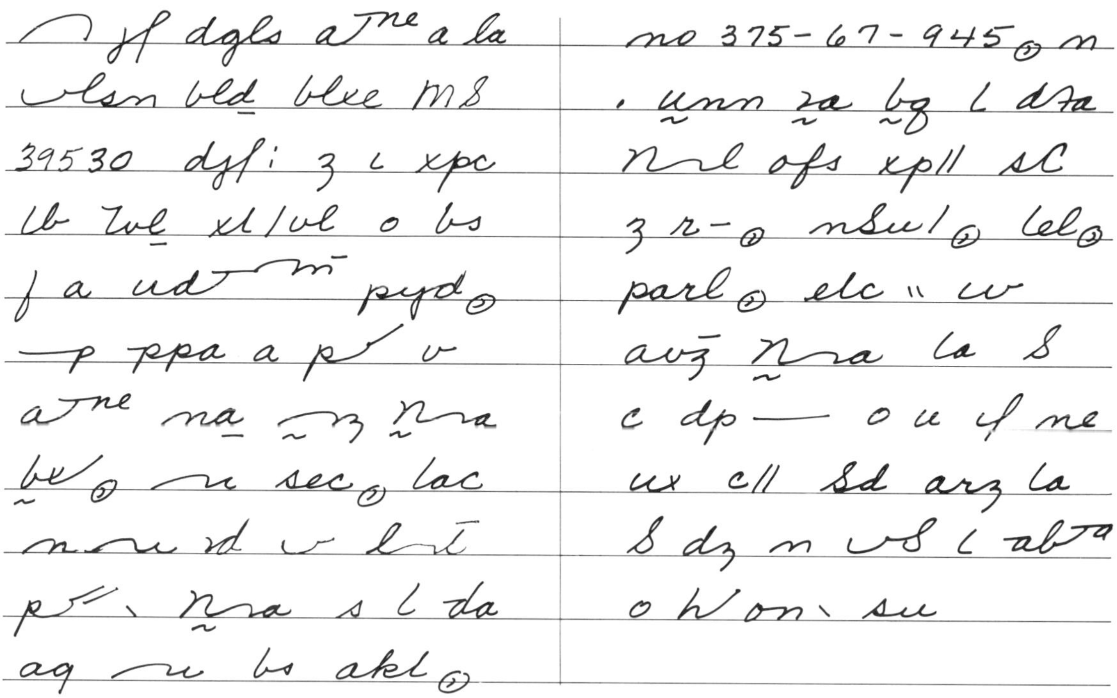

4.4 VOCABULARY BUILDING

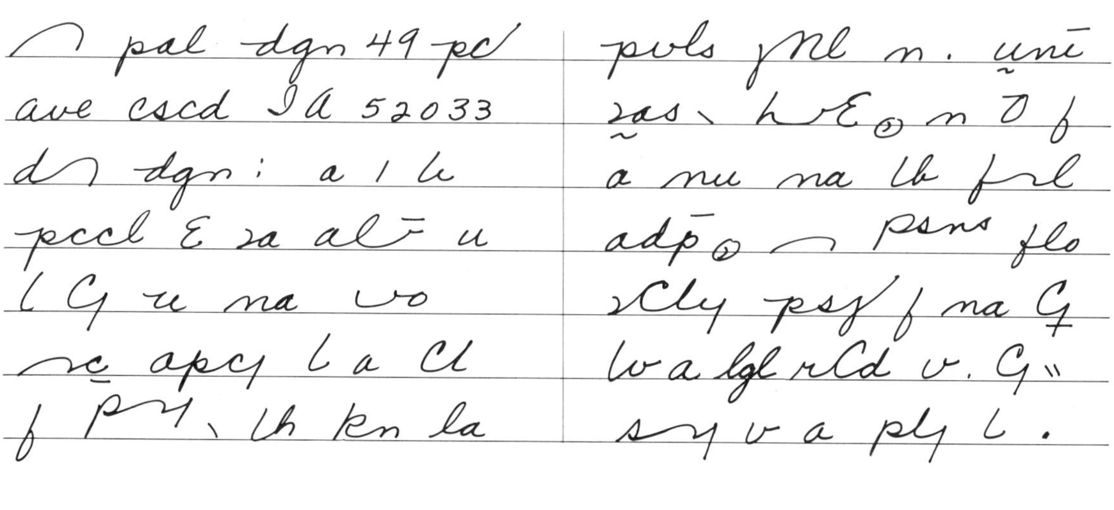

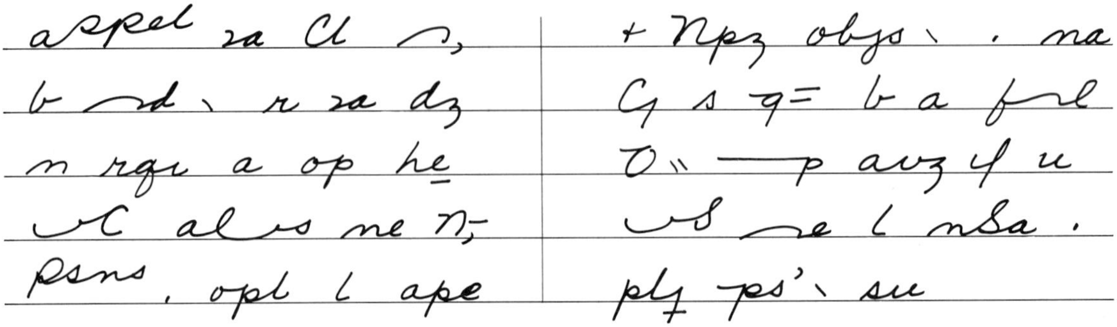

5.1 THEORY REVIEW

1. *āve*
2. *āte*
3. *ōry*
4. Initial *gr*
5. *ūre*

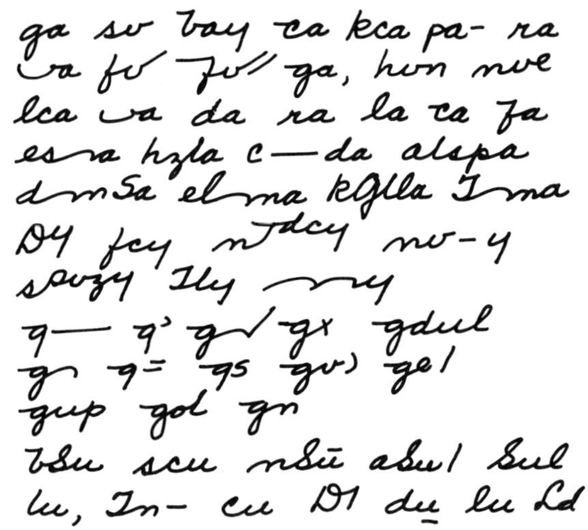

KEY 1. gave; save; bravery; crave; concave; pavement; rave; wave; favor; flavors; gravest; haven; navy 2. locate; wait; date; rate; late; create; freight; estimate; hesitate; candidate; anticipate; demonstrate; eliminate; congratulate; terminate 3. directory; factory; introductory; inventory; supervisory; territory; memory 4. grand; greatness; grammar; gracious; gradual; gram; granted; grasp; gravity; grievance; group; growth; green 5. brochure; secure; insured; assurance; surely; tourist; tournament; cure; duration; during; lure; lurid

5.2 TRANSCRIPTION SKILL BUILDING

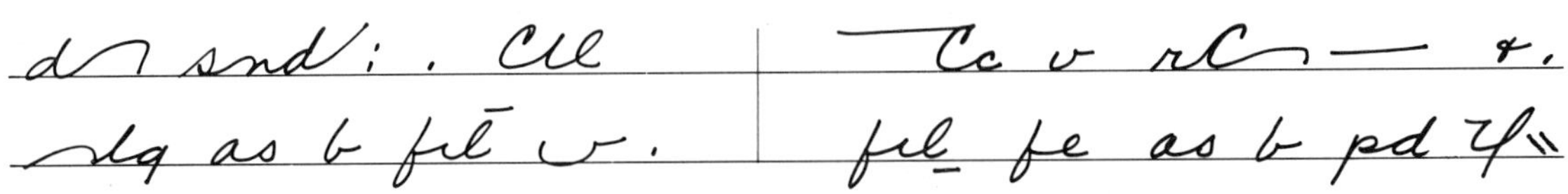

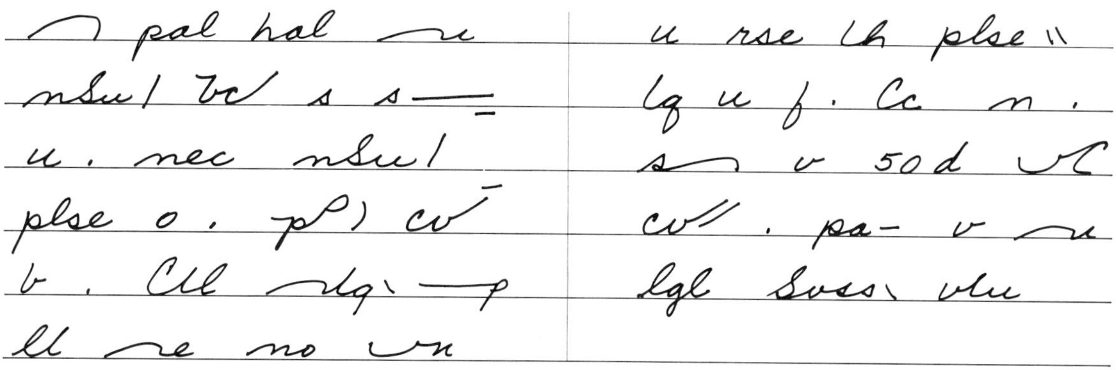

GUIDE Insert one conjunction comma, two apposition commas, and one parenthetical comma.

5.3 SPEED BUILDING

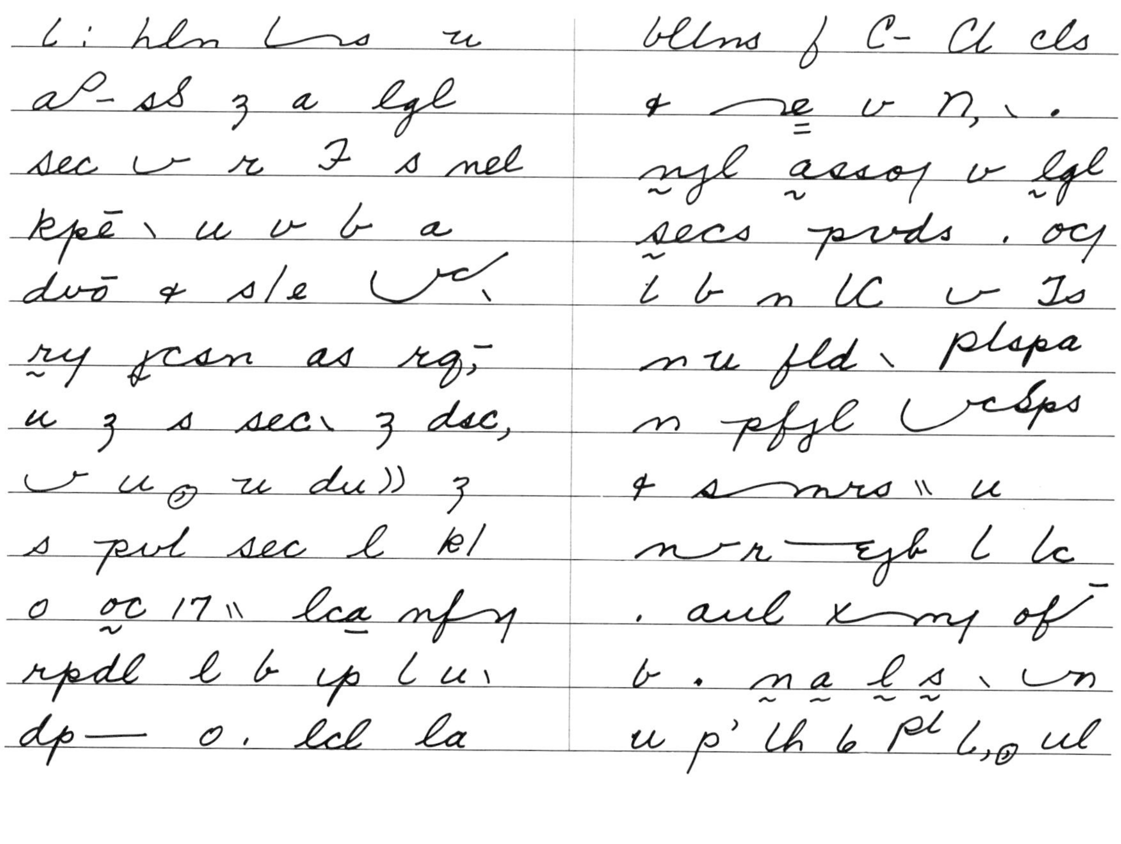

v. ttl v cert
pfyl lgl sec \ el
riBs ri lol xpl// a
la li \

5.4 VOCABULARY BUILDING

. lgl sec ⌒, b
nlyb l aCll kpe
dVs fs + dcu--\
lz ⌒a nolv ss Kcy
ls cperus afdvls
o pxes \ ⌒ lus S
l b rqī l vl'.
sin v a nS-\\
if a sec s n a
nly pb S ⌒a
b xpc̄ l ary l v
pp// nT3, f kvnl
S ⌒a b sc̄ lsec

a nly kp \ pC v a
nly pb sel + a
rb ⌒p l b nec \
. sel Sos . k) n
vC a nly s aT3
l ac + . rb ⌒p
Sos . da v xP1 v
. kp \ a nly s n
kSn̄ v . pp//
nolv̄ \ W nl fqp
s l cerl . vld) v
sig \ S ⌒a lso
a nS ols \ eC za

InSs nlys u
ruls u uC ly

n, kpe \

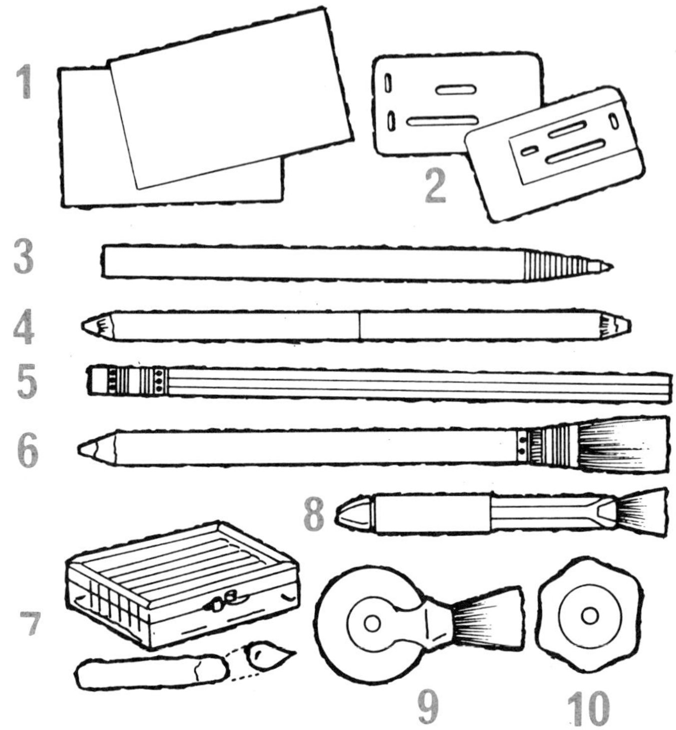

ERASING SUPPLIES

1. Cards (5″ x 3″) for protection of copies behind error being erased.

2. Eraser shield for protection of typed copy around letter or letters being erased.

3. Pencil-type eraser that is sharpened by unwrapping or "peeling back."

4. Pencil-type eraser that has an eraser for originals on one end and a softer one for carbon copies on the other.

5. Regular pencil eraser (good for carbon copies, especially on 9-pound paper).

6. Pencil-type eraser with brush.

7. Plastic type cleaner to take off "top" (excess ink) of error so that smearing will be eliminated and amount of erasing necessary reduced.

8. Fiberglass eraser.

9. Circular eraser with brush.

10. Circular eraser without brush.

CORRECTION TECHNIQUES

Before erasing, move the carriage or the carrier to the right if the error is on the right side of the paper; move to the left if the error is on the left side. Do not erase over the typing mechanism.

Place an eraser shield, plastic or metal, behind the original copy so that the carbon copy is not smeared. Erase one letter at a time.

As you near the end of a page, place a sheet of blank paper under the bottom of the page and the back of the platen. This helps to maintain the alignment of the typing if a correction needs to be made in the last three or four lines.

Brush the eraser crumbs away with a brush or cleansing tissue and then roll the paper back to typing position. Strike the correct letter with a light stroke. Backspace and strike over the correction until it matches the surrounding copy.

UNIT 13

FINANCE

1.1 THEORY REVIEW

1. *nt*
2. *shun*
3. Initial *pr*
4. Past tense
5. Brief forms

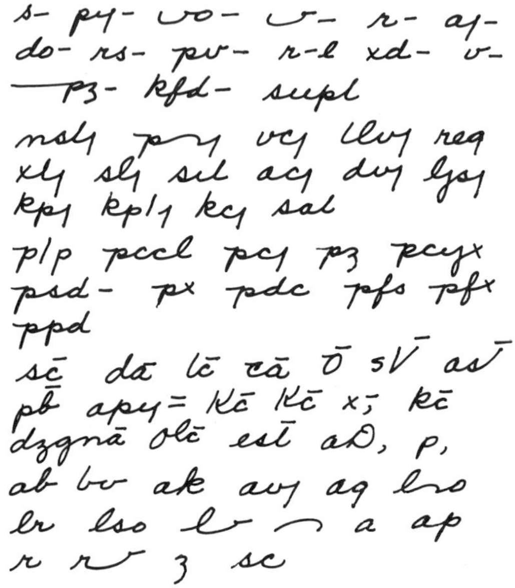

KEY 1. sent; point; won't; went, want; rent; agent; don't; recent; prevent; rental; accident; haven't; pleasant; confident; superintendent 2. institution; promotion; vacation; television; regulation; extension; solution; situation; action; division; legislation; completion; compensation; connection; satisfaction 3. principal, principle; practical; precaution; praise; precarious; precedent; precious; product; preface; prefix; prepaid 4. asked; dated; talked; created; ordered; sponsored; answered; published; appointed; contracted; corrected; existed; connected; designated; overlooked; established; addressed; passed 5. about; above; acknowledge; advantage; again, against; almost; already; also; always; am; at, an; appreciate; are; around; as, was; ask

1.2 TRANSCRIPTION SKILL BUILDING

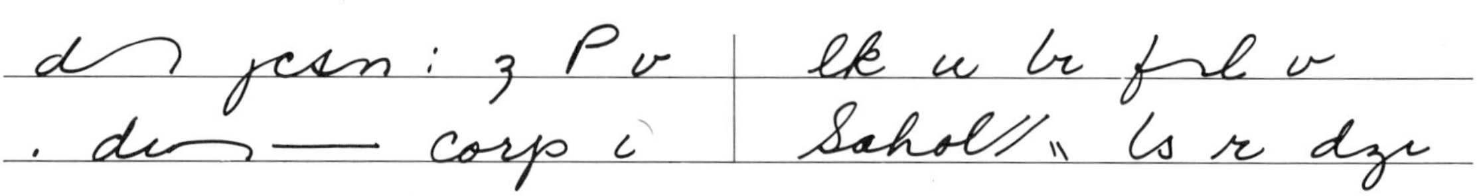

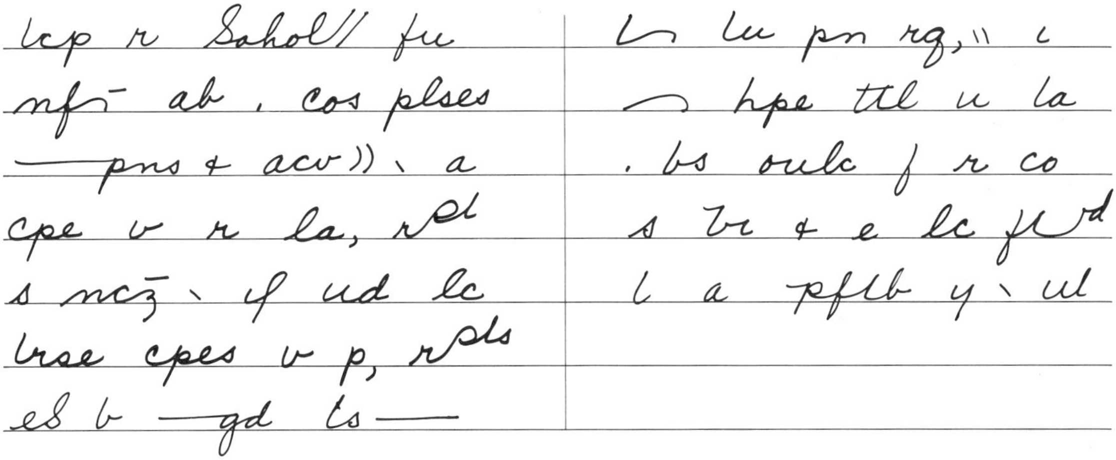

GUIDE Insert two introductory commas, two series commas, one conjunction comma, and one possessive apostrophe.

1.3 SPEED BUILDING

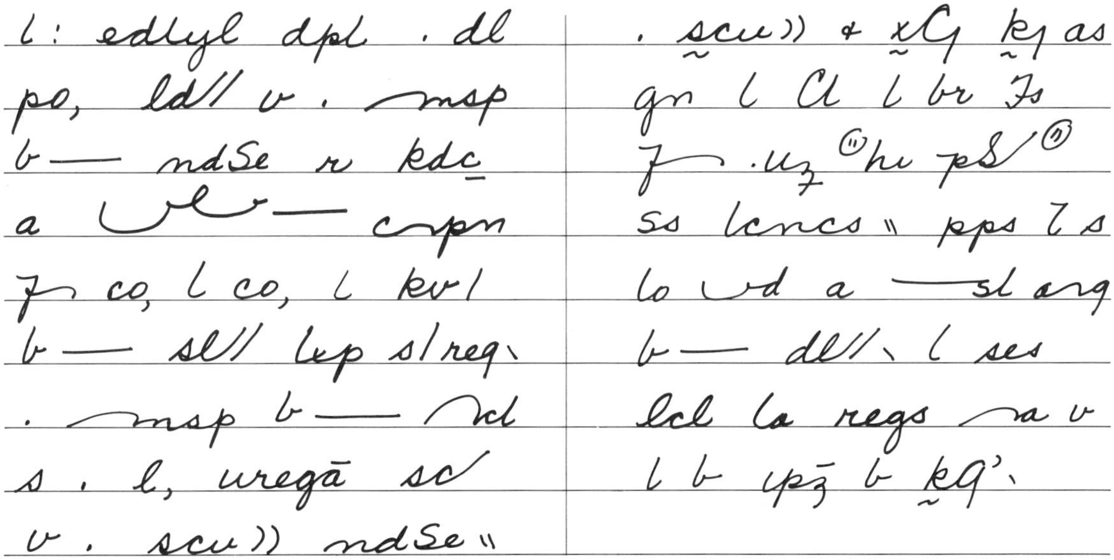

1.4 VOCABULARY BUILDING

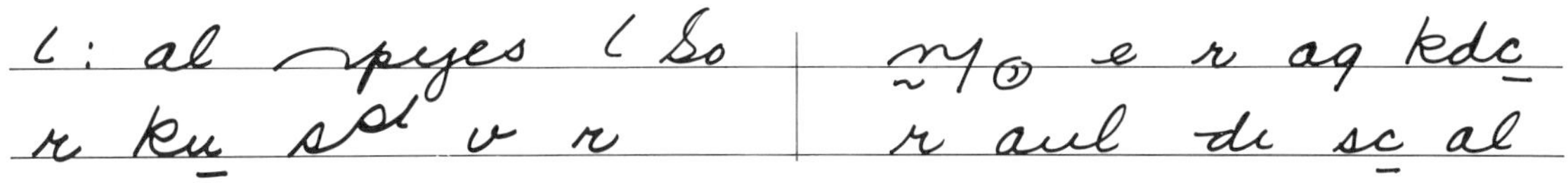

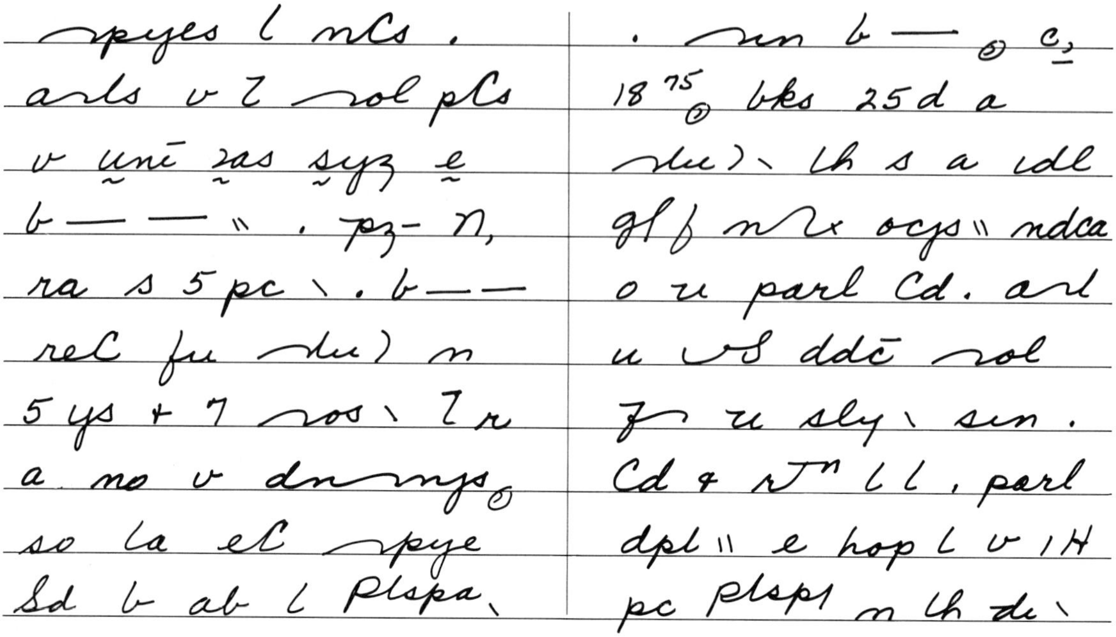

2.1 THEORY REVIEW

1. *bē*
2. *rē*
3. *dē*
4. Initial *spr*
5. Compound words

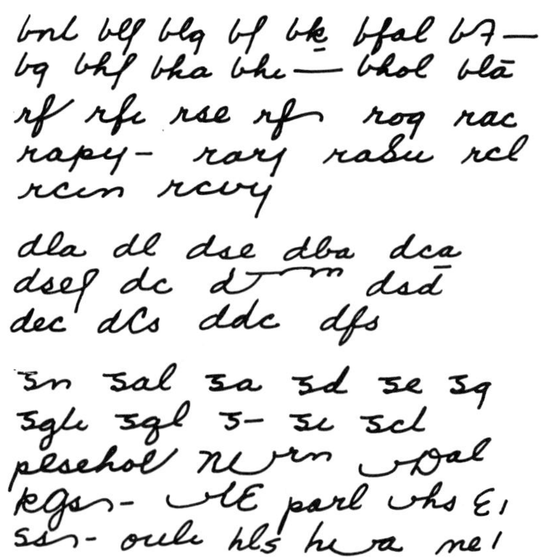

KEY 1. beneath; belief; belong; before; becoming; befall; befriend; begin; behalf; behave; behind; behold; belated 2. refer; refine; receipt, receive; reform; reorganize; react; reappoint; rearrange; reassure; recall; recline; recovery 3. delay; delivery; deceive; debate; declaim; deceitful; December; determine; decided; declare; decrease; deduct; deface 4. sprain; sprawl; spray; spread; spree; spring; springtime;

sprinkle; sprint; sprite; sprocket 5. policyholder; northwestern; withdrawal; congressman; whatever; payroll; warehouse; everyone; salesman; outline; wholesale; highway; anyone

2.2 TRANSCRIPTION SKILL BUILDING

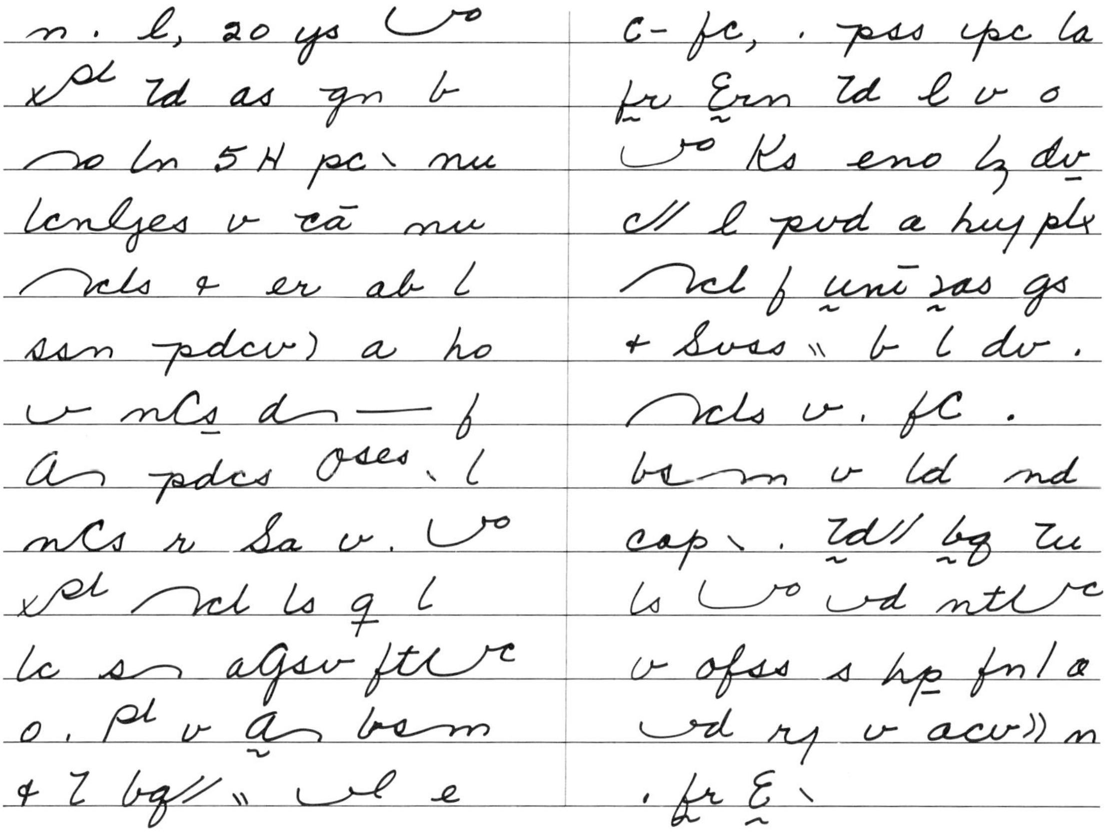

GUIDE Insert four introductory commas, one conjunction comma, two parenthetical commas, three contraction apostrophes, and one compound adjective hyphen.

2.3 SPEED BUILDING

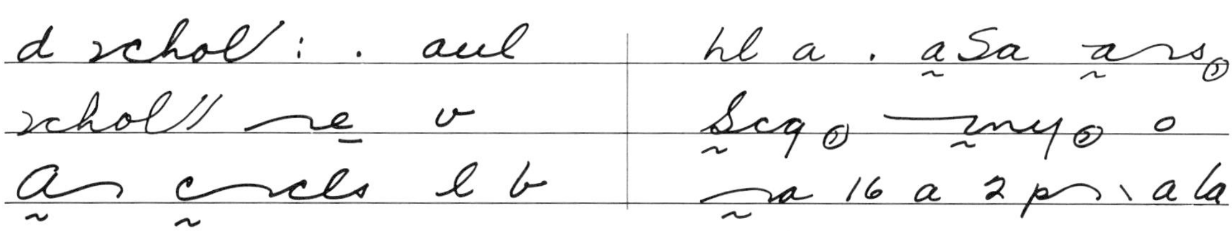

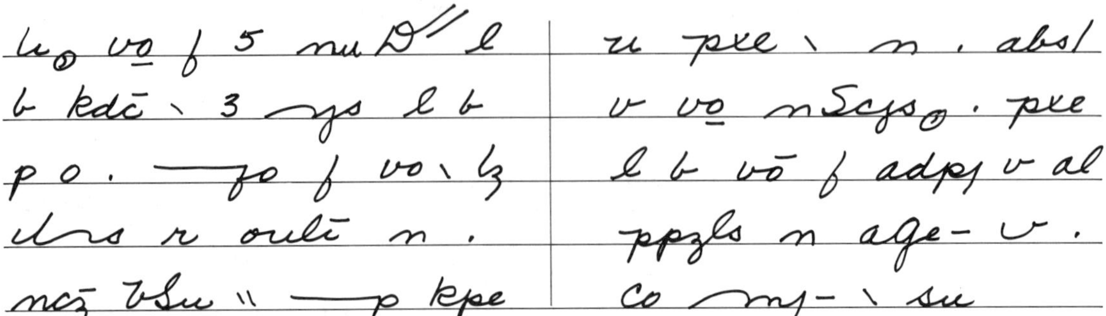

2.4 VOCABULARY BUILDING

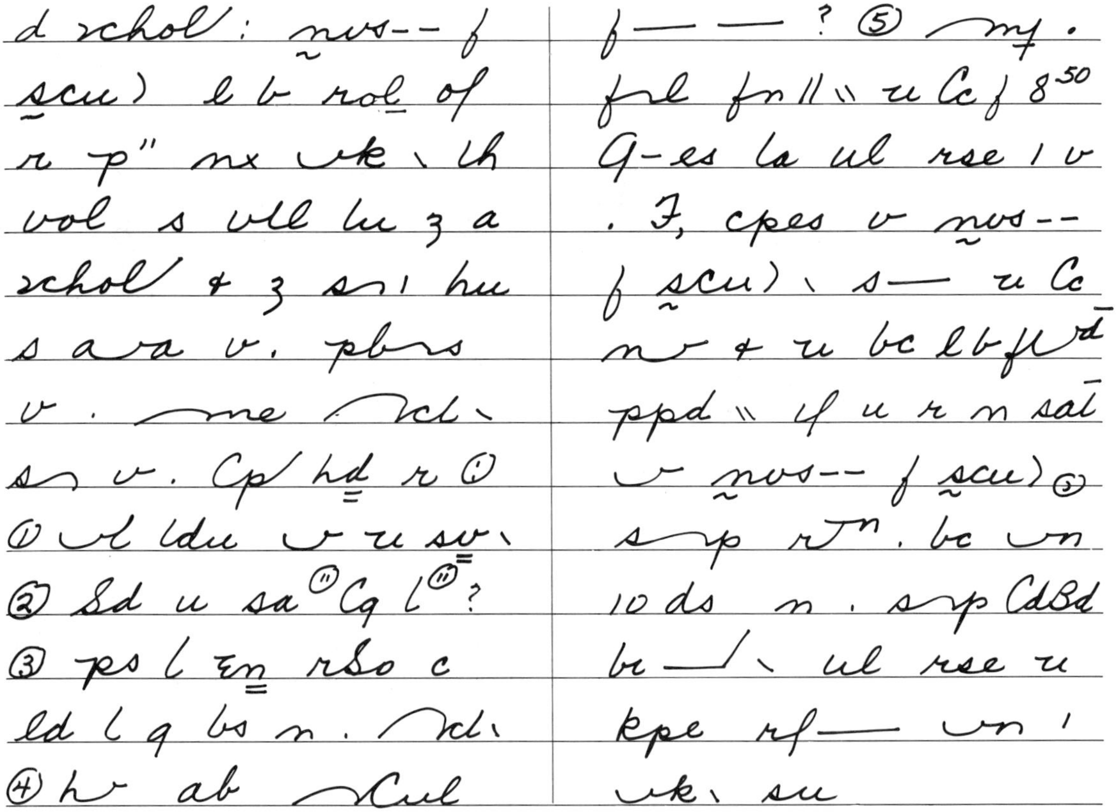

3.1 THEORY REVIEW

1. Initial *kr*

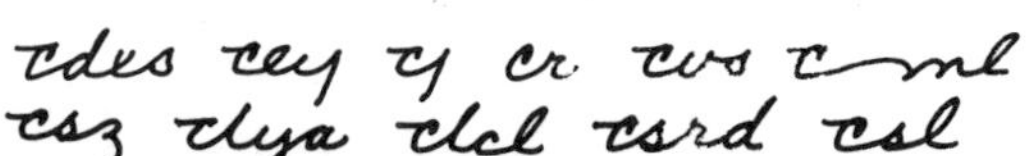

2. *dis* 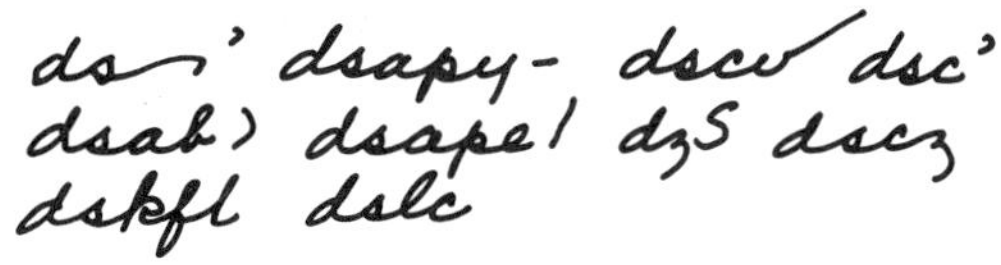

3. *des* 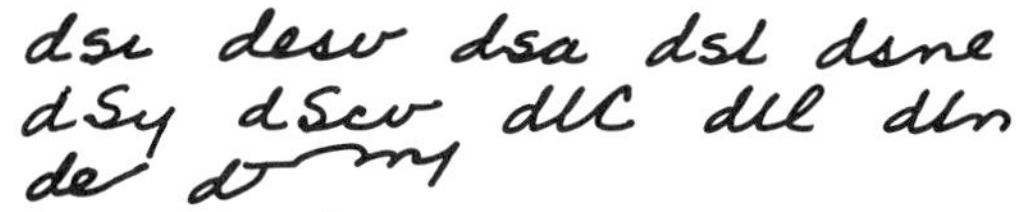

4. *mis* 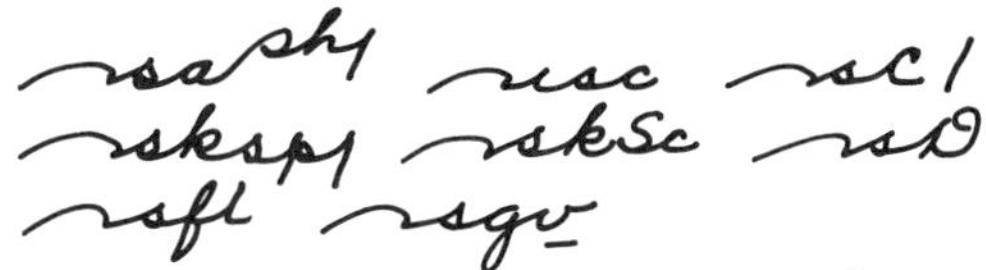

5. Brief forms 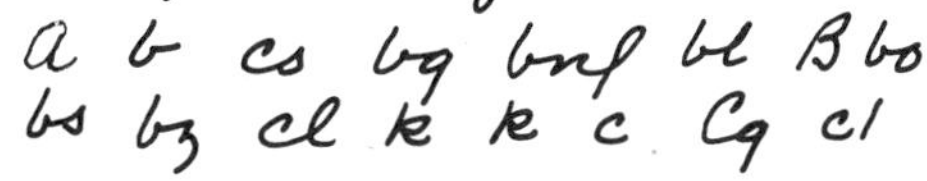

KEY 1. credentials; creamery; creation; credit; crevice; criminal; crises; criteria; critical; crossroad; crystal 2. dismiss; disappoint; discover; discuss; disability; disappearance; disaster; disclose; discomfort; dislike 3. despite; descriptive; despair; despot; destiny; destroy; destructive; detach; detail; detain; deter; determination 4. misapprehension; miscellaneous; mischance; misconception; misconstruct; misdirect; misfit; misgiving 5. auto; be, by, buy, but, been; because; began, begin; benefit; between; billion; both; business; busy; call; came, come; committee; can, cents; charge; once, circumstance

3.2 TRANSCRIPTION SKILL BUILDING

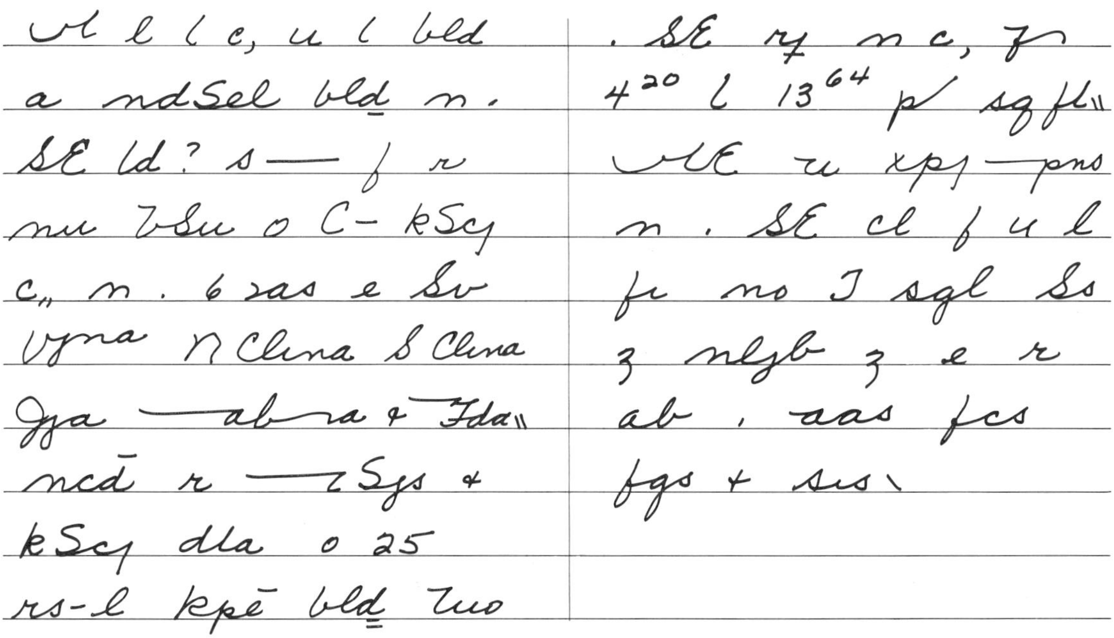

GUIDE Insert one enumeration colon, seven series commas, one parenthetical comma, one introductory comma, one contraction apostrophe, and one possessive apostrophe.

3.3 SPEED BUILDING

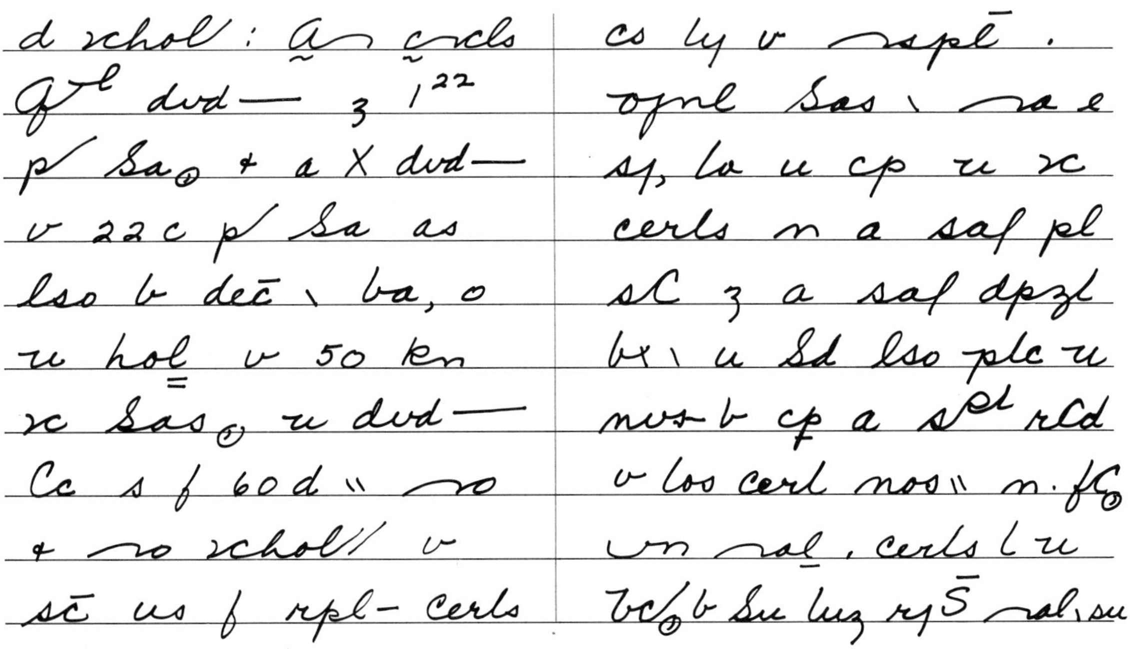

3.4 VOCABULARY BUILDING

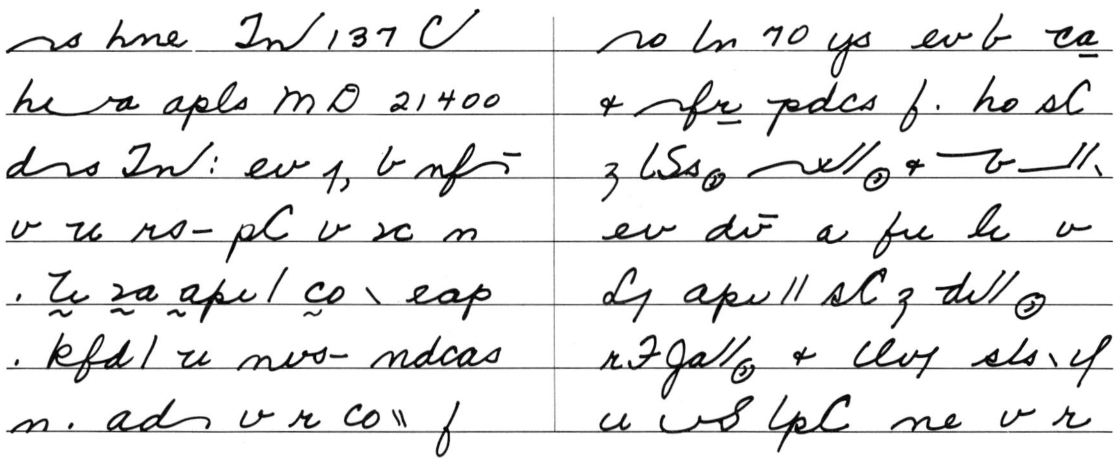

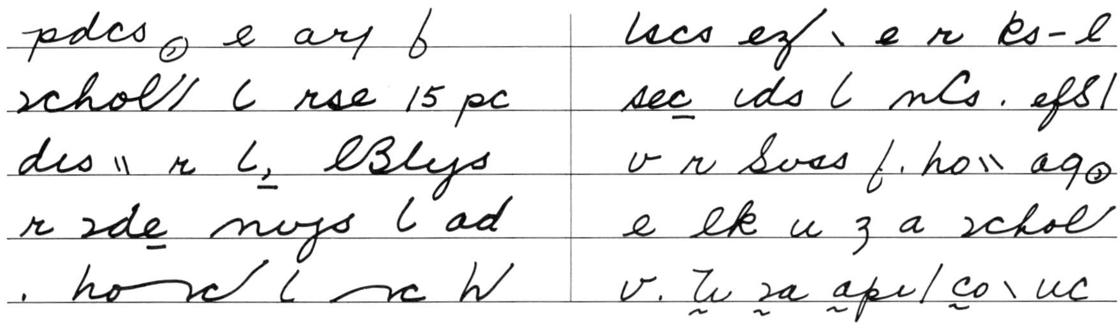

4.1 THEORY REVIEW

1. Initial *fr*

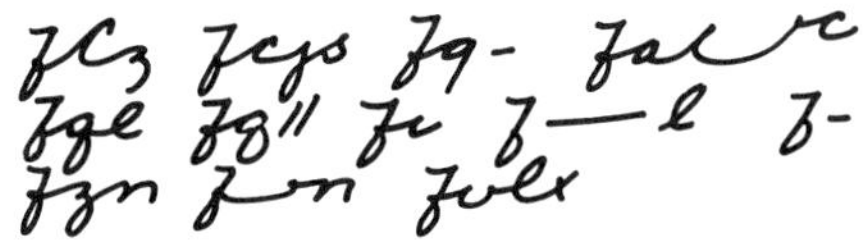

2. Plurals

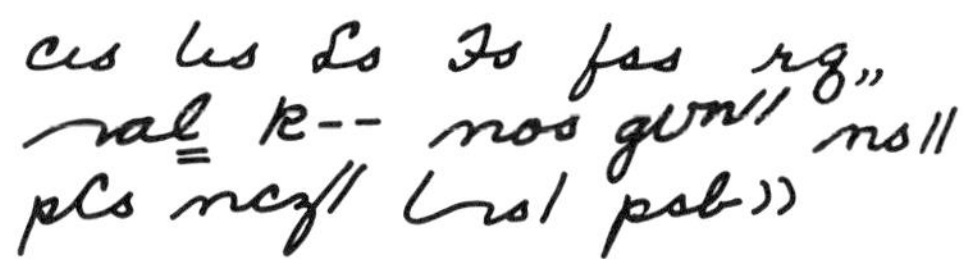

3. *ex*

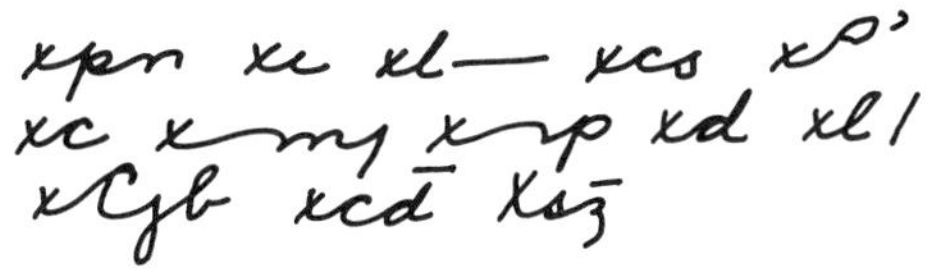

4. *com*

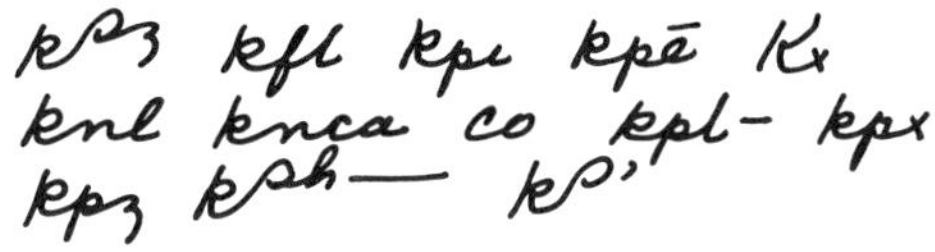

5. Brief forms

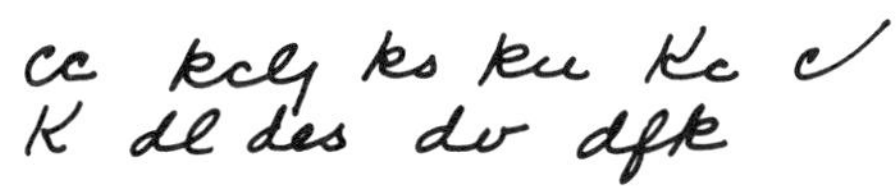

KEY 1. franchise; fractions; fragment; framework; frankly; frequencies; fright; friendly; front; frozen; frown; frivolous 2. kinds; times; letters; firms; forces; requests; mailings; comments; numbers; governors; instances; purchases; enclosures; themselves; possibilities 3. explain; excite; extend; excuse; express; exact; examination; example; exceed; excellence; exchangeable; excluded; exercised 4. comprise; comfort; comply; completed; commercial; commonly; communicate; company; competent; complex; compose; comprehend; compress 5. collect; conclusion; consider; continue; contract, correct; country; customer; deal, deliver, delivery; describe, description; develop; difficult, difficulty

4.2 TRANSCRIPTION SKILL BUILDING

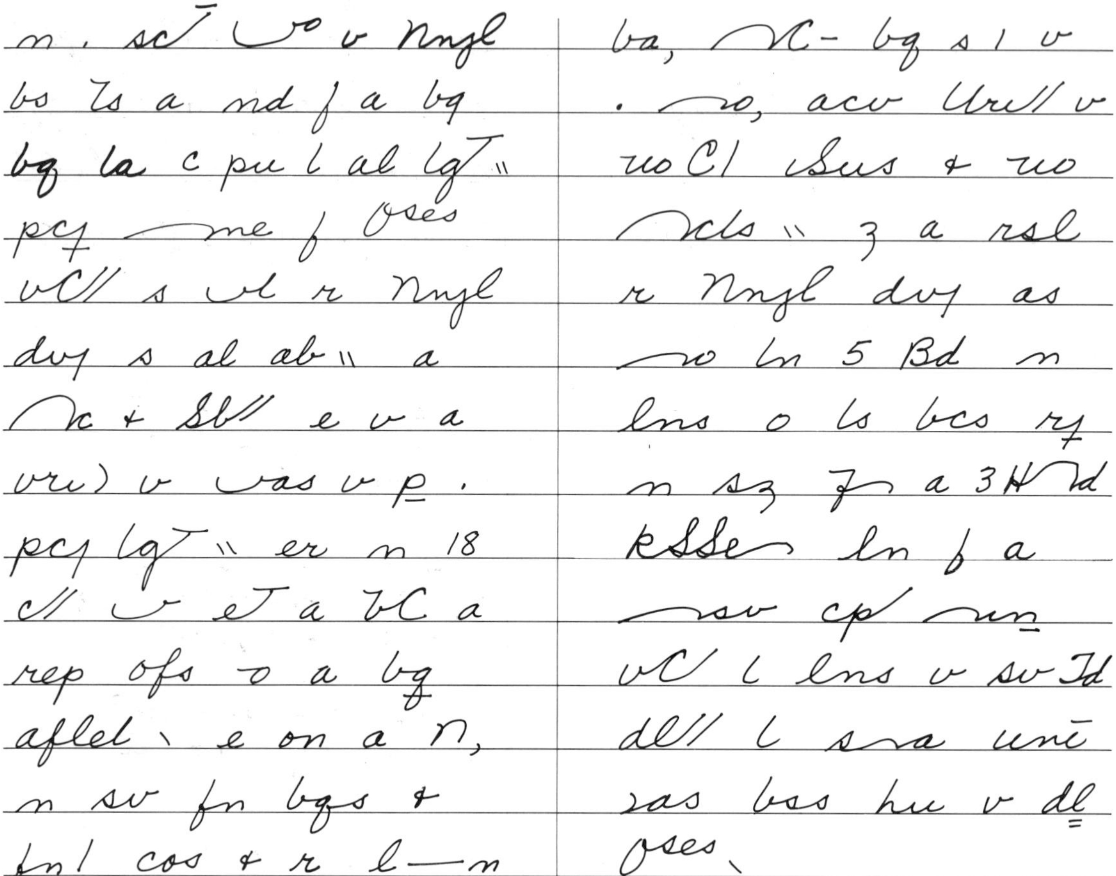

GUIDE Insert three introductory commas, one conjunction comma, one parenthetical comma, two series commas, five numbers commas, two contraction apostrophes, and three compound adjective hyphens.

4.3 SPEED BUILDING

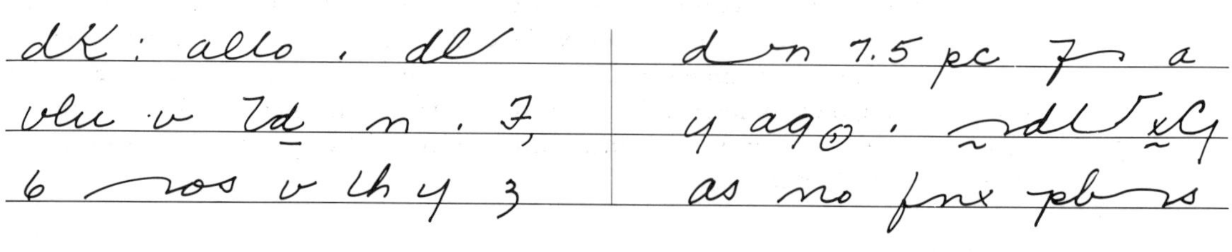

cs c,, v b cp n li
o vol " lh xC 3
est 20 ys aq & as
h a rde xl- gol
ra sa P aT /ln
n a rs- Nor \ . xC

as rn n . bc sl
ls nspj \ l as 2
ssdys \ 1 s a kpe
akl ss l B bc/&
. Ts a dpzly & ce
ss f xc certs \ cu

4.4 VOCABULARY BUILDING

Bd v D" sun ml
ls mCS WI 53945
1: 3 a rchol v . sun
ml ls rq u
lP u opn o .
ppz pn l lgda
. mCS ml l "
ible la Tf ajs-- l
b d b . fed dpl
v Ks al adjl
sls v l \ rT
ln lgda ufl la 3
lq 3 l s sl hop f
. l lgl bc l Nl

pdcj u fv . rk- j
v apl f a Srl Ts ln
v 2 H Tdd " a i lso
sj, la u rSC dpl
nvsga nu fBcs vC
d kbin vl v nCrl
fb \ allo a pz- l
s a Srlj v l .
ds f nt gs s
a a al li hi \ lh
cd op p a nu li
& al . l l
w bc nl fu
pdcj \ su

5.1 THEORY REVIEW

1. *con*
2. *sub*
3. *al*
4. *fur*
5. Brief forms

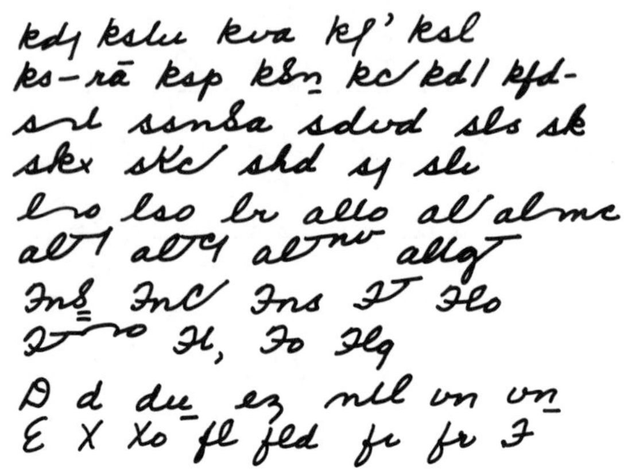

KEY 1. condition; constitute; convey; confess; console; concentrated; concept; concerning; concur; condense; confident 2. submit; substantiate; subdivide; sublease; subcommittee; subconscious; subcontractor; subhead; subject; sublime 3. almost; also; already; although; alter; almanac; alteration; altercation; alternative; altogether 4. furnishings; furniture; furnace; further; furlough; furthermore; furthest; furrow; furlong 5. direct; dollar, s; during; easy; entitle; even; evening; ever, every; extra; extraordinary; fail, feel; field; fine, find; fire; firm

5.2 TRANSCRIPTION SKILL BUILDING

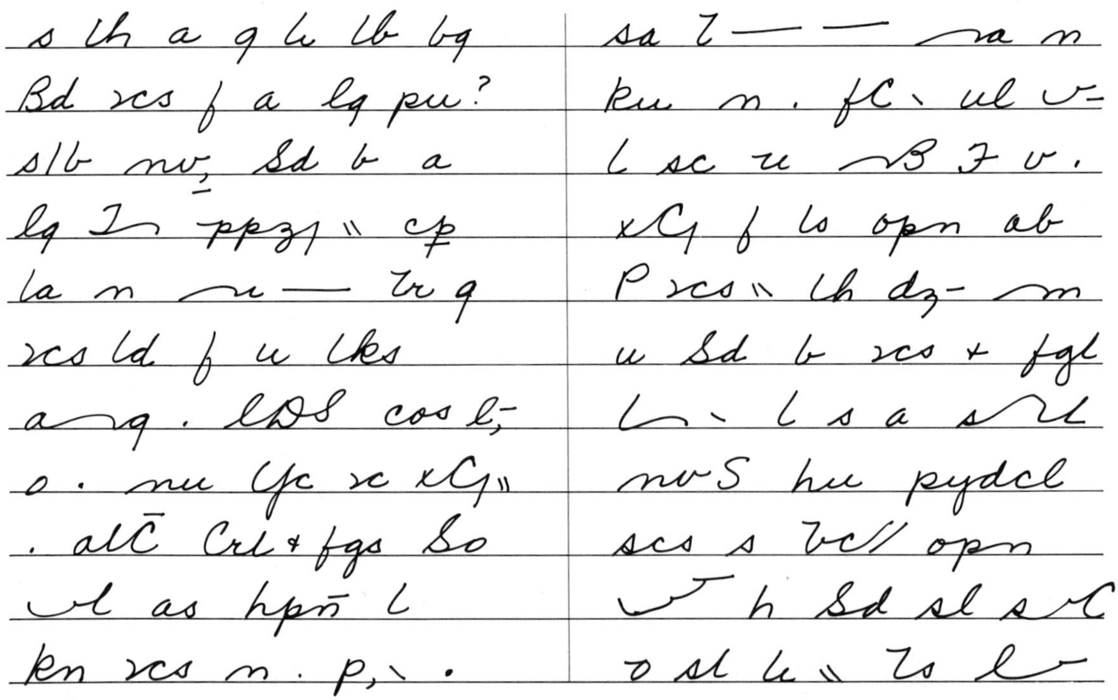

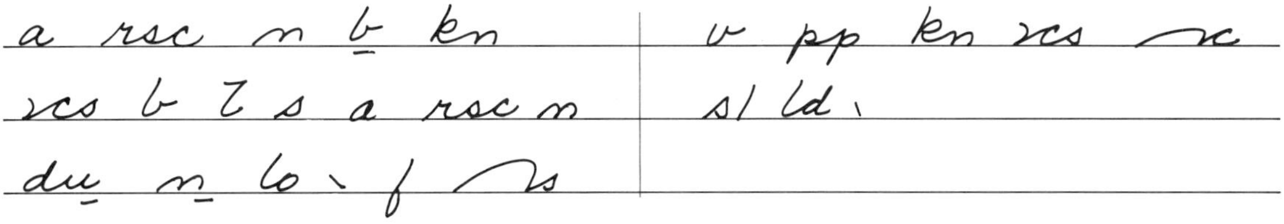

GUIDE Insert two introductory commas, two series commas, one parenthetical comma, one compound adjective hyphen, five contraction apostrophes, one possessive apostrophe, and one internal punctuation semicolon.

5.3 SPEED BUILDING

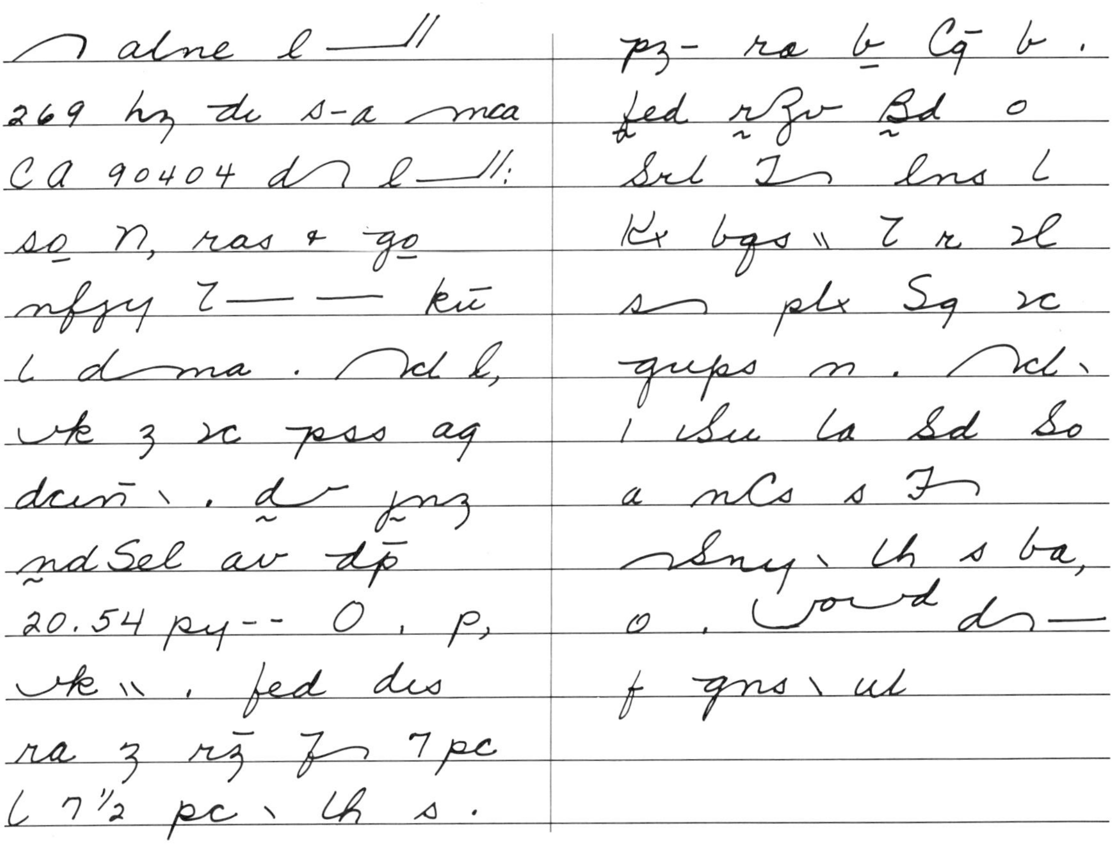

5.4 VOCABULARY BUILDING

1 N, asc. v . secs
asin-- ra b a kSn
v W spyfl nvs-
pflo, vn if . xcv
kvls s on rcl
nvs-- s sec Sd
frLz Hs/ v rcl
Imlze & S Sd
bk kflb v nvs-
psfl + fnx rPls
xc s. rro, kn pC
n. rcl + s evdl
v oNS n a co,
vn xc s pC u
rse a pp/ no z
a xc cerl , . xchol
ra rse dvd——
o N, cs v s nvs-
n a corp, lz
dvd—— r pd

f . En v . co
xc s csf n 2
vas kn + pf,
if u b pf xc
I s a fi dvd—
ra, pf xchol
rse pa-- v
dvd—— o co
asls bf kn xchol
vT l s a Nl
dvd— dSby o
if a co s Ug
lgdj psd pf
xc ra v , ru
v kUT la s l
kvl. pf xc l kn
xc a ne lu . on/Cgs,
rro, pf xcs r clb
vC nsly r rdeb
a, opj v . iSu co,

ENCLOSURES

References to enclosures should be circled in red in the notes as the dictation is being given, so that they will not be forgotten.

If any item is to be enclosed in the envelope with the letter, indicate this by using an enclosure notation, "Enc." or "Enclosure." The purpose of this notation is to remind the person who puts the letter into the envelope to insert the enclosures too. It also aids the person who opens the envelope by reminding him to look for the enclosures.

The older practice is to double space after the reference initials before typing the enclosure notation. The common practice today is to place the enclosure notation at the left margin on the line below the reference initials.

If the writer is sending a copy of the letter to another person and wishes the addressee to know that it is being sent, make a carbon copy notation at the left margin on the line below the reference initials or below the enclosure notation if it is used.

If more than one person is to receive a carbon copy, the names should be listed alphabetically.

When the writer does not intend to let the addressee know that anyone else is receiving a copy of the letter, type "bcc" (blind carbon copy) on the upper left corner of the carbon copies only. This notation is never typed on the original copy.

UNIT 14

TRAVEL

1.1 THEORY REVIEW

1. *oi*

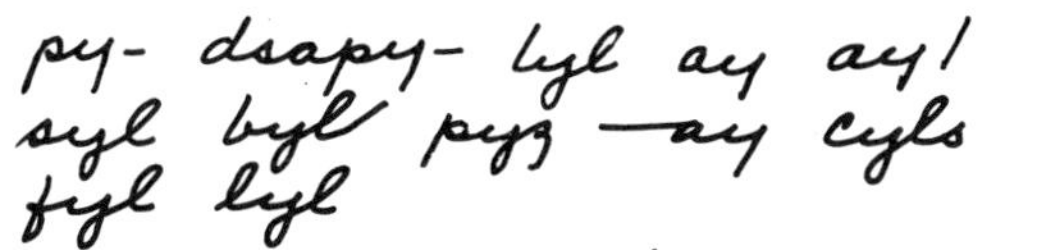

2. *ow*

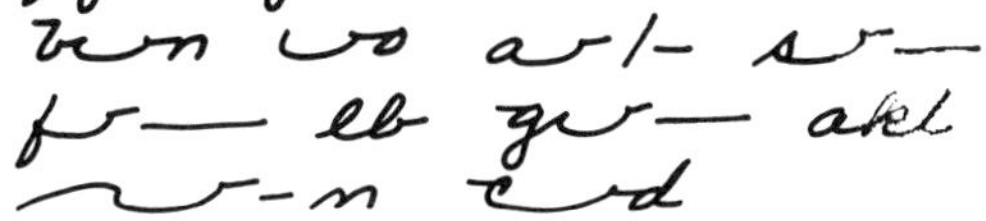

3. *ū*

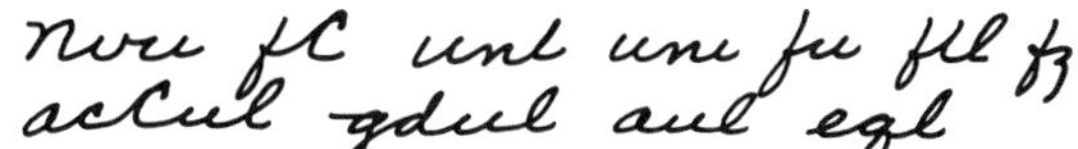

4. *ī*

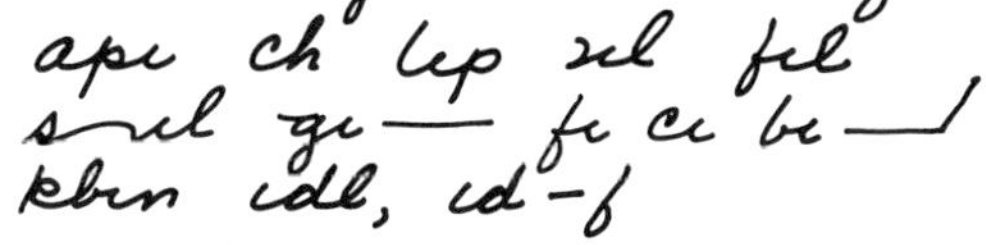

5. Brief forms

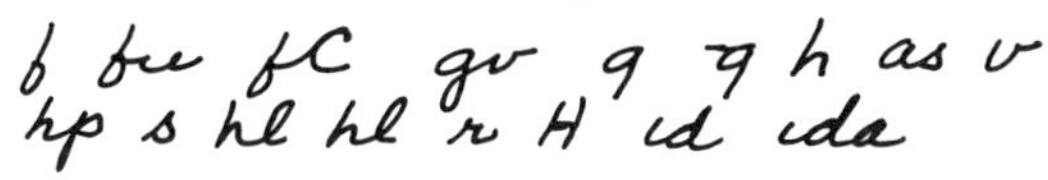

KEY 1. point; disappoint; toil; annoy; annoyance; soil; boiler; poise; alloy; coils; foil; loyal 2. brown; without; announcement; sound; found; pound; ground; account; mountain; crowd 3. interview; future; unit; unite; few; futile; fuse; actual; gradual; annual; equal 4. apply; child; type; style; file; smile; grind; find; kind; binder; combine; idealist; identify 5. for; full, fully; future; given; go, good; great; he, had, him; has; have, of, very; help; his, is; held; hole, whole; are, our, hour; hundred; idea; immediate, immediately

1.2 TRANSCRIPTION SKILL BUILDING

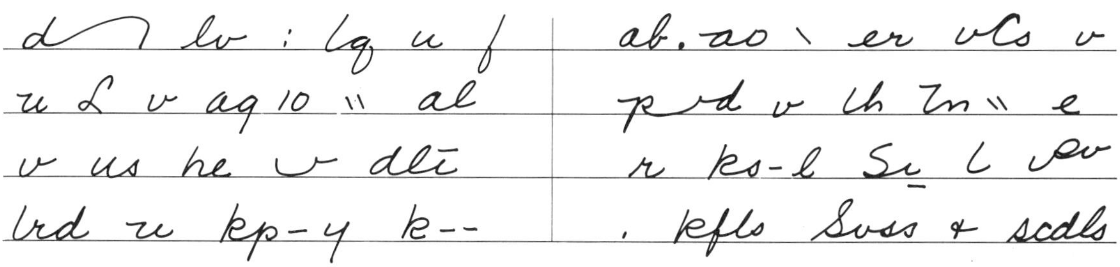

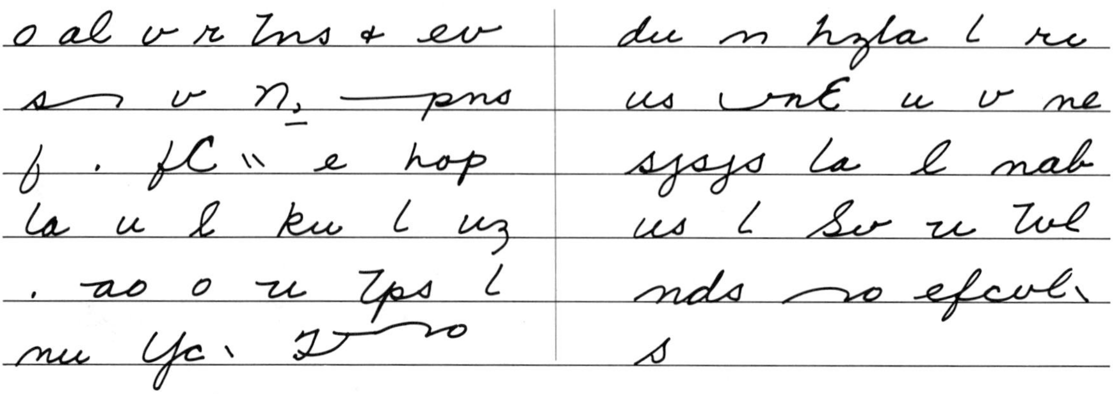

GUIDE Insert two parenthetical commas, two series commas, one internal punctuation semicolon, and one introductory comma.

1.3 SPEED BUILDING

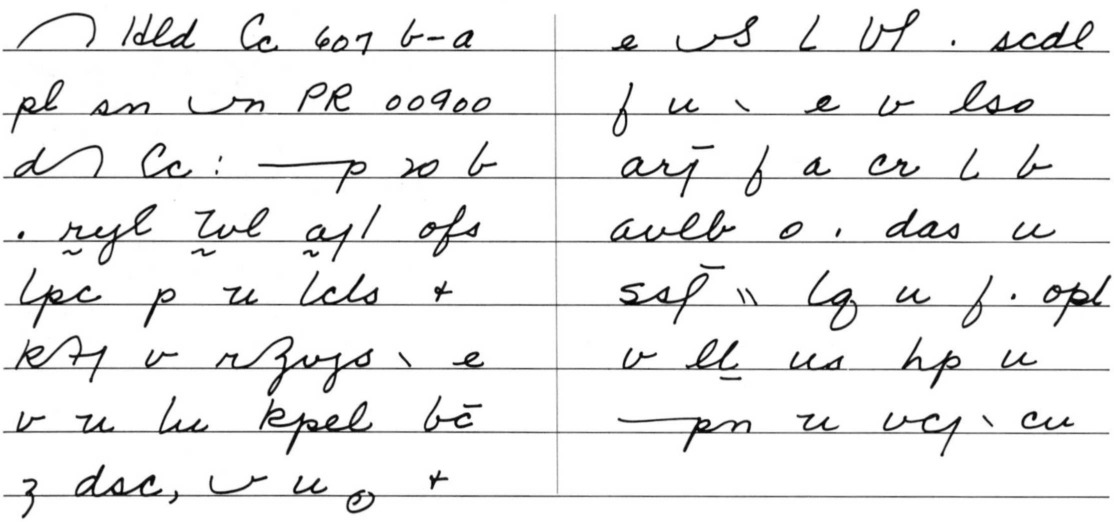

1.4 VOCABULARY BUILDING

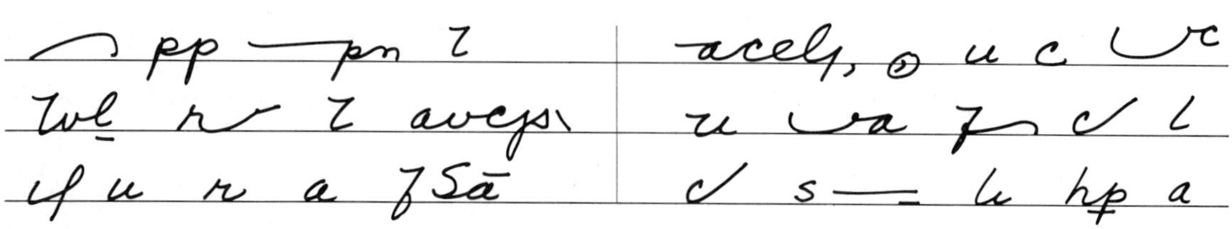

dgs vr 7 s lro
l a nd f a X
pr v h — — " St
n nu h S uc
d m . la v
ocpf v pv nhbl--
z u zde . gf
pls o 7d rus v
ndens hu vC
7 cda alq .
klcl rv vl l
p nu lfc za , u
c dq f nden rlcs
v . ll no gln
7lb hu rzd n
ula , hpl 7bln l
SC 7u sllc runs
o sec sins v .
nvf v . r—
ocpf lyns n apx
12 H ad " . Bdo ca
sus bcn . 7vl l
7/o vr uc fu El
ru + pcC Ses o
. ca vals , ull +
ges r ddca 7 efls
l . Vc v pzv .
sins v 7 Hl " a
vcq galfd n
dnk as Sā ls
sCls v El byl
csns , a no v
nus a va alq .
arben glf uc hp
sf El a . dlm
nden su — a h
uno clC n vn q,
a " a —sul l'
sd-y vcln so
Vc o acelycl sus
s a dnsc aC l Sn
ab. Hly v a c/ ,

2.1 THEORY REVIEW

1. *ble*

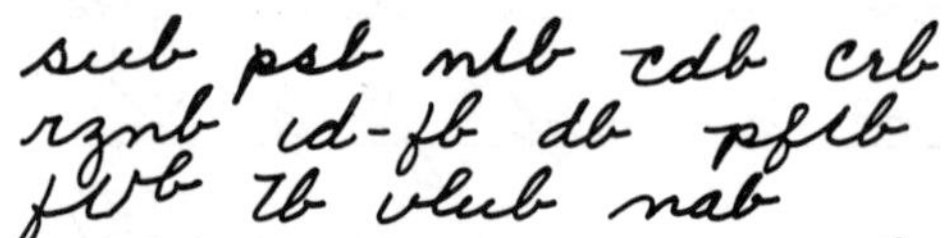

2. *hood*

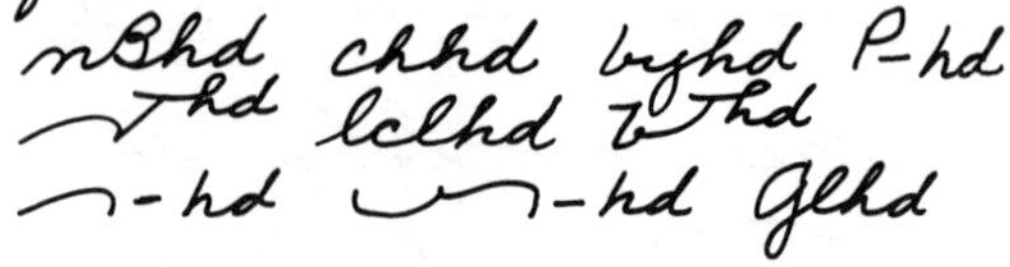

3. *ple*

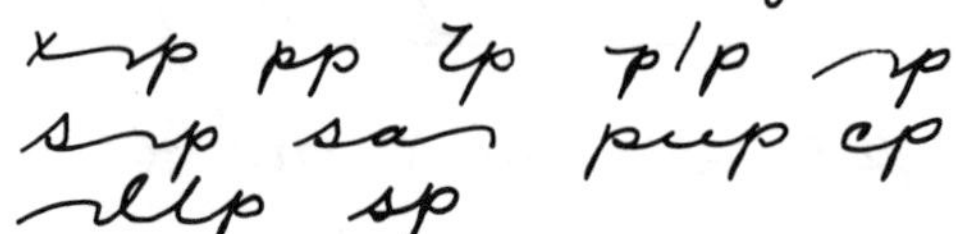

4. *bility*

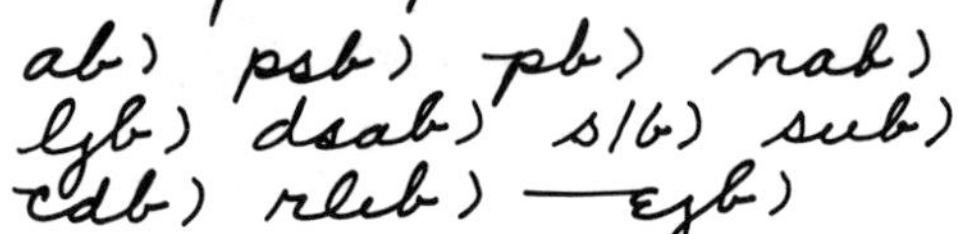

5. Brief forms

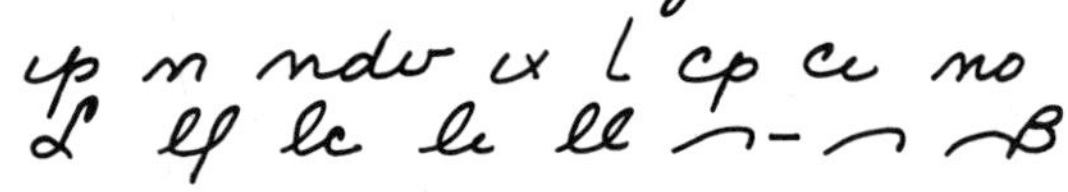

KEY 1. suitable; possible; notable; credible; creditable; reasonable; identifiable; double; profitable; favorable; trouble; valuable; enable 2. neighborhood; childhood; boyhood; parenthood; motherhood; likelihood; brotherhood; manhood; womanhood; girlhood 3. example; people; triple; principle, principal; ample; simple; sample; pupil; couple; multiple; supple 4. ability; possibility; probability; inability; legibility; disability; sensibility; suitability; credibility; reliability; eligibility 5. important; in, not; individual, ly; initial, ly; it, to; keep; kind; known; letter; life; like; line; little; man; many; member

2.2 TRANSCRIPTION SKILL BUILDING

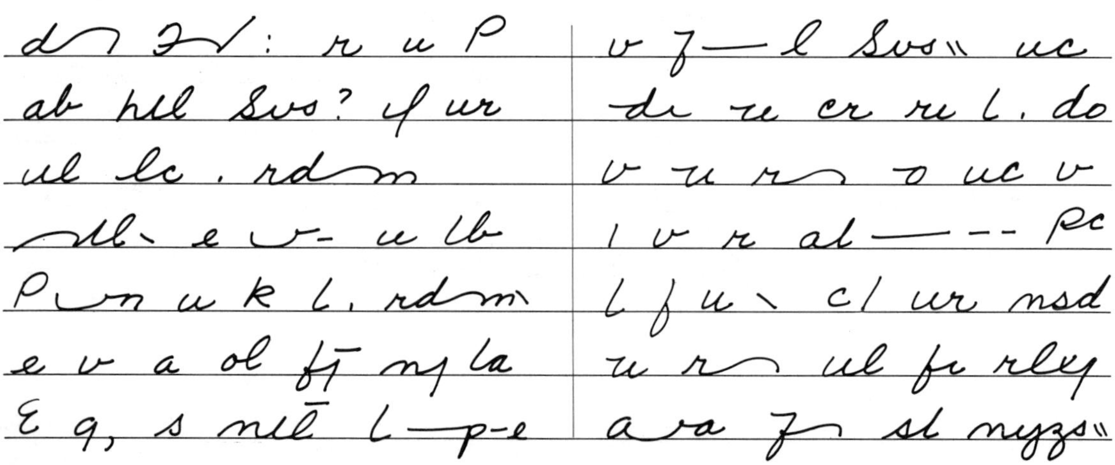

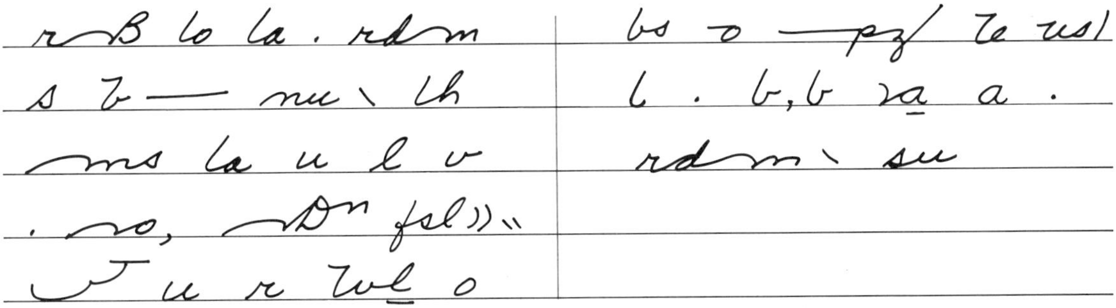

GUIDE Insert three introductory commas, one conjunction comma, two parenthetical commas, and one compound adjective hyphen.

2.3 SPEED BUILDING

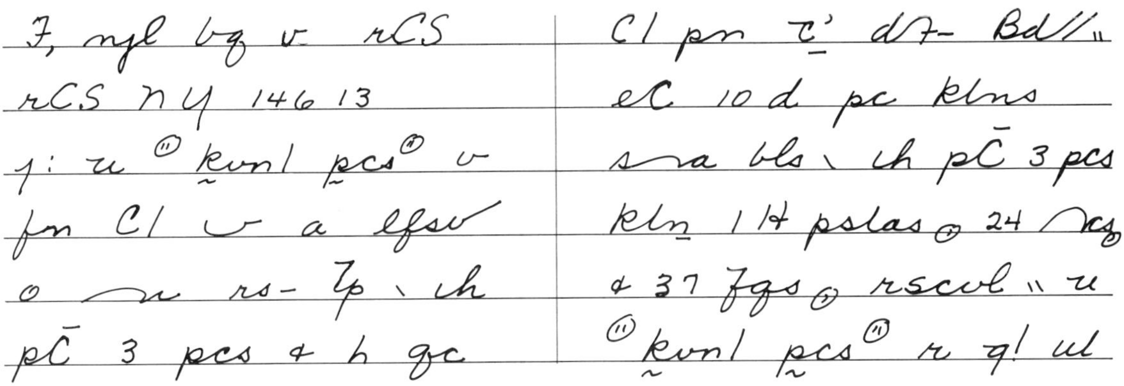

2.4 VOCABULARY BUILDING

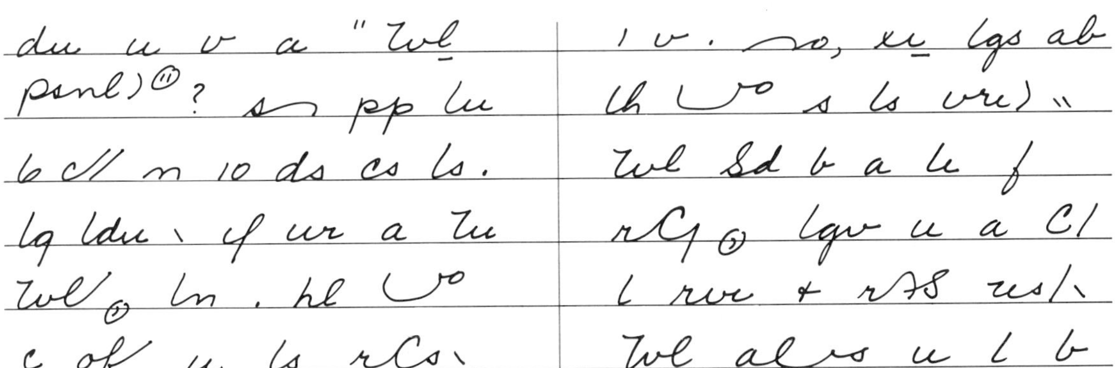

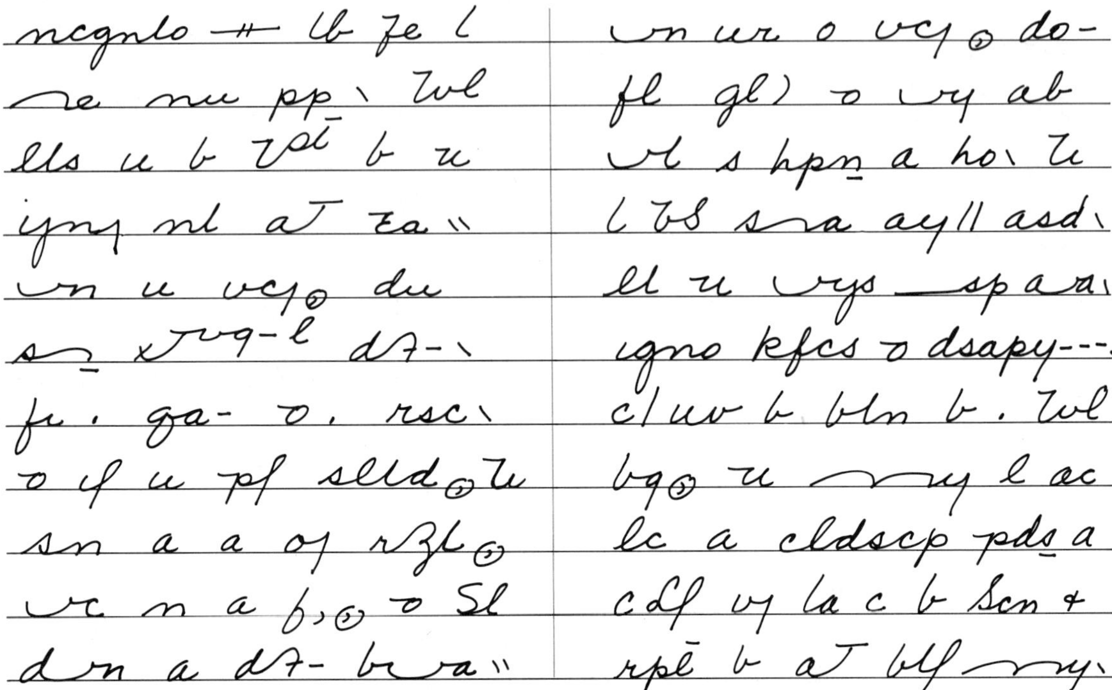

3.1 THEORY REVIEW

1. *vity*

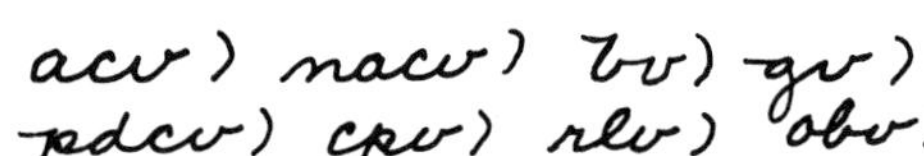

2. *sup*

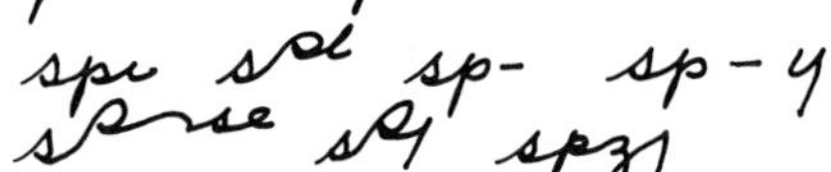

3. *ng*

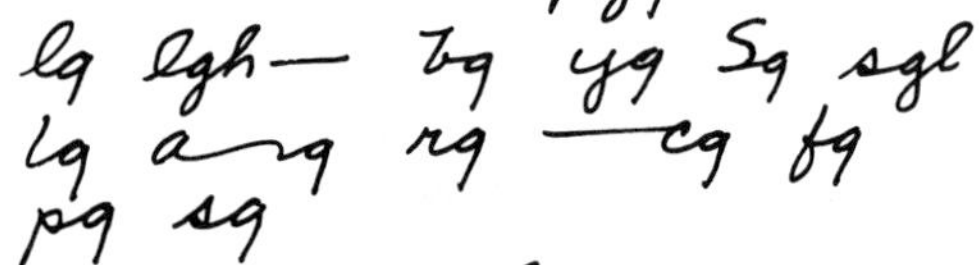

4. *nk*

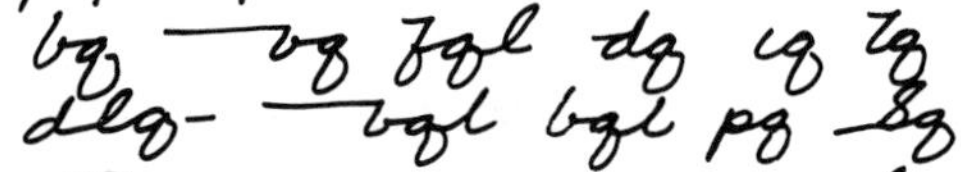

5. Brief forms

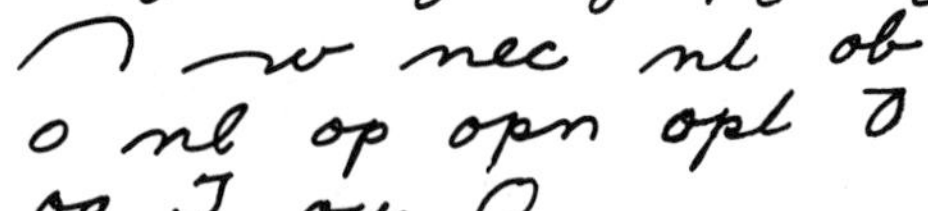

KEY 1. activity; inactivity; brevity; gravity; productivity; captivity; relativity; objectivity 2. supply; support; supplement; supplementary; supremacy; suppression; supposition 3. long; longhand; bring; young; strong; single; thing; among; ring,

wrong; clang; fang; pang; sing 4. bank; blank; frankly; drink; ink; trunk; delinquent; blanket; banquet; pink; shrink 5. million; move; necessary, necessarily; note; object; on; only; open; opinion; opportunity; order; organize, organization; other; out; over

3.2 TRANSCRIPTION SKILL BUILDING

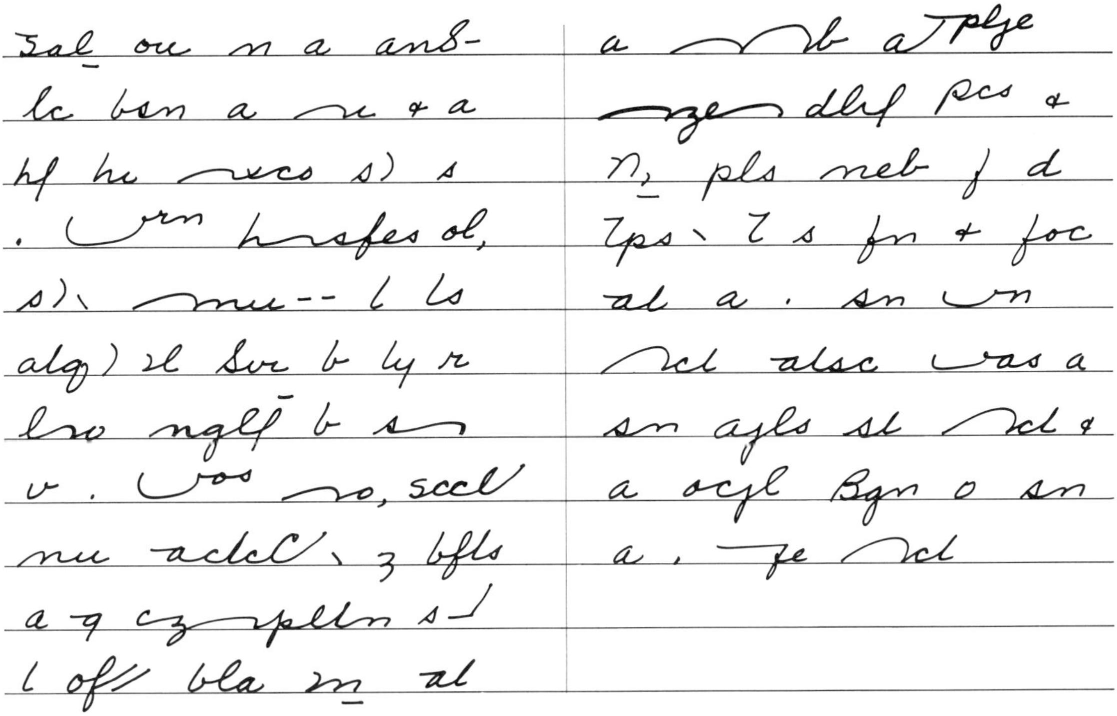

GUIDE Insert two introductory commas, one conjunction comma, six series commas, two possessive apostrophes, and one contraction apostrophe.

3.3 SPEED BUILDING

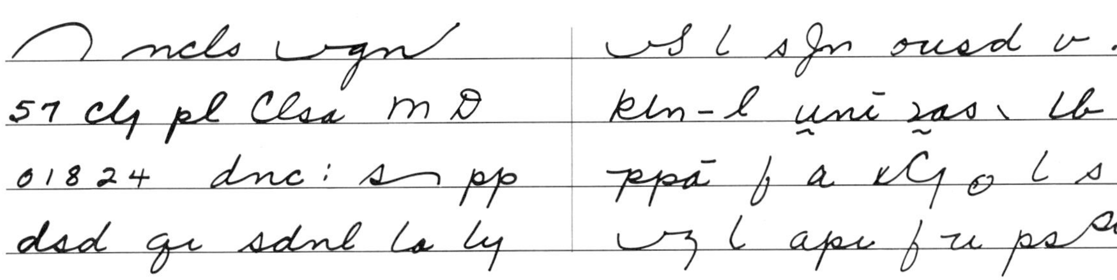

ru a ra " apc f a
psSl s , lsc a
adll —, du f hsl \
kpe . rqi s—p
f—s + s—l l—l
a —Cc v a fed o
ra Cl v a psSl
apl \ pz- puf v u
uni zas slzns " 2

dpcl flGfs no s—al
ln 2½ x 2½ ins + nofl
ln 3 x 3 ins r rqi \ lz
—, ncd . apc-- sig
o . lf h— sd " a 12d
fe s Cq f a psSl vC
s vld f 7 ys \ zsnz u
rse u psSl sin l vr
ndca \ Iz ls n lgl \ su

3.4 VOCABULARY BUILDING

pp Tvl cs ly v- dt-
xpyll \ ly v- l 2—
a hScl sls \ ly v- l
rde dt- ssu)) \ ly
—a Tvl cs ly vS l
nyy . fed— v v—!
Tu vr —= sls v fn
s)) " f . h— cp psn
Tvl z a 7Sa upz-
hsl z h Ti l —cl
ol bss v hu rps o
z uab lgl nsd —zers

v —fs v rps cs v
b kfi l a vlCa "
—pn lus r n— dzin
f . Tb— + h— cp la
r z dVs z 9 o a aTcn
sTe l dun a . ufl
V \ bss r dzin v
r—ps + vd —rs
l akda vlCas o
rCs \ lz r hpfl kdjs
f a no v sr slzns
hu vS l Tvl a a

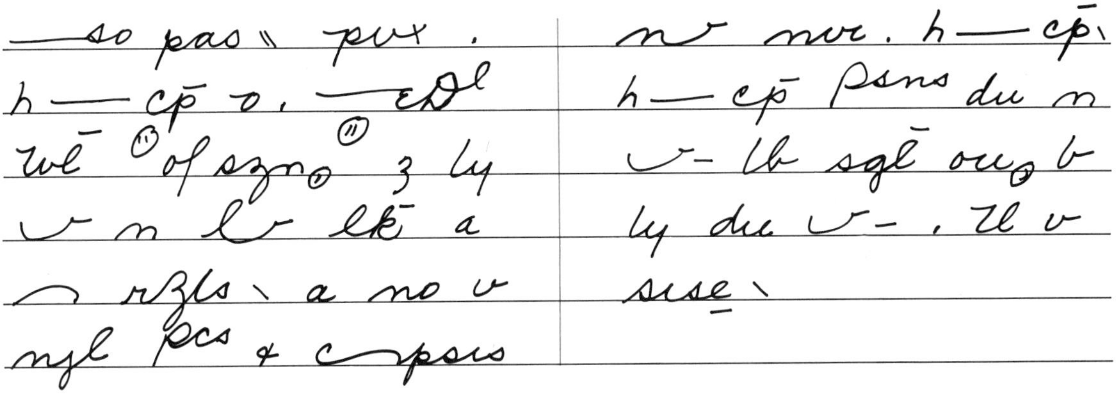

4.1 THEORY REVIEW

1. *circum* 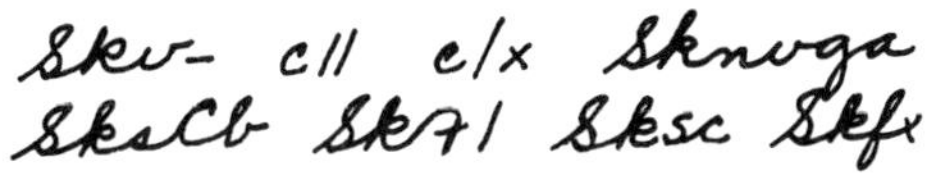

2. *work* 

3. *man* 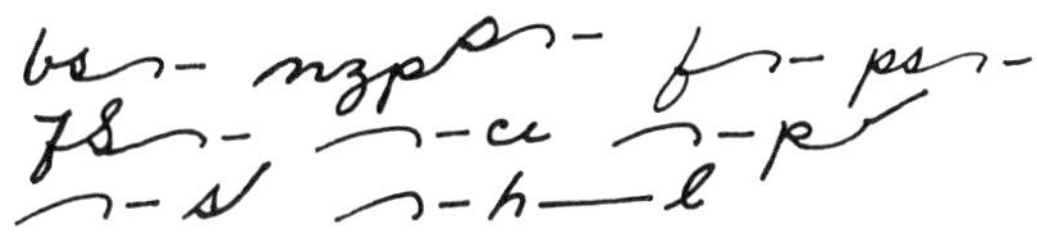

4. *super* 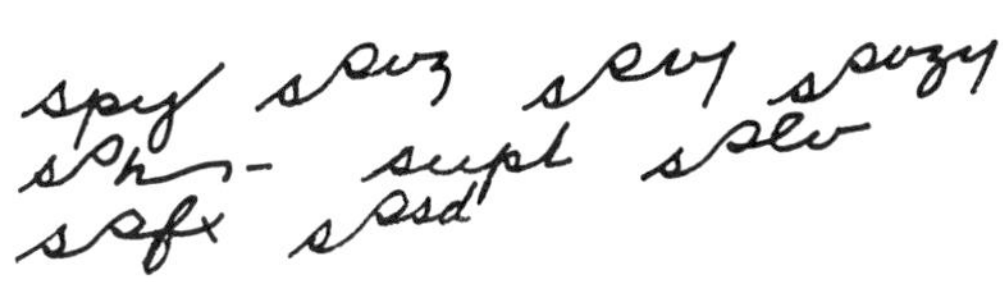

5. Brief forms 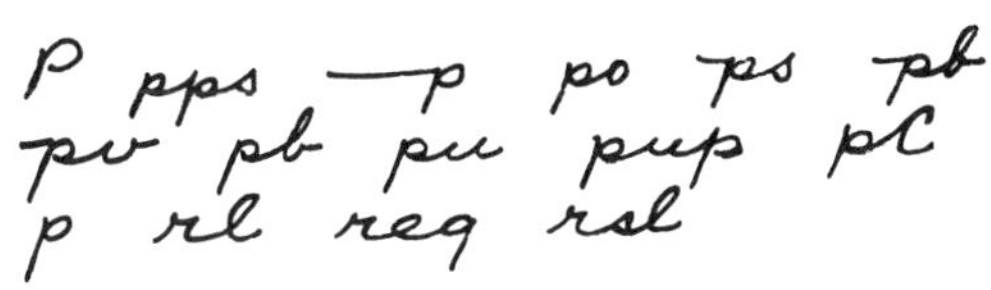

KEY 1. circumvent; circumstances; circumstantial; circumnavigate; circumscribe; circumference; circumspect; circumflex 2. network; framework; overwork; teamwork; guesswork; workmen; workers; workout; workshop 3. businessman; newspaperman; foreman; postman; freshman; mankind; manpower; manslaughter; manhandle 4. superior; supervise; supervision; supervisory; superhuman; superintendent; superlative; superficial, superfluous; supersede 5. particular, ly; perhaps; please; poor; price; probable, ly; prove; public, publish; pull; pupil; purchase; put, up; real, ly; regular, ly, regulation; result

4.2 TRANSCRIPTION SKILL BUILDING

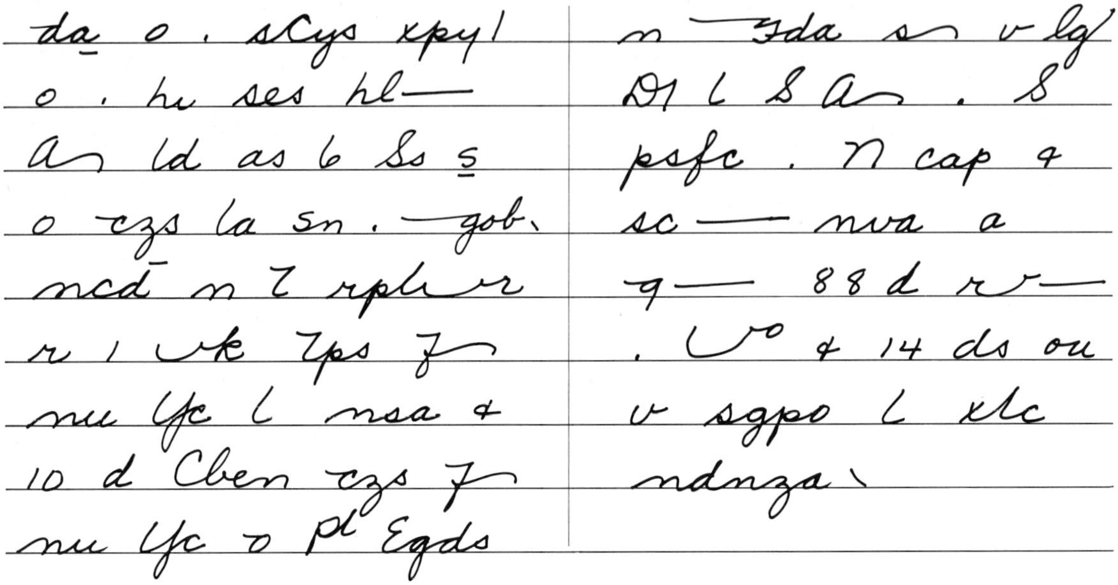

GUIDE Insert one introductory comma, three series commas, one possessive apostrophe, three compound adjective hyphens, and three internal punctuation semicolons.

4.3 SPEED BUILDING

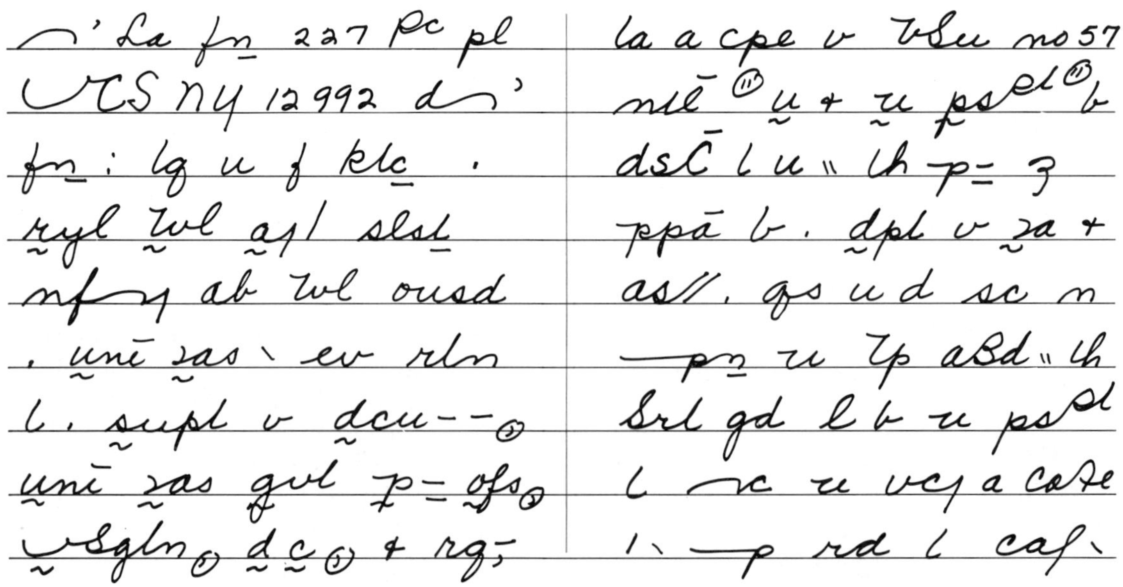

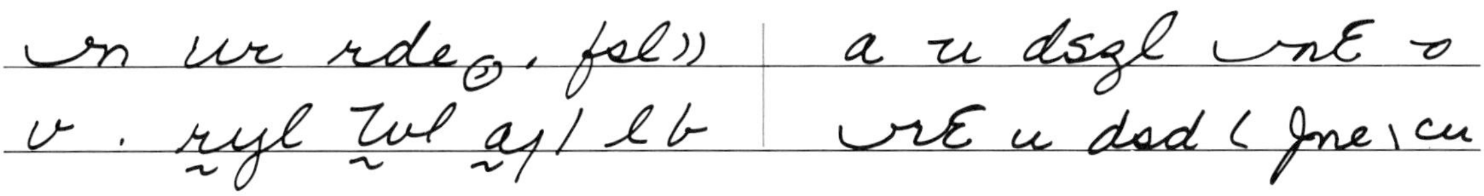

4.4 VOCABULARY BUILDING

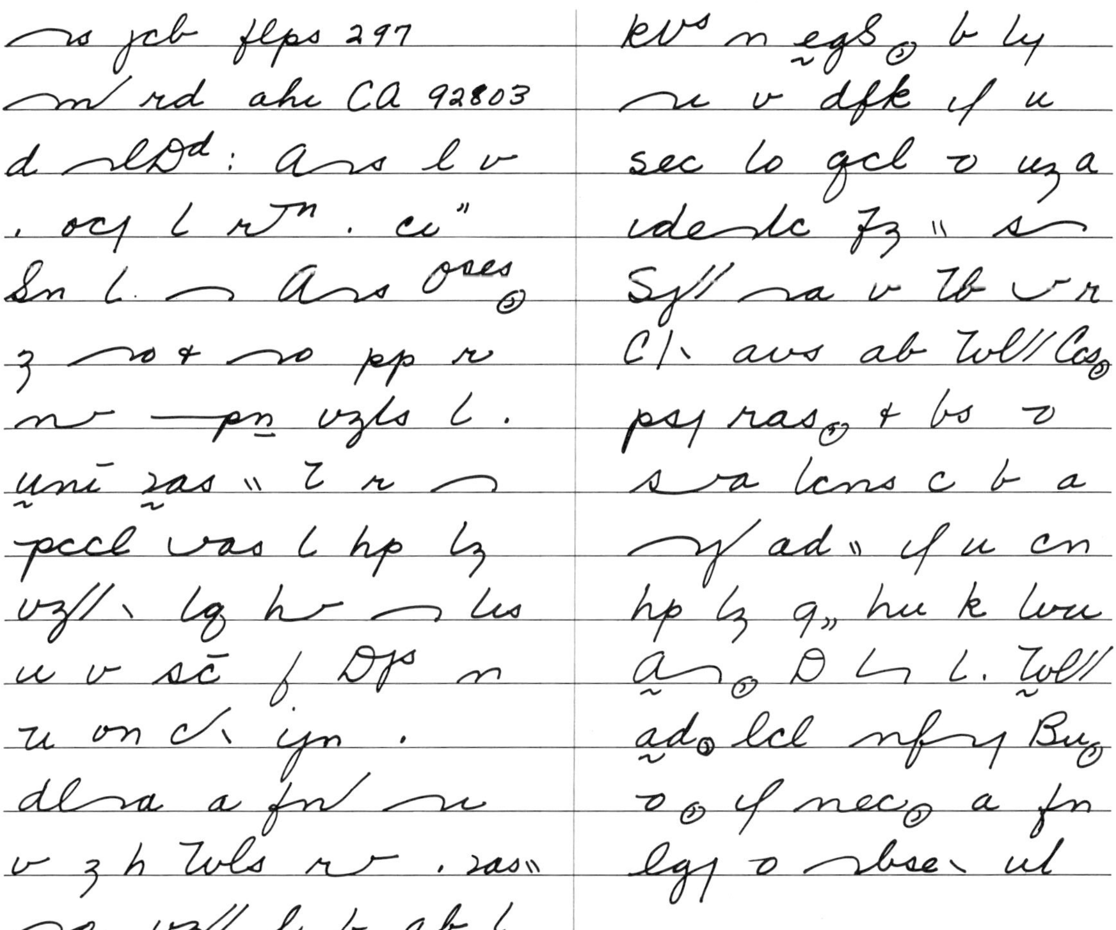

5.1 THEORY REVIEW

1. *post*

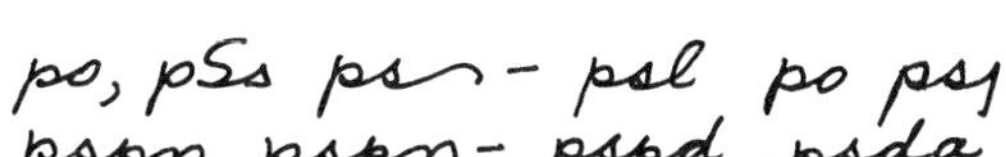

2. *fer*

3. *ish*

4. *ser*

5. Brief forms

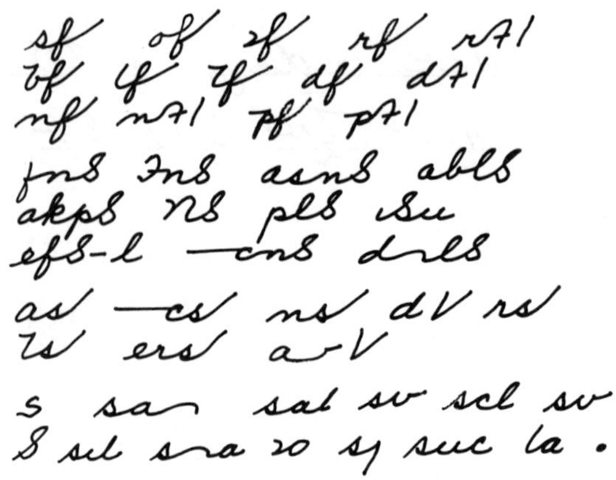

KEY 1. post; posters; postman; postal; post office; postage; postpone; postponement; postpaid; postdate 2. suffer, safer; offer; stuffer; rougher, refer; reference; briefer; tougher; transfer; differ; difference; infer; inference; prefer; preference 3. finish; furnish; astonish; abolish; accomplish; nourish; polish; issue; efficiently; clannish; demolish 4. answer; closer; nicer; dancer; racer; tracer; eraser; announcer 5. sale, sail; sample; satisfy, satisfactory, satisfaction; save; school; several; she, shall, ship; situation; small; stop; subject; success, successful, ly; that; the

5.2 TRANSCRIPTION SKILL BUILDING

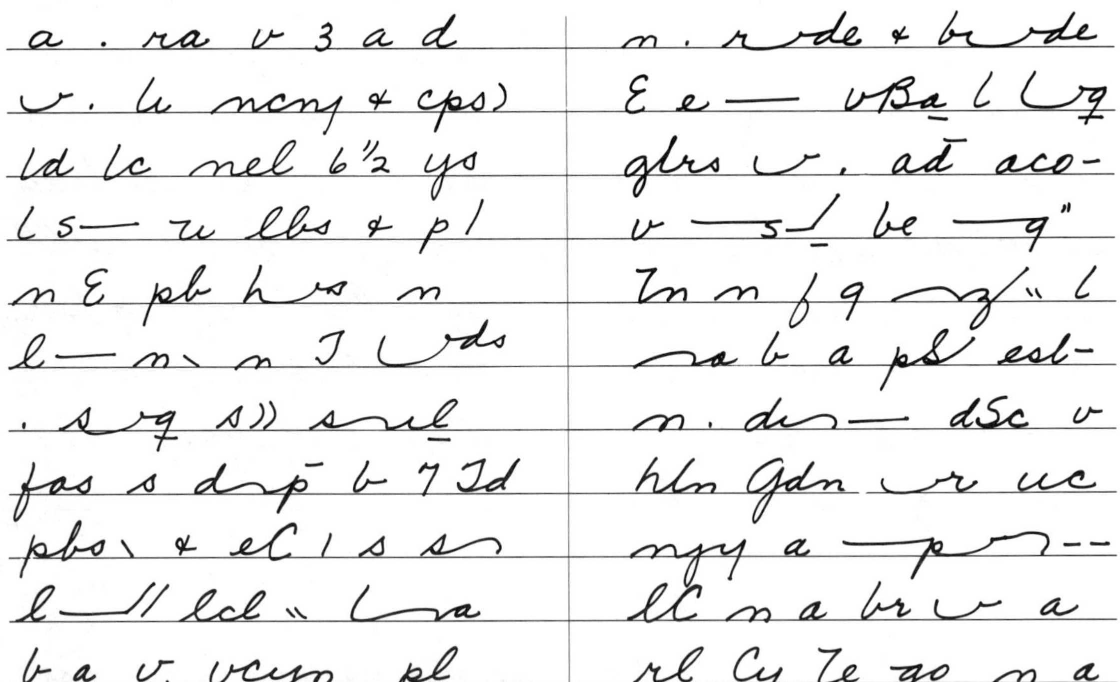

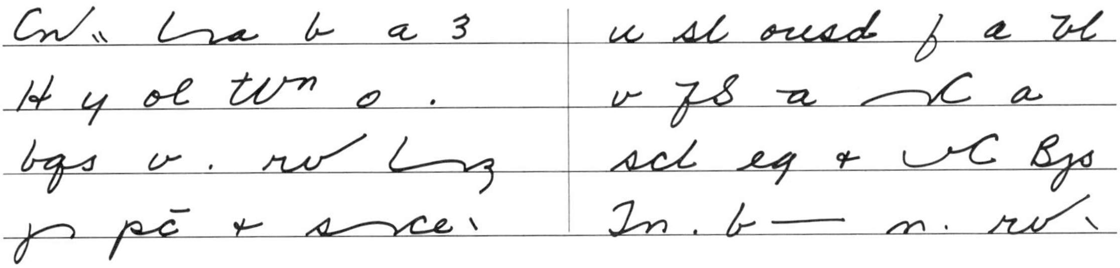

GUIDE Insert four series commas, two introductory commas, three parenthetical commas, one numbers comma, three possessive apostrophes, and two compound adjective hyphens.

5.3 SPEED BUILDING

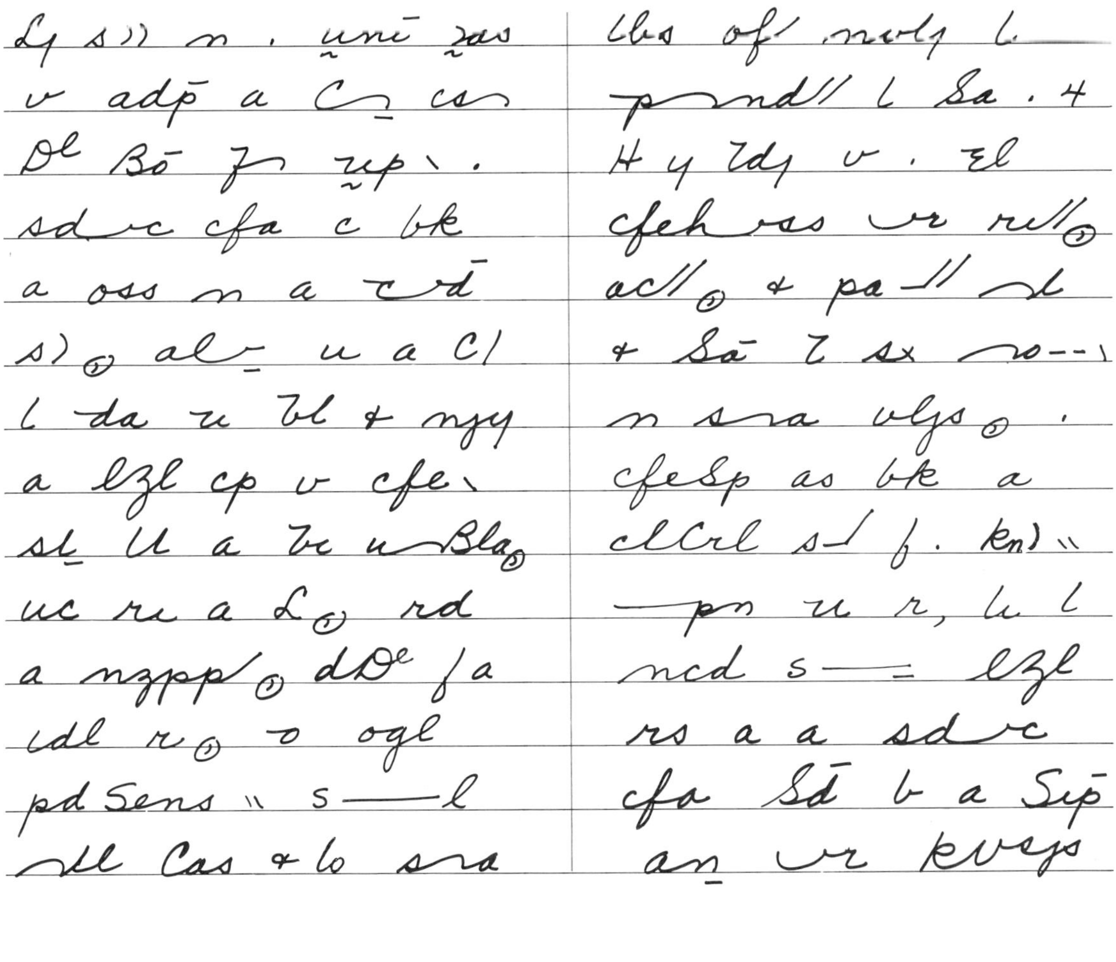

5.4 VOCABULARY BUILDING

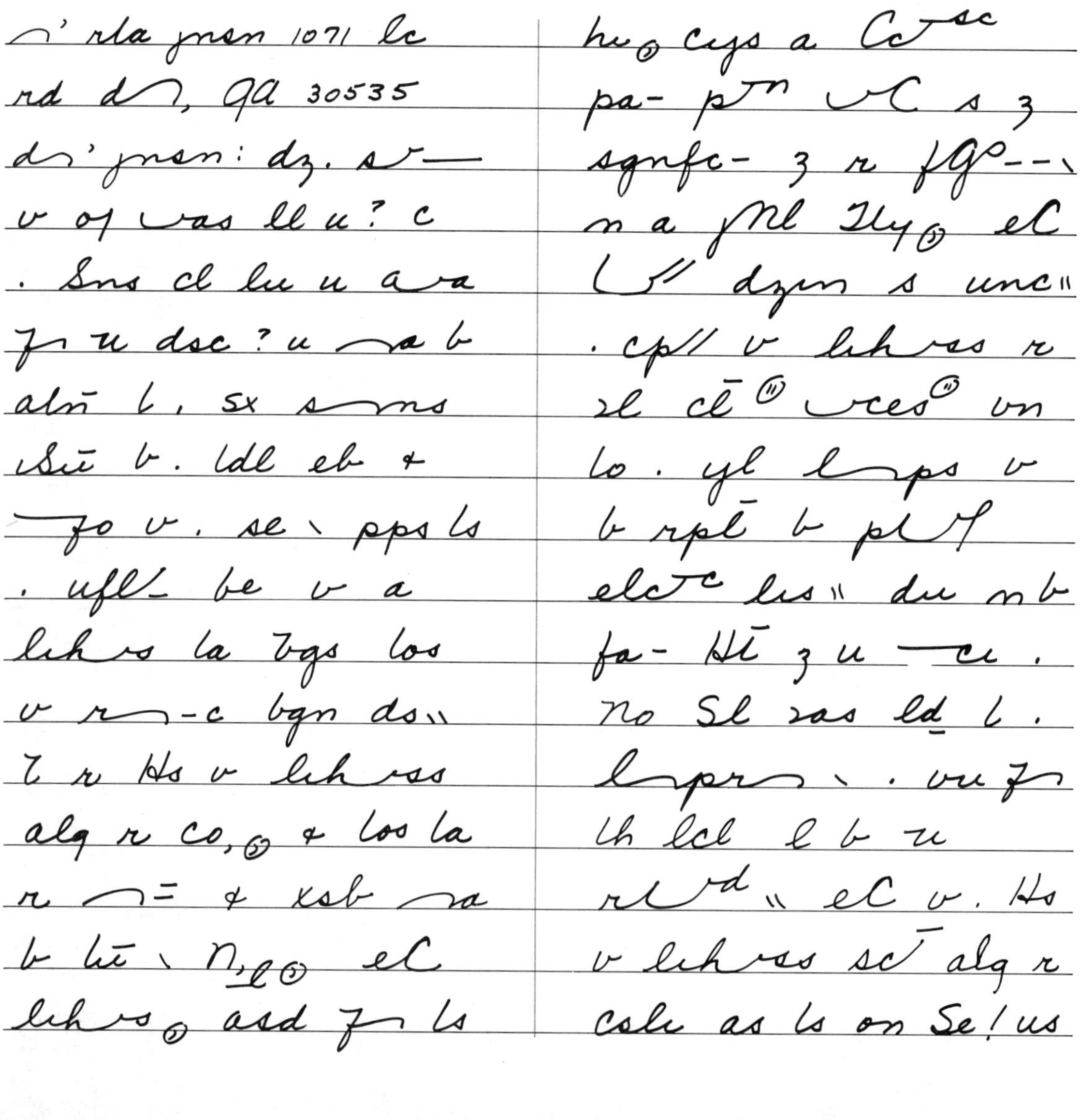

SMITH, KING & COMPANY
BROADWAY AND RIVER STREET
CAMBRIDGE, MASSACHUSETTS 02100

Niagara Prospect Company
Attention: Mr. Norman Chambers
105 32d Street
Niagara Falls, NY 14305

Niagara Falls, NY 14305

Attention: Mr. Norman Chambers

Gentlemen:

SUBJECT: Care of typewriters

I am glad to learn that the trouble you have had with your new machines has been corrected and that they are now in good working order.

May I suggest that you consider our annual maintenance service. This contract not only covers emergency calls but also provides for periodic inspection by one of our factory-trained men, who will clean and oil your machines and maintain them in tiptop condition.

A booklet describing this plan is enclosed. If you have any questions after reading it, please feel free to call.

Sincerely yours,

SMITH, KING & COMPANY

L. R. Barnum, President

LRB:hr
Enclosure

SUBMITTING LETTERS FOR SIGNATURE

Place the envelope face up over the top of the letter with enclosures attached for presentation to the dictator for signing.

File copies are stapled on top of the letters being answered. If the executive likes to have the carbon copies submitted with originals, they are placed under the originals.

Urgent letters are submitted as soon as they are finished; others are submitted several times a day, rather than all at once.

UNIT 15

DECORATING AND DESIGN

1.1 THEORY REVIEW

1. *ort*
2. *sive*
3. *tract*
4. *th*
5. Brief forms

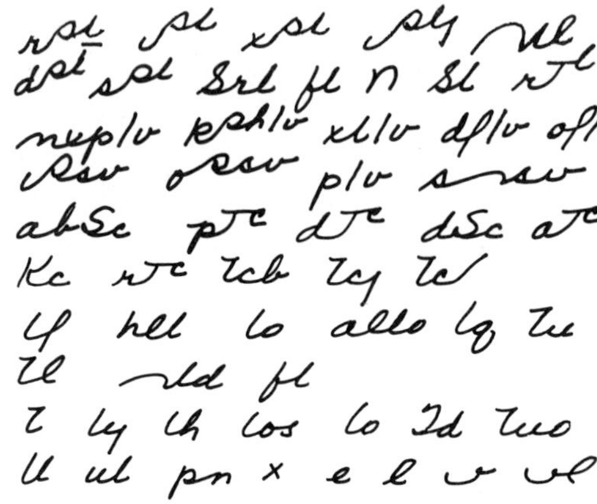

KEY 1. reporting; import; export; importation; mortal; deport; support; short; fort; north; sort; retort 2. inexpensive; comprehensive; extensive; defensive; offensive; impressive; oppressive; pensive; submissive 3. abstract; protract; detract; distract; attract; contract; retract; tractable; traction; tractor 4. theft; health; though; although; think; through; thrill; method; forth 5. their, there; they; this; those; too, thought; thousand; throughout; under; until; upon; usual, ly; we; will, well; were, with; while

1.2 TRANSCRIPTION SKILL BUILDING

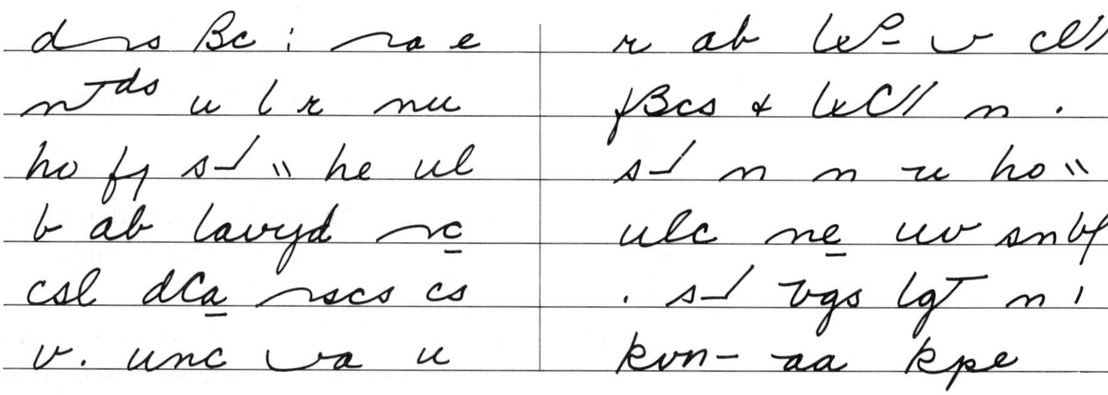

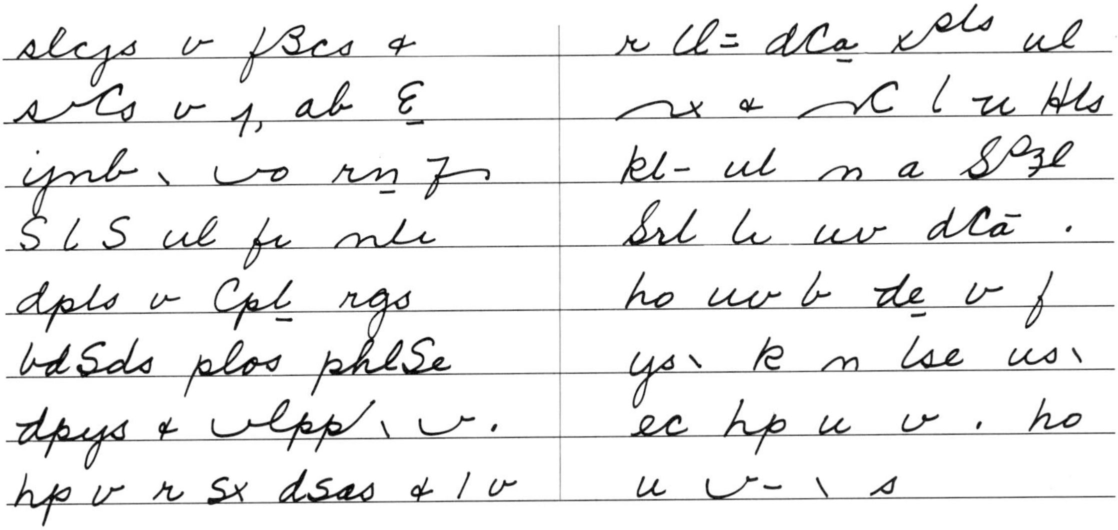

GUIDE Insert one possessive apostrophe, eight series commas, three parenthetical commas, and three introductory commas.

1.3 SPEED BUILDING

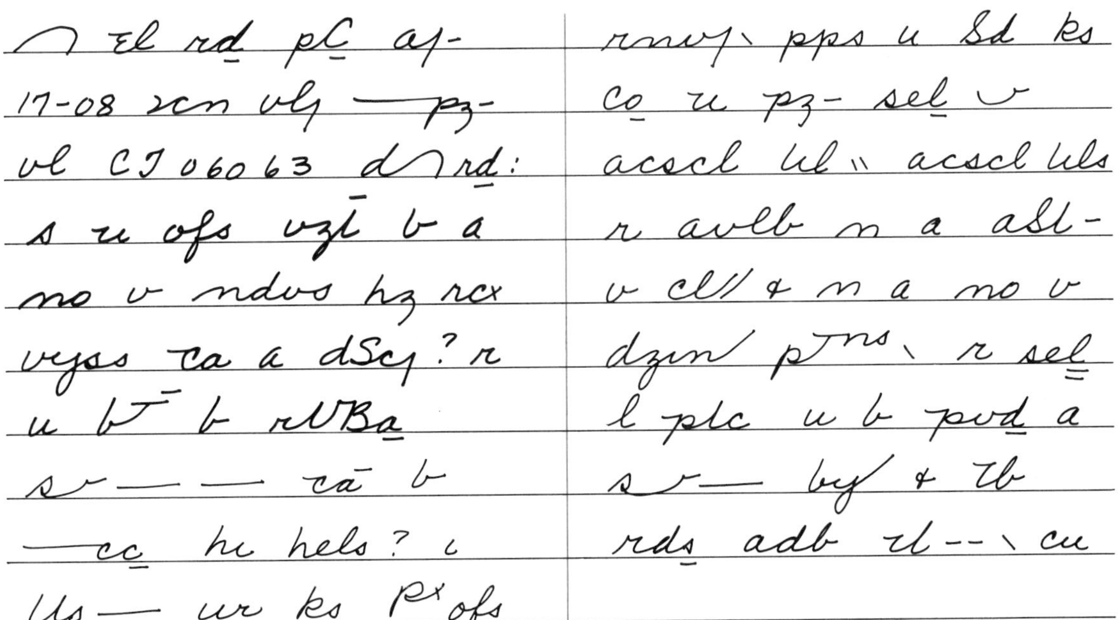

1.4 VOCABULARY BUILDING

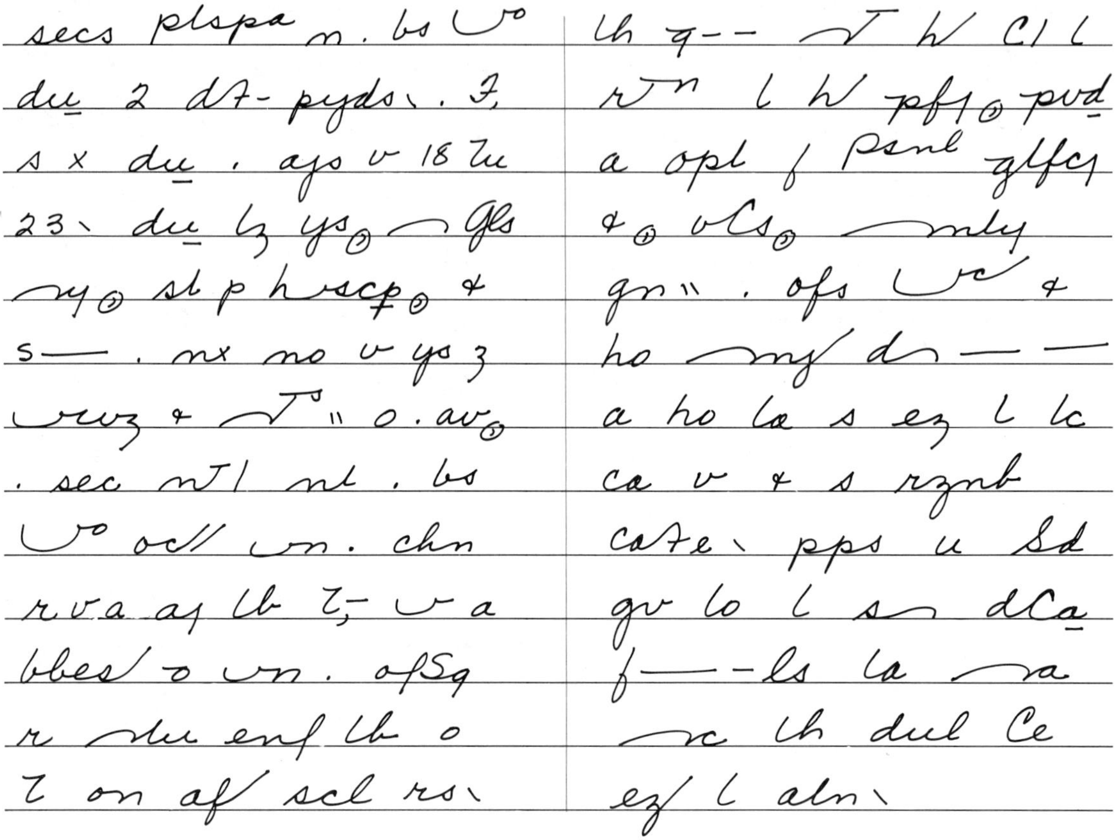

2.1 THEORY REVIEW

1. *sist*
2. *ward*
3. *inter*
4. *ness*
5. Brief forms

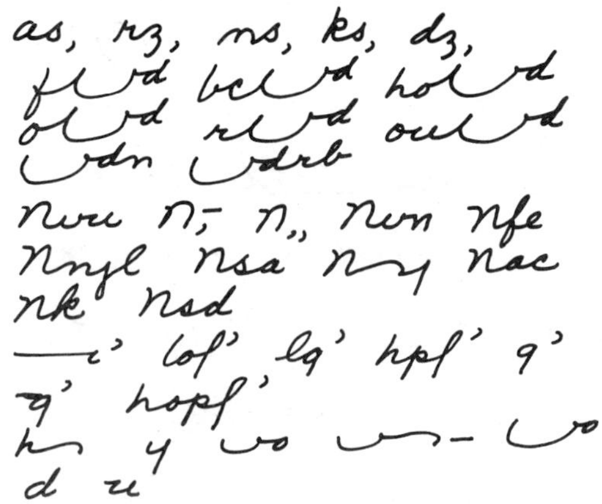

KEY 1. assist; resist; insist; consist; desist 2. forward; backward; homeward; onward; reward; outward; warden; wardrobe 3. interview; interested; interests; intervene; interfere; international; interstate; intermission; interact; intercom; intercede 4. illness; thoughtfulness; willingness; helpfulness; goodness; greatness; hopefulness 5. whom; why; without; woman; world; would; your

2.2 TRANSCRIPTION SKILL BUILDING

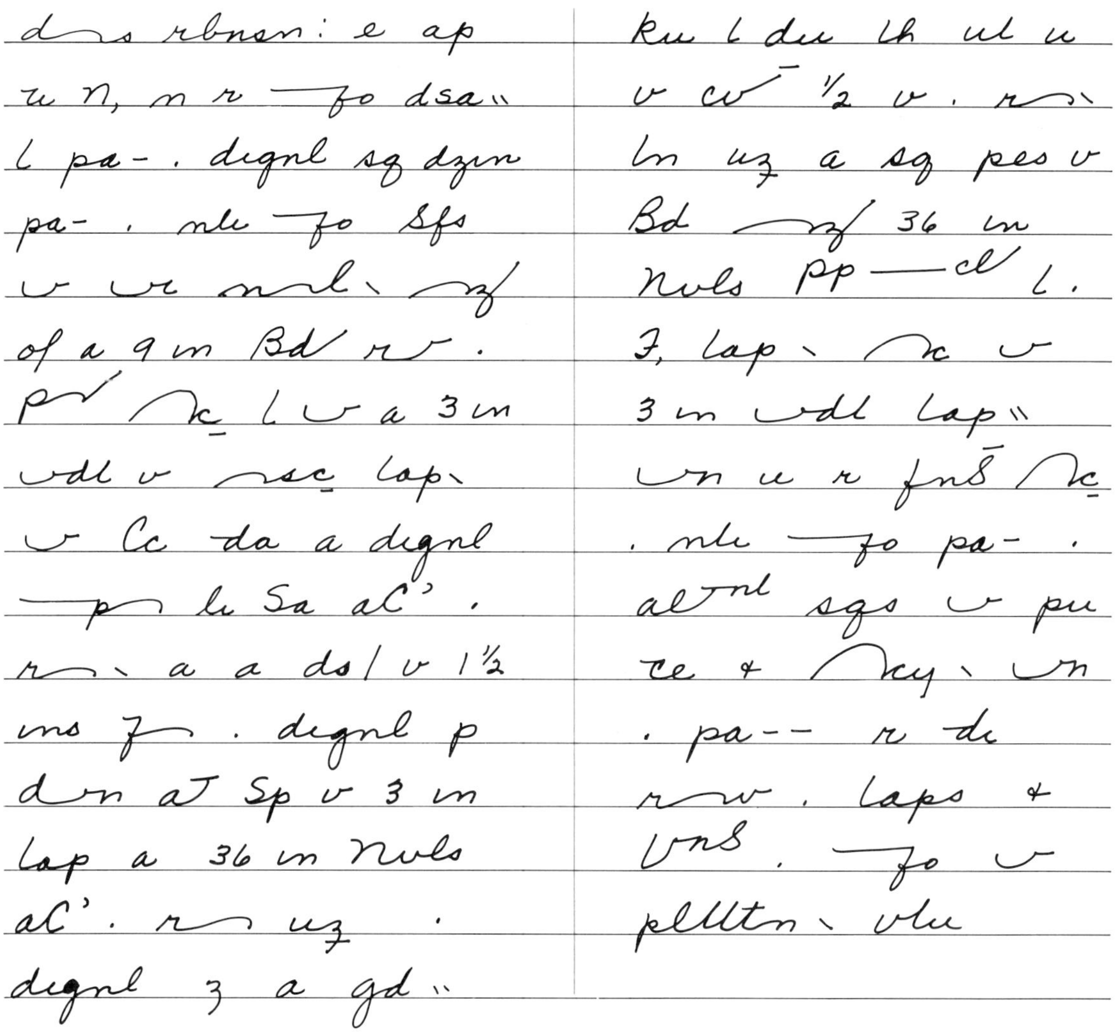

GUIDE Insert six introductory commas, three parenthetical commas, and six compound adjective hyphens.

2.3 SPEED BUILDING

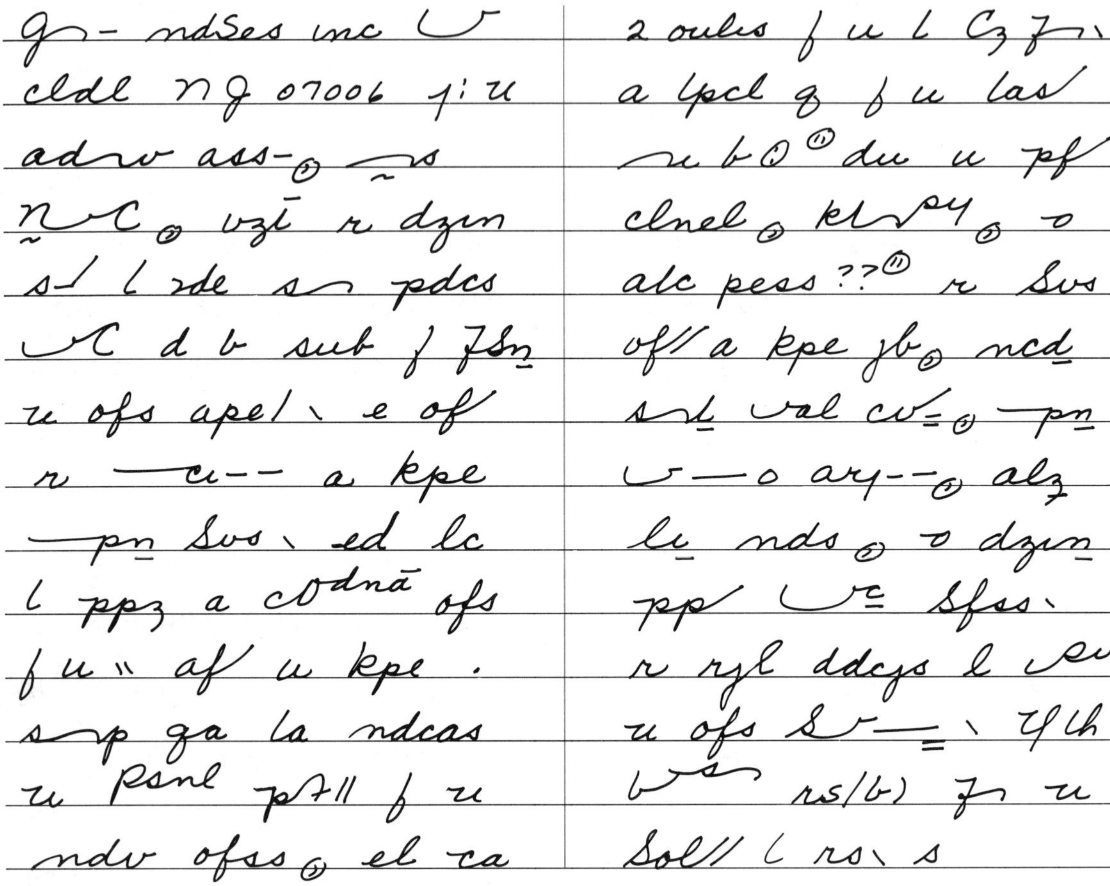

2.4 VOCABULARY BUILDING

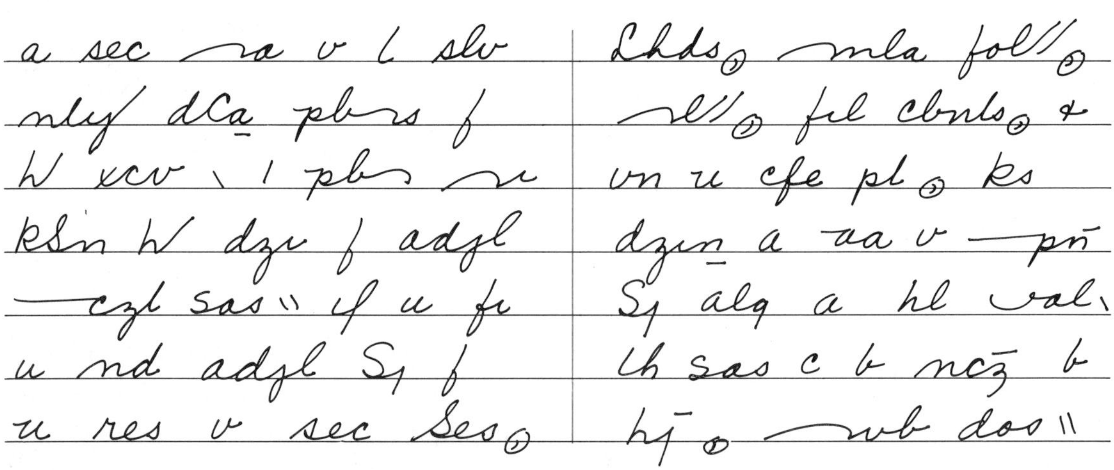

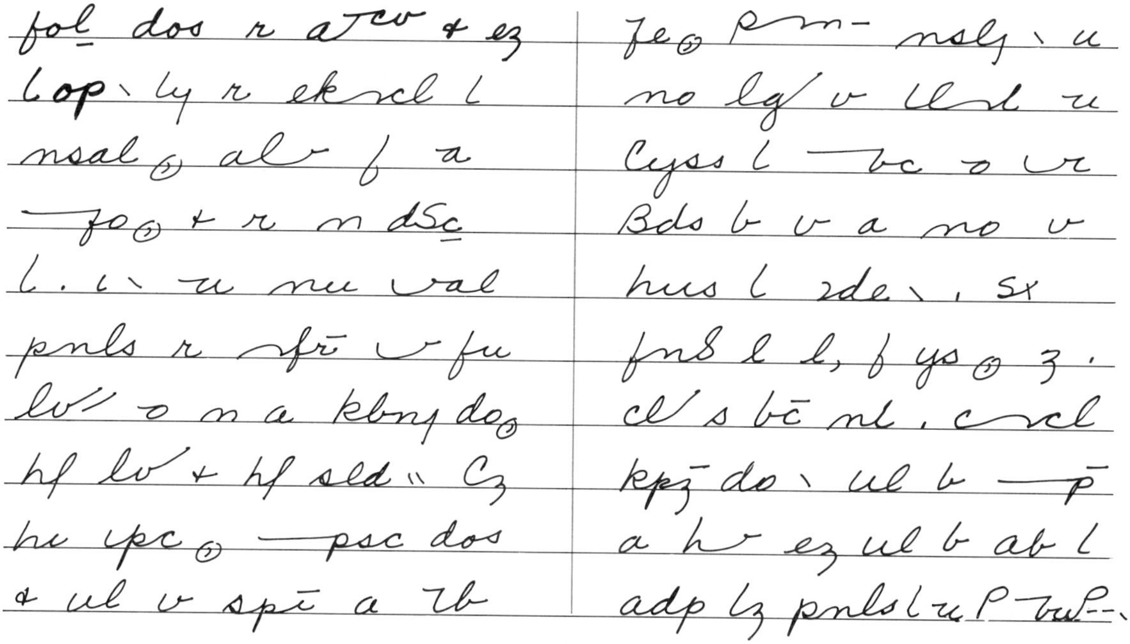

3.1 THEORY REVIEW

1. *vent* 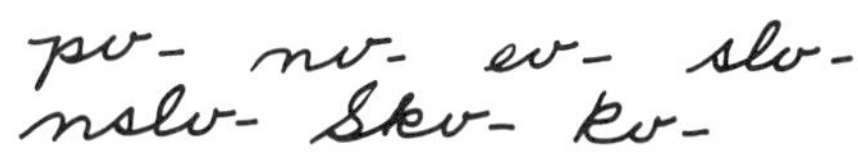

2. *point* 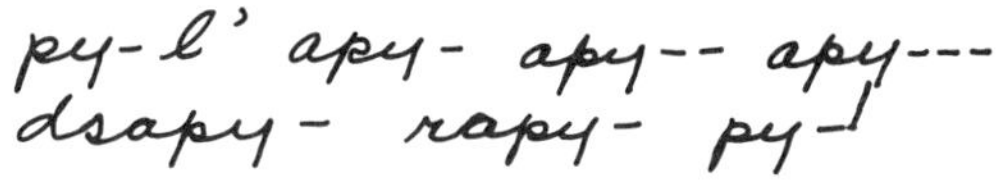

3. *gram* 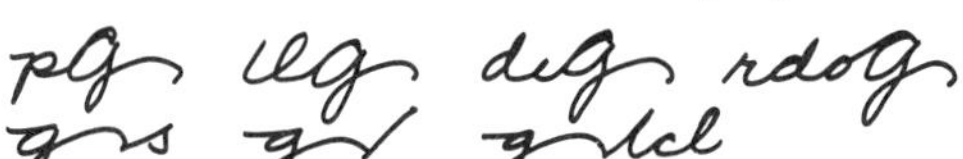

4. *shully* 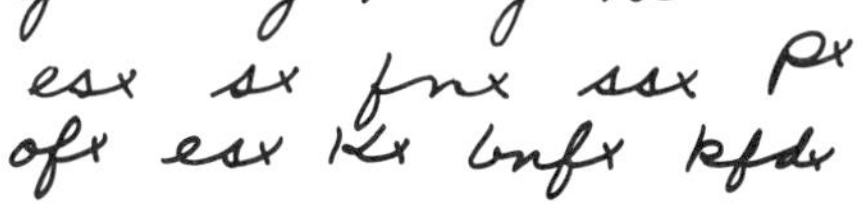

5. *us* 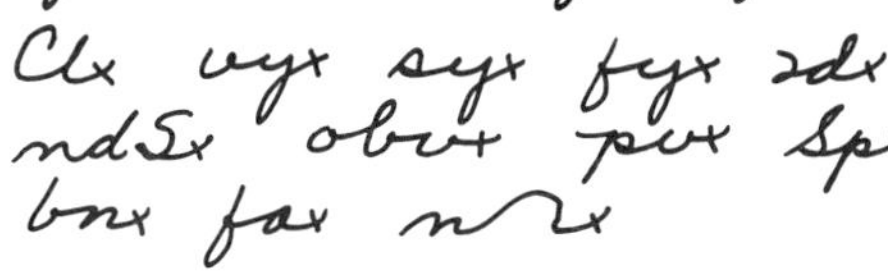

KEY 1. prevent; invent; event; solvent; insolvent; circumvent; convent 2. pointless; appoint; appointment; appointments; disappoint; reappoint; pointer 3. program; telegram; diagram; radiogram; grams; grammar; grammatical 4. essentially; socially; financially; substantially; partially; officially; essentially; commercially; beneficially; confidentially 5. courteous; various; serious; furious; studious; industrious; obvious; previous; surplus; bonus; famous; numerous

3.2 TRANSCRIPTION SKILL BUILDING

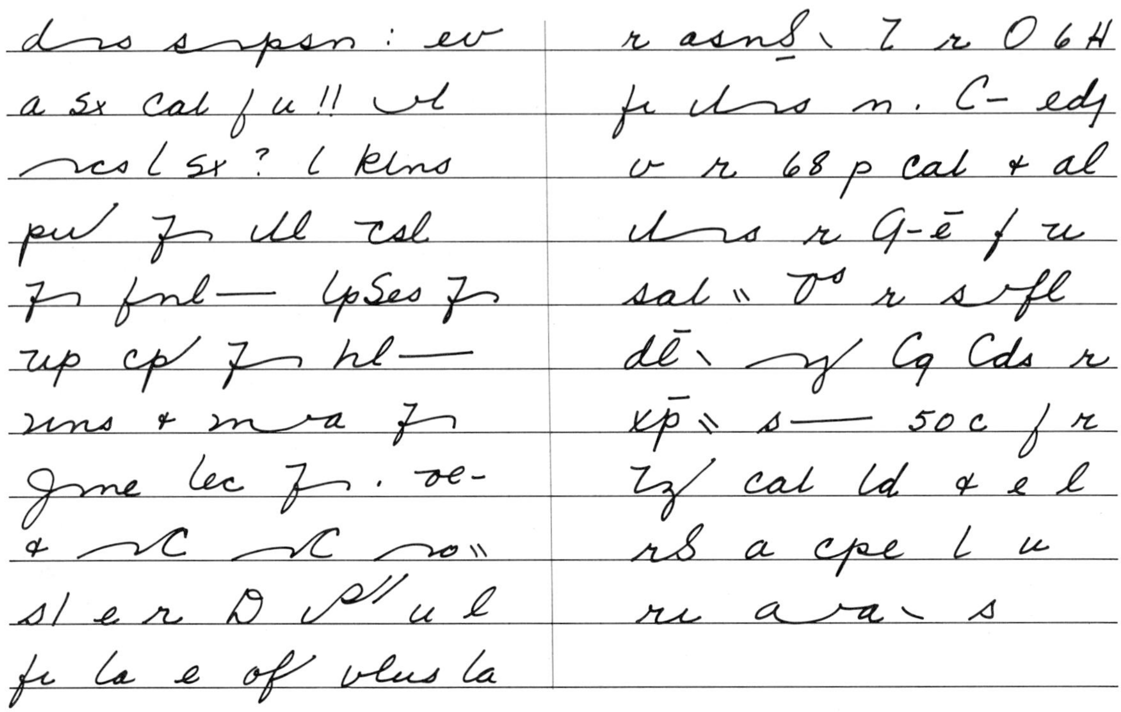

GUIDE Insert six series commas, two conjunction commas, one adjective comma, one introductory comma, and one compound adjective hyphen.

3.3 SPEED BUILDING

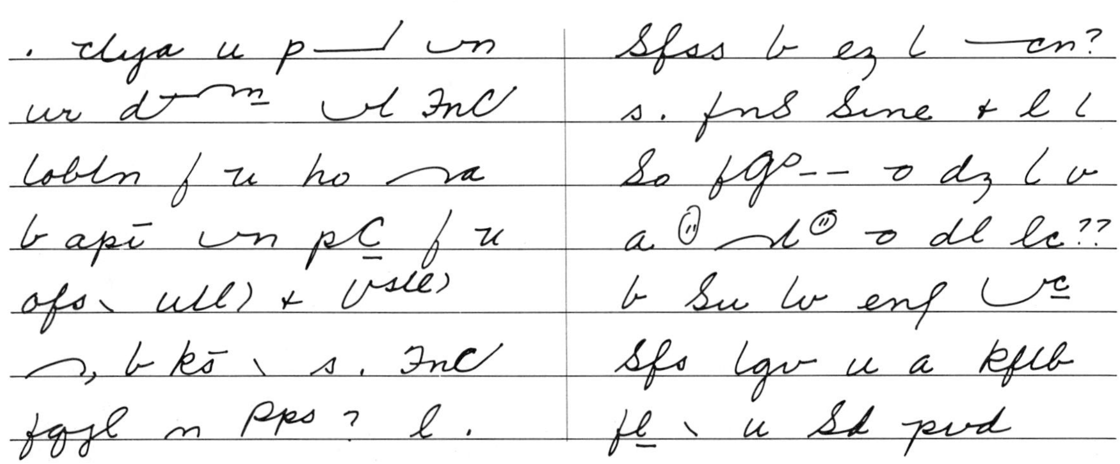

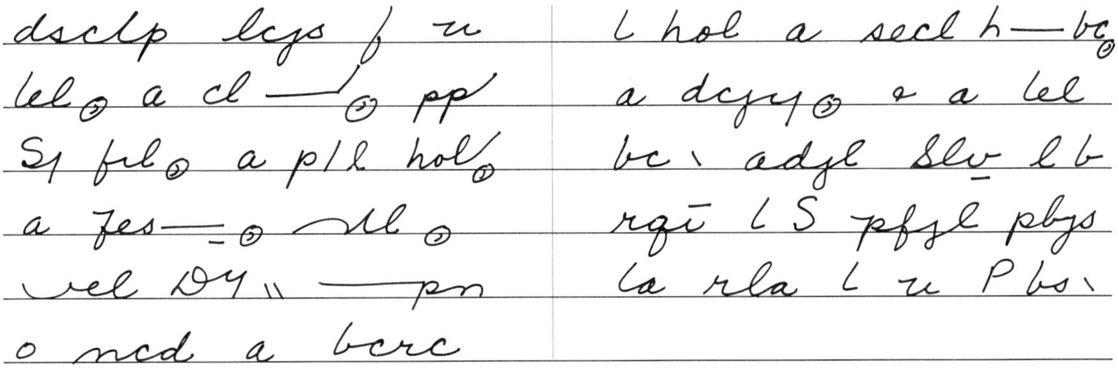

3.4 VOCABULARY BUILDING

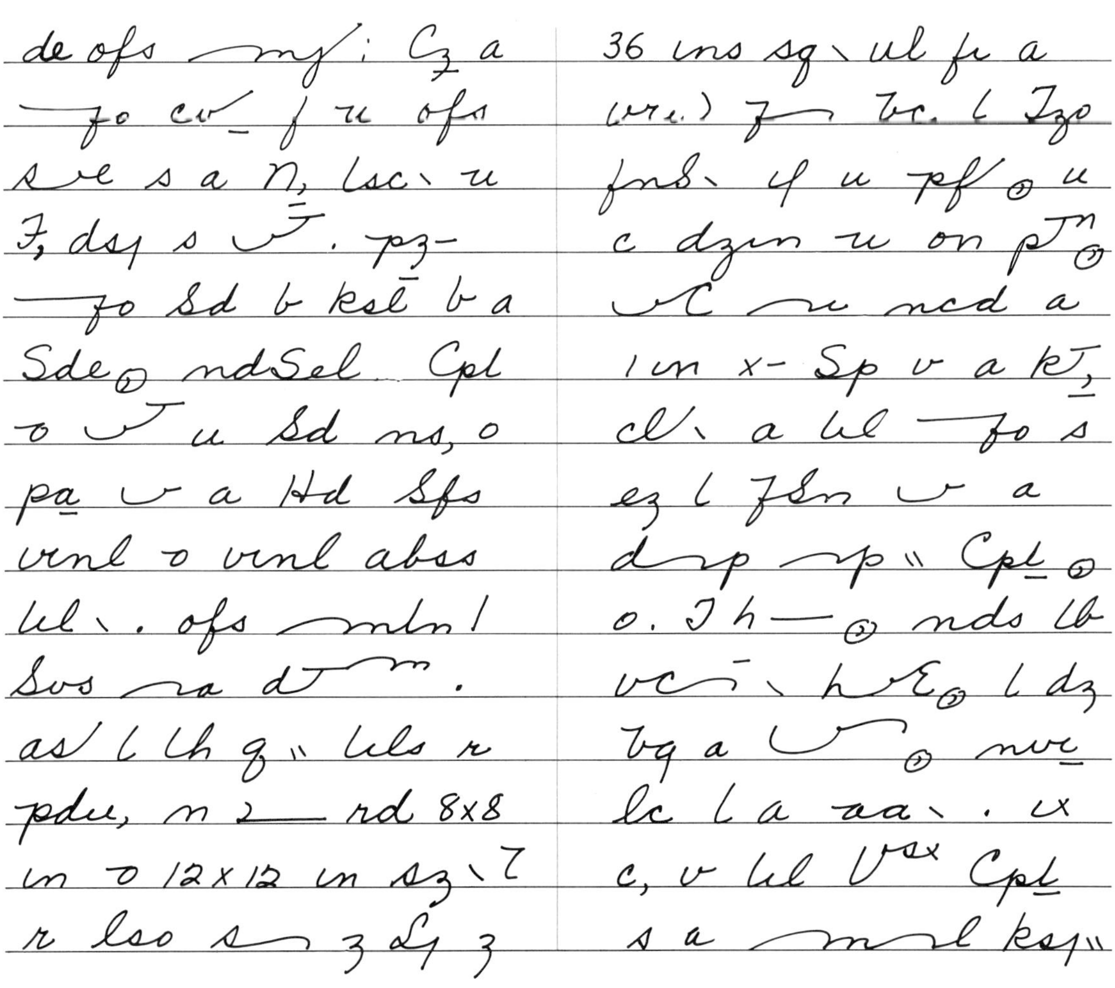

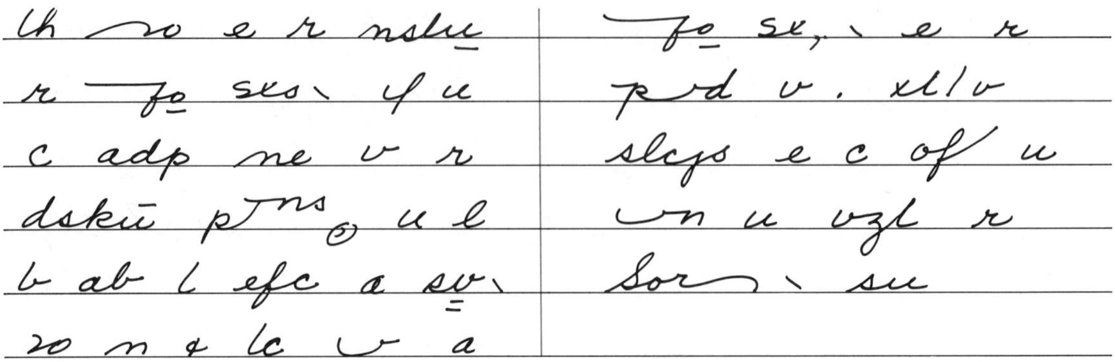

4.1 THEORY REVIEW

1. *fy*
2. *ize*
3. *tee*
4. *th*
5. *fer*

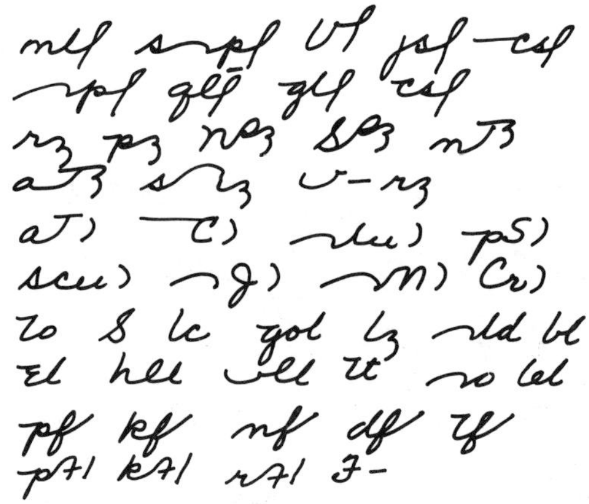

KEY 1. notify; simplify; verify; justify; classify; amplify; qualified; gratify; crucify 2. rise; prize; enterprise; surprise; notarize; authorize; summarize; winterize 3. authority; clarity; maturity; prosperity; security; majority; minority; charity 4. throw; south; thick; growth; these; method; bath; earth; health; wealth; threat; month; teeth 5. prefer; confer; infer; defer; transfer; preference; conference; reference; ferment

4.2 TRANSCRIPTION SKILL BUILDING

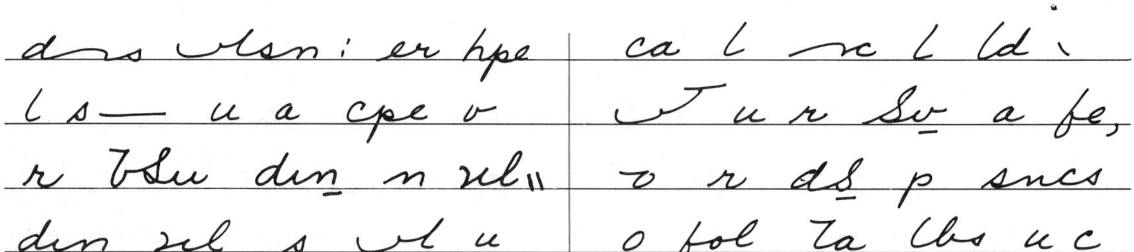

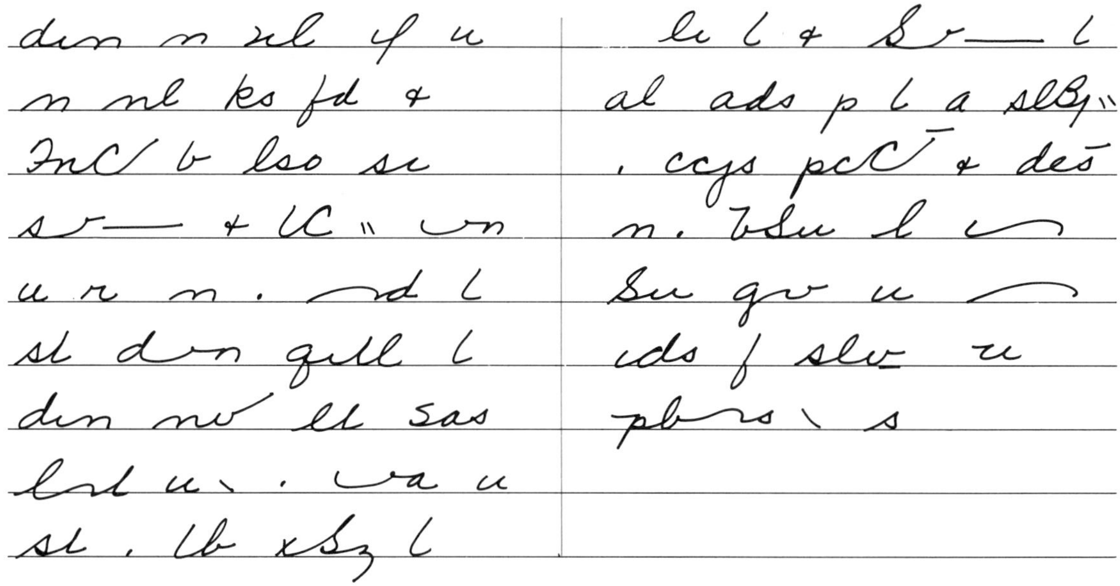

GUIDE Insert one apposition comma, three introductory commas, two parenthetical commas, and five series commas.

4.3 SPEED BUILDING

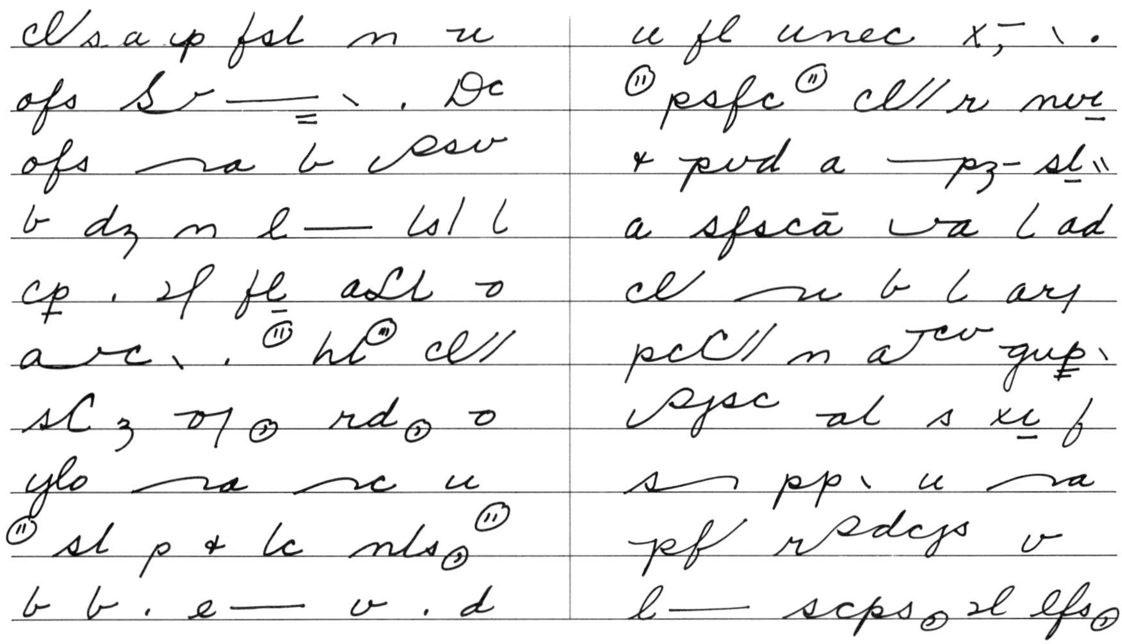

o ptas , Cz u al
caf r B la ul

b lv v los pc//
f 9 l 5 5 ds a vk.

4.4 VOCABULARY BUILDING

a lC v gny c
bq . oudos nl
u ho al y r— ,
ul nyy v a —p-
n u ofs f . sa
ryn " ul n vS
l s— xl/v lu v—
pt —p---, u na
fu la scl-- c b
sal l go , scl--
vC ncd . ccu
frl r dvyd v
les, ly rqu a
du al sfe lsi
v & s— e syl,
ly na sfl b lf
f . vks u —pn
lb o vcy & l
n rqu ca z lq

z ly r n a du &
lu sl " . nas v
scl-- r v pcCrsc
& desv, u nu
vS lon a bne Es
bv lal gzl ba
goln Ss s—
dl S ccx o
pncy " a no v
lz scl-- pds
—f// s n nl
a sgl —bs
& Is Su ou a
pfy v cl, ccu
c b —p= n Cqs
v vlcnc rc ca
a drc lC o u
bccs,

5.1 THEORY REVIEW

1. *ow*
2. *oi*
3. *ashun*
4. *son zon*
5. *olve*

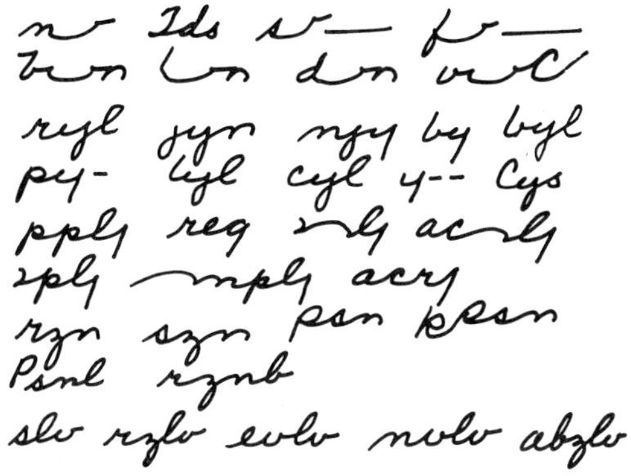

KEY 1. now; thousands; sound; found; brown; town; down; voucher 2. royal; join; enjoy; boy; boil; point; toil; coil; ointment; choice 3. population; regulation; stimulation; accumulation; stipulation; manipulation; accreditation 4. reason; season; person; comparison; personal, personnel; reasonable 5. solve; resolve; evolve; involve; absolve

5.2 TRANSCRIPTION SKILL BUILDING

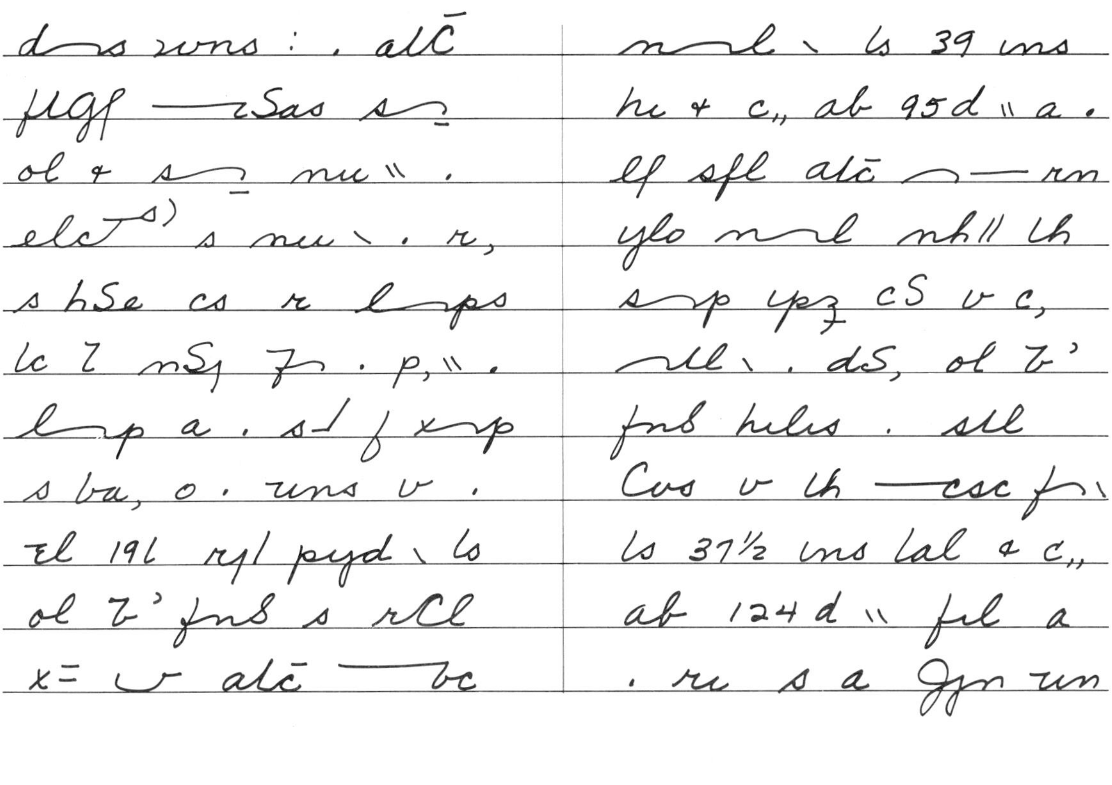

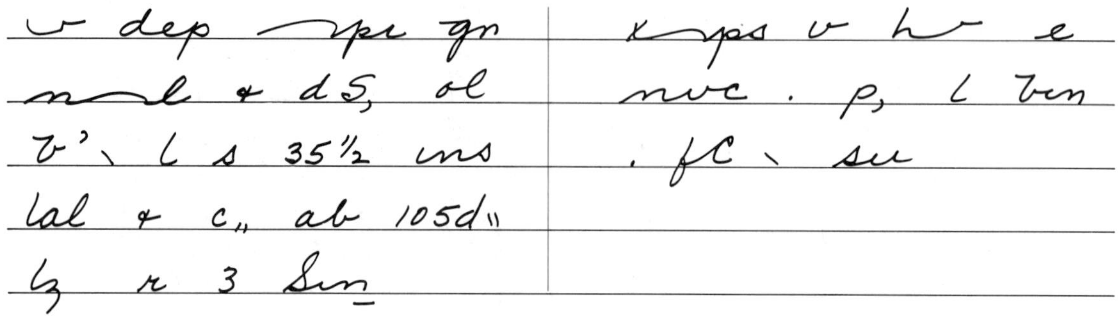

GUIDE Insert four parenthetical commas, two introductory commas, and one adjective comma.

5.3 SPEED BUILDING

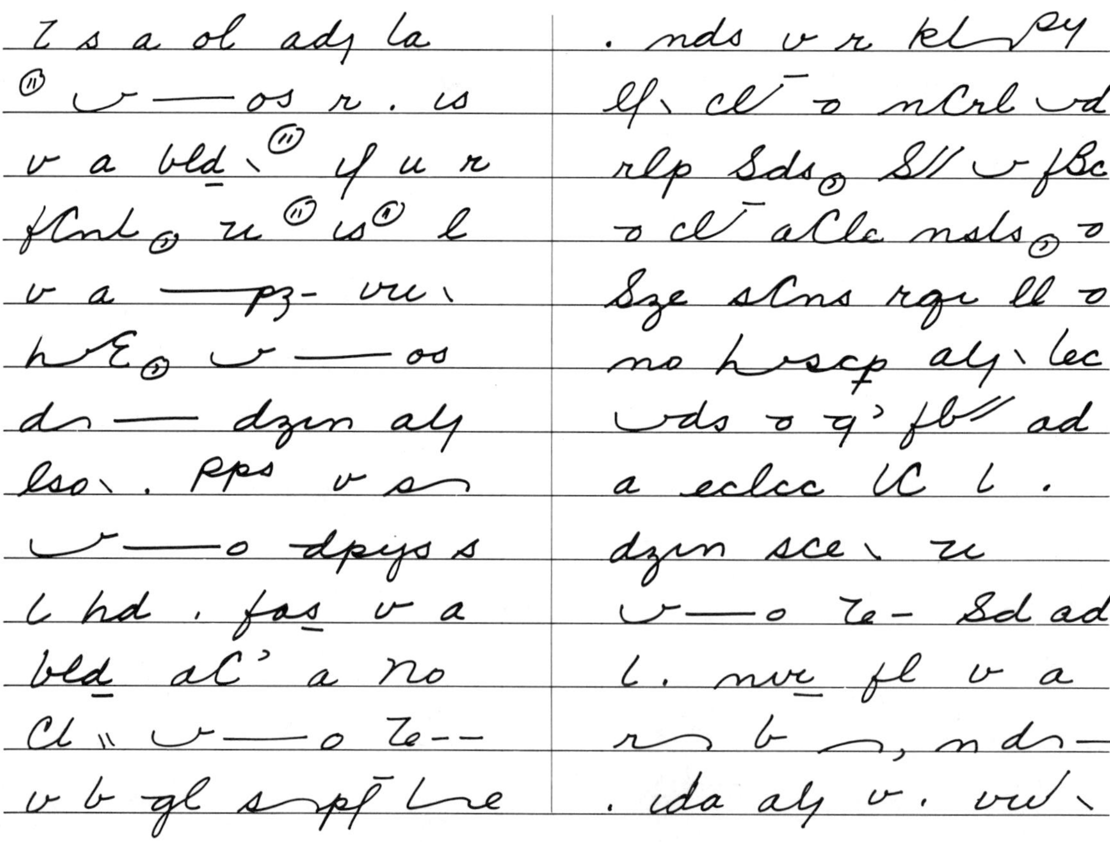

5.4 VOCABULARY BUILDING

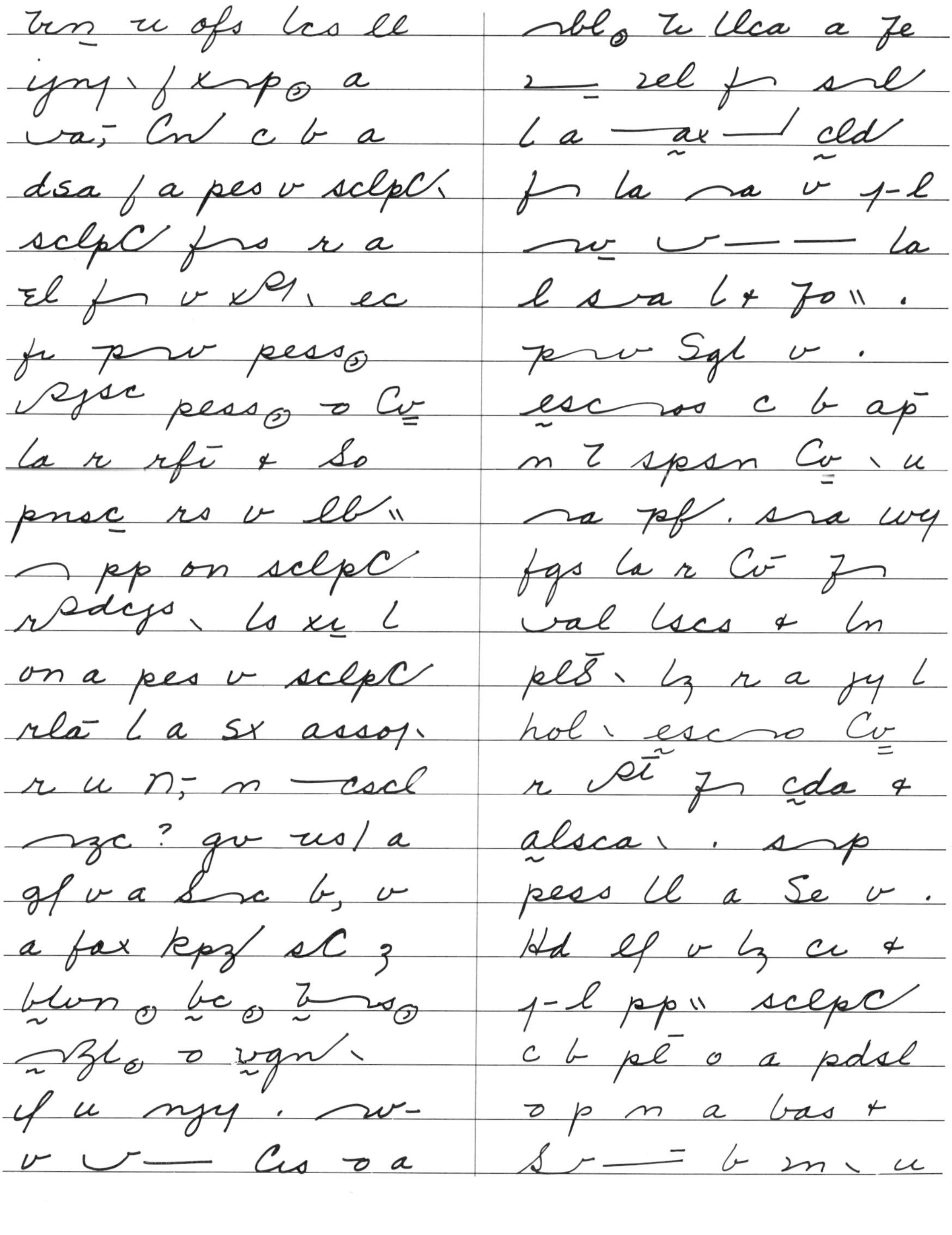

c nyy ls bu) cda\ | b lC + h — l̄ \ a sp
sclpC/ s sal cs l c | sclpC/ c fl nl ne bs ofs\

FOLDING AND INSERTING LETTERS

Before folding your letter for insertion into an envelope, make a final check to be sure that the letter is signed, that all corrections have been made, that all enclosures have been included, and that you have the correct envelope.

Follow the steps shown in the illustrations.

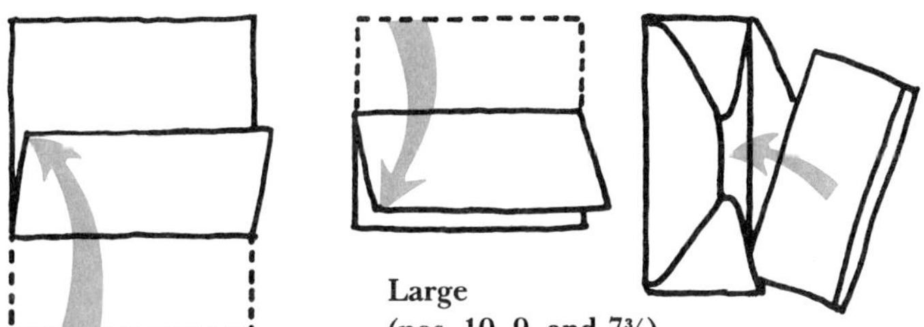

Large
(nos. 10, 9, and 7¾)

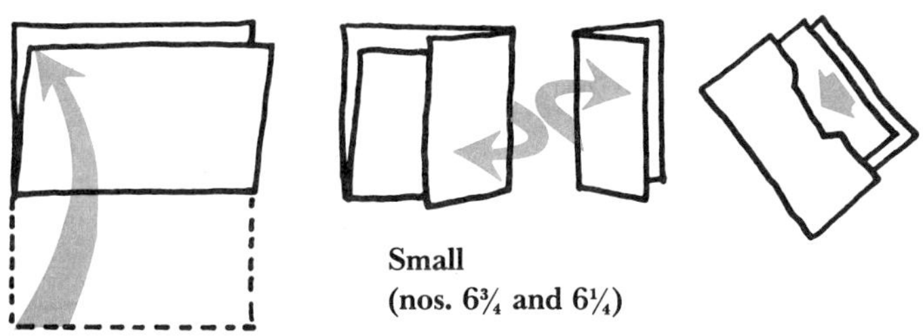

Small
(nos. 6¾ and 6¼)

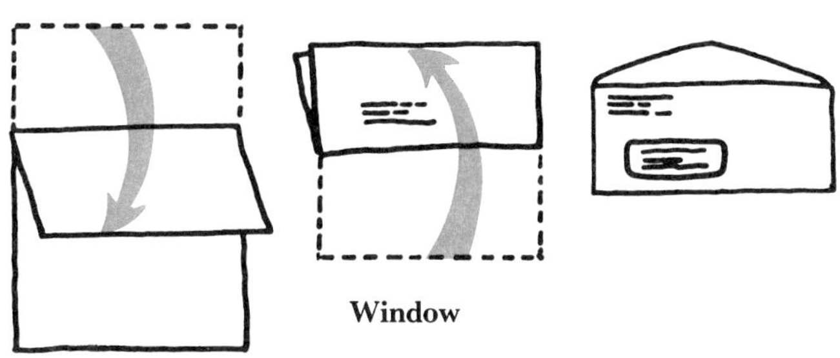

Window

UNIT 16

HOBBIES/HANDCRAFTS

1.1 THEORY REVIEW

1. *ō*
2. *self*
3. *ington*
4. *plī*
5. *long*

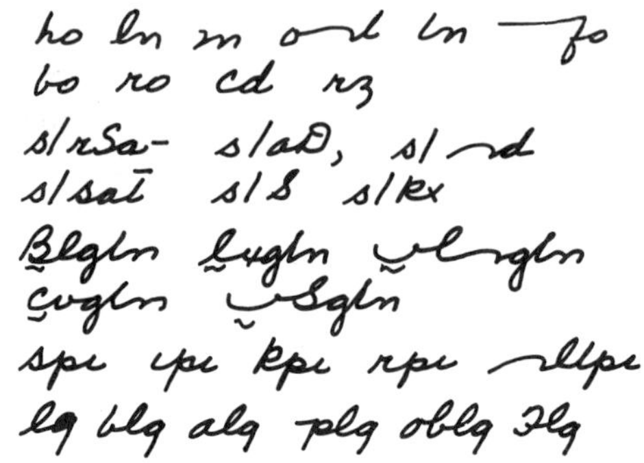

KEY 1. home; loan; stone; omit; tone; floor; boat; roam; code; rose 2. self-restraint; self-addressed; self-made; self-satisfied; selfish; self-conscious 3. Burlington; Lexington; Wilmington; Covington; Washington 4. supply; imply; comply; reply; multiply 5. long; belong; along; prolong; oblong; furlong

1.2 TRANSCRIPTION SKILL BUILDING

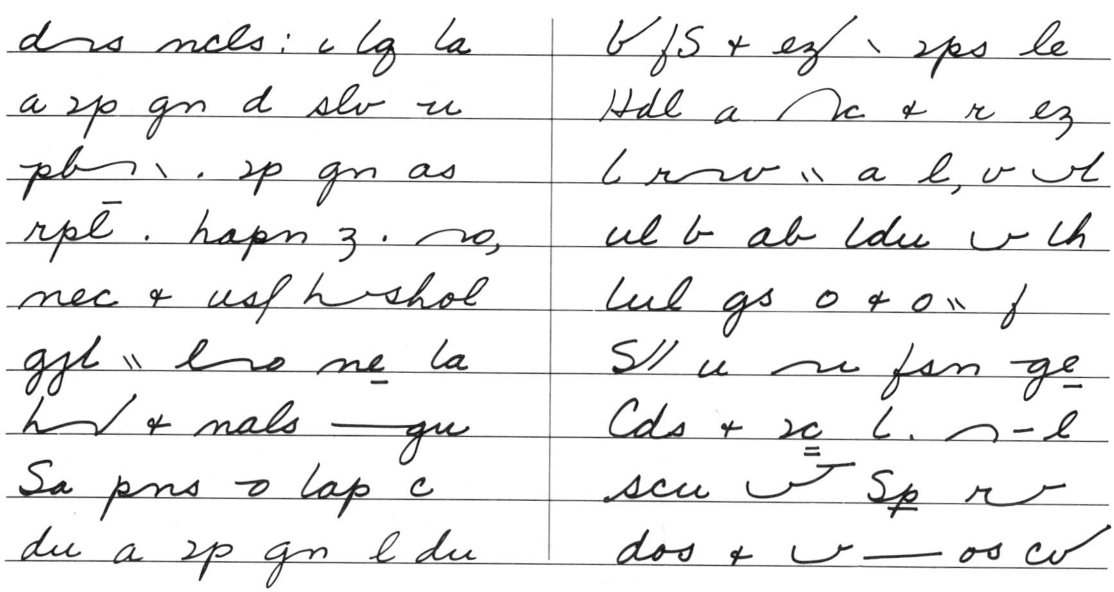

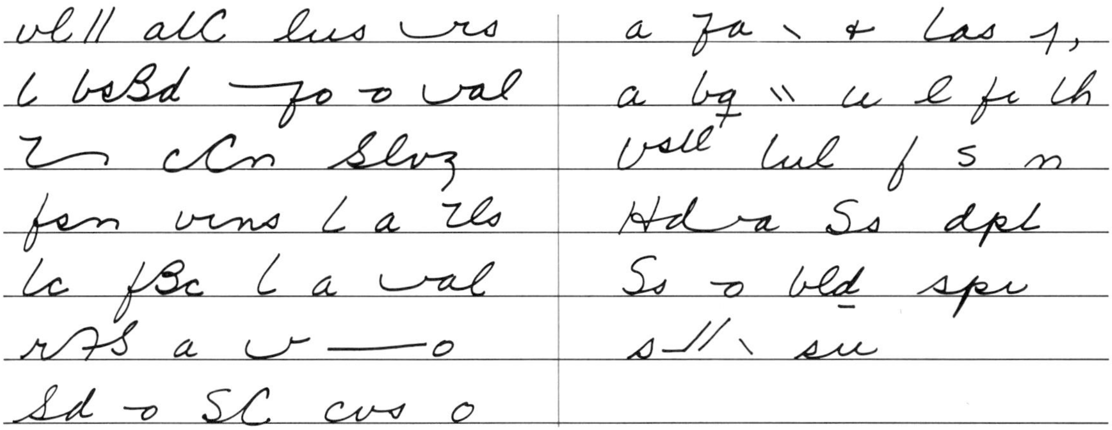

GUIDE Insert nine series commas, one introductory comma, one enumeration colon, eight internal punctuation semicolons, one contraction apostrophe, and one compound adjective hyphen.

1.3 SPEED BUILDING

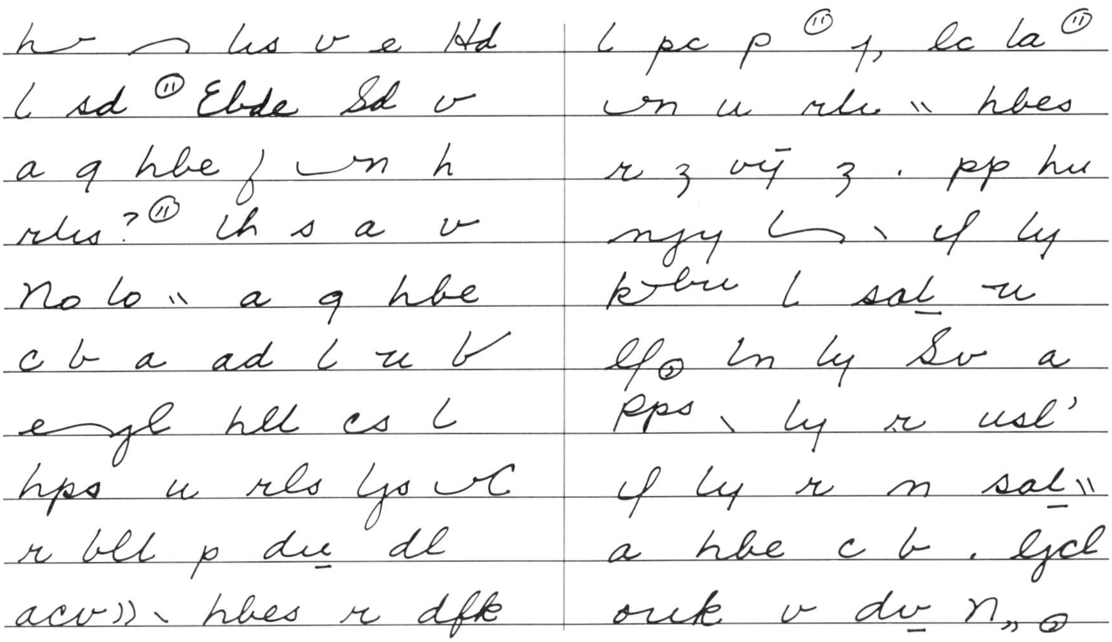

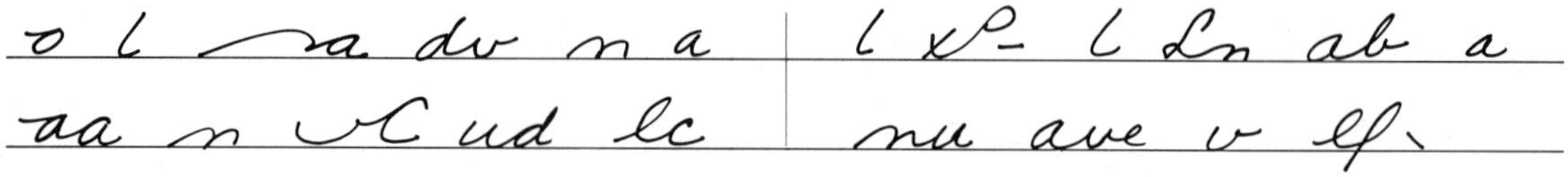

1.4 VOCABULARY BUILDING

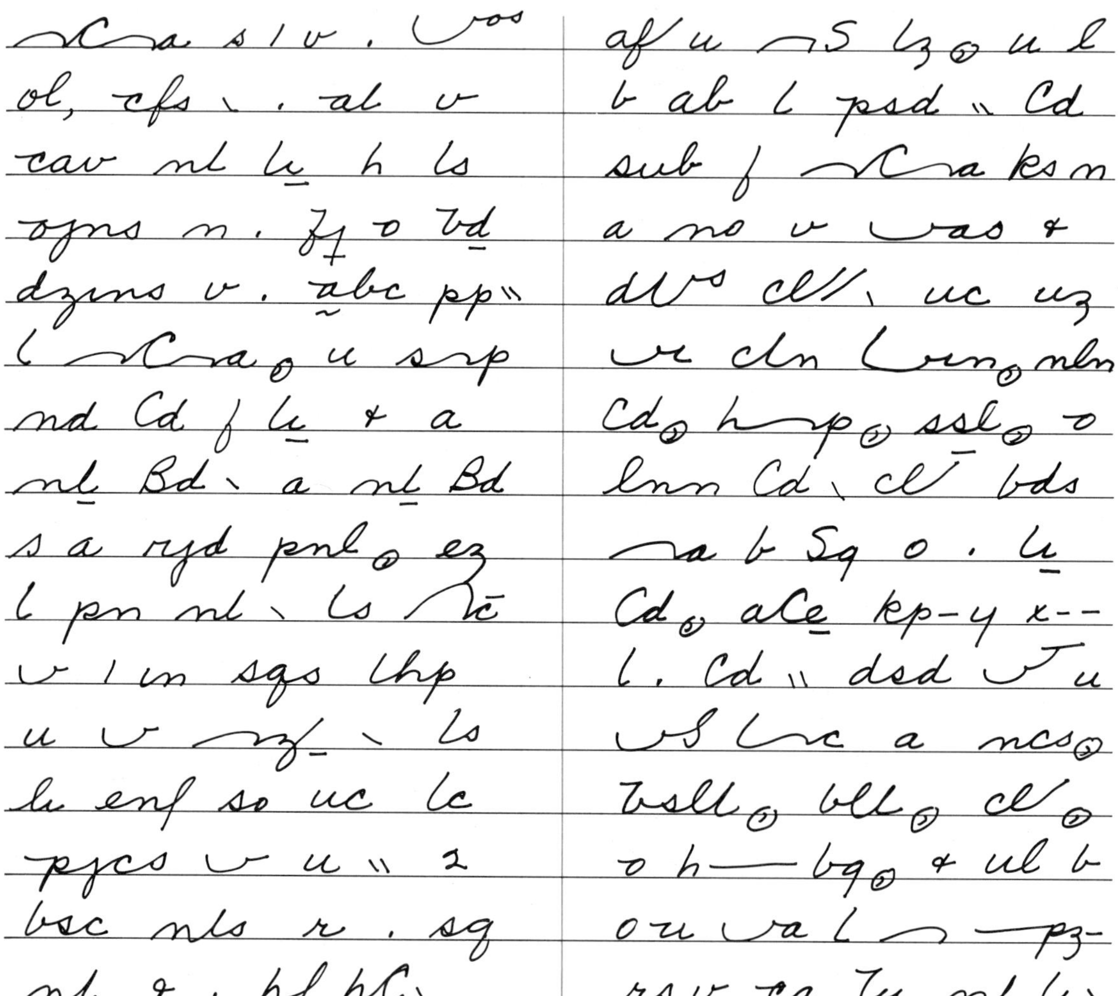

2.1 THEORY REVIEW

1. *serve zerve*

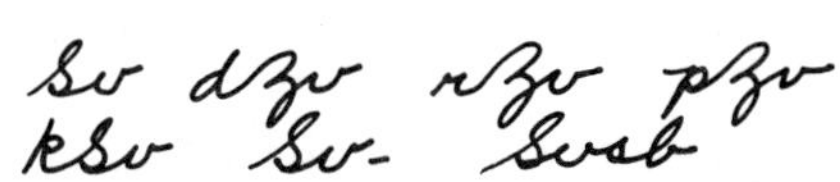

2. *st*

3. Final *ate*

4. *shul*

5. Initial *en*

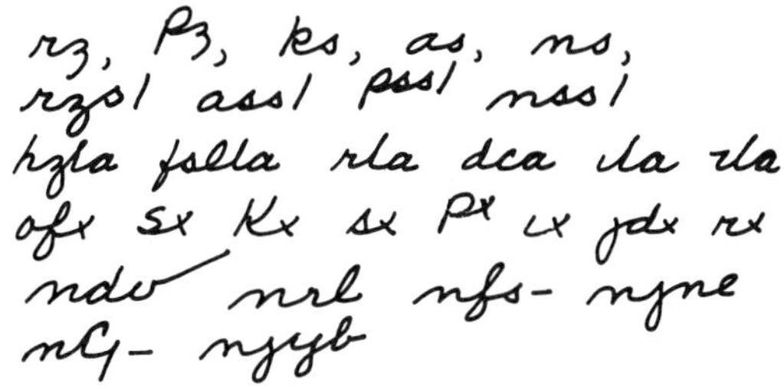

KEY 1. serve; deserve; reserve; preserve; conserve; servant; serviceable 2. resist; persist; consist; assist; insist; resistance; assistance; persistence; insistence 3. hesitate; facilitate; rotate; dictate; imitate; irritate 4. official; special; commercial; social; partial; initial; judicial; racial 5. endeavor; enroll; enforcement; engineer; encouragement; enjoyable

2.2 TRANSCRIPTION SKILL BUILDING

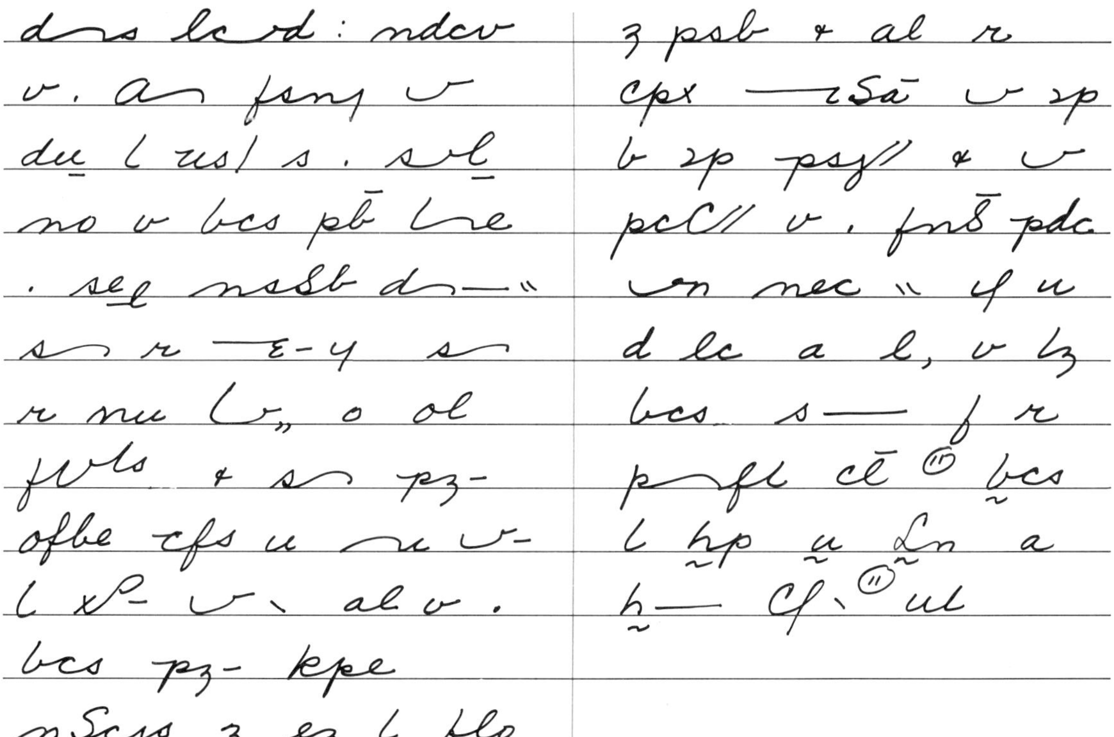

GUIDE Insert four compound adjective hyphens, two series commas, one parenthetical comma, one internal punctuation semicolon, and one introductory comma.

2.3 SPEED BUILDING

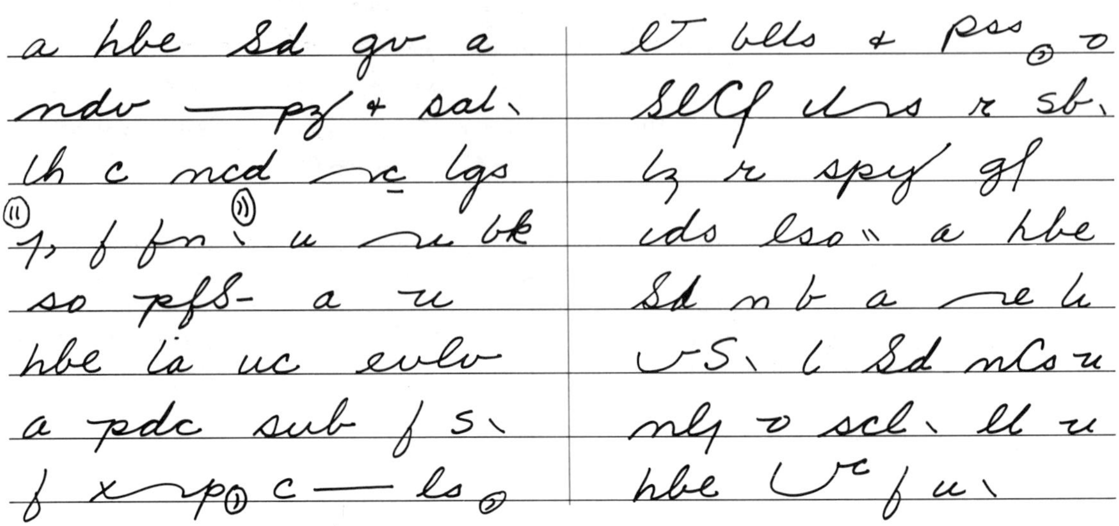

2.4 VOCABULARY BUILDING

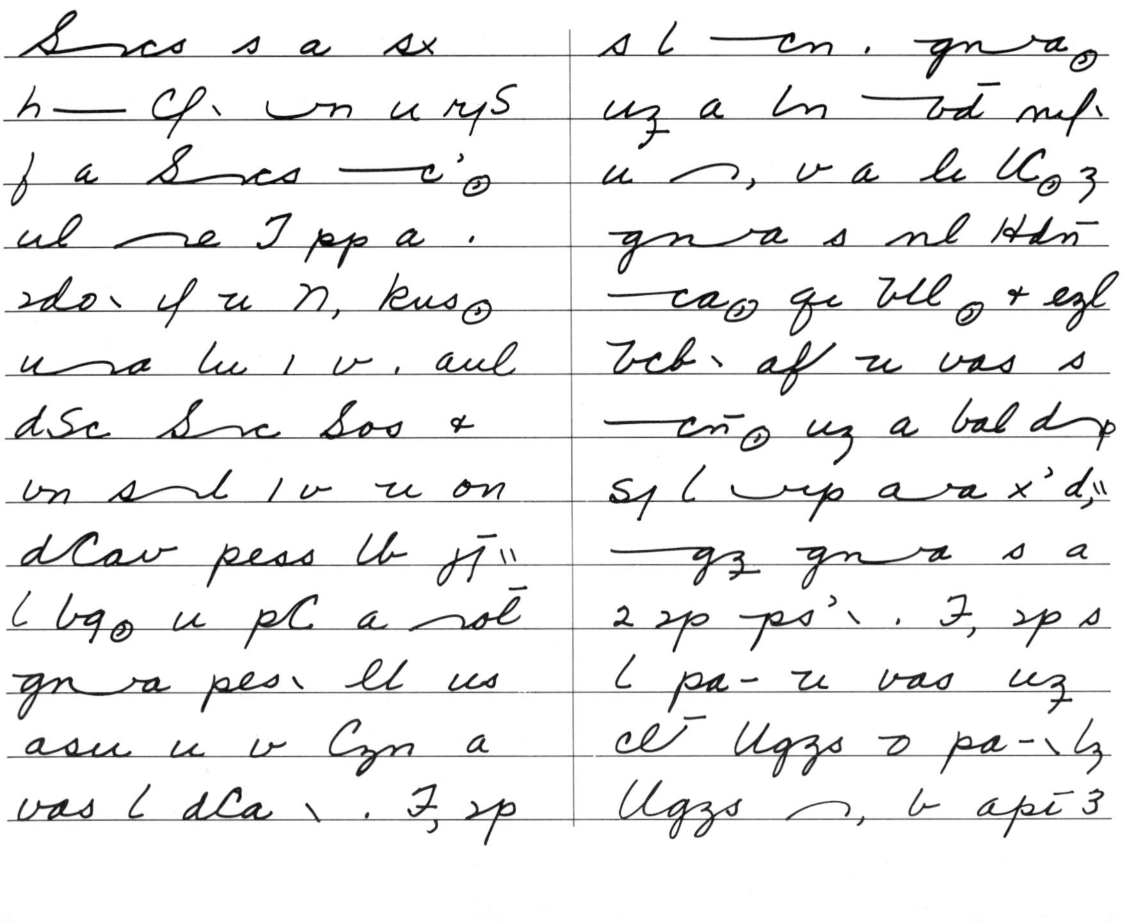

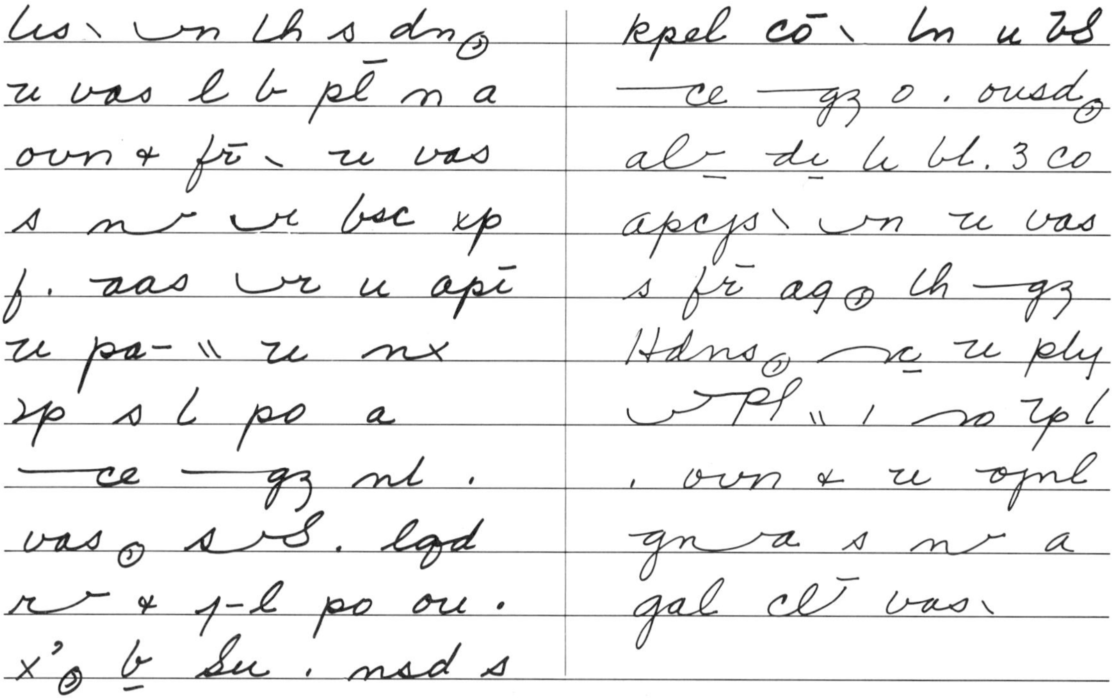

3.1 THEORY REVIEW

1. Initial *ex*

2. *less*

3. *īve*

4. *ple*

5. *dent*

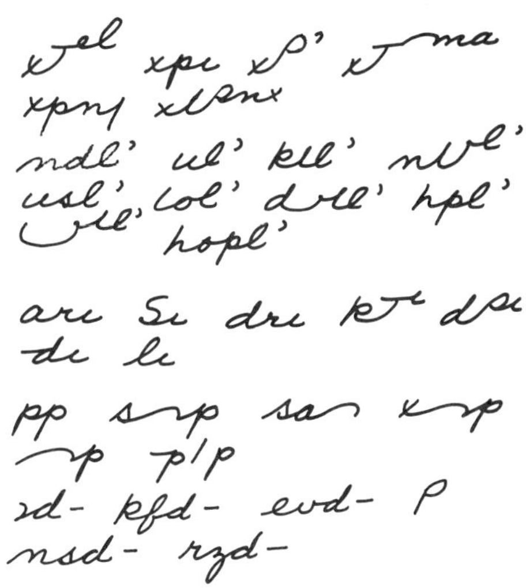

KEY 1. extremely; expire; express; exterminate; explanation; extemporaneous 2. needless; unless; countless; nevertheless; useless; thoughtless; doubtless; helpless; worthless; hopeless 3. arrive; strive; derive; contrive; deprive; drive; live 4. people; simple; sample; example; ample; principle, principal 5. student; confident; evident; president; incident; resident

3.2 TRANSCRIPTION SKILL BUILDING

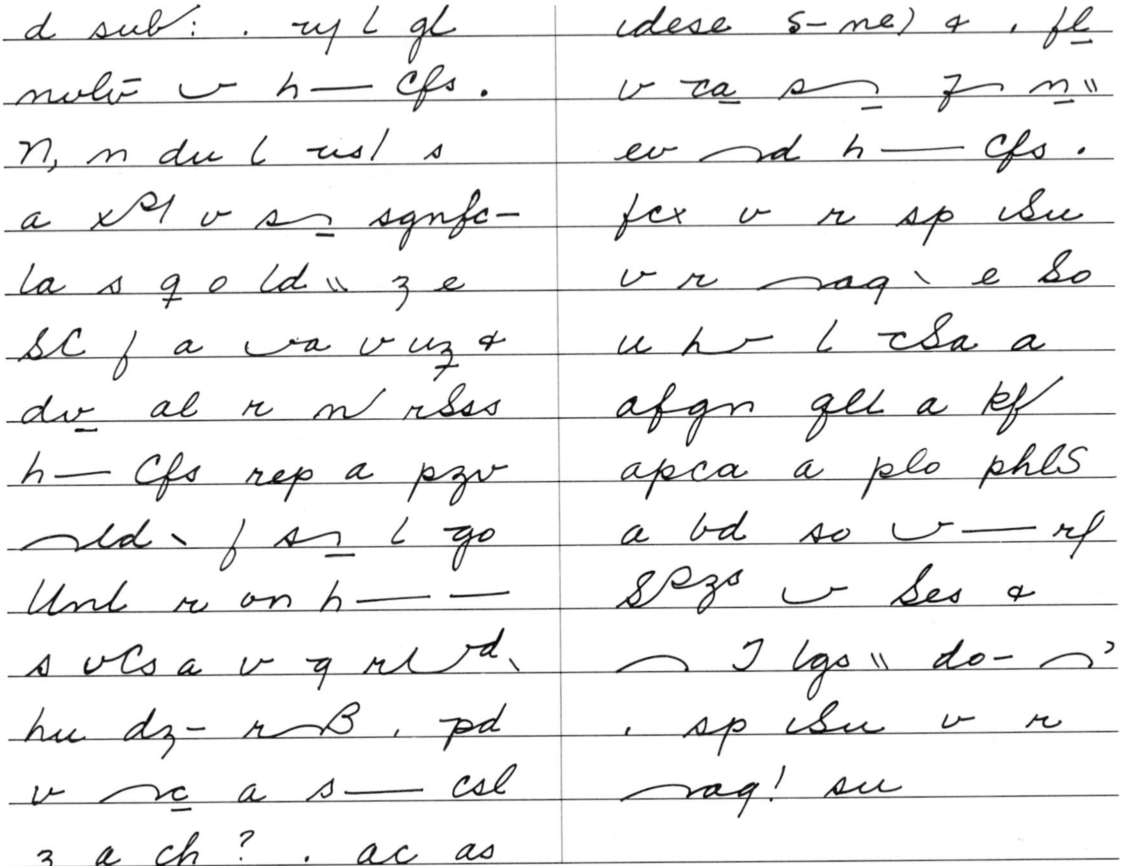

GUIDE Insert four parenthetical commas, one introductory comma, seven series commas, two compound adjective hyphens, and two contraction apostrophes.

3.3 SPEED BUILDING

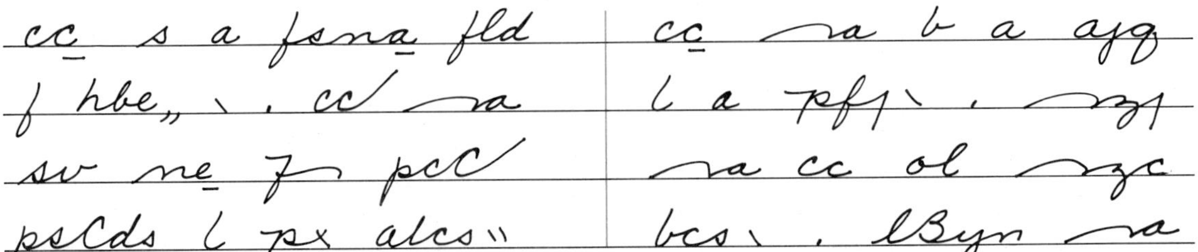

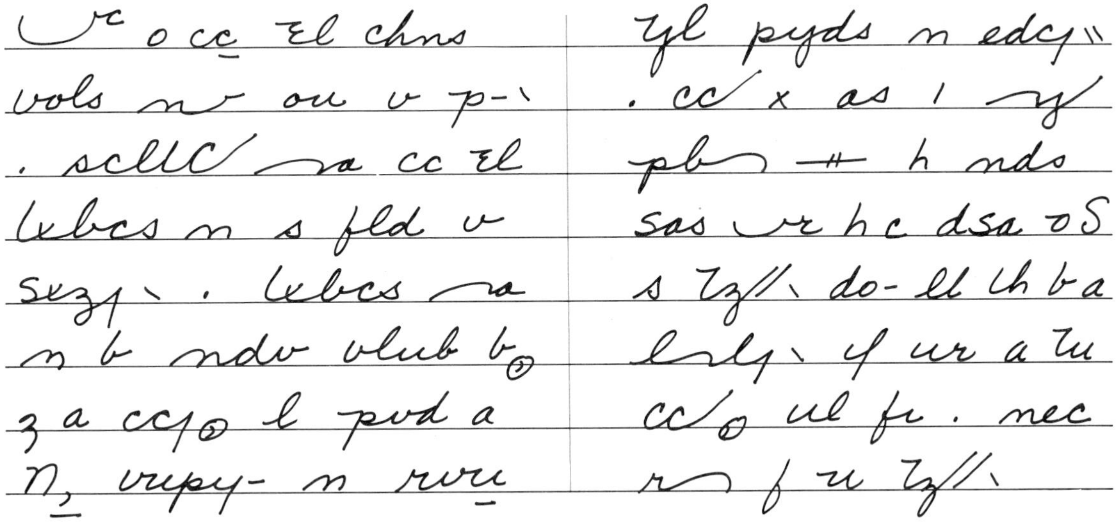

3.4 VOCABULARY BUILDING

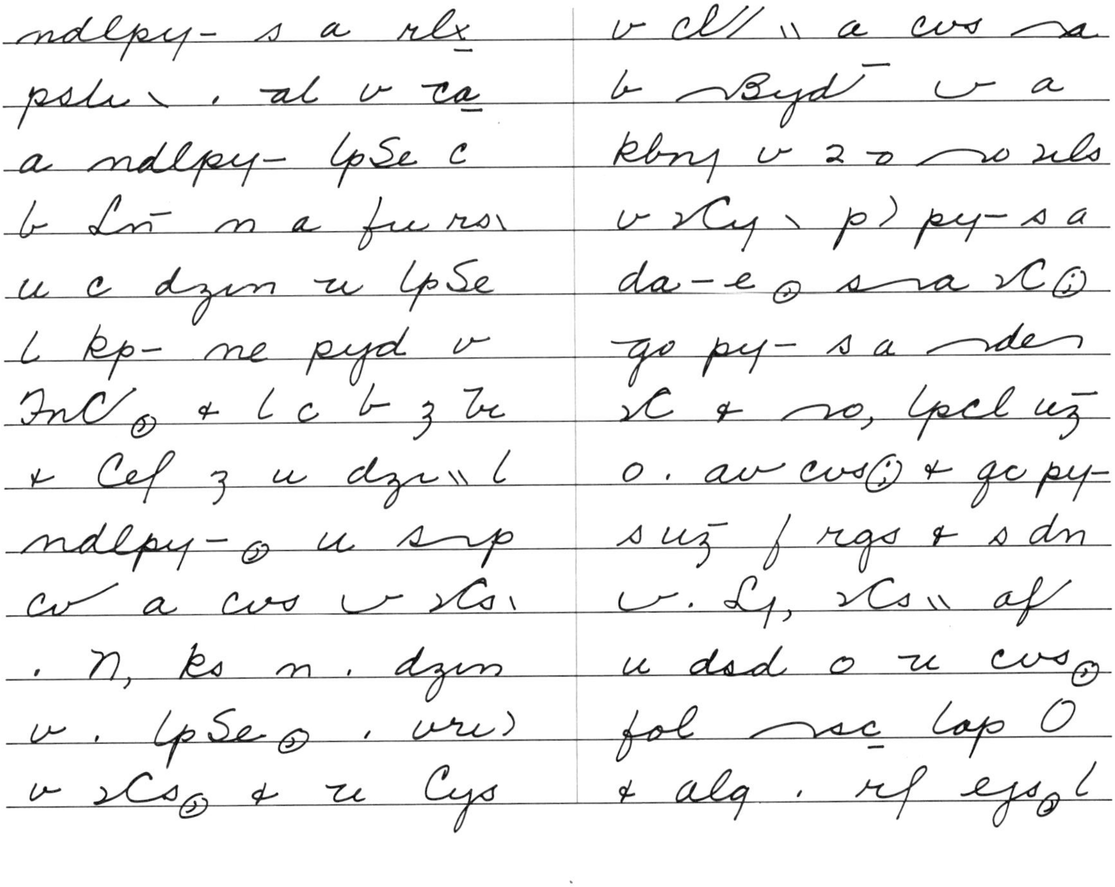

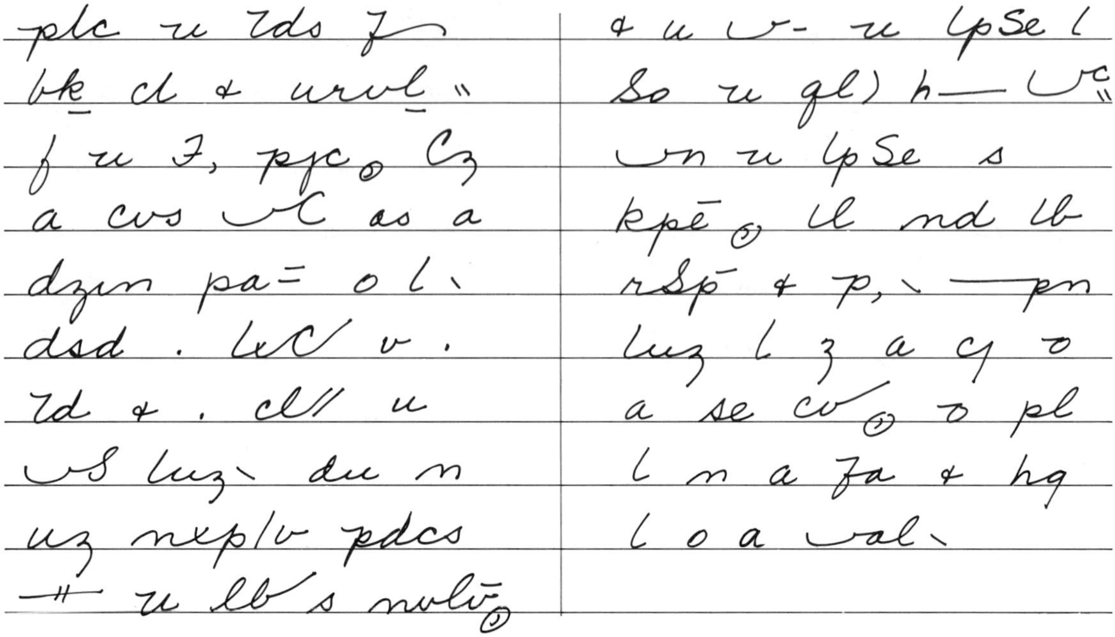

4.1 THEORY REVIEW

1. *fication*

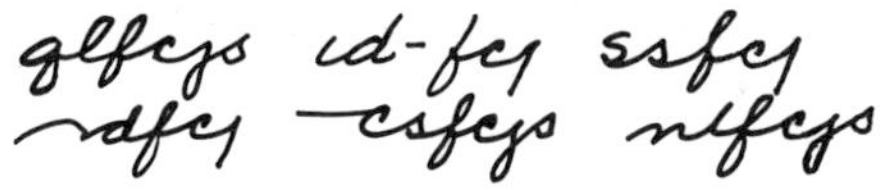

2. *x*

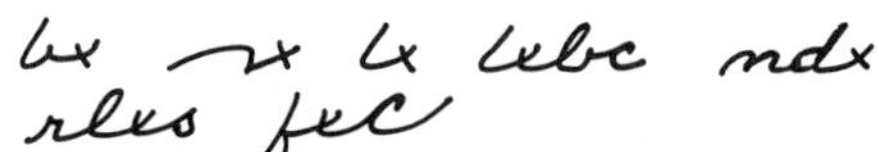

3. *tem*

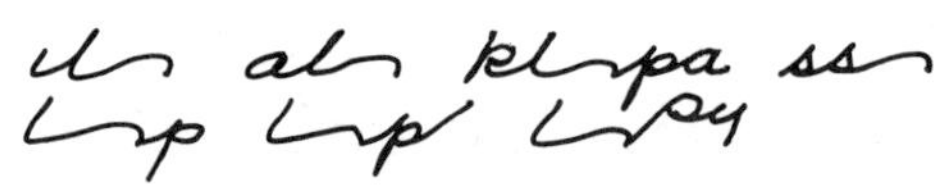

4. *shun*

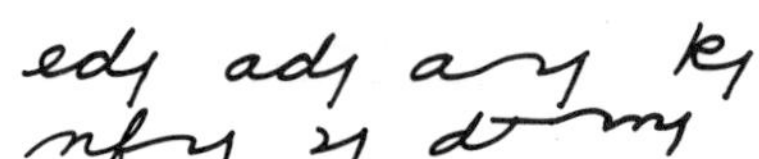

5. *kle*

KEY 1. qualifications; identification; specification; modification; classifications; notifications 2. box; mix; text; textbook; index; relaxes; fixture 3. item; attempt; contemplate; system; temple; temper; temporary 4. edition; addition; admission; commission; information; station; determination 5. technical; medical; practical; chemical; logical; political

4.2 TRANSCRIPTION SKILL BUILDING

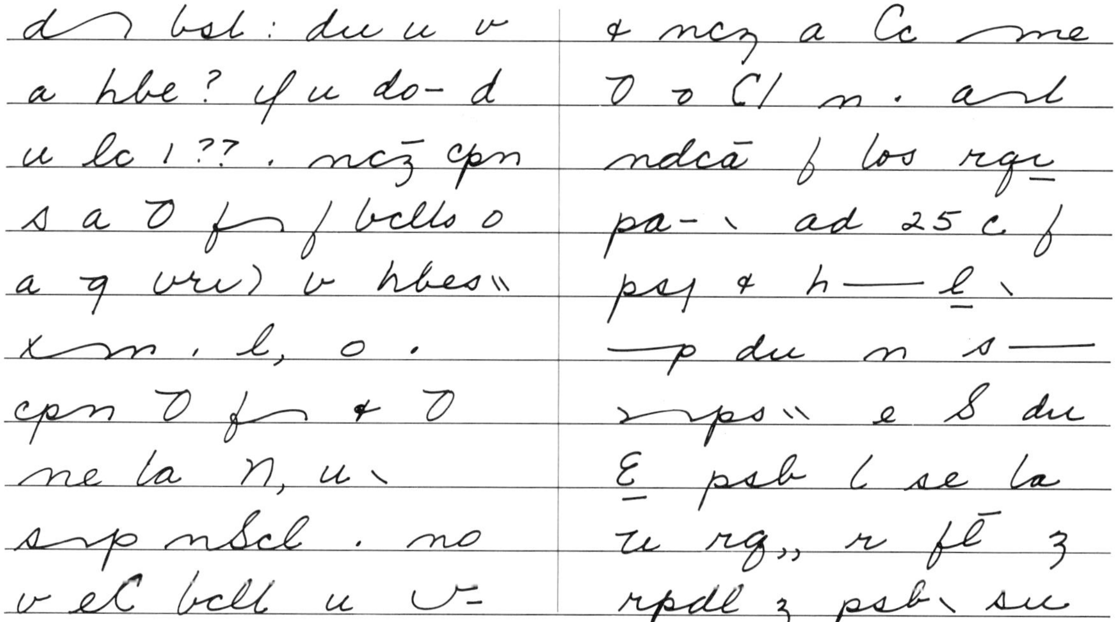

GUIDE Insert one introductory comma, two series commas, and one contraction apostrophe.

4.3 SPEED BUILDING

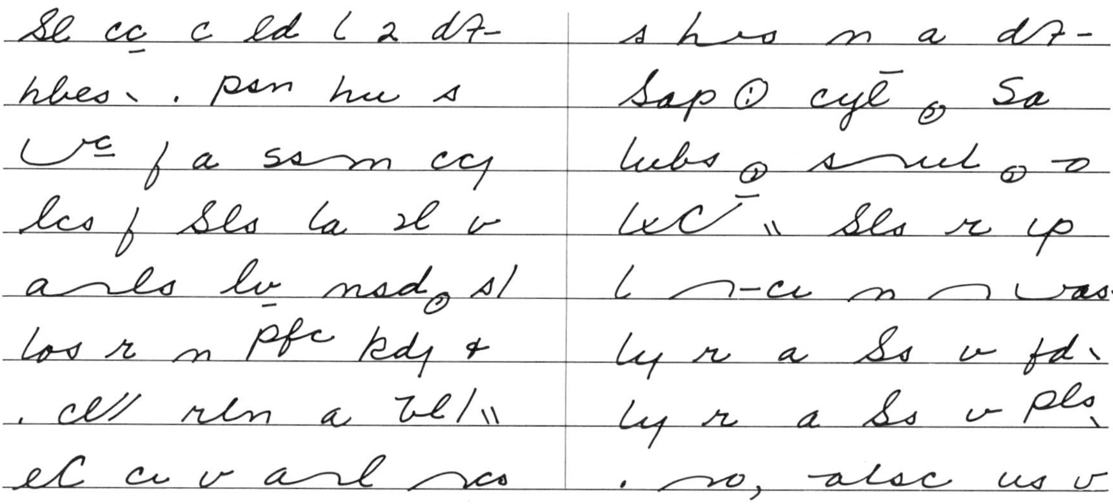

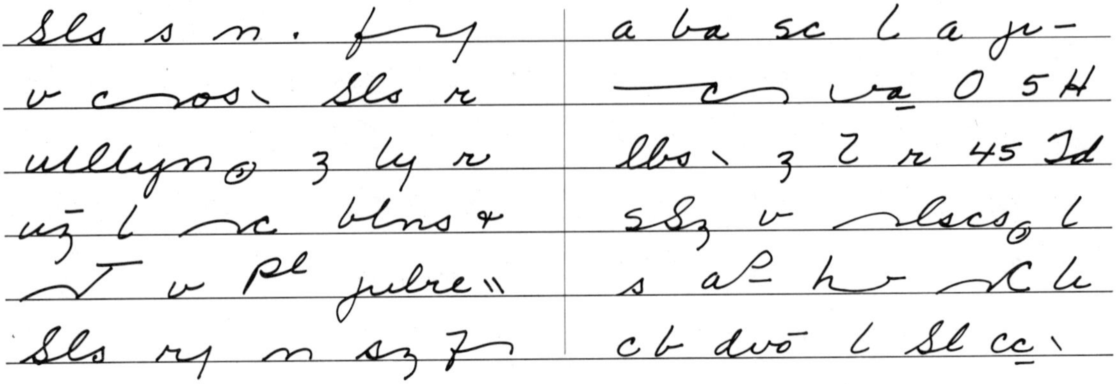

4.4 VOCABULARY BUILDING

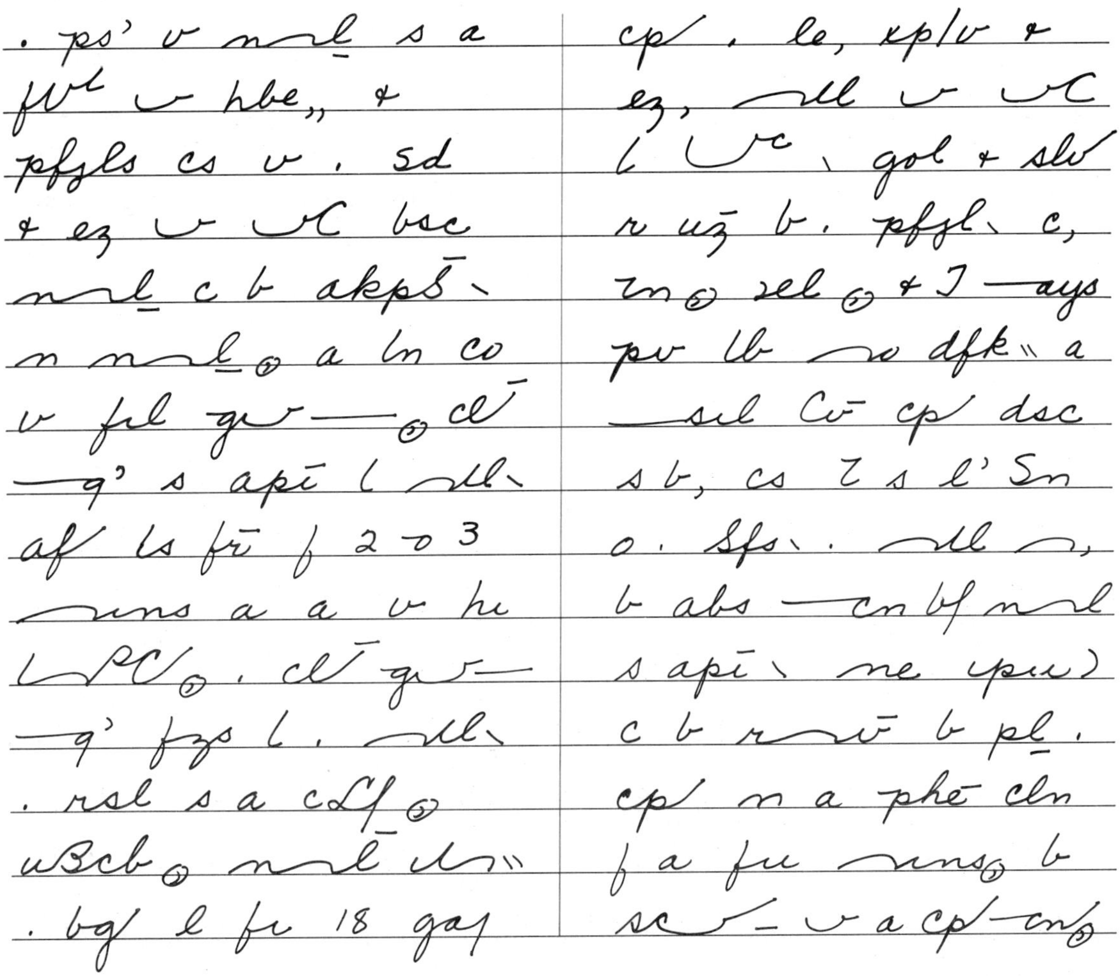

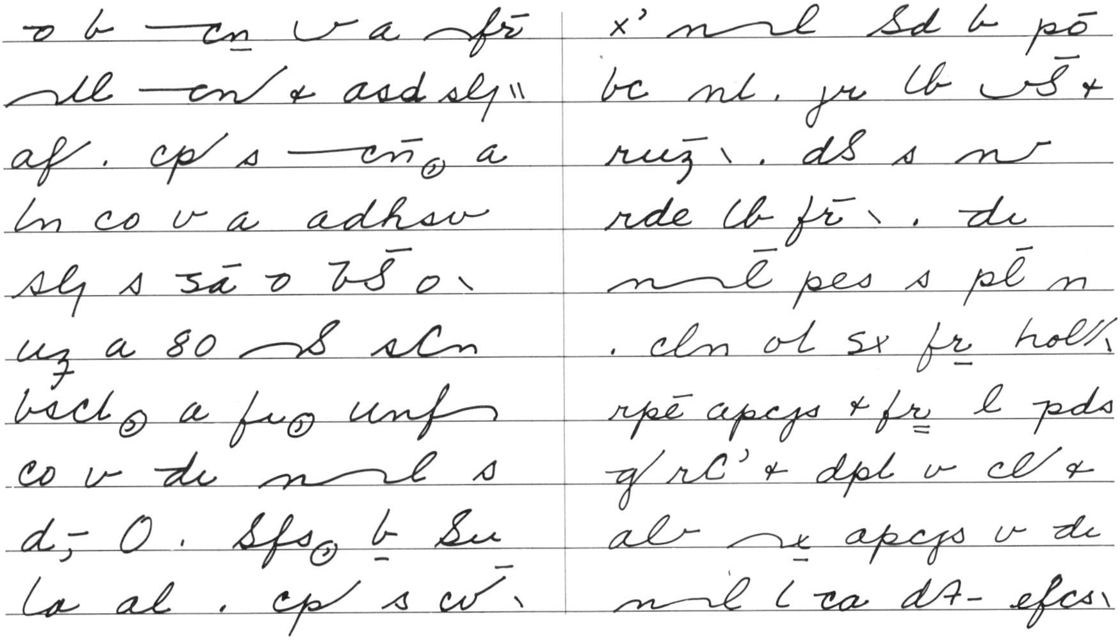

5.1 THEORY REVIEW

1. *ship*

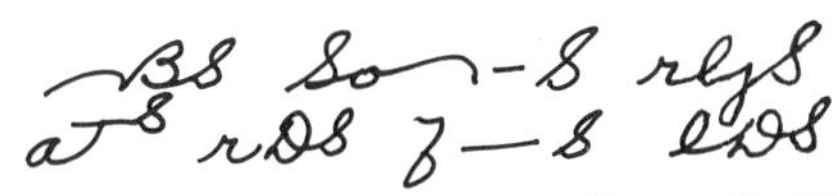

2. *ther*

3. *super*

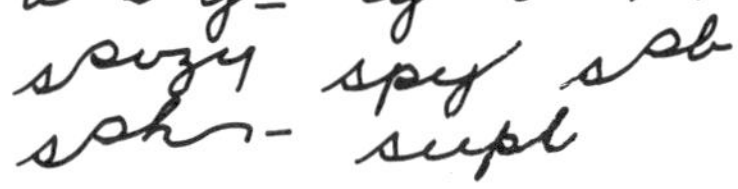

4. *pect*

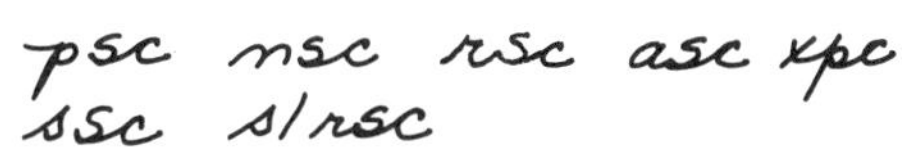

5. *ble*

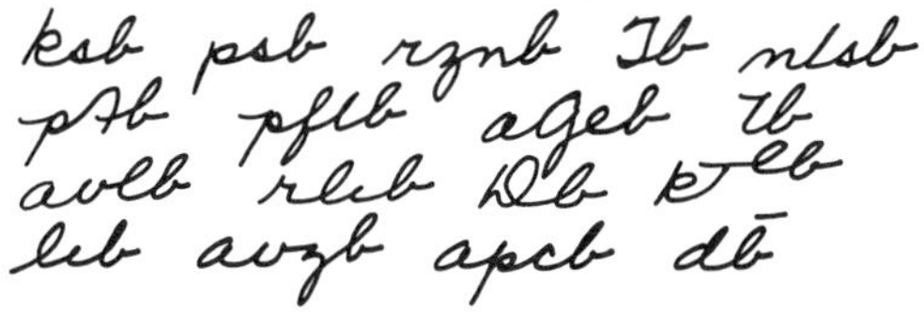

KEY 1. membership; showmanship; relationship; authorship; readership; friendship; leadership 2. another; other; gathering; together; brother; mother; further; farther 3. supervisory; superior; superb; superhuman; superintendent 4. prospect; inspect; respect; aspect; expect; suspect; self-respect 5. considerable; possible; reasonable; terrible; noticeable; preferable; profitable; agreeable; trouble; available; reliable; durable; controllable; liable; advisable; applicable; doubled

5.2 TRANSCRIPTION SKILL BUILDING

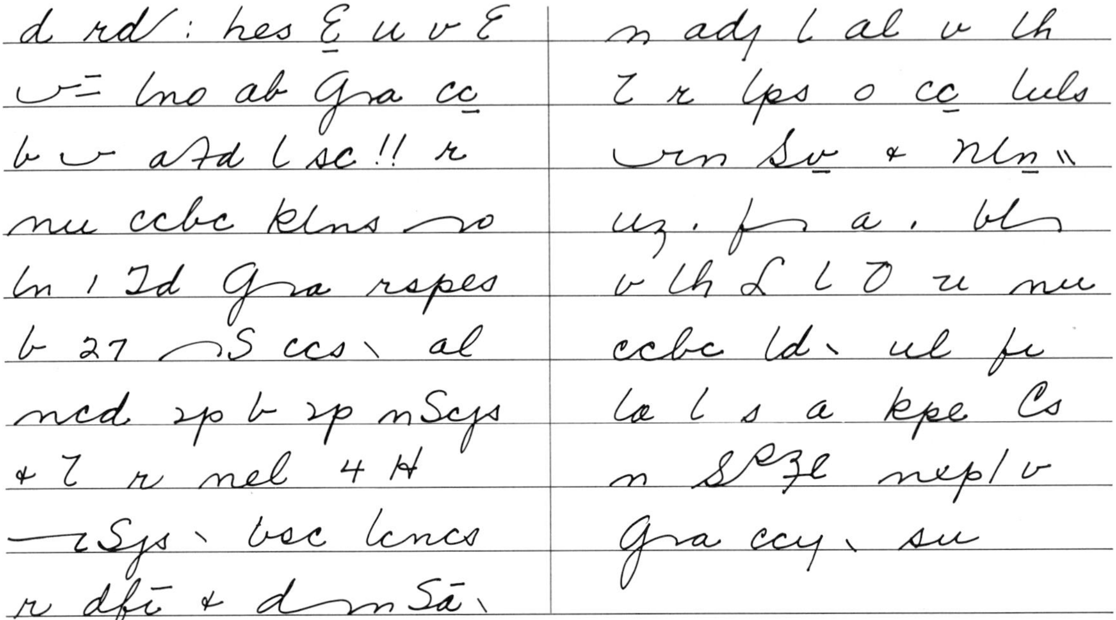

GUIDE Insert one conjunction comma, one introductory comma, two series commas, one number comma, two contraction apostrophes, two compound adjective hyphens.

5.3 SPEED BUILDING

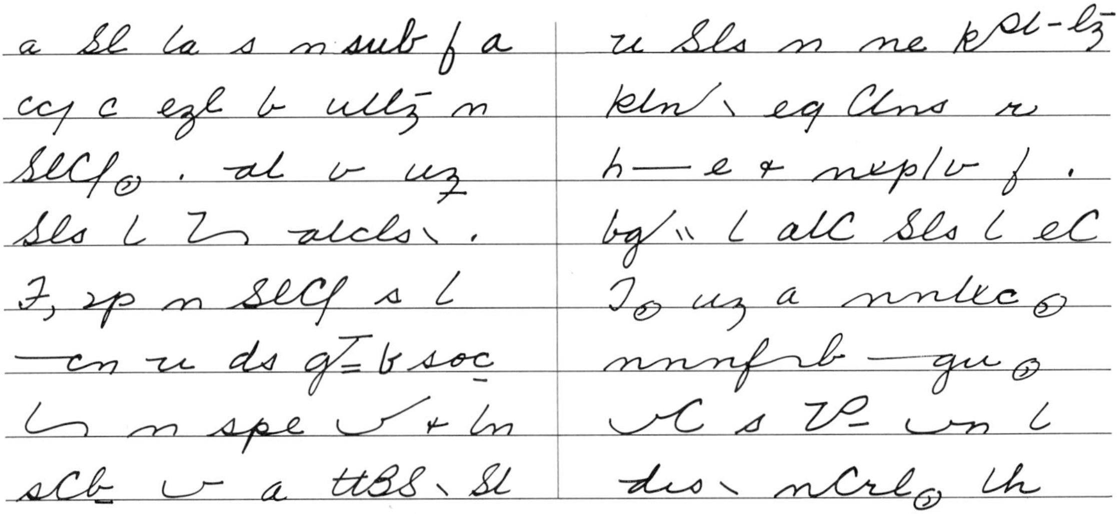

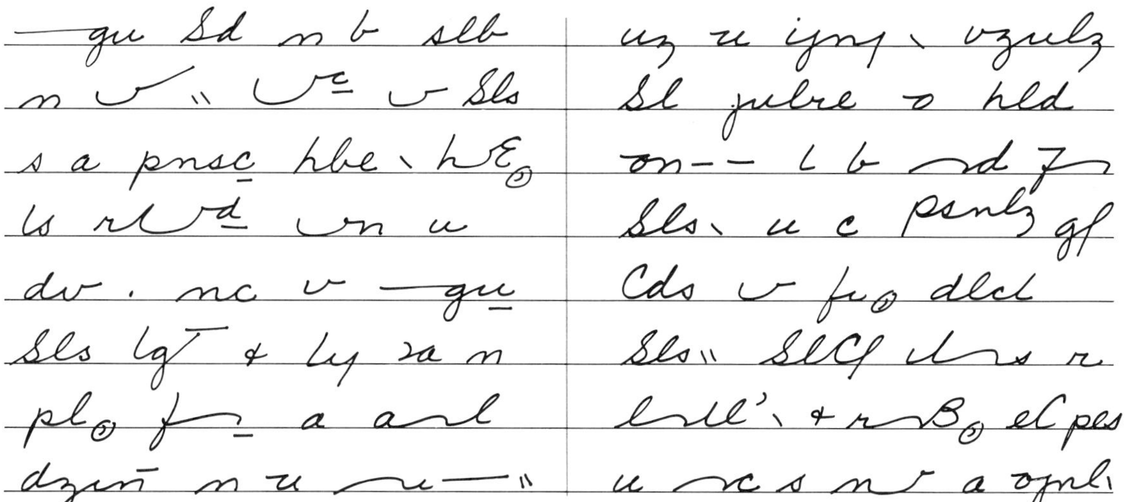

5.4 VOCABULARY BUILDING

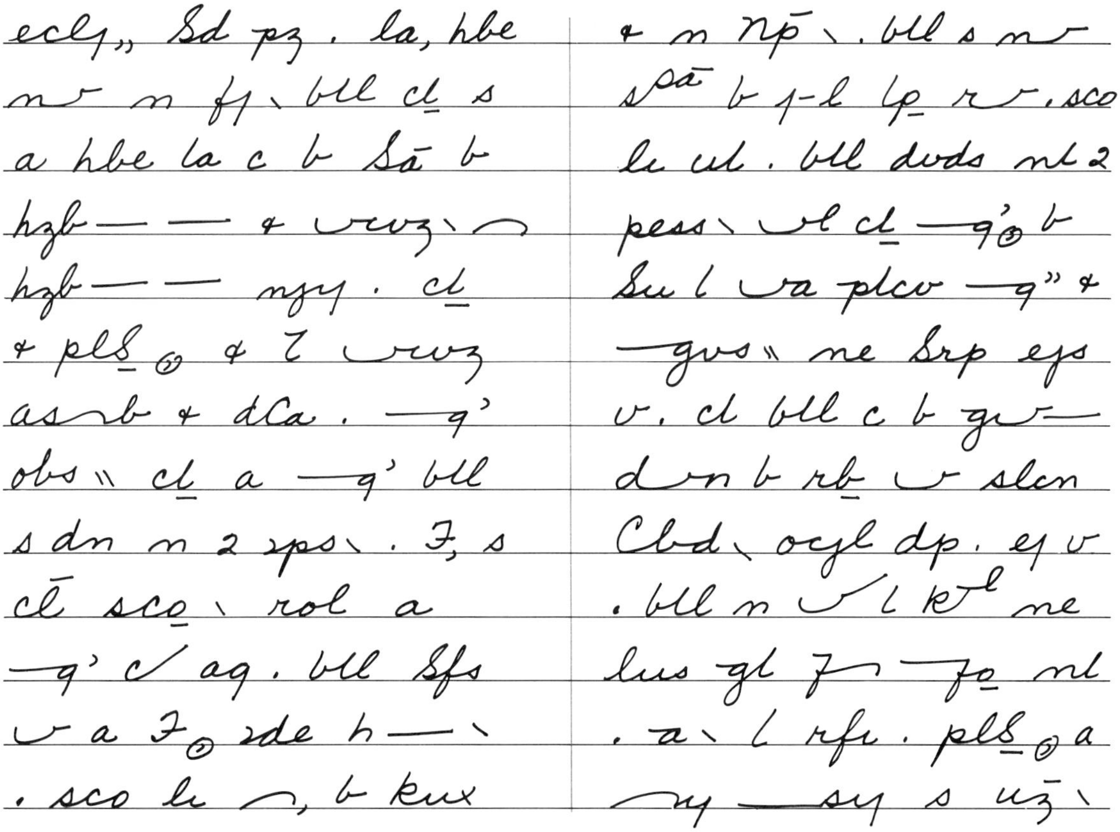

DICTIONARIES

The English language is not a static thing; it changes to reflect the usage of the people. Some words drop out of common usage and become archaic. Others are created to give names to the new procedures and the new discoveries of our age. Modern science and technology coin new words constantly.

Not only are new words born, but old ones are subject to change. Nearly everyone wrote "catalogue" a short time ago instead of "catalog," which we use today. Not long ago, you always found a hyphen in such words as "non-profit," which is now written "nonprofit."

American and British lexicographers are constantly revising, adding, deleting, and compiling the results into new, up-to-date dictionaries. (The latest Italian dictionary was based on Dante's *Inferno* and was published in 1811.)

There are countless dictionaries on the market today—college dictionaries, high school dictionaries, pocket dictionaries, office dictionaries. It's important to pick one that is up to date and thumb-indexed for quick reference, and it's equally important to know how to use it.

Examine the table of contents and look through the book. You may be amazed to find such a wide range of information available at your fingertips. There are biographical and geographical listings, tables of weights and measures, rules for spelling and pronunciation, foreign words and phrases, and signs and symbols.

UNIT 17

DATA PROCESSING

1.1 THEORY REVIEW

1. *ik*
2. *gāte*
3. *ng*
4. *nj*
5. *nch*

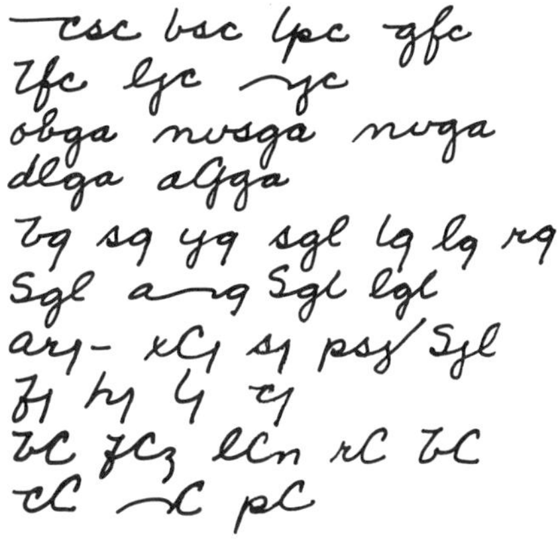

KEY 1. classic; basic; topic; graphic; traffic; logic; magic 2. obligate; investigate; navigate; delegate; aggregate 3. bring; sing; young; single; thing; long; ring, wrong; strongly; among; strength; length 4. arrangement; exchange; singe; passenger; strangely; fringe; hinge; tinge; cringe 5. branch; franchise; luncheon; ranch; branch; crunch; munch; punch

1.2 TRANSCRIPTION SKILL BUILDING

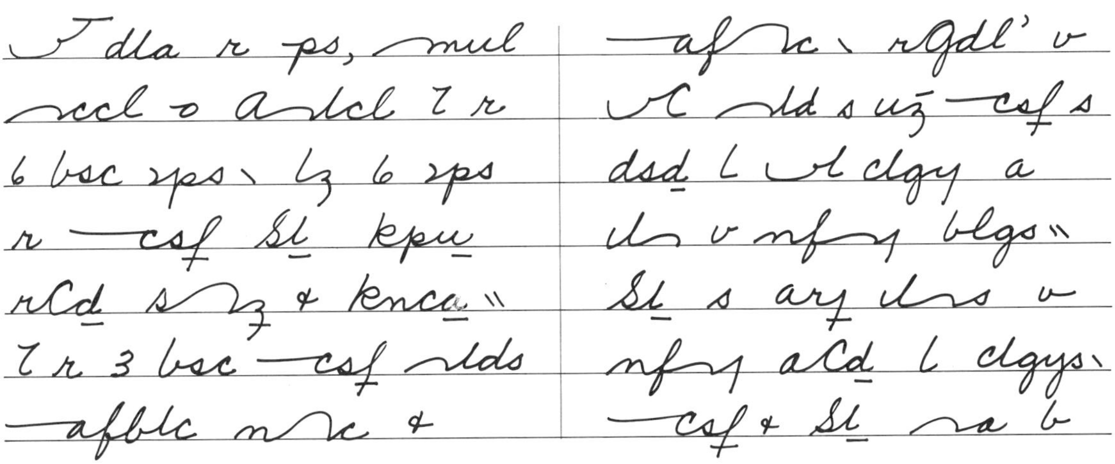

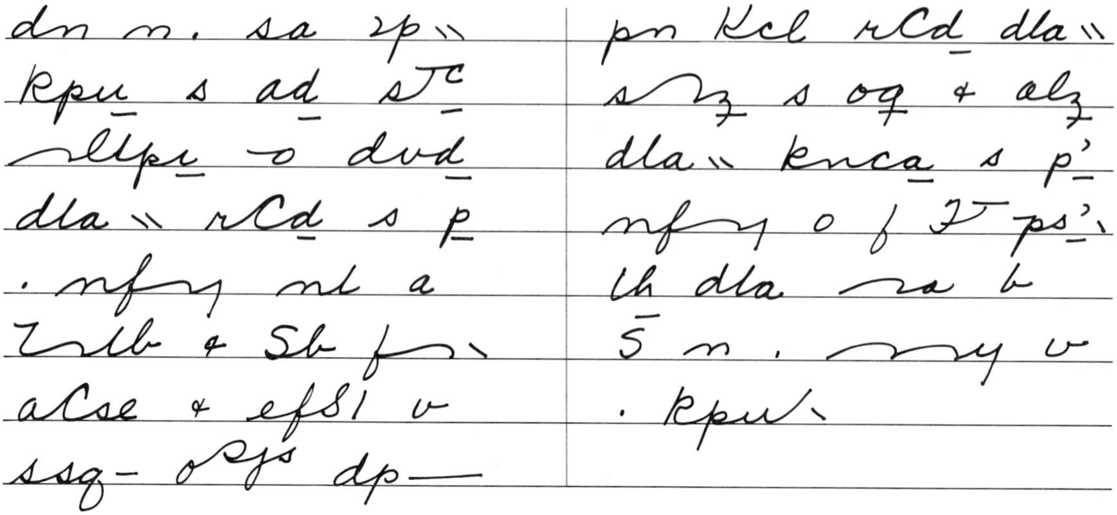

GUIDE Insert twelve series commas, two introductory commas, and two enumeration colons.

1.3 SPEED BUILDING

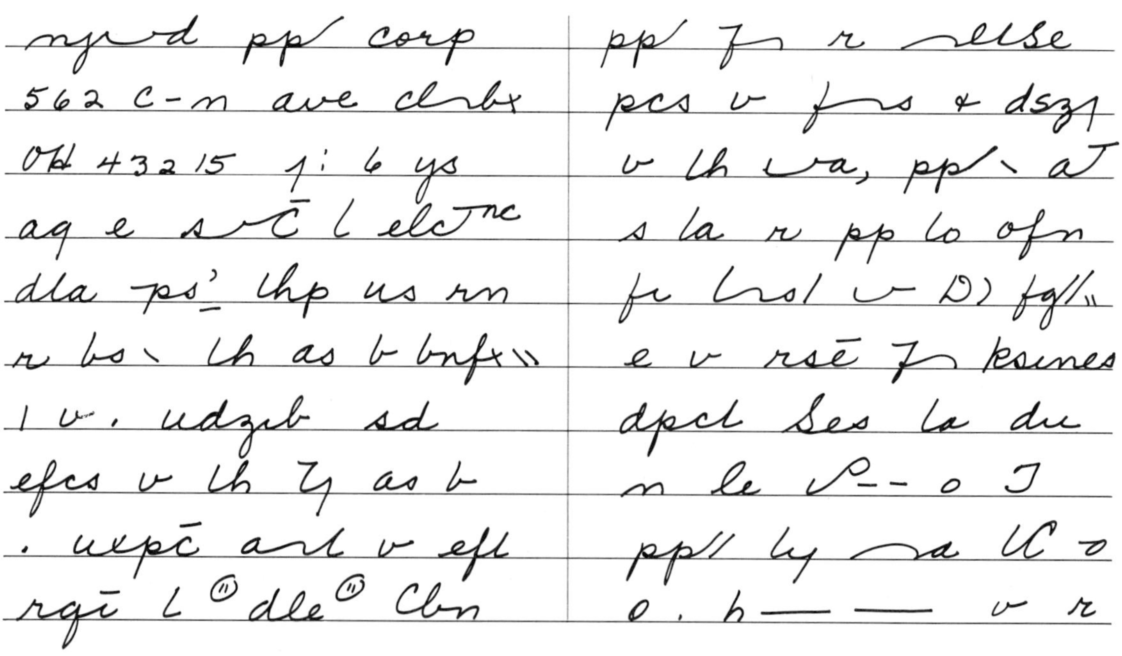

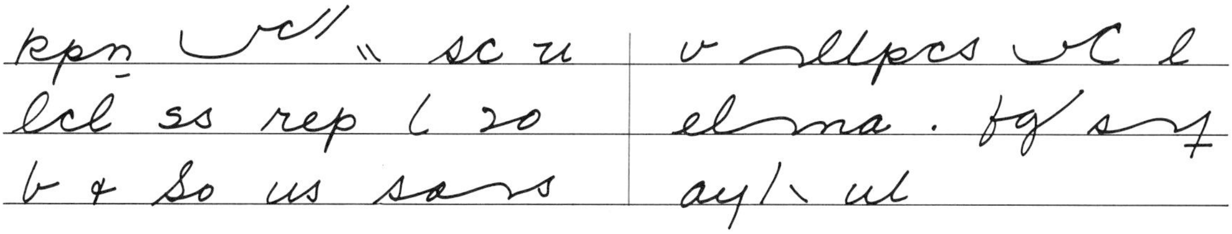

1.4 VOCABULARY BUILDING

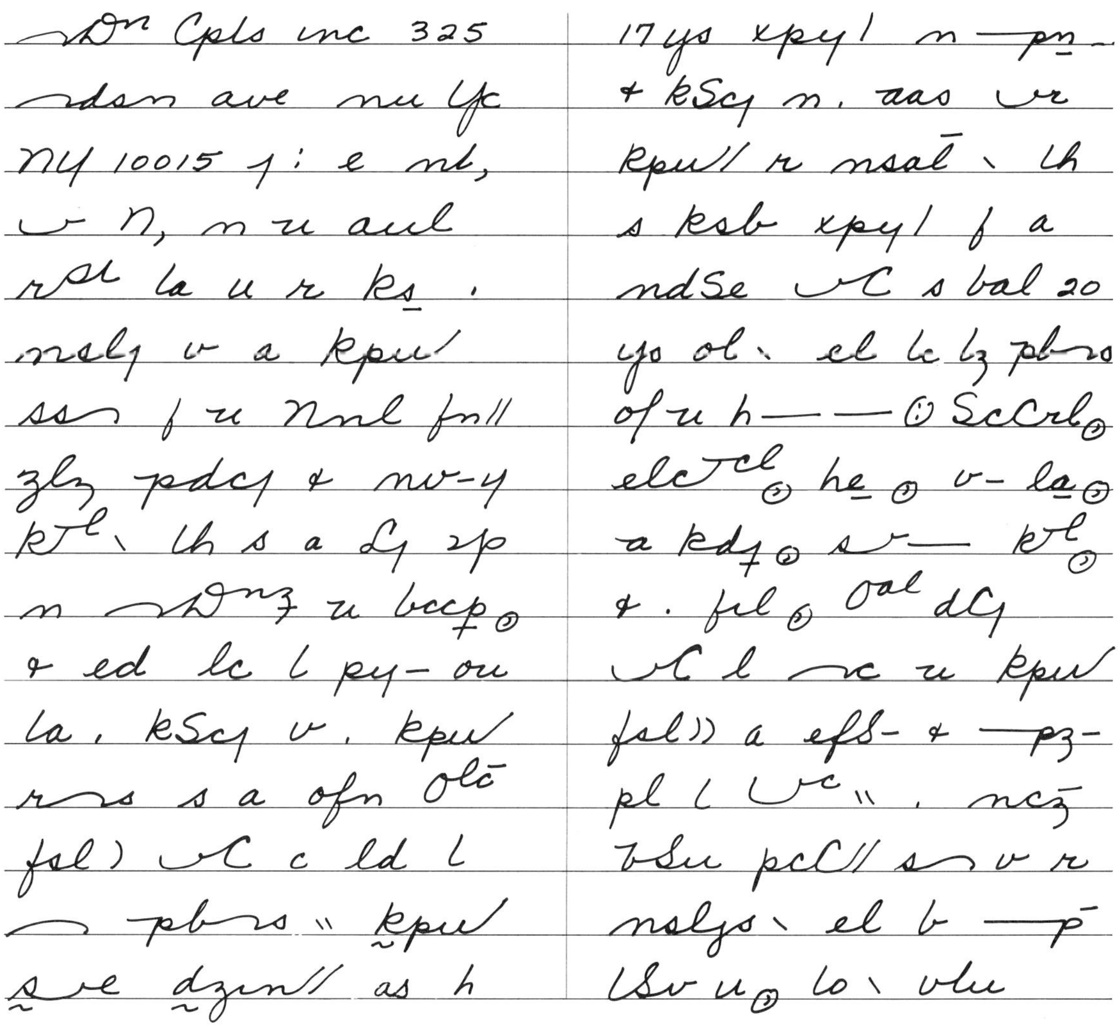

2.1 THEORY REVIEW

1. *ūre*

2. *ingly* 

3. *lee* 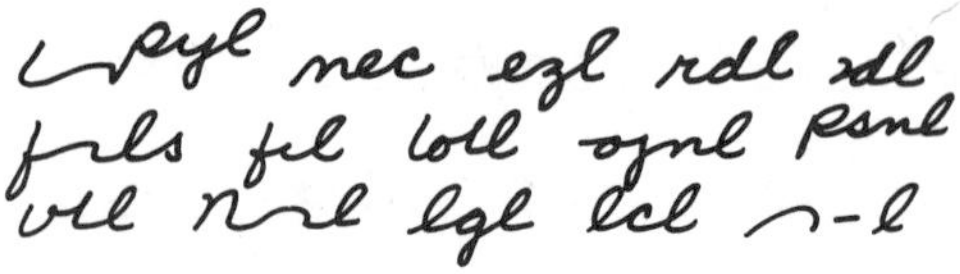

4. *tive* 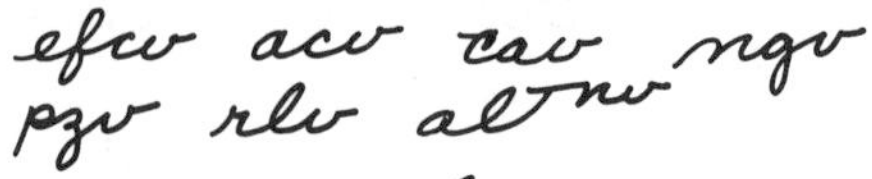

5. *prove* 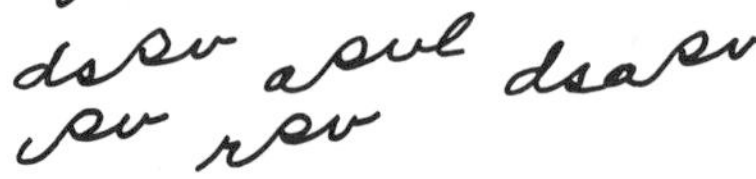

KEY 1. endure; mature; pure; cure; sure; brochure; duration; lure; secure 2. exceedingly; willingly; knowingly; seemingly; convincingly; surprisingly 3. temporarily; necessarily; easily; readily; steadily; families; finally; totally; originally; personally; vitally; normally; legally; locally; mentally 4. effective; active; creative; negative; positive; relative; alternative 5. disprove; approval; disapprove; improve; reprove

2.2 TRANSCRIPTION SKILL BUILDING

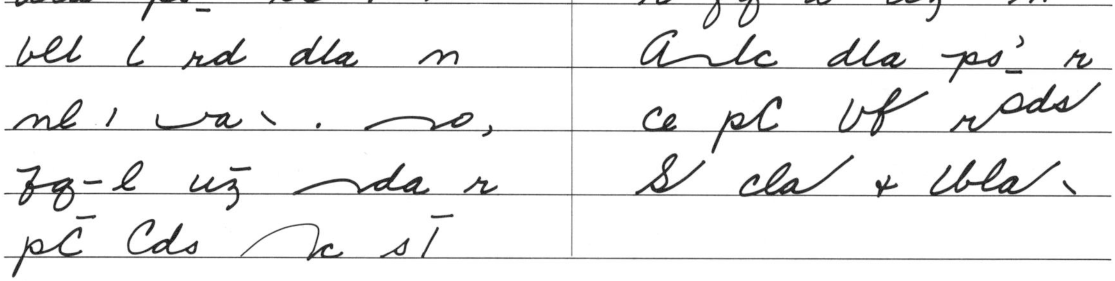

GUIDE Insert one conjunction comma, nine series commas, two compound adjective hyphens, and two enumeration colons.

2.3 SPEED BUILDING

acd-c ali inc
42-13 scili ave
vlPzo IN 46383 ȷ:
aCd l ndSe nfyo
ev Ln- la u r- .
Ovl- no v a Qf
v a ⌒ acd-c
robs eC y \ u ⌒,
cp Tc n nl v s—
. g-ns ou Kc f
sz lgl + cl b
lso v l r-n " e v

hp- ⌒ Is lfi a nuplo
sly l nv-y dfks
srl l us\. sly s.
elc-nc akl -Sn f
u sz I pC Cd ps:
s Sde aCl + efcv"
akl -Sns inc
pvds kpel rkdj
akl -Sns vC r
fcy 9-e \ ly -Sns
r ukdjl 9-e f a
pyd v 6 -os\ vlu

2.4 VOCABULARY BUILDING

Uo fnx rP 480 K
st N U vSgln DC
20033 ȷ: Uo fnx rP
s bq . -pn v a nu
-aq lb -dl af
u pz- suc Uo
rP\ uv pb Uo
rP f 32 ys + l
as b so pflb la

u r nfy . scop
v ls cV1 " ul v-
lreC . Tul nfx v
. Nngl fnx kn)\ e
v n r fils . Ly,
kply v nas n. nk
Uo\ ly nas r n-
kpuT3 so la e c
slcvl spi u U

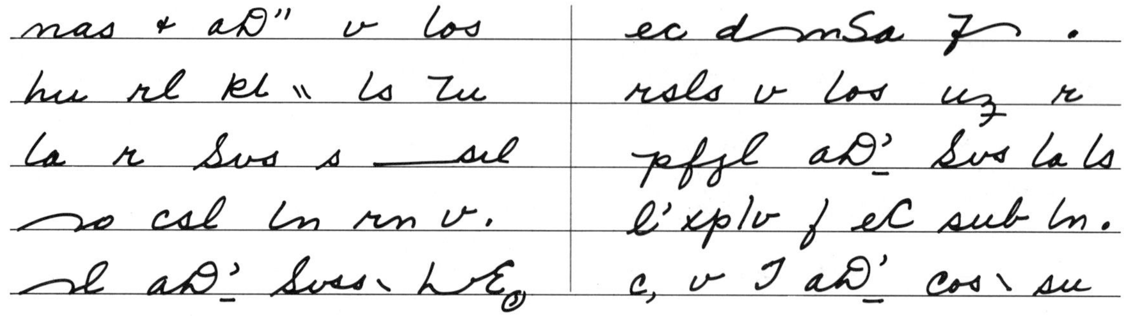

3.1 THEORY REVIEW

1. *ia ea*
2. Initial *ŭn*
3. *ful*
4. *enter*
5. *entr*

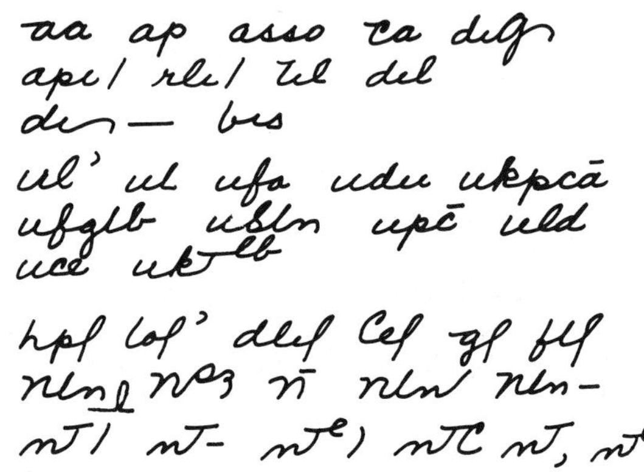

KEY 1. area; appreciate; associate; create; diagram; appliance; reliance; trial; dial; diamond; bias 2. unless; until; unfair; undo; uncomplicated; unforgettable; uncertain; unpacked; unload; unclear; uncontrollable 3. helpful; thoughtfulness; delightful; cheerful; grateful; faithful 4. entertainingly; enterprise; entered; entertainer; entertainment 5. entrance; entrant; entreaty; entrench; entrust; entry

3.2 TRANSCRIPTION SKILL BUILDING

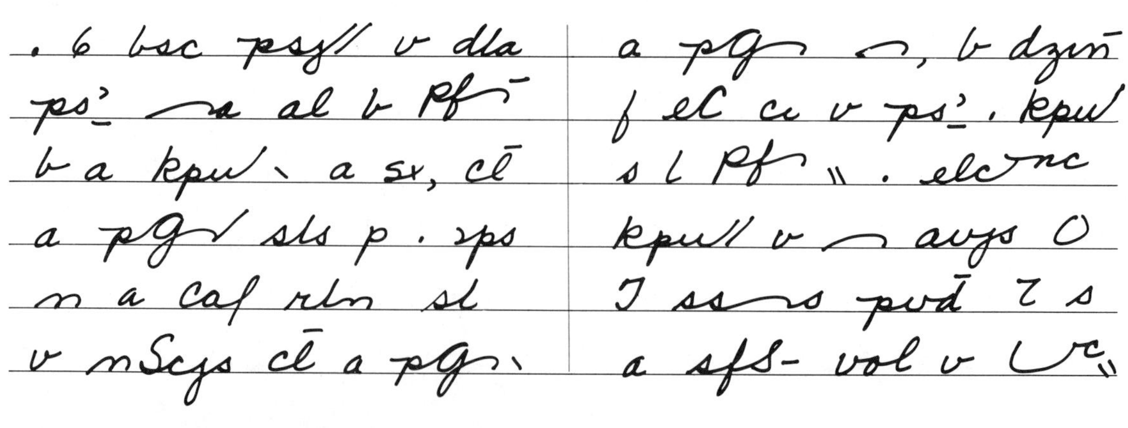

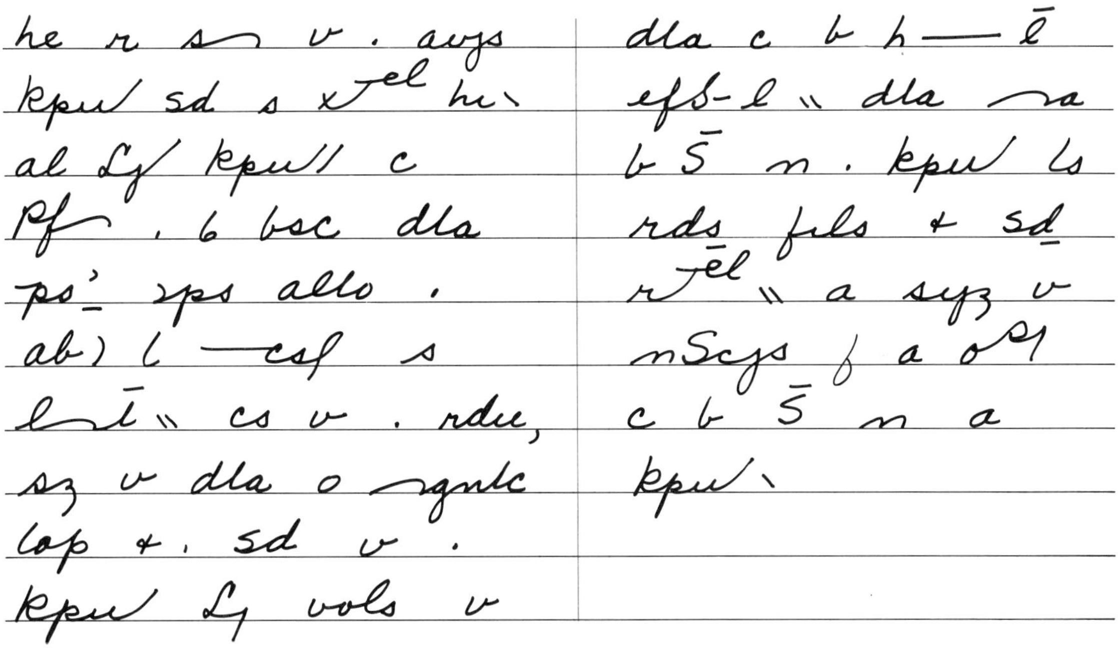

GUIDE Insert three parenthetical commas, one introductory comma, and one enumeration colon.

3.3 SPEED BUILDING

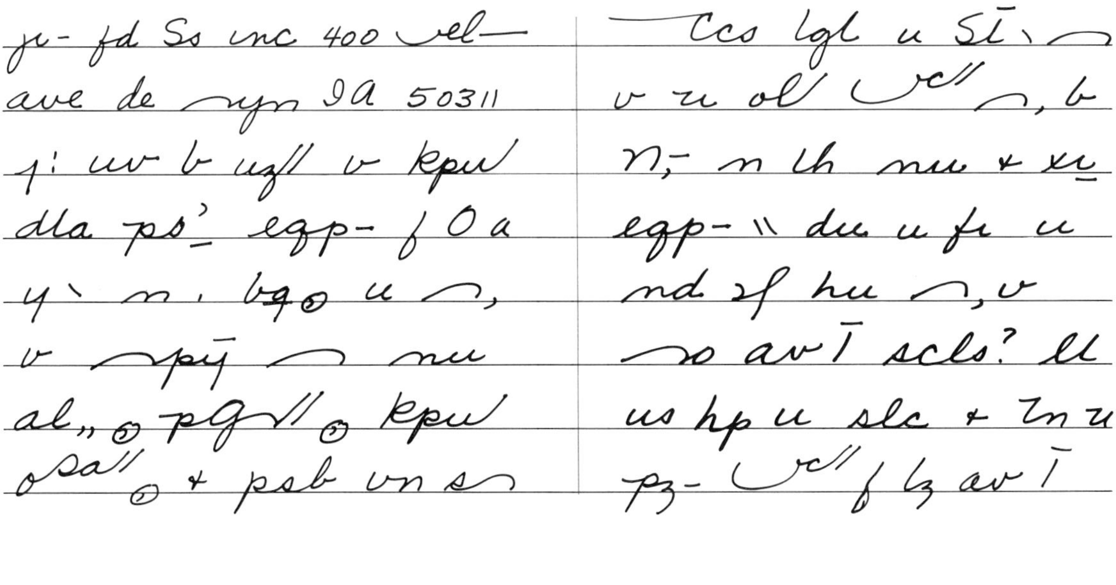

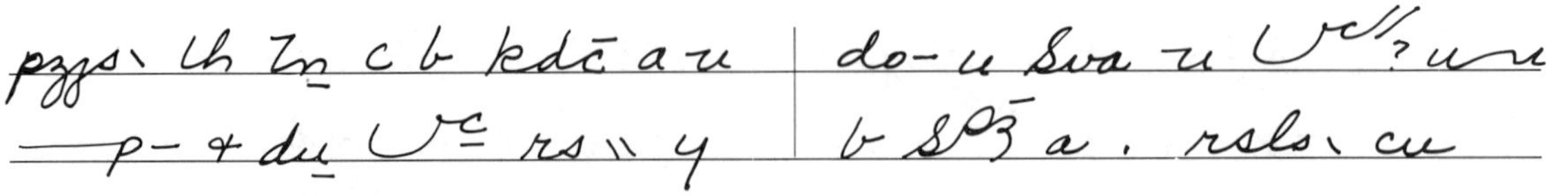

3.4 VOCABULARY BUILDING

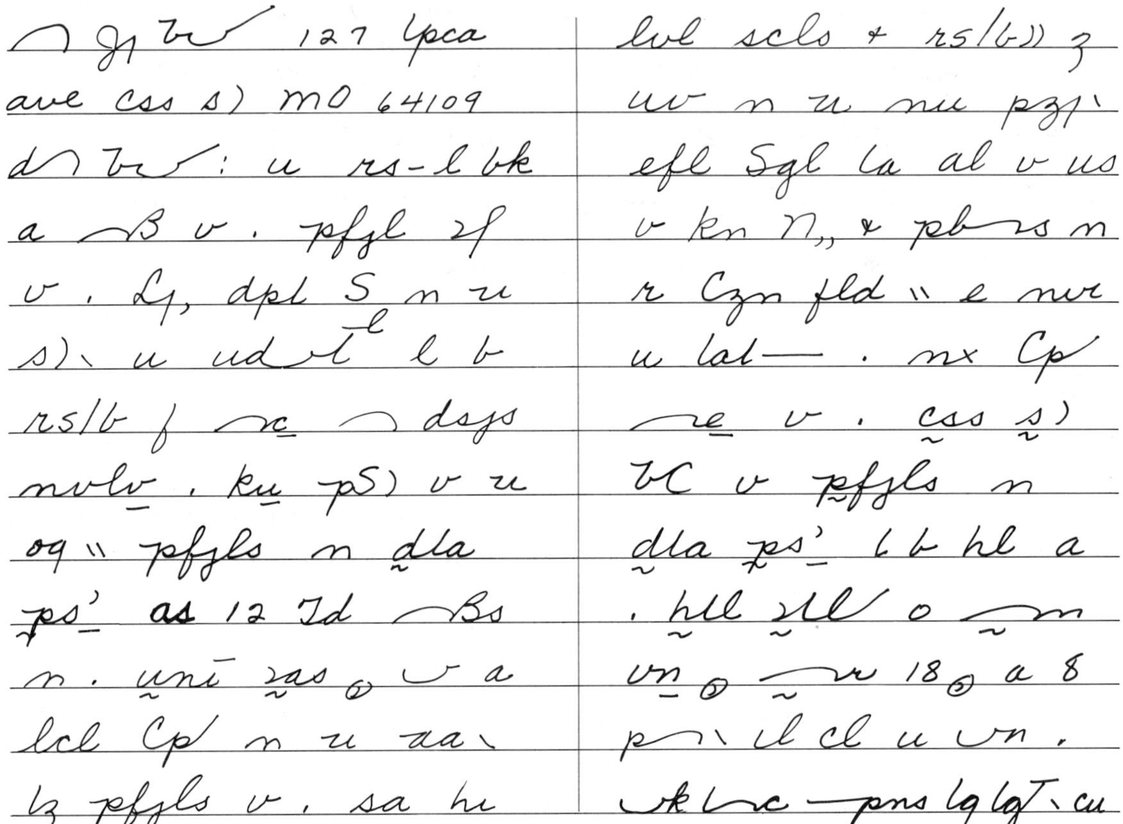

4.1 THEORY REVIEW

1. *cum*
2. *āne*
3. *kw*
4. *ow*
5. *ū*

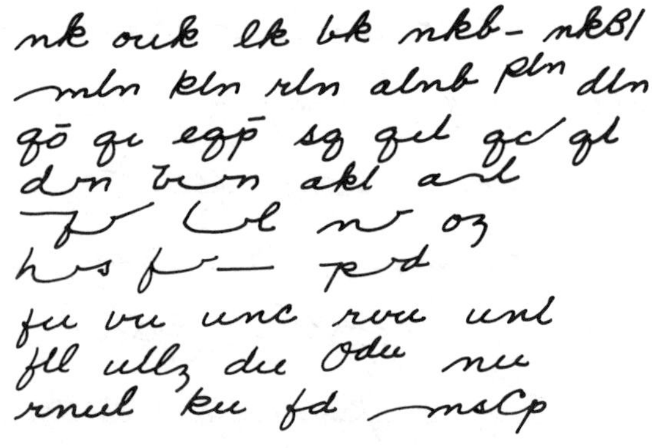

KEY 1. income; outcome; welcome; become; incumbent; encumbrance 2. maintain; contain; retain; attainable; pertain; detain 3. quoted; quite; equipped; square; quiet; quicker; quit 4. down; brown; account; amount; flower; towel; now; ounce; house; found; proud 5. few; view; unique; review; unit; unite; futile; utilize; do; overdue; new; renewal; continue; feud; manuscript

4.2 TRANSCRIPTION SKILL BUILDING

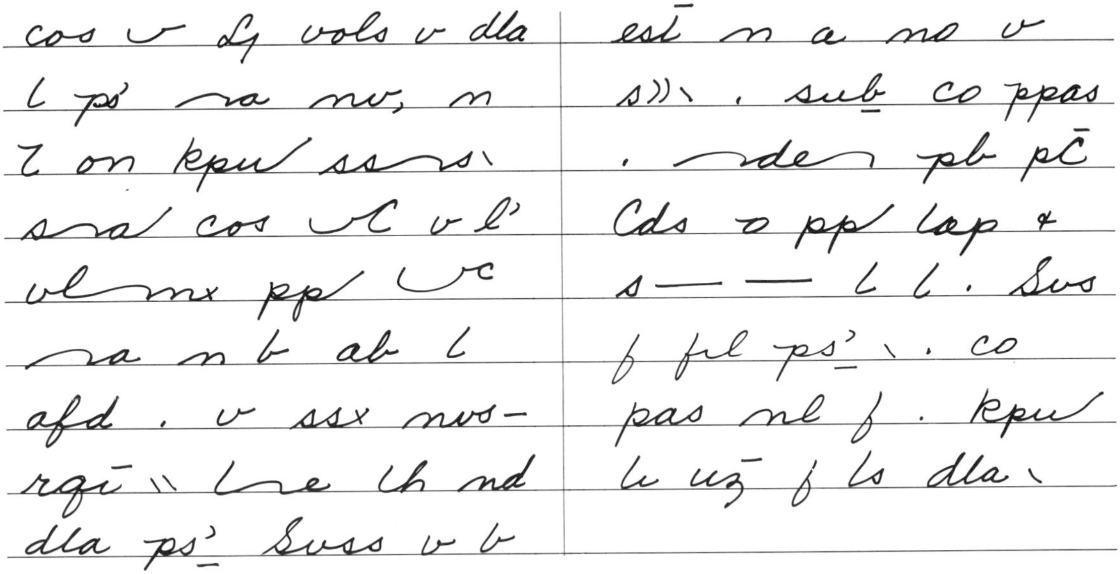

GUIDE Insert one introductory comma and four parenthetical commas.

4.3 SPEED BUILDING

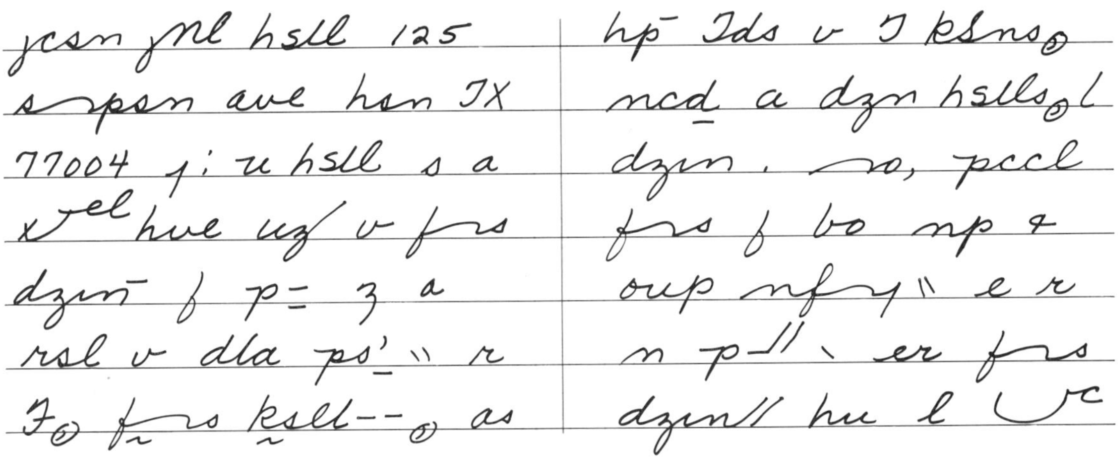

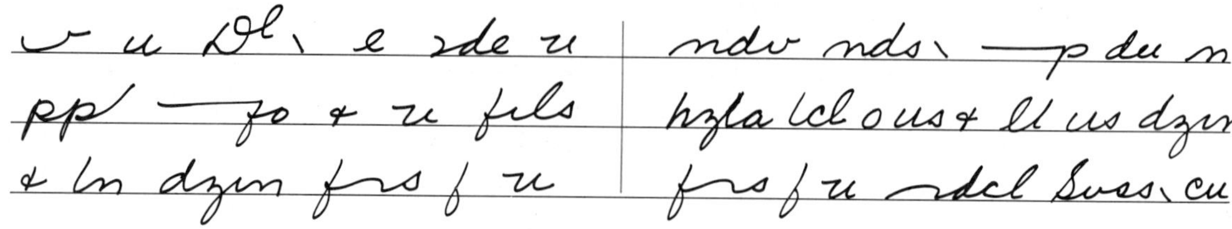

4.4 VOCABULARY BUILDING

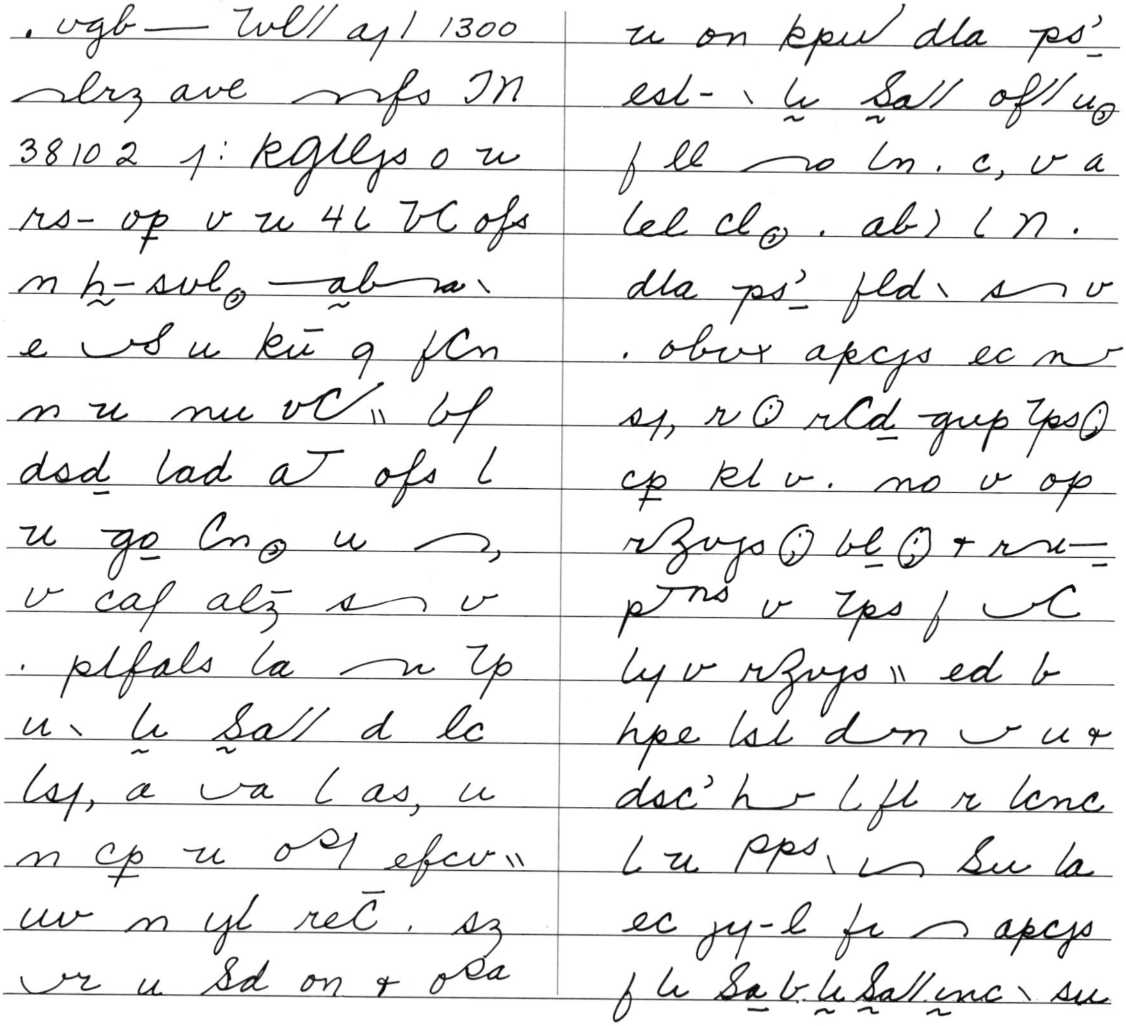

5.1 THEORY REVIEW

1. *oi* 

2. *īde*
3. *nk*
4. *ter*
5. *trans*

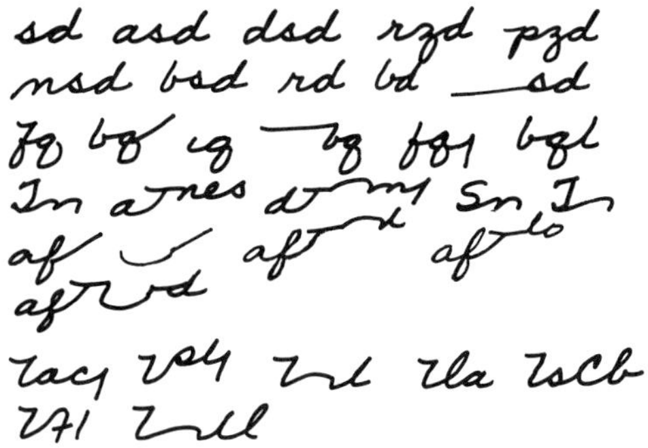

KEY 1. point; invoice; toil; enjoyed; boil; join; voice; avoid 2. side; aside; decide; reside; preside; inside; beside; ride; bide; slide 3. frank; banker; ink; blank; function; banquet 4. turn; attorneys; determination; stern; term; after; water; aftermath; afterthought; afterward 5. transaction; transportation; transmit; translate; transcribe; transference; transmittal

5.2 TRANSCRIPTION SKILL BUILDING

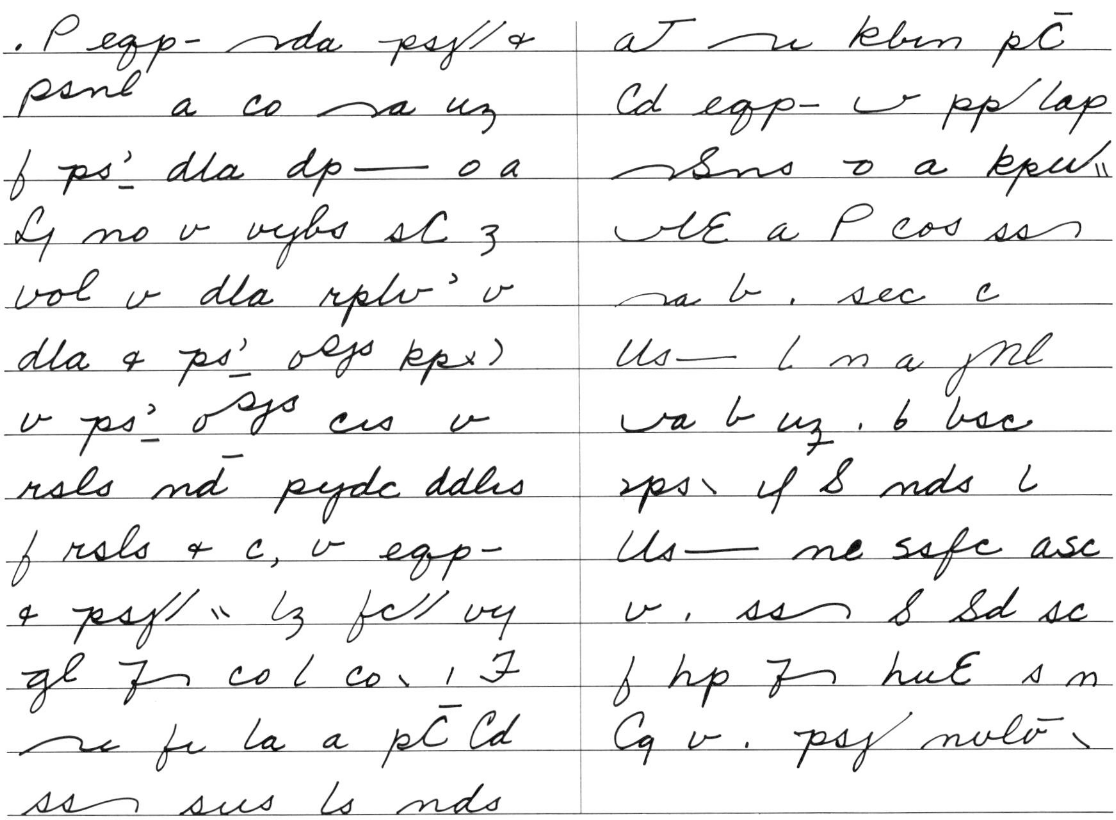

GUIDE Insert eight series commas, one parenthetical comma, two introductory commas, one enumeration colon, one no conjunction semicolon, three compound adjective hyphens, and one possessive apostrophe.

5.3 SPEED BUILDING

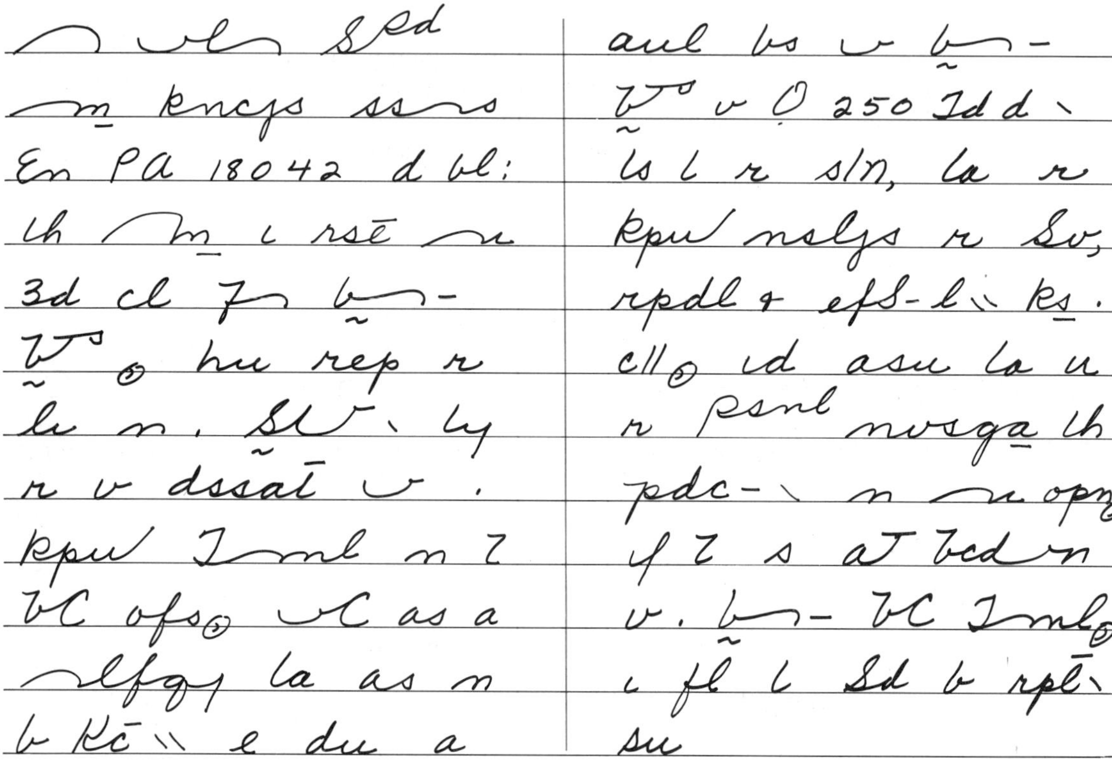

5.4 VOCABULARY BUILDING

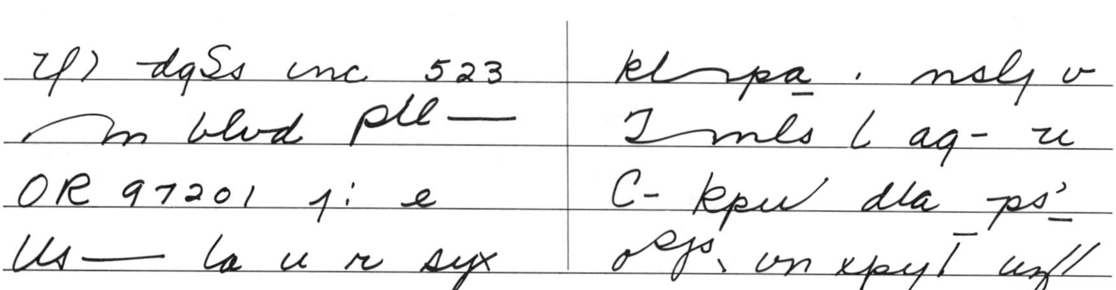

v kpull lc usll
Olc, fc la elc
pr sub f hrshol
& ndSel Ppss s
ofn n sf8-l rlib
f rl lu dla ps: "
nDa pr as d
. nds v nu
uz// v kpu Imls.
e Q-e la nDa Ks
c ssn l dla ps'
n a kl va vn
vn Nl elc

pr fls. d n
av/ h c lu ul
nd n. ev-v pr
fl. nDa l spe
u pr rqe-- f a
gdul sod n
pyd v 3 ns l
3 rs " jyn r l, v
pGsv e--. ksll
us lhp u pn lh
f zp l pds.
Cp, + o, efcv
rsls. su

REFERENCES

A secretary is not expected to have all information at his fingertips, but he is expected to know where to find it.

Buy a new and up-to-date desk dictionary every five or six years. In addition every office should have an unabridged dictionary.

Many technical dictionaries are available, such as financial, medical, law, and chemical. If there is no need for a technical dictionary, an alphabetical list of words peculiar to the business should be compiled.

In addition to dictionaries, every office should have a good atlas and a map of the city as well as a current statistical almanac.

Other valuable reference books are a book of quotations, a secretarial handbook, an office manual, and a thesaurus.

UNIT 18

GENERAL BUSINESS

1.1 THEORY REVIEW

1. *con*
2. *com*
3. *old*
4. *ual*
5. *re*

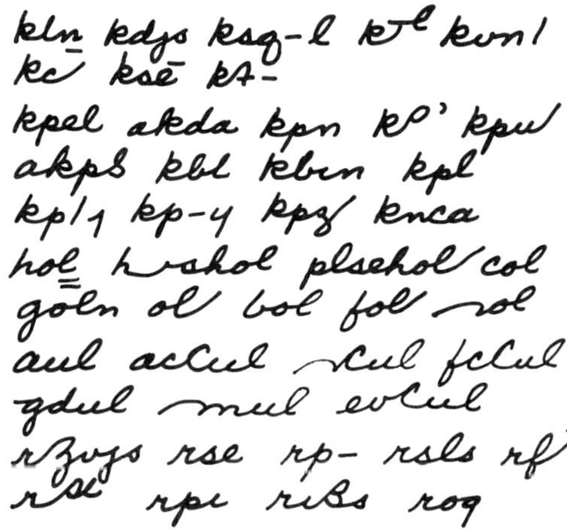

KEY 1. containing; conditions; consequently; control; convenience; concur; conceived; confront 2. completely; accommodate; complain; compress; computer; accomplish; combat; combine; compel; compensation; complimentary; compositor; communicate 3. holdings; household; policyholder; cold; golden; older; bold; folder; mold; 4. annual; actual; mutual; factual; gradual; manual, eventual 5. reservations; receive; repent; results; referred; report; reply; reimburse; reorganize

1.2 TRANSCRIPTION SKILL BUILDING

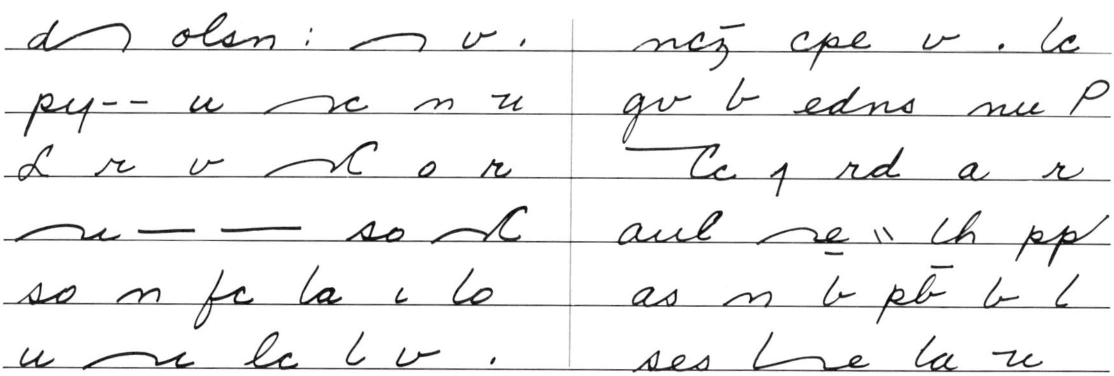

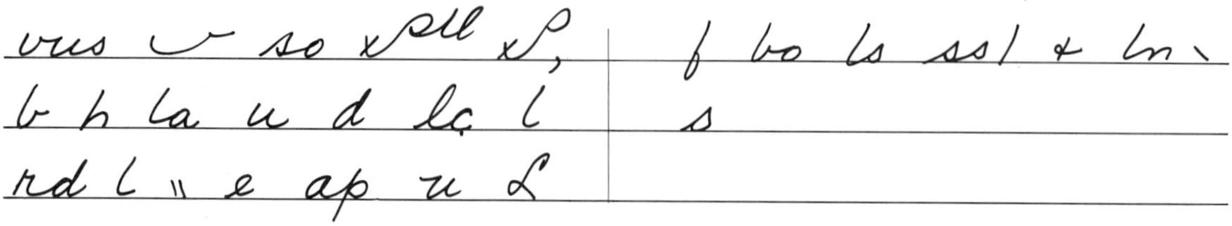

GUIDE Insert one dash, two parenthetical commas, two apposition commas, one conjunction comma, and one possessive apostrophe.

1.3 SPEED BUILDING

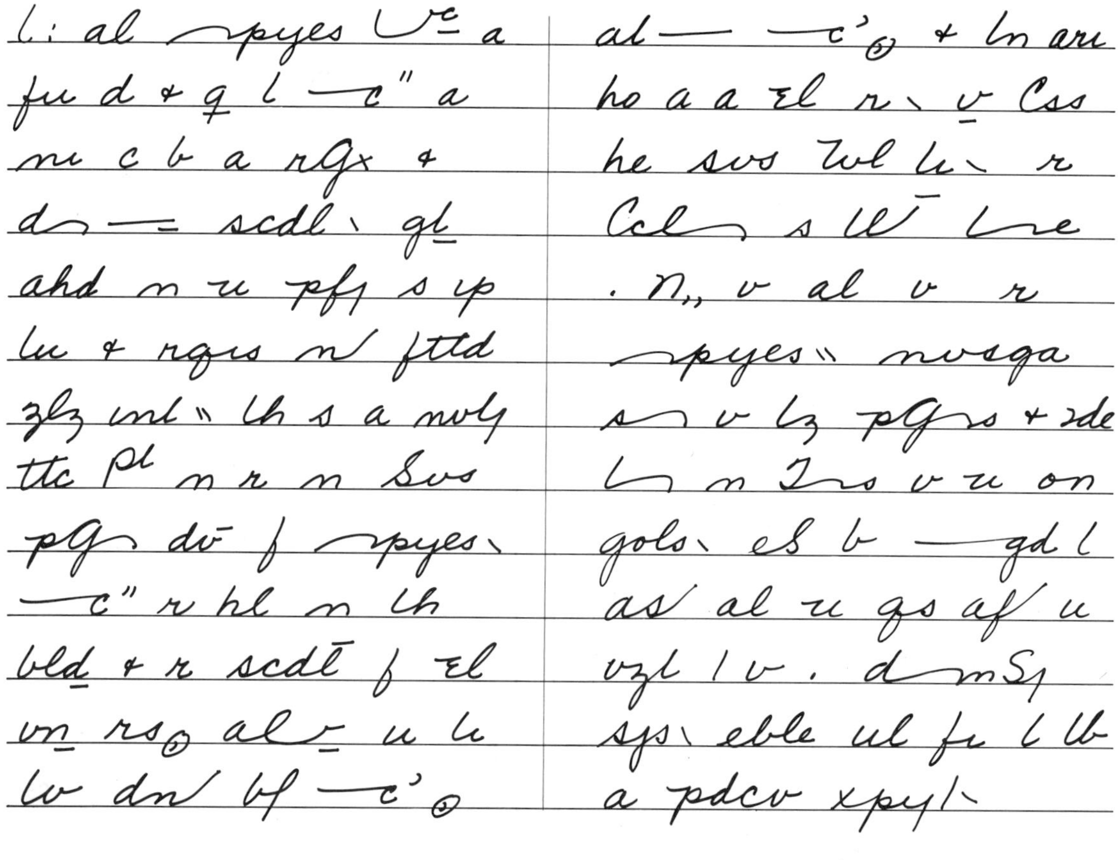

1.4 VOCABULARY BUILDING

d' cml —f— 69
gnt blvd lq Bec CA
90806 dr' —f—: Bs
v. fC secs —cb v
Ern hi scl r —pn
a nfy Ucsp, er
ntds lh lup v scl
acv) f. F, lu, .
Ucsp s scdl f
sl ap 27 & l ncd
a lCn" r Pps sl
gv secl rd-- a opl
lre v pfyl secs
Uc n vyx ofss hu
d b gx enf l dsc'
s pzv los ab 7
ofs suls" z u r a
cert pfyl sec hu
gda f Ern hi
& r a xcv sec
l. VP v u co

u qlfcys pl u F,
o r l, v secs l
b nvi l sec l us"
e r nvi rd--
f 4 J hi scls l,
b v us, r pG
s —pn f 9 a
l 2 p, r 9,,
a Cz vC lpcs
ly d lc l lsn l,
e hop l v a no
v scl l e v
rd-- n s a
s mr r s" e
hop u l sa ys
& s— lh lu v
us, e d lc l
ppa a pG gd
& r p= a DY v
9,, a e v. ttl
v u 20 un aD'? s

2.1 THEORY REVIEW

1. *im*
2. *de*
3. *em*
4. *for*
5. *fur*

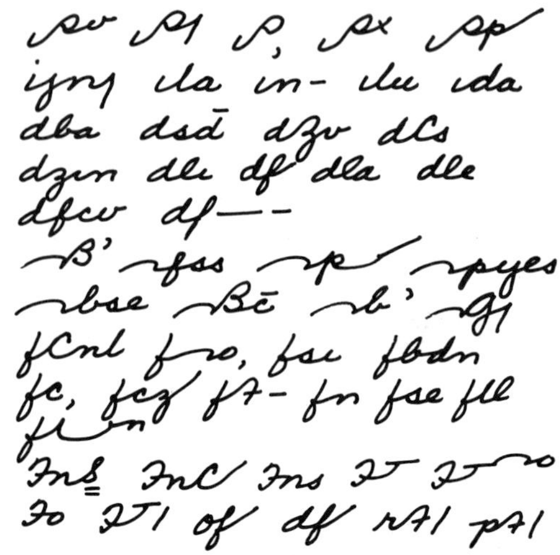

KEY 1. improve; impression; impressed; impartial; improper; imagination; imitate; imminent; immature; immediate 2. debate; decided; deserve; decrease; design; delight; defer; delay; delete; defective; defendent 3. embarrass; emphasis; empower; employees; embassy; embarked; emboss; emigration 4. fortunate; foremost; foresight; forbidden; forecast; foreclosure; forefront; foreign; foresee; foretell; forewarn 5. furnishings; furniture; furnace; further; furthermore; furrow; furtherance; offer; defer; reference; preference

2.2 TRANSCRIPTION SKILL BUILDING

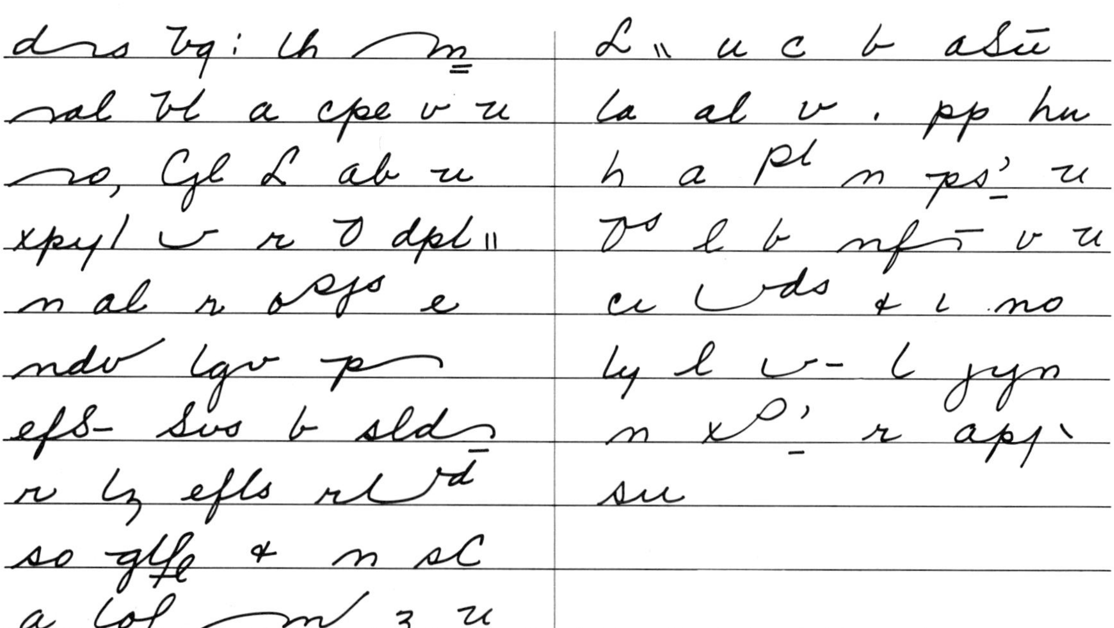

GUIDE Insert one possessive apostrophe, one introductory comma, one adjective comma, and two conjunction commas.

2.3 SPEED BUILDING

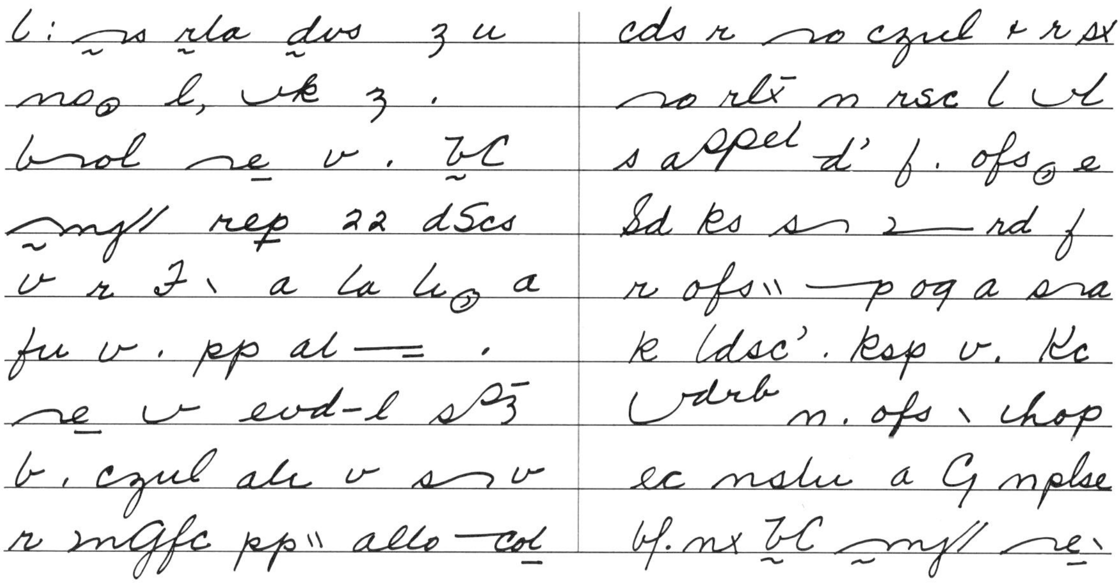

2.4 VOCABULARY BUILDING

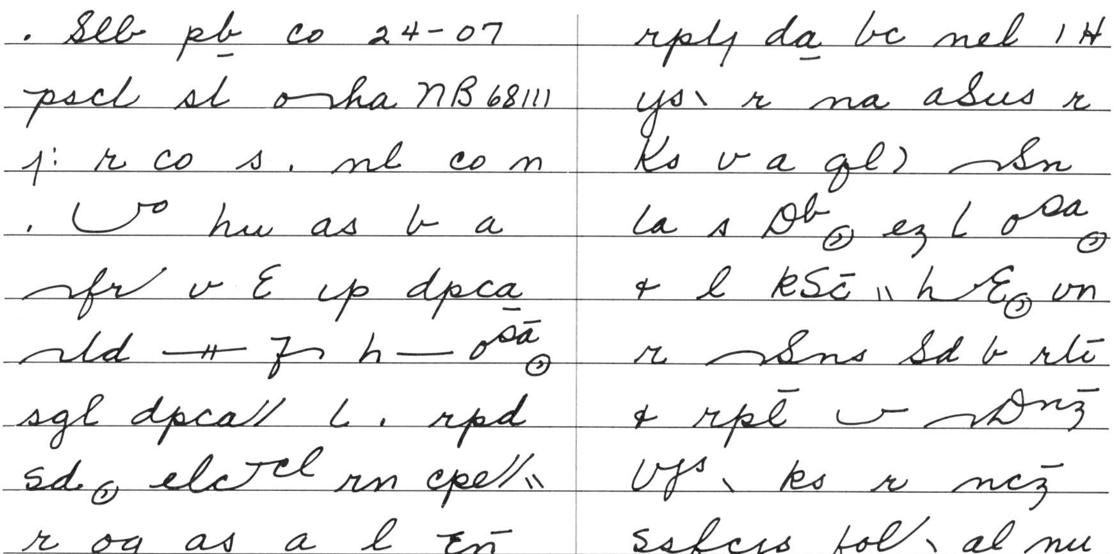

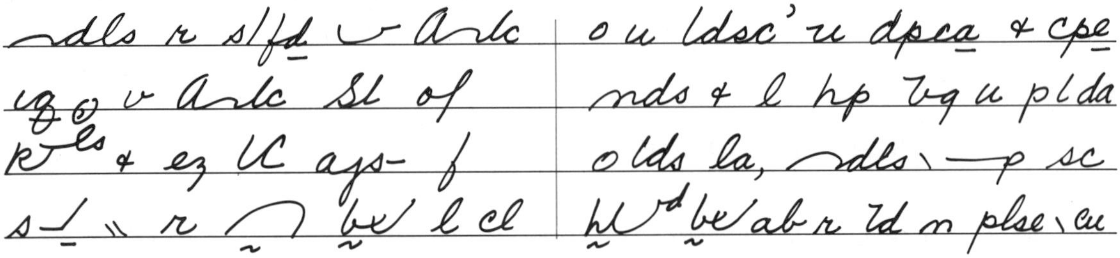

3.1 THEORY REVIEW

1. *in*
2. *mis*
3. *over*
4. *post*
5. *under*

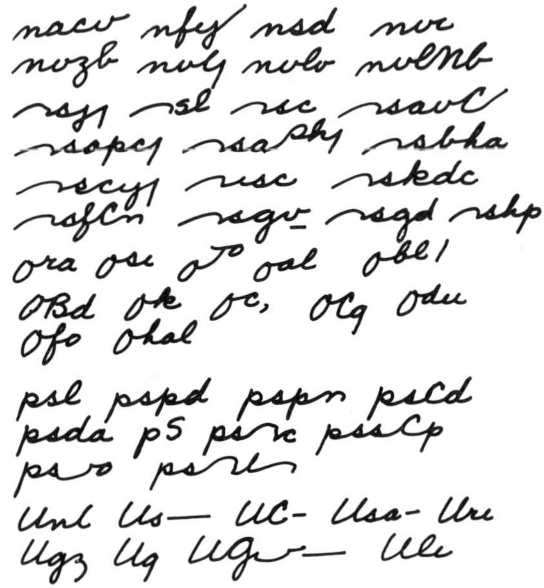

KEY 1. inactive; inferior; inside; invite; invisible; invitation; involve; invulnerable 2. misjudge; misspell; mistake; misadventure; misapplication; misapprehension; misbehave; miscarriage; miscellaneous; misconduct; misfortune; misgiving; misguide; mishap 3. overrate; oversight; overthrow; overall; overbalance; overboard; overcome, overcame; overcast; overcharge; overdo, overdue; overflow; overhaul 4. postal; postpaid; postpone; postcard; postdate; poster; postmark; postscript; postwar; postmortem 5. underneath; understand; undercurrent; understatement; underwrite; underglaze; undergo; underground; underline

3.2 TRANSCRIPTION SKILL BUILDING

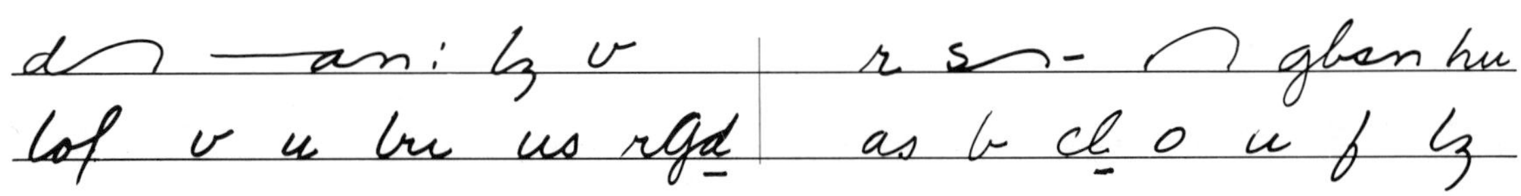

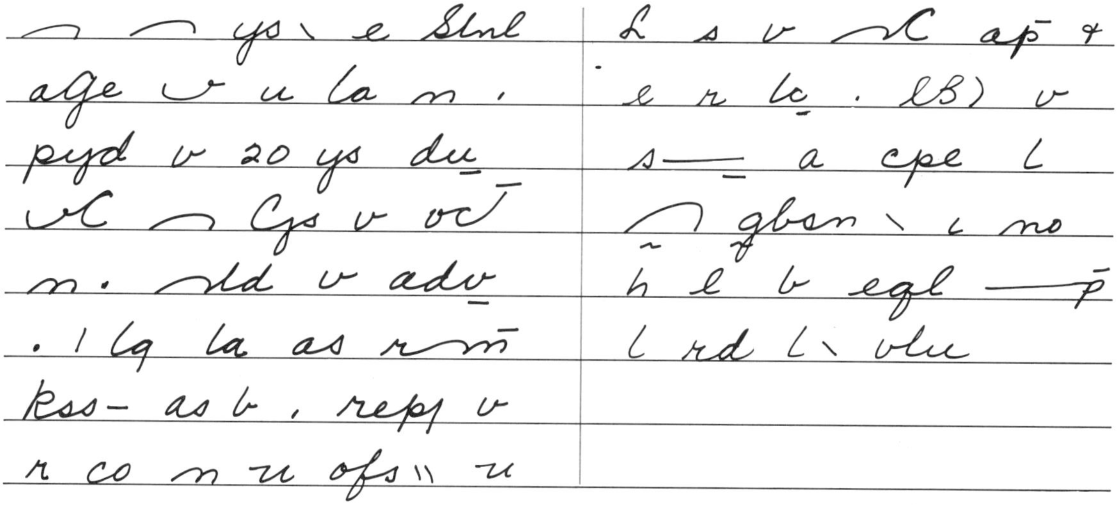

GUIDE Insert two apposition commas, one adjective comma, two parenthetical commas, and one conjunction comma.

3.3 SPEED BUILDING

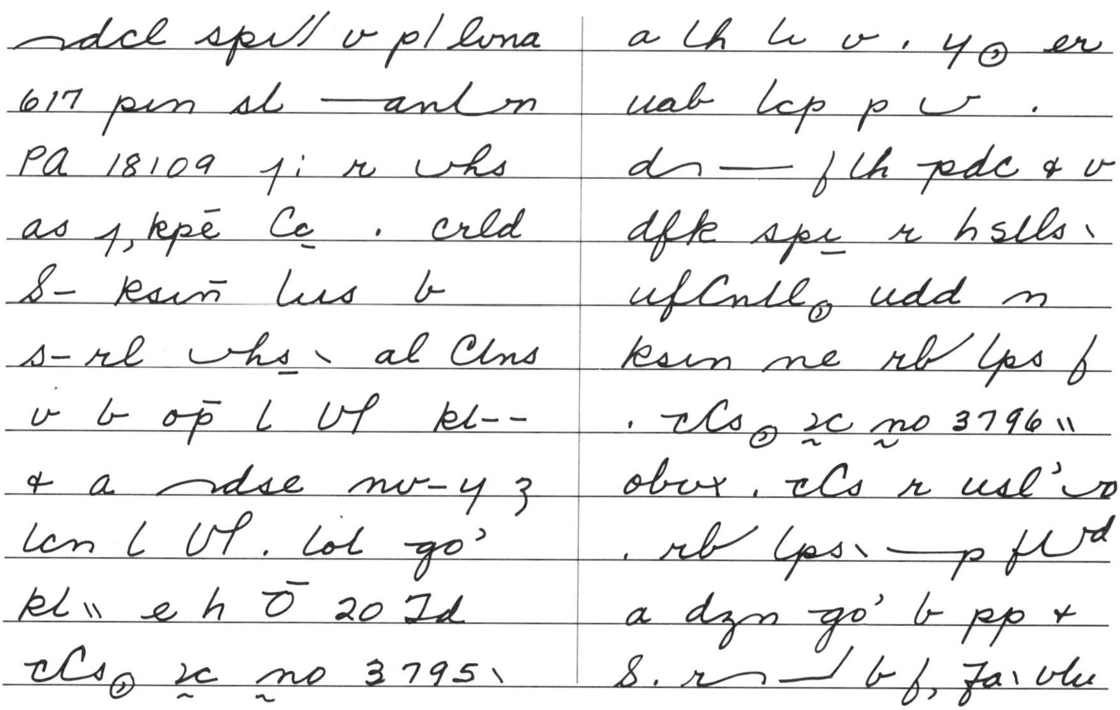

3.4 VOCABULARY BUILDING

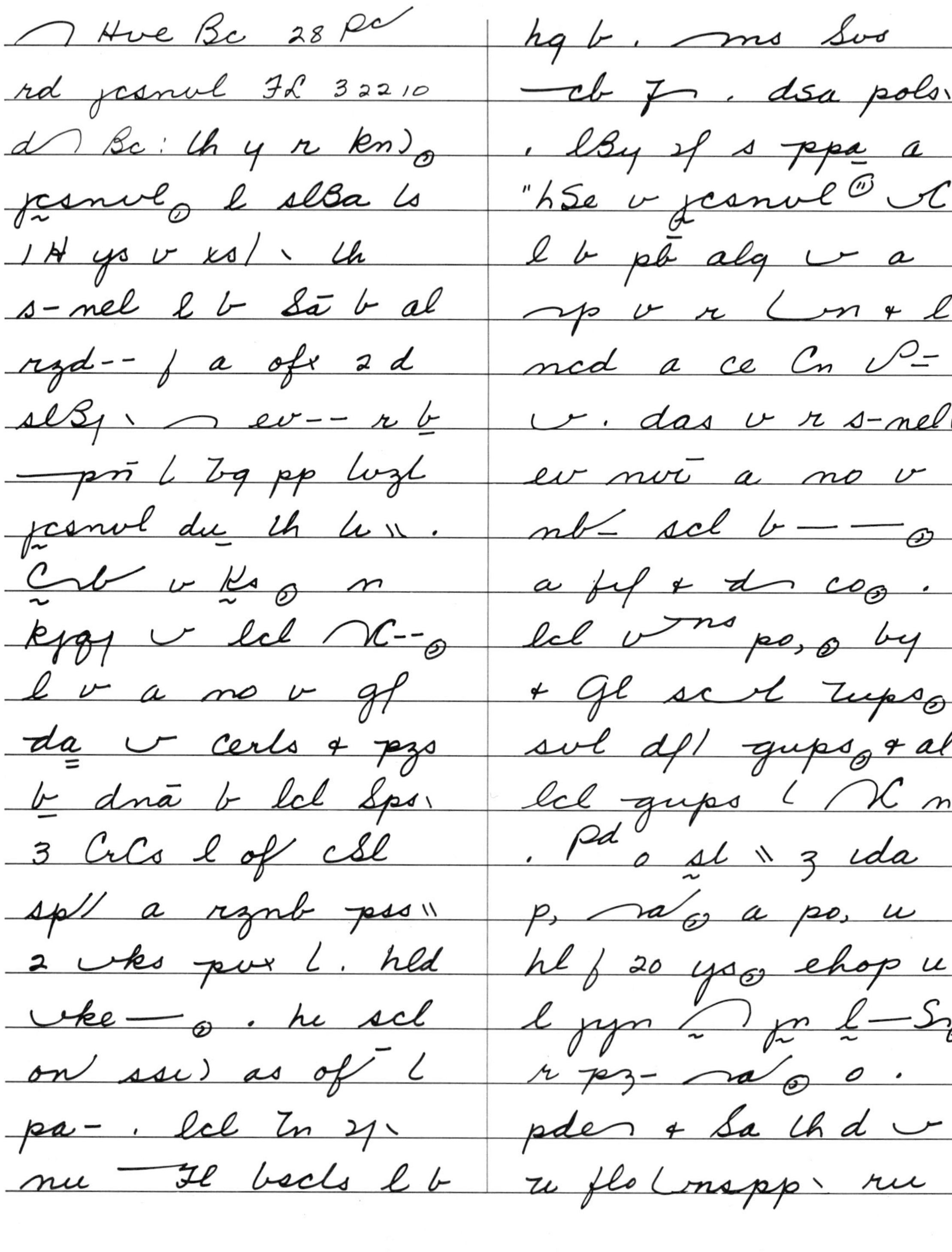

4.1 THEORY REVIEW

1. *eet*
2. *ame*
3. *ake*
4. *wh*
5. Abbreviations

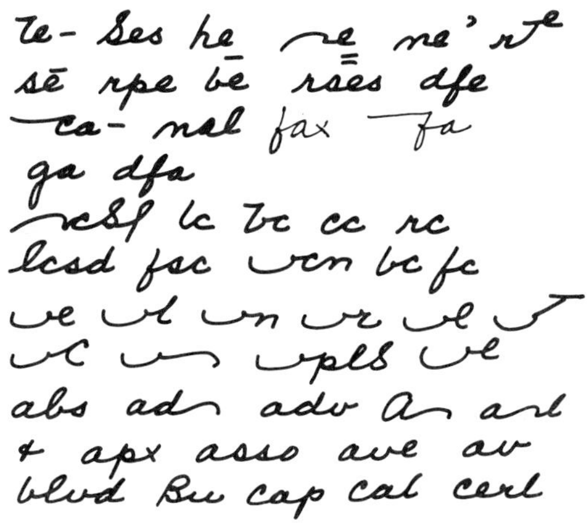

KEY 1. treatment; sheets; heating; meetings; neatness; retreat; seated; repeat; beat; receipts; defeat 2. claimant; namely; famous; flame; game; defame 3. makeshift; take; break, brake; cake; rake; lakeside; forsake; waken; bake; fake 4. wheat; what; when; where; while; whether; which; whim; whiplash; whirl 5. absolute, ly; administrate, administration; advertise; America, n; amount; and; approximate, ly; associate; avenue; average; boulevard; bureau; capital; catalog; certify, certificate

4.2 TRANSCRIPTION SKILL BUILDING

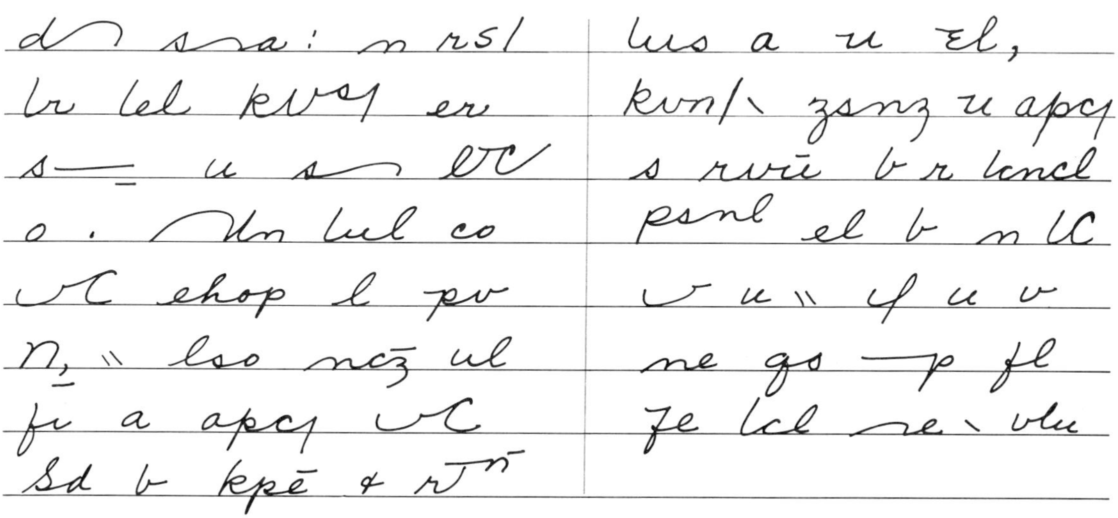

GUIDE Insert four introductory commas and two parenthetical commas.

4.3 SPEED BUILDING

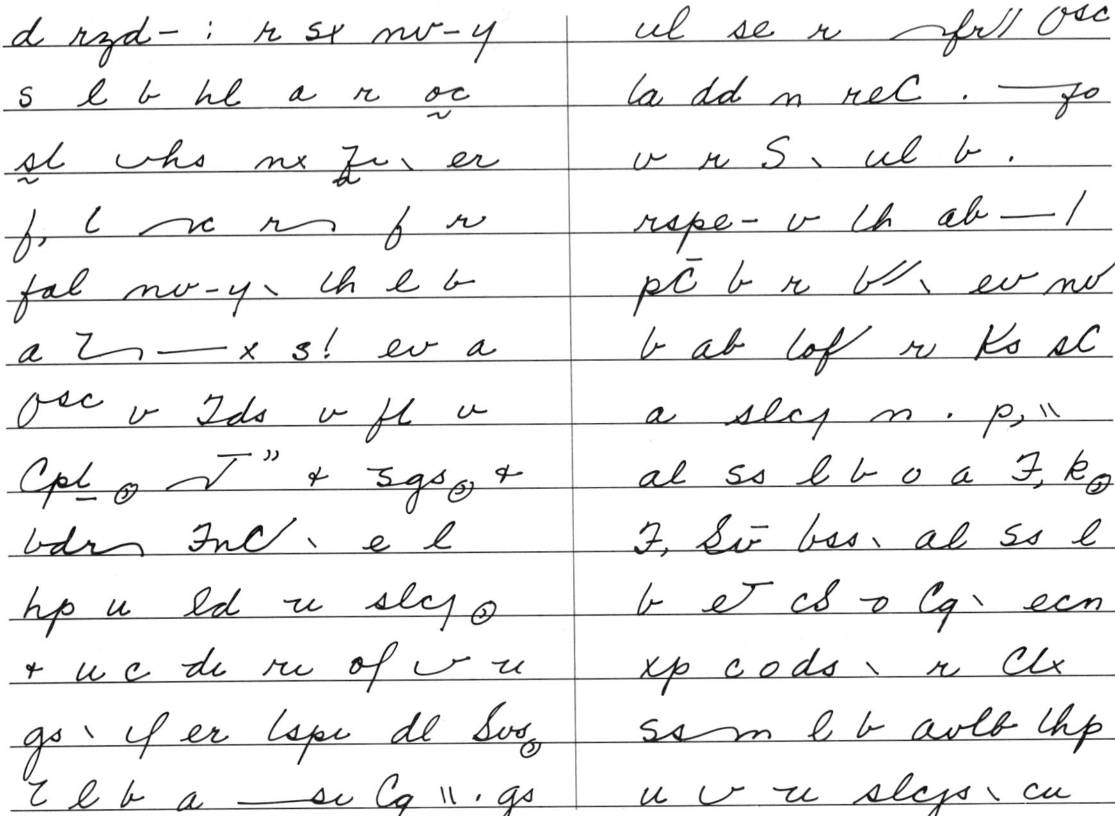

4.4 VOCABULARY BUILDING

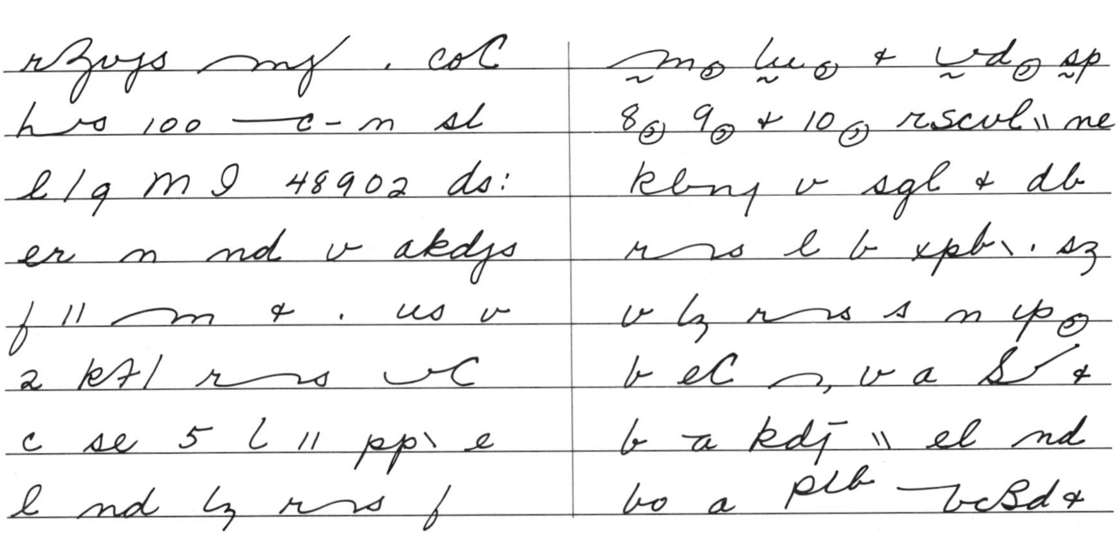

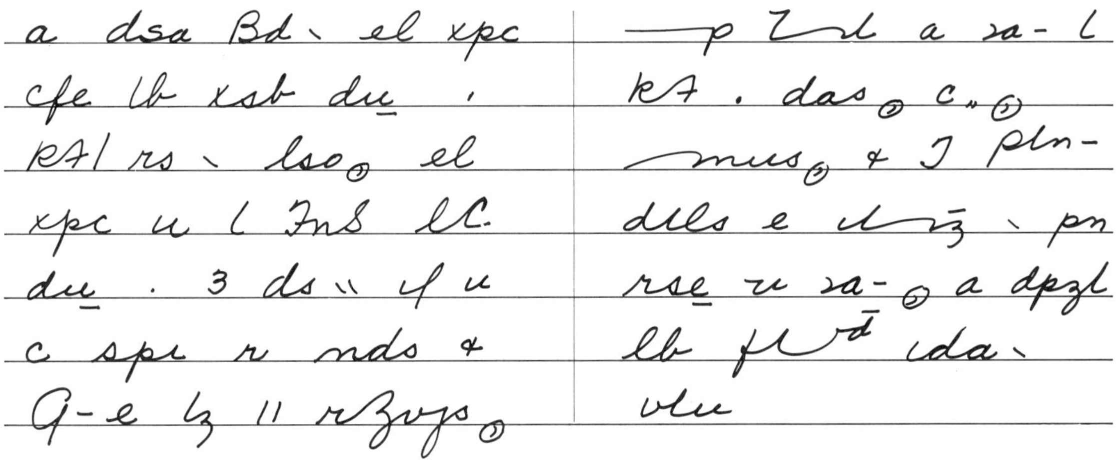

5.1 THEORY REVIEW

1. *ite*
2. *eem*
3. *ede*
4. *ch*
5. Abbreviations

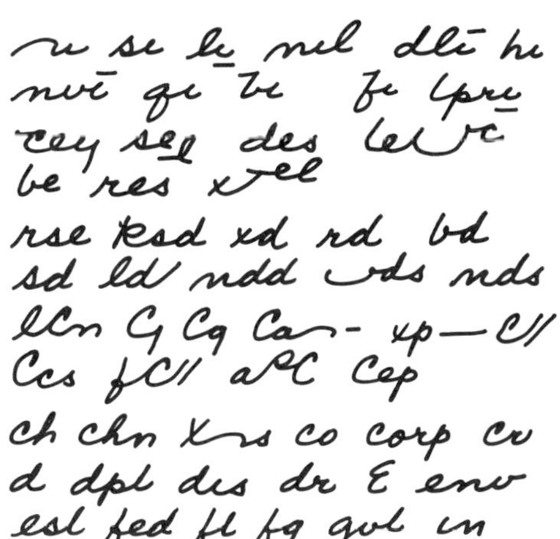

KEY 1. might; sight; lighting; nightly; delighted; height; invited; quite; bright; fright; typewriting 2. creamery; seemingly; deems; teamwork; beam; reams; extremely 3. recede; concede; exceed, accede; read; bead; seed, cede; leader; indeed; weeds; needs 4. luncheon; change; charge; chairman; expenditures; checks; features; approach; cheap 5. child; children; Christmas; company; corporation; credit; day; department; discount; doctor; east; envelope; establish; federal; foot, feet; figure; government; inch

5.2 TRANSCRIPTION SKILL BUILDING

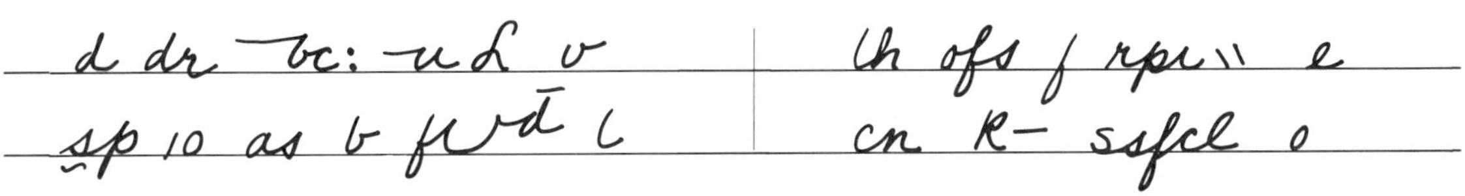

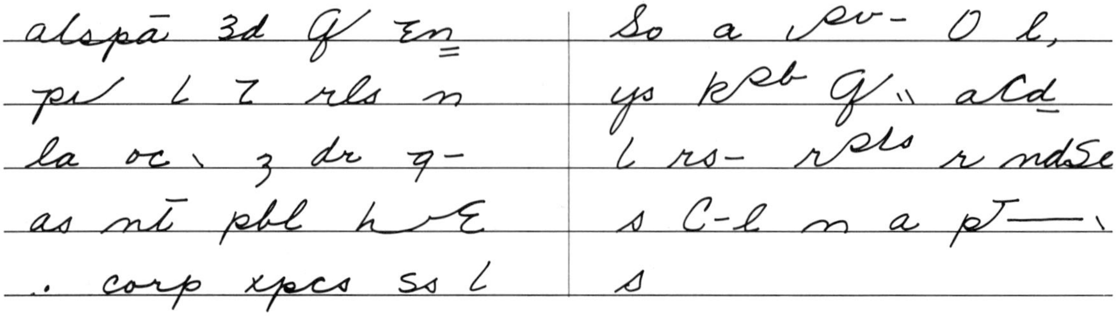

GUIDE Insert two parenthetical commas, one introductory comma, and one possessive apostrophe.

5.3 SPEED BUILDING

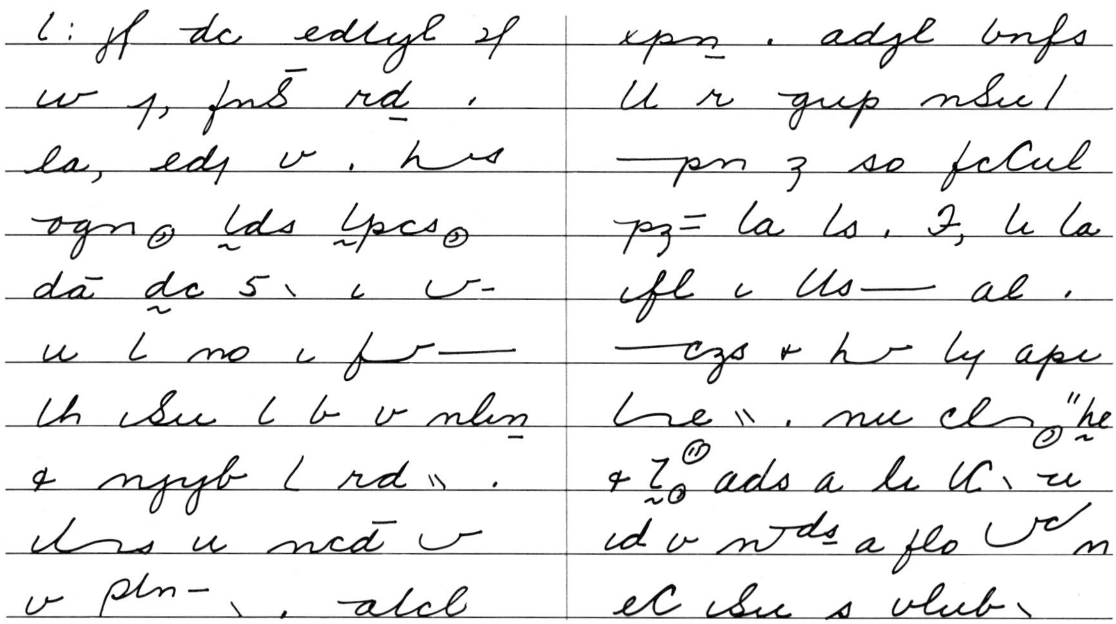

5.4 VOCABULARY BUILDING

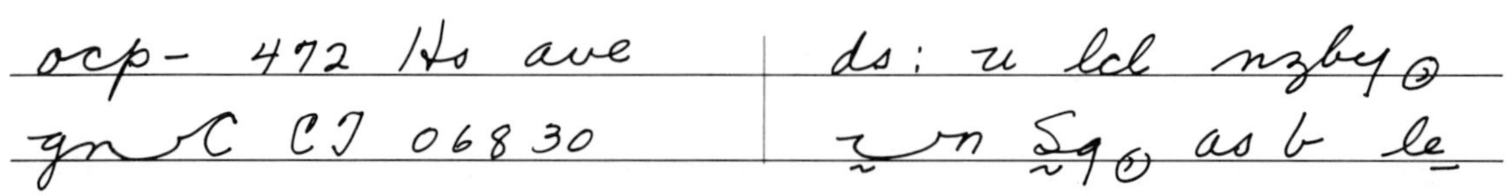

u a cpe v . gnC
rCd eC m e
xpc u v fr-l
o u dosp z u v
b le f Lvc .
gnC rCd s a
nzpp f . fsl e
p-nyl & Nnyl
nz a fsl p Sls
& kcs edlyls b
nyl fgs llvy
rdo & lecl l
& clCrl acv)) e
nvi nlss F
lcl grups er l
sst b lcl bsm
hu ap r xl/v sub
l, z ur a nu
rzd- n l dl

a ze cpe v . rCd
lu f a adyl vk
1 vn h l so b l
nTds hsl lu e hop
u v nyj rd .
gnC rCd & v
fr- l a Ss v
nfy lu z a nu
B v . kn)) r
sub ras r rznb
e pd rsl o r dl
Svs n as b 1
v r so, rlib dl
bys y n ll h
of u s cpb Svs
& sa ys n
h sos b l sc u
l bk 1 v r sub//?
s

WORD DIVISION

Whenever possible, avoid dividing words at the end of a line. Why? Word divisions detract from the appearance of the letter and they slow down and sometimes confuse the reader.

A line may be approximately five strokes longer or shorter than the desired line length. Therefore, the guiding rule for every typist should be to divide words only when it is absolutely necessary in order to maintain a reasonably even right margin.

A condensed list of rules for word division is given in the introduction to your *Speedwriting Dictionary*.

In addition to these rules, here are a few more suggestions:

One-syllable words must never be divided because a word may be divided only between syllables.

Words containing prefixes and suffixes are usually divided after the prefix or before the suffix. However, examine the word *practicable.* The suffix is *able* but the word is divided *prac-ti-cable.* Always check a dictionary when you are not certain of the division.

A punctuation mark must never be separated from the word it follows.

Avoid separating the parts of a word group that are ordinarily read together, such as: *on March 10, at 10:30 a.m.,* and *at 60 West Street.*

UNIT 19

SECRETARIAL CHECKLIST

1.1 THEORY REVIEW

1. *ote*
2. *ime*
3. *ude*
4. *sp*
5. Abbreviations

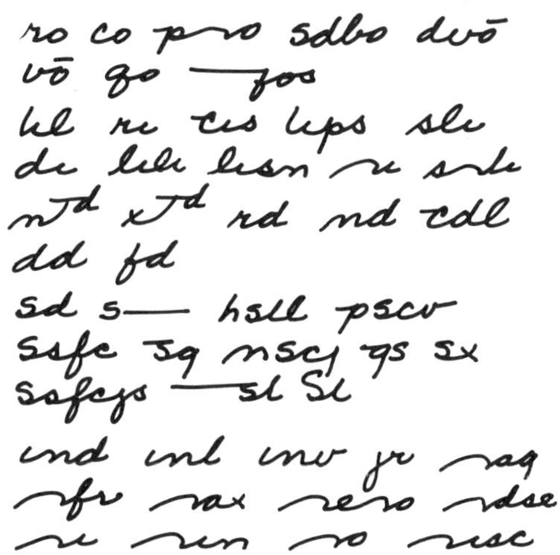

KEY 1. wrote; coat; promote; speedboat; devoted; voted; quote; floats 2. timely; rhyme; crimes; timepiece; sublime; dime; limelight; limestone; mime; sometime 3. intrude; extrude; rude; nude; crudely; dude; feud 4. speed; spend; hospital; prospective; specific; spring; inspection; grasp; special; specifications; split; sport 5. independent; intelligent, intelligently, intelligence; invoice; junior; magazine; manufacture; maximum; memorandum; merchandise; mile; minimum, minute; month; miscellaneous

1.2 TRANSCRIPTION SKILL BUILDING

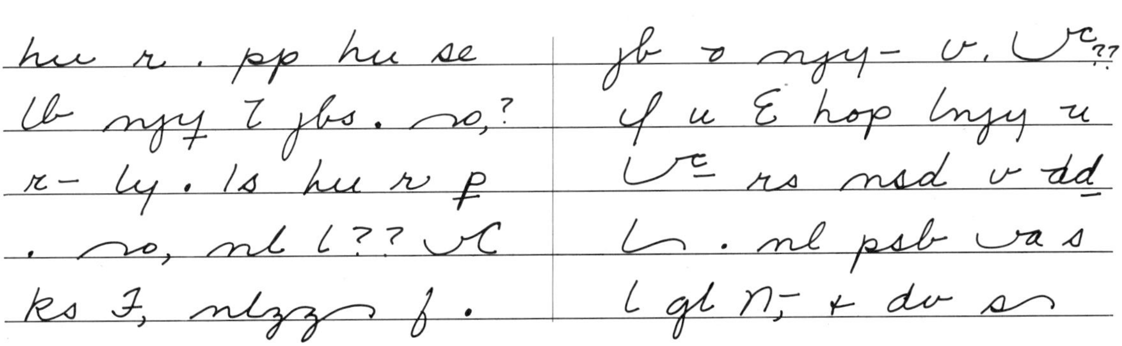

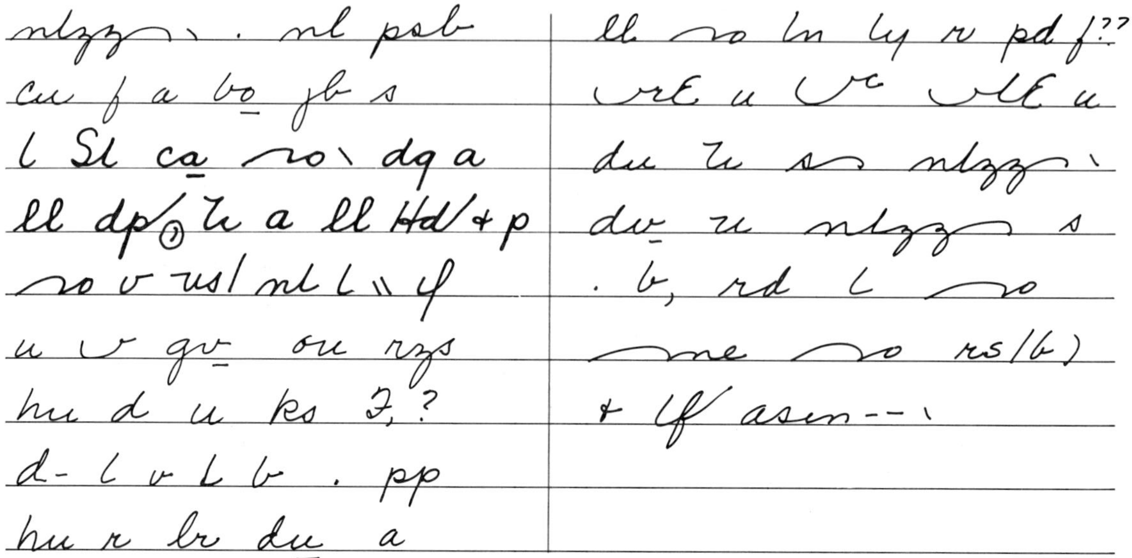

GUIDE Insert two contraction apostrophes, one parenthetical comma, four introductory commas, and four series commas.

1.3 SPEED BUILDING

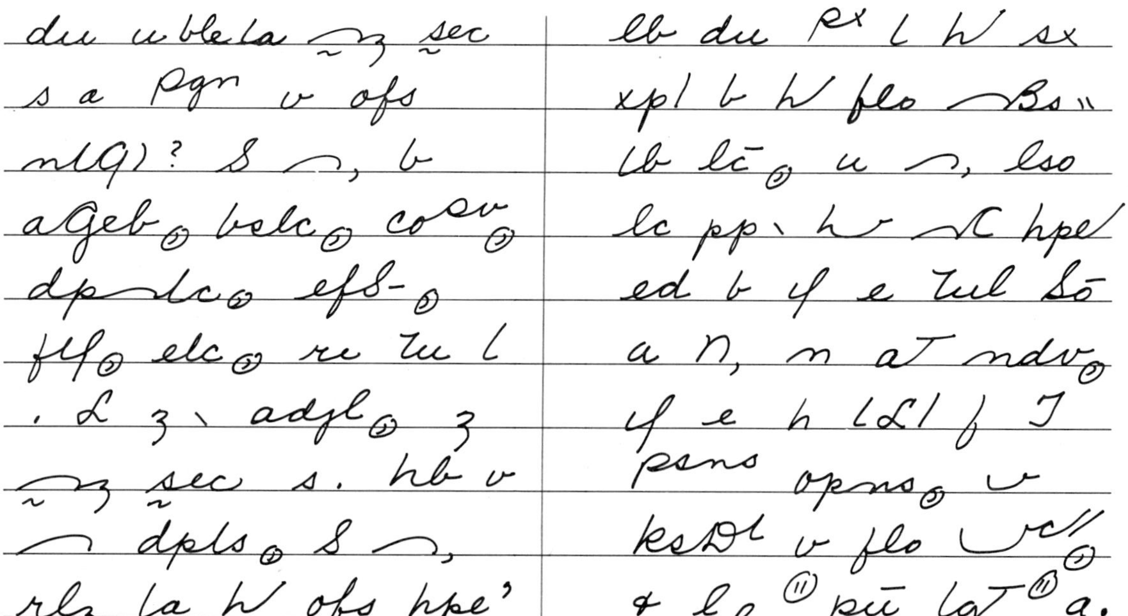

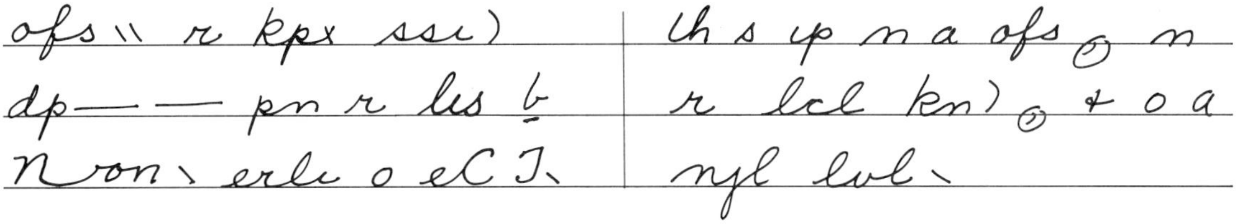

1.4 VOCABULARY BUILDING

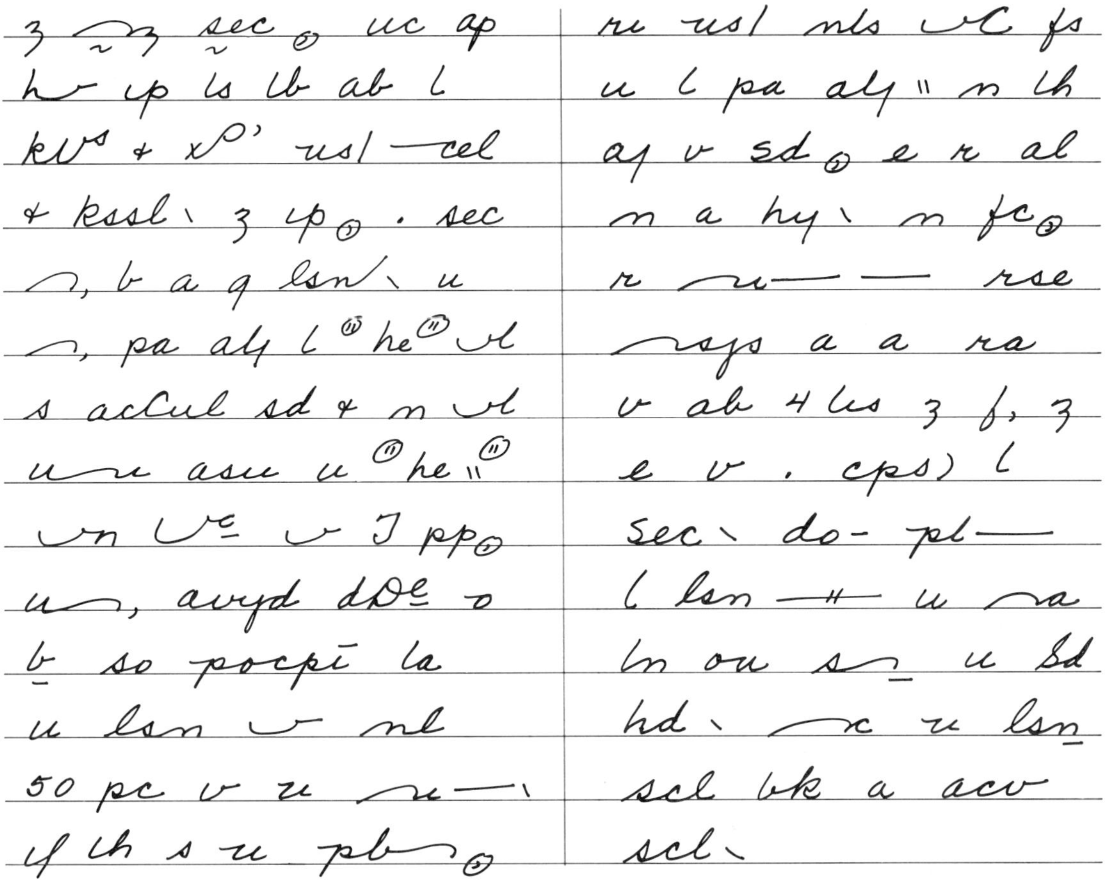

2.1 THEORY REVIEW

1. *ute* 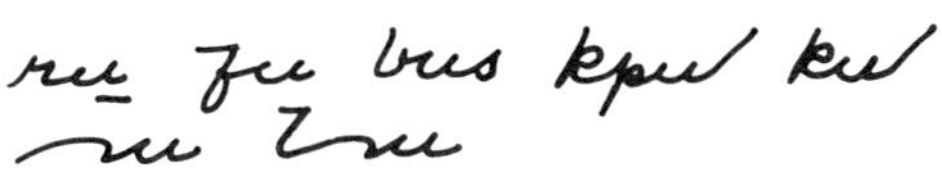

2. *ome*
3. *aze*
4. *nse*
5. *nsy*

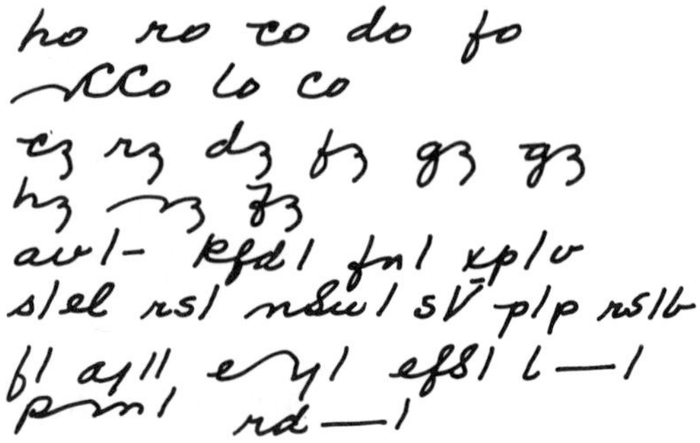

KEY 1. routing; fruit; boots; computer; commuter; mute; transmute 2. home; roam; chrome; dome; foam; Mercurochrome; tome; comb 3. craze; raise; daze; faze; gaze; graze; haze; maze; phrase 4. advancement; confidence; finance; expensive; sincerely; response; insurance; sponsored; principal, principle; responsible 5. fancy; agencies; emergency; efficiency; tendency; permanency; redundancy

2.2 TRANSCRIPTION SKILL BUILDING

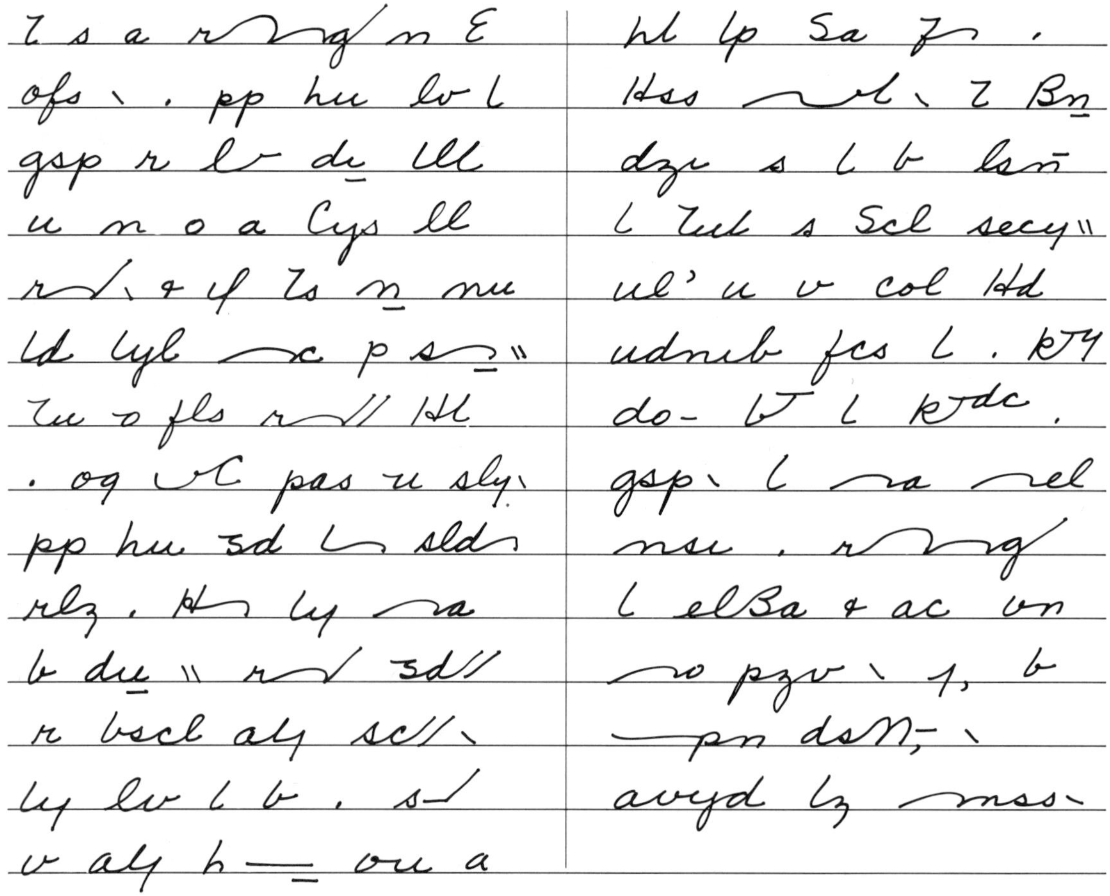

GUIDE Insert one possessive apostrophe, three contraction apostrophes, three introductory commas, one parenthetical comma, two adjective commas, and one no conjunction semicolon.

2.3 SPEED BUILDING

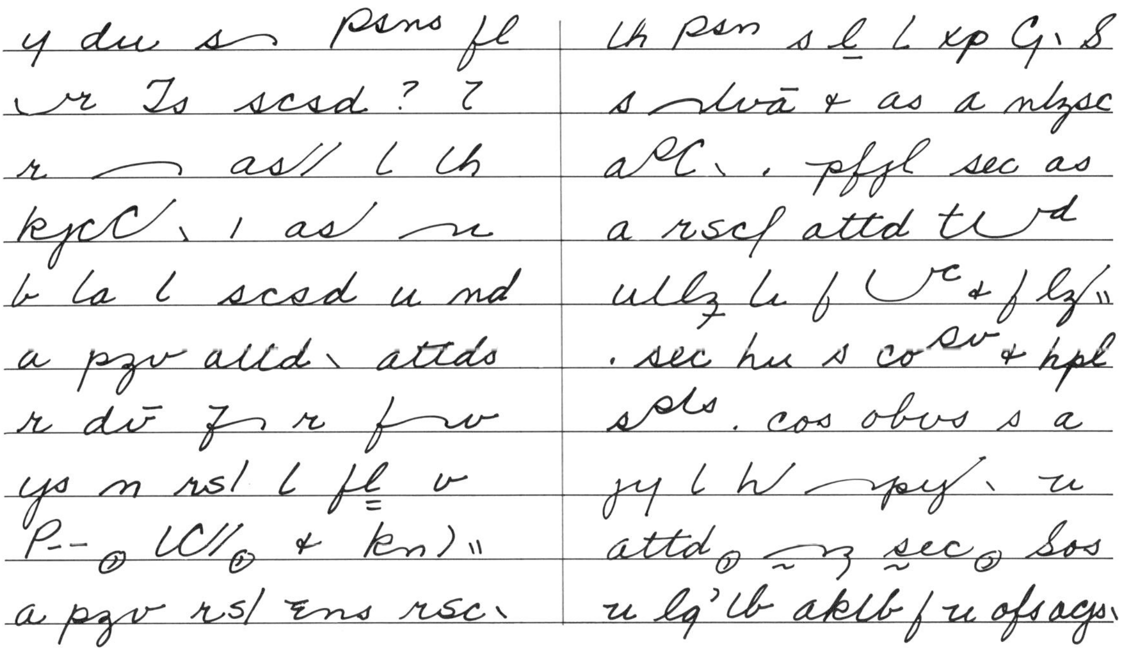

2.4 VOCABULARY BUILDING

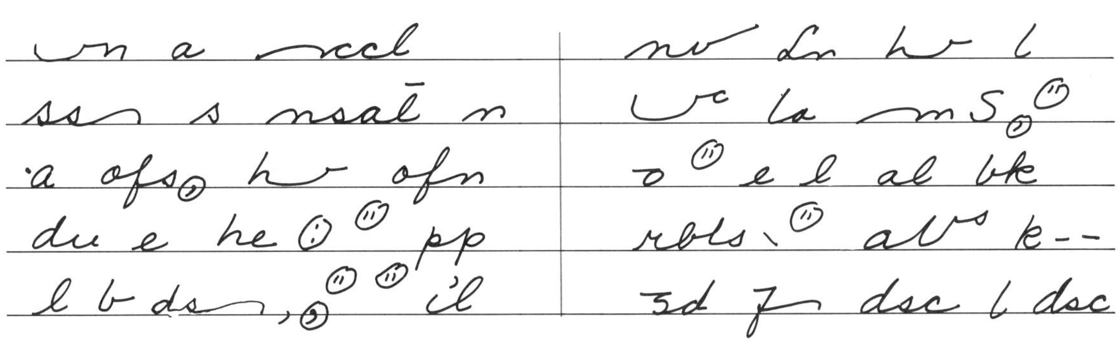

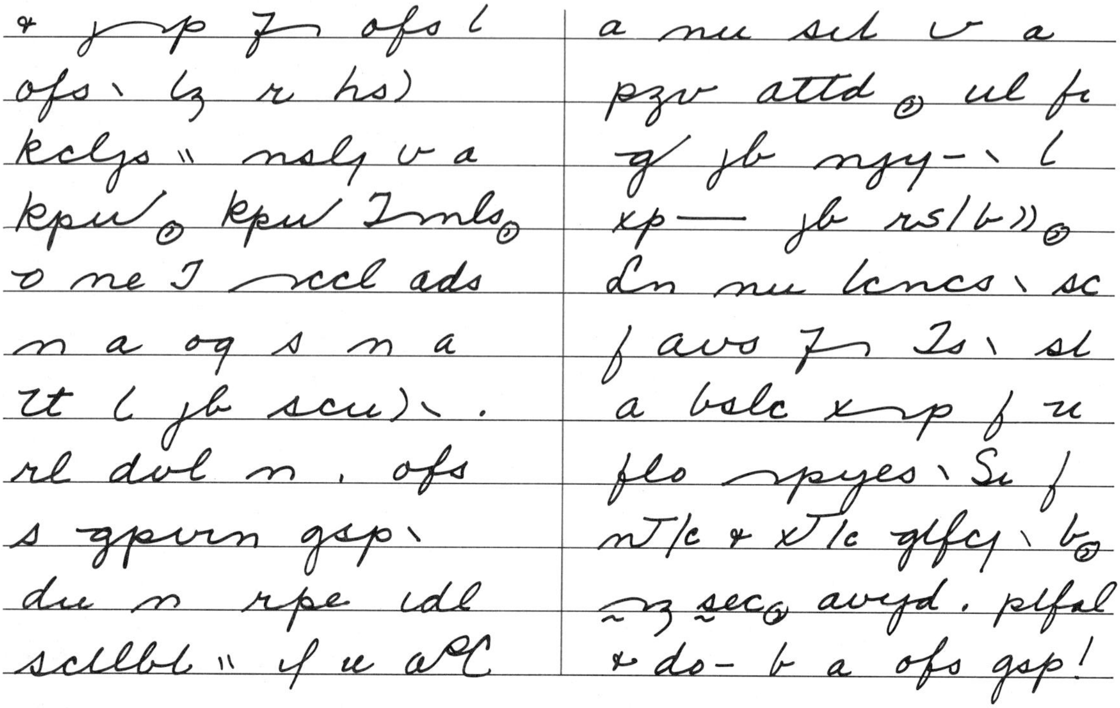

3.1 THEORY REVIEW

1. *eve*
2. *eze*
3. *zh*
4. *str*
5. *stor*

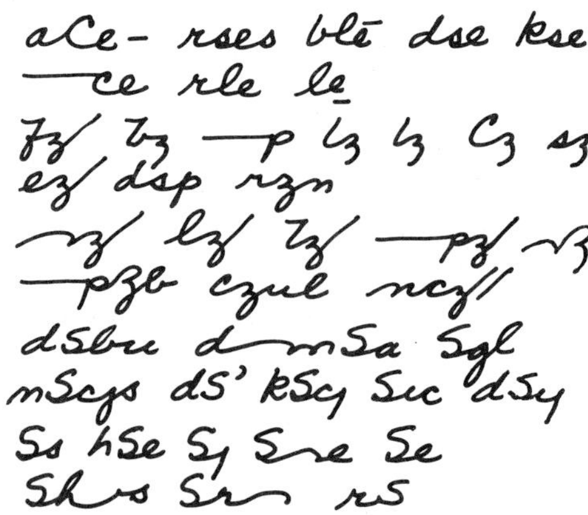

KEY 1. achievement; receives; believed; deceive; conceive; cleave; relieve; leaving 2. freezer; breeze; please; these; tease; cheese; seize; easier; displease; reason 3. measure; leisure; treasure; pleasure; measurement; pleasurable; casual; enclosures 4. distribute; demonstrate; strongly; instructions; distress; construction; strike; destroy 5. stores; history; storage; stormy; story; storehouse; storeroom; restore

3.2 TRANSCRIPTION SKILL BUILDING

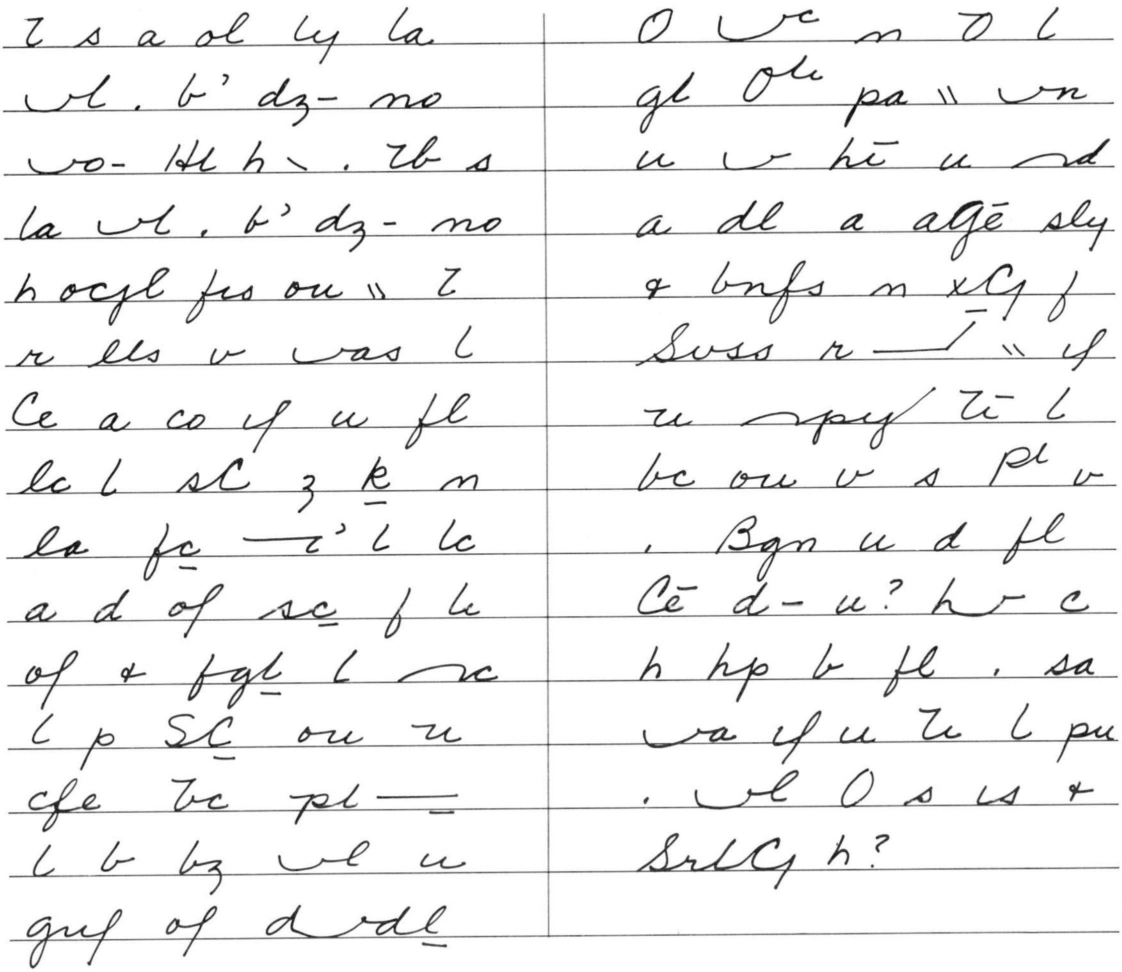

GUIDE Insert four contraction apostrophes, one enumeration colon, two parenthetical commas, five series commas, two introductory commas, and one question comma.

3.3 SPEED BUILDING

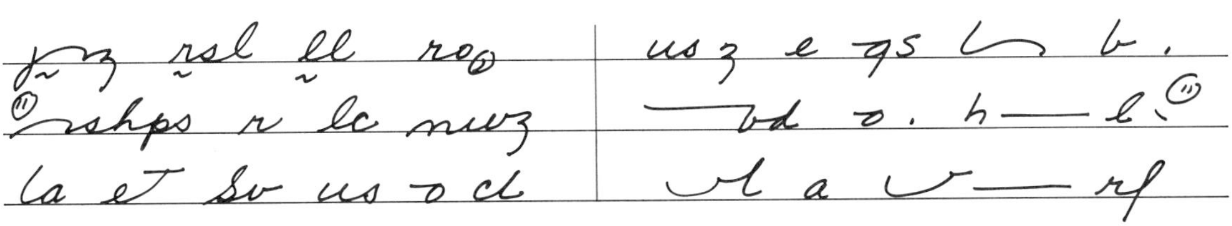

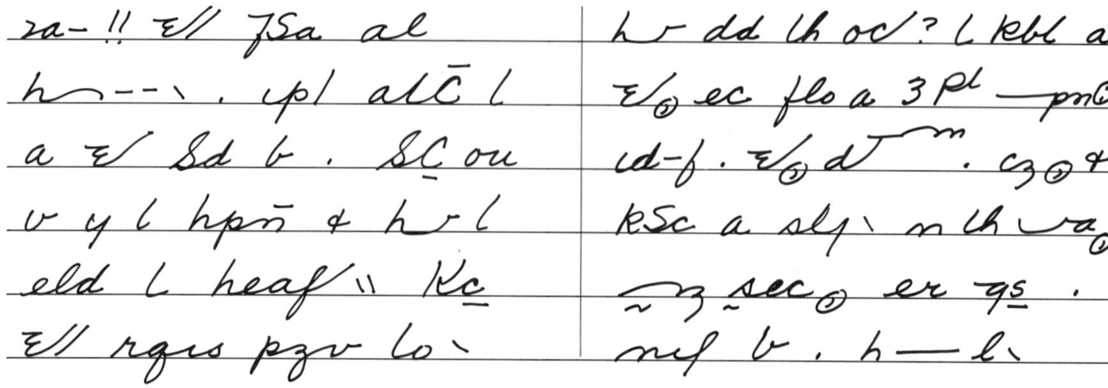

3.4 VOCABULARY BUILDING

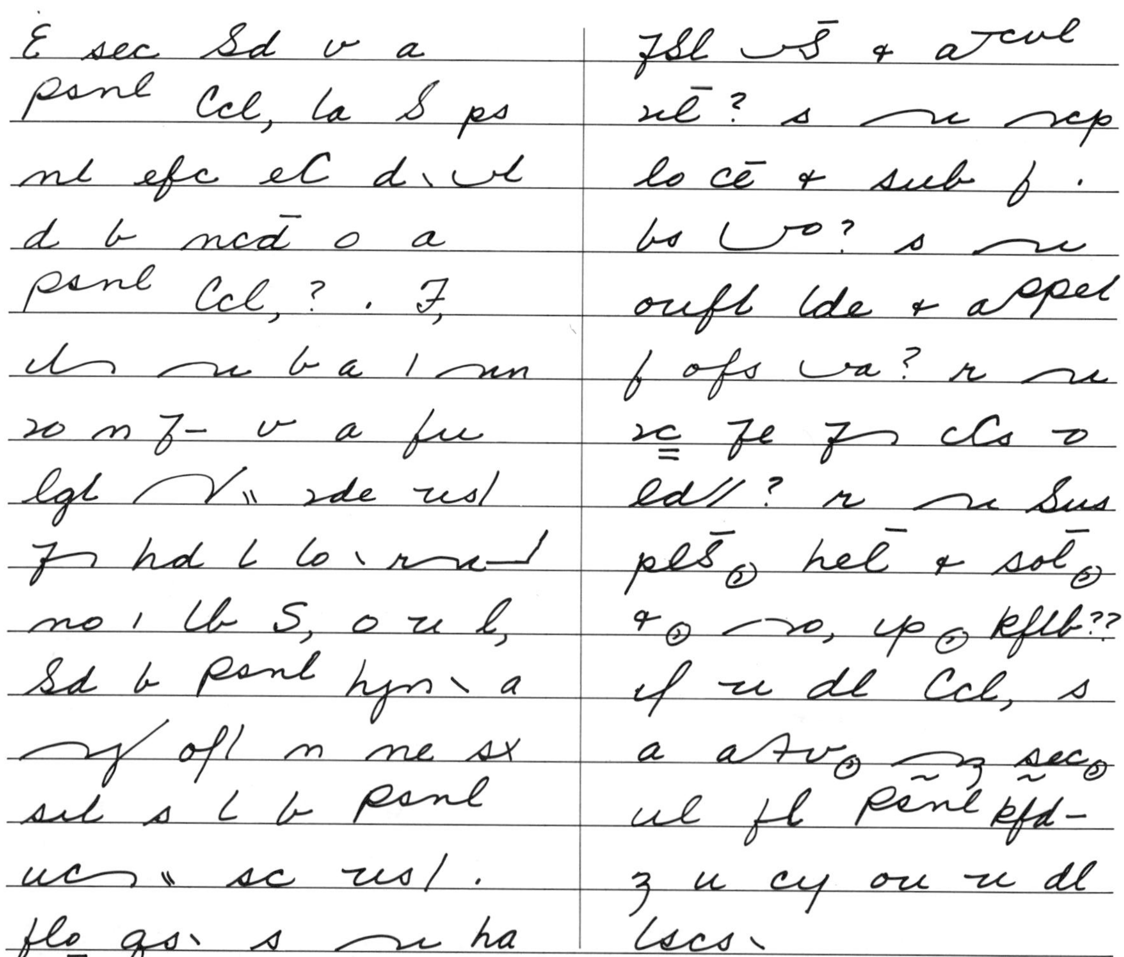

4.1 THEORY REVIEW

1. *ove*
2. *oze*
3. *star*
4. *ary*
5. *ad*

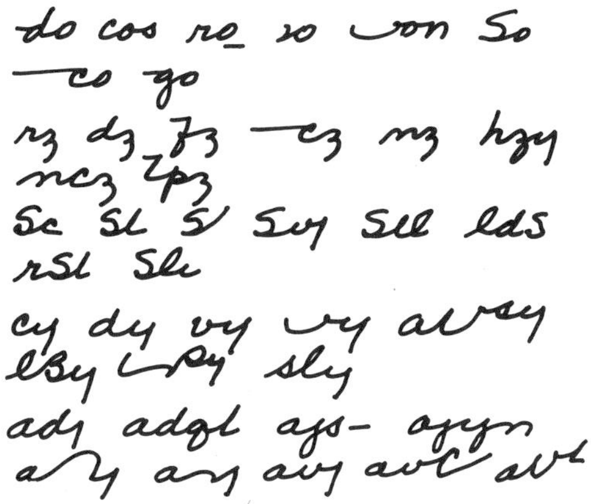

KEY 1. drove; coves; roving; stove; woven; strove; clove; grove 2. rose; doze; froze; close; nose; hosiery; enclose; transpose 3. stark; start; starter; starvation; startle; lodestar; restart; starlight 4. carry; dairy; vary; wary; adversary; library; temporary; salary 5. addition; adequate; adjustment; adjoin; admiration; admission; advantage; adventure; advert

4.2 TRANSCRIPTION SKILL BUILDING

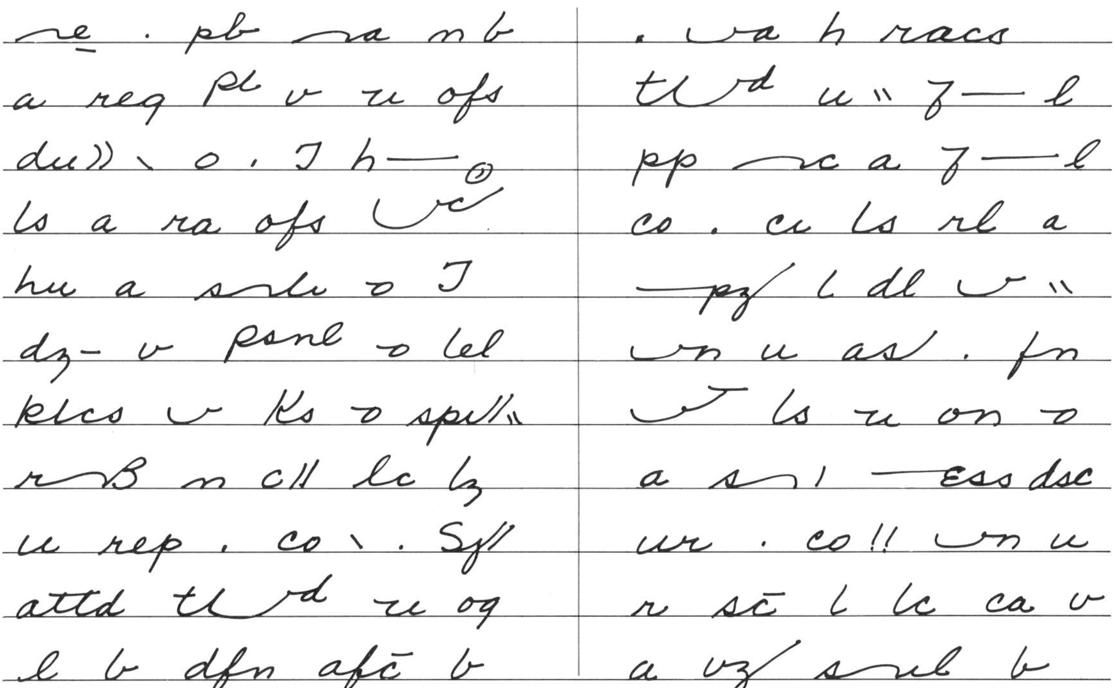

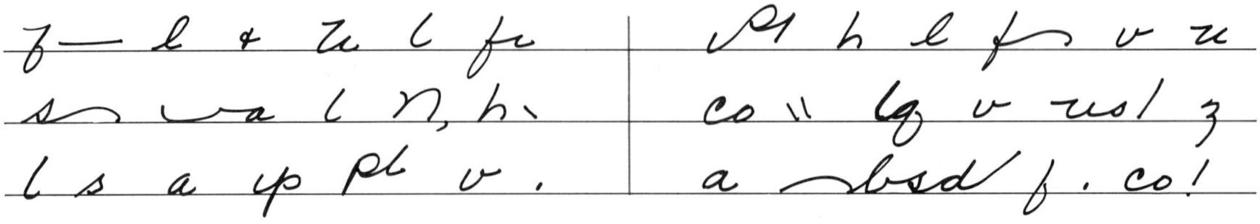

GUIDE Insert five contraction apostrophes, two possessive apostrophes, four introductory commas, five parenthetical commas, and two series commas.

4.3 SPEED BUILDING

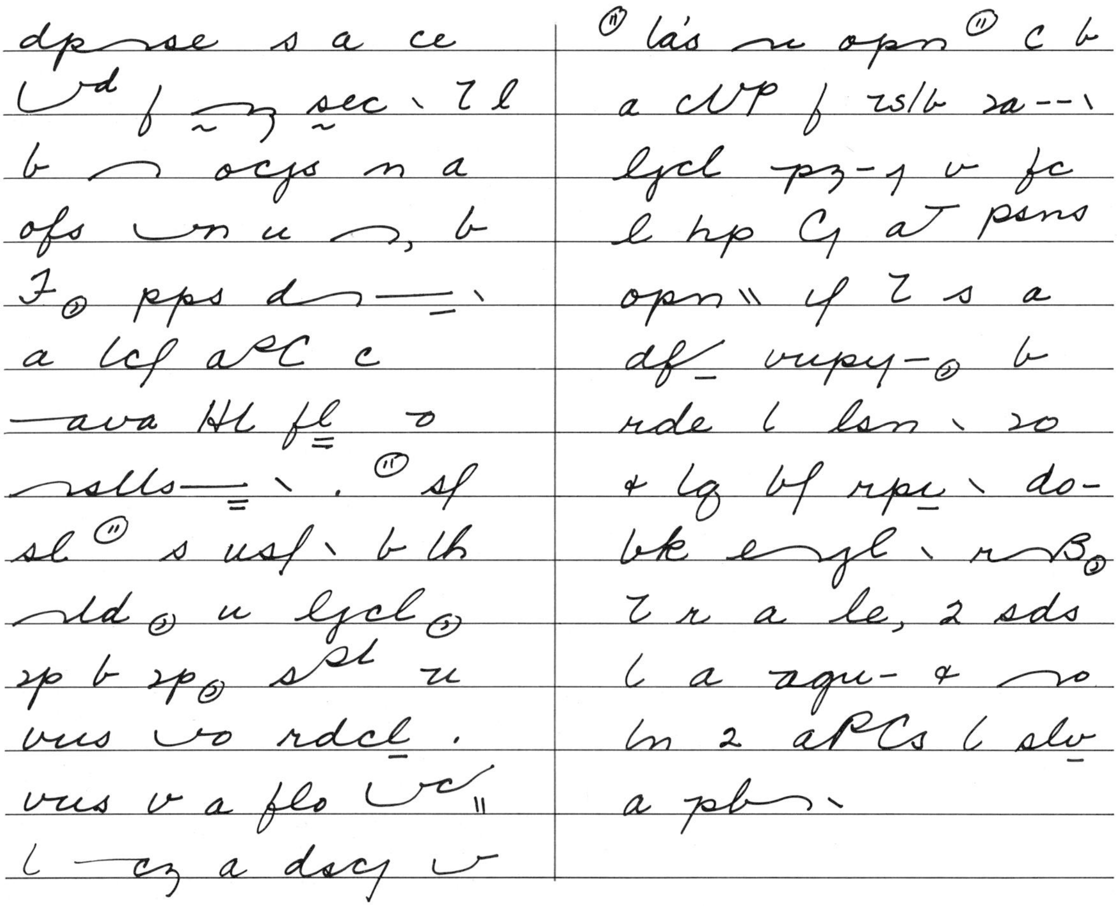

4.4 VOCABULARY BUILDING

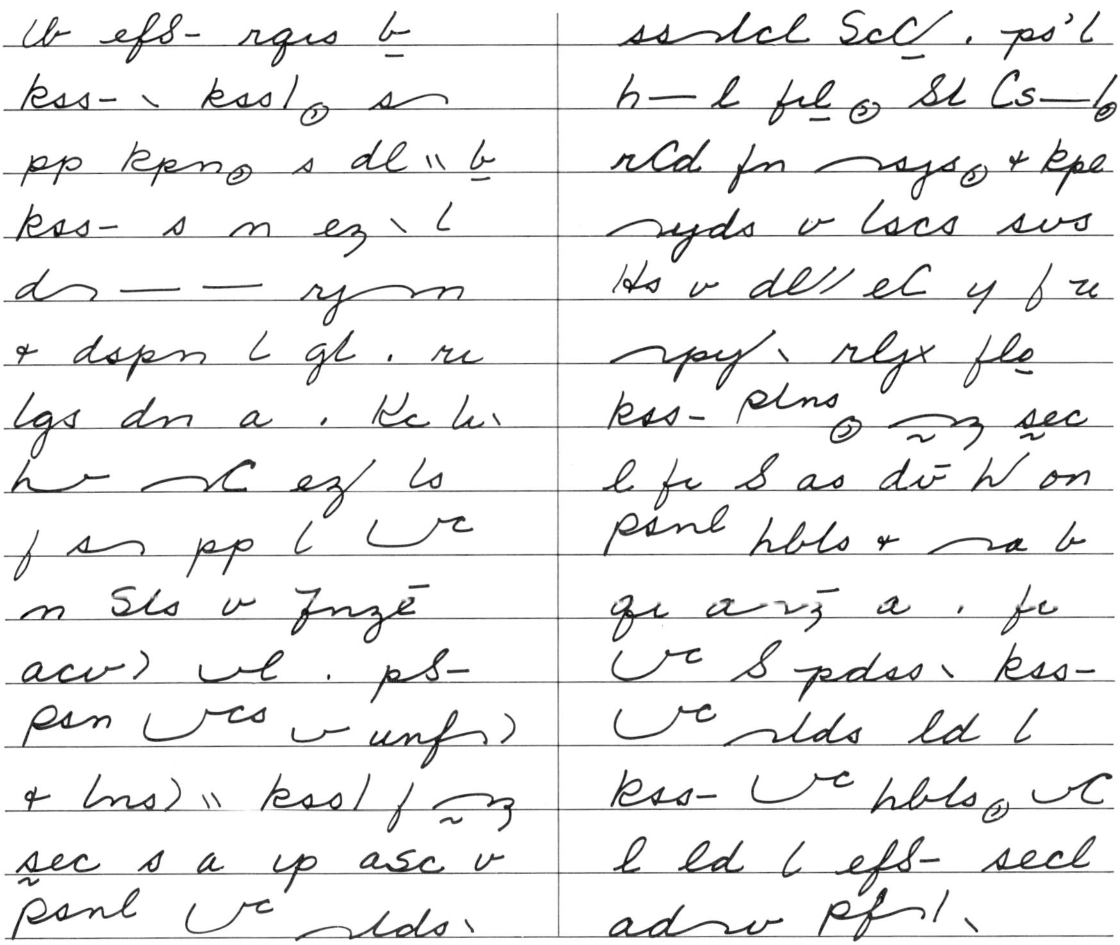

5.1 THEORY REVIEW

1. *uze*
2. *ster*
3. *ery*
4. Abbreviations

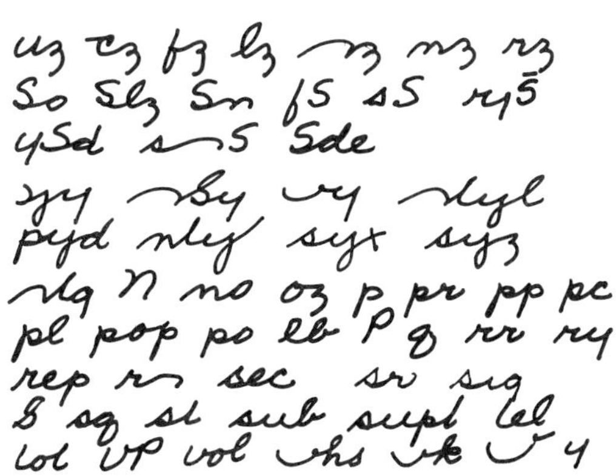

KEY 1. use; cruise; fuse; lose; muse; news; ruse 2. stereo; sterilize; stern; faster; sister; registered; yesterday; semester; sturdy 3. stationary, stationery; machinery; weary; material; period; interior; serious; series 4. mortgage; north; number; ounce; page; pair; parcel post; percent; place; popular; post office; pound; president; question; railroad; railway; represent, representative; room; secretary, second; senior; signature; south; square; street; subscribe, subscription; superintendent; telephone; total; vice-president; volume; warehouse; week; west; year

5.2 TRANSCRIPTION SKILL BUILDING

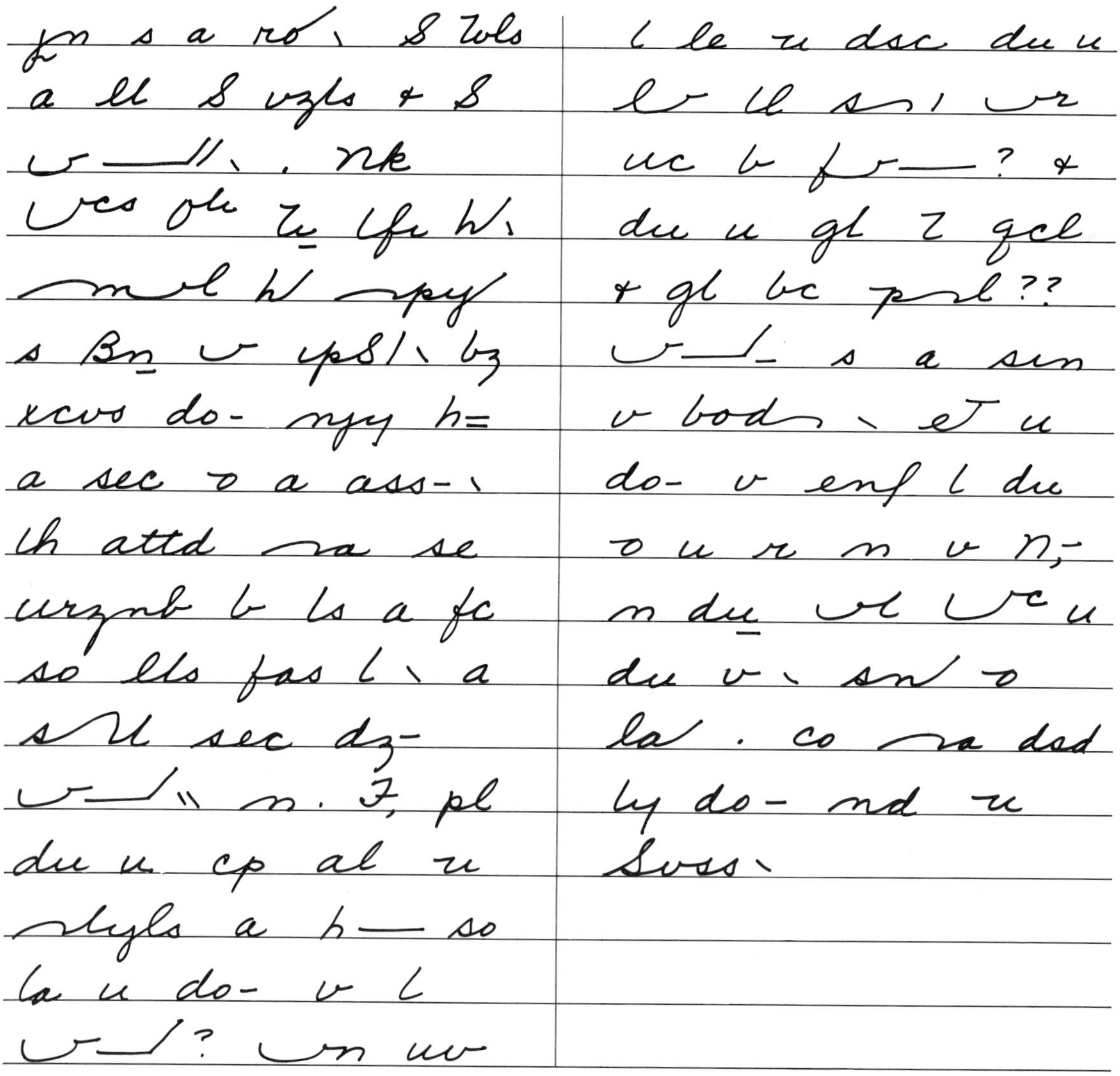

GUIDE Insert seven contraction apostrophes, two series commas, four introductory commas, and two conjunction commas.

5.3 SPEED BUILDING

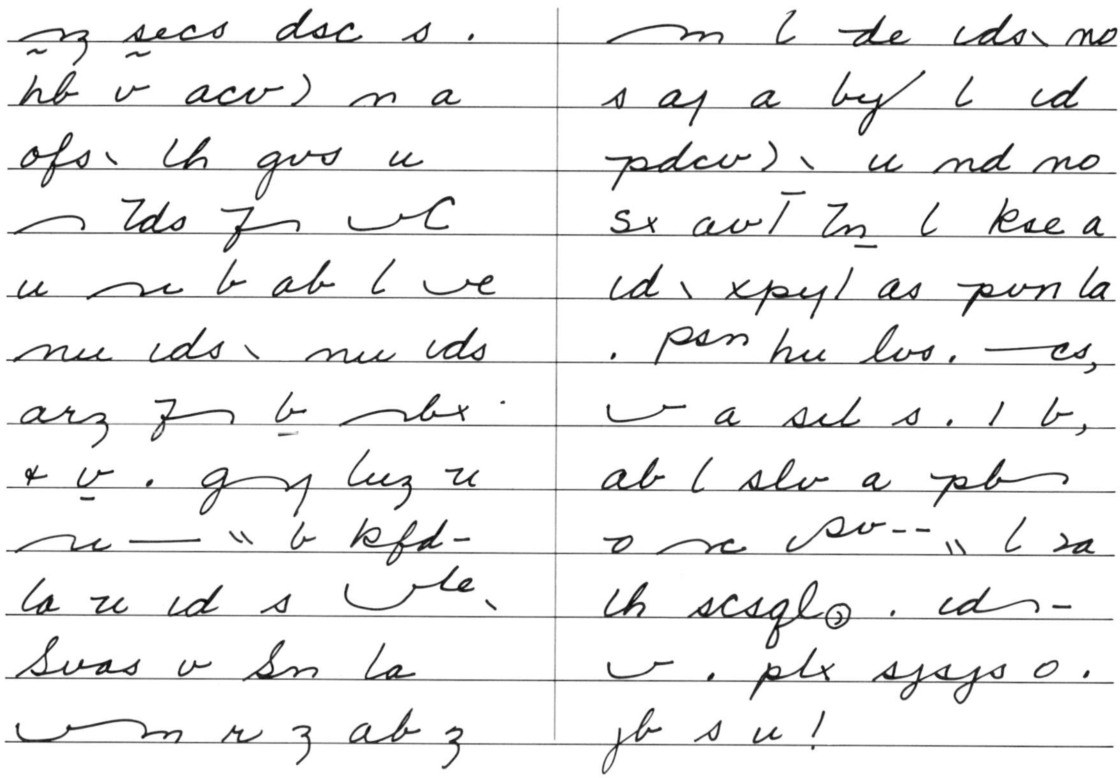

5.4 VOCABULARY BUILDING

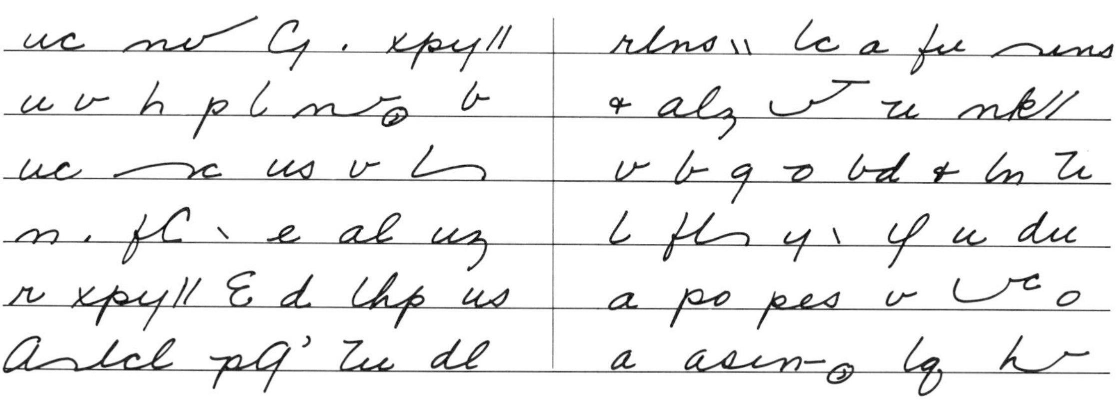

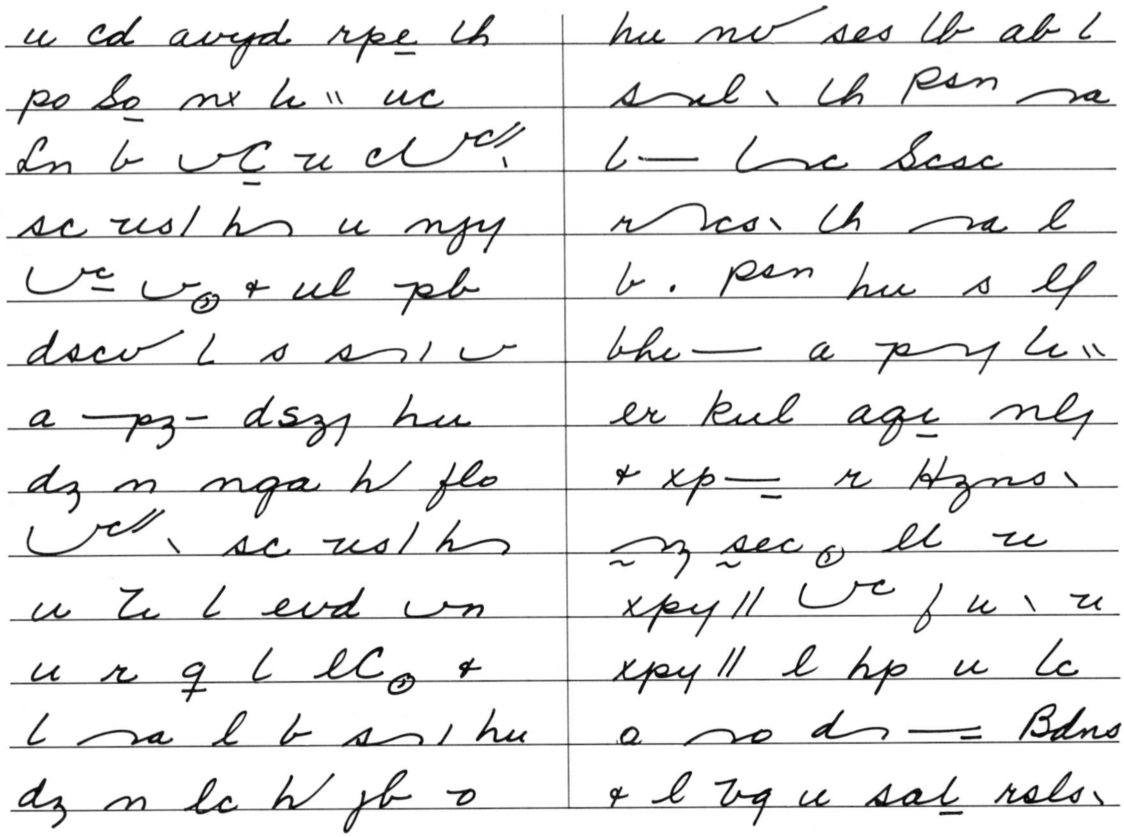

APPENDIX A

SUMMARY OF PRINCIPLES

WRITING VOWELS

1. Write long vowels in one-syllable words: *goal* gol ; *huge* huj ; *wife* yf ; *league* leg

2. Write INITIAL and FINAL short vowels: *asset* asl ; *egg* eg ; *ice* is ; *quota* goa ; *editor* ed/ ; *formula* fla

3. When a word ends in the sound *ate, eet, ite, ote,* or *ute,* write the vowel and omit the *t: date* da ; *meet* me ; *light* li ; *vote* vo ; *suit* su

4. When a word ends in the sound of *ave, eve, ive, ove,* or *uve,* write the vowel and omit the *v: gave* ga ; *leave* le ; *arrive* arv ; *drove* do ; *groove* gu

5. When a word ends in the sound of *ame, eem, ime, ome,* or *ume,* write the vowel and omit the *m: same* sa ; *extreme* xe ; *lifetime* lfl ; *home* ho ; *presume* pzu

6. When a word ends in the sound of *air, eer, ire, ore,* or *ure,* write the vowel and omit the *r: repair* rpa ; *appear* ape ; *acquire* agi ; *explore* xpo ; *insure* nsu

7. When *ing* or *ed* is added to an outline that contains a long vowel, retain the vowel in the outline: *hoping* hop ; *teaching* leC ; *filed* fil (Recap and Prevue: Vowels).

8. When the outline of a root word begins or ends in a vowel, retain that vowel when a prefix or suffix is added to it: *high* hi ; *highly* hil ; *true* tu ; *truly* tul ; *pay* pa ; *payroll* parl ; *renew* rnu ; *renewal* rnul; *react* rac ; *reelect* relc ; *reopen* rop

9. When a long vowel is followed by a mark of punctuation, retain the vowel: *moment* mo- ; *truant* tu- ; *duty* du) ; *consumer* ksu

10. Write ol for the sound of *old: golden* goln ; *boulder* bol/ ; *folder* fol/

11. Write i for the INITIAL sound of *im: imitate* ila ; *impossibility* ipsb)

12. Write u for the INITIAL sound of *un: undoubtedly* udtl ; *unfortunately* ufCnll

13. Write in for the sound of *ine: combine* kbin ; *consignee* ksne

14. When a word contains two MEDIAL pronounced consecutive vowels, write the first vowel only: *trial* til ; *annual* aul ; *diameter* de/

15. When a word contains two FINAL pronounced consecutive vowels, write the last vowel only: *create* ta ; *graduate* gda

16. Write al for the FINAL sound of *all: install* nsal ; *football* ftbal

17. Write a for the INITIAL and FINAL sound of *aw: all* al ; *alter* al/ ; *law* la ; *saw* sa

OMITTING VOWELS

1. Omit all MEDIAL short vowels: *citizenship* stzns ; *finish* fns ; *yellow* ylo ; *knowledge* nlj

2. Omit all MEDIAL long vowels in words of more than one syllable: *obtain* obtn ; *procedure* psj/ ; *belief* blf

3. Write c for the MEDIAL and FINAL sounds of *ake: make* mc ; *lakeside* lcsd ; *taking* lc

4. Omit the vowel and write d for the MEDIAL and FINAL sounds of *ade, ede, ide, ode,* and *ude: made* md ; *cede* sd ; *side* sd ; *reload* rld ; *crudely* cdl

5. Omit the vowel and write z for the MEDIAL and FINAL sounds of *aze, eze, ize, oze,* and *uze: phase* fz ; *reason* rzn ; *wisely* wzl ; *chosen* Czn ; *chooses* Czs

6. Write m for the prefix *em: emphatic* mflc ; *emblem* mbl ; *employer* mpy/

7. Omit the vowel and write *n* for the sounds of *ane, een, one,* and *une: train* tn ; *seen* sn ; *loan* ln ; *soon* sn

8. Write **y** for the MEDIAL or FINAL sound of a vowel + *ry: various* **vyx** ; *machinery* **mSny**, *inquiry* **nqy** ; *territory* **Tly** ; *hurry* **hy**

9. Write **n** for the prefix *en: enclosure* **ncz**; *endure* **ndu**; *engine* **njn**

10. When a word contains two MEDIAL pronounced consecutive vowels, omit the second vowel: *trial* **Tel** ; *annual* **aul**; *diameter* **dmt**

11. When a word contains two FINAL pronounced consecutive vowels, omit the first vowel: *create* **ca** ; *graduate* **gda**

12. Write **l** for the FINAL sound of *lee: efficiently* **efS-l**; *originally* **ojnl**; *early* **El**

13. Write **y** for the MEDIAL or FINAL sounds of a vowel + *shun: qualifications* **qlfcys**; *completion* **kpy** ; *competition* **kpty** ; *promotions* **pmys**

14. Write a **)** for the FINAL sound of *tee: duty* **du)**; *quantities* **g-))** ; *ability* **ab)** ; *authority* **aT)**

COMBINATION SOUNDS

1. Write **w** for the sound of *wh: what* **wl** ; *when* **wn** ; *which* **wC**

2. Write **C** for the sound of *ch: attachment* **atC-**; *chiefly* **Cfl** ; *much* **mC** ; *nature* **nC/**

3. Write **S** for the sound of *sh: issuing* **iSu** ; *insurance* **nSu/**; *sufficient* **sfS-**

4. Write **w** for the MEDIAL and FINAL sounds of *ow: allowance* **alw/**; *doubt* **dwl** ; *now* **nw**

5. Write **l** for the sound of *th: them* **ln** ; *method* **mld**; *health* **hll**

6. Write a hyphen on the INITIAL letter of an outline to indicate the INITIAL combination-*r* sounds: *broke* **boc**; *crashed* **cS** ; *dropped* **dp** ; *free* **fe** ; *group* **gup**; *privilege* **pvlj** ; *travel* **tvl** ; *through* **tu** ; *argue* **agu** ; *earn* **En** ; *or* **o** ; *urge* **uj** ; *shred* **Sd**

To express a MEDIAL combination-*r* sound, capitalize the letter that precedes the *r* and omit the *r* from the outline: *fabric* fbc ; *increase* ncs ; *refresh* rfs ; *agreement* age- ; *approach* apc ; *attractive* atcv

7. Write y for the sound of *oi: appointment* apy-- ; *oil* yl ; *toy* ty

8. Write g for the sound of *kw: frequently* fg-l ; *acquainted* aga= ; *quit* gl ; *quite* gi ; *adequate* adgl

9. Write a dash on the INITIAL letter of an outline to indicate the INITIAL combination-*l* sounds: *block* —bc ; *clients* —ci-- ; *element* —e- ; *flight* —fi ; *glad* —gd ; *ill* —i ; *plan* —pn ; *slow* —so ; *ultimate* —ulml ; *alibi* —ab ; *else* —es

When the combination-*l* sound is MEDIAL, omit the *l* and write the letter that precedes it: *application* apcj

10. Write a comma (,) for the INITIAL and FINAL sound of *st: largest* lj, ; *listings* l,= ; *introduced* ntdu, ; *study* ,de ; *stands* ,— —

11. Write s for the MEDIAL sound of *st: mistake* msc ; *instead* nsd

12. Write g for the sound of *nk: frankly* fgl ; *thinking* tg

13. Write b for the FINAL sounds of *bul* and *blee: able* ab ; *favorably* fvb

14. Write p for the FINAL sounds of *pul* and *plee: simple* sp ; *simply* sp

15. Write a small printed s for the sound of *sp: spend* s— ; *respect* rsc ; *grasp* gs

16. Write a disjoined slant for the sounds of *nse* and *nsy: expense* xp/ ; *responsible* rs/b ; *fancy* f/

17. Write z for the sound of *zh: treasure* tz/ ; *treasury* tzy

18. Write a capital printed S for the sound of *str: distribute* dSbu

19. Write a dash (—) for the MEDIAL or FINAL *nd: recommend* rk— ; *brand* b—

20. Write s for *sub: submit* sml

21. Write t for *trans: transfer* tf

PUNCTUATION MARKS

1. Use an underscore to indicate the addition of *ing* or *thing* to a word: *getting* gt̲ ; *recommending* rk—̲; *anything* ne̲

2. Use an overscore to indicate the addition of *ed* to form a past tense: *added* ad̄ ; *occurred* oc̄ ; *wanted* w= ; *mended* m—= ; *announced* an̄

3. Use a hypen for the MEDIAL and FINAL sounds of *nt* and *ment:* *resident* rzd-; *didn't* dd-; *judgment* jj- ; *rental* r-l

4. Use a joined slant to indicate the FINAL sounds of *er* and *ter: favor* fv/ ; *feature* fC/ ; *officers* ofs//; *errors* e// ; *center* s-/

5. Use a dash for the sound of *nd: recommend* rk—; *brand* b—

6. Use an apostrophe to indicate a FINAL *ss* and *ness: regardless* rgdl'; *addresses* aD" ; *illness* —l'

7. Use a quotation mark to indicate a FINAL *ssness: hopelessness* hopl"; *helplessness* hpl"

8. Use a comma to indicate the INITIAL and FINAL sounds of *st: largest* lj, ; *listings* l,̲ ; *introduced* ntdu,; *study* ,de ; *stands* ,— —

9. Use a blend ( )) to indicate the FINAL sound of *tee: duty* du) ; *abilities* ab))

10. Use a disjoined slant to indicate the sounds of *nse* and *nsy: expense* xp/ ; *responsible* rs/b ; *fancy* f/ and s/ for *self* and *selves: selfish* s/s ; *myself* ms/; *themselves* Ls/

CAPITALIZATION

1. To express a MEDIAL combination-*r* sound, capitalize the letter that precedes the *r* and omit the *r* from the outline: *fabric* fBc ; *increase* nCs ; *refresh* rFs ; *agreement* aGe-

2. To express the MEDIAL vowel and *r*, capitalize the outline that precedes the sound: *liberally* lBl ; *report* rPl ; *accordingly* aCdl, ; *modern* mDn; *furniture* FnC ; *regard* rGd ; *certainly* Snl; *determine* dTm; *converse* kVs ; *reserved* rZv̄ ; *thorough* To

3. For the FINAL sound of *ther* write a capital *t: author* aT ; *farther* fT
4. Write C for the sound of *ch: cheap* Cep ; *reach* reC
5. Write ʃ for the sound of *sh: issue* iʃu ; *rush* rʃ
6. Write N for the sounds of *enter* and *inter: entertain* Ntn ; *interest* N,

MISCELLANEOUS

1. Write s to form plurals of outlines ending in a letter of the alphabet: *groups* gups ; *today's* tds ; *joins* jyns
2. Repeat the punctuation mark to form plurals of outlines ending in punctuation marks: *mailings* mal= ; *events* ev-- ; *abilities* ab)) ; *expenses* xp// ; *invests* nv,,
3. Write c for the sound of *k: cashier* cʃe ; *keynote* cenl ; *booklet* bcll ; *walk* wc
4. Write v for MEDIAL and FINAL *tiv: effective* efcv ; *tentative* t-v ; *positively* pzvl
5. Write k for the sounds of *com, con,* and *coun: combination* kbnj ; *convenient* kvn- ; *counters* k//
6. Write S for the sounds of *str, star, ster,* and *stor: distribute* dSbu ; *start* St ; *registered* rjS̄ ; *story* Se
7. Write x for the sounds of *aks, eks, iks, oks,* and *uks: accident* xd- ; *extent* xt- ; *fix* fx ; *box* bx ; *deluxe* dlx
8. Write j for the sounds of MEDIAL and FINAL *shun,* vowel + *shun,* and *nshun: national* njl ; *invitations* nvtjs ; *attention* atj
9. Omit *n* before the sounds of *g, j,* and *ch: bring* bg ; *length* lgt ; *exchange* xCj ; *ranch* rC
10. Write x for MEDIAL and FINAL sounds of *us, usly, shus, shusly, shul, shully, nshul,* and *nshully* in words of more than one syllable: *bonus* bnx ; *officially* ofx ; *anxious* agx ; *financially* fnx
11. Omit *t* after the sounds of *k, p, f,* and *x* and omit *pt* after *m: act* ac ; *except* xp ; *draft* df ; *next* nx ; *prompt* pm
12. Omit *d* before *m* and *v: admit* amt ; *advance* av/
13. Write *f* for *ful, fully,* and the final sound of *fy: carefully* caf ; *beautiful* bf ; *notify* ntf

WRITING SPECIFIC SOUNDS IN DIFFERENT POSITIONS

1. Write a hyphen on the INITIAL letter of an outline to indicate the INITIAL combination-*r* sound; capitalize the letter that precedes this sound in a MEDIAL position: *brick* -bc ; *fabric* fBc ; *crease* -ces ; *increase* nCs ; *drama* -dra ; *melodrama* mlDra ; *fresh* -fs ; *refresh* r-fs ; *gram* -gm ; *program* pGm ; *print* -p- ; *reprint* rP-

2. Write a dash on the INITIAL letter of an outline to indicate the INITIAL combination-*l* sound; omit the *l* and write the letter that precedes the MEDIAL combination-*l* sound: *block* —bc ; *glad* —gd ; *plan* —pn ; *apply* apl ; *duplicate* dpca

3. INITIAL *er* is indicated E ; FINAL *er* and *ter* are indicated with a joined slant; and MEDIAL vowel + *r* is indicated by capitalizing the letter that precedes the sound: *earn* En ; *cover* cv/ ; *after* af/ ; *different* dF-

4. INITIAL and FINAL *st* are indicated by a comma; MEDIAL *st* is indicated by writing , : *style* ,sl ; *just* j, ; *mistake* msc

APPENDIX B

SUMMARY OF BRIEF FORMS

about	ab
above	bv
acknowledge	ak
advantage	avj
again, st	ag
almost	lmo
already	lr
also	lso
always	lw
am	m
an	a
appreciate	ap
are	r
around	rw
as	z
ask	sc
at	a
auto	a
be	b
because	cs
been	b
began	bg
begin	bg
benefit	bnf
between	bt
both	bo
business	bs
busy	bz
but	b
buy	b
by	b
call	cl
came	k
can	c
charge	Cg
circumstance	c/
collect	cc
come	k
committee	k
conclusion	kclj
consider	ks
continue	ku
contract	Kc
correct	Kc
country	c/
customer	K
deal	dl
declare	dec
definite, ly	dfn
deliver	dl
delivery	dl
describe	des
description	des
develop	dv
difficult	dfk
difficulty	dfk
direct	D
during	du
easy	ez
entitle	ntl

even
evening
ever
every
extra
extraordinary
fail
feel
field
find
fine
fire
firm
for
full
fully
future
given
go
good
great
had
has
have
he
held
help
him
his
hole
hour
idea
immediate, ly
important
in
individual, ly
initial, ly

is
it
keep
kind
known
letter
life
like
line
little
man
many
member
move
necessarily
necessary
not
note
object
of
on
once
only
open
opinion
opportunity
order
organization
organize
other
our
out
over
particular, ly
perhaps
please
poor

price
probable, ly
prove
public
publish
pull
pupil
purchase
put
real, ly
reel
regular, ly
regulation
result
sale
sample
satisfaction
satisfactory
satisfy
save
school
several
shall
she
ship
situation
small
stop
subject
success
successful, ly
that

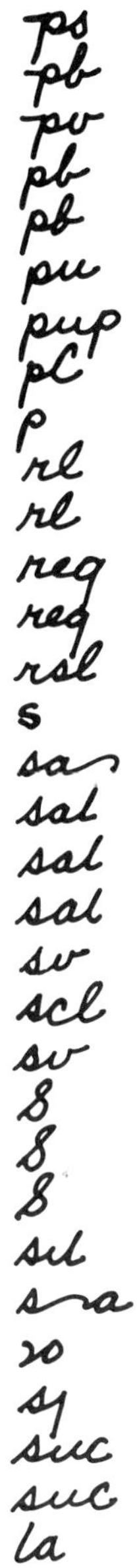

the
their
there
they
this
those
thought
throughout
to
too
under
until
up
upon
usual, ly
very
was
we
well
were
where
while
whole
whom
why
will
with
without
woman
world
would
your

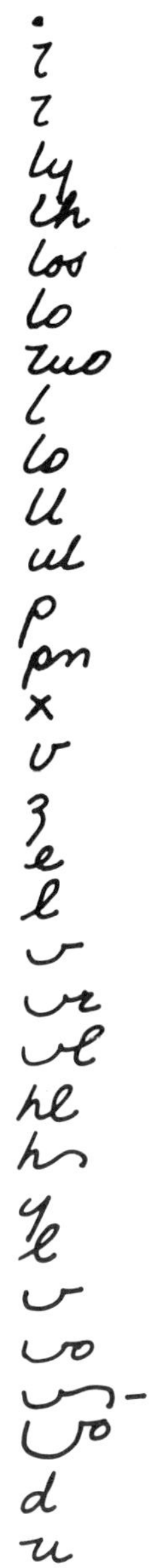

APPENDIX C

SUMMARY OF STANDARD ABBREVIATIONS

absolute, ly	abs
administrate	adm
administration	adm
advertise	adv
America, n	am
a.m.	am
amount	amt
and	&
approximate, ly	apx
associate	asso
avenue	ave
average	av
billion	B
boulevard	blvd
bureau	Bu
capital	cap
catalog	cat
cent, s	c
certificate	cert
certify	cert
child	ch
children	chn
Christmas	Xms
company	co
corporation	corp
credit	cr
day	d
department	dpt
discount	dis
doctor	dr
dollar, s	d
East	E
envelope	env
establish	est
federal	fed
feet	ft
figure	fg
foot	ft
government	gvt
hundred	H
inch	in
independent	ind
intelligence	int
intelligent, ly	int
invoice	inv
junior	jr
magazine	mag
manufacture	mfr
maximum	max
memorandum	memo
merchandise	mdse
mile	mi
million	M
minimum	min
month	mo
minute	min
miscellaneous	misc
mortgage	mtg
Mr.	M
Mrs.	ms

North	N
number	no
o'clock	o
ounce	oz
page	p
paid	pd
pair	pr
parcel post	pp
percent	pc
place	pl
p.m.	pm
popular	pop
post office	po
pound	lb
president	P
question	q
railroad	rr
railway	ry
represent	rep
representative	rep
room	rm
second	sec
secretary	sec
senior	sr
signature	sig
South	S
square	sq
street	st
subscribe	sub
subscription	sub
superintendent	supt
telephone	tel
thousand	Td
total	tot
vice-president	VP
volume	vol
warehouse	whs
week	wk
West	W
year	y

APPENDIX D

SUMMARY OF GEOGRAPHICAL TERMS

THE UNITED STATES

Alabama (AL)
Alaska (AK)
Arizona (AZ)
Arkansas (AR)
California (CA)
Colorado (CO)
Connecticut (CT)
Delaware (DE)
District of Columbia (DC)
Florida (FL)
Georgia (GA)
Hawaii (HI)
Idaho (ID)
Illinois (IL)
Indiana (IN)
Iowa (IA)
Kansas (KS)
Kentucky (KY)
Louisiana (LA)
Maine (ME)
Maryland (MD)
Massachusetts (MA)
Michigan (MI)
Minnesota (MN)
Mississippi (MS)
Missouri (MO)
Montana (MT)
Nebraska (NB)
Nevada (NV)
New Hampshire (NH)
New Jersey (NJ)
New Mexico (NM)
New York (NY)
North Carolina (NC)
North Dakota (ND)
Ohio (OH)
Oklahoma (OK)
Oregon (OR)
Pennsylvania (PA)
Rhode Island (RI)
South Carolina (SC)
South Dakota (SD)
Tennessee (TN)
Texas (TX)
Utah (UT)
Vermont (VT)
Virginia (VA)
Washington (WA)
West Virginia (WV)
Wisconsin (WI)
Wyoming (WY)

AMERICAN CITIES

Akron
Albany
Albuquerque
Amarillo
Annapolis
Atlanta
Augusta
Austin
Baltimore
Baton Rouge
Birmingham
Bismarck
Boise
Boston
Bridgeport
Buffalo
Cambridge
Camden
Carson City
Charleston
Chattanooga
Cheyenne
Chicago
Cincinnati
Cleveland
Columbia
Columbus
Concord
Dallas
Dayton
Denver
Des Moines
Detroit
Dover
El Paso
Erie
Evansville
Flint
Fort Wayne
Fort Worth
Frankfort
Gary
Grand Rapids
Greensboro
Harrisburg
Hartford
Helena
Honolulu
Houston
Indianapolis
Jacksonville
Jefferson City
Jersey City
Juneau
Kansas City
Lansing
Lincoln
Little Rock
Long Beach
Los Angeles
Louisville
Madison
Memphis
Miami
Milwaukee
Minneapolis
Montgomery
Montpelier
Nashville
Newark
New Haven
New Orleans

New York	nu Yc
Norfolk	nfc
Oakland	ocl—
Oklahoma City	och a s)
Olympia	—o pa
Omaha	o ha
Paterson	pt sn
Philadelphia	fldlfa
Phoenix	fnx
Pierre	pa
Pittsburgh	plsBg
Portland	pll—
Providence	pvd/
Raleigh	rl
Richmond	rC—
Rochester	rCS
Sacramento	sC-o
St. Louis	sa-lus
St. Paul	sa-pal
St. Petersburg	sa-pt sBg
Salem	sl
Salt Lake City	sll lc s)
San Antonio	sn alno
San Diego	sn deq
San Francisco	sn fnsco
San Jose	sn hza
Santa Fe	s-a fa
Savannah	svna
Seattle	sell
Shreveport	Svpl
South Bend	S b—
Spokane	sc
Springfield	sgfld
Syracuse	Scz
Tacoma	lc a
Tallahassee	llhse
Toledo	lldo
Trenton	l-n
Tucson	lsn
Tulsa	llsa
Washington	vSgln
Wichita	vCla
Worcester	vS
Yonkers	yg//
Youngstown	ygsln

CANADIAN PROVINCES AND TERRITORIES

Alberta	abla
British Columbia	bt8 clmba
Manitoba	mlba
New Brunswick	nu bnzvc
Newfoundland	nf—l—
Northwest Territory	nv Tly
Nova Scotia	nva scSa
Ontario	o-yo
Prince Edward Island	p/ edvd il—
Quebec	qbc
Saskatchewan	sscCvn
Yukon Territory	uk Tly

CANADIAN CITIES

Alma	ama
Amherst	H,
Arvida	avda
Barrie	by

Belleville	blvl
Brampton	b-m
Brandon	b—n
Brantford	b-Fd
Brockville	bcvl
Calgary	clgy
Cap-de-la-Madeleine	cpdl-dln
Charlottetown	Sltt-n
Chicoutimi	Sct-e
Cornwall	Cn-al
Cote-St.-Michel	clsa-Sl
Dartmouth	D-t
Drummondville	d—vl
Edmonton	ed-n
Edmundston	ed—sn
Fairville	Fvl
Flin Flon	fn fn
Forest Hill	f, hl
Ft. William	ft wl
Ft. William-Pt.	ft wl, pt
Arthur	aT
Fredericton	FDcn
Galt	glt
Glace Bay	gas ba
Granby	grnb
Guelph	gwlf
Halifax	hlfx
Hamilton	hmltn
Hull	hl
Jacques-Cartier	zcCla
Jasper-Place	jSpl
Joliette	zlet
Jonquiere	zce
Kenogami	cngme
Kenora	cNa
Kingston	cgsn
Kirkland Lake	Ccl— lc
Kitchener	cCn
Lachine	lSn
LaSalle	lsl
La Tuque	la luc
Lauzon	lzn
Laval-des-Rapides	lvldrpd
Leaside	lsd
Lethbridge	lLBj
Lindsay	l—ze
London	l—n
Long Branch	lg bC
Magog	mgg
Medicine Hat	mdsn ht
Mimico	mmco
Moncton	mgn
Montreal	mnTal
Moose Jaw	mus ja
Nanaimo	nnmo
New Toronto	nu T-o
New Westminster	nu Wmns
Niagara Falls	nega fals
North Bay	N ba
North Vancouver	N vncv
Orillia	ola
Oshawa	oSa
Ottawa	olwa
Owen Sound	on s—
Pembroke	pmBc
Penticton	p-cn
Peterborough	pTBo
Pointe-aux-Trembles	p-o Tmb
Pointe-Claire	p-ca
Portage la Praire	plzlby
Port Alberni	pt aBne
Port Arthur	pt aT
Port Colborne	pt clBn
Prince Albert	p/ aBl

Prince George
Prince Rupert
Quebec
Red Deer
Regina
Rimouski
Riverside
St. Boniface
St. Catharines
St. Hyacinthe
St. James
St. Jean
St. Jerome
St. John's
St. Lambert
St. Laurent
St. Michel
St. Thomas
Ste. Foy
Sarnia
Saskatoon
Sault Sainte Marie
Shawinigan Falls
Sherbrooke
Sillery

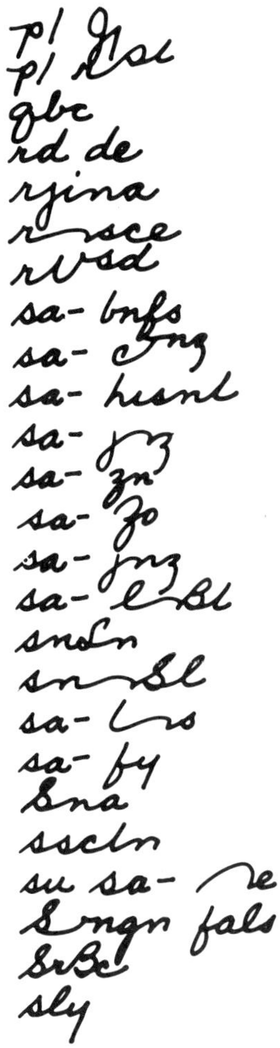

Sorel
Stratford
Sudbury
Swift Current
Sydney
Thetford Mines
Timmins
Toronto
Trail
Trenton
Trois-Rivieres
Truro
Valleyfield
Vancouver
Verdun
Victoria
Victoriaville
Ville-Jaques-Cartier
Waterloo
Welland
Whitehorse
Windsor
Winnipeg
Woodstock

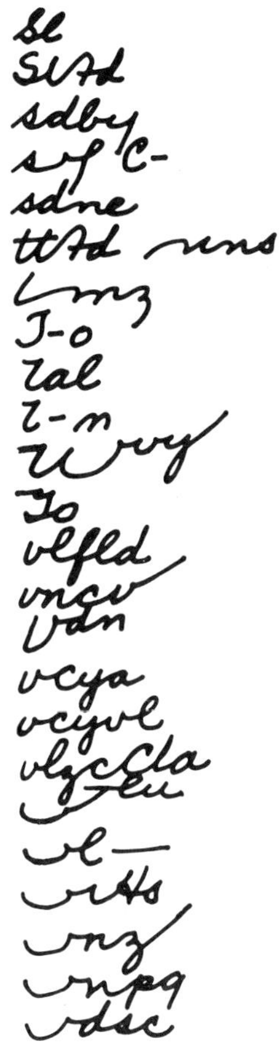

APPENDIX E

SUMMARY OF PUNCTUATION RULES

This is a summary of the rules for punctuation that you will encounter most frequently. They account for about 98 percent of the punctuation in business correspondence. Each rule is followed by the name label used in the Transcription Skill Building drills.

1. It is cold. I need a coat.

   Here are two simple sentences. They are always correctly written as two sentences, but they could also be written together, as in 2. (Statement Period)

2. It is cold; I need a coat.

   Here the two sentences are joined by a semicolon because they are so obviously related. (No Conjunction Semicolon)

3. It is cold, and I need a coat.

   The two sentences have been joined by the conjunction *and* as well as by a comma. Please keep in mind that pros and cons are irrelevant; if you get this point accurately, then 4, 5, and 6 will be understood. (Conjunction Comma)

4. However, it is cold; and I need a coat.
5. It is cold; and therefore, I need a coat.
6. However, it is cold; and, therefore, I need a coat.

   When there are two sentences joined by a conjunction and one has a comma, the comma before the conjunction turns into a semicolon. The same is true if both sentences have commas; the comma before the conjunction becomes a semicolon. (Internal Punctuation Semicolon)

7. I know it is so and that you love me.

   No comma here. The first sentence, up to *and,* is correct without punctuation and is complete; after *and,* however, "that you love me" is not a complete sentence. The word *that* is not a conjunction. Therefore, in such a sentence as "I know that it is so," no punctuation will appear because there is no conjunction. Conjunctions in addition to *and* are *but* and occasionally *or* and *for; so* and *because* are sometimes treated as conjunctions even though technically they are not.

In the following series, we no longer have two complete sentences:

8. *Since it is cold,* I need a coat.
9. *Because it is cold,* I need a coat.
10. *When it is cold,* I need a coat.

Each underscored portion is incomplete and cannot stand alone; it is subordinate. The only complete sentence is "I need a coat," and all others introduce it.

11. *As it is cold,* I need a coat.
12. *If it is cold,* I need a coat.
13. *While it is cold,* I need a coat.
14. *Now that it is cold,* I need a coat.

As a rule, whatever precedes the subject and verb of a sentence is introductory and should be a signal to us to set it off by a comma. (Introductory Comma)

15. I need a coat *when it is cold.*
16. I need a coat *because it is cold.*
17. I need a coat *if it is cold.*

No comma is needed when the subordinate clause follows the main clause.

In the following sentences, we demonstrate other introductories:

18. *However,* it is cold.
19. *Furthermore,* it is cold.
20. *Unfortunately,* it is cold.
21. *Moreover,* it is cold.
22. *Therefore,* I need a coat.
23. *However,* is it cold?

In each of these cases, the word preceding the subject and verb is introductory and set off by a comma. (Introductory Comma)

Commas are also called for in these circumstances:

24. Our anniversary is Monday, May 4.

Separating day from date. (Apposition Comma)

25. On April 8, 1972, the shop opened.

Separating month and day from year. (Parenthetical Comma)

26. The store will close on November 25, Thanksgiving Day.

27. Our president, John Smith, will be present.

These two sentences illustrate the comma used in apposition; i.e., when we say the same thing in different ways. (Apposition Comma)

28. I see, though, that she is here.

29. This is my sample, however.

30. Joan, who dresses well, was promoted.

Parenthetical commas are identified as commas setting material off which could be included in parentheses and therefore omitted. (Parenthetical Comma)

31. Our flag is red, white, and blue.

32. The sweaters were green, brown, yellow, and white.

Place a comma before the *and,* just as we did in 3. (Series Comma)

33. Here is a stamped, self-addressed envelope. It is a beautiful blue color.

We need a comma in the first sentence because *and* sounds right between the two adjectives. (Adjective Comma)

Do you know about the period which is acceptable following a courteous request?

34. May we have your check by return mail.

35. May we have your check by return mail?

We expect the check in reply, not an answer saying "Yes, you may have our check by return mail." However, the question mark is always correct.

Commas and periods always go inside quotation marks in business correspondence.

36. "Yes," he said.

37. I have your book, "Better Days."

If, however, your employer insists on their going outside, do it. This is not a life-and-death matter.

Use of the hyphen:

38. Here is a self-addressed envelope.
39. Your past-due account totals $40.
40. Your account for $40 is past due.
41. This book is well known.
42. This well-known book belongs to me.

All expressions which include *self* are hyphenated. Use a hyphen when the noun follows a compound expression; when no noun follows, there is no hyphen. (Compound Adjective Hyphen)

43. It is a nationally known product.
44. It is a newly painted room.

There is no hyphen when the first part of the compound expression ends in *ly*.

These illustrate apostrophes showing possession:

45. That one sheep's wool is black.
46. That one woman's hair is brown.
47. That one mouse's tail is curly.
48. That one boy's tie is red.

All singulars call for the apostrophe + *s*. All you have to know is whether it is singular or not.

In the following sentences, assume three of everything, so we have plurals:

49. The sheep's wool is black.
50. The women's dresses were all blue.
51. The mice's tails were cut off.

Just take the plural form and add apostrophe + *s*. (Possessive Apostrophe)

52. The boys' ties were red.

except here: We would add apostrophe + *s* but it sounds strange to say *boys's;* so we remove the *s* which follows the apostrophe.

53. These are yours.

54. Ours is here; theirs is there.

55. Here is its label.

Pronouns do not require any apostrophe to show possession.

APPENDIX F

KEY

UNIT 1

1.2 Dear Mrs. White: Our monthly bulletin presents current news, trends, and developments of interest to advertising[20] concerns. We wish to compile a mailing list for distribution of this publication. It will stimulate[40] interest in progressive advertising campaigns. (P) Will you please fill out the enclosed blank, place it in the stamped envelope,[60] and return it to us. We shall appreciate your cooperation. Sincerely, (73 words)

1.3 Miss Shirley Martin, 28-06 Court Street, Trenton, NJ 18619 Dear Miss Martin: We are happy to inform you that you have won first prize in our contest. (P) Plans for a wonderful [20] three-week vacation have been made through the Acme Travel Agency. They are sending you the itinerary,[40] and they are available to discuss any questions you may have. (P) The enclosed check for $250 [60] is to cover any incidental expenses. Sincerely, (71 words)

1.4 Have you considered the fact that there are 110 additional days of vacation in each year? There are[20] 52 weekends a year, which gives you 104 days plus our six national holidays. That is a real[40] bonanza of leisure time without being away from your desk during the working day. (P) We would like you to share your[60] leisure time with us. Our easy-care A-frames and Swiss chalets are nestled in the foothills of the Poconos[80]—easy to reach by car, bus, or train. Outside your door are year-round activities: skiing, ice skating, hiking, golfing,[100] swimming, boating, fishing, and much more. (P) Our central lodge is the meeting place for you and your neighbors to socialize.[120] Our snack bar has become the hangout for our teenagers. (P) Let us show you how to turn your weekends into fun[140] days. Read our brochure and picture yourself and your family sharing in our year-round fun world. On your next free weekend [160] bring your family and look us over. We think you will like what you see! (174 words)

2.2 Dear Mr. Allen: Thank you for your order for one dozen file boxes. (P) As you requested, we will imprint the[20] name of your organization on the cover of each box. When this work has been completed, we will ship the boxes[40] by air express. Cordially, (46 words)

2.3 Mr. Joseph Friend, 17 Maple Street, Phoenix, AZ 85021 Dear Mr. Friend: We have been wondering why you have not used your credit card recently. (P) Some people save their cards[20] just for travel, but actually they are a great convenience in your daily life. Our monthly statements will give[40] you a complete record of your purchases. Let your credit card work for you. Sincerely yours, (56 words)

2.4 Mrs. Steven Doyle, 685 Hedman Place, Kingston, MA 01522 Dear Mrs. Doyle: We have asked our head counselor, Paul Finch, to call you and meet with you to discuss Frank's interest in[20] spending the summer at Camp Cayuga. Paul will show you slides of the campgrounds and some of the activities of[40] last year's campers. (P) Camp Cayuga has been a summer home for boys for 37 years, and we are proud of our[60] reputation of offering the best of care to our campers. (P) The camp is located near two lakes, offering[80] excellent opportunities for canoeing, boating, sailing, and fishing. We have many planned hiking trails, and[100] our campers often have the opportunity to leave camp for a few days to sleep out in the open. A large[120] stone fireplace near the main hall is the gathering place for outdoor sings and entertainment of varied nature. (P) As[140] you will see from our slides, we offer all the activities expected in a camp program. As we have a number[160] of campers with diverse interests, we let our students plan their weekly activities individually.[180] (P) The enrollment at Cayuga is limited and open only to boys from ten to sixteen years of age. There[200] are still several vacancies available. (P) We invite investigation. We are proud of our staff, who are well[220] qualified to take charge of active boys. Sincerely yours, (231 words)

3.2 Dear Customer: Our lease will expire next month, and we shall be moving to a new location. Consequently, we[20] are placing all of our garden equipment on sale. All purchases will represent a great savings. (P) Come in soon,[40] before all the best merchandise is gone. Yours very truly, (51 words)

3.3 Mr. Gus Lawson, 39-38 Sycamore Drive, Shreveport, LA 71101 Dear Mr. Lawson: As a long-time subscriber to the Star Herald, we know you do not want to miss even one[20] issue while you are on vacation. (P) Before you get involved in the packing rush, just sign the official[40] notification form and list your mailing address so you will not miss one issue. (P) Let us be responsible for all[60] the details. We will hold your billings until you return from your vacation. Sincerely yours, (73 words)

3.4 Miss Rita Connors, Apartment 12, Sunnyside Towers, 235-618 Sunnyside Drive, Lansing, MI 48905 Dear Miss Connors: We are pleased to forward our most recent booklet about travel conditions in Europe. We can[20] offer you a variety of trips, depending on the amount of time you will have available for your[40] vacation. (P) Some of our tours are based on visiting five major cities and spending approximately three days[60] in each city. Some people prefer to visit only one or two major areas and tour those areas[80] in detail after establishing residence at one hotel. This avoids the nuisance of packing and unpacking[100] as well as some of the problems of purchasing different currencies. (P) At the present time, because of the[120] national economic situation, we feel duty bound to advise our clients that travel in Europe[140] is more expensive than it was three months ago and costs have risen between 15 to 20 percent. We have[160] tried to offset some of this problem by increasing our recommended list of hotels and restaurants to include[180] those we feel are more reasonable and still offering quality service. (P) Our office will be glad to supply[200] you with any information concerning passports, customs regulations, and transportation facilities[220] available in any country in Europe. If you have any additional questions after reading[240] our booklet, please call 767-6500. We shall be glad to handle your reservations.[260] Sincerely yours, (262 words)

4.2 If a letter, memorandum, or any other kind of written communication is to convey the writer's[20] meaning and make sense to the reader, it must contain correctly used punctuation marks. Since very few[40] businessmen dictate punctuation, secretaries, stenographers, and other office workers must know how to use[60] commas, periods, and other marks of punctuation. (70 words)

4.3 Mr. Robert Marshall, Director, Camp Cayuga, Blue Lake, N.Y. 12812 Dear Mr. Marshall: We enjoyed meeting Mr. Finch and viewing the slides of Camp Cayuga. If the pictures do[20] true justice, your camp should provide an exciting adventure for the summer. (P) As this will be our son's first summer[40] at camp, we want the experience to be a satisfying one. We have been very interested in your camp,[60] not only from your brochure and slides but also from the comments we have heard from friends whose sons have spent their summers[80] with you. (P) Frank has gotten out his fishing rod preparatory to spending the summer at Blue Lake. He filled out[100] the enclosed application himself. Our check for $300 is the deposit you requested. The[120] medical forms will be in the mail by the end of the week. Cordially yours, (133 words)

4.4 The National Hosteling Association offers your youngster an exciting and different experience.[20] Your son or daughter will be able to spend his summer participating in a planned bicycling tour[40] throughout our countryside. There are a number of hosteling trips planned to different corners of our country,[60] varying from three to six weeks. (P) The hostelers bicycle on the average of 30 to 35 miles a[80] day, stopping at prearranged meeting places along the way. The trip does allow for visiting national and[100] historic spots of interest. (P) We recommend a lightweight, English-style bicycle equipped with a 10-gear speed[120] assembly and hand brakes. Each hosteler is responsible for keeping his bicycle in good repair and will need[140] to carry one spare tire with him. (P) To prepare for this somewhat arduous tour, each hosteler should bicycle at[160] least 5 miles daily over varied terrain to strengthen his leg muscles. Without this preparation, the beginning[180] hosteler may find the first three or four days to be very uncomfortable until his leg muscles adjust[200] to this enforced exercise. (P) Talk with your child and see if he does not indicate that, when the school year ends, he[220] wants to be a member of a hosteling group traveling along the Eastern seaboard. (236 words)

5.2 Dear Mr. Adams: Because you are a person who does a great deal of traveling in the course of your business[20] activities, we want to bring to your attention the many excellent Crown Motels. (P) When you make your next[40] business trip, see for yourself, Mr. Adams, the outstanding accommodations and services that are provided[60] by a Crown Motel. After you have enjoyed our hospitality, I am sure you, like so many others, will[80] start to make staying at the Crown a delightful habit. Sincerely yours, (93 words)

5.3 Mr. Philip Yarby, 267 Hayes Avenue, Springfield, MA 01125 Dear Mr. Yarby: Our membership committee has just established a special six-month's winter special to run[20] from November 15 to April 15. The dues are $75 plus tax. (P) We are planning a fine[40] winter program. Music and dancing will be available at the club every evening except Monday. (P) Look[60] over our schedule. I think you will find the club a delightful place to spend your weekends during the winter.[80] Cordially yours, (82 words)

5.4A The Burgess Family, 23 Orchard Place, Mayfair, MD 21106 Dear Campers: The perfect family fun summer can be found camping at one of our country sites. This is a[20] wonderful way of rekindling your enjoyment of our natural environment. (P) Our camping fields offer you a[40] choice of pitching your own tent or of hooking your trailer to one of our many water and electrical sources.[60] (P) Bring back the joy of the simple life. Cast your fishline into a stream that meanders only a few hundred [80] yards from your campsite; cook your evening meal over an open fire; then relax at night in the satisfying[100] shadowy warmth of the pine forest. (P) Yes, we have painted an inviting scene. Picture yourself and your family[120] in this lovely setting. Join us for one of the most enjoyable summers you will experience as a[140] family. (P) Please plan to be with us and share your summer joys with us. We will be looking for you! Sincerely yours, (159 words)

5.4B Mr. Irwin Singer, 14-07 Craig Road, Ridgefield, OH 43345 Dear Mr. Singer: This wet spring offers you the unusual chance to organize your outdoor equipment,[20] to plan your necessary purchases, to charge them, and to have them delivered immediately. In this way, you[40] will be prepared for the first fine weekend when this rainy spell is over. (P) Ralph's Sporting Goods Store can supply you with[60] fine quality, utilitarian goods which should last for years under normal situations and usage.[80] For example, our nylon tents are designed with zipper windows and door flaps which can be quickly sealed to protect you[100] from the elements. These tents are bright orange and easily noticeable in the deep woods. (P) Study our[120] extraordinary samples. We have hundreds of regulation items that will add to your future good times. Yours[140] cordially, (141 words)

UNIT 2

1.2 Dear Mrs. Curtis: If you have read the catalog we sent you a few days ago, you realize how entertaining,[20] practical, and economical our handcraft kits are. (P) As a matter of fact, we have received hundreds[40] of letters from thoroughly satisfied customers. (P) Honestly, it wouldn't surprise us at all to receive a[60] note of satisfaction from you, too, as soon as you have finished your first handcraft kit. Sincerely yours, (78 words)

1.3 Mr. Robert Fenton, Fenton Photography Studio, 244 Main Street, Painted Post, NY 14870 Dear Bob: This morning's newspaper described the damage your photo shop suffered in the recent floods. Let me assure[20] you that I am ready to help you in these difficult times. (P) Just advise me what stock you will need and how soon you[40] want delivery, and I shall have our warehouse fill your order to replenish your shelves immediately.[60] (P) Pay for this merchandise when you can spare the cash. We have always enjoyed a fine business relationship with you and [80] hope it will continue for years to come. Yours sincerely, (90 words)

1.4 TO: ALL CLUB MEMBERS OF THE SKYWATCH CLUB The National Bird Watchers Association has invited us to[20] participate in the annual summer bird census. Our task is to watch for flocks of birds that will pass through[40] predetermined and designated altitudes as they migrate southwards. We are expected to estimate the numbers[60] in each flock. (P) To conduct this census, 60 x 60 power telescopes will be mounted on tripods at[80] the ranger station on Hawk Mountain. Members of the local ornithological club will help us identify[100] the different species. (P) Please call Miss Wilson at the Skywatch Club and register the hours you will be willing[120] to volunteer your help. We are depending upon all members to support our efforts on behalf of the[140] National Bird Watchers Association. (147 words)

2.2 Dear Mrs. Small: Think of the richness and beauty a brand new rug or wall-to-wall carpeting would bring to your[20] living room. (P) We are inviting you to trade in your old, out-of-date floor covering for a new, luxurious rug[40] or a carpet that covers your floor from wall to wall. (P) Mail the postage-free card today for full details about this[60] reclamation plan that saves you money. Sincerely yours, (70 words)

2.3 Mr. Joe Sharp, The Daily Herald, New London, CT 06301 Dear Joe: The annual New England Newspaper Reporters Association reunion will be meeting this[20] year on November 14 in Boston. (P) This is an invitation for you to be our guest speaker. We would like[40] you to consider speaking on some of your on-the-scene shots for which you are justly famous. We will be glad to[60] supply any "blowups" of any of the photographs you would like. (P) If you accept this assignment, we know you[80] will provide us with one of the most stimulating talks ever planned for our annual banquet. Sincerely yours,[100] (100 words)

2.4A Photography has become one of America's most popular hobbies. The novice starts with family shots[20] using a box camera and, with practice, usually promotes himself to using a double-reflex model.[40] (P) No matter where you live you can find a different subject for your viewer any way you turn. Do you live[60] in the city? There are numerous exciting subjects available. For example, you can "shoot" statuary[80] in museum gardens, children at play, people in all poses, ships being unloaded, a simple fountain[100] in a park, or you might spot a gargoyle perched on a rooftop. Each change of season brings a new scene to be caught by[120] the camera. The list of subjects is endless. (P) Many hours will slip by as you study your photos to determine[140] how to improve your photographic technique. Your pictures will delight you with many memories. (158 words)

2.4B Mrs. Paul Gates, 278 Anderson Avenue, Oneonta, NY 13820 Dear Mrs. Gates: Are you starting to plan your holiday gift list? Are you searching your mind for the gift that is[20] different? Are you trying to avoid the usual? Would you like to surprise someone special with an oil painting[40] of his favorite photograph? (P) We can solve your gift problem for you. We are the originators of "Paintings from Pictures." We can produce rich, glowing oil paintings[60] from a favorite picture. The method is quite simple but is time consuming. (P) We make an enlarged duplicate[80] of your picture. The outline of the subject is projected into textured, canvaslike material. Then[100] our skilled artists apply oil paint to this outline. The warmth of the colors of the rainbow bring your favorite picture[120] to life. (P) Come to our studio and let us show you how your black and white print can become the gift of the year[140]—to be enjoyed for years to come. Cordially yours, (149 words)

3.2 Dear Mrs. Gardner: Two weeks from today we will be celebrating our company's 25th year in business.[20] Wouldn't you like to celebrate the occasion by taking part in our special sale of men's, women's, and children's[40] clothing? (P) Bargains will be available on all clothing, and there will be a selection wide enough to satisfy[60] everyone. (P) To make the occasion a really gala affair, we will give a surprise gift to each customer[80] at the sale. Yours is waiting for you. Sincerely, (89 words)

3.3 Mr. John Crosby, 253 Madison Avenue, Fargo, ND 58105 Dear Mr. Crosby: At this time of the year many of our friends find that their daily activities are beginning[20] to lose their appeal. A change of scenery for at least a few days seems to be uppermost in their thoughts. We[40] suspect that you, too, may be having this urge. (P) The Ramsey Travel Bureau offers a choice of several delightful[60] tours. The most popular of these are described in the enclosed booklet. You will find pleasure in reading about[80] the exciting and colorful places that are within your reach because of the speed and convenience of today's[100] planes. (P) Won't you call at our office for a detailed description of the trip of your choice. Very truly yours,[120] (120 words)

3.4A Mr. Paul Meyer, M & S Suppliers, La Porte, IN 46350 Dear Mr. Meyer: We thank you again for the most recent filmstrips that you forwarded to be viewed by the[20] adult education senior citizens photography class. The group studied your examples in depth before they[40] began their latest assignments to produce stories on film. (P) All the scenarios were written by club members.[60] The imaginative filming effects were created by spending many hours planning, filming, and then splicing[80] the film together into a finished package. Sound effects were added and the projects completed. (P) Some of these[100] efforts appear so professional that you might wish to preview some of these original efforts. You might[120] even wish to incorporate them with some of the new strips you mentioned you were preparing. Cordially yours, (139 words)

3.4B To add to the pleasure of his hobby, the amateur photographer will often spend hours in a darkroom[20] processing his own film. This effects an economy, as professional processing is expensive. Home processing[40] allows the photo bug the chance to see his handiwork as soon as a roll of film is completely exposed.[60] (P) To process film, the exposed roll is dipped into a solution of developer which brings out the latent[80] images on the negative film. Then the film is submerged in a solution of stopbath, which finalizes the[100] process of the developer bath. The film is slipped into a container of fixer in order to make the[120] film permanent. The film is then hung to dry. This whole operation may take a total of three minutes. (P) After[140] the film is completely dried, it can be handled. The strips are cut into individual prints ready to be[160] mounted in an album or tucked into a plastic pocket to be kept handy so that the pictures can be shared [180] or studied by other people. (186 words)

4.2 Dear Mr. Carter: You know by now that our magazine, *Views*, is interestingly written and authoritative.[20] Moreover, you know that it is a medium through which you can keep up to date on all areas of modern[40] life. (P) Many exciting topics are planned for the months ahead, and we do not want you to miss any of them.[60] Consequently, we are offering special renewal rates of one year for $6, two years for $11,[80] and three years for $15. (P) Simply fill in and mail the enclosed card to receive this special offer.[100] Cordially yours, (102 words)

4.3 Mr. Paul Meyer, M & S Suppliers, La Porte, IN 46350 Dear Mr. Meyer: Our classes were very impressed with the filmstrips that were rented from you. The

"Language of the[20] Camera" was particularly informative. (P) Our students gained insight into the working parts of the[40] camera and in analyzing the balance between shutter speed, amount of light (f/stop), and focal distance.[60] (P) Color film helps to produce pleasant shots, but black and white filming encourages attempts to achieve special effects[80] by varying speed, light, and focal distance relationships. (P) Our adult education senior citizens' [100] photography class will be producing film stories. Do you have any additional filmstrips that would be[120] useful for this assignment? Sincerely yours, (126 words)

4.4 Shipman Film and Photo Supply Co., 147 South Street, Pueblo, CO 81007 Gentlemen: Thank you for considering my store as headquarters for the picture contest that you are planning for[20] the month of October. This should help to encourage sales of photographic supplies during this normally[40] quiet month. (P) In preparing for this contest, the newspaper announcements are written; flyers and handbills are printed [60] and are ready for distribution. The rules have been carefully reviewed and will be posted in the center store[80] window as well as being included in all the publicity. (P) We have rented some easels to help make the[100] display of early submissions easier to be viewed. A local decorator has volunteered to arrange the[120] window and change the pictures every few days. This will help by having the window become a focal point on[140] this shopping thoroughfare. (P) Please fill the enclosed order as rapidly as possible. My supplies of developer,[160] fixer, and stopbath are very low. Very truly yours, (171 words)

5.2 Dear Mr. Hansen: In Mr. Baker's absence, I am acknowledging receipt of your book, *Tracy's Plight*, that you[20] sent to him. As soon as Mr. Baker returns, I know he will thank you personally for the book. (P) I have taken[40] the liberty of reading the book, and I find it fascinating. Sincerely yours, (56 words)

5.3 Mr. Harold Jones, 143 West Wabash Avenue, Terre Haute, IN 47801 Dear Mr. Jones: Thank you for your invitation to take part in your conference on photography. I am[20] happy to accept, but I shall not be able to give you a definite date until next month. (P) I can definitely[40] say that I will come on either June 20 or August 2. I will write you again as soon as I am able[60] to tell you which date is possible. Sincerely yours, (70 words)

5.4 The New City Photographers Club is pleased to announce that it will sponsor its fifteenth annual photography[20] contest. The contest is open to anyone who wishes to submit entries. Each registrant will be given[40] a contestant number, and he may register up to seven entries. (P) Black and white entries will be judged [60] separately from color prints. All entries will be categorized under major headings such as still lifes, children,[80] people, animals, architecture, landscapes, or seascapes. (P) All entries must be received by Wednesday, June 14, at[100] noon. They will be put on display for public viewing at the club building on Orchard Street. (P) Prizes and ribbons will [120] be awarded on Saturday, June 17, between 3 and 5 p.m. (134 words)

UNIT 3

1.2 Dear Miss Nelson: Two months ago we entered your order for the special eight-month subscription to *Fashion Monthly*.[20] We hope that you have enjoyed the copies you have received. (P) We have not, however, received your check for $6,[40] the price of this special subscription. Won't you take a moment now to write a check for $6 and mail it to[60] us in the enclosed envelope. Yours truly, (68 words)

1.3 Ward Bent Company, 842 Northumberland Street, Fredericton, New Brunswick, Canada Gentlemen: Thank you for your letter of March 21. (P) Our Shipping Department informed us this morning that your[20] annual order will be ready for shipment on Thursday, March 25. You should, therefore, have your new[40] stock within a few days. Sincerely yours, (46 words)

1.4A In order to place local and long distance calls efficiently and rapidly, you must be able to place your[20] calls quickly. Learn to use the telephone directories. (P) The telephone directory has two parts. The white pages[40] include the alphabetical listing of subscribers, their addresses, and their telephone numbers. (P) The yellow[60] pages, which include the listing of names of businesses, are categorized alphabetically by product[80] or by service offered. These pages are a helpful reference and guide for the office workers. (P) Commonly used [100] telephone numbers should be recorded on a separate desk file so that they are immediately at hand [120] and can be located within 30 seconds. (129 words)

1.4B Mr. Tice Alexanders, 310 Bellair Avenue, Manhasset, NY 11030 Dear Mr. Alexanders: Your application for a telephone credit card has been approved and will be placed [20] in the mail to you within ten days' time. (P) This card has your private code number on it, which allows you to charge your[40] long distance calls with ease while traveling. The charges will be itemized on your monthly bills. Sincerely yours, (59 words)

2.2 Dear Mr. Jackson: We had not seen the clipping you sent us, and we appreciate your thoughtfulness in sending[20] it. (P) While we realize the value of advertising in your magazine, we are not in a position to[40] expand our advertising at this time. (P) We shall, however, keep your magazine in mind when we plan next year's[60] advertising budget. Sincerely yours, (66 words)

2.3 General Publishing Company, 91 State Street, Jersey City, NJ 07309 Gentlemen: Thank you for the examination copy of the latest edition of *English for Business.* I [20] think you have done a fine job in revising the book. (P) I felt that the following lessons were weak: Lesson 7 [40] on prepositions, Lesson 9 on conjunctions, and Lesson 11 on punctuation. The new edition[60] represents a great improvement in these lessons. (P) If we adopt this new edition for our classes, will you give[80] us full credit for the copies of the old edition that we have in stock? Sincerely yours, (96 words)

2.4 Miss Joan Adler, c/o The Rapid Line Answering Service, 448 Hillman Drive, Pierce, ID 83546 Dear Miss Adler: There are an average of 400 million telephone calls made each day. Business offices make[20] and receive numerous calls daily. (P) As a secretary for a telephone answering service, you certainly[40] recognize how important are good telephone manners. Your telephone voice must be friendly and pleasing because[60] a secretary is the initial telephone representative for a company. Your good manners[80] show in your telephone personality. (P) I enjoyed speaking with you this morning and learning about the thoughtful [100] methods employed by The Rapid Line Answering Service. Sincerely yours, (114 words)

3.2 Dear Mr. Bates: The Insurance Report is the leading magazine in the insurance industry, Mr. Bates.[20] It is read by thousands of life insurance agents throughout the country. (P) Isn't this a good reason why you should [40] place your advertising in our magazine? If you will return the enclosed card, we shall be glad to send you our[60] advertising rates. Yours truly, (66 words)

3.3 Trade Manufacturing Company, 13 West 15 Street, Wilmington, DE 19806 Gentlemen: In order that you may learn about our newspaper, we shall send it to you free for a month. We hope[20] that you will find it interesting and helpful in your work. (P) The news is reported in full in the *Post*. The financial [40] page will keep you up to date on the stock market because we make it a point to include a full listing of [60] all stocks. (P) Read the *Post* for a month at our expense; then send us an order for daily delivery. Yours very[80] truly, (81 words)

3.4 Mr. Edward Martinson, 642 Godwin Avenue, Muskogee, OK 74401 Dear Mr. Martinson: In our present study we are concerned with the problem of how effectively and [20] rapidly mail is being delivered in the average office. (P) Mail should be sorted as speedily as possible[40] into three general classifications: (1) business, (2) personal, and (3) direct mail. (P) Certified letters,[60] special delivery, airmail, and first-class mail should be set aside in a separate pile to be processed [80] immediately. All of these letters except those marked personal should be opened, the contents quickly scanned,[100] enclosures verified, date and time stamped, and finally placed on the executive's desk ready for action. (P) Direct[120] mail, which is often composed of advertising materials, can be opened and sorted after the handling[140] of the first-class mail has been completed. (P) If you have questions on this problem of rapid mail handling, please do not[160] hesitate to contact us to help you. Sincerely yours, (170 words)

4.2 Dear Mr. Black: This year's edition of National Sports will keep football fans up to date on what's going on in[20] one of the country's most popular sports. (P) The book covers more than 300 squads, and it contains all of the records[40] of professional players. (P) You can obtain your copy by filling out the enclosed form and returning it[60] with your check for $9. Sincerely yours, (68 words)

4.3 Mr. Ralph A. Winslow, 89 Grandview Avenue, Portland, ME 04106 Dear Mr. Winslow: We are glad to send you a copy of the radio address of Mr. Howard Clark,[20] president of the National Association of Savings Institutions, which you recently requested. (P) It[40] is a pleasure to learn that you are listening to our radio hour, and we hope that you will find the programs[60] sufficiently enjoyable to tune in every Wednesday evening. (P) These talks cover a wide variety[80] of subjects. We are sure you will find them interesting and helpful. Very truly yours, (95 words)

4.4A To: Patricia Young, Sales Department Welcome to you as the newest member of our firm! The attached handbook is[20] our most recent edition. I know you will find it to be a useful guide, informative as to your benefits,[40] and helpful to you in making your adjustment to our business organization. Please spend some time studying[60] this handbook, as it will outline the procedures we follow in our daily routine. (P) If you have any questions,[80] please do not hesitate to contact Miss Hartley, our secretarial staff adviser. (96 words)

4.4B Home Aluminum Products, 118 Forest Avenue, Saddle Brook, NJ 07662 Gentlemen: The telegram is an inexpensive and dramatic method of sending a brief informative[20] message. Because of its brevity, the telegram is an effective attention getter. It requires the[40] writer to limit the message and include only necessary information. (P) When you need to send a short,[60] concise message, just call your local Western Union office and say, "I want to send a telegram, please." Yours truly, (80 words)

5.2 To the Staff: Please note that our textbook, *Essentials of Grammar*, will be out of print as soon as we have disposed of[20] our present stock. There is sufficient stock, we believe, to carry us through June or July. (P) For your information, sales have[40] dropped so much that it is not worthwhile to reprint the book. In other words, we cannot afford to carry[60] it any longer. (64 words)

5.3 Mr. John R. Myers, 25 State Street, Hartford, CT 06105 Dear Mr. Myers: Thank you for your application for fire insurance, which we received today from our agent,[20] Mr. James Quinn. You may be sure that we shall make every effort to give you the best service possible under the[40] terms of the policy. (P) The enclosed binder confirms your coverage. This is effective as of noon, January[60] 29. We are preparing a policy that you will receive before the binder period expires.[80] Very truly yours, (84 words)

5.4A To: All Members of Secretaries International When you sit down at your typewriter to transcribe your[20] employer's dictation, you want each letter that he signs to look like "a picture in a frame." (P) One way to be sure your[40] transcribed material will be eye catching is to keep your typewriter in good repair. Your letters will look[60] professional if the typewriter impressions are clean and even when struck. *A*'s and *o*'s should be open circles[80]—not ink-filled, shadowy letters. (P) Five minutes spent on Monday morning quickly brushing and cleaning your typewriter will[100] help you produce satisfying copy all week long. (107 words)

5.4B Aetna Roofing Company, 17-08 Plaza Road, Driftwood, TX 78619 Gentlemen: We know you will be pleased to receive the revised Postal Manual of the United States Post Office[20] Department, which explains in detail the postal services available. This manual lists the charges[40] and mailing costs for all classes of mail. Additionally, we are including a paper-bound copy of zip[60] code listings. We know your secretary will find this a handy reference and will include a zip code on every[80] letter she mails for you. (P) If you have any questions not covered by the Postal Manual, do not hesitate[100] to call your local postmaster. Cordially yours, (109 words)

UNIT 4

1.2 Dear Mr. Horn: Our records indicate that your child's policy expires on September 1. (P) The enclosed renewal[20] notice will give your child protection for a full 12 months, in school and out. (P) The premium for this coverage is[40] $30. (P) Please return the renewal notice, together with your check, in the enclosed envelope.[60] Sincerely yours, (62 words)

1.3 Mr. David Roth, 36-05 High Street, Santa Fe, NM 87501 Dear Sir: Do you have difficulty remembering whether you have paid the premiums on your insurance[20] policies? Do you receive notices that you are on your 30 days of grace? (P) We are preparing a summary[40] record for each of our customers so that this will no longer be a problem. Your secretary will be able[60] to provide you with ready information upon your request as to premium-payment dates and amounts.[80] (P) This is just one of the helpful ideas we will initiate for you when you are protected by our nationwide[100] insurance organization. Sincerely yours, (109 words)

1.4 Insurance may be classified in two broad groups. Personal insurance includes life, accident, disability,[20] health, and social insurance. Property insurance covers losses from fire, marine, casualty, loss from[40] impairment, liability, destruction of property, burglary, and automobile claims. (P) An individual [60] or business purchases insurance and receives a policy which is a written contract between the buyer[80] and the insurance company. The buyer is called a policyholder and the insurance company[100] is called the underwriter. (P) The policyholder makes regular payments to the insurance company and,[120] therefore, guarantees continuing protection. These payments or premiums are payable in advance and can[140] be made monthly, quarterly, semiannually, or annually. (P) To assist her employer, the secretary[160] must accept three responsibilities. Her first responsibility is to see that premiums are paid [180] promptly so that there is no lapse in protection. The second responsibility is to keep informative[200] records summarizing the kinds of insurance purchased. Lastly, the secretary must be sure that the policies[220] are stored in a safe, fireproof place. (226 words)

2.2 Dear Mr. Walters: Today you can buy up to $30,000 of straight life insurance at the City[20] Savings Bank at surprisingly low cost. (P) At age 25, for example, the rate for a $5,000 [40] policy is only $7.50 a month. At other ages, rates are correspondingly low.[60] (P) Join the thousands of smart accountants, lawyers, and engineers who are taking advantage of this protection. To[80] learn what the rates are at your age, return the enclosed card. Sincerely yours, (93 words)

2.3 Mr. Rodney Harris, 7 Ashburn Place, Troy, NY 21804 Dear Mr. Harris: Re: Automotive Policy No. 605 S87 1605 Your[20] automotive insurance agent, Mr. Earl Dean, has advised us that he has written you several times regarding[40] the overdue premiums on the above-listed policy covering your station wagon for the[60] current year. (P) We are including copies of the letters written by Mr. Dean to you on October 12 and [80] October 25, which state most clearly that your policy will lapse unless you forward a certified check in[100] the amount of $164.80. (P) Unless we receive the complete charge of [120] $164.80 by November 2, this policy will be canceled immediately.[140] Very truly yours, (144 words)

2.4 Reed Brothers, Inc., 248 Rose Place, Chicago, IL 60681 Gentlemen: The fire losses in our nation have increased steadily, and statistics indicate that they are still [20] on the increase. (P) When valuable records are lost as a result of fire, two out of every five firms fail within[40] a brief period of time thereafter. (P) You can protect your business papers by installing a Champion[60] Safety System. Our metal cabinets have a two-hour fire rating. If you are unfortunate and do[80] experience a fire, we are able to guarantee that you will find your vital papers intact and usable.[100] (P) Come in and look at our "before and after" exhibition of papers that were in fires and were not destroyed because[120] they were protected by a Champion Safety System. Sincerely yours, (133 words)

3.2 Dear Mr. Wait: Would you like a complete record of your family's insurance? I shall be glad to review your[20] policies at no cost to you. (P) There are certain questions about your insurance that should be checked from time to time.[40] (P) Remember, there is no charge for this service. You will, of course, not be under any obligation by taking[60] advantage of it. Yours very truly, (67 words)

3.3 Mr. Mark Hammond, President, Office Specialists, Incorporated, 12 Miller Plaza, Raleigh, WV 25911 Dear Mr. Hammond: The executive advisory service of the Mutual Insurance Co. offers[20] you our experts to plan your insurance needs. Our basic policy in the executive group is for a[40] minimum of $100,000 protection, which, I am sure, should be of interest to you. (P) A well-planned[60] insurance portfolio depends upon your having a diversified financial plan. One of our specialists[80] will be pleased to visit you to study your present holdings. The needs of each client and his family are[100] considered on a completely individual basis. (P) The data you share with us are treated as privileged[120] information. We respect your privacy. Do not hesitate to contact our executive advisory[140] service to review your insurance program. Cordially yours, (151 words)

3.4 Mr. and Mrs. Nat Wilson, 6-33 Manfield Drive, Hazelton, PA 18201 Dear Mr. and Mrs. Wilson: We offer a special policy designed to protect your college student while[20] he is traveling to and from school as well as while he is enrolled and living at college. This policy is[40] offered at the exceptionally low rate of $15 per school year from September 1 through June 15.[60] (P) We are able to offer this benefit because our policy is bought by so many concerned parents across[80] the country. This floater has two major protective clauses: (1) payment in case of accident if your child[100] is maimed or killed; (2) payment for theft or damage to possessions. (P) To have the coverage for your college-bound student,[120] complete the simple application form and forward it together with your check for $15. The[140] policy will go into effect as of September 1. Very truly yours, (154 words)

4.2 Dear Mr. Link: If you do not pay the premium on your insurance policy by January 17,[20] the policy will lapse; and your family will be without protection. (P) If you permit this policy to[40] lapse, you will never again be able to obtain insurance at such low cost. (P) Won't you please send your check now or[60] at least tell me why you cannot pay. If you are short of funds at this time, perhaps some plan can be arranged that will[80] enable you to keep this insurance in force. Sincerely yours, (91 words)

4.3 Mr. Peter Kempner, Kempner Construction Company, 39-46 Sunderland Drive, Watertown, SD 57201 Dear Mr. Kempner: Next year our company will celebrate 150 years of writing insurance.[20] Originally founded to insure ships against risks on the high seas, our organization writes nearly every[40] kind of insurance, except life. (P) Through varying economic periods, our company has met every[60] obligation to protect property owners throughout the state. In your profession, this should be a most important[80] consideration. (P) At Shield Insurance, we have been pioneers in occupational safety. Our specialized[100] services have given attention to helping provide safe working environments and, when necessary, have[120] aided in rehabilitation training for the worker. (P) The name, Shield Insurance, stands for reliability[140] and dependability in this difficult and changing world. Sincerely yours, (155 words)

4.4 Day Steel Fabricators, Corner of Smith Street and Underhill Road, Bethlehem, PA 18015 Attention: Mr. George Day, President Gentlemen: Today a number of discussions that take place between management and labor are concerned with the[20] group insurance that is to be provided for all employees. (P) Before you can participate in a discussion[40] on the subject, you should be prepared with factual research to answer basic questions. What benefits must[60] be considered to be a well-rounded and protective umbrella for your employees? What have similar firms[80] in this area done to furnish security for their laborers? What will a complete proposal cost Day[100] Steel Fabricators? (P) Our trained representatives will be able to supply you with all the latest developments[120] relative to group insurance in your general locality. They will outline a schedule that you will[140] be able to afford and under which all claims will be disposed of quickly and fairly. This will be beneficial[160] to both management and labor in your workshop. Yours sincerely, (173 words)

5.2 Dear Mr. Massey: Thank you for your check for $75 renewing your policy No.[20] 14982. (P) You can, if you wish, include public liability and property damage with this policy for an[40] additional $35 annually. (P) In view of the new law that went into effect last[60] June, I strongly advise this additional protection. (P) If you would like to include this extra protection, sign[80] and return the enclosed form. Very truly yours, (89 words)

5.3 Mr. Irwin Marshall, 20-08 Carlton Place, Columbia, SC 29204 Dear Mr. Marshall: As personnel director of Knight Publishing Co., the enclosed factual guide should[20] be of unique importance to you. This is a frank discussion of your responsibility to keep yourself[40] in good physical condition and thereby set an example for every one of your coworkers. (P) Follow the[60] simple rules to help you cultivate daily good living habits. You will find you will enjoy following the easy[80] program of mild exercise, controlled diet, and good health habits suggested in this outline because you will[100] feel so well. (P) Take 15 minutes from your busy schedule and skim this pamphlet now! We think you will agree that[120] this may be one of the most important publications you have ever read. Cordially yours, (136 words)

5.4 Mr. Roger Kaufman, 70-25 Richard Terrace, Pine Bluff, AR 71601 Dear Mr. Kaufman: As secretary to Mr. Jess Harper, I am taking the liberty to write to you,[20] as I thought you would be interested in the attached copy of an article which was printed in the National[40] Insurance Reporter. (P) As you will note, this article traces the history of the Harper Insurance[60] Agency from its inception over 50 years ago to its present successful existence. (P) The Harper[80] Insurance Agency has built its fine reputation because each client is treated as if he were the first[100] customer to walk through our door. (P) Because you are an old and valued policyholder and a personal[120] acquaintance of Mr. Harper, I felt sure you would be pleased to read about his recognition in this national[140] publication. I am sure Mr. Harper would be most flattered if you mentioned this article at the next[160] Chamber of Commerce meeting. Sincerely, (169 words)

UNIT 5

1.2 Dear Mr. Shaw: I was very much impressed, Mr. Shaw, by the complimentary comments contained in the[20] letters you sent to me. (P) In the future, will you please pass on to me any similar letters that you receive. (P) I [40] will use extracts from them in June, July, and August advertising in several national magazines.[60] Sincerely yours, (62 words)

1.3 Mr. Charles Drake, 41 West Fourth Street, Kingston, TN 37763 Dear Mr. Drake: Have you been postponing the purchase of a postage meter because it did not fit into your[20] budget? Well, now the Acme Postage Meter Company can offer you a postage meter to fit the needs of [40] your particular mailing department. (P) The Acme Postage Meter will print postage on your letters, circulars,[60] and advertising mail efficiently and rapidly and will give you control over your postage expenditures.[80] (P) Our special trial offer will allow you to use the Acme Postage Meter of your choice for a full week. Come[100] in today, make your selection, and let us deliver a postage meter direct to your office. Yours sincerely, (120 words)

1.4 There are a number of categories of advertising media: billboards, mailers, throwaways, newspapers,[20] magazines, radio and television commercials. All of these categories are employed by the[40] advertising industry in their efforts to have the public become aware of and then purchase a particular[60] product. We only have to look around to find other methods of advertising which affect our daily living:[80] signs in windows, neon lights, carcards in buses and subways, and even messages written across the sky.[100] (P) Advertising was originally thought of as "selling through print." Advertising, today, uses any method [120] of communication to have the consumer accept an idea to lead to the purchase of a product.[140] By reading the "blurb" printed on a book jacket, the customer is being invited to read the book. The[160] customer's interest is heightened by an attractively colored cover and by the brief resume of the story.[180] (P) Planned advertising intends for the public to consider and then purchase a particular brand article.[200] In fact, campaigns have been so effective that many of us ask for a product by its brand name rather than[220] just asking for an article such as toothpaste, detergent, or cat food. (P) Advertising has become a strong force[240] in our society. (246 words)

2.2 Dear Miss Martin: On April 10 we sent you our advertising rate card, a brochure, and a copy of our March[20] issue. We hoped that your request for this material, Miss Martin, indicated your interest in renewing[40] your advertising in our magazine. (P) However, we have not received an order for space. May we look forward [60] to an order soon? Yours truly, (66 words)

2.3 Mr. William Grand, The Grand Department Store, 135 South Street, Livingston, NY 12541 Dear Mr. Grand: The spot commercials you forwarded to be broadcast for eight consecutive weeks have been recorded [20] by Ralph Meadows, our electrical engineer, who specializes in disk records. We have found that radio[40] spot commercials are an effective sales media and reasonable to produce. (P) Mr. Paul Simmons has[60] recently joined our staff, and he will be aiding our clients in coordinating their advertising campaigns. Please[80] call him direct at 748-3700 to assist you with any of your future advertising[100] problems. Cordially yours, (105 words)

2.4 Chase Printing Corporation, 7 South Square, Grand Forks, ND 58201 Gentlemen: Will you please quote a price on printing a magazine for our high school junior class[20] association. We shall require 1,700 copies. (P) As planned, the publication will be standard 8½[40] x 11 inches and include approximately 35 pages. The magazine will have a two-column[60] setup and will include 14 photographs. There will be a number of commercial-style cuts from local [80] advertisers, as we are depending upon this revenue to help us underwrite the costs of publication.[100] The logo for the cover will be supplied by us and will be a two-color run. (P) The printed material [120] will be composed of short stories, poems, and essays submitted by students from the English classes. We will include[140] a class history as well as some opinions from class members in response to questions by the "Crusading[160] Columnist." (P) We expect to complete the rough copy before February 1. Can you submit galley proofs for[180] verification three weeks later—by February 22? We are hoping to have the magazine on[200] sale by March 14. Very truly yours, (207 words)

3.2 Dear Mr. Webster: Thank you for the copy of your brochure, "A Career in Advertising." I have read it[20] carefully and have decided that my students, especially those in our General Business Course, would find it helpful.[40] (P) Please consider this my order for 50 copies. According to your letter of April 17, the enclosed [60] check for $12.50 covers the cost of this order. Sincerely yours, (73 words)

3.3 Mr. John Tyler, The Broadway Shop for Men, 749 Seventh Avenue, Albany, NY 12216 Dear Mr. Tyler: We are sorry if there was a misunderstanding concerning the advertising copy[20] submitted to the *Daily Tribune* which was printed last Thursday. If there was an error on our part, a retraction[40] will be printed immediately. (P) Our understanding was that this was to be a one-day sale of men's suits[60] with stated discounts of 25 to 40 percent. This allowed for reductions of $35 to[80] $70, depending upon the garment sold. (P) We are returning a copy of your original [100] advertising copy, which had been rechecked and thoroughly verified by our copywriter before he sent the[120] copy to press. Sincerely yours, (126 words)

3.4 Miss Jean Marder, 431 Harrison Avenue, Fort Worth, TX 76109 Dear Jean: Yes, it is true that consumer surveys are more effective when conducted by personal interview[20] rather than depending on mailed returns. We will be interviewing a number of candidates to help us[40] conduct our next survey. (P) Our Market Research Department presently will complete the pretesting program[60] evaluating the questionnaire to be used in surveying and studying six well-known brands of frozen fruit juices.[80] (P) This will be a more complicated project, as it will involve distribution of samples on one day and a[100] return visit to the interviewee three days later to complete the questionnaire. As this is a new testing[120] method using a personalized approach, we are hopeful that we will receive a higher percentage of returns[140] completed in more detail than usual. The results of this survey will take careful tabulating. The[160] findings will be submitted to the ABC Institute no later than May 14. (P) As you have conducted surveys[180] for us before, I know you will find this to be an exciting new approach to meeting the American[200] consumer. Sincerely yours, (205 words)

4.2 Dear Mr. Crenshaw: Your clients know what's happening in today's business world, but are you equally well informed? [20] (P) If you read the *Advertisers' Review* each week, you can be confident your business information is accurate[40] and up to the minute. The *Advertisers' Review* gives you business and financial news as it happens, long[60] before your clients become aware of it. (P) Call us for complete information about the *Advertisers' Review.*[80] Sincerely yours, (84 words)

4.3 Denver Lithographers, Inc., 48-37 North Haven Square, Darien, CT 06820 Gentlemen: We are proud of our years of leadership in the advertising and publishing fields, and we are[20] especially proud of the workers whose efforts aided us to achieve our reputation. (P) Please join us on Thursday,[40] May 25, as we honor those employees who have been with us for 25 years. We are enclosing a[60] schedule of the tentative program. Sincerely, (79 words)

4.4 Mr. Barton Peterson, 27 LaSalle Street, Deer Park, WI 54007 Dear Mr. Peterson: We appreciate your confidence and thank you for designating us to take charge of[20] lithographing the pictures for your yearbook. We are confident that you will be satisfied with the[40] reproductions. (P) As we are not equipped to bind these books, we subcontract this work. As we have dealt with the Blackston Binding[60] Company for many years, we are more than willing to guarantee the quality of their work. We will forward[80] samples of their leather bindings at your request. (P) Please have your photographer supply us with glossy prints of all your[100] photographs as soon as possible. We will put them into production immediately. Very truly yours, (120 words)

5.2 Dear Mr. Rankin: At the beginning of each year we set aside the amount to be spent on advertising,[20] and the advertising department decides how best to spend this amount. (P) Our advertising for this year has[40] already been planned. We cannot, therefore, consider any additional advertising programs at this time. We[60] feel it would be a waste of your time and ours if your representative were to call on us now. (P) May we suggest,[80] however, that your representative postpone his visit until near the end of the year. We shall then be in a[100] better position to consider any plan you may have. Yours very truly, (114 words)

5.3 Mr. John Durand, World Services, Inc., 24 West Boulevard, Tarrytown, NY 10591 Dear Mr. Durand: Recently we published a book of sample letters which many firms have successfully used[20] to increase circulation by the hundreds. These letters are appropriate in numerous situations. (P) We[40] are sure you will agree that this little volume will benefit every man and woman in your organization.[60] (P) The unusually low price of only $3.50 will satisfy your advertising[80] budget. Sincerely, (84 words)

5.4 Mrs. Albert Franklin, 329 Broad Street, Austin, TX 78705 Dear Mrs. Franklin: Thank you for your order for the evening gown advertised in the Herald. The demand for this[20] dress was so great that we immediately sold out our whole line. (P) We are holding your order as we will be able[40] to ship this gown within ten days. We hope this will be satisfactory. (P) The enclosed brochure describes eight outfits[60] to be featured in our fall showings. These will give you, a valued customer, the opportunity to select[80] any of these items before they are advertised in the local newspapers. (P) Please let us help you in planning[100] and selecting your fall wardrobe. Cordially yours, (109 words)

UNIT 6

1.2 Dear Mr. Powers: We are glad to learn that you are again considering the organization of a[20] driver-training program. (P) We are happy, Mr. Powers, to give you permission to use any of our materials.[40] It will be our pleasure, furthermore, to send you cuts of charts and drawings. (P) Will you please examine our booklets[60] and then let us know what will help you. Cordially yours, (69 words)

1.3 Miss Ruth Long, 188 Spring Street, Shreveport, LA 71118 Dear Miss Long: Every automobile owner knows how necessary it is to equip his car with seat covers[20] in order to beautify and protect the interior. (P) If you are among those who demand the best in fashion[40] and wearing quality, we suggest that you inspect the various styles available at National Service[60] Stations. (P) These covers are made of a plastic-coated material in red, blue, or green; and they are expertly[80] tailored. You will be delighted to know that the bright, new look can be easily maintained with soap and water.[100] (P) We urge you to make your purchase within the next two weeks while our sale prices are still in effect. Sincerely yours, (120 words)

1.4 Skilled workers in the automotive field earn excellent salaries. We are proud of the number of our students[20] who have successfully completed our one-year program and have entered the automotive industry in a[40] number of technical positions. (P) Our program is a combination of classroom study, laboratory[60] work, and an apprenticeship in the field in some phase of automobile work. (P) The automotive courses start with[80] a very basic study of the auto and its moving parts. Then the course progresses to an analytic[100] study of the engine system, the transmission system, and the electrical system. Emphasis is also[120] placed on the study of the materials found in an automobile: metals; glass; numerous forms of plastic;[140] and different fabrics such as cotton, nylon, and wool. (P) Come in and discuss your needs with us. We invite you to[160] talk with our students. Study our curriculum. Visit our up-to-date laboratories and garage center.[180] Let us help you fill your needs with our planned programs. (P) We are sure you will find that your career will start in our[200] automotive classrooms. (203 words)

2.2 Gentlemen: After reviewing the report of our men who attended your factory demonstration, we believe[20] that we are justified in adding your equipment to our line. (P) We are, therefore, enclosing an order to[40] confirm the tentative one Mr. Black gave you. (P) If you can arrange to have a factory mechanic here[60] about May 15, we shall be ready to profit from his visit. Sincerely yours, (74 words)

2.3 Logan's Automotive Service Center, 68-47 Maple Avenue, Elmhurst, NY 11319 Dear Mr. Logan: I have had my car, which I purchased from you, serviced at your Center twice in the last three weeks.[20] I have had trouble starting it. (P) Your mechanic was certain the problem was a defective ignition switch. This[40] switch has been replaced twice, and I have been charged a total of $37.85 for parts[60] and labor. (P) This condition is still not corrected. Please arrange for a factory engineer to look at my[80] car and see if he can solve this problem. Yours truly, (89 words)

2.4 Mr. Donald Johnson, 62 Wilson Drive South, Rumfield, RI 02873 Dear Sir: Did you realize that, after you purchase a home, your second largest expense is the initial cost[20] of the family auto? You depend on your automobile for transportation to work, for shopping, for visits[40] to the doctor, for taking your youngsters to and from school, and for a vacation vehicle. (P) Our Automotive[60] Car Check Center is located in the center of Rumfield. This next week only we are offering our special [80] spring saver—at the very low cost of $22. This is a sound preventive measure for avoiding[100] car problems and includes checking wheel alignment, complete brake testing, checking engine compression, adjusting[120] headlights, determining steering accuracy, and engine tuneup. We also check the levels of transmission[140] and hydraulic brake fluids, inspect all hoses, and lastly, road test your brakes. (P) Come in today and schedule your[160] car for this spring-saver checkup and then have a summer of carefree traveling. Sincerely, P.S. When you[180] register your car for our checkup, be sure to pick up your free copy of our latest travel guide. (197 words)

3.2 Gentlemen: When we received your telegram on December 8, we immediately telephoned our Mr.[20] Watson, who was in Atlanta. We are glad such a capable man was so near when your trouble developed.[40] Without doubt he has your machine back in service by this time. (P) Our experts will be at your plant for the first inspection[60] on Monday, April 21, at 10 a.m. (P) Trips must be carefully planned. In this way, a small number of trained[80] men can give excellent service at regular intervals to many plants. Sincerely yours, (96 words)

3.3 Mr. Harold Roberts, 49 Madison Avenue, Lincoln, NB 68506 Dear Mr. Roberts: I am sorry you have had so much difficulty with your car. It can be a very[20] frustrating experience when a new automobile does not start as readily as it should. (P) Mr. John Lukas,[40] a factory representative, will be here on Thursday. Would it be convenient for you to bring your car in[60] around 9:30 a.m.? Please telephone my secretary to confirm if you will be able to be here[80] at that time. Sincerely yours, (85 words)

3.4 Mr. Dean Jackson, 37-28 Holly Drive, Greensburg, LA 70441 Dear Mr. Jackson: Every week we offer the residents of Greensburg a special $1 discount coupon[20] for our regular car-washing service. (P) Our service includes washing the car windows on the inside, vacuuming[40] the seats and floor, and removing and washing the floor mats. After your car is washed, two men will completely hand dry the car.[60] (P) A hot wax protective coating spray is available at a slight extra charge. This really adds[80] protection and life to the body of your automobile. (P) Look for our advertisement in the *Record.* Bring in your[100] discount coupon the next time your car needs a thorough cleaning and washing. Very truly yours, (116 words)

4.2 Dear Mr. Barton: We have asked our factory representative in Chicago, Mr. Fred Bradley, to take[20] care of your equipment as soon as possible. (P) Although our force of trained men is being increased as rapidly[40] as possible, we are still unable to meet the demands as promptly as we should like. Since all of our men have[60] crowded schedules, we hope you will be patient about any delay. You may feel certain, however, that we are[80] doing everything in our power to give good service. (P) We are glad your Wilson equipment has given[100] satisfaction for so many years because our reputation is built upon the quality of our products, our[120] excellent service, and the praise of our customers. Very sincerely yours, (134 words)

4.3 Ms. Jane Sherman, Abbott Court Apartments, Falmouth Avenue, Harrisburg, PA 17113 Dear Ms. Sherman: The itinerary you requested has been marked on the enclosed map and [20] incorporated in the spiraled trip guide. In the front of this booklet is a listing of your guaranteed accommodations[40] according to the dates you specified. (P) We know this travel guide will help make your trip more pleasant and enjoyable[60] as you depend upon the accurate detailed road information which we have supplied. You can depend on the[80] recommended up-to-date listings of places of national interest to visit to add to the enjoyment[100] of your travels. Cordially yours, (106 words)

4.4 Mr. Carl Archer, 24 Chittenden Road, Elmwood, WV 25072 Dear Mr. Archer: The members of the Elmwood Board of Education as well as the residents of this[20] community sincerely appreciate your annual loan of two new-model sedans to be used by our students[40] in the driver-training program. Your thoughtfulness in outfitting these cars with dual controls and safety[60] harnesses indicates to our young people how dedicated you are to their learning safe driving practices. (P) As[80] you know, our classroom road-preparation course is required before any student sits behind the wheel. Teachers and [100] students discuss state traffic rules based on the motor vehicle handbook for new drivers. Each student must pass an[120] examination on this material with a grade of 80 percent. Also, a series of films of [140] actual accidents is viewed by all students, which certainly reminds them of the terrible hazards of careless driving.[160] (P) Please use any of the enclosed cuts of our students in your campaign for safe and sane driving. Sincerely yours, (180 words)

5.2 Gentlemen: More than three million automobiles rode to market last year on rack-car freight trains; and they arrived [20] swiftly, safely, and at far less cost. (P) If these autos had been moved over highways, one such shipment would have required [40] 300 trucks. (P) The rack-car train is an example of how the taxpaying railroads are shaping the transportation[60] future, how they are winning new business with new and better ideas, and how they are giving you better[80] service and lower costs. (P) We will gladly make a cost analysis for your firm, at no obligation of course.[100] Sincerely yours, (102 words)

5.3 Mr. David Cummings, R.F.D. 4, Lynch, MD 21646 Dear Mr. Cummings: Have you checked the brakes on your car recently? (P) The brakes are evenly adjusted if your car[20] comes to a straight smooth stop. However, some cars that are neglected will have brakes that "pull" left or right. This is difficult[40] to adjust, and driving becomes a dangerous situation when the pavement is wet and slippery. (P) Our[60] electric brake-testing machine will show you how well adjusted your brakes are. We will be glad to check your car brakes[80] for you. Our modern service station is equipped with the most recent testing machinery available. Let[100] our trained mechanics keep your car in safe driving condition. Very truly yours, (114 words)

5.4A Mr. Elliot Scott, Richter Building, 487 Eastern Parkway, Bradford, NH 03221 Dear Mr. Scott: One of our services is sending you biweekly bulletins containing recommendations[20] and suggestions to follow which should help your car give you better service. (P) With the addition of the antipollution[40] devices, extra attention should be given to "warming" the car engine. This allows the oil to[60] circulate through the engine fully. Driving at high speeds before your automobile is sufficiently warmed causes[80] unnecessary wear. (P) Try to drive at a steady speed. Try to avoid stepping on the gas pedal with too much[100] force; avoid jamming on your brakes. (P) Remember, if you want to lengthen the life of your car, try to follow good [120] driving practices. Very truly yours, (126 words)

5.4B Mr. Daniel Blake, Flint Tire Co., 112 Naples Street, Lewiston, ID 83501 Dear Mr. Blake: We are conducting a survey of stocks of tires that merchants have on hand. Our sales department is[20] trying to determine how fast our tires are moving in the retail market, especially in comparison[40] to our nearest three competitors. (P) We would appreciate your completing the enclosed reports and mailing them[60] to us at the end of each week. We are asking you to do this for only the next four weeks. (P) Our office force will [80] tabulate the results, so we ask you to be as exacting as possible in your figures. (P) We appreciate[100] your help and we do realize that we may be imposing on you. We thank you for supporting this[120] survey. Sincerely yours, (123 words)

UNIT 7

1.2 Gentlemen: Because of the rising cost of raw materials, we are obliged to increase the prices of our[20] leather products. This increase will apply to all orders received after March 1. (P) So that you may take advantage[40] of this opportunity to save money, we are sending you advance notice. We suggest, therefore, that you place[60] your order while the current lower prices are still in effect. (P) A large volume of business will no doubt reach us[80] before the end of next month, and there may be a delay in some of our deliveries. Won't you determine your[100] requirements within the next ten days and let us fill your needs at once. Yours truly, (114 words)

1.3 To: District Managers Eight district planning sessions are being projected for the months of April and May.[20] (P) Traditionally sales decrease during the summer months. It is expected that, with modifications and restructuring[40] of our sales promotions, we could change this trend. Our present strong economy will also encourage[60] consumer spending. (P) At our planning sessions, accepted leaders in marketing techniques will talk on such topics as[80] "How to Reduce Overhead Costs" and "Implementation of Sales Promotions." Time will be allotted for a question[100] and answer period. (P) Lodgings will be secured by the central reservations clerk. Tentative schedules[120] are being duplicated and will be distributed next week. (131 words)

1.4 The production of goods for society is the result of hours and years of experimentation and [20] scientific technology. Search your surroundings and you will agree. The furniture we sit on, the light fixtures[40] we use, the cars we drive, and the clothes we wear are the results of machine operation. (P) Years ago the home was the center[60] of preparing the necessities that people depended on. Fabrics were homespun, kitchen utensils[80] and furniture were carved from wood, light was supplied by handmade candles, and travel depended on animal [100] power. (P) Manufactured products help the secretary in the busy office. There are dictating and transcribing[120] machine systems, electric typewriters, copying and duplicating machines, interoffice[140] communication systems, and air-conditioning units to keep the office comfortable. (P)

In every profession, we[160] rely on the imagination and greatness of an inventive society. (175 words)

2.2 Dear Mr. Bassett: As you have already been informed, our seminars will be held in August this year. We are[20] not sure, however, whether we shall meet in Chicago or Detroit. You will be informed of the city as soon[40] as we reach a decision. (P) Regardless of the city chosen, I shall stop in Ohio, Indiana, and [60] Michigan to call on some of our potential member firms. Will you, therefore, send me a list of any of those[80] you know who have expressed interest. (P) I don't expect to get all of them as members, but I want to see as many[100] as possible. Sincerely yours, (106 words)

2.3 Adams Heating Service, 83 Bridge Street, Buffalo, NY 14206 Gentlemen: We are sending you a supply of booklets that will explain to your customers how[20] simple it is to modernize their homes with Parker equipment. (P) We shall be glad, of course, to work out time-payment plans to meet the[40] needs of the customers. (P) We are eager to do everything we can to bring comfort and economy to the[60] homes of your customers because we believe modern homes are the best investments in the nation. Sincerely yours, (80 words)

2.4A Chamber of Commerce, Manchester, NH 03111 Gentlemen: My brother and I are seeking a locale zoned for light industry. We intend to start a knitting[20] mill. (P) Manchester is near a number of industrialized communities and yet does not have an overwhelming[40] number of factories drawing off the potential labor force we will need. We expect to employ[60] 180 people at top capacity. (P) We are studying a few areas that could offer us a[80] one-story building, concrete floor, containing about 500,000 square feet. The mill must be encompassed by enough[100] land to allow for expansion, and we will need parking facilities for our employees. We are also[120] dependent upon a ready supply of water. (P) Do you have any recommendations? Yours truly, (131 words)

2.4B Mr. Samuel Miles, Box 1172, Central Station, Chicago, IL 60628 Dear Mr. Miles: Your letter inquiring about an industrial site reached us at an opportune time. We can[20] suggest two possible neighborhoods that might meet your needs. Both of these buildings are empty at this time. Either plant[40] is available on a rental basis or a rental with option to buy. (P) If you advise our secretary[60] when you plan to visit Manchester, she will arrange to introduce you to the realtor who has the two[80] listings. (P) Please consider Manchester before you travel to other areas. We are sure you will find it to[100] be the ideal location for your needletrade plant. (P) You will also find that our progressive city has a fine[120] school system for your children. Sincerely yours, (131 words)

3.2 Dear Mr. Harding: As you will recall, you telephoned to say that you did not receive credit for the payment[20] of $40 that you sent on Thursday, May 13. We were delayed in crediting you with this payment[40] because you did not give us your membership number. (P) Whenever the membership number is not listed with the[60] payment, it takes us a few days to complete the record. May we suggest, therefore, that you include your membership number[80] on each check that you send. If you will do so, we can instantly credit your payments promptly; and then you will [100] not find it necessary to take time to check on them. Sincerely yours, (113 words)

3.3 Mr. Harold Strong, The T. Eaton Co., 560 Yonge Street, Belleville, Ontario, Canada Dear Mr. Strong: We welcome the opportunity to work with you in planning the reception room of the new[20] office building of the Hall Lumber Company. (P) Complete information concerning our modern equipment[40] appears in the catalog that we are sending to you today. (P) You will find styles and materials that fit every need [60] and give charm to any interior. No extra charge will be made for the use of more than one color. (P) Please let[80] us know when we can help you, Mr. Strong. Sincerely yours, (90 words)

3.4 To: Department Foremen Dr. Chester, director of our first-aid emergency center, has advised me that[20] during the month of January there was an increase of industrial accidents by 14 percent. This[40] is a disturbing statistic. Review and reemphasize safety measures in your departments! (P) Please consider[60] the following suggestions which might prevent some of the minor accidents: 1. Double check to be sure that hand [80] tools are in good condition; that protective goggles are worn whenever necessary; that gloves or asbestos mitts are disposed of when they are too thin. 2. Wipe up oil spills[100] quickly. Thickly coat slippery areas with sand. 3. Ask your machine operators to check their machines[120] carefully before turning them on. Watch for frayed pulley belts or for bolts that have loosened and should be replaced. 4. Be[140] sure that deliveries of supplies do not block passageways. 5. Do not leave rolling carts unattended in an[160] aisle. 6. Ask your workers to form a "safety committee" to offer their recommendations to management for[180] improving safety conditions and to act as protective "watchdogs" during the working hours. (196 words)

4.2 Dear Mr. Marsh: As you know, your account is now more than 60 days past due. When you are behind in paying your[20] account, you may become hesitant about placing further orders. Consequently, both of us lose. We lose the[40] business you would give us, and you lose the profit that this merchandise would bring. (P) Why not take a few minutes today,[60] Mr. Marsh, to check your stock. Then send us your order and your check in the envelope that is enclosed. Yours very[80] truly, (82 words)

4.3 Mr. Max Black, High Point Road, Windham, NY 12496 Dear Mr. Black: Hardwood floors will be an attractive and durable feature of your new home. However, lumber[20] prices have increased sharply. If you are forced to cut back on expenses, you may restrict hardwood to the main entrance,[40] the living room, and the first floor halls. If you have any intention of using tile in the entrance, then, of course,[60] hardwood would be wasted and an unnecessary expense. (P) When you are placing your order for board feet, you[80] will save money if you use shorter and narrower board lengths. To gain the best price, give your cutting sizes to the[100] lumber yard. This will enable them to better fill your order. (P) Do allow extra time for shipments coming from[120] the Southwest. Sincerely yours, (125 words)

4.4 Grant Products, Cincinnati, OH 45233 Gentlemen: Over three years ago your concern hired us to study the needs of your stenographic and duplicating[20] departments. You indicated you were very satisfied with the redesign of these departments. The[40] machines we installed have been in steady usage functioning an average of 40 hours a week. Are they beginning[60] to show signs of "battle fatigue"? (P) We would like to reexamine the original goals of your stenographic[80] pools and see if your equipment meets your operating needs for the future. (P) Our engineers have not been standing[100] still. There have been many alterations to our standard machine since the time of your purchases. Trade-in[120] agreements are also available. (P) Modernize your office machinery. We are sure you will find a definite[140] increase in productivity in producing the typed word. Sincerely yours, (154 words)

5.2 Dear Mr. Lennox: May I express my appreciation for the courtesy you showed me last Monday, June 15,[20] when we discussed the cost of the direct mail project you are planning. Although you chose another company[40] for the job, I appreciate your considering the use of our company. (P) As I am sure you realize,[60] the Independent Advertising Company will be glad to work with you on any of your mailing needs in[80] the future. We pride ourselves in our high quality work, prompt service, and reasonable rates. (P) When you again plan[100] a mailing project, please give us an opportunity to serve you. Sincerely yours, (115 words)

5.3 Miss Roberta Welch, 422 Tenth Avenue, Monson, ME 04464 Dear Miss Welch: The clock that you forwarded to us for repair was received on January 27, and [20] we have spent some time examining it. Your clock appears to have been dropped. The main stem is cracked, the hands are bent, and [40] some of the gears are missing teeth. The wooden case can be reglued and touched with paint. (P) We are proud of the timepieces[60] that we manufacture. The steel gears are ground and polished and put in place by hand. Our designers and skilled workers[80] have a heritage of producing quality timekeepers and have years of training in the repair of these items.[100] When our craftsmen are finished revitalizing your clock, we guarantee that it will run with precision. (P) The[120] cost for these repairs, including parts and labor, would be approximately $30. Notify us if [140] you wish us to make these repairs. Respectfully yours, (149 words)

5.4 Rockwell Distributors, 1120 Montgomery Road, Savannah, GA 31406 Gentlemen: With the opening of our third factory in Houston, we can furnish our customers any[20] assortment of extruded aluminum shapes at affordable prices and allow you, our distributors, to[40] realize attractive profits. (P) The Houston plant is the third point in the triangle of factories. Our other[60] two are located, as you know, in Niagara and on Lake Huron. Because of the mileage between factories,[80] you can promise your customers the items they want knowing you can effect extensive savings for them because[100] of sharply lowered freight charges. (P) To aid you in promoting sales, a colorful brochure was prepared that you can[120] mail to your purchasers. This brochure details our complete line of home products fabricated from extruded [140] aluminum: storm windows, porch enclosures, tool sheds, shutters, and house siding. Each of these items can be fabricated [160] to meet individual needs. Cordially yours, (169 words)

UNIT 8

1.2 Dear Mr. Dash: Where do you keep your valuable papers such as birth certificates, insurance policies,[20] stocks, and bonds? Are you keeping them in a desk drawer or filing cabinet? If so, you are increasing the risk[40] of loss by fire or theft. (P) Why not store your valuable papers in a safe-deposit box in our bank? (P) The cost[60] of a safe-deposit box at our bank is very little. Isn't 5 cents a day a small price to pay for the[80] peace of mind that a safe-deposit box provides? Very truly yours, (93 words)

1.3 Mr. Harold Bruce, 95 Dearborn Avenue, Pittsburgh, PA 15216 Dear Mr. Bruce: Thank you for your telephone order for 500 shares of Madison Company stock at[20] $35. We were able to buy this stock at that price today. (P) The stock certificate will be mailed as soon[40] as we receive it. (P) We appreciate this opportunity to serve you. If there is any other way in[60] which we can help you with your investments, please let us know. Sincerely yours, (73 words)

1.4A Mr. Walter Fredericks, 7-18 Manor Avenue, Flint, MI 48501 Dear Mr. Fredericks: If your family income is $15,000 or more, you will qualify for[20] one of our new educational loans. You can borrow up to $20,000 at any one time to send your[40] child to an educational institution whether it be elementary, secondary,[60] preparatory, vocational, or college. You can spread monthly repayments over as long as seven years. (P) There[80] are two scholastic plans for you to choose from. One plan helps you meet current educational bills. Under this plan,[100] if you are under sixty, you are eligible to receive life insurance coverage at no extra cost.[120] (P) Our other plan will cover a full four-year period. Just estimate your total needs, establish a line of[140] credit, and then each year for four years you will automatically receive the financing you need for the amount[160] you arranged for. (P) Insurance at a low rate is available, which protects your child by guaranteeing that he will[180] have money to complete his education in the event of your death. Just advise us which plan interests you. The[200] forms are not complex. Sincerely, (206 words)

1.4B The Independence Commercial Bank, 10 Park Way, Milwaukee, WI 53221 Gentlemen: I have had excessive difficulty attempting to reconcile my bank statements based on your three-month,[20] quick-check account. Not receiving a statement every month is a nuisance and creates a definite hardship.[40] My account is evidently too active to continue using the quick-check system. (P) Am I correct in[60] believing that the Independence Commercial Bank requires a balance of $400 in a regular[80] checking account? If this condition still prevails, I will have to transfer my funds to another location less[100] accessible but more economical. There are other banking organizations who do offer regular[120] checking accounts without any minimum balance being left on deposit. With the present savings interest[140] rate of 5½ percent, my $400 can earn an additional $22 in[160] interest per year. Very truly yours, (166 words)

2.2 Dear Mr. Clayton: When your cash is lost or stolen, it is gone forever. When your Midstate Traveler's Checks are[20] lost or stolen, you can get them replaced at any one of our 10,000 banks around the world. (P) Midstate Traveler's Checks[40] are honored all over the world. You can spend them as easily in Rome as in Atlanta. (P) Use Midstate[60] Traveler's Checks on your next business or pleasure trip. Sincerely yours, (73 words)

2.3 Mrs. Kenneth Strong, 7821 River Road, Covington, KY 41011 Dear Neighbor: We are pleased to announce the opening of a new Merit Finance Corporation office in your[20] community. (P) In case you have never borrowed from Merit Finance Corporation before, it is known among[40] two million customers as the company where families can borrow with confidence. (P) When you need a loan,[60] today or tomorrow, choose your lending company as you would choose a doctor—by reputation. Choose Merit Finance! [80] (P) Drop in or phone and ask to speak to the manager. Cordially, (93 words)

2.4A Mr. and Mrs. Louis Harrison, 8-03 Hopper Place, Savannah, GA 31405 Dear Mr. and Mrs. Harrison: Thank you for thinking of County Trust Bank when you were placing the mortgage for[20] your new home. The interest rate of 8 percent is the best rate available for 25-year mortgages.[40] (P) The enclosed payment cards are to be presented monthly when making your mortgage payments. At the end of each fiscal [60] year, our bookkeeping department will send you an itemized report showing a schedule of monthly payments[80] made, interest paid, and amortization of your mortgage. Save these reports, as they will be necessary when you[100] are completing your income tax reports. Very truly yours, (111 words)

2.4B Mr. and Mrs. Lionel Fletcher, 91 Blue Hill Road, Niagara Falls, NY 14302 Dear Mr. and Mrs. Fletcher: Now that the remodeling at our Prospect Street Branch is completed, we are able[20] to offer our customers another convenience service, a drive-in window. Without even getting out[40] of your car, you will be able to make deposits and withdrawals, cash checks, or make payments on loans. (P) To serve all [60] our customers, the drive-in window will be open from 7 a.m. to 7 p.m., Monday through Friday.[80] We hope these hours will meet the needs of our commuting public. (P) Our official grand opening day is this Friday.[100] Stop in and admire our new facility. Pick up your ticket for our big drawing. The lucky winner will receive[120] an 18-inch color television. Most cordially, (131 words)

3.2 Dear Miss Green: A statement of interest earned on your account last year is enclosed with this letter. (P) Beginning next year,[20] this statement will be expanded to show not only the total interest earned but the quarterly interest as well.[40] The account balance as of December 31, your passbook balance as of that date, and the total of any[60] interest earned but not yet recorded in your book will also be indicated. (P) Since the annual statement,[80] which will be mailed to you each January, will provide you with a record of quarterly interest, our tellers[100] will record all unposted interest in your passbook as one total. This will enable them to process your[120] transactions more quickly and efficiently. (P) We appreciate your continued patronage. Very truly yours, (139 words)

3.3 Mrs. Robert Ford, 316 Center Street, East Orange, NJ 07017 Dear Mrs. Ford: Why waste precious hours going from place to place to pay your bills when you can open a special checking[20] account at the Central Bank? (P) You may open an account with any amount from $1 up. No minimum[40] balance is required. It will cost you only 50 cents a month for maintenance, plus 10 cents a check. There is[60] no charge for deposits. Your canceled checks and statement are sent to you monthly. (P) If it is not convenient to come[80] to one of our banks in person, we can arrange your account for you by mail. Cordially yours, (96 words)

3.4A To: Testing Laboratories During the past four months, we have noted that a number of monthly checks have been[20] handled incorrectly. (P) The problem seems to be prevalent mainly when an employee is absent. If an[40] employee is absent on payday, checks should be returned to the Payroll Department promptly rather than being held [60] pending the employee's return. (P) When a check cannot be delivered to an employee on the payment day, the[80] envelope should be returned to the Payroll Department the same day. Please attach a note to each individual [100] paycheck indicating why it could not be delivered. Payroll envelopes should not be left lying around [120] on a desk or even placed in a desk drawer. In fact, payroll envelopes should be handed directly to each[140] employee. (P) Please discuss this memorandum with your payroll distribution clerk and please make a special point about[160] the responsibility of returning checks immediately to the Payroll Department. (177 words)

3.4B Dear Customer: For years you have enjoyed joining the annual Christmas Club with us. As you know, our Christmas Club[20] starts as low as 50 cents per week. No matter how small or how large a club you choose, if you have deposited [40] the amount agreed upon by November 12, you will be among the growing number of depositors who[60] complete their Christmas Clubs and receive 5 percent interest. (P) This year we are adding another exciting form of [80] savings for you. We are inviting you to join our Vacation Club. The Vacation Club is just like a Christmas[100] Club except that it will begin July 1, and you will receive your check by June 15—in time to help pay[120] for your summer fun. (P) Come in and sign our simple Vacation Club card and receive your coupon book on the spot. Start[140] saving for your vacation now! Sincerely yours, (149 words)

4.2 To: The Board of Directors and Shareholders We have examined the statement of net assets of the Mutual [20] Investors, Inc., a Delaware corporation, including the schedule of holdings, the related [40] statements of net income, changes in net assets, and supplementary information for the year. (P) In our[60] opinion, the enclosed statements present fairly the financial position of the company on December[80] 31 and the results of these operations for the year then ended. (94 words)

4.3 Mr. Carl Baxter, 316 Center Street, Edmonton, Alberta, Canada Dear Mr. Baxter: Do you want to make sure that you don't lose your money? If you do, here are three steps to follow:[20] 1. Avoid carrying large amounts of cash. 2. Avoid exposing your money in public. 3. Pay your bills by[40] check. (P) If you follow these three steps, you will decrease the hazards that lead to the loss of money. (P) Checking accounts are[60] available at our bank. We invite you to stop in to learn about our services. Cordially yours, (79 words)

4.4A Mr. Donald Grayson, 247 Rochelle Parkway, Gary, IN 46401 Dear Mr. Grayson: One of the problems you should be facing is planning the distribution of your estate as[20] well as naming your executor, particularly if you have minor-aged children. Depending on the size[40] of your estate, the executor's job can be a burden and not an honor for a personal friend. (P) The Watson[60] National Trust can function as your executor or coexecutor. If you study the enclosed pamphlet,[80] you will find that the duties of an executor can be quite imposing. We have specially trained [100] professionals to deal with investment, tax, trust, and estate issues. Few individuals possess the expertise that[120] we can offer. It is important for you to have advice in order to gain full tax relief allowed at death.[140] (P) We manage nearly 4 billion dollars' worth of individual trusts and estates. Our trust department officers[160] are completely familiar with the problems of estate taxation. You will find the officer in charge of[180] your folio to be understanding and capable of giving you impartial, knowledgeable judgments. (P) The[200] services of the bank are always available and fiscally accountable. Our commission costs for[220] executor services are tax deductible from either estate or inheritance taxes. Very truly[240] yours, (241 words)

4.4B Mr. William Kennedy, 95 Hamilton Avenue, Montgomery, AL 36100 Dear Mr. Kennedy: The safest way to take cash on your trip is in the form of traveler's checks. The advantage[20] of traveler's checks is that they are acceptable in almost all places in the world. The most common amounts[40] of traveler's checks are usually in $10 or $20 blocks. The charge for this service is[60] $1 per $100 worth of checks purchased. (P) If you are planning to locate in one area for[80] a long period of time, you might prefer either a bank draft or a cashier's check. These can be cashed at any[100] bank. This form of protection is quite inexpensive compared to the purchase of a number of checks. Let us aid [120] you with the first step toward a financially secure vacation and let us furnish you with either traveler's[140] checks, a bank draft, or a cashier's check. Respectfully yours, (154 words)

5.2 Dear Shareholder: Mutual Investors' net asset value per share increased 14.9 percent during the[20] year. As you know, the Board of Directors declared a capital gains distribution of 36 cents per share[40] on December 31. (P) Last year was one of the most prosperous years our company has experienced.[60] Over the long term, we are confident that the upward trend of our economy will continue. (P) We want to thank[80] the many shareholders who, through their investments, have helped build our assets to a record level. (P) From time to time,[100] questions may occur to you about the operation of your fund. We shall be happy to answer your inquiries[120] at any time. Sincerely, (126 words)

5.3 Mr. Arnold Jensen, 24 King Street, Montreal, Quebec, Canada Dear Mr. Jensen: On Saturday, April 6, we celebrate an important event; namely, the tenth[20] anniversary of our operation as a commercial bank. (P) We started with assets of $75,000.[40] For ten years we have safeguarded the savings of the people of this province. We have played a major role[60] in assisting thousands of people to own their own homes through our financing plans. (P) Today our assets exceed [80] $15,000,000, and we have six branches throughout the province. (P) The directors and officers of the bank pledge[100] themselves to even greater service in the future for the people of this province. Cordially yours, (138 words)

5.4A Miss Cynthia Grant, 31-11 Garfield Place, Dover, NJ 07801 Dear Miss Grant: Having a checking account is safer than carrying a large amount of cash with you. Having a[20] checking account is an easy and meticulous way to keep control of your major expenses. Your canceled [40] checks give you a permanent record of your purchases and expenditures and are easier to keep than receipts[60] of all differing sizes. (P) Our regular checking account tenders another privilege. The overdraft[80] option lets you write a check for more cash than you actually have in your account. We pledge to cover your[100] overdraft for you at a predetermined sum. (P) Compare our services with those of other banks. When you have decided [120] affirmatively, ask for Miss Dane, our account officer. She will help you complete our signature forms. As[140] soon as you make your first deposit, your account will be in effect. Cordially yours, (155 words)

5.4B Mrs. Robert Oliver, 97 MacArthur Drive, Long Beach, CA 90810 Dear Madam: Do you worry about the safety of your valuables? Are your important papers well organized [20] and kept in a fireproof and theftproof drawer? Are you satisfied with your safeguards for your insurance policies,[40] your automobile certificate of ownership, your stocks, your bonds, your birth registration form, your marriage license,[60] and all the other important papers that would be such trouble to replace? The Williamson Savings and Loan[80] Company has just expanded their safety deposit vaults and have boxes available for rental. Our smallest[100] safety deposit box carries an annual fee of only $7.50 plus tax. (P) By using a[120] safety deposit box to store your important documents, you keep your future free from concern and anxiety.[140] Your personal vault needs two keys to unlock it; you retain one and we have the other. Both keys must be turned [160] in two individual locks to allow entry into your vault. (P) When you wish to examine your papers in[180] privacy, step into an individual air-conditioned booth fitted to meet your needs from paper clips to[200] scissors for clipping coupons. (P) You will sleep better at night knowing we are keeping your valuables under our[220] protective safety system. Cordially yours, (228 words)

UNIT 9

1.2 The letters of professional men are written in dignified, faultless English. The snappy, glib style effected [20] by publications today has no place in scientific and professional writing. The essence of good [40] professional style is clarity, simplicity, and coherence. (P) Hackneyed words and trite phrases must be avoided.[60] Sentences should be short. This, of course, is not always possible in scientific writing; but a short sentence[80] should be interposed now and then to avoid tiring the reader. On the other hand though, many short sentences[100] may result in monotony. One good way to achieve variety is to begin sentences with different[120] parts of speech such as with an adverb, an adjective, a verb, a preposition. (135 words)

1.3 Bruce Book Store, Inc., 95 Dearborn Avenue, Pittsburgh, PA 15204 Gentlemen: An examination copy of the sixth edition of *Your Health and Your Food* is in the mail. Read [20] it and we know you will agree with us that at last the relation of food to health appears in language that can[40] be understood by everyone. (P) This book is full of useful information; the technical terms have been avoided.[60] The author has no product to sell except health and happiness. Sincerely yours, (95 words)

1.4A Miss Joan Roberts, 29 University Place, Baltimore, MD 21254 Dear Miss Roberts: Ragweed season is here and it is predicted that this will be one of the worst periods for[20] allergy sufferers in years. Your original scratch tests showed a high propensity to react to the[40] ragweed pollens. (P) You have missed your last two appointments for injections. Unless you receive your injections on a[60] regular schedule, you will lose the immunity you have developed to this point. You will have to start your series[80] of vaccine at a lower tolerance. (P) Antihistamine will give you temporary relief but does have[100] some side effects that you may find distressing. Yours truly, (110 words)

1.4B Dr. Paul Ramsey, 458 Prospect Street, Jacksonville, FL 32208 Dear Dr. Ramsey: No medical library is complete without copies of our *Medical Digest.* This[20] publication is designed for medical practitioners who desire to keep up with developments in the[40] medical world but are limited in the time they can spend scanning the numerous outpourings printed annually. (P) The[60] *Medical Digest* is unique. It is a card index of articles published monthly. Each card is[80] color coded and carries a file number so it can be located or filed rapidly. Title, author, publisher,[100] summary, and commentary appear on a separate card. A complete reprint of any article[120] is sent you by return mail when we receive your request card. (P) We know you will find the *Medical Digest* to be[140] a necessity for the busy M.D. If you place your order for a three-year subscription, we will supply[160] you with a file cabinet designed to hold 1,000 cards. Very truly yours, (174 words)

2.2 A method should be devised to keep before one's attention letters requesting a reply. Correspondence in[20] a doctor's office rarely is large enough to require a tickler file. Carbon copies of letters to which a[40] reply is expected can be placed in a folder for pending material, and this folder should be consulted [60] every day. If a letter has not been answered within a reasonable time, a follow-up letter[80] should be sent. It is one of the duties of the secretary to remind the doctor to do this; or, if he[100] wishes, the secretary may send an answer over her own signature. (114 words)

2.3 Mrs. Leon Chalmers, 1423 Mountaintop Drive, Wilkes-Barre, PA 18711 Dear Mrs. Chalmers: We need your assistance to carry on the great work of this hospital. Our appeal is in[20] behalf of those who are dependent on the specialized services that we provide. (P) Most of our clinic patients[40] are in the low-income bracket, with no money to go to private specialists. Our hospital is their only[60] hope. (P) This appeal is made to you so that you can express your sympathy for those less fortunate. One practical [80] way to do so is to aid the work which our hospital is doing. (P) Please send whatever sum you can. It will be[100] gratefully received. Sincerely yours, (106 words)

2.4A To: Editor, *Youngstown Eagle* When my husband tripped on the stairs last Sunday morning and I was unable to[20] rouse him, I called the Police Department. Before I had barely hung up the telephone, an ambulance was at[40] my door. The men from our volunteer ambulance service were so effective and handled the whole frightening plight[60] so skillfully, they gave me the strength to maintain my self-control. (P) My husband suffered a hairline fracture and was[80] in a state of concussion for 24 hours. Because the ambulance reached the hospital speedily, my husband [100] received professional treatment far faster than if he had had to rely on having a doctor come to[120] our home on a Sunday. (P) I am sorry it took an emergency for me to acknowledge how fortunate[140] Youngstown is to have a volunteer ambulance service staffed by such diligent and conscientious members. (159 words)

2.4B Dear Parents: Our state law requires that every student under 16 years of age have a biennial ocular[20] and audio examination. These eye and ear tests will be conducted by our school nurses. Gym classes[40] will be suspended for two days while the gymnasium is temporarily converted into a testing[60] center. All classes will be released during class time to participate in this program. (P) If a student is absent[80] or if you wish the testing to be done privately, we will supply the forms to be completed by the doctor[100] you choose. (P) All reports will be recorded onto master files in our office. All parents will be[120] notified of the results of their children's tests. Cordially yours, (129 words)

3.2 The medical secretary, like the secretary in any other office today, may have occasion[20] to use one of the many dictation and transcription machines. While the doctor dictates into the machine, his[40] secretary can be doing other work. (P) The machines differ in that they use records, belts, tapes, or wire for[60] recording. The reproduction process is the same for all practical purposes. A microphone is built into[80] the machine, and the secretary uses a loudspeaker or headphones. (93 words)

3.3 Dr. William Davis, 419 Doctor's Building, Ogden, UT 84401 Dear Doctor: You are cordially invited to attend the dinner honoring Dr. Arthur Carey, the noted [20] neurologist. This dinner will take place at our School of Medicine on Monday, January 5. (P) Dr.[40] Carey is being honored with the award of the Institute of Medicine in recognition of his research[60] on cerebral palsy. (P) We are sure that you will want to attend this dinner. Details are given on the enclosed [80] program. Sincerely yours, (85 words)

3.4A Mr. John Baxter, 14 Barry Place, Jersey City, NJ 07301 Dear Mr. Baxter: My consultation with Dr. Rose verifies his original findings. The X rays do[20] show impacted wisdom teeth on both sides of your lower jaw. (P) You have been suffering from food-filled gum pockets next[40] to these impacted teeth. The food remains in the pockets, creating infections. You will continue to have painful [60] bouts as the infection occurs periodically. Removal of your impacted teeth will allow you[80] to reach the pockets and free them of nondigested foods. (P) Surgery at your age will be less painful before the[100] bone matter calcifies. We have scheduled oral surgery for Thursday, August 10, at 9 a.m. You will [120] be able to leave about two hours later. Plan to bring a companion with you to escort you home. (P) As I do not foresee any unusual conditions, you should [140] return to your office on Monday. Sincerely yours, (149 words)

3.4B Mrs. Mary Alexanders, Assistant Superintendent of Nurses, Rosemont Hospital, Trenton, NJ 08610 Dear Mary: During our weekly staff meeting, a lengthy discussion centered on the fact that medical services[20] are hampered in emergencies because we do not contact nurses quickly or easily. We also have[40] difficulty finding nurses to serve on private duty on the night shifts. We have a full staff for our daytime[60] hours but coverage at night should be improved. (P) We would like you to try to work out solutions for the following[80] two problems: (1) Establish an agency to act as an in-hospital nurses' registry. Encourage our[100] nurses to advise the registry of their whereabouts and how to contact them quickly, particularly in[120] an emergency. (2) Look for additional sources of nursing personnel. We would be willing to conduct[140] in-service classes to encourage licensed nurses to return to hospital work. (P) Keep me posted on your tentative[160] work plans. Sincerely yours, (165 words)

4.2 Where case histories are kept on cards, the filing will depend on the type of card used. At present, three card filing[20] systems are in use. These are: (1) the vertical filing system, (2) the visible filing system, and (3) the[40] rotary filing system. Cards to fit any one of these three systems may be had specially printed for a[60] doctor's requirements, or they may be printed to order if a sufficiently large quantity is needed. (79 words)

4.3 Miss Audrey Sherman, 675 Mockingbird Lane, Dallas, TX 75215 Dear Miss Sherman: Opportunities for work in the mental health field are numerous and steadily growing. (P) Young[20] men and women who enter any of the professions related to mental health can choose the section of the[40] country in which they would like to work. (P) If you will complete the enclosed questionnaire and return it to me, I shall [60] be glad to arrange for an interview with you. Sincerely yours, (71 words)

4.4A More and more demands are being made on the medical secretary. Many times she performs functions that are[20] the duties of a medical office assistant. (P) The tasks of the medical secretary are many. She[40] must be able to perform her office routines with competence. Accuracy is her keyword. (P) The medical [60] secretary is receptionist, appointment maker, bookkeeper, office supervisor, librarian, and [80] public relations agent. Persons coming to a doctor's office often have a problem, and so the medical [100] secretary is constantly required to be gentle and tactful. (P) The medical secretary must remain[120] in full control of herself no matter what traumatic conditions might prevail. Her calm manner reassures her[140] coworkers and patients. (144 words)

4.4B To: Dr. Albert Stone, Medical Director, Ohio General Hospital In studying the case[20] histories of the emergency room for the past six months, we noted that there has been an increase of 17 [40] percent of industrial burn patients. At your request, we undertook a study to plan how we could best use[60] the hospital facilities to cope with future increases. (P) We determined that allocating additional [80] space for the stockpiling of vaseline dressings and pressure dressings was warranted. We also need extra[100] bed space in an isolated area where burn patients could be watched for respiratory complications[120] which would require either placement in an oxygen tent or a tracheotomy operation. Intravenous[140] feedings would be ordered for severely burned patients. Replacement of fluids is critical in the[160] 24- to 48-hour period after receiving the burn. (P) If there is a continuing increase of industrial [180] burn victims, our medical facility will be overburdened. However, if there is any[200] sort of mass disaster, we do have adequate supplies to institute immediate basic first aid procedures[220] for burn patients. (224 words)

5.2 Case histories and other material relating to the patients should be kept entirely separate from[20] any other material. If possible, such material should be contained in a special filing[40] cabinet; but certainly a special drawer should be set aside for it. There should be a separate folder for each[60] patient, and this folder should contain all the material relating to a particular patient: case history,[80] progress reports, laboratory reports, correspondence with the patient, and correspondence with doctors,[100] relatives, or friends regarding the patient. (P) Filing cabinets should have a lock, especially those holding[120] patients' material. (124 words)

5.3 Dr. Phillip Bryan, Medical Building, 6841 Far Hills, Dayton, OH 45422 Dear Doctor Bryan: Doctor Matthews has been closely associated with me for several years here at the[20] Shore Medical School. He is a thoroughly trained surgeon capable of performing all types of eye surgery.[40] (P) He holds the rank of Assistant Professor here at the school and is in complete charge of our research programs.[60] (P) Doctor Matthews is highly ethical. I recommend him for a fellowship in the Academy. Sincerely[80] yours, (81 words)

5.4 Mr. Clifford Farmer, 89 Fairmont Avenue, Newport, RI 02842 Dear Cliff: I have studied the X rays taken after you broke your right thighbone. The break was a closed fracture. The skin[20] was not punctured. Your leg appears to be healing normally. (P) There are some facts that you should know which might make you a[40] little more cautious instead of overtaxing your body. The femur is the largest, longest, and strongest of[60] all bones and carries the most body weight. Your bones contain virtually all of the body's mineral supply;[80] and most of the white blood cells, which protect you from infection, are produced within the bone marrow. Your bones store and[100] release calcium into the bloodstream in exact and controlled amounts. (P) During childhood, our bones support our body[120] and also continue to grow. As we age, cartilage forms at the ends of each bone. As the cartilage[140] between bones hardens, no further growth is possible. (P) The approach to treating broken bones has changed radically. No[160] longer does a broken leg mean a long recuperation period in bed. Orthopedic surgeons try to[180] have their patients function as normally as possible. They use pins, screws, plates, artificial joints, and will install[200] a new ball and socket, if necessary. (P) Now that you are in your mid-twenties, your bones have reached their peak density[220] and strength. Now the bone strength diminishes at a very slow rate. The minerals stored in the bone marrow[240] begin to diminish also. Your bones are growing less rugged. Give them more respect. Sincerely, (256 words)

UNIT 10

1.2 Dear Miss Simmons: The position for which you applied has not been filled. Mr. Baxter, the man for whom you would work[20] if employed, is out of town. However, it might expedite matters if you would send me another copy of your[40] resume; and I will forward it to Mr. Baxter and get his reaction by telephone. (P) In addition,[60] will you please send another personal reference. I will check on it in Mr. Baxter's absence. (P) You will,[80] no doubt, know our decision within a week. Sincerely, (90 words)

1.3 Miss Marjorie Howe, 77 Parkwood Avenue, Lincoln, NB 68508 Dear Miss Howe: Are you interested in making some extra money between now and Christmas? We shall be needing many[20] temporary workers because people will be doing their Christmas shopping during the next two months. (P) If you[40] are interested in part-time work of this type, please come in to see our Personnel Manager. Sincerely yours, (59 words)

1.4 The advantage of secretarial work is that it offers diversification of activity. To[20] mention a few responsibilities, there will be dictation, transcription, mail processing, filing, record keeping,[40] and purchasing of supplies. Another strong advantage of secretarial work is that there are positions[60] open in almost every type and size of community. There are, of course, benefits to each location,[80] urban or suburban. (P) For the secretary entering the field, perhaps the first interview is the most difficult[100] step. For this first interview, the beginning applicant can help herself by preparing a personal[120] resume to outline her qualifications. The resume will help give the secretary support during the[140] interview. (P) The secretary working in the large city will find her clothing budget is higher than in the[160] suburban world. Food, transportation, and entertainment on the average will be more expensive in the city.[180] (P) The secretary in the suburban areas will find a slower pace with lower costs and more casual dress.[200] In these communities, offices will probably have fewer employees. (P) The alert secretary[220] will find dozens of opportunities for variety during each business day. (233 words)

2.2 To Alice White: The reason your payroll check this week was a few dollars less than the previous week is that[20] beginning the first of each year we are required to deduct for your Social Security benefits. In your case, this[40] deduction does not have to be made throughout the year. (P) So that you fully understand the deductions from your[60] paycheck, I have attached an itemized breakdown. This shows your deductions for income taxes, Workmen's Compensation[80] taxes, and Social Security. If this is not clear, come to my office and we will talk about it. (99 words)

2.3 Miss Cynthia Grover, 400 Bedford Street, Ashland, KY 41101 Dear Miss Grover: May I remind you that when you accepted employment with the Wright Insurance Agency you[20] had a signed agreement with this employment agency that clearly outlined the amount of our fee and the method[40] in which it was to be paid. (P) It has now been two weeks since you began the job, and we have not received either[60] of the two installments that were due. When we talk with job applicants and send them on interviews, we act in good[80] faith. We feel we have a right to similar treatment from successful job candidates. Yours very truly, (99 words)

2.4 In large organizations, there are many potential steps for advancement. A secretary can rise to[20] supervisory or administrative positions. Many companies offer fringe benefits to their employees.[40] Fringe benefits are financial advantages above a salary. One benefit could be[60] hospitalization insurance which covers a percentage of hospital and medical fees. Another protection[80] is group life insurance. The rate for insurance coverage becomes quite reasonable because it is obtained[100] for many employees. (P) Stock-purchase plans and pension plans allow the employee to have money deducted from[120] the salary toward purchase of company stock or for pension payments upon retirement. (P) In some companies,[140] bonuses are given at the end of successful years where profits were high. Bonuses may be in the form of[160] cash or company stock. (P) The secretary must weigh the advantages and offerings of more than one job to[180] find the one that she feels will be the most suitable, interesting, and challenging. (194 words)

3.2 Dear Miss James: Thank you for your inquiry concerning classified ads. (P) Display advertising costs only[20] $25 per column inch. A regular classified ad, with a minimum of four lines, costs[40] $1.45 per line. This allows for 42 upper- or lower-case characters or 31 all-cap[60] characters. A box number is included at no charge. (P) Remember, our magazine has an audience of more than[80] 50,000 subscribers. Total estimated readership of each issue is over 150,000[100] people. (P) To place your classified ad, either send copy to the above address or come in person to[120] Room 807. Yours truly, (126 words)

3.3 The Finch Institute, 157 Cambridge Avenue, Nashville, TN 37211 Gentlemen: Our company is enlarging its office force; and we are seeking a young woman who can do filing, is[20] an accurate typist, and can operate an adding machine. (P) If we were to advertise this position in[40] the newspaper, we are sure we would receive several hundred resumes, letters of application, and phone[60] calls. Thus we are contacting your business school because of its fine reputation of graduating trustworthy[80] personnel. (P) For this position, experience is not required. We prefer to teach our own office routine to[100] our staff. The young woman must be pleasant and neat in appearance and must be diligent. Yours sincerely, (119 words)

3.4A Mr. Raymond Lampron, Personnel Director, Dixon Fabric Co., Burlington, VT 05401 Dear Mr. Lampron: The Finch Institute suggested that I contact you in response to your recent inquiry[20] for an applicant to join your office force. Your letter indicated that you are seeking someone who is[40] capable of following general office routine, is an accurate typist, and can operate an adding[60] machine. I believe I can fulfill these requirements. (P) I will be receiving my certificate from Finch Institute[80] on Friday, May 24. My class schedule ends at two o'clock every day, and I am available[100] for an interview every afternoon after 2:30 p.m. I will call your office on Tuesday to[120] discuss which afternoon would be most convenient for you to interview me. If that is not satisfactory, please[140] call me at home any weekday after 3 p.m. Sincerely yours, (153 words)

3.4B Mr. Morris Dixon, Dixon Fabric Co., Burlington, VT 05401 Dear Mr. Dixon: As you know, yesterday was my first job interview, and you and Mr. Lampron were very[20] kind and made our hour together a very easy and pleasant experience. I appreciated the time[40] you spent with me outlining your office routine. I am sure I would not have any problem following your[60] procedures. (P) Working at Dixon Fabric Co. would be a satisfying situation. I would like to be[80] associated with your firm. If there is any additional information you would like me to supply,[100] I will forward it to you as soon as possible. Yours sincerely, (111 words)

4.2 Dear Miss Harvey: Your business skills tests indicate that you have the typing and shorthand abilities required for[20] the position for which you applied, even though you have no specific experience in this business. However,[40] do not let this discourage you, Miss Harvey. (P) We would like to have you come in next Wednesday, May 12, at nine o'clock[60] to take a brief aptitude test. This test gives us a clearer picture of your qualifications. (P) If you cannot[80] make the appointment at this time, please call me and we will reschedule it. Cordially, (96 words)

4.3 Ms. Ethel Brennan, The Tool and Machine Corporation, Yakima, WA 98901 Dear Ms. Brennan: Mrs. Nora Livingston has given us your name as reference. She advised us that you were[20] her immediate supervisor, and she felt you would be willing to answer questions concerning her employment[40] with your firm. (P) Very often people attempt to be kind and glorify the person wishing the letter of reference.[60] However, in all fairness, a reference should include the individual's strong and weak points. We[80] would appreciate this frankness as you complete the enclosed questionnaire. Sincerely yours, (96 words)

4.4A Austin Motors, 1784 Highway 17, Yakima, WA 98901 Gentlemen: We have been the recipient of a number of references when hiring new employees and are[20] well aware that people tend to be too kind when writing references. In fairness to everyone involved, frankness[40] on everyone's part would avoid disappointments as well as frequent failure of a person to hold a position[60] that may be beyond his ability. (P) This, however, is not the case with Nora Livingston. She is an[80] excellent secretary. Her daily office work was superior. Nora had access to confidential [100] data, and we never doubted her ability to restrict her business life to our office. (P) Nora has the[120] qualities and capabilities that will lead her to the administrative level. Sincerely, (138 words)

4.4B Miss Anne Pine, 16 Chelsea Drive, Framingham, MA 01701 Dear Miss Pine: Your request in regard to mailing out your college transcript will be fulfilled in three days. This is a[20] busy time for our office. We receive the greatest concentration of requests for mailings in June as people[40] apply for various jobs after their graduation. (P) We will be pleased to forward your records. There is no charge[60] for this first service. In the future, we are compelled to charge $3 for each duplication that we put in[80] the mail for you. (P) As soon as you have accepted employment, please let us know; and we will make the required changes[100] in your folder. We shall be interested to hear of your progress in your new surroundings. Yours sincerely, (119 words)

5.2 To Mr. Atkins: Will you begin looking for a good overall assistant to supplement our staff? (P) This person[20] should be a good writer, preferably experienced in the preparation of news releases, booklets,[40] speeches, and broadcast copy. Any experience in writing film sequences, product information sheets, and [60] trade paper and magazine articles will be helpful, but not absolutely required. Eventually, we[80] want to work this employee into the editing of publications and news letters. (P) Since we will be adding[100] two new clients next month, we urgently need someone within the next two weeks. (114 words)

5.3 The Jaffee Agency, 11-30 Norma Avenue, Akron, OH 44302 Gentlemen: This letter will introduce Mrs. Mary Lane who has been employed by us for the past three years. Our[20] company is closing its Akron office, and Mrs. Lane does not wish to transfer to our central offices[40] in Chicago. (P) Mrs. Lane has been a definite asset to our company, having absorbed routine[60] responsibilities with ease. She is an excellent secretary, and we recommend her to you most highly. It[80] is with sincere regret that we have to allow Mrs. Lane to leave our employ. Sincerely yours, (97 words)

5.4A The Placement Office, Richmond Collcgc, Richmond, VA 23217 Gentlemen: We will be formally opening our new department store on October 1, and we will presently[20] be interviewing applicants for positions that are open in our book department. The staff must be able[40] to speak with people easily and be alert to keeping up to date on new publications. In time, these[60] salespeople will have complete charge of ordering stock, arranging counter displays, preparing sales promotions, and [80] assisting guest authors who make public appearances at the store. (P) We need candidates who are knowledgeable[100] and, therefore, are limiting our interviewing to college students who majored in either English or Library[120] Science. (P) Previous sales experience would be helpful but not necessary, as we have a two-week training[140] period for all new employees. Our company offers an excellent employee benefits plan. (P) We[160] hope you will be able to encourage some interesting young people to talk with us. Sincerely yours, (178 words)

5.4B Let us study some amazing facts which have recently been published about the outlook for the working woman[20] in the labor market. (P) In the next five years, nearly half of all women between thirty-five and sixty-five will [40] be employed or looking for employment, with the largest proportion of workers coming from the forty-five to[60] fifty-four age group. This should be quite evident when we realize that numbers of women worked for a few years,[80] married, raised families, and, in their forties, realized that they no longer wished to remain at home. They can then[100] reenter their chosen field with relatively little retraining. (P) A competent secretary not only[120] can offer good shorthand and typewriting skills but also is an expert in public relations. She is her[140] administrator's right hand and is an assistant to all the employees in the organization. (P) The[160] secretarial field has long appealed to college women, as it allows for entry into many[180] organizations and provides the opportunity to work to supervisory or administrative positions. (199 words)

UNIT 11

1.2 Dear Mr. Parker: Thank you for all the help you gave in making it possible to photograph the loading of[20] our three reels of cable from your terminal dock last Tuesday. (P) I was there with our photographer, Mr. John Rogers,[40] and did meet with Mr. Garrick, superintendent of the terminal facility, who was most cooperative.[60] (P) Prior to the use of any photographs taken at your facility, I shall submit them to you,[80] together with caption material, for your complete review and approval. As you requested, I shall allow[100] a minimum of two weeks for your review. (P) Again, Mr. Parker, many thanks for all your help. Sincerely, (120 words)

1.3 Chief Robert Case, Camp Arrowhead, Blue Island, IL 60406 Dear Chief Case: Camp Arrowhead will again have its own private coach on the Illinois Ltd. It is a pleasure[20] to reserve a coach for your boys as we have done for the past 20 years. (P) There is a fine dining car on the[40] Limited, but box lunches can also be made available upon request. Please advise if you prefer us[60] to supply box lunches and how many will be needed. (P) The cost of the ticket for each passenger will be[80] $8.65. Yours truly, (87 words)

1.4 Congressman Benjamin Edmunds, Rayburn Building, Pennsylvania Avenue, Washington, DC 20001 Dear Congressman Edmunds: More than $600 million for research and development and more than[20] $2 billion for equipment and facilities must be spent by the Federal Flight Agencies over the next[40] decade. Aside from federal funding, part of the cost of these additional benefits must be paid by a[60] new-user charge program. (P) This projection includes increasing long-range radar and replacing older systems;[80] installation of collision avoidance systems; relocating radar and beacon systems; and increasing[100] navigational aids at terminals and while planes are en route. Simulators and trainers will also be needed.[120] (P) Communication lines need to be extended. Future communication plans call for satellite development[140] and automatic air-ground interchanges of information. (P) Therefore, Mr. Congressman, please consider[160] adding your support to bill No. 17481 to further the work of the national safety flight[180] planning committee. Yours truly, (186 words)

2.2 Dear Mr. Barnes: In response to your recent letter, I am pleased to send you a copy of our booklet, "Century[20] Milepost," which contains information about our railroad, along with a brochure called "The Great Southwest." (P) I hope[40] you will find this material satisfactory as a teaching aid, and we appreciate your interest.[60] Sincerely, (61 words)

2.3 Dear Traveler: The next trip you plan, be sure to fly from the new Northfields

Terminal, which has been completely[20] redesigned for passenger comfort. (P) You will find abundant parking under the terminal, baggage loaders which[40] deliver your luggage directly to your plane, and X-raying of your suitcases rather than hand inspection to[60] speed you through the security checkline. (P) Boarding lines have been eliminated by our new seat assignment method.[80] Just step onto your plane and the stewardesses will seat you promptly. (P) We believe we have smoothed out the annoyances[100] so that you will find flying from Northfields Terminal to be relaxing and pleasurable. Sincerely, (120 words)

2.4 Have you ever pictured yourself at the stick of an airplane? Would you like the freedom of being your own pilot? [20] Would you like to avoid the problem of crowded highways and traveling at inconvenient times? More and more[40] people are breaking out of their ruts and spending their spare time qualifying for pilot's licenses. (P) The Delta[60] Flying School offers you private lessons. An individual instructor is assigned to you personally and [80] arranges your step-by-step flight plan for you. (P) Our one-engine cruisers are designed for easy maneuverability[100] for the novice. Our trainee airplanes are soundproofed so you have no trouble hearing your instructor. These planes[120] are fitted with dual controls. On a clear day, you could cruise up to 900 miles without even refueling.[140] (P) Come in and let Delta help you fly into the sky. (150 words)

3.2 Dear Mr. Turner: A brochure on the 747, which includes the information you requested [20] in your letter, is enclosed. The first 747, which is operating in the North Atlantic, has[40] done extremely well in service. It makes at least four round trips a week between Frankfurt and New York, and it carries[60] substantial payloads. (P) For more information about the 747 in service, you should look up recent[80] issues of *Aviation Week*, which carries a series on this airliner. Yours very truly, (99 words)

3.3 Mr. and Mrs. William Brill, 324 Dayton Avenue, Camden, NJ 08106 Dear Mr. and Mrs. Brill: Reservations for family and automobile train transportation from Washington,[20] D.C., to Florida on Amtrak have a waiting list; and we are sorry that we cannot accept the[40] reservation you wished to make for December. (P) The first open date at this time is March 18, and this is for coach[60] seating only. Reservations for roomettes are available as of April 23. A deposit of [80] $100 is required when making your reservations. Very truly yours, (95 words)

3.4 Warner Airports, Inc., High Meadows Road, Rockland, DE 19732 Gentlemen: If you study your competitors in the aviation industry, you will see the spread of [20] nonmetallic substances used as structural materials. More than 1,000 different reinforced plastic[40] designs for airplane parts have been fabricated. The reason for this is that plastic materials have a low[60] specific gravity, high strength, and are immune to environmental changes. (P) Substituting reinforced plastic[80] molding compounds for your present glass laminates can cut production costs up to 35 percent.[100] Horizontal stabilizer tips, engine nose cups, propeller spinners, and air ducts are typical uses of [120] reinforced plastic. (P) Our design engineers will help you update your production using easy-to-handle plastic resins.[140] Yours truly, (143 words)

4.2 Dear Mr. Freeman: Your letter of June 21, addressed to our office in San Francisco, has been brought to[20] my attention. (P) We have a large selection of photographs showing both past and present locomotives,[40] which we make available at $1 a print. A complete list is attached for your perusal. Should you decide to[60] order some, please send a check with your order; and the pictures will be forwarded promptly. (P) Because of your interest,[80] I am including several posters, which you may find suitable for display. It is a pleasure to be of[100] assistance, Mr. Freeman. Sincerely, (106 words)

4.3 Department of Transportation, State Capitol, Boston, MA 02113 Gentlemen: The Coast Railway has requested permission of the Interstate Commerce Commission to discontinue[20] railway service between Northampton, Massachusetts, and Lewiston, Maine. (P) If this service is suspended, our[40] 800 residents will be without public transportation. Produce will have to be moved by truck. Commuters[60] will not have public service. This will create a number of hardships for people who have depended on Coast Railway[80] for years. (P) We earnestly ask you to reconsider denying us this service. Yours truly, (97 words)

4.4 Park Freight Services, Jackson Terminal, Marshall, WI 53559 Gentlemen: Our annual Skyways Association meeting is to be held in Wichita starting Saturday,[20] July 17, at 10 a.m. Of special interest on the agenda will be the topic of[40] agricultural aviation. (P) Past president, Jim Halliday, will discuss the modifications of the Britt Air[60] Services which have made them number one in demand for crop-dusting and airlifting food for animals in[80] out-of-the-way locations not reachable by truck. (P) A special ladies' day program has been prepared for wives while the[100] business meetings are in session. Cordially yours, (109 words)

5.2 Dear Mr. Scott: The two ads on used tanks that you ran in your local paper are great; and, of course, they qualify[20] for reimbursement under the terms of our dealer advertising plan. (P) So that we can submit your claim as quickly[40] as possible, will you please send us photocopies of both sides of the check you wrote to pay the newspaper[60] for the ad. (P) I am returning one of the copies of the newspaper's invoice you submitted to help you[80] identify your check. (P) Keep up the good work, Mr. Scott. Sincerely, (91 words)

5.3 Chamber of Commerce, Lewiston, ME 04240 Gentlemen: The Interstate Commerce Commission will conduct a hearing on November 18 to consider[20] the problems related to discontinuance of railway service between Northampton, Massachusetts, and [40] Lewiston, Maine. Three delegates from each community will be allowed 15 minutes each to present their arguments[60] for maintaining services. (P) Four days after this hearing, all communities on this line will be notified [80] of the decision of the Interstate Commerce Commission. Sincerely yours, (94 words)

5.4 The Net Shop, Highway Plaza, Brewster, MA 02631 Gentlemen: We do not know what happened to your shipment of tennis rackets and tennis balls for Mr. J. Brewster[20] of Springfield. A tracer has been placed on your lost shipment, and we have alerted our station agents to check[40] consignments of that weight that were handled by the railway express offices between March 16 and March 19.[60] (P) We checked with Mr. Brewster and he does not have a bill of lading from you. Please send it to him so he will be[80] able to identify the package. (P) There are 14 communities in the United States named Springfield. It[100] will take a few days to contact each agent to trace your shipment. We are sure it will be located shortly.[120] Cordially yours, (122 words)

UNIT 12

1.2 Dear Mr. Hatfield: Enclosed you will find a Proof of Debt and Power of Attorney in the Johnson matter. (P) Please[20] execute this document in the usual way, making sure your signature is acknowledged before a[40] notary public. Do not forget to affix the corporate seal in the proper place. (P) If the debtor issued [60] any notes or checks to you, you must attach such notes or checks to the Proof of Debt. (P) I cannot impress upon you too[80] greatly, Mr. Hatfield, the importance of having a properly executed Proof of Debt; and I shall[100] appreciate your returning these papers to me promptly. Yours very truly, (114 words)

1.3 Mr. Walter Hunt, 643 Chestnut Drive, Wallace, SD 57272 Dear Mr. Hunt: If you wish some additions to be written into your will, you can do so by simply including[20] a codicil, if these additions are not too extensive. (P) A codicil is material that is added [40] to a will but does not require that the will be completely rewritten. The codicil will require your[60] signature, which will have to be witnessed, following a procedure similar to the original signing of [80] your will. (P) After you decide what you wish to include in a codicil, I will review the matter with you and [100] have the matter prepared for your signature. Yours sincerely, (111 words)

1.4 Mr. Herbert Nash, 137 White Birches Drive, Erie, PA 16502 Dear Mr. Nash: Our register reveals that you have disregarded our recent communications. The last two[20] letters were certified mail with return signature receipts signed by you. (P) These mailings were reminders that your payments[40] are long overdue on the "family entertainment center," which you purchased from us. At the time of the sale,[60] you signed an agreement signifying your intention to make regular payments on this account. You have failed [80] to meet this agreement for the last four months, and you have not answered any of our dispatches. (P) Our Legal [100] Department will now have to manage this matter for us. They have two choices. Either they reclaim the merchandise at[120] which time you will forfeit all previous monies paid, or they will be forced to institute suit against you. (P) Any[140] further exchange on this topic will have to be conducted by contacting our Legal Department. Very truly[160] yours, (161 words)

2.2 Dear Mr. Hickson: When I was in Court this morning, I notified the Referee that you would submit a bid [20] of $2,500 pursuant to the terms and conditions contained in the letter to the trustee.[40] (P) Will you please sign the enclosed bid in duplicate and return it to me, together with your check in the sum[60] of $250 payable to Henry Watson as trustee. Very truly yours, (77 words)

2.3 Mr. Bennett Lipton, Hampshire Hotel, Buffalo, NY 14210 Dear Mr. Lipton: Many people have commented about the informative discussion you gave at the high[20] school PTA meeting on the topic of "Understanding the Legal Responsibilities of the Eighteen-Year[40] Old." (P) Would you be willing to repeat your talk on Tuesday evening, November 16, for the Men's Community[60] Service Club? Prior to the meeting, please be our guest for dinner at 6:30 at the Manor House. (P) Our budget[80] allows for a donation of $40 to our speakers. Would this be satisfactory? Cordially[100] yours, (101 words)

2.4 Mrs. Alice Norton, 59-84 Northvale Road, Independence, MO 64051 Dear Madam: It is a simple process to transfer title of stocks presently held by you to another[20] individual. First complete the lined form on the reverse side of the security being sure to fill in all [40] the information requested. (P) Your signature on these papers will have to be authenticated by an[60] officer of a commercial bank registered with the Stock Clearing House Association in Chicago. There is[80] a stock transfer fee of 4 cents per share of stock. (P) Forward your endorsed certificates and the transfer fee with a[100] letter of instructions to the stock exchange office of the firm whose stock you own. Be sure to register this letter[120] at the post office. New securities will be returned to you within 14 days. (P) If you have any[140] difficulty transferring your stock, do not hesitate to contact this office for further assistance. Cordially[160] yours, (161 words)

3.2 Dear Mr. Simpson: Prior to the adjourned meeting of September 9, you told me that you would have a plan for[20] presentation within the next few days. No plan has yet been forthcoming, and the new date of September 23 [40] is only a week away. (P) It was made perfectly clear to you, I believe, that no plan will be acceptable[60] to my client unless it contains a provision for a substantial payment on account and a workable[80] schedule for paying the balance. (P) Unless an acceptable plan is presented prior to September[100] 23, I shall proceed with the liquidation. Yours very truly, (113 words)

3.3 Men's Community Service Club, c/o Mr. Arthur Hadwen, 24 Hazelton Drive, Buffalo, NY 14212 Gentlemen: I accept with pleasure your invitation to repeat my recent talk about "Understanding the[20] Legal Responsibilities of the Eighteen-Year Old." (P) The evening of November 16 will be reserved for[40] you, and I will be pleased to join you at the Manor House for dinner. (P) Rather than pay me any speaker's fee, please[60] donate the $40 to the Storefront Legal Office situated on Culver Street. These devoted young[80] legal practitioners need all the support we can give them. Sincerely, (93 words)

3.4 Mr. and Mrs. Gus Pomeroy, 20-48 Maitland Road, Lincoln, NB 68504 Dear Mr. and Mrs. Pomeroy: Your joint wills have been prepared and are ready for your signatures. I am[20] enclosing a photocopy of the wills. Please study these sheets to be certain your will frames your full intentions. (P) If [40] you are satisfied with the photocopies and have no immediate additions or corrections, please telephone[60] my secretary for an appointment for an official signing. (P) After you have signed your wills and your[80] signatures have been witnessed by two adults, we will catalog and then file one copy of each document in our[100] fireproof vault. You will retain two copies. I suggest one of your copies should be placed in a fireproof safe. Sincerely, (120 words)

4.2 Dear Mr. Moore: In my opinion, the above-named debtor is avoiding payment of your claim of [20] $156. (P) I have, therefore, prepared papers for summary judgment. Will you sign the enclosed affidavit,[40] have it acknowledged before a notary public, and return it to me as soon as possible so[60] that I may proceed with the litigation. Sincerely yours, (71 words)

4.3 Mr. Jeff Douglas, Attorney-at-Law, Wilson Building, Biloxi, MS 39530 Dear Jeff: As I expect to be traveling extensively on business for an undetermined period, please[20] prepare a power of attorney naming Ms. Norma Baxter, my secretary, to act in my stead with[40] limited powers. Norma is to draw against my business account, No. 375-67-945,[60] in the Union State Bank to defray normal office expenses such as rent, insurance, telephone, payroll,[80] etc. (P) I have advised Norma that she can depend on you if any unusual circumstances should [100] arise that she does not wish to arbitrate on her own. Sincerely yours, (113 words)

4.4 Mr. Paul Dragon, 49 Proctor Avenue, Cascade, IA 52033 Dear Mr. Dragon: At one time practically every state allowed you to change your name without making application[20] to a court for permission. This common law prevails generally in the United States. However, in[40] order for a new name to be formally adopted, many persons follow statutory procedure for[60] name changing to have a legal record of the change. (P) Submission of a petition to the appropriate state[80] court must be made. Our state does not require an open hearing which allows any interested persons the[100] opportunity to appear and interpose objections. The name change is granted by a formal order. (P) Please advise[120] if you wish me to initiate the petitioning process. Sincerely yours, (134 words)

5.2 Dear Mr. Snyder: The chattel mortgage has been filed with the clerk of Richmond, and the filing fee has been paid therefor.[20] (P) Mr. Paul Hall, my insurance broker, is sending you the necessary insurance policy on the[40] property covered by the chattel mortgage. Please let me know when you receive this policy. (P) Thank you for the check[60] in the sum of $50, which covers the payment of my legal services. Very truly yours, (79 words)

5.3 To: Helen Thomas Your apprenticeship as a legal secretary with our firm is nearly completed. You[20] have been a devoted and sincere worker. Roy Jackson has requested you as his secretary. As discussed [40] with you, your duties as his private secretary will commence on October 17. (P) Locating[60] information rapidly will be important to you. Depend on the local law bulletins for current court calls and[80] meetings of interest. The National Association of Legal Secretaries provides the occasion to[100] be in touch with others in your field. Participate in professional workshops and seminars. (P) You now are[120] eligible to take the annual examination offered by the NALS. When you pass this six-part[140] test, you will have the title of Certified Professional Legal Secretary. We will reimburse your total[160] expenses at that time. (165 words)

5.4 The legal secretary must be knowledgeable to accurately complete diverse forms and documents. These[20] may involve sales contracts, wills, copyrights, affidavits, or proxies. Many times she will be required to witness[40] the signing of an instrument. (P) If a secretary is not a notary public, she may be expected [60] to arrange to have papers notarized. For convenience, she may be asked to seek a notary commission.[80] Purchase of a notary public seal and a rubber stamp will be necessary. The seal shows the county in which[100] a notary is authorized to act, and the rubber stamp shows the date of expiration of the commission.[120] A notary is not concerned with the papers involved. Her only function is to certify the validity[140] of signature. She may also administer oaths. Each state furnishes notaries with rules with which they must[160] comply. (161 words)

UNIT 13

1.2 Dear Mr. Jackson: As president of the Diamond Corporation, I welcome you to our family of[20] shareholders. (P) It is our desire to keep our shareholders fully informed about the company's policies, plans, and[40] activities. A copy of our latest report is enclosed. If you would like to receive copies of past reports,[60] we shall be glad to send them to you upon request. (P) I am happy to tell you that the business outlook for[80] our company is bright, and we look forward to a profitable year. Yours truly, (95 words)

1.3 To: Editorial Department, *The Daily Post* Leaders of the municipal bond industry are conducting[20] a whirlwind campaign from coast to coast to convince bond sellers to accept self-regulation. The municipal[40] bond market is the last unregulated sector of the securities industry. (P) The Securities[60] and Exchange Commission has gone to court to bar firms from using "high pressure" sales techniques. (P) Perhaps there is too wide[80] a split among bond dealers. It seems likely that regulations may have to be imposed by Congress. (98 words)

1.4 To: All Employees To show our continuing support of our Nation, we are again conducting our annual[20] drive asking all employees to increase the amounts of their monthly purchases of United States Series[40] E bonds. (P) The present interest rate is 5 percent. The bonds reach full maturity in five years and seven months. There[60] are a number of denominations, so that each employee should be able to participate. The minimum[80] bond, costing $18.75, becomes $25 at maturity. This is[100] an ideal gift for numerous occasions. (P) Indicate on your payroll card the amount you wish deducted monthly[120] from your salary. Sign the card and return it to the payroll department. (P) We hope to have 100 percent[140] participation in this drive. (146 words)

2.2 In the last 20 years, world export trade has grown by more than 500 percent. New technologies have created[20] new markets, and we're able to sustain productivity at home with increasing demand for American[40] products overseas. To increase our share of the world export market, it's going to take some aggressive footwork[60] on the part of American businessmen and their bankers. (P) While we can't forecast the precise impact that Far[80] Eastern trade will have on world customers, we know these developing countries will provide a huge potential market[100] for United States goods and services. (P) But to develop the markets of the future, the businessmen of[120] today need capital. The Traders Bank, through its world-wide network of offices, is helping finance a wide range[140] of activities in the Far East. (146 words)

2.3 Dear Stockholder: The annual stockholders meeting of American Chemicals will be held at the[20] Astoria Arms, Chicago, Illinois, on May 16 at 2 p.m. At that time, voting for five new directors[40] will be conducted. Three motions will be put on the floor for vote. These items are outlined in the enclosed brochure.[60] (P) Please complete your proxy. In the absence of voting instructions, the proxy will be voted for adoption of[80] all proposals in agreement with the company management. Sincerely yours, (94 words)

2.4 Dear Stockholder: *Investments for Security* will be rolling off our presses next week. This volume is vital [20] to you as a stockholder and as someone who is aware of the problems of the money market. Some of the[40] chapter headings are: 1. What to do with your savings. 2. Should you say "Charge it?" 3. Price-to-earnings ratio can lead [60] to good buys in the market. 4. How about mutual funds? 5. Managing the family finances. (P) Your check[80] for $8.50 guarantees that you will receive one of the first copies of *Investments for*[100] *Security*. Send your check now and your book will be forwarded prepaid. (P) If you are not satisfied with *Investments*[120] *for Security*, simply return the book within ten days in the simple cardboard binder. You will receive your[140] complete refund within one week. Sincerely yours, (149 words)

3.2 What will it cost you to build an industrial building in the Southeast today? Send for our new brochure on current[20] construction costs in the six states we serve: Virginia, North Carolina, South Carolina, Georgia, Alabama,[40] and Florida. (P) Included are illustrations and construction data on 25 recently[60] completed buildings throughout the Southeast, ranging in cost from $4.20 to $13.64 [80] per square foot. (P) Whatever your expansion plans in the Southeast call for, you'll find no other single source[100] as knowledgeable as we are about the area's facts, figures, and sites. (114 words)

3.3 Dear Stockholder: American Chemicals' quarterly dividend was $1.22 per share,[20] and an extra dividend of 22 cents per share has also been declared. Based on your holdings of 50 [40] common stock shares, your dividend check is for $60. (P) More and more stockholders have asked us for replacement[60] certificates because they have misplaced the original shares. May we suggest that you keep your stock certificates[80] in a safe place such as a safe-deposit box. You should also protect your investment by keeping a[100] separate record of those certificate numbers. (P) In the future, when mailing the certificates to your broker,[120] be sure to use registered mail. Sincerely yours, (129 words)

3.4 Mrs. Honey Turner, 137 Carter Highway, Annapolis, MD 21400 Dear Mrs. Turner: We have just been informed of your recent purchase of stock in the Tri-State Appliance Company.[20] We appreciate the confidence your investment indicates in the administration of our company.[40] (P) For more than 70 years we have been creating and manufacturing products for the home such as[60] toasters, mixers, and blenders. We have developed a full line of large appliances such as dryers, refrigerators,[80] and television sets. If you wish to purchase any of our products, we arrange for stockholders to receive[100] 15 percent discount. (P) Our testing laboratories are studying innovations to aid the homemaker[120] to make her tasks easier. We are constantly seeking ideas to increase the efficiency of our[140] services for the home. (P) Again, we welcome you as a stockholder of the Tri-State Appliance Company. Yours[160] cordially, (161 words)

4.2 In the scattered world of international business, there's a need for a big bank that can pull it all together.[20] (P) Packaging money for overseas ventures is what our international division is all about. (P) At Mark[40] and Serbers, we have a variety of ways of putting the package together. (P) We're in 18 countries with[60] either a branch, a representative office, or a banking affiliate. We own an interest in several [80] foreign banks and finance companies, and our London-based Merchant Bank is one of the most active underwriters[100] of Euro-currency issues and Euro-markets. (P) As a result, our international division has[120] more than $5,000,000,000 in loans on its books, ranging in size from a $300,000,000 consortium[140] loan for a massive copper mining venture to loans of several thousand dollars to small U. S. businesses[160] who have dealings overseas. (166 words)

4.3 Dear Customer: Although the dollar value of trading in the first six months of this year was down 7.5[20] percent from a year ago, the Midwest Exchange has no financial problems because costs have been kept in line[40] on volume. (P) "This Exchange was established 20 years ago and has had a steady, excellent growth rate," stated [60] President Arthur Winston in a recent interview. The exchange has run in the black since its inception. It[80] has two subsidiaries. One is a complete accounting system to member brokers and the other is a[100] depository and clearing system for stock certificates. Cordially yours, (114 words)

4.4 Board of Directors, Sexton Knitting Mills, Manchester, WI 53945 Gentlemen: As a stockholder of the Sexton Knitting Mills, I am writing you to express my opinion on[20] the proposed plan to liquidate the Manchester Knitting Mill. (P) I believe that tariff adjustments will be made by[40] the Federal Department of Commerce, allowing additional imports of wool. Rather than liquidate, I[60] feel that as long as there is still hope for the mill to get back to normal production, I favor the recommendation[80] of applying for a short-term loan of $200,000. (P) May I also suggest that your Research[100] Department investigate new fabrics which would combine wool with natural fiber. Although at present there[120] is a shortage of wool, the demand for knitted goods is at an all-time high. This could open up a new line and [140] allow the mill to move back into full production. Sincerely yours, (153 words)

5.2 Is this a good time to buy Big Board stocks for a long pull? Sensible investing should be a long-term proposition.[20] (P) Keeping that in mind, there are good stocks today for you to consider among the leadership companies listed [40] on the New York Stock Exchange. (P) The attached chart and figures show what has happened to common stocks in the past. The[60] same trends may not continue in the future. You'll want to ask your member firm of the Exchange for its opinion[80] about particular stocks. (P) This doesn't mean you should buy stocks and forget them. It's a smart investor who periodically[100] asks his broker's opinion whether he should sell, switch, or sit tight. (P) There's always a risk in buying common[120] stocks; but there's a risk in doing nothing, too. For millions of people, common stocks make sense today. (138 words)

5.3 Mr. Anthony Landers, 269 Hayes Drive, Santa Monica, CA 90404 Dear Mr. Landers: Soaring interest rates and growing inflationary trends continued to dominate the[20] market last week as stock prices again declined. The Dow-Jones Industrial average dropped 20.54 [40] points over the past week. (P) The federal discount rate was raised from 7 percent to 7½ percent. This[60] is the present rate being charged by the Federal Reserve Board on short-term loans to commercial banks. (P) There are still [80] some potentially strong stock groups in the market. One issue that should show an increase is farm machinery. This[100] is based on the worldwide demand for grains. Yours truly, (109 words)

5.4 One interesting aspect of the secretary's assignments may be a concern with her employer's investment[20] portfolio. Even if the executive controls his own market investments, his secretary should [40] familiarize herself with market "terminology," and she should become comfortable with investment[60] procedures and financial reports. (P) Stock is the most common purchase in the market and is evidence of ownership[80] in a company. When stock is purchased, you receive a paper known as a stock certificate. The stockholder[100] may receive dividends or interest because of his investment in a corporation. These dividends are[120] paid from the earnings of the company. (P) Stock is classified in two ways: common and preferred. If you buy preferred [140] stock, there is a fixed dividend rate. Preferred stockholders receive payments of dividends or company assets[160] before common stockholders, whether it is a normal dividend distribution or if a company is[180] undergoing liquidation proceedings. (P) Preferred stock may have the right of conversion; that is, to convert the[200] preferred stock to common stock at any time the owner chooses. Most preferred stocks are callable, which means they are[220] redeemable at the option of the issuing company. (231 words)

UNIT 14

1.2 Dear Mr. Love: Thank you for your letter of August 10. (P) All of us here were delighted to read your complimentary[20] comments about the Arrow. We are, of course, very proud of this train. (P) We are constantly striving to improve[40] the comforts, services, and schedules on all of our trains; and we have some very interesting plans for the future.[60] (P) We hope that you will continue to use the Arrow on your trips to New York. Furthermore, do not hesitate[80] to write us whenever you have any suggestions that will enable us to serve your travel needs more[100] effectively. Sincerely, (104 words)

1.3 Mr. Harold Kirk, 607 Banta Place, San Juan, PR 00900 Dear Mr. Kirk: Please stop by the Royal Travel Agency office to pick up your tickets and confirmation[20] of reservations. We have your tour completely booked as discussed with you, and we wish to verify the schedule[40] for you. We have also arranged for a car to be available on the dates you specified. (P) Thank you for the[60] opportunity of letting us help you plan your vacation. Cordially yours, (74 words)

1.4 Many people plan their traveling around their avocations. If you are a frustrated archeologist,[20] you can work your way from country to country spending time helping at digs where there is almost always a need for[40] an extra pair of hands. (P) Starting in New Hampshire, you can determine the layers of occupation of previous[60] inhabitants as you study the migration paths or trade routes of Indians who marched from Canada along[80] the Connecticut River Valley to upper New York State. You can dig for Indian relics of the little-known[100] Mogollon tribe who resided in Utah. Hop to Britain to search through Celtic ruins or seek signs of the[120] invasion of the Roman Occupation Legions in approximately 1200 A.D. (P) The Bordeaux cave[140] sites beckon the traveler to France, where you can find early writings and picture stories on the cave walls. Italy[160] and Greece are dedicating their efforts to the work of preserving the signs of their heritage. (P) A Viking[180] graveyard in Denmark has shared its secrets of early burial customs. A number of miles away along the[200]

Arabian Gulf, you can help sift earth at the Dilmun Indian site—a hitherto unknown culture not even[220] guessed at. (P) A slightly less sedentary vacation than some, working on archeological sites is a[240] dynamic approach to learning about the heritage of a country. (253 words)

2.2 Dear Mr. Farmer: Are you particular about hotel service? If you are, you will like the Redmon Motel.[20] We want you to be particular when you come to the Redmon. We have an old-fashioned notion that every guest[40] is entitled to plenty of friendly service. (P) You can drive your car right to the door of your room, or you can have[60] one of our attendants park it for you. Once you are inside your room, you will find relaxation away from street[80] noises. (P) Remember, too, that the Redmon is brand new. This means that you will have the most modern facilities. (P) Whether[100] you are traveling on business or pleasure, treat yourself to the best by staying at the Redmon. Sincerely[120] yours, (121 words)

2.3 First National Bank of Rochester, Rochester, NY 14613 Gentlemen: Your "Convenience Paks" of foreign currency were a lifesaver on my recent trip. I had purchased [20] three paks and had quick currency upon crossing different borders. (P) Each $10 pak contains small bills. I had [40] purchased three paks containing 100 pesetas, 24 marks, and 37 francs, respectively. (P) Your[60] "Convenience Paks" are great! Yours truly, (66 words)

2.4 Do you have a "traveling personality"? Some people tour six countries in ten days because it is the thing[20] to do. If you are a true traveler, then the whole world can offer you its riches. One of the most exciting[40] things about this world is its variety. (P) Travel should be a time for recreation, to give you a chance to[60] revive and refresh yourself. Travel allows you to be incognito—to be free to meet new people. Travel [80] lets you be transported by your imagination into another era. (P) When you vacation, do something[100] extravagantly different. Find the quaint or the rustic. Or if you prefer solitude, try sun at an ocean[120] resort, walk in a forest, or stroll down a different byway. (P) When you are on vacation, don't feel guilty or[140] worry about what is happening at home. Try to brush small annoyances aside. Let your worries slip away.[160] Ignore conflicts or disappointments. (P) Once you have been bitten by the travel bug, your memory will act like a[180] kaleidoscope producing a colorful vision that can be shaken and replaced by another beautiful[200] memory. (282 words)

3.2 Sprawling out in an ancient lake basin a mile and a half high, Mexico City is the Western Hemisphere's[20] oldest city. Monuments to its antiquity still survive, but they are almost engulfed by some of the world's[40] most spectacular new architecture. As befits a great cosmopolitan center, it offers ballet,[60] stunning art, a memorable anthropology museum, delightful parks, and interesting places nearby for[80] day trips. There's fun and folk art at the San Juan market, artistic wares at San Angeles Street Market, and an[100] occasional bargain on Sunday at the flea market. (109 words)

3.3 Mr. Nicholas Wagner, 57 Cottage Place, Chelsea, MD 01824 Dear Nick: Some people decide quite suddenly that they wish to sojourn outside of the continental U.S.[20] To be prepared for an excursion, it is wise to apply for your passport right away. (P) Applying for a[40] passport is one task an adult must do for himself. Complete the required simple forms and submit them to a clerk[60] of a federal or state court having a passport agency. Present proof of your United States citizenship.[80] (P) Two duplicate photographs no smaller than 2½ x 2½ inches and no larger than[100] 3 x 3 inches are required. These must include the applicant's signature on the left-hand side. (P) A $12 [120] fee is charged for a passport which is valid for seven years. As soon as you receive your passport, sign it where[140] indicated. Otherwise, it is not legal. Sincerely yours, (151 words)

3.4 People travel because they want different experiences. They want to stand at historical spots. They want[20] to study different societies. They may travel because they wish to enjoy the freedom of wandering through[40] winding streets of foreign cities. (P) For the handicapped person, travel was a frustrating, unpleasant hassle[60] as he tried to clamber onto buses with high steps or was unable to get inside museums with flights of[80] steps because of being confined to a wheelchair. (P) Planned tours are now designed for the blind and handicapped that are as[100] diverse as going on an African safari to dining at the Eiffel Tower. Buses are designed with[120] ramps and wider aisles to accommodate wheelchairs or crutches. These are helpful conditions for a number of senior[140] citizens who wish to travel at a slow pace. (P) Previously the handicapped or the elderly traveled [160] "off-season," as they were not always welcomed at many resorts. A number of national parks and campsites now[180] invite the handicapped. Handicapped persons do not want to be singled out, but they do want the thrill of sightseeing. (200 words)

4.2 Drawing on the century's experience on the high seas, Holland American today has six ships sailing[20] on cruises that span the globe. Included in their repertoire are one-week trips from New York to Nassau and ten-day[40] Caribbean cruises from New York or Port Everglades in Florida; some of longer duration to South[60] America, the South Pacific, the North Cape, and Scandinavia; a grand 88-day round the world; and [80] 14 days out of Singapore to exotic Indonesia. (91 words)

4.3 Miss Laura Fanning, 227 Park Place, Westchester, NY 12992 Dear Miss Fanning: Thank you for contacting the Royal Travel Agency soliciting information about[20] travel outside the United States. We have written to the Superintendent of Documents, U.S.[40] Government Printing Office, Washington, D.C., and requested that a copy of brochure No. 57 [60] entitled "You and Your Passport" be dispatched to you. (P) This printing was prepared by the Department of State and [80] answers the questions you would ask in planning your trip abroad. (P) This short guide will be your passport to make your vacation[100] a carefree one. Please read it carefully. When you are ready, the facilities of the Royal Travel [120] Agency will be at your disposal whenever or wherever you decide to journey. Cordially yours, (139 words)

4.4 Mrs. Jacob Phillips, 297 Manor Road, Anaheim, CA 92803 Dear Mildred: Americans will have the occasion to return the kindnesses shown to many Americans[20] overseas, as more and more people are now planning visits to the United States. (P) There are many practical [40] ways to help these visitors. Think how many times you have asked for directions in your own country. Imagine the[60] dilemma a foreigner might have as he travels around the states. (P) Most visitors will be able to converse[80] in English, but they might have difficulty if you speak too quickly or use an idiomatic phrase. (P) Some strangers[100] may have trouble with our currency. Advice about traveler's checks, postage rates, and bus or subway tokens[120] can be a major aid. (P) If you cannot help these guests who come to view America, direct them to the Traveler's[140] Aid, local information bureau, or, if necessary, a foreign legation or embassy. Yours truly, (160 words)

5.2 At the rate of three a day with the time, inclination, and capacity, it would take nearly 6½[20] years to spend your pounds and pence in every public house in London. In other words, the swinging city's smiling face[40] is dimpled by 7,000 pubs. And each one is some Londoner's local. (P) It may be a vast Victorian[60] place in the rowdy and bawdy East End, vibrating to twanging guitars with the added accompaniment of[80] splintering beer glasses thrown in for good measure. (P) It may be a posher establishment in the diamond district[100] of Hatton Garden, where you can enjoy a plowman's lunch in a bar with a real cherry tree growing in a corner.[120] (P) It may be a 300-year old tavern on the banks of the River Thames, jamb-packed and smokey. You sit outside[140] for a breath of fresh air, munch a Scotch egg, and watch the barges turn the bend in the river. (156 words)

5.3 Large cities in the United States have adopted a charming custom directly borrowed from Europe. The sidewalk[20] cafe can become an oasis in a crowded city, allowing you a chance to draw your breath and enjoy[40] a leisurely cup of coffee. Sitting under a bright umbrella, you can write a letter, read a newspaper,[60] daydream for an idle hour, or ogle pedestrians. (P) Spindly metal chairs and too small tables offer[80] invitation to promenaders to share the 400-year tradition of the early coffeehouses where writers,[100] actors, and painters met and shared their social moments. In small villages, the coffeeshop has become a[120] cultural center for the community. (P) Plan your rest time to include spending leisurely hours at a sidewalk cafe[140] shaded by a striped awning where conversations can be exciting—or nonexistent. (156 words)

5.4 Miss Rita Johnson, 1071 Lake Road, Demorest, GA 30535 Dear Miss Johnson: Does the sound of ocean waves lull you? Can the sirens' call lure you away from your desk? You may be[20] attuned to the special summons issued by the tidal ebb and flow of the sea. Perhaps it is the unfaltering[40] beam of a lighthouse that brings thoughts of romantic bygone days. (P) There are hundreds of lighthouses along our coast,[60] and those that are manned and accessible may be toured. Interestingly, each lighthouse, aside from its height, carries a[80] characteristic paint pattern which is as significant as are fingerprints. In a general territory,[100] each tower's design is unique. (P) The keepers of lighthouses are still called "wickies" even though the oil lamps have[120] been replaced by powerful electric lights. (P) Do not be faint-hearted as you climb the narrow spiral stairs leading[140] to the lamproom. The view from this locale will be your reward. (P) Each of the hundreds of lighthouses scattered along[160] our coastline has its own story! Yours sincerely, (169 words)

UNIT 15

1.2 Dear Mrs. Burke: May we introduce you to our new Home Fashion Center. (P) Here you will be able to avoid making[20] costly decorating mistakes because of the unique way you are able to experiment with colors,[40] fabrics, and textures in the Center, not in your home. (P) Unlike anything you have seen before, the Center brings[60] together in one convenient area complete selections of fabrics and swatches of just about everything[80] imaginable. Without running from store to store, you will find entire departments of carpeting, rugs, bedspreads,[100] pillows, upholstery, draperies, and wallpaper. (P) With the help of our special displays and one of our talented [120] decorating experts, you will mix and match to your heart's content until, in a surprisingly short time, you have[140] decorated the home you have been dreaming of for years. (P) Come in to see us. We can help you have the home you want.[160] Sincerely, (162 words)

1.3 Mr. Earl Redding, Purchasing Agent, 17-08 Stockton Village, Pleasant Valley, CT 06063 Dear Mr. Redding: Is your office visited by a number of individuals whose raucous voices create[20] a distraction? Are you bothered by reverberating sounds created by clicking high heels? I understand [40] you are considering partial office renovation. Perhaps you should consider coating your present ceiling[60] with acoustical tile. (P) Acoustical tiles are available in an assortment of colors and in a number[80] of designer patterns. Our ceilings will protect you by providing a sound barrier and thereby reducing[100] audible irritants. Cordially yours, (108 words)

1.4 Secretaries participate in the business world during two different periods. The first is usually[20] during the ages of 18 through 23. During these years, many girls marry, set up housekeeping, and [40] spend the next number of years as wives and mothers. (P) On the average, the second entrance into the business world [60] occurs when the children are of an age to be trusted with a babysitter or when the offspring are mature[80] enough to be on their own after school hours. This grants mother her chance to return to her profession, providing[100] an opportunity for personal gratification and, of course, monetary gain. (P) The office worker[120] and home manager demands a home that is easy to take care of and is reasonably carefree. Perhaps you[140] should give thought to some decorating fundamentals that may make this dual career easier to attain. (160 words)

2.2 Dear Mrs. Robinson: We appreciate your interest in our floor display. (P) To paint the diagonal square design,[20] paint the entire floor surface with white enamel. Measure off a 9-inch border around the perimeter,[40] marking it with a 3-inch width of masking tape. With chalk, draw a diagonal plumb line straight across the room. At[60] a distance of 1½ inches from the diagonal, put down another strip of 3-inch tape at[80] 36-inch intervals across the room, using the diagonal as a guide. (P) Continue to do this until [100] you have covered ½ of the room. Then, using a square piece of board, measure 36-inch intervals[120] perpendicular to the first tape. Mark with 3-inch width tape. (P) When you are finished marking the entire floor, paint the alternate[140] squares with pure cream and mercury. When the paints are dry, remove the tapes and varnish the floor with polyurethane.[160] Very truly yours, (164 words)

2.3 Gorman Industries, Inc., West Caldwell, NJ 07006 Gentlemen: Your administrative assistant, Mrs. Norwich, visited our design center to study some[20] products which would be suitable for freshening your office appearance. We offer our clients a complete planning[40] service. We would like to propose a coordinated office for you. (P) After you complete the simple[60] questionnaire that indicates your personal preferences for your individual offices, we will create two[80] outlines for you to choose from. A typical question for you to answer might be: "Do you prefer colonial,[100] contemporary, or antique pieces?" (P) Our service offers a complete job, including submitting wall coverings,[120] planning window arrangements, analyzing lighting needs, or designing proper working surfaces. Our[140] rational deductions will improve your office surroundings. Transfer this bothersome responsibility from your[160] shoulders to ours. Sincerely, (165 words)

2.4 A secretary may have to solve interior decorating problems for her executive. One problem[20] might concern her desire for additional closet space. (P) If you find you need additional storage for your reams[40] of second sheets, letterheads, manila folders, mailers, file cabinets, and even your coffee pot, consider[60] designing an area of planned storage along a whole wall. This space can be enclosed by hinged, movable doors.[80] (P) Folding doors are attractive and easy to open. They are economical to install, allow for air flow,[100] and are not distracting to the eye. Your new wall panels are manufactured with full louvres or in a[120] combination door, half louvre and half solid. (P) Choose high-impact, plastic doors and you will have supplied a trouble-free,[140] permanent installation. You no longer have to limit your choices to black or white boards but have a number of[160] hues to study. The special finish will last for years, as the color is baked into the chemically composed[180] door. You will be pleased at how easy you will be able to adapt these panels to your particular blueprints. (200 words)

3.2 Dear Mrs. Simpson: We have a special catalog for you! (P) What makes it special? It contains pewter from Italy,[20] crystal from Finland, tapestries from Europe, copper from Holland, steins and stoneware from Germany, teak from the[40] Orient, and much, much more. (P) Since we are direct importers, you will find that we offer values that are astonishing.[60] There are over six hundred fine items in the current edition of our 68-page catalog,[80] and all items are guaranteed for your satisfaction. (P) Orders are swiftly delivered. Major charge cards are[100] accepted. (P) Send 50 cents for our treasure catalog today, and we will rush a copy to you right away.[120] Sincerely, (122 words)

3.3 The criteria you ponder when you are determining what furniture to obtain for your home may be applied[20] when purchasing for your office. Utility and versatility must be considered. Is the furniture[40] functional in purpose? Will the surfaces be easy to clean? Is the finish shiny and will it show[60] fingerprints or does it have a "mat" or dull look? (P) Be sure to have enough working surface to give you a comfortable[80] feeling. You should provide desktop locations for your telephone, a calendar, paper storage file, a pencil[100] holder, a freestanding, metal, wheel directory. (P) Plan on including a bookrack to hold a secretarial[120] handbook, a dictionary, and a telephone book. Additional shelving will be required to store[140] professional publications that relate to your particular business. (153 words)

3.4 Dear Office Manager: Choosing a floor covering for your office suite is an interesting task. Your first decision[20] is whether the present floor should be concealed by a sturdy, industrial carpet or whether you should[40] insist on paving with a hard-surface vinyl or vinyl asbestos tile. The office maintenance service may[60] determine the answer to this question. (P) Tiles are produced in standard 8- x 8-inch or 12- x 12-inch size. There[80] are also some as large as 36 inches square. You will find a variety from brick to terrazzo finish.[100] If you prefer, you can design your own pattern, which might include a 1-inch accent strip of a contrasting[120] color. A tile floor is easy to freshen with a damp mop. (P) Carpeting, on the other hand, needs to be vacuumed.[140] However, it does bring a warm, inviting look to an area. The initial cost of tile versus carpeting[160] is a minimal consideration. (P) This month we are instituting our flooring specials. If you can adapt[180] any of our discontinued patterns, you will be able to effect a savings. Stop in and talk with a[200] flooring specialist. We are proud of the extensive selections we can offer you when you visit our showroom.[220] Sincerely yours, (223 words)

4.2 Dear Mrs. Watson: We are happy to send you a copy of our brochure, "Dining in Style." (P) Dining style is what[20] you care to make it today. Whether you are serving a feast or are dishing up snacks on folding tray tables, you[40] can dine in style if you not only consider food and furniture but also sight, sound, and touch. (P) When you are in[60] the mood to sit down quietly to dine, never let space limit you. The way you set the table, accessorize[80] it, light it, and surround it, all adds up to a celebration. (P) The collections pictured and described in the brochure[100] will, I am sure, give you many ideas for solving your problems. Sincerely, (115 words)

4.3 Color is an important facet in your office surroundings. The dark office may be impressive but does not[20] lend itself to keeping the staff feeling alert or awake. The "hot" colors such as orange, red, or yellow may[40] make you "sit up and take notice," but by the end of the day you feel unnecessarily exhausted. The[60] "Pacific" colors are inviting and provide a pleasant setting. (P) A sophisticated way to add color might[80] be to arrange pictures in attractive groupings. Impressionistic art is exciting for some people. You may[100] prefer reproductions of landscapes, still lifes, or portraits. Choose your art carefully, remembering that you will be[120] living with those pictures from nine to five, five days a week. (130 words)

4.4 A touch of greenery can bring the outdoors into your home all year round. You will enjoy having a plant in your[20] office for the same reason. (P) You will not wish to spend extensive time watering potted plants. You may find that[40] succulents can be satisfying to grow. Succulents, which include the cacti family, are devoid of leaves. They[60] require a dry atmosphere, limited water, and sandy soil. They may safely be left for the weeks you plan to[80] be on vacation and will not require care as long as they are in a dry and light spot. (P) The names of succulents[100] are very picturesque and descriptive. You might wish to own a Bunny Ears, Beaver Tail, Grizzly Bear, Golden Stars,[120] Sand Dollar, Star Cactus, or Pincushion. (P) A number of these succulents produce flowers, some only a single[140] blossom, and others shoot out a profusion of color. Cacti can be planted in chunks of volcanic rock,[160] creating a dramatic touch on your bookcase. (168 words)

5.2 Dear Mrs. Stevens: The attached photograph illustrates something old and something new. (P) The electricity is[20] new. The rest is history, because our lamps take their inspiration from the past. (P) The lamp at the center, for[40] example, is based on the urns of the early 19th Regency period. Its old brass finish is richly[60] accented with antiqued black enamel. It is 39 inches high and costs about $95. (P) At the[80] left, softly antiqued Mandarin yellow enamel enhances this simple, imposing canister of cast metal.[100] The distressed old brass finish highlights the subtle curves of this classic form. It is 37½ [120] inches tall and costs about $124. (P) Finally, at the right, is a Georgian urn with deep[140] Empire green enamel and distressed old brass. It is 35½ inches tall and costs about[160] $105. (P) These are three shining examples of how we invoke the past to brighten the future. Sincerely[180] yours, (181 words)

5.3 There is an old adage that "windows are the eyes of a building." If you are fortunate, your "eyes" will have a pleasant[20] view. However, windows demand design attention also. The purpose of some window draperies is to[40] hide the facing of a building across a narrow court. (P) Window treatments have been greatly simplified to meet the[60] needs of our contemporary life. Colored or natural wood roll-up shades, shutters with fabric or colored [80] acrylic insets, or shoji screens require little or no housekeeping attention. Teak woods or grass fibers add an[100] eclectic touch to the design scheme. Your window treatment should add to the inviting feel of a room but must[120] not demand the immediate attention of the viewer. (131 words)

5.4 Brightening your office takes little imagination. For example, a wasted corner can be a display[20] for a piece of sculpture. Sculpture forms are an early form of expression. We can find primitive pieces,[40] impressionistic pieces, or carvings that are refined and show painstaking hours of labor. (P) Many people own sculpture[60] reproductions. It is exciting to own a piece of sculpture related to a special association.[80] Are you interested in classical music? Give yourself a gift of a ceramic bust of a famous composer[100] such as Beethoven, Bach, Brahms, Mozart, or Wagner. If you enjoy the movement of wind chimes or a mobile, try[120] to locate a free standing steel form similar to an Alexander Calder form that may have gently moving[140] wands that will sway to and fro. (P) The primitive strength of the Eskimos can be appreciated in their soapstone[160] carvings. You may prefer the small ivory figures that are carved from whale tusks and then polished. These are a joy to[180] hold. Eskimo carvings are imported from Canada and Alaska. The simple pieces tell a story of [200] the hard life of these kind and gentle people. (P) Sculpture can be placed on a pedestal or put in a base and [220] surrounded by stone. You can enjoy its beauty immediately. Sculpture is satisfying because it can be[240] touched and handled. A simple sculpture can fit into any business office. (254 words)

UNIT 16

1.2 Dear Mrs. Nichols: I think that a staple gun would solve your problem. The staple gun has replaced the hairpin as[20] the most necessary and useful household gadget. (P) Almost anything that hammer and nails, glue, straight pins, or tape[40] can do, a staple gun will do better, faster, and easier. Staples leave hardly a mark and are easy to[60] remove. (P) A list of what you will be able to do with this tool goes on and on. (P) For starters: you might fasten[80] greeting cards and stockings to the mantel; secure weather stripping around doors and windows; cover valences; attach[100] loose wires to baseboard, floor, or wall; trim kitchen shelves; fasten vines to a trellis; tack fabric to a wall; refresh a[120] window shade; or stretch canvas on a frame. And that's just a beginning. (P) You will find this versatile tool for sale in[140] hardware stores, department stores, or building-supply centers. Sincerely yours, (153 words)

1.3 How many times have we heard it said "everybody should have a good hobby for when he retires?" This is a[20] very narrow thought. (P) A good hobby can be an aid to your better emotional health because it helps you release[40] tensions which are built up during daily activities. Hobbies are difficult to pick up "just like that" when[60] you retire. (P) Hobbies are as varied as the people who enjoy them. If they contribute to satisfying your[80] life, then they serve a purpose. They are useless if they are not satisfying. (P) A hobby can be the logical [100] outcome of developing interests, or it may develop in an area in which you would like to[120] experiment to learn about a new avenue of life. (129 words)

1.4 Macrame is one of the world's oldest crafts. The art of creative knot tying had its origins in the fringing[20] or braiding designs of the Arabic people. (P) To macrame, you simply need cord for tying and a[40] knotting board. A knotting board is a rigid panel, easy to pin into. It is marked with 1-inch squares to help you[60] with measuring. It is light enough so you can take your projects with you. (P) Two basic knots are the square knot and the[80] half hitch. After you master these, you will be able to proceed. (P) Cord suitable for macrame comes in a number[100] of weights and diverse colors. You can use white cotton twine, nylon cord, hemp, sisal, or linen cord. Colored beads[120] may be strung on the tying cord, achieving complimentary accents to the cord. (P) Decide whether you wish to[140] make a necklace, bracelet, belt, collar, or handbag, and you will be on your way to many pleasant hours of [160] creating through knot tying. (164 words)

2.2 Dear Mrs. Lockwood: Indicative of the American fascination with doing-it-yourself is the swelling[20] number of books published to meet the seemingly insatiable demand. (P) Some are elementary, some are[40] new twists on old favorites, and some present offbeat crafts you might want to experiment with. All of the books present[60] complete instructions as easy to follow as possible; and all are copiously illustrated with[80] step-by-step procedures and with pictures of the finished product, when necessary. (P) If you would like a list of [100] these books, send for our pamphlet called "Books to Help You Learn a Handcraft." Yours truly, (114 words)

2.3 A hobby should give an individual pleasure and satisfaction. This can include making things "just for fun." [20] You might become so proficient at your hobby that you can evolve a product suitable for sale. For example,[40] candles, leather belts and purses, or shellcraft items are saleable. These are superior gift ideas[60] also. (P) A hobby should not be a mere time waster. It should increase your knowledge or skill. Let your hobby work for you. (80 words)

2.4 Ceramics is a social handcraft. When you register for a ceramics class, you will meet other people at[20] the studio. If your interest continues, you may tour one of the annual district ceramic shows and [40] even submit one of your own decorative pieces to be judged. (P) To begin, you purchase a molded greenware piece.[60] Let us assume you have chosen a vase to decorate. The first step is to clean the greenware, using a thin-bladed [80] knife. You must have a light touch, as greenware is only hardened clay, quite brittle, and easily breakable. After[100] your vase is cleaned, use a barely damp sponge to wipe away excess dust. (P) Glazing greenware is a two-step process.[120] The first step is to paint your vase using colored underglazes or paint. These underglazes must be applied three times.[140] When this is done, your vase will be placed in an oven and fired. Your vase is now white bisque except for the areas[160] where you applied your paint. (P) Your next step is to pour a clear glaze into the vase, swish the liquid around and gently[180] pour out the excess, being sure the inside is completely coated. Then you brush clear glaze on the outside, allowing[200] drying time between the three-coat applications. When your vase is fired again, this glaze hardens, making your[220] pottery waterproof. (P) One more trip to the oven and your original greenware is now a gaily colored vase. (240 words)

3.2 Dear Subscriber: The urge to get involved with handcrafts, the interest in do-it-yourself, is an expression of something[20] significant that is going on today. (P) As we search for a way of using and developing all our[40] inner resources, handcrafts represent a positive method. For something to grow underneath our own hands is,[60] of course, a very great reward. Who doesn't remember the pride of making a sand castle as a child? The act[80] has immediacy, spontaneity, and the feeling of creating something from nothing. (P) We have made handcrafts[100] the focus of our September issue of our magazine. We show you how to crochet an afghan, quilt a[120] comforter, applique a pillow, upholster a bed, sew wonderful surprises with sheets, and many other[140] things. (P) Don't miss the September issue of our magazine! Sincerely yours, (153 words)

3.3 Collecting is a fascinating field for hobbyists. The collector may save anything from picture postcards[20] to precious antiques. (P) Collecting may be an adjunct to a profession. The musician may collect old music[40] books. The librarian may work on collecting early children's volumes now out of print. The schoolteacher may collect[60] early textbooks in his field of specialization. The textbooks may not be individually valuable[80] but, as a collection, will provide an interesting viewpoint in reviewing transitional periods[100] in education. (P) The collector usually has one major problem—he needs space where he can display or[120] store his treasures. Don't let this be a limitation. If you are a true collector, you will find the necessary[140] room for your treasures. (144 words)

3.4 Needlepoint is a relaxing pastime. The art of creating a needlepoint tapestry can be learned in a[20] few hours. You can design your tapestry to complement any period of furniture, and it can be as[40] bright and cheerful as you desire. (P) To needlepoint, you simply cover a canvas with stitches. The interest comes in[60] the design of the tapestry, the variety of stitches, and your choice of colors. (P) A canvas may be[80] embroidered with a combination of two or more styles of stitchery. Petit point is a dainty, small stitch; gros[100] point is a medium stitch and most typically used on the average canvas; and quick point is used for rugs and [120] is done with the largest stitches. (P) After you decide on your canvas, fold masking tape over and along the rough[140] edges, to protect your threads from becoming caught and unraveling. (P) For your first project, choose a canvas which has[160] a design painted on it. Decide the texture of the thread and the colors you wish to use. Do not use[180] inexpensive products—your labor is involved, and you want your tapestry to show your quality handwork. (P) When your tapestry[200] is completed, it will need to be reshaped and pressed. Plan to use it as a cushion or a seat cover, or place[220] it in a frame and hang it on a wall. (227 words)

4.2 Dear Mr. Bassett: Do you have a hobby? If you don't, would you like one? (P) The enclosed coupon is an order form[20] for booklets on a great variety of hobbies. (P)

Examine the list on the coupon order form and order[40] any that interest you. Simply encircle the number of each booklet you want and enclose a check, money order,[60] or currency in the amount indicated for those requiring payment. Add 25 cents for postage[80] and handling. Please do not send stamps. (P) We shall do everything possible to see that your requests are filled as rapidly[100] as possible. Sincerely yours, (106 words)

4.3 Shell collecting can lead to two different hobbies. The person who is working for a specimen collection[20] looks for shells that still have animals living inside, since those are in perfect condition and the colors retain[40] a brilliancy. (P) Each kind of animal makes his house in a different shape: coiled, straight tubes, smooth, or textured. (P) Shells[60] are important to mankind in many ways. They are a source of food. They are a source of pearls. The most artistic[80] use of shells is in the formation of cameos. Shells are utilitarian, as they are used to make buttons[100] and mother-of-pearl jewelry. (P) Shells range in size from a bare speck to a giant clam weighing over 500 [120] pounds. As there are 45,000 species of mollusks, it is apparent how much time can be devoted [140] to shell collecting. (144 words)

4.4 The process of enameling is a favorite with hobbyists and professionals because of the speed and [20] ease with which basic enameling can be accomplished. In enameling, a thin coat of finely ground, colored [40] glass is applied to metal. After it is fired for two to three minutes at a very high temperature, the[60] colored ground glass fuses to the metal. The result is a colorful, unbreakable, enameled item. (P) The[80] beginner will find 18-gauge copper the least expensive and easiest metal with which to work. Gold and [100] silver are used by the professional. Cast iron, steel, and other alloys prove to be more difficult. (P) A slightly[120] curved copper disk is best because there is less strain on the surface. The metal must be absolutely clean before[140] enamel is applied. Any impurity can be removed by placing the copper in a preheated kiln[160] for a few minutes, by scouring with a copper cleaner, or by cleaning with a manufactured metal cleaner[180] and acid solution. (P) After the copper is cleaned, a thin coat of an adhesive solution is sprayed or brushed [200] on. Using an 80-mesh screen basket, a fine, uniform coat of dry enamel is dusted over the surface,[220] being sure that all the copper is covered. Excess enamel should be poured back into the jar to be washed [240] and reused. The dish is now ready to be fired. The dry enameled piece is placed in the kiln onto special firing[260] holders. Repeated applications and firings will produce greater richness and depth of color and allow[280] mixing applications of dry enamel to create different effects. (294 words)

5.2 Dear Reader: Here's everything you have ever wanted to know about gourmet cooking but were afraid to ask! (P) Our[20] new cookbook contains more than 1,000 gourmet recipes by 27 master cooks. All include step-by-step[40] instructions, and there are nearly 400 illustrations. Basic techniques are defined and demonstrated.[60] (P) In addition to all of this, there are tips on cooking tools, wine serving, and entertaining. (P) Use the form at the[80] bottom of this letter to order your new cookbook today. You will find that it's a complete course in surprisingly[100] inexpensive gourmet cookery. Sincerely yours, (110 words)

5.3 A shell that is not suitable for a collection can easily be utilized in shellcraft, the art of using[20] shells to trim articles. The first step in shellcraft is to clean your day's gatherings by soaking them in soapy[40] water and then scrubbing with a toothbrush. Sort your shells in any compartmentalized container. Egg cartons are[60] handy and inexpensive for the beginner. (P) To attach shells to each other, use a nontoxic, noninflammable[80] glue, which is transparent when it dries. Naturally, this glue should not be soluble in water. (P) Working[100] with shells is a painstaking hobby. However, it is rewarding when you develop the knack of gluing[120] shells together and they stay in place, forming an animal designed in your mind. (P) Use your imagination.[140] Visualize shell jewelry or holiday ornaments to be made from shells. You can personalize gift cards with fine,[160] delicate shells. (P) Shellcraft items are limitless. And remember, each piece you make is now an original. (180 words)

5.4 Ecologists should praise the latest hobby now in fashion. Bottle cutting is a hobby that can be shared by[20] husbands and wives. Many husbands enjoy the cutting and polishing, and their wives assemble and decorate the[40] glass objects. (P) Cutting a glass bottle is done in two steps. The first is called scoring. Roll a glass cutter against the[60] bottle surface with a firm, steady hand. The score line must be continuous and not interrupted. The bottle[80] is now separated by gently tapping around the score line until the bottle divides into two pieces.[100] While cutting glass, be sure to wear protective glasses and gloves. (P) Any sharp edges of the cut bottle can be ground[120] down by rubbing with silicon carbide. Occasionally dip the edge of the bottle in water to control[140] any loose grit from floating into the air. To refine the polishing, an emery slurry is used. (157 words)

UNIT 17

1.2 Whether data are processed manually, mechanically, or automatically, there are six basic[20] steps. These six steps are: classifying, sorting, computing, recording, summarizing, and communicating. (P) There[40] are three basic classifying methods: alphabetic, numeric, and alphameric. Regardless of which method[60] is used, classifying is deciding to what category an item of information belongs. (P) Sorting[80] is arranging items of information according to categories. Classifying and sorting[100] may be done in the same step. (P) Computing is adding, subtracting, multiplying, or dividing data. (P) Recording[120] is putting the information into a transmittable and storable form. Accuracy and[140] efficiency of subsequent operations depend upon correctly recording data. (P) Summarizing is[160] organizing and analyzing data. (P) Communicating is passing information on for further processing.[180] This data may be stored in the memory of the computer. (193 words)

1.3 Nationwide Paper Corporation, 562 Canton Avenue, Columbus, OH 43215 Gentlemen: Six years ago we switched to electronic data processing to help us run our business. This has[20] been beneficial. (P) One of the undesirable side effects of this transition has been the unexpected[40] amount of effort required to "deleave" carbon paper from our multisheet packs of forms and disposition of[60] this waste paper. Another is that our people too often find themselves with dirty fingers. (P) We have received from[80] consignees duplicate sheets that do not leave imprints on other papers they may touch or on the hands of our[100] complaining workers. (P) Ask your local sales representative to stop by and show us samples of multipacks which will [120] eliminate the finger smudging annoyance. Yours truly, (131 words)

1.4 Modern Carpets, Inc., 325 Madison Avenue, New York, NY 10015 Gentlemen: We noticed with interest in your annual report that you are considering the installation[20] of a computer system for your internal finances as well as production and inventory control.[40] This is a large step in modernizing your bookkeeping, and we would like to point out that the construction of the[60] computer rooms is an often overlooked facilty which can lead to many problems. (P) Computer Suite[80] Designers has had 17 years' experience in planning and construction in the areas where computers[100] are installed. This is considerable experience for an industry which is barely 20 years old. We[120] will take these problems off your hands: structural, electrical, heating, ventilating, air-conditioning, sound control,[140] and the final, overall decoration which will make your computer facilities an efficient and [160] pleasant place to work. (P) The enclosed brochure pictures some of our installations. We will be pleased to serve you, too.[180] Very truly yours, (183 words)

2.2 A secretary can interpret and process information from any source, but each machine in a data[20] processing system is built to read data in only one way. The most frequently used media are: punched cards,[40] mark-sensed cards, paper tape, magnetic tape, and magnetic-ink characters. (P) Machines that are frequently used in[60] automatic data processing are: key punch, verifier, reproducer, sorter, collator, and tabulator. (80 words)

2.3 Academic Attire, Inc., 42-13 Skyline Avenue, Valparaiso, IN 46383 Gentlemen: According to industry information, we have learned that you rent the overwhelming number of [20] a quarter of a million academic robes each year. You must keep track not only of sending the gowns out,[40] correct for size, length, and color, but also of their return. (P) We have helped many firms to find an inexpensive[60] solution to inventory difficulties similar to yours. The solution is the electronic accounting[80] machine. For your size firm, punched card processing is speedy, accurate, and effective. (P) Accounting Machines,[100] Inc., provides completely reconditioned accounting machines which are factory guaranteed. These machines[120] are unconditionally guaranteed for a period of six months. Very truly yours, (137 words)

2.4 *World Financial Reporter*, 480 K Street, NW., Washington, DC 20033 Gentlemen: *World Financial Reporter* is beginning the planning of a new magazine to be modeled after[20] your present successful *World Reporter.* You have published *World Reporter* for 32 years, and it has been[40] so profitable that you are enlarging the scope of its coverage. (P) You will want to reach the truly[60] influential of the international financial community. We have in our files the largest compilation[80] of names in the entire world. These names are now computerized so that we can selectively supply you with names[100] and addresses of those who really count. (P) It is true that our service is slightly more costly than run-of-the-mill [120] addressing services. However, we can demonstrate from the results of those using our professional [140] addressing service that it is less expensive for each subscription than the cost of other addressing companies.[160] Sincerely yours, (163 words)

3.2 The six basic procedures of data processing may all be performed by a computer. A specialist called [20] a programmer sets up the steps in a carefully written set of instructions called a program. A program must[40] be designed for each kind of processing the computer is to perform. (P) The electronic computers have many[60] advantages over other systems, provided there is a sufficient volume of work. (P) Here are some of [80] the advantages: (P) Computer speed is extremely high. (P) All larger computers can perform the six basic[100] data processing steps, although the ability to classify is limited. (P) Because of the reduced size of [120] data on magnetic tape and the speed of the computer, large volumes of data can be handled efficiently.[140] (P) Data may be stored in the computer, thus reducing files and speeding retrieval. (P) A series of instructions[160] for an operation can be stored in a computer. (171 words)

3.3 Giant Food Stores, Inc., 400 Wheatland Avenue, Des Moines, IA 50311 Gentlemen: You have been users of computer data processing equipment for over a year. In the[20] beginning, you must have employed many new analysts, programmers, computer operators, and possibly[40] even some clerks to get you started. Many of your older workers must be interested in this new and exciting[60] equipment. (P) Do you find you need staff who must have more advanced skills? Let us help you select and train your present[80] workers for these advanced positions. This training can be conducted at your plant and during working hours. (P) Why don't you[100] survey your workers? You might be surprised at the results. Cordially yours, (113 words)

3.4 Mr. George Brower, 127 Topeka Avenue, Kansas City, MO 64109 Dear Mr. Brower: You recently became a member of the professional staff of the largest department[20] store in your city. You undoubtedly will be responsible for making many decisions involving the[40] continuing prosperity of your organization. (P) Professionals in Data Processing has twelve thousand [60] members in the United States, with a local chapter in your area. These professionals have the same[80]high-level skills and responsibilities as you have in your new position. We feel strongly that all of us[100] have common interests and problems in our chosen field. (P) We invite you to attend the next chapter meeting of the[120] Kansas City branch of Professionals in Data Processing to be held at the Hotel Statler on Monday[140] evening, March 18, at 8:00 p.m. I will call you within the week to make plans to go together. Cordially[160] yours, (161 words)

4.2 Companies with large volumes of data to process may invest in their own computer systems. Smaller companies,[20] which have less voluminous paper work, may not be able to afford the very substantial investment[40] required. (P) To meet this need, data processing services have been established in a number of cities. The[60] subscribing company prepares the medium, probably punched cards or paper tape, and sends it to the service for[80] final processing. The company pays only for the computer time used for its data. (96 words)

4.3 Jackson General Hospital, 125 Sampson Avenue, Houston, TX 77004 Gentlemen: Your hospital is an extremely heavy user of forms designed for printing as a result of [20] data processing. (P) Our firm, Forms Consultants, has helped thousands of other concerns, including a dozen hospitals,[40] to design the most practical forms for both input and output information. (P) We are not printers. We are[60] forms designers who will work with you directly. We study your paper flow and your files and then design forms for your[80] individual needs. Please do not hesitate to call on us and let us design forms for your medical [100] services. Cordially yours, (105 words)

4.4 The Vagabond Travelers Agency, 1300 Melrose Avenue, Memphis, TN 38102 Gentlemen: Congratulations on your recent opening of your fourth branch office in Huntsville, Alabama.[20] We wish you continued good fortune in your new venture. (P) Before deciding to add another office to your[40] growing chain, you must have carefully analyzed some of the pitfalls that might trap you. Time-Sharers would like to[60] suggest a way to assist you in keeping your operation effective. (P) You have not yet reached the size where you should [80] own and operate your own computer data processing establishment. Time-Sharers offers you, for little[100] more than the cost of a telephone call, the ability to enter the data processing field. Some of the[120] obvious applications we can now suggest are: recording group trips; keeping count of the number of open[140] reservations; billing; and reminding patrons of trips for which they have reservations. (P) We would be happy to[160] sit down with you and discuss how to fit our technique to your purpose. I am sure that we can jointly find many[180] applications for time-sharing by Time-Sharers, Inc. Sincerely yours, (195 words)

5.2 The particular equipment, media, procedures, and personnel a company may use for processing[20] data depend on a large number of variables, such as: volume of data, repetitiveness of data and [40] processing operations, complexity of processing operations, kinds of results needed,[60] periodic deadlines for results, and cost of equipment and procedures. (P) These factors vary greatly from company[80] to company. One firm might find that a punched-card system suits its needs; another might combine punched-card equipment[100] with paper-tape machines or a computer. (P) Whatever a particular company's system may be, the[120] secretary can understand it in a general way by using the six basic steps. If she needs to[140] understand any specific aspect of the system, she should ask for help from whoever is in charge of the[160] procedure involved. (163 words)

5.3 Mr. William Shepard, Manning Communication Systems, Easton, PA 18042 Dear Bill: This morning I received my third call from Bowman Brothers, who represent our line in the Southwest. They are[20] very dissatisfied with the computer terminal in their branch office, which has a malfunction that has not[40] been corrected. (P) We do an annual business with Bowman Brothers of over $250,000.[60] It is to our self-interest that our computer installations are serviced rapidly and efficiently.[80] (P) Considering the circumstances, I would assume that you are personally investigating this[100] predicament. In my opinion, if there is another breakdown of the Bowman branch terminal, I feel it should be[120] replaced. Sincerely yours, (124 words)

5.4 Thrifty Drugstores, Inc., 523 Marine Boulevard, Portland, OR 97201 Gentlemen: We understand that you are seriously contemplating the installation of terminals to[20] augment your current computer data processing operations. Even experienced users of computers,[40] like yourselves, overlook the fact that electric power suitable for household and industrial purposes[60] is often not sufficiently reliable for real-time data processing. (P) Endura Power has met[80] the needs of many new users of computer terminals. We guarantee that Endura customers can sustain[100] their data processing in a controlled way even when normal electric power fails. Determine in advance[120] how much time you will need in the event of power failure. Endura will supply your power requirements[140] for a gradual slowdown period of three minutes to three hours. (P) Join our list of progressive clients. Consult[160] us to help you plan this major step to produce the cheapest and most effective results. Sincerely yours, (180 words)

UNIT 18

1.2 Dear Mr. Olsen: Many of the points you make in your letter are very much on our minds—so much so, in fact,[20] that I thought you might like to have the enclosed copy of the talk given by Eden's new president, Clark J. Read,[40] at our annual meeting. (P) This paper has not been published, but it seems to me that your views were so expertly[60] expressed by him that you would like to read it. (P) We appreciate your letter for both its substance and tone. Sincerely, (80 words)

1.3 To: All Employees Working a full day and going to classes at night can be a rigorous and demanding schedule. Getting[20] ahead in your profession is important to you and requires inner fortitude as well as intelligence.[40] (P) This is an invitation to take part in our in-service program developed for employees. Classes are held[60] in this building and are scheduled for early evening hours, allowing you time to have dinner before class,[80] attend class, and then arrive home at an early hour. Having courses here saves travel time. Our curriculum is[100] tailored to meet the interests of all of our employees. (P) Investigate some of these programs and study them in terms[120] of your own goals. We shall be glad to answer all your questions after you visit one of the demonstration sessions.[140] We believe you will find it to be a productive experience. (153 words)

1.4 Miss Camille Flemming, 69 Granite Boulevard, Long Beach, CA 90806 Dear Miss Flemming: The members of the Future Secretaries Club of Eastern High School are planning an information[20] workshop. We are introducing this type of school activity for the first time. The workshop is scheduled[40] for Saturday, April 27, and will include a luncheon. (P) Our purpose is to give secretarial[60] students an opportunity to meet with professional secretaries working in various offices[80] who would be gracious enough to discuss some positive thoughts about their office situations. (P) As you are a[100] Certified Professional Secretary who graduated from Eastern High and are an executive[120] secretary to the vice-president of your company, your qualifications place you first on our list of[140] secretaries to be invited to speak to us. (P) We are inviting students from four other high schools to be with[160] us. Our program is planned for 9 a.m. to 2 p.m. Our guests may choose which topics they would like to listen to.[180] We hope to have a number of speakers to meet with students in smaller seminar rooms. (P) We hope you will say "yes"[200] and spend this time with us. We would like to prepare a program guide and are printing a directory of guests. May[220] we have the title of your 20-minute address? Sincerely, (231 words)

2.2 Dear Mrs. Bragg: This morning's mail brought a copy of your most cordial letter about your experience with our[20] order department. (P) In all our operations, we endeavor to give prompt, efficient service, but seldom are[40] these efforts rewarded so gratifyingly and in such a thoughtful manner as your letter. (P) You can be[60] assured that all of the people who had a part in processing your orders will be informed of your kind words, and I [80] know they will want to join in expressing our appreciation. Sincerely yours, (94 words)

2.3 To: Mrs. Rita Davis As you know, last week was the bimonthly meeting of the Branch Managers representing[20] 22 districts of our firm. At that time, a few of the people attending the meeting were evidently[40]surprised by the casual attire of some of our stenographic people. (P) Although clothing codes are more[60] casual and are socially more relaxed in respect to what is appropriate dress for the office, we should [80] consider some standard for our office. (P) Please organize a small committee to discuss the concept of the correct[100] wardrobe in the office. I hope we can institute a change in policy before the next Branch Managers' meeting. (120 words)

2.4 The Shelby Publishing Company, 24-07 Prescott Street, Omaha, NB 68111 Gentlemen: Our company is the only company in the world who has been a manufacturer of every[20] important duplicating method—from hand-operated, single duplicators to the rapid-speed,[40] electrically run copiers. (P) Our organization has a well-earned reputation dating back nearly one[60] hundred years. Our name assures our customers of a quality machine that is durable, easy to operate,[80] and well constructed. (P) However, even our machines should be retired and replaced with modernized versions.[100] Consider our enclosed specifications folder. All new models are self-feeding with automatic inking, have[120] automatic shut-off controls and easy touch adjustment for centering. (P) Our Mr. Baxter will call on you[140] to discuss your duplicating and copying needs and will help bring you up to date on today's latest models.[160] Please ask Howard Baxter about our trade-in policy. Cordially yours, (173 words)

3.2 Dear Mr. Allen: It was very thoughtful of you to write us regarding our salesman, Mr. Gibson, who has[20] been calling on you for these many, many years. We certainly agree with you that in the period of [40] 20 years, during which many changes have occurred in the method of advertising, the one thing that has[60] remained consistent has been the representation of our company in your office. (P) Your letter is very much[80] appreciated, and we are taking the liberty of sending a copy to Mr. Gibson. I know he[100] will be equally pleased to read it. Very truly yours, (110 words)

3.3 Medical Suppliers of Pennsylvania, 617 Pine Street, Allentown, PA 18109 Gentlemen: Our warehouse has just completed checking the carload shipment consigned to us by central warehousing.[20] All cartons have been opened to verify contents and a merchandise inventory was taken to verify[40] the total gross count. (P) We had ordered 20,000 crutches, Stock No. 3795. At this time of [60] the year, we are unable to keep up with the demand for this product and have difficulty supplying our[80] hospitals. Unfortunately, you did not consign any rubber tips for the crutches, Stock No. 3796.[100] (P) Obviously, the crutches are useless without the rubber tips. Please forward a dozen gross by parcel [120] post and ship the remainder by fast freight. Very truly yours, (131 words)

3.4 Mr. Harvey Burke, 28 Parker Road, Jacksonville, FL 32210 Dear Mr. Burke: This year our community, Jacksonville, will celebrate its one hundred years of existence. This[20] centennial will be shared by all residents for an official two-day celebration. Many events are[40] being planned to bring people to visit Jacksonville during this time. (P) The Chamber of Commerce, in conjunction with local [60] merchants, will have a number of gift drawings with certificates and prizes being donated by local shops.[80] Three churches will offer casserole suppers at reasonable prices. (P) Two weeks previous to the holiday[100] weekend, the high school honor society has offered to paint the local train station. New floral baskets will [120] be hung by the men's service club from the display poles. The library staff is preparing a "History of [140] Jacksonville" which will be published along with a map of our town and will include a key chain imprinted with the dates[160] of our centennial. (P) We have invited a number of neighboring school bands, a fife and drum corps, the local [180] veterans post, boy and girl scout troops, civil defense groups, and all local groups to march in the parade on Saturday.[200] (P) As immediate past mayor, a post you held for 20 years, we hope you will join Mr. John Lindstrom, our[220] present mayor, on the podium and share this day with your fellow townspeople. Respectfully yours, (237 words)

4.2 Dear Mr. Small: In response to our telephone conversation, we are sending you some literature on the[20] Martin Tool Company, which we hope will prove interesting. (P) Also enclosed, you will find an application, which should [40] be completed and returned to us at your earliest convenience. As soon as your application is reviewed [60] by our technical personnel, we will be in touch with you. (P) If you have any questions, please feel free to call me.[80] Very truly yours, (84 words)

4.3 Dear Resident: Our special inventory sale will be held at our Oak Street warehouse next Friday. We are forced to[20] make room for our fall inventory. This will be a tremendous sale! We have an overstock of thousands of feet[40] of carpeting, mattresses and springs, and bedroom furniture. We will help you load your selection, and you can drive[60] right off with your goods. If we are to supply delivery service, there will be a slight charge. (P) The goods you[80] will see are manufacturers' overstock that did not reach the floor of our store. You will be the recipient[100] of this abundance purchased by our buyers. We have never been able to offer our customers such a[120] selection in the past. (P) All sales will be on a first come, first served basis. All sales will be either cash or charge. We cannot[140] accept c.o.d.'s. Our courteous salesmen will be available to help you with your selections. Cordially[160] yours, (161 words)

4.4 Reservations Manager, The Coach House, 100 Clinton Street, Lansing, MI 48902 Dear Sir: We are in need of accommodations for 11 men and the use of 2 conference rooms which can[20] seat 5 to 11 people. We will need these rooms for Monday, Tuesday, and Wednesday, September 8, 9, and 10,[40] respectively. (P) Any combination of single and double rooms will be acceptable. The size of these rooms[60] is not important, but each must have a shower and be air-conditioned. (P) We will need both a portable blackboard [80] and a display board. We will expect coffee to be accessible during the conference hours. Also, we will [100] expect you to furnish lunch during the three days. (P) If you can supply our needs and guarantee these 11 [120] reservations, please transmit a statement to confirm the dates, costs, menus, and other pertinent details we itemized.[140] Upon receiving your statement, a deposit will be forwarded immediately. Very truly yours, (160 words)

5.2 Dear Dr. Block: Your letter of September 10 has been forwarded to this office for reply. (P) We cannot comment[20] specifically on anticipated third quarter earnings prior to their release in late October. As[40] Dr. Grant has noted publicly, however, the corporation expects sales to show an improvement over[60] last year's comparable quarter. (P) According to recent reports, our industry is currently in an uptrend.[80] Sincerely, (82 words)

5.3 To: Jeff Drake, Editorial Staff I have just finished reading the latest edition of the house organ,[20] *Today's Topics*, dated December 5. I want you to know I found this issue to be very enlightening and [40] enjoyable to read. (P) The items you included were very pertinent. The article explaining the[60] additional benefits under our group insurance plan was so factually presented that it is the first[80] time that I feel I understand all the clauses and how they apply to me. (P) The new column, "Here and There," adds[100] a light touch. Your idea of introducing a fellow worker in each issue is valuable. (119 words)

5.4 Occupant, 472 Harris Avenue, Greenwich, CT 06830 Dear Sir: Your local newsboy, Irwin Strong, has been leaving you a copy of the *Greenwich Record* each morning. We[20] expect you have found it on your doorstep as you have been leaving for work. (P) The *Greenwich Record* is a newspaper[40] for the family. We print national and international news, a family page, sports and comics,[60] editorials by national figures, television, radio, and theatrical listings, and cultural [80] activities. We invite notices from local groups. We are well supported by local businessmen, who appreciate[100] our extensive subscription list. (P) As you are a new resident, Irwin will deliver a free copy[120] of the *Record* to you for an additional week. One evening he will stop by to introduce himself to[140] you. We hope you have enjoyed reading the *Greenwich Record* and have found it a source of information to you[160] as a new member of the community. (P) Our subscription rates are reasonable. We pride ourselves on our[180] delivery service. Irwin has been one of our most reliable delivery boys. Why not let him offer you[200] his capable service and say "yes" when he stops by to ask you to become one of our subscribers? Sincerely, (220 words)

UNIT 19

1.2 Who are the people who seem to be enjoying their jobs the most? Aren't they the ones who are putting the most[20] into it? (P) Which comes first, enthusiasm for the job or enjoyment of the work? (P) If you ever hope to enjoy[40] your working hours instead of dreading them, the only possible way is to get interested and develop some[60] enthusiasm. The only possible cure for a boring job is to start caring more. Dig a little deeper,[80] try a little harder, and put more of yourself into it. (P) If you were giving out raises, who would you[100] consider first? Wouldn't it have to be the people who are already doing a little more than they are paid for? [120] (P) Wherever you work, whatever you do, try some enthusiasm. Developing your enthusiasm is[140] the best road to more money, more responsibility, and tougher assignments. (154 words)

1.3 Do you believe that Ms. Secretary is a paragon of office integrity? She must be agreeable,[20] businesslike, cooperative, diplomatic, efficient, faithful, etc., right through to the letter *z*.[40] Additionally, as Ms. Secretary is the hub of many departments, she must realize that her office[60] happiness will be due partially to her social acceptance by her fellow members. (P) To be liked, you must[80] also like people. How much happier we would be if we truly showed an interest in another individual,[100] if we had tolerance for other persons' opinions, were considerate of fellow workers, and [120] willingly "pulled together" at the office. (P) Our complex society depends upon our lives being interwoven.[140] We rely on each other. This is important in an office, in our local community, and on a[160] national level. (164 words)

1.4 As Ms. Secretary, you can appreciate how important it is to be able to converse and express[20] yourself clearly and concisely. As important, the secretary must be a good listener. You must pay[40] attention to "hear" what is actually said and not what you might assume you "hear." (P) When working with other people,[60] you must avoid daydreaming or being so preoccupied that you listen with only 50 percent of your[80] mind. If this is your problem, write yourself notes which force you to pay attention. (P) In this age of speed, we are all in[100] a hurry. In fact, our minds receive messages at a rate of about four times as fast as we have the capacity[120] to speak. Don't pretend to listen—you may tune out something you should heed. Make your listening skill become an[140] active skill. (142 words)

2.2 There is a rumormonger in every office. The people who love to gossip are always dying to let you[20] in on a choice little rumor. And if there's nothing new today, they'll make up something. (P) True or false, rumors hurt the[40] organization which pays your salary. People who spread them seldom realize the harm they may be doing.[60] (P) Rumor spreaders are basically attention seekers. They love to be the center of attention, handing out a[80] hot tip straight from the horse's mouth. Their burning desire is to be listened to; truth is strictly secondary.[100] (P) Unless you have cold, hard, undeniable facts to the contrary, don't bother to contradict the gossip. It may[120] merely incite the rumormonger to elaborate and act even more positive. Just be plain disinterested.[140] Avoid these menaces. (145 words)

2.3 Why do some persons fail where others succeed? There are many answers to this conjecture. One answer might be that[20] to succeed you need a positive attitude. Attitudes are developed from our formative years in response[40] to feelings of parents, teachers, and community. (P) A positive response earns respect. This person is willing[60] to accept change. She is motivated and has an enthusiastic approach. The professional secretary[80] has a respectful attitude toward utilizing time for work and for leisure. (P) The secretary who is[100] cooperative and happily supports the company's objectives is a joy to her employer. Your attitude,[120] Ms. Secretary, shows your willingness to be accountable for your office actions. (136 words)

2.4 When a mechanical system is installed in an office, how often do we hear: "People will be dismissed," "I'll [20] never learn how to work that monster," or "We will all become robots." Adverse comments spread from desk to desk and jump[40] from office to office. These are hasty conclusions. (P) Installation of a computer, computer terminals,[60] or any other mechanical aids in an organization is not a threat to job security. The[80] real devil in the office is grapevine gossip. Do not repeat idle scuttlebutt. (P) If you approach a new[100] situation with a positive attitude, you will find greater job enjoyment. To expand job responsibilities,[120] learn new techniques. Ask for advice from others. Set a businesslike example for your fellow employees.[140] Strive for intrinsic and extrinsic gratification. But, Ms. Secretary, avoid the pitfall and don't be[160] an office gossip! (164 words)

3.2 There is an old theory that what the boss doesn't know won't hurt him. The trouble is that what the boss doesn't know he[20] occasionally finds out. (P) There are lots of ways to cheat a company if you feel like it, such as: coming in[40] late, faking illness to take a day off, asking for time off and forgetting to make it up, stretching out your coffee[60] break, pretending to be busy while you goof off, dawdling over work in order to get overtime pay. (P) When you[80] were hired, you made a deal, an agreed salary and benefits in exchange for services rendered. (P) If your[100] employer tried to back out of his part of the bargain, you would feel cheated, wouldn't you? How can he help but feel the[120] same if you try to pull the wool over his eyes and shortchange him? (131 words)

3.3 James Russell Lowell wrote, "Mishaps are like knives that either serve us or cut us as we grasp them by the blade or the handle." [20] What a wonderful statement! (P) Errors frustrate all humans. The importance attached to an error should be the[40] searching out of why it happened and how to elude it hereafter. (P) Correcting errors requires positive thought.[60] How did this occur? To combat an error, we can follow a three-part plan: identify the error, determine[80] the cause, and construct a solution. In this way, Ms. Secretary, we are grasping the knife by the handle. (100 words)

3.4 Every secretary should have a personal checklist that she puts into effect each day. What would be included [20] on a personal checklist? The first item might be a one-minute stop in front of a full-length mirror. (P) Study[40] yourself from head to toe. Reminder No. 1 to be stressed on your list should be personal hygiene. A major[60] offense in any social situation is to be personally unkempt. (P) Ask yourself the following[80] questions. Is my hair freshly washed and attractively styled? Is my makeup low-keyed and suitable for the business[100] world? Is my outfit tidy and appropriate for office wear? Are my stockings free from catches or ladders? Are[120] my shoes polished, heeled and soled, and, most important, comfortable? (P) If your daily checklist is an affirmative, Ms.[140] Secretary, you will feel personally confident as you carry out your daily tasks. (156 words)

4.2 Meeting the public may not be a regular part of your office duties. On the other hand, it's a rare office[20] worker who, at sometime or other, doesn't have personal or telephone contacts with customers or[40] suppliers. (P) Remember, in circumstances like these, you represent the company. The stranger's attitude toward your[60] organization will be definitely affected by the way he reacts toward you. (P) Friendly people make a[80] friendly company, the kind it's really a pleasure to deal with. (P) When you answer the phone, whether it's your own or[100] at someone else's desk, you are the company! (P) When you are asked to take care of a visitor, smile, be friendly,[120] and try to find some way to interest him. It's an important part of the impression he will form of your company.[140] (P) Think of yourself as an ambassador for the company! (151 words)

4.3 Diplomacy is a key word for Ms. Secretary. There will be many occasions in an office when you[20] must be firm, perhaps demanding. A tactful approach can alleviate hurt feelings or misunderstandings. The[40] "soft sell" is useful. By this method, you logically, step-by-step, support your views without ridiculing the views[60] of a fellow worker. (P) To close a discussion with "that's my opinion" can be a coverup for[80] irresponsible statements. Logical presentation of fact will help change another person's opinion. (P) If there is a[100] differing viewpoint, be ready to listen. Stop and think before replying. Don't become emotional. Remember,[120] there are at least two sides to an argument and more than two approaches to solving a problem. (138 words)

4.4 To be efficient requires being consistent. Consistency, some people complain, is dull. (P) Being consistent[20] is not easy. It demands regimen and discipline to get the right things done at the correct time. How much[40] easier it is for some people to work in spurts of frenzied activity while the patient person works with[60] uniformity and tenacity. (P) Consistency for Ms. Secretary is an important aspect of[80] personal work methods. Systematically structuring the process to handle filing, sort correspondence, record[100] phone messages, and complete myriads of tasks saves hundreds of dollars each year for your employer. Religiously[120] following consistent patterns, Ms. Secretary will find she has developed her own personal habits and[140] may be quite amazed at the fine work she produces. Consistent work methods lead to consistent work habits, which[160] will lead to efficient secretarial administrative performance. (174 words)

5.2 Jane is a roamer. She travels a lot, she visits, and she wanders. The intercom works overtime trying to[20] find her. Meanwhile, her employer is burning with impatience. (P) Busy executives don't enjoy hunting a[40] secretary or an assistant. This attitude may seem unreasonable, but it's a fact so let's face it. A[60] smart secretary doesn't wander. (P) In the first place, do you keep all your materials at hand so that you don't[80] have to wander? When you have to leave your desk, do you always tell someone where you can be found? And do you get there[100] quickly and get back promptly? (P) Wandering is a sign of boredom. Either you don't have enough to do, or you are[120] not very interested in doing what work you do have. Sooner or later, the company may decide they don't[140] need your services. (144 words)

5.3 Ms. Secretary's desk is the hub of activity in an office. This gives you many threads from which you might be[20] able to weave new ideas. New ideas arise from being ambitious and having the gumption to use[40] your mind. (P) Be confident that your idea is worthy. Surveys have shown that women are as able as men to[60] dream ideas. Nor is age a barrier to idea productivity. You need no special advanced training[80] to conceive an idea. Experience has proven that the person who lives the closest with a[100] situation is the one best able to solve a problem or make improvements. (P) To state this succinctly, the ideaman[120] with the potential suggestions on the job is you! (130 words)

5.4 You can never change the experiences you have had up to now, but you can make use of them in the future.[20] We all use our experiences every day to help us automatically progress through daily routines. (P) Take[40] a few minutes and analyze whether your encounters have been good or bad and then try to fathom why. If you[60] do a poor piece of work on an assignment, think how you could avoid repeating this poor showing next time. (P) You can learn[80] by watching your coworkers. Ask yourself whom you enjoy working with, and you will probably discover it is[100] someone with a pleasant disposition who does not negate her fellow workers. Ask yourself whom you try to evade[120] when you are going to lunch, and it may well be someone who does not like her job or who never seems to be[140] able to smile. This person may tend to make sarcastic remarks. This may well be the person who is left behind [160] at promotion time. (P) We are continually acquiring knowledge and expanding our horizons. Ms.[180] Secretary, let your experiences work for you. Your experiences will help you take on more demanding burdens[200] and will bring you satisfying results. (208 words)